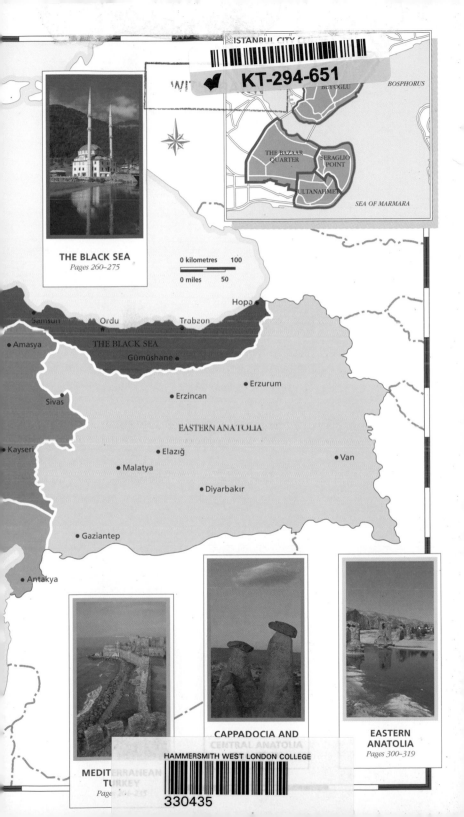

ISTANBUL CITY

KT-294-651

BOSPHORUS

BEYOGLU

THE BAZAAR
QUARTER

SERAGLIO
POINT

SULTANAHMET

SEA OF MARMARA

THE BLACK SEA
Pages 260–275

0 kilometres   100

0 miles   50

Hopa

Samsun   Ordu   Trabzon

Amasya   THE BLACK SEA

Gümüshane

Erzurum

Erzincan

Sivas

EASTERN ANATOLIA

Kayseri

Elazığ   Van

Malatya

Diyarbakır

Gaziantep

Antakya

**CAPPADOCIA AND
CENTRAL ANATOLIA**

**EASTERN
ANATOLIA**
Pages 300–319

**MEDITERRANEAN
TURKEY**
Pages

TURKEY

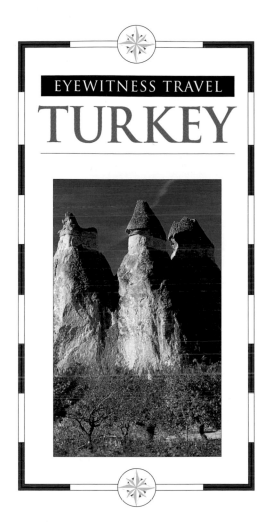

EYEWITNESS TRAVEL

TURKEY

MAIN CONTRIBUTOR: SUZANNE SWAN

DK

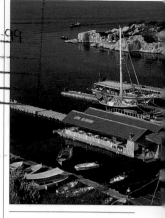

DK

LONDON, NEW YORK
MELBOURNE, MUNICH AND DELHI
www.dk.com

PRODUCED BY Struik New Holland Publishing (Pty) Ltd,
Cape Town, South Africa

MANAGING EDITORS Alfred LeMaitre, Laura Milton
MANAGING ART EDITOR Steven Felmore
EDITORS Amichai Kapilevich, Anna Tanneberger
EDITORIAL ASSISTANT Christie Meyer
DESIGNER Peter Bosman
MAP CO-ORDINATOR John Loubser
CARTOGRAPHER Carl Germishuys
PICTURE RESEARCHERS Sandra Adomeit, Karla Kik
DTP CHECK Damian Gibbs
PRODUCTION MANAGER Myrna Collins

MAIN CONTRIBUTOR
Suzanne Swan

OTHER CONTRIBUTORS
Rosie Ayliffe, Rose Baring, Barnaby Rogerson, Canan Sılay, Dominic Whiting

PHOTOGRAPHERS
Kate Clow, Terry Richardson, Anthony Souter, Dominic Whiting, Linda
Whitwam, Francesca Yorke

ILLUSTRATORS
Richard Bonson, Stephen Conlin, Gary Cross, Bruno de Robillard, Richard
Draper, Steven Felmore, Paul Guest, Ian Lusted,
Maltings Partnership, Chris Orr & Associates, David Pulvermacher, Paul
Weston, John Woodcock

Reproduced by Colourscan, Singapore
Printed and bound in Malaysia by Vivar Printing Sdn. Bhd.

First published in Great Britain in 2003
by Dorling Kindersley Limited
80 Strand, London, WC2R 0RL

11 12 13 14 10 9 8 7 6 5 4

Reprinted with revisions 2006, 2008, 2010

Copyright 2003, 2010 © Dorling Kindersley Limited, London
A Penguin Company

A CIP CATALOGUE RECORD IS AVAILABLE FROM THE BRITISH LIBRARY.

ISBN 978 1 40535 206 2

FLOORS ARE REFERRED TO THROUGHOUT IN ACCORDANCE WITH EUROPEAN
USAGE; I.E. THE "FIRST FLOOR" IS THE FLOOR ABOVE GROUND LEVEL.

Front cover main image: Blue water along the coast, Lycia region.

MIX
Paper from
responsible sources
FSC™ C018179

**The information in this
DK Eyewitness Travel Guide is checked regularly.**
Every effort has been made to ensure that this book is as up-to-date
as possible at the time of going to press. Some details, however,
such as telephone numbers, opening hours, prices, gallery hanging
arrangements and travel information are liable to change. The
publishers cannot accept responsibility for any consequences arising
from the use of this book, nor for any material on third party
websites, and cannot guarantee that any website address in this
book will be a suitable source of travel information. We value the
views and suggestions of our readers very highly. Please write to:
Publisher, DK Eyewitness Travel Guides,
Dorling Kindersley, 80 Strand, London WC2R 0RL, Great Britain.

CONTENTS

INTRODUCING
TURKEY

Commagene stone head on Mount
Nemrut (Nemrut Dağı)

◁ Dramatic light accentuates the İshak Paşa Sarayı near Doğubeyazıt

The village of Üçağız, on the Mediterranean coast

Vendor selling *boza*, a drink made from lightly fermented grain

Emblems of Istanbul, the Haghia Sophia and Blue Mosque

Example of Turkish weaving with geometric design

Sumela Monastery *(see p272)*

HOW TO USE THIS GUIDE

This guide helps you to get the most from your stay in Turkey. It provides expert recommendations and detailed practical advice. *Introducing Turkey* locates the country geographically, and sets it in context. *Istanbul Area by Area* and *Turkey Region by Region* are the main sight-

seeing sections, giving information on major sights, with photographs, maps and illustrations. Suggestions for restaurants, hotels, entertainment and shopping are found in *Travellers' Needs*, while the *Survival Guide* contains useful advice on everything from changing money to travelling by bus.

ISTANBUL AREA BY AREA

Turkey's largest city has been divided into four sightseeing areas. Each has its own chapter opening with a list of the sights that are described. The *Further Afield* section covers many peripheral places of interest. All sights are numbered and plotted on an *Area Map*. Information on the sights is easy to locate as it follows the numerical order used on the map.

Sights at a Glance lists the chapter's sights by category, such as Museums and Galleries, Mosques, Parks and Gardens and Historic Buildings.

2 Street-by-Street Map
This gives a bird's-eye view of the key areas in each sightseeing area.

Stars indicate the sights that no visitor should miss.

Story boxes explore specific subjects in detail.

All pages relating to Istanbul have red thumb tabs.

A locator map shows clearly where the area is in relation to other areas of the city.

1 Area Map
For easy reference, sights are numbered and located on a map. City centre sights are also marked on the Istanbul Street Finder maps (see pp135–40).

A suggested route for a walk covers the more interesting streets in the area.

3 Feature
Each feature looks in detail at an important attraction, tracing its history or cultural context, and providing detailed information on what can be seen today.

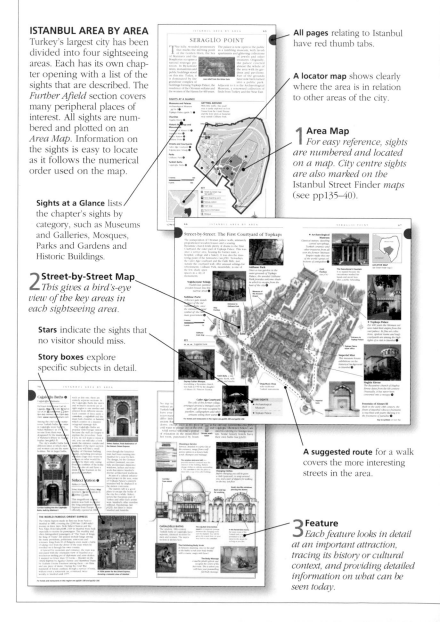

THE AEGEAN

Discovering the Aegean region of Turkey takes visitors on a panoramic, classical journey, from Çanakkale on the Dardanelles (the ancient Hellespont) to the finger of land off Marmaris known as the Datça Peninsula. Together, the coast and hinterland tell a story spanning some 5,000 years of Greek and Roman history. This is where Homer's myths and heroes come to life.

1 Introduction

A general account of the landscape, history and character of each region is given here, explaining both how the area has developed over the centuries and what attractions it has to offer visitors today.

TURKEY REGION BY REGION

Apart from Istanbul, the rest of the country is divided into seven regions, each with a separate chapter. The most interesting towns and sights to visit are numbered on a *Regional Map* at the beginning of each chapter.

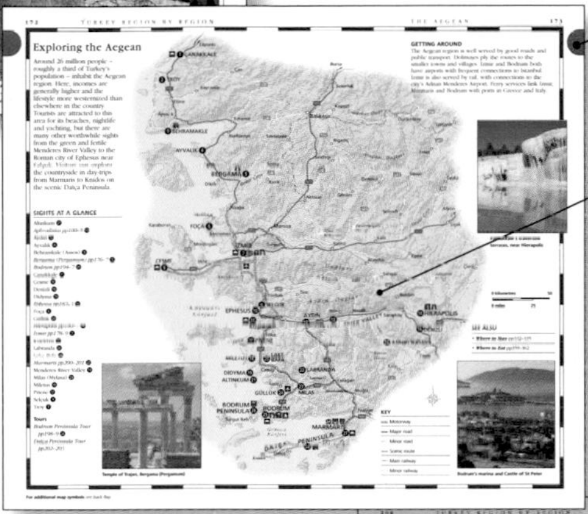

Exploring the Aegean

Each area of Turkey can be easily identified by its colour coding, shown on the inside front cover.

2 Regional Map

This shows the main road network and gives an illustrated overview of the whole region. All interesting places to visit are numbered and there are also useful tips on getting to, and around, the region.

A town map shows the locations of all the sights described in the text.

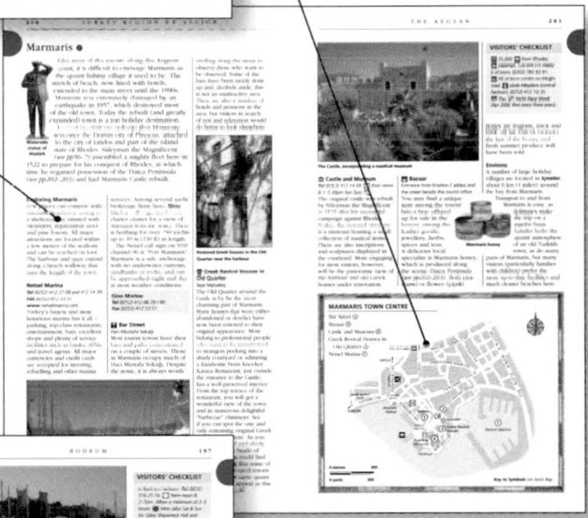

3 Detailed information

All the important towns and other places to visit are described individually. They are listed in order, following the numbering on the Regional Map. Within each entry, there is further detailed information on important buildings and other sights.

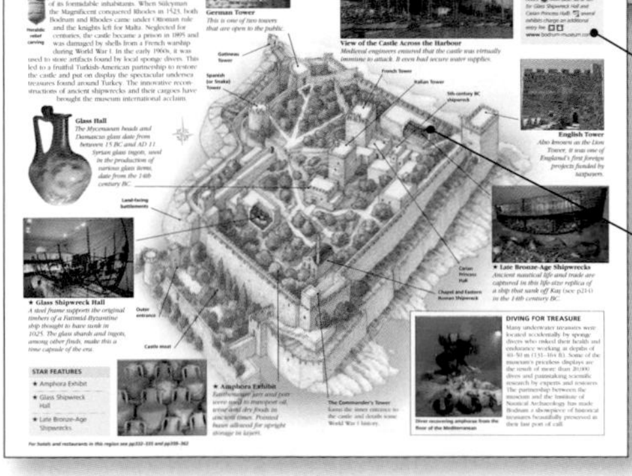

Marmaris

VISITORS' CHECKLIST

For all the top sights, a Visitors' Checklist provides the practical information you will need to plan your visit.

Castle of St Peter

4 Turkey's Top Sights

The historic buildings are dissected to reveal their interiors; important archaeological sites have maps showing key sights and facilities. The most interesting towns or city centres have maps, with sights picked out and described.

INTRODUCING TURKEY

DISCOVERING TURKEY

From prehistory to the present, numerous ingenious and civilized cultures have emerged and declined within Turkey's present-day borders, such as the pre-Biblical Hittites, and the Byzantine and Ottoman empires. The country possesses rich layers of history, ancient palaces and museums, impressive mosques and churches

16th-century
İznik tiles

and remarkable ruins – Turkey is home to ten World Heritage Sites. Turkey also offers a range of invigorating outdoor activities, particularly in the Black Sea and Eastern Anatolian areas, where visitors can walk, hike, kayak, sail, horse ride, ski and more. Beautiful, sandy beaches along the Mediteranean and Aegean coasts offer relaxing surroundings.

Elegant domes and minarets of the Blue Mosque, Istanbul

ISTANBUL

- **Historic Blue Mosque**
- **Sizzling nightlife and café society**
- **The Grand Bazaar**

The name Constantinople, or Istanbul, stirs visions of Ottoman sultans, harems and palaces. **Topkapı Palace** museum *(see p68–71)* built by the conquerer Mehmet II in the 14th century, offers an intriguing insight into a part of the city's rich history.

The iconic Blue Mosque *(see p88–9)*, a dignified contour on Istanbul's skyline, is one of Islam's most revered holy sites.

Modern Istanbul is an eminently sophisticated city which also has a bohemian side. The **Beyoğlu** district *(see p106–11)* pulses with night life in the jazz and rock clubs and *mayhane* or tavernas.

Committed shoppers will love the energy that per-

meates the labyrinthine **Grand Bazaar** *(see pp104–05)*. Thousands of booths sell a staggering array of wares.

THRACE & SEA OF MARMARA

- **Byzantine capital Iznik**
- **Poignant World War 1 battleground Gallipoli**
- **Peaceful island retreat**

One of the most glorious Byzantine capitals in the 6th century, **İznik** *(see pp160–1)* produced exquisite ceramic tiles in the 16th century and still retains its original layout.

The annual Gallipoli ceremony on **ANZAC Day** in April *(see p34)* commemorates the courage of World War I soldiers on both sides and the Kabatepe Information Centre houses poignant memorabilia *(see p168)*.

The cool and verdant **Princes' Islands** *(see p158)* have lovely beaches and offer respite from Istanbul's bustle.

AEGEAN

- **Fantastic beaches**
- **Legendary Greek and Roman cities**
- **Pamukkale hot springs**

Beaches, yachts and fun in the sun are a major draw for visitors to this region. **Bodrum** *(see p194)* was Turkey's first tourist resort and the Castle of St Peter is its most distinctive landmark.

An incredible amount of remains of Classical Greek and Roman civilizations are scattered across the region. The Greco-Roman ruins at Ephesus *(see pp182–3)* are a dramatic sight, and the city also played an important role in the spread of Christianity.

The terraced pools and springs at **Pamukkale** *(see p186)* are one of the country's most popular natural attractions. The unusually shaped formations were created by limestone-laden thermal springs.

Spectacular white travertine terraced pools at Pamukkale

◁ A close-up of an İznik tile panel, showing the intricate floral motifs known as arabesques

Picturesque lagoon and beach at Ölü Deniz

MEDITERRANEAN TURKEY

- **Ölü Deniz lagoon**
- **Legends of St Nicholas**
- **Timeless Antakya**

Sweeping sandy beaches, warm sun, golf and leisurely cruising on *gület* (wooden boats) are the notable attractions of Mediterranean Turkey. The most dramatic stretch of sand is at **Ölü Deniz** *(see pp212–3)*, while the compelling backdrop of the Toros Mountains, cool streams and forests and the 350 km (217 mile) **Lycian Way** *(see p216)*, a long-distance footpath, offer an invigorating alternative.

St Nicholas was the 4th-century Christian bishop of **Myra** *(see p216)*, and Demre's church bears his name. **Antakya** *(see pp234–5)*, called the "Turkish Riviera", has French colonial architecture and a beautiful coastline.

ANKARA & WESTERN ANATOLIA

- **Steaming geothermal spas**
- **Bronze Age Çatalhöyük**
- **Home of the Whirling Dervishes**

The dignified air of **Ankara**, *(see pp240–7)*, Turkey's capital city, adds to its shopping opportunities, cosmopolitan restaurants and lively nightlife. An hour's drive away is the opportunity to picnic in national parks such as **Soguksu** *(see p246)* or enjoy the hot springs at **Kızılcahamam** or **Haymana**

(see p246). Of particular note are the Bronze Age settlements of **Çatalhöyük** *(see p254)*; however, the best finds are displayed in the Museum of Anatolian Civilizations *(see pp242–3)*. The Whirling Dervishes are celebrated in Konya's **Mevlâna Museum** *(see pp252–3)*.

Traditional Whirling Dervish

BLACK SEA

- **Exhilarating outdoor sports**
- **Ottoman town Safranbolu**
- **Sumela Monastery**

The Black Sea is Turkey's wettest and most temperate region and it is ideal for rafting and trekking or just enjoying simple village life. In **Safranbolu's** *(see pp 268–9)* market area, traditional trades and crafts are still practised by local artisans as they were

Stone heads of Zeus and the other gods at Mount Nemrut

in Ottoman times. The frescoes of **Sumela Monastery** *(see p272)*, although badly damaged, are worth seeing.

CAPPADOCIA & CENTRAL ANATOLIA

- **Surreal volcanic formations**
- **Göreme Open-Air Museum**
- **Seat of Pontic Kings**

The bizarre **rock formations** and "'fairy chimneys" *(see pp280–81)* of the Cappadocia region offer bewitching natural beauty. Below ground, early Christian churches with Byzantine frescoes can be discovered at the **Göreme Open-Air Museum** *(see pp 284–5)*. Secluded **Amasya** *(see pp298–9)* has a long and prominent history. Settled first by the Hittites, the town became the capital of the Roman Pontus Kings; their graves are carved out of the cliff faces, which tower over the town.

EASTERN ANATOLIA

- **Mystical site of Mt Nemrut**
- **Restored Roman mosaics**
- **World's oldest functioning monastery**

This region is relatively undeveloped and unspoiled. Little can rival the Greco-Persian cult site of **Mount Nemrut** *(see p306)*. Vistas of the enormous terraces and stone heads at sunrise or sunset are dramatic.

The exquisite Roman mosaics of Zeugma (Belkis) on display at the **Gaziantep Archaeological Museum** *(see pp308–9)* are one of Turkey's most thrilling finds in 50 years. The Syrian Orthodox monastery of **Mor Gabriel** *(see p307)*, near Mardin, is the oldest surviving monastery in the world, having practised devout monastic traditions for over 1,600 years.

Putting Turkey on the Map

Lying between Europe, Asia and the Middle East, Turkey is located midway between the equator and the North Pole. It covers an area of 814,578 sq km (314,533 sq miles). A small area (3 per cent) called Thrace forms part of the European continent, while the larger section, Anatolia, forms part of Asia. The city of Istanbul is situated at the meeting point of Europe and Asia and is divided by the Bosphorus, the strait linking the Black Sea and the Sea of Marmara. Countries bordering Turkey are Greece and Bulgaria on the European side, and Georgia, Armenia, Iran, Iraq, Syria and Nakhichevan to the east and southeast.

KEY

✈ Airport

═ Motorway

▬ Major road

═ Secondary road

— Railway

-·- International boundary

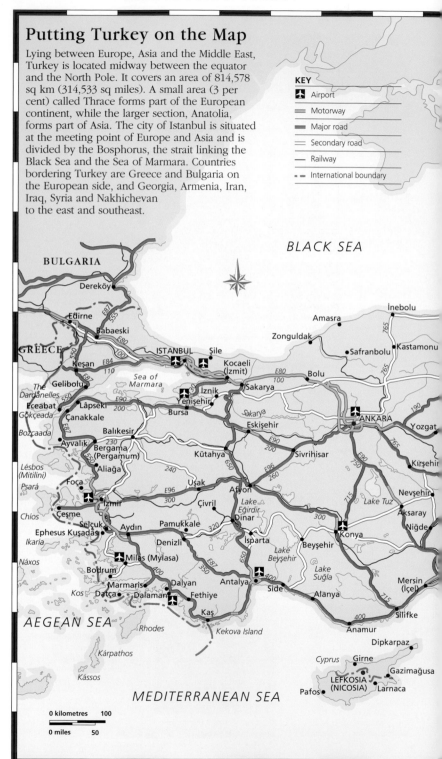

BLACK SEA

BULGARIA

Dereköy

Edirne

Babaeski

GREECE

Keşan

İnebolu

Amasra

Zonguldak

Safranbolu

Kastamonu

The Dardanelles

Gelibolu

ISTANBUL

Şile

Kocaeli (İzmit)

Bolu

E80

Eceabat

Gökçeada

Lâpseki

Çanakkale

İznik

Yenişehir

Bursa

Sakarya

Sakarya

ANKARA

Bozcaada

Balıkesir

Eskişehir

E90

Ayvalık

Bergama (Pergamum)

Kütahya

Sivrihisar

Yozgat

Lésbos (Mitilini)

Aliağa

240

650

E90

Kırşehir

Psará

Foça

Uşak

Afyon

E96

Lake Tuz

Nevşehir

Chios

Çeşme

İzmir

E96

Çivril

Lake Eğirdir

Dinar

Aksaray

Ephesus

Kuşadası

Selçuk

Aydın

Pamukkale

Konya

Niğde

Ikaria

Denizli

Isparta

Beyşehir

Náxos

Milas (Mylasa)

Lake Beyşehir

Mersin (İçel)

Bodrum

Lake Suğla

Marmaris

Dalyan

Antalya

Side

Alanya

Kos

Datça

Dalaman

Fethiye

Kaş

Silifke

AEGEAN SEA

Rhodes

Kekova Island

Anamur

Dipkarpaz

Kárpathos

Cyprus

Girne

Gazimağusa

Kássos

LEFKOSIA (NICOSIA)

Larnaca

Pafos

MEDITERRANEAN SEA

0 kilometres   100

0 miles   50

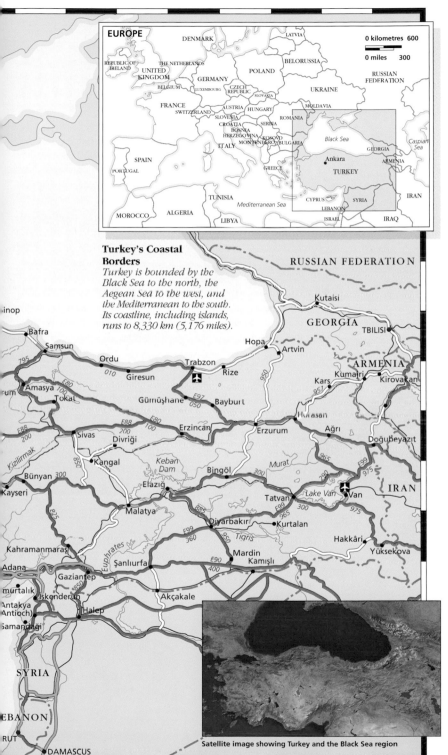

EUROPE

LATVIA
DENMARK
REPUBLIC OF IRELAND
THE NETHERLANDS
BELORUSSIA
UNITED KINGDOM
GERMANY
POLAND
BELGIUM LUXEMBOURG
CZECH REPUBLIC
RUSSIAN FEDERATION
UKRAINE
SLOVAKIA
FRANCE
AUSTRIA HUNGARY
SWITZERLAND
MOLDAVIA
SLOVENIA
ROMANIA
CROATIA
BOSNIA
HERZEGOVINA
SERBIA
Black Sea
GEORGIA
Caspian Sea
ITALY
MONTENEGRO/ BULGARIA
KOSOVO
ARMENIA
SPAIN
Ankara
PORTUGAL
GREECE
TURKEY
IRAN
TUNISIA
Mediterranean Sea
CYPRUS
SYRIA
MOROCCO
ALGERIA
LEBANON
ISRAEL
IRAQ
LIBYA

0 kilometres 600
0 miles 300

Turkey's Coastal Borders

Turkey is bounded by the Black Sea to the north, the Aegean Sea to the west, and the Mediterranean to the south. Its coastline, including islands, runs to 8,330 km (5,176 miles).

RUSSIAN FEDERATION

inop
Bafra
Samsun
Ordu
795
010
Giresun
Kutaisi
GEORGIA
TBILISI
Hopa
Artvin
Trabzon
Rize
um
Amasya
Tokat
E80
700
E97
Gümüşhane
050
Bayburt
950
Kars
Kumajri
Kirovakan
957
ARMENIA
Erzincan
Erzurum
Husasan
E88
E88
100
E80
200
100
Sivas
Divriği
200
Ağrı
Doğubeyazıt
850
Kangal
Keban Dam
Bingöl
Murat
965
E99
975
Bünyan
300
Elazığ
290
Kayseri
895
Tatvan
Lake Van
Van
IRAN
Malatya
300
975
E99
Diyarbakır
Kurtalan
965
Tigris
Hakkâri
Kahramanmaraş
Euphrates
E99
360
Mardin
Yüksekova
Adana
Şanlıurfa
Kamışlı
murtalık
Gaziantep
E90
400
İskenderun
Akçakale
Antakya (Antioch)
Halep
Samandağı
SYRIA

LEBANON
RUT
DAMASCUS

Satellite image showing Turkey and the Black Sea region

A PORTRAIT OF TURKEY

The popular image many visitors have of Turkey is one of idyllic Mediterranean beaches lapped by an azure sea. Sun and sand, however, barely hint at the riches this country has to offer. A bridge between Asia and Europe, Turkey is one of the great cradles of civilization – a proud country whose cultural and historic treasures will delight and inspire even seasoned travellers.

Contrasts between old and new add greatly to the fascination that overwhelms visitors to Turkey. Istanbul, the metropolis of this fast-changing nation, displays all the hustle and bustle of a great world city, while only a few hours away rural people congregate around communal water supplies and collect wood to light their fires.

Tulips in bloom

The superb scenery and landscape reflect a remarkable geographical diversity. Beguiling seascapes, soft beaches and brooding mountains along the Mediterranean coast yield to the tranquillity of Turkey's Lake District, while the deep forests and cool *yayla* (plateaux) of the Black Sea region leave visitors unprepared for the vast empty steppes of the eastern provinces. Pictures can only hint at the enchantment that awaits travellers in Cappadocia. Here, centuries of underground activity have resulted in entire cities carved deep into the porous tuff, while aeons of erosion have carved the landscape into fantastic fairytale-like mushroom formations.

Many of Turkey's national parks and wetland sanctuaries are a last refuge for species that are almost extinct elsewhere in Europe, and for botanists there is an amazing display of flora.

Add to this countless ancient ruins, and the friendliness and hospitality of the Turkish nation, and you are guaranteed an unforgettable holiday.

Looking out over the Bosphorus from Sultanahmet

◁ **Prayer on a holy Friday during Ramazan**

The Library at Ephesus *(see pp182–3)*, one of the most famous Roman sites in Turkey

HISTORICAL FRAMEWORK

Anatolia has seen the rise and fall of sophisticated civilizations, including that of the great Assyrians, Hittites, Phrygians and Urartians. Over the centuries, this land was populated almost continuously. The Hellenistic period produced some of the finest sites. Near Çanakkale, on the Aegean coast, lie the remains of ancient Troy *(see p174)*, and in the mountainous southwest are the ruined settlements of Lycia *(see p215)*, whose inhabitants left behind an assortment of unusual rock tombs.

In the early Christian era, St Paul travelled through Asia Minor, then part of the Roman empire, to preach the Gospel. Between the 3rd and 7th centuries, Christianity was a central force in the development of Anatolia. This was the period when the Byzantine empire attained the pinnacle of its glory. The Romans and Byzantines endowed Turkey with glorious archi-

Ottoman tilework at the Topkapı Palace, Istanbul

tectural masterpieces, which can still be seen at places like Ephesus *(see pp182–3)*, Aphrodisias *(see pp188–9)*, and in Istanbul, where the former church of Haghia Sophia has stood for more than 14 centuries *(see pp82–5)*.

The Seljuk Turks added their superb architectural legacy, as did the Ottomans, whose empire at one point stretched from Hungary to Iraq. Many other peoples, among them Jews, Russians, Armenians and Greeks, have played an important part in Turkey's complex history. The fruits of this diversity can be seen in superb mosaics and frescoes, colourful tilework, underground cities, interesting historic and biblical sights, city walls and fortresses.

Turks are proud of the modern nation Atatürk *(see p58)* forged out of the ruined Ottoman empire. *"Ne Mutlu Türküm Diyene"* is a common Turkish phrase that means "happy is the person who can say he is a Turk."

RELIGION

Most of Turkey's population of 71 million people follow the Sunni branch of Islam, but one quarter of the population are Alevis, Mevlevis *(see p225)* or other Muslim sects.

Because the Turkish Republic is founded on secular principles, religion does not seem to hold the significance that it does in other Muslim countries. The devout do attend prayer times in the mosque five times daily as laid down by the Koran, but some Turkish Muslims do not go to mosque at all.

A department of religious affairs exists and carries out the function of exercising control over family morals and to safeguard the principles of Islam. Mosque and state are not separated by statute, and so the boundaries between them can be unclear at times. Invariably, Atatürk's principles are invoked as sacred when religion appears to steer too close to politics. The issue of Islamic dress is emotionally charged and a subject of debate.

Approximately 130,000 non-Muslims, including Greek and Armenian Orthodox, are found in larger cities, and members are allowed to worship freely within their own communities.

A card game interrupted for a tray of *simit*

SOCIETY

The Turkish language is of Central Asian origin but uses the Latin alphabet. It has a natural vowel harmony that makes it sound melodic and soft. Turkish terms such as *divan* and *ottoman* have entered the English vocabulary, while Turkish borrows words like *tren* and *randevu* from English and French.

Byzantine mosaic, Haghia Sophia

Turks have an uninhibited body language that is as emphatic as speech. They are unrestrained about enjoying themselves, but traditional segregation of the sexes means that groups of men sitting around smoking, drinking endless cups of *çay* (tea) and playing dominoes, cards or *tavla* (backgammon) are a common sight. A pronounced family ethos cements the generations, and festivals unite the extended family. It is all bound together by hospitality, an age-old Turkish tradition, in which food and drink play a central role.

Children are regarded as national treasures, but many families blame the advent of television and the Internet for eroding the discipline and respect for elders that were once sacred.

The Blue Mosque *(see pp88–9)* in Istanbul

Turkey's gradual transition to a modern, Western society received a major boost in 1952 when it became a member of the North Atlantic Treaty Organization (NATO). This brought advances in communications, transport and its defence policy. New roads, highways and projects to improve the tourism infrastructure changed the face of the country.

Traditional juice vendor

Modernization is, more than ever, the hallmark of Turkish society. Today, remote villages can boast of high-speed, fibre-optic telephone connections, but may lack adequate water or reliable electricity supplies. The Internet and mobile telephones have become essential accessories, and new housing projects are quickly festooned with satellite TV dishes.

MODERN TURKEY

For most Turks, the modern version of their ancient country dates from the founding of the Turkish Republic in 1923. Its architect was Mustafa Kemal – better known as Atatürk – a decorated former army officer who became Turkey's first President.

Atatürk set Turkey on the road to becoming a modern state. His reforms, strictly enacted, steered Turkey towards becoming European rather than Asian, and his status in the eyes of the Turkish nation has scarcely dimmed since his death. His picture is everywhere and his statue adorns almost every village square. Few statesmen have matched his integrity and style, and the soldier-turned-politician model still appeals strongly to Turks.

Democracy has proved much more difficult to implement than Western theoretical models. Turkey's military leaders, who intervened in politics in 1960, 1971 and 1980, keep a close eye on political life. In 1997, democratically elected prime minister, Necmettin Erbakan, was ousted from office for his overt religious leanings, but few Turks challenge the idea of a secular safety net. In November 2002 an Islamic party scored a victory in national elections, sweeping aside a decade of coalition party alliances whose populist tendencies overshadowed democratic reforms.

Soldiers mounting guard at the Atatürk Mausoleum *(see p244)*, **Ankara**

Children hard at work in school

Turks consider themselves Europeans, despite income gaps and social inequalities.

POPULATION MOVEMENT

In the 1960s, many Turks left for Germany to work under a government scheme offering remittances in foreign currency – an important source of export income. Many settled there, and 2.2 million Turks now call Germany their home. There are large Turkish communities in other EU states, too.

In Ottoman times, the state provided an all-encompassing social service to its citizens, who willingly complied with its ordered governance. Today, the role of the state is being redefined. Officials are elected and democracy is the goal of society. Many state-owned joint-stock companies and monopolies that put Turkey on its feet are scheduled for privatization. Several are well prepared for global competition but others view change as eroding a comfortable status quo.

Within Turkey, the trend has been for rural people to leave the land and seek a more stable life in urban areas. Few plan to return, even if city life is not what they hoped for. Some of Turkey's best-known films, such as *Sürü* (The Herd), and *Eşkıya* (The Bandit), highlight the common themes of identity, lifestyle and poverty. Turkey's indomitable spirit and vitality are best seen and appreciated in its proud people. Journeys invariably result in friendships. If a Turk declares himself your *arkadaş* (friend), he will be a steadfast soulmate long after your holiday memories have faded.

Folk dancers from the Black Sea

Maintaining a centralized state has placed a huge financial burden on Turks. Interest on international loans consumes a large chunk of public money, while the military budget exceeds that of health, social services and education. Since 2002, political and economic reforms have transformed Turkey. Inflation, running at 100 per cent in 2001, is now in single digits and the Turkish Lira has shed its awkward zeros (*see p397*). Many

Fish sold on the quayside along Istanbul's Golden Horn *(see p99)*

Landscape and Geology

Mountain ranges are Turkey's most distinctive
geographic feature, with the Taurus and Pontic
ranges enclosing the high Anatolian Plateau. The
mountains are geologically young, and the many
faulting and folding areas indicate that mountain
building is still active. In fact, 80 per cent of the
country lies in an extremely active tectonic zone,
and earthquakes are frequent. Turkey has eight
main drainage basins but the most important ones
are the Euphrates (Fırat) and the Tigris (Dicle).
About one quarter of Turkey is covered with forest,
with stands of pine, spruce and cedar, as well as
deciduous trees. About 13 per cent of this area
is productive; erosion, logging and fires have all
depleted forested areas.

Saklıkent Gorge *is typical of the
Mediterranean coastal region,
where steep valleys and gorges
bisect elongated mountain ridges.*

**İzmit, east of
Istanbul,** *was the
epicentre of the
1999 earthquake
that measured 7.4
on the Richter scale
and claimed the
lives of at least
25,000 people.*

PLATE MOVEMENTS

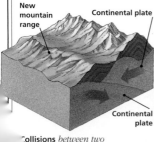

Strike-slip faulting *is found along
the North Anatolian Fault. When
rocks suddenly shift or move along
such fault lines, the tension is
released as an earthquake.*

Collisions *between two
continental plates result in crust
being pushed upwards to form
mountain ranges.*

KEY

— Fault line

→ Direction of plate
movement

The Mediterranean
*and Aegean coasts
are characterized by
mountain soils which
are clay-based and
red, brown and grey in
colour. Plains around
Adana and Antalya
support extensive food,
crop and horticultural
production.*

Lake Van *lies in a crater-like depression that became landlocked when lava flows from the adjacent Pleistocene-era volcano blocked the flow of water. Today, drainage from feeder streams fills the lake and only evaporation sustains a constant water level. It has a surface area of 3,713 sq km (1,440 sq miles) and a very high level of sodium carbonate.*

Pontic Mountains

BLACK SEA

Erzurum

Erzincan

Lake Van

Arabian Plate

Antakya

Adana

NEAN SEA

Taurus Mountains

GEOLOGY AND EARTHQUAKES

Turkey lies between three converging continental plates – the Anatolian, Eurasian and Arabian plates. As the Arabian plate moves northward into the Eurasian plate, it pushes the Anatolian plate westward, causing earthquakes along the North Anatolian Fault. Further west, the African plate pushes beneath the Anatolian plate, stretching the crust under the Aegean Sea. Tectonic activity is prevalent throughout Turkey.

East of Adıyaman, *the alluvial Mesopotamian plain lies between the Tigris and Euphrates rivers. This fertile area produces much of Turkey's wheat and cotton.*

Isolated Mediterranean bays *were, for centuries, havens for pirates. The Taurus Mountains made sections of the coast inaccessible, allowing peoples like the Lycians (1st and 2nd century BC) to resist Roman rule and retain their own language and culture. As harbours silted up, such civilizations declined.*

SOUTHEAST ANATOLIAN PROJECT (GAP)

This showpiece project was conceived during the 1980s to produce hydroelectric power by harnessing the flow of the Tigris and Euphrates rivers. Plans involve the building of 22 dams and 19 power plants spread over more than 1.7 million hectares (4.2 million acres) of land. The project is intended to help develop Turkey's poor eastern provinces, but critics argue that flooding 300,000 sq km (115,800 sq miles) will submerge ancient cultural treasures and displace local people.

The massive Atatürk Dam

Flora and Fauna of Turkey

Poppies,
central
Anatolia

Turkey offers much for the naturalist, with rich marine ecosystems, abundant birdlife and elusive larger mammals. The rugged eastern provinces still harbour large mammals such as bear, jackal, and wolf. The country is also floristically rich, with more than 11,000 plant species recorded. The tulip is perhaps the most famous of these. The great diversity of plants stems from the variety of habitats – from arid plains to mountains and temperate woodland – but also from Turkey's position as a "biological watershed" at the crossroads of Europe and Asia. There are huge tracts of unspoiled countryside, some of which have been set aside as national parks.

The Anatolian lynx *can still be found in upland areas, although its habitat is under threat.*

THE MEDITERRANEAN COAST

Large areas of the Mediterranean and Aegean coast are dominated by evergreen scrub, with Jerusalem sage, kermes oak, broom and sun roses among the common species. More open scrub areas contain orchids, bulbs and annuals. Tucked under bushes are hellebores and Comper's orchid with its distinctive trailing tassels. Arum lilies exude a fetid odour to entice pollinators. Late summer brings the spires of sea squill and sea daffodil. The carob tree sheds its pods in autumn while colchicum and sternbergias unfold.

Common sternbergia

WETLANDS

Here, dragonflies hover over flowering rush, waterlilies and irises, while water meadows fill with buttercups, bellevalia, marsh orchids and pale blue asyneumas. Despite international recognition of their diversity, Turkish wetlands are under threat from dams, drainage, pollution and climatic change. Surviving examples are Sultansazlığı near Niğde (see p289), Kuşcenneti National Park near Bursa (see p157), and the Göksu Delta (see p229).

Marsh orchid

WOODLANDS

Coniferous forests harbour stands of peonies, orchids, foxgloves, fritillaries and golden peas. The western Taurus range has an endemic subspecies of cedar of Lebanon, and in the north are forests of Oriental beech and fir, with rhododendron, ferns, lilies, primulas and campanulas. In autumn cyclamen and edible mushrooms appear. There are giant cedar at Dokuz Göl near Elmalı, endemic oak species at Kasnak near Eğirdir (see p254), and ancient mixed woodland, now threatened by a dam, in the Fırtına valley.

Peony

STEPPE

Despite their sparse appearance, the broad expanses of the Anatolian Plateau support many flowering plants. Highlights include stately asphodelines, which reach 1.8 m (6 ft) in height, purple gladioli, flax in yellow, pink or blue and the colourful parasite *Phelypaea coccinea*. On the eastern steppe are found the lovely white, purple or blue oncocyclus iris. Göreme National Park in Cappadocia and Nemrut Dağı National Park *(see p306)* are good places to see this flora. Deforestation and erosion have greatly altered the steppe, and intensive farming practices have accelerated this process.

Iberian oncocyclus

MOUNTAINS

In spring, subalpine meadows are carpeted with buttercups. Above the treeline, snow-drops, winter aconite and crocus crowd together near the snowmelt. These are followed by star-of-Bethlehem, grape hyacinth, fritillaries, foxtail lilies, asphode-lines and bright red tulips. Scree and rocky slopes are dotted with colourful alpine flowers like iris, rock jasmine and aubretia. Important mountain reserves include Kaçkar Mountains National Park near the Black Sea coast, Aladağlar National Park, Beyşehir Gölü National Park near Eğirdir *(see p254)* and the ski centres at Uludağ *(see p157)* and Erciyes *(see p288)*.

Snowdrop

BIRDS OF ANATOLIA

More than 440 species of bird have been recorded in Turkey, which offers a range of habitats from woodlands and mountains to wetlands and steppe. The country's position on the migratory flyways makes its a paradise for bird-watchers. Autumn offers the spectacle of vast flocks of migrating storks and raptors over the Bosphorus. In winter, lakes and wetlands hold thousands of wintering wildfowl.

Alpine chough *can be seen in the mountains, where they nest on ledges, nooks and crevices. They store food in cracks, which they cover with stones.*

Adult golden eagles *are resident, but the young of northern Europe migrate south in winter to the mountainous areas of the Mediterra-nean.*

Chukar partridge *is one of many game birds in Turkey, where hunting is a popular pastime.*

Serin *live in woodlands and vine-yards. Local populations are augmented by migra-tory birds in autumn.*

Hans and Caravanserais

Carved detail from the Sultanhanı

Dotted across Anatolia are many *hans* (storage depots) and *caravanserais* (hostelries) built in Seljuk and Ottoman times to protect merchants travelling the caravan routes that crossed Anatolia along the Roman-Byzantine road system. From the 13th century, the Seljuks built more than 100 *hans* to encourage trade.

It was under the Ottomans, though, that *hans* and *caravanserais* became a part of the state-sponsored social welfare system and played a key role in expanding Ottoman territory and influence. Several of these facilities can be visited today, and some have been turned into hotels or restaurants.

LOCATOR MAP

← *Major trade routes*

Camel caravans *laden with silks and spices from China made their way through Anatolia to the great commercial centre of Bursa (see pp162–7). Slaves from the Black Sea hinterland were another important trading commodity.*

Portal of the storage hall

A small mosque raised on arches stands in the centre of the courtyard.

A thick curtain wall surrounded the *caravanserai.*

The central gate provided the only entry to the fortified structure.

The central courtyard, *surrounded by arcades, provided shelter from the hot sun and contained apartments and a* hamam *(Turkish bath) to revive weary travellers.*

Corner turret for defence

The stone bridge *over the Köprü River near Antalya was built by the Seljuks near the site of a Roman bridge. The structure has been restored.*

Barrel-vaulted ceiling

A caravanserai at Mylasa, *a bustling commercial centre in western Anatolia, is shown in this 19th-century oil painting by the English artist, Richard Dadd.*

The octagonal lantern tower let light into the interior.

THE SULTANHANI

The Sultanhanı, near the central Anatolian city of Aksaray *(see pp292–3)*, is one of the best-preserved Seljuk *caravanserais*. Built between 1226 and 1229 for Sultan Alaeddin Keykubad *(see p250)*, the complex consisted of a courtyard surrounded by various amenities – stables, mosque, Turkish bath and accommodation – for the use of travellers, and a covered hall in which trade goods could be safely stored.

Five-aisled storage hall

The Cinci Hanı (see p268) *was an important fixture of the busy trading centre of Safranbolu, which lay on the key Black Sea caravan route.*

Accommodation for travellers was provided in two tiers of rooms.

The Kızlarağası Hanı *in İzmir* (see p178) *is an Ottoman han dating from 1744. Hans had the same amenities found at a caravanserai, together with storerooms, offices and rows of cell-like workshops, all grouped around a courtyard. The restored Kızlarağası Hanı houses a variety of cafés, shops and craft workshops.*

Customs and Traditions

Turkish customs have been passed down from generation to generation and are integrated into contemporary life. Climate, geography and ethnic background play a significant role, but many customs have their origins in Islam and have changed little over the years. An enduring faith is attached to the blue bead, or *mavi boncuk*, an amulet that protects the wearer from the evil eye. It may be seen dangling wherever good luck is needed.

Mavi boncuk

Religious and social mores dictate separate lives for many men and women, so customs bring them together for celebrations such as weddings, births and rites of passage. Family life is pivotal to Turkish culture, and communities are strengthened by the social and economic ties of the extended family.

In **Karagöz** *shadow puppet theatre, a cast of stock characters enact satiric themes. The puppets are three-dimensional cut-outs made from camel skin.*

CIRCUMCISION

For the celebration of his *sünnet*, or circumcision ritual, a boy is dressed in the satin uniform of a sergeant major, and his parents throw as lavish a celebration as they can afford. Relatives and friends proffer money as gifts for the young man, and the whole event is often photographed for the family album.

Gold coins attached to ribbons

Offerings *pinned to a pillow symbolize the gifts the young man will take into manhood.*

In line with Islamic tradition, *Turkish boys are circumcised between the ages of seven and 10. A lavish uniform is worn for this special occasion.*

VILLAGE WEDDINGS

Celebrations such as weddings may last for several days and involve a number of individual rituals. In the rural areas, families often approve and sanction wedding partners. The bride always has a *çeyiz* (trousseau) comprising lovely, handcrafted articles she and her mother have made for the new home.

Headscarves are worn by many rural women.

Village square (meydan)

Making flat bread *for the marriage feast is the responsibility of the women of the family. The tradition of making* katmer *or* gözleme *(crepes) is being revived in some parts of Turkey.*

Wedding festivities *in the picturesque village of Midyat, near the Syrian border, bring a large and appreciative crowd out to watch dancers performing.*

HANDICRAFTS

Craft skills were handed down from the Ottoman guild system, and Turkey has many skilled craftspeople. One example is *oya*, or needle lace, which is noted for its intricate floral designs crocheted in silk. These were originally crafted for a bride's trousseau. As late as the 1920s, wives crocheted them as part of their husband's headdress. Quilt-making, on the other hand, was traditionally passed down from the father.

Weaving *is a rural tradition and done mainly by women. Designs of carpets and* kilims *(see pp358–9) are handed down from one generation to the next.*

Copper and brass ware, *worked by hand, is an integral part of the Turkish household.*

Local markets *are the best places to look for traditional crafts. Shown here are handmade linens in Kalkan.*

Hand-printed textiles, *known as* yazma, *are a proud and venerable craft tradition in central Anatolian towns such as Tokat.*

Woodworking skills *were handed down from the Ottomans. Unique wooden walking sticks are made in Devrek, near the Black Sea. These wooden bowls were produced near Adana.*

TRADITIONAL DRESS

Traditionally, Turkish women wove their clothing according to individual designs, and dyed them using plant extracts. Today, each region has its own styles of *şalvar* (trousers worn by women) and head coverings such as *başörtüsü* (scarves).

A group of folk dancers *wears the traditional costume of the Van region. Folk dancing is hugely popular, with regional costumes as much a part of the show as music and laughter.*

Printed skirt

Full robe

Decorative headdress

NATIONAL SERVICE

All men over the age of 20 must serve 15 months of compulsory military service, and Turkish society still considers this to be a fundamental rite of passage to manhood. For rural youths, this may be their first time away from home, and *askerlik* (military service) fulfils a social role as a bridge to adulthood. The departing conscript may be required to visit friends and relatives to ask forgiveness for any wrongdoings and be presented with gifts and money before he reports for duty.

Young soldiers of the Turkish Army on duty

Islamic Art in Turkey

Tile detail

In Islamic art, the highest place is held by calligraphy, or the art of beautiful writing. This is because a calligrapher's prime task is writing the Holy Koran, believed by Muslims to be the word of God. In the purest forms of Islam, the use of animal forms in works of art is regarded as detracting from pious thoughts. Thus artists and craftsmen turned their talents to designs featuring geometric motifs and intricate foliage designs known as arabesques. As well as calligraphy, these highly disciplined forms included miniature paintings, jewellery, metal, tiles and ceramics, stone-carving and textiles. Under the Ottomans, the finest creations came from the Nakkaşhane, or sultan's design studio. Here, an apprentice system that lasted up to 10 years maintained the imperial traditions of excellence and innovation.

Ceramic tile panels contain messages taken from the Koran, executed in Arabic or Kufic script.

Calligraphic inscription in embossed metal

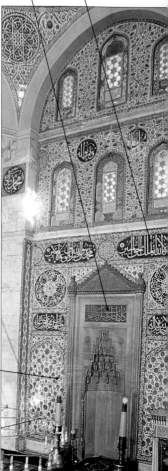

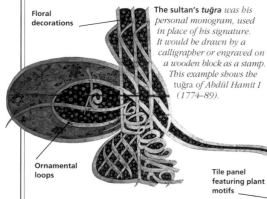

Floral decorations

The sultan's *tuğra* *was his personal monogram, used in place of his signature. It would be drawn by a calligrapher or engraved on a wooden block as a stamp. This example shows the tuğra of Abdül Hamit I (1774–89).*

Ornamental loops

Tile panel featuring plant motifs

Floral tile motif

Koranic texts *provided templates for woodcarvers, metal-workers, weavers and ceramic painters. Although highly decorative, Islamic art is filled with meaning: the tulip (lâle), a much-used motif, is an anagram for Allah.*

SOKOLLU MEHMET PAŞA MOSQUE IN KADIRGA, ISTANBUL

Designed by Sinan (1577–8) for a distinguished grand vizier, the prayer hall features a beautiful *qibla* (wall of the mosque at right angles to the direction of Mecca). The calligraphic decoration includes exquisite tilework and stone-carving.

Inscription in metal

Tilework on squinches supporting the dome

The minaret *of the Green Mosque (Yeşil Camii) in İznik (see p160) features complex patterns of coloured tiles. The mosque, which was completed in 1378, takes its name from the richly decorated minaret.*

This tile panel is set into the the stone wall.

The conical roof of the *minbar (see p32)* features polychrome tiling.

Stained-glass windows

THE ART OF THE OTTOMAN MINIATURE

Ottoman miniature painting was primarily a courtly art form, which reached a peak of development in the late 16th century during the rule of Süleyman the Magnificent *(see p55)*. Miniature painting was influenced by Persian art, with many of the finest Persian minaturists being brought to work at the court workshops of Topkapı Palace *(see pp68–71)*. As well as illustrations for manuscripts of Koranic texts and Persian epics – Persian was the language of the Ottoman court – a unique style was developed to record the history of the dynasty. This included battle scenes, palace rituals, major festivals and topographical scenes. By the 17th century, miniature painters had mastered three-dimensional representation, while the 18th century heralded a more naturalistic style and a broadening of subjects to include landscapes, still lifes and portraits. Although there were a number of celebrated miniature artists, these exquisite works were, for the most part, neither signed nor dated.

An Arabic inscription *winds around a gravestone in the grounds of the Alanya Museum (see p226).*

A tile panel *over the entrance to the Mausoleum of Selim II, in the precincts of Haghia Sophia in Istanbul, shows a masterful integration of calligraphy and organic motifs.*

Early 17th-century miniature showing Hasan, grandson of Mohammed, on his deathbed

Ottoman Architecture

İznik tile detail

From Albania to Tripoli, and from Baghdad to Bosnia, the Ottomans left superb examples of their architectural skills. Nowhere is this more apparent than in Istanbul, where the sultans built beautiful mosques, palaces and *külliyes* (Islamic charitable institutions).

Ottoman architecture is marked by a strict hierarchy of forms, scales and materials, reflecting the rank of a building's patron. Mosques commissioned by members of the Ottoman family, for example, were the only ones entitled to two or more minarets. Another distinguishing feature is the influence of Byzantine architecture. Many architects, among them Mimar Sinan *(see p101)*, were of Greek or Armenian origin.

Ornamental fountains (*çeşme*) *were built in busy central squares or markets. This example is in the bazaar in Kayseri* (see pp290–91).

THE EARLY OTTOMAN MOSQUE

The earliest form of the Ottoman mosque consisted of a single large prayer hall covered by a hemispheric dome, with a covered porch and minaret outside. The Junior Hacı Özbek Mosque (1333) in İznik is considered the earliest example of this form. It was modified by adding bays (often covered by small domes) around the central dome, and by the addition of a covered portico and arcaded courtyard.

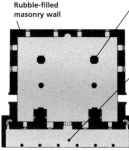

Rubble-filled masonry wall

A pier supports the central dome.

The pillared portico is covered by seven domes.

A ground plan of the Selimiye Mosque shows the domed bays surrounding the central hall.

The Selimiye Mosque, *in Konya (see pp250–51), was started in 1558 by Sultan Selim II when he was governor of Konya. It was finished in 1587. Clearly visible is the bulk of the central prayer hall, which is topped by a hemispheric dome. The mosque adjoins the Mevlâna Museum.*

THE LATER OTTOMAN MOSQUE

The form of the Ottoman mosque underwent a dramatic evolution in the years following the conquest of Constantinople. The Ottomans frequently converted Orthodox churches, notably Haghia Sophia *(see pp82–5)*, into mosques. Under the influence of such models, architects began to create higher, single-domed mosques, and greatly open up the interior space.

The Şehzade Mosque *(also called the Prince's Mosque) in Istanbul was the first imperial mosque built by the architect, Mimar Sinan (see p101). It was commissioned in 1543 by Süleyman the Magnificent.*

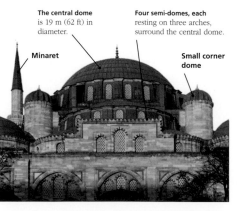

The central dome is 19 m (62 ft) in diameter.

Four semi-domes, each resting on three arches, surround the central dome.

Minaret

Small corner dome

FOUNTAINS (ŞADIRVAN)

Based on the Koranic principle that water is the source of life, the provision of public water supplies was a civic duty. Every town had its *çeşme* (public fountain), and *külliyes* offered *sebil* (free distribution of water). The *şadırvan* was placed in a mosque courtyard for the performance of ritual ablutions.

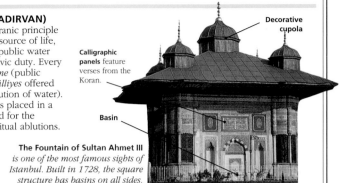

Decorative cupola

Calligraphic panels feature verses from the Koran.

Basin

The Fountain of Sultan Ahmet III *is one of the most famous sights of Istanbul. Built in 1728, the square structure has basins on all sides.*

THE KONAK

Like many other Ottoman buildings, the *konak* (mansion house) consisted of a wooden structure built on a foundation of stone and brick to withstand the cold Anatolian winter. The ground floor contained granaries, stables and storage areas. The kitchens and public rooms were on the first floor, with the private quarters on the top floor.

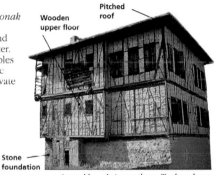

Pitched roof

Wooden upper floor

Living areas *had sofas (upholstered benches) along the walls. The nook shown here is in a konak that has been turned into a hotel in Safranbolu (see pp268–9).*

Stone foundation

A rural konak *in northern Turkey shows the typical three-storey form. Some had separate entrances for the* harem *(women's quarters) and* selamlık *(men's quarters).*

YALI

The *yalı* (waterfront villa), is found along the Bosphorus. Most *yalıs* were built during the 18th and 19th centuries as grand summer residences for wealthy citizens of Ottoman Istanbul. Sited to make maximum use of the waterside location, they also incorporated boathouses or moorings.

Wood was the main building material.

Decorative pilasters

The waterside location provided easy access and maximum visibility.

Yalıs were built *in a variety of forms and architectural styles, from simple wooden structures to this lavish Russian-style mansion.*

BUILDING TYPES

Bedesten Covered stone market

Çeşme Public water fountain

Daruşşifa Hospital

Hamam Bath house *(see p//)*

İmaret Soup kitchen

Külliye Educational/charitable complex surrounding a major mosque *(see pp32–3)*

Medrese Theological college *(see pp32–3)*

Mescit Small prayer hall

Tekke Dervish lodge

Tımarhane Lunatic asylum

Türbe Tomb

Exploring Mosques

Five times a day throughout Istanbul a chant is broadcast over loudspeakers set high in the city's minarets to call the faithful to prayer. Over 99 per cent of the population is Muslim, though the Turkish state is officially secular. Most belong to the Sunni branch of Islam, but there are also a few Shiites. Both follow the teachings of the Koran, the sacred book of Islam, and the Prophet Mohammed (c.570–632), but Shiites accept, in addition, the authority of a line of 12 imams directly descended from Mohammed. Islamic mystics are known as Sufis *(see p255)*.

Overview of the impressive Süleymaniye Mosque complex

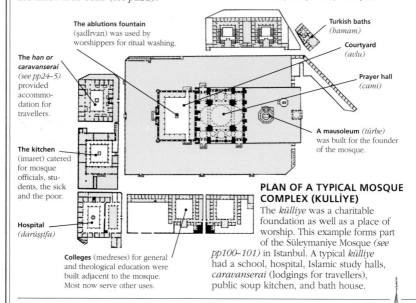

The ablutions fountain (şadırvan) was used by worshippers for ritual washing.

The *han or caravanserai* (see pp24–5) provided accommodation for travellers.

The kitchen (imaret) catered for mosque officials, students, the sick and the poor.

Hospital (*darüşşifa*)

Colleges (medreses) for general and theological education were built adjacent to the mosque. Most now serve other uses.

Turkish baths (*hamam*)

Courtyard (*avlu*)

Prayer hall (*cami*)

A mausoleum (*türbe*) was built for the founder of the mosque.

PLAN OF A TYPICAL MOSQUE COMPLEX (KULLİYE)

The *külliye* was a charitable foundation as well as a place of worship. This example forms part of the Süleymaniye Mosque *(see pp100–101)* in Istanbul. A typical *külliye* had a school, hospital, Islamic study halls, *caravanserai* (lodgings for travellers), public soup kitchen, and bath house.

INSIDE A MOSQUE

The prayer hall of a great mosque can offer visitors a soaring sense of space. Islam forbids images of living things (human or animal) inside a mosque, so there are never any statues or figurative paintings, but the geometric and abstract architectural details of the interior can be exquisite. Men and women pray separately. Women often use a screened-off area or a balcony.

The *müezzin mahfili* *is a platform found in large mosques. The* muezzin *(mosque official) stands on this when chanting responses to the prayers of the* imam *(head of the mosque).*

The *mihrab*, *a niche in the wall, marks the direction of Mecca. The prayer hall is laid out so that most people can see the mihrab.*

The *minbar* *is a lofty pulpit to the right of the mihrab. This is used by the imam when he delivers the Friday sermon (khutba).*

MUSLIM BELIEFS AND PRACTICES

Muslims believe in God (Allah), and the Koran shares many prophets and stories with the Bible. However, whereas for Christians Jesus is the son of God, Muslims hold that he was just one in a line of prophets – the last being Mohammed, who brought the final revelation of God's truth to mankind. Muslims believe that Allah communicated the sacred texts of the Koran to Mohammed through the archangel Gabriel.

Muslims have five basic duties. The first of these is the profession of faith: "There is no God but Allah, and Mohammed is his Prophet". Muslims are also enjoined to pray five times a day, give alms to the poor, and fast during the month of Ramazan (see p36). Once during their lifetime, if they can afford it, they should make the pilgrimage (haj) to Mecca (in Saudi Arabia), the site of the Kaaba, a sacred shrine built by Abraham, and also the birthplace of the Prophet.

The call to prayer *used to be given by the muezzin from the balcony of the minaret. Now-adays loudspeakers broadcast the call. Only imperial mosques have more than one minaret.*

PRAYER TIMES

The five daily prayer times are calculated according to the times of sunrise and sunset, and thus change throughout the year. Exact times are posted on boards outside large mosques. Those given here are a guide.

Prayer	Summer	Winter
Sabah	5am	7am
Öğle	1pm	1pm
İkindi	6pm	4pm
Akşam	8pm	6pm
Yatsı	9:30pm	8pm

When praying, *Muslims face the Kaaba in Mecca, even if they are not in a mosque, where the mihrab indicates the right direction. Kneeling and lowering the head to the ground are gestures of humility and respect for Allah.*

Ritual ablutions *must be undertaken before prayer. Worshippers wash their head, hands and feet either at the fountain in the courtyard or at taps set in a wall of the mosque.*

VISITING A MOSQUE

Visitors are welcome at any mosque in Turkey, but non-Muslims should avoid visiting at prayer times, especially the main weekly congregation and sermon on Fridays. Take off your shoes before entering the prayer hall. Shoulders and knees should be covered. In remote areas women should cover their head with a scarf but main touristic mosques insist less on this. Do not eat, take photographs with a flash or stand very close to worshippers. A contribution to a donation box or mosque official is courteous.

Board outside a mosque giving times of prayers

The loge (hünkar mahfili) *provided the sultan with a screened-off balcony where he could pray, safe from would-be assassins.*

The kürsü, *seen in some mosques, is a throne used by the imam while he reads extracts from the Koran.*

TURKEY THROUGH THE YEAR

Turkey's national and regional holidays fall into three categories: religious feasts celebrated throughout the Islamic world, festivities associated with events or people in Turkish history, and traditional festivals, usually with a seasonal theme. The joyful spirit is tangible on public holidays and religious feast days when old and young, rich and poor unite and extended families gather.

Folk dancers

Regional events celebrate Turkey's diverse origins in terms of music, folklore, sport and the performing arts. Urban centres like İzmir and Istanbul host well-publicized festivals, but smaller towns also stage lively celebrations. *Luna park* (fun fairs) are wildly popular. The passage of the seasons is important, as many venues are outdoors. In the eastern provinces, harsh winters restrict the types of events that can be staged.

SPRING

This is the best season for visiting Turkey. Temperatures are comfortable and the days longer and warmer. Many places receive a facelift after winter and restaurants arrange their tables outdoors. This is also the time to see Turkey's wild flower displays. Most tourist attractions, such as the historic sights, are far less crowded and thus more peaceful at this time of year.

Turkish children paying their respects to the memory of Atatürk

MARCH

International Film Festival *(late Mar–mid-Apr)*, Istanbul. Various cinemas in the city screen a selection of Turkish and foreign films.

APRIL

Tulip Festival *(Apr–May)*, Emirgan, Istanbul. A colourful celebration of the flower that originated in Turkey, held in a chic suburb north of the Fatih Bridge.

Tulips in Emirgan Park, scene of the Tulip Festival in spring

National Sovereignty and Children's Day *(23 Apr)*. Anniversary of the first Grand National Assembly that convened in Ankara in 1920. Children from all around Turkey commemorate the life of the revered Atatürk.
ANZAC Day *(24–25 Apr)*, Çanakkale and Gallipoli Peninsula *(see pp168–9)*. Representatives from Australia, New Zealand and Turkey commemorate the courage in battle displayed by both sides in World War I.

MAY

Yunus Emre Culture and Art Week *(6–10 May)*, Eskişehir *(see p257)*. A week-long commemoration of the life and devotional love poetry of the 13th-century mystic, Yunus Emre.

Memorial at Gallipoli

Marmaris International Yachting Festival *(2nd week in May)*, at Marmaris *(see pp200–201)*. Mainly a convention for yacht owners, brokers and buyers, this event fills the marina with all kinds of vessels and is sure to appeal to anyone interested in yachting.
National Youth and Sports Day *(19 May)*. Celebrated all over the country to mark Atatürk's birthdate in 1881 and the anniversary of his arrival in the town of Samsun *(see p265)* in 1919 to plan the War of Independence.
Conquest of Istanbul *(May 29)*, Istanbul. The anniversary of Constantinople's capture by Sultan Mehmet the Conqueror in 1453.
Cirit Games *(May–Sep; see September p36)*.

Turkey's beaches, popular with locals and visitors in summer

SUMMER

Turks take their holidays seriously, and summer sees coastal areas of the Aegean and Mediterranean, in particular, crowded with university students and families on the move. Those city-dwellers lucky enough to own a summer house usually move to the coast to escape the oppressive heat when the school holidays begin in June.

Turkey's beaches offer opportunities for all kinds of activities, and resorts such as Bodrum and Marmaris are renowned for their active nightlife. Be on the look-out for impromptu festivals involving grease-wrestling or folk dancing, for example. Although local tourist offices have information on events in their area, these may not be well publicized and full details may be unavailable until just prior to the event.

JUNE

Kafkasör Culture and Arts Festival *(second week Jun)*, Artvin *(see p275).* A festival in an alpine meadow that offers country handicrafts, folk dancing and singing, as well as bull wrestling.
Istanbul Festival of Arts and Culture *(mid-Jun–mid-Jul),* venues around the city. A prestigious event for opera, theatre and ballet performances. Both Turkish and Western classical music are featured and the highlight is a one-night performance of Mozart's *Abduction from the Seraglio,* which is authentically staged at the Topkapı Palace.
Kırkpınar Festival and Grease Wrestling Championship *(last week Jun),* Edirne *(see pp152–3).* A popular event with men, in which the contenders, in *kıspet* (leather breeches) and smeared with olive oil, compete for the coveted honour in this traditional national sport.
International Opera and Ballet Festival *(Jun–mid-Jul),* Aspendos *(see p221).* The Roman amphitheatre is the venue for thrilling, open-air performances of opera, ballet and orchestral music. Visitors can also enjoy a picnic at the site before performances.

International Opera and Ballet Festival poster, Aspendos

JULY

Navy Day *(1 Jul).* This holiday has some symbolism for Turks as it commemorates the anniversary of the end of the capitulations, or trade concessions, granted by the Ottoman sultans to a number of European powers from the mid-16th century onwards.
International Hittite Festival *(first week Jul),* Çorum *(see p294).* Students of Hittite art and culture and enthusiasts from around the globe gather for this annual event to attend lectures, debates and related outings.

AUGUST

Troy Festival *(10–15 Aug),* Çanakkale *(see p174).* Dance, theatre and art events that attract foreign performers.
Hacı Bektaş Commemorative Ceremony *(mid-Aug),* Avanos *(see p283).* Annual ceremony held in remembrance of Hacı Bektaş Veli, the mystic and philosopher who founded an Islamic sect based on the principles of unity and human tolerance.

Grease-wrestling tournament

Turkish Grand Prix *(third week Aug),* Otodram, Tuzla and Istanbul. One leg of this Formula One racing event is held at the purpose-built Grand Prix Circuit.
International İzmir Festival *(last week Aug–early Sep),* İzmir *(see pp178–9).* An excellent programme for connoisseurs of music, ballet and theatre. Some performances also take place at Çeşme and Ephesus.
Victory Day *(30 Aug).* This day, known as Zafer Bayramı, is celebrated throughout Turkey. It celebrates the victory of the Turkish Republican army over the Greeks at the battle of Dumlupınar in 1922 during the War of Independence.

Racing yachts competing in Marmaris Race Week

AUTUMN

Autumn is an ideal time for visiting Turkey. The rural regions have grape or wine festivals and many villages celebrate their successful harvests of wheat, apricots, cotton or other crops. In coastal regions, the sea is still warm and watersports can continue well into October. Along the south coast, warm weather can last until quite late in November.

Watermelon cart, Diyarbakır

SEPTEMBER

Cirit Games *(May–Sep)*, Erzurum *(see pp318–319)*. Cirit originated with nomads from Central Asia. It is a rough-and-tumble cross between polo and javelin-throwing in which horse and rider enjoy equal prestige. The games take place every Sunday. **Kaş-Lycia Culture and Art Festival** *(first week Sep)*, Kaş. Renowned for its superb performances of contemporary dance and theatre, as well as painting exhibits. **Tango Festival** *(second week in Sep)*, in Marmaris *(see pp200–201)*. A popular six-day event in which couples follow the lead of professional dance couples. **Watermelon Festival** *(16–23 Sep)*, Diyarbakır *(see pp310–311)*. One of only a few festivals in eastern Turkey, this one focuses on the gigantic watermelons grown by the local farmers. **Cappadocia Grape Harvest Festival** *(mid-Sep)*, Ürgüp *(see p283)*. Celebration of local food and wine in an area that has been called the birthplace of viticulture.

OCTOBER

Golden Orange Film Festival *(first week Oct)*, Antalya *(see pp218–19)*. Turkish-language films and those with a local flavour now feature more prominently in this festival that has been going for over 20 years. **International Bodrum Cup Regatta** *(third week of Oct)*,

Horse and rider at the Cirit Games in Erzurum

Bodrum *(see pp198–9)*. This regatta is open to several classes of wooden yachts only. Both Turkish and foreign yachtsmen compete. **Race Week** *(last week Oct to first week Nov)*, Marmaris *(see pp200–201)*. In-and offshore races held in three divisions under authority of the Turkish Sailing Federation. There is also a fancy-dress night, and cocktail and dinner parties. **Republic Day** *(29 Oct)*. This important national holiday commemorates the proclamation of the Turkish Republic in 1923.

NOVEMBER

Atatürk Commemoration Day *(10 Nov)*. Atatürk's death in 1938 is recalled each year with a poignant one-minute silence. This show of respect is observed throughout the country at 9:05am, the exact moment the revered leader passed away in Istanbul's Dolmabahçe Palace. Everything in the country grinds to a halt – people and even the traffic stops.

MUSLIM HOLIDAYS

The dates of the Muslim calendar and its holy days are governed by the phases of the moon and therefore change from year to year. In the holy month of **Ramazan**, Muslims do not eat or drink between dawn and dusk. Some restaurants are closed during the day and tourists should be discreet when eating in public. Straight after this follows the three-day **Şeker Bayramı** (Sugar Festival), when sweetmeats are prepared. Two months and 10 days later, a four-day celebration, **Kurban Bayramı** (Feast of the Sacrifice), commemorates the Koranic version of Abraham's sacrifice. This is the main annual public holiday in Turkey, and hotels, trains and roads are packed.

Whirling Dervishes at the Mevlevi Monastery in Istanbul

WINTER

When the street vendors begin roasting chestnuts in Ankara and Istanbul, it is a sign that winter is near. Both cities can be damp and cold. Ankara frequently has temperatures below freezing and much snow. This is when coastal regions have their rainy season. Winter is a good time for visitors to explore Turkey's museums, as major sights are open and uncrowded. The ski centres (*see p384*) at Palandöken (*see p319*) and Uludağ (*see p157*) have their busiest season from December to April, and offer activities both on and off the slopes.

Turks do not celebrate Christmas, but most hotel chains offer a special menu on the day. New Year's Day, however, is an official holiday throughout Turkey. It is celebrated heartily in restaurants and at home, and a lavish meal is served. Often the main course is turkey! Visitors are always welcome to join in these celebrations, but advance booking is advisable for popular places. Some establishments that close for the winter open again just for the New Year's Eve celebrations.

DECEMBER

St Nicholas Symposium and Festival (*first week Dec*), Demre (*see p216*). Visitors who have an interest in the legend of Santa Claus will not want to miss this symposium and the discussions and ceremonies that accompany it. A host of related debates is organized, and pilgrimages are made to the 4th century church of St Nicholas in Demre, located near Antalya, and to the birthplace of Nicholas in Patara, near Kaş.
Mevlâna Festival (*10–17 Dec*), Konya (*see pp250–51*). A festival that commemorates Celaleddin Rumi (*see p255*),

the mystic who founded the Mevlevi order. This is the only time that the whirling dervishes are in residence in their home city and offers one of the best performances anywhere in Turkey.

JANUARY

New Year's Day (*1 Jan*). A national holiday.
Camel Wrestling (*mid-Jan*), Selçuk (*see p180*). Premier championship event held in the ruined Roman theatre at Ephesus (*see pp182–3*).

FEBRUARY

Camel Wrestling (*through Feb*), Aydın, İzmir and other Aegean towns. Impromptu camel wrestling bouts (*deve güreşi*) that coincide with the mating season (Dec–Feb), after which male camels become docile again.

A champion camel, adorned with tassels and rugs

NATIONAL HOLIDAYS
New Year's Day (1 Jan)
National Sovereignty and Children's Day *Ulusal Egemenlik ve Çocuk Bayramı* (23 Apr)
National Youth and Sports Day *Gençlik ve Spor Günü* (19 May)
Conquest of Istanbul (May 29)
Navy Day *Denizcilik Günü* (1 Jul)
Victory Day *Zafer Bayramı* (30 Aug)
Republic Day *Cumhuriyet Bayramı* (29 Oct)
Atatürk Commemoration Day (10 Nov)

New Year's celebrations in Istanbul

The Climate of Turkey

Turkey's mountainous terrain and maritime influence have created diverse climatic regions. The Aegean and Mediterranean coasts enjoy mean temperatures of 29°C (84°F) in July and 9°C (48°F) in January. Rain falls mainly in winter; Antalya receives an annual average of 991 mm (39 in). Along the Black Sea, rainfall is heavier, averaging 2,438 mm (96 in) a year. The rugged northeast has warm summers, but severe winters, with temperatures averaging -9°C (16°F). Precipitation is more evenly spread throughout the year, and snow lasts 120 days. The central plateau has hot, dry summers averaging 23°C (73°F) and cold, moist winters, when temperatures average below 0°C (32°F).

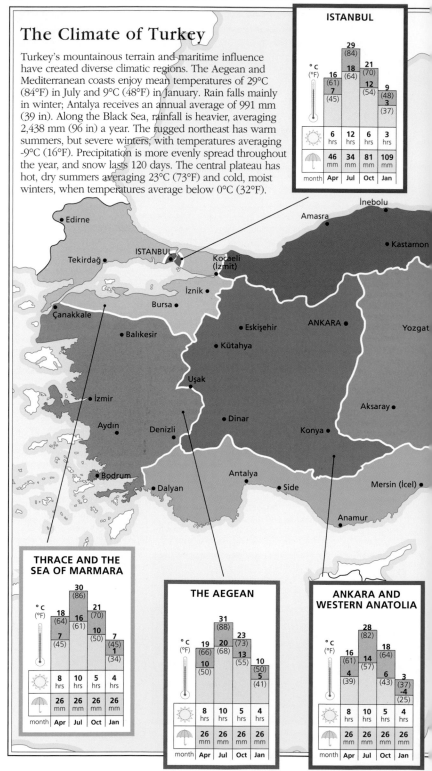

ISTANBUL

°C (°F)			
16 (61)	29 (84)	21 (70)	
7 (45)	18 (64)	12 (54)	9 (48)
			3 (37)

month	Apr	Jul	Oct	Jan
☀	6 hrs	12 hrs	6 hrs	3 hrs
☂	46 mm	34 mm	81 mm	109 mm

İnebolu

Amasra

• Kastamon

• Edirne

Tekirdağ •

ISTANBUL

Kocaeli (İzmit)

İznik •

Bursa •

Çanakkale

• Balıkesir

• Eskişehir

ANKARA •

Yozgat

• Kütahya

Uşak •

• İzmir

Aydın

Denizli

• Dinar

Aksaray •

Konya •

• Bodrum

• Dalyan

Antalya

• Side

Mersin (İcel) •

Anamur

THRACE AND THE SEA OF MARMARA

°C (°F)			
18 (64)	30 (86)	21 (70)	
7 (45)	16 (61)	10 (50)	7 (45)
			1 (34)

month	Apr	Jul	Oct	Jan
☀	8 hrs	10 hrs	5 hrs	4 hrs
☂	26 mm	26 mm	26 mm	26 mm

THE AEGEAN

°C (°F)			
19 (66)	31 (88)	23 (73)	
10 (50)	20 (68)	13 (55)	10 (50)
			5 (41)

month	Apr	Jul	Oct	Jan
☀	8 hrs	10 hrs	5 hrs	4 hrs
☂	26 mm	26 mm	26 mm	26 mm

ANKARA AND WESTERN ANATOLIA

°C (°F)			
16 (61)	28 (82)	18 (64)	
4 (39)	14 (57)	6 (43)	3 (37)
			-4 (25)

month	Apr	Jul	Oct	Jan
☀	8 hrs	10 hrs	5 hrs	4 hrs
☂	26 mm	26 mm	26 mm	26 mm

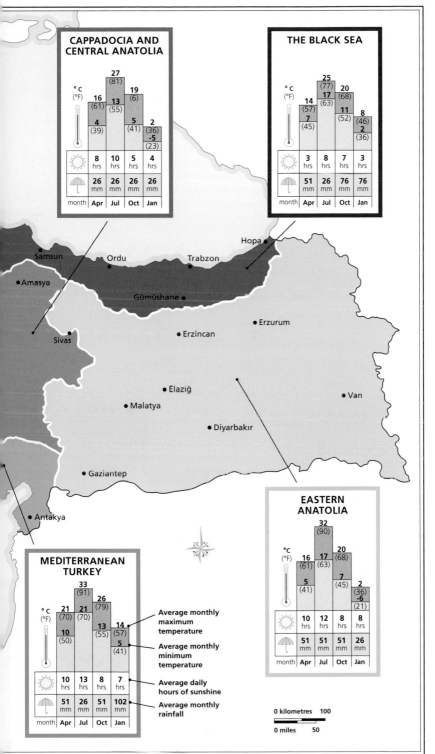

CAPPADOCIA AND CENTRAL ANATOLIA

°C (°F)

16 (61)	27 (81)	19 (6)	
4 (39)	13 (55)	5 (41)	2 (36)
			-5 (23)

month	Apr	Jul	Oct	Jan
☀	8 hrs	10 hrs	5 hrs	4 hrs
☂	26 mm	26 mm	26 mm	26 mm

THE BLACK SEA

°C (°F)

14 (57)	25 (77)	20 (68)	
7 (45)	17 (63)	11 (52)	8 (46)
			2 (36)

month	Apr	Jul	Oct	Jan
☀	3 hrs	8 hrs	7 hrs	3 hrs
☂	51 mm	26 mm	76 mm	76 mm

Hopa

Samsun   Ordu   Trabzon

Amasya

Gümüşhane

Erzurum

Sivas   Erzincan

Elazığ   Van

Malatya

Diyarbakır

Gaziantep

Antakya

MEDITERRANEAN TURKEY

°C (°F)

21 (70)	33 (91)	26 (79)	
10 (50)	21 (70)	13 (55)	14 (57)
			5 (41)

Average monthly maximum temperature

Average monthly minimum temperature

month	Apr	Jul	Oct	Jan
☀	10 hrs	13 hrs	8 hrs	7 hrs
☂	51 mm	26 mm	51 mm	102 mm

Average daily hours of sunshine

Average monthly rainfall

EASTERN ANATOLIA

°C (°F)

16 (61)	32 (90)	20 (68)	
5 (41)	17 (63)	7 (45)	2 (36)
			-6 (21)

month	Apr	Jul	Oct	Jan
☀	10 hrs	12 hrs	8 hrs	8 hrs
☂	51 mm	51 mm	51 mm	26 mm

0 kilometres   100

0 miles   50

THE HISTORY OF TURKEY

*T*he history of Turkey is as ancient as that of humankind. Known as Anatolia and previously as Asia Minor, this land has witnessed the rise and fall of many great and advanced civilizations, from the early Hittites to the Persians, Lydians, Greeks, Romans, Byzantines and Ottomans. A singular heritage of splendid art and architecture bears the mark of an often tumultuous past.

Long before great empires such as the Persian, Roman, Byzantine and Ottoman began to exploit the strategic position of Asia Minor, important ancient civilizations flourished in the fertile river valleys, on the windswept, arid interior plains and along the southern coastline of Anatolia. The early communities were replaced by successive waves of migration that saw the rise and fall of new cultures, each of which left reminders of its dominance and glory and contributed to the astoundingly varied cultural tapestry that forms the basis of today's proud, modern republic.

Female figurine,
Alacahöyük
(c.1270 BC)

PREHISTORIC TURKEY
Stone tools as well as various other crude artifacts, animal bones and food fossils from the Old Stone Age that were found near Burdur north of Antalya *(see pp218–19)*, prove that people have lived in Turkey since 20,000 BC. The earliest inhabitants were nomadic hunter-gatherers who migrated in response to changing weather patterns and seasons. They followed the wild animal herds they depended upon for their sustenance, clothing, tools and weapons.

THE FERTILE CRESCENT
The earliest permanent settlers were the prehistoric farming communities of Mesopotamia, living in the well-watered stretch of land between the Tigris and Euphrates rivers in what is now northern Syria and Iraq.

Around 10,000 BC groups of people began to settle in Anatolia, where they raised crops of wheat and barley. They also kept domestic animals such as sheep, goats and cattle, and used dogs to protect and herd their livestock. These early farmers were the first to venture beyond the boundaries of the Fertile Crescent, establishing communities along the Mediterranean and Red Sea, as well as around the Persian Gulf. Here, the archaeological remains of Neolithic villages date back to 8000 BC, and by 7000 BC countless thriving settlements had sprung up.

It was during this period that people discovered how to smelt metal and work with it. They developed methods of extracting and casting various useful objects such as weapons, as well as ornamental items. The earliest items cast from copper were made in Anatolia around 5000 BC.

TIMELINE

20,000 BC Old Stone Age settlement north of Antalya			*Hand axe*		**10,000 BC** End of Old Stone Age in Anatolia	
20,000 BC	18,000 BC	16,000 BC	14,000 BC	12,000 BC	10,000 BC	8000 BC

Flint spear tips

17,000 BC Paleolithic hunter-gatherers fashion flint spear tips

9000 BC Emergence of modern humans in Anatolia

◁ **Constantine IX Monomachus, ruler of the Byzantine Empire from 1042 to 1055**

THE FIRST TOWN

Together with Hacılar, Çatalhöyük *(see p254)* near Konya was possibly the world's first town. It had a population of around 5,000 people and is thought to have been the largest settlement at the time. Most of its inhabitants were farmers, but there was also brisk trade in obsidian (volcanic glass), brought into workshops from nearby volcanoes and used to fashion sharp cutting tools.

Archaeologists have been able to determine with certainty that Çatalhöyük's houses were sturdy structures built of brick and timber. The architectural designs also reflect the demands of an advanced culture that valued comfort. They typically feature separate living quarters and cooking areas, as well as several sheds and a number of store rooms.

Cattle seem to have played a rather important part in this ancient culture of Anatolia. This is evident from the fact that many of the rooms that were excavated at Çatalhöyük were decorated with elaborate wall paintings depicting cows, as well as clay heads with real horns moulded in relief onto the walls. Since Çatalhöyük's people had animistic beliefs, it has been suggested that the murals and bull's-head emblems could point to the practice of ritual or cult activities. Similarly, small terracotta figurines of a voluptuous female deity (the mother goddess) probably played a part in fertility rites, offerings or other religious ceremonies.

Flint dagger with bone handle

THE COPPER AGE

By the Copper Age (from about 5500 to 3000 BC), farming had become a way of life and people were raising crops and animals for a living. The increase in agricultural activity created a growing need for tools and implements. Methods for ore extraction and smelting were refined and passed on from father to son. Copper implements were widely used. Focal points of this period were Hacılar and Canhasan, both of which also manufactured fine pottery items, using advanced techniques. Their attractive clay vessels were decorated with distinctive multicoloured backgrounds.

THE BRONZE AGE

Between 3000–1200 BC, the Anatolian metalworkers began to experiment with various techniques and developed new skills. Their workshops produced a surplus of goods and a brisk trade began to flourish. Among these items were gold jewellery, ornaments, belts, drinking vessels and statuettes of the mother goddess.

Artist's impression of Çatalhöyük, possibly the world's first town

TIMELINE

8000 BC Start of the Neolithic period in Anatolia

Statuette of mother goddess, Çatalhöyük

5600 BC Fertility figurines made of terracotta at Hacılar and Çatalhöyük

8000 BC	7000 BC	6000 BC	5000 BC

7250–7500 BC Community at Cayonu near Diyarbaklr farms with sheep and goats

6800 BC Çatalhöyük develops into a farming town of 5,000 people

Terracotta jar from Canhasan

5000 BC Pottery begins to combine functionality with attractive design

THE ASSYRIANS

The empire of Assyria developed in northern Mesopotamia sometime in the 3rd millennium BC. It expanded and, by about 1900 BC, a network of Assyrian trading colonies had been established. Commerce between northern Mesopotamia and Anatolia began to take shape.

As trade goods circulated, the demand for them quickly grew and merchants found themselves catering to a rapidly expanding market.

The Assyrians grasped the importance of keeping track of their transactions, and developed a writing system using cuneiform symbols to represent words. Their trade agreements and accounts were imprinted on clay tablets, several of which have been preserved. The commercial records that were found at the Assyrian trading colony at Kanesh (modern Kültepe, see p291)

Assyrian clay 'letter' and envelope

are the earliest examples of writing to have been discovered in Anatolia.

Lively trade meant increased travel and demands on transport. Some areas saw the introduction of simple taxation systems. For the first time in history, money came to be regarded as the primary source of wealth, and envy, conflict and violence ensued as communities sought to protect territories, routes and resources from outsiders.

Not all inhabitants of the area presently occupied by Turkey gathered in central Anatolia. The city of Troy, immortalized by Homer and Virgil, stood at the strategic entrance to the Dardanelles Straits (see p168). Some scholars believe that the fall of Troy, as told in Homer's *Iliad*, coincides with the end of the Bronze Age, an era that had helped to establish an artistic and civilized culture in which the next civilization, the Hittites, would thrive and flourish.

HELEN OF TROY

According to Greek mythology Helen was the most beautiful woman of the ancient world. She was the daughter of King Tyndareus and Leda, who had been seduced by Zeus. In childhood, Helen was abducted by Theseus, who hoped to marry her when the time came. After having been rescued by her twin brothers Castor and Pollux, King Tyndareus decreed that Helen should marry the man of her choice. Helen chose Menelaus, king of Sparta, and lived happily at his side until she met Paris. Her elopement with the Trojan prince resulted in a heated battle between Greece and Troy as Menelaus fought to free his wife. After nine years of futile warfare Menelaus and Paris agreed to meet in single combat. Paris died as a result of his wounds; the victorious Menelaus reclaimed his Helen and returned with her to Sparta, where they lived happily to an old age.

Beautiful Helen of Troy with Paris

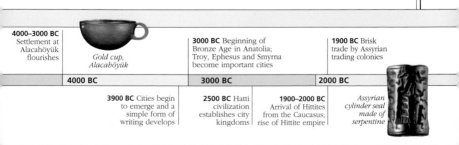

4000–3000 BC Settlement at Alacahöyük flourishes		3000 BC Beginning of Bronze Age in Anatolia; Troy, Ephesus and Smyrna become important cities	1900 BC Brisk trade by Assyrian trading colonies
Gold cup, Alacahöyük			
4000 BC	**3000 BC**	**2000 BC**	
3900 BC Cities begin to emerge and a simple form of writing develops	2500 BC Hatti civilization establishes city kingdoms	1900–2000 BC Arrival of Hittites from the Caucasus; rise of Hittite empire	*Assyrian cylinder seal made of serpentine*

THE HITTITES

Historians are uncertain about the origins of the Hittites and how they got to Anatolia. It is clear that they arrived some time before the second millennium BC and were established at the time of the Assyrian trading colonies. Theirs was the first powerful empire to arise in Anatolia. Its capital was at Hattuşaş, present-day Boğazkale *(see pp296–7)*.

The Hittite language, which was written in both cuneiform script and hieroglyphics, is believed to be the oldest of the Indo-European languages and was deciphered only in 1915. Large collections of Hittite writings were discovered at Hattuşaş. They contained cuneiform texts on various subjects, such as religious rituals, omens, myths and prayers, as well as royal annals, state treaties and diplomatic letters. Religion and appeasing the gods played an important role in Hittite life. They worshipped the "Thousand Gods of the Land of Hatti", an impressive pantheon of semitic deities, chief among whom were the Weather or Storm god, and his wife, the Sun goddess.

An advanced people, Hittites knew the art of forging iron, an advantage

Remains of Hittite relief, Boğazkale

that made them a powerful military force. Their cuneiform texts also revealed a complex legal system and their remarkably fair treatment of criminals and prisoners.

King Anitta conquered large parts of central Anatolia, including the Assyrian trading colony at Kanesh. His conquests increased the might of the kingdom, but also led to decentralization. The empire splintered into several city-states, until King Huzziya began to reunite the independent elements and fought to regain parts of Anatolia.

One of King Huzziya's successors, Labarna Hattushili I, is considered to be the founder of the Old Hittite Empire. He had his eye on wealthy Syria, then an important centre of trade, crafts and agriculture, and in an effort to annex its city-states he began to extend his campaigns into northern Syria. One of his grandsons finally managed to conquer Babylon around 1530 BC, but the constant wars made expansion difficult, and in general, Hittite rulers repeatedly gained, lost and regained territories throughout the duration of their empire.

GOLDEN AGE OF THE HITTITES

The Hittite empire reached its peak around 1260 BC, when Hattushili III and Ramses II, the ruler of Egypt, signed an agreement of peace and friendship. As a result of this treaty, Hittite culture could flourish and the city of Hattuşaş grew rapidly. The Hittite empire entered its Golden Age. Hattuşaş grew into a large city. It was surrounded by sturdy walls and had an impressive temple and palace complex. The columns of the royal palace

Carved reliefs on the Sphinx Gate at Alacahöyük

TIMELINE

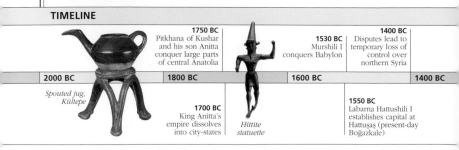

2000 BC | **1800 BC** | **1600 BC** | **1400 BC**

Spouted jug, Kültepe

1750 BC
Pitkhana of Kushar and his son Anitta conquer large parts of central Anatolia

1700 BC
King Anitta's empire dissolves into city-states

Hittite statuette

1530 BC
Murshili I conquers Babylon

1550 BC
Labarna Hattushili I establishes capital at Hattuşaş (present-day Boğazkale)

1400 BC
Disputes lead to temporary loss of control over northern Syria

were supported on bases in the shape of bulls and lions, while the city gates were decorated with elaborate relief sculptures of fantastic sphinxes and armed gods.

Relative peace and stability saw a flowering of Hittite culture. Elegant pottery items, metal figures, animal-shaped vessels and stamp seals bearing royal symbols were produced. They also collected the documents in cuneiform

Croesus, the wealthy king of the Lydians

script that now provide valuable information about their culture for archaeologists. According to records written at the time, Hittite kingdoms flourished throughout Anatolia.

DECLINE OF THE HITTITES

In the early 12th century BC, an indistinct group of maritime marauders known as the "Sea Peoples" migrated to the eastern Mediterranean, and the collapse of the Hittites is attributed to their warring tactics. Around 1205 BC, Mediterranean pirates harried the boundaries of the empire, while the empire was suffering under a terrible famine. Many people died or fled, leaving only vestiges of the former empire in Syria and southern Anatolia. The Assyrians used the sufferings of the Hittites to their advantage and incorporated many of their kingdoms. The remaining pieces of the former Hittite empire were occupied by the Phrygians, a Balkan tribe, who had invaded from the northwest.

TOWARDS THE HELLENISTIC AGE

During the 7th century BC, Anatolia gradually became dominated by the Lydians, while the Lycian civilization flourished along the Mediterranean coastline. Their rock tombs *(see p215)* can still today be seen between Fethiye and Antalya *(see pp218–19)*.

The Lydians, a powerful Hittite-related tribe, settled in western Anatolia. Under the leadership of their king, Croesus, they conquered and annexed many Anatolian city-states around 700 BC. Renowned silversmiths, they are credited with the invention of coinage.

Lydian coin from 700 BC

In the meanwhile, the Ionian Renaissance saw a flowering of Greek culture and economy along the Aegean coast. Pioneers from Miletus *(see pp190–91)* established colonies along the shores of the Mediterranean and Black Sea. City-states such as Knidos and Halicarnassus flourished, setting the stage for the next act in Anatolia's history.

1274 BC War between Syria and Egypt	1000 BC Urartians establish a state near Lake Van	*Assyrian-influenced statue of King Tarhunza*	700 BC Remaining Hittite kingdoms annexed by Assyria
1200 BC	**1000 BC**	**800 BC**	
1259 BC War with Egypt ends with the first written peace treaty signed by Ramses II and Hittite king Hattushili III	*Urartian gold button*	800 BC Phrygians rise to power in central and southeastern Anatolia	

The Hellenistic Age

Eastward expansion of Greek influence, roughly between 330 BC and 132 BC, was led by Alexander the Great (356–324 BC). After the assassination of his father, Philip II of Macedon, the young Alexander first consolidated his position in Europe and then took on the might of the Persian Empire, which had absorbed most of Anatolia during the 5th century BC. He first invaded Anatolia and Phoenicia, proceeding on to Egypt and India, setting up cities and leaving garrisons behind as he went. In Anatolia, the new colonists soon became the ruling class and imposed laws to promote Hellenization.

Alexander the Great

ALEXANDER'S EMPIRE

→ *Alexander's campaigns*

Sarisses (spears) used by the Macedonian phalanx (battle formation) were 5.5 m (18 ft) long.

Pergamum
This artist's impression shows what the hilltop city would have looked like in 200 BC. It depicts the magnitude of Alexander's vision to create Pergamum as the perfect Greek city.

Alexander is on his stallion, Bucephalus.

Perge
The city of Perge, reputedly founded by two Greek seers after the Trojan War, welcomed Alexander the Great in 333 BC and gave him guides for his journey from Phaselis to Pamphylia.

THE BATTLE AT ISSUS

After campaigning in Asia Minor for just one year, Alexander won his first major battle. In November 333 BC, he and the Persian king, Darius III, clashed for the second time. At a mountain pass at Issus (near İskenderun), Macedonian troops managed to encircle the Persian cavalry. When Darius saw Alexander cut through his men and head straight for him, he fled the field leaving his troops in disarray and his mother, wife and children as hostages. Victorious Alexander pressed on to Egypt and then across Persia to the Himalayas until a mutiny by his exhausted soldiers in 324 BC forced him to turn back. He died of a sudden fever in Babylon the following year, at the age of 32.

Alexander Sarcophagus
Dating from the late 4th century BC, this sarcophagus is named after Alexander because he is depicted in the battle scene friezes. The carvings are regarded as being among the most exquisite examples of Hellenistic art ever discovered.

Gold Octodrachma
This coin was minted by one of Alexander's successors, King Seleukos III of Syria, who ruled from 226–223 BC.

Darius III

Golden chariot

The Lycian Sarcophagus and Harpy Tomb at Xanthos
Xanthos was the chief city of ancient Lycia. Ravaged by the Persians around 540 BC, it was rebuilt and soon regained its former prominence. The Lycian sarcophagus and the Harpy Tomb shown here date from this period. Together with Pinara and many other Lycian cities, Xanthos surrendered to Alexander the Great in 334 BC.

THE GORDIAN KNOT

Zeus, the father of the gods, had decreed that the people of Phrygia should choose as their king the first person to ride a wagon to his temple. The unlikely candidate, according to legend, was a peasant by the name of Gordius. Hardly able to believe his good fortune, the newly crowned king dedicated his wagon to Zeus, tying it to a pillar of the temple with an intricate knot. A subsequent oracle prophesied that the person who managed to untie it would become ruler of all Asia. That honour fell to Alexander the Great, who cheated the oracle by using his sword to cut the strands.

Alexander and the Gordian knot

ROME MOVES EASTWARD

The Roman Republic, established in central Italy around 500 BC, began a rapid expansion to the east during the 2nd century BC. After defeating their old enemies and rivals, the Carthaginians, the Roman armies defeated the Greeks at Corinth and Galatian forces in northern Anatolia. While the Romans were victorious in battle, the civilization of the Greeks in time exerted a great influence on Rome. This led the poet Horace to write *"Graecia capta ferum victorum cept"* (Greece took her fierce conqueror captive).

Marble head of a Greek youth

Greek art and culture dominated the Roman way of life. The Romans even adopted Greek as lingua franca in their newly acquired territories east of the Adriatic Sea.

Roman rule brought the benefits of Roman civilization, such as law, better hygiene and civil engineering. As they advanced, Roman armies built impressive military roads. These were of vital importance for trade. At the height of the Roman empire, it was possible to travel from the Adriatic coast to Syria on well-constructed, wide stone roads. The Stadiusmus (guidepost) monument at Patara (near Kalkan), possibly erected by Claudius, displays an inventory of roads and distances throughout Lycia.

19th-century depiction of Mithradates VI of Pontus

ROMAN EXPANSION

The short-lived empire of Alexander the Great produced a number of successor states, including the Seleucid empire, which controlled much of Anatolia by the 2nd century BC. In two wars, known as the First and Second Macedonian Wars, Rome gained control of key city-states and kingdoms on the Mediterranean coast and in the Anatolian interior. Most submitted without resistance; others were simply handed over. King Atallus III of Pergamum, for example, simply left his kingdom to Rome in 133 BC when he realized that resistance was futile. Those who fought back, such as Mithridates VI of Pontus, were eventually defeated. But the wars against Mithridates marked the beginning of the turbulent Roman civil wars.

In 31 BC, Octavian, the nephew of Julius Caesar, emerged as victor of the civil wars. As a sign of its gratitude, the Roman Senate declared him emperor, and he was henceforth known as Augustus. Apart from extending the Roman territory and reorganizing the army, Octavian also established *colonia*, communal villages for retired soldiers. Examples of these can still be seen today, at Sagalassos and Antiocheia-in-Pisidia (near modern-day Eğirdir).

ROMAN RELIGION

The Romans worshipped an impressive array of gods. The greatest were Jupiter, his wife Juno, Minerva, the goddess of wisdom, and Mars, god of war. Apart from their own deities, the Romans also adopted those of the people they conquered, and allowed the

---

Cyrus the Great

546 BC Sardis, captial of the Lydian Empire, is overthrown by the Persians under Cyrus the Great

130 BC The Roman province of Asia is created

AD 96–180 Five good emperors rule Rome

Emperor Hadrian

| 600 BC | 400 BC | 200 BC | AD 1 |

560–546 BC King Croesus rules the Lydian empire

334 BC Alexander the Great claims Anatolian peninsula from the Persians

68 BC Pompey defeats the pirates

St Paul's Well in Tarsus

AD 1 St Paul (Saul of Tarsus) born in Cilicia

local customs to continue. The people of Anatolia, therefore, continued to perform the fertility rites that were associated with the mother goddess, Cybele. Other, smaller sects and cults also flourished. Mithraism, originating with the Zoroastrian religion that was practised in Persia, was extremely influential, particularly among the soldiers of the Roman army. Many people, especially the poor, were drawn to the popular cult of the Egyptian god, Osiris.

Statuette of the Mother Goddess, Cybele

FIVE GOOD EMPERORS

By the 2nd century AD, peace and order again prevailed in Rome's outlying provinces. At home, the empire prospered under the rule of the "five good emperors" (Nerva, Trajan, Hadrian, Antonius Pius, and Marcus Aurelius with Lucius Verus). During this period of relative peace and prosperity, the Romans endowed their far-flung territories with countless sophisticated aqueducts and *nymphaea* (reservoir systems) to distribute fresh water and remove waste products. Theatres and council chambers were built, as were *stadia* and *gymnasia* to host the popular sporting events. When emperor Hadrian (AD 117–138) toured the remote provinces, the delighted citizens of Attaleia (modern Antalya) *(see p218–9)*, Termessos *(see p220)* and numerous

Hadrian, one of the "five good emperors"

other towns erected elaborate, beautiful memorial arches to honour the emperor and commemorate his visit.

CHRISTIANITY

St Paul, born Saul of Tarsus around AD 1, established the first churches in Asia Minor. Early Christian communities soon came into conflict with Roman authorities when they refused to make sacrifices to the emperor. However, all this changed in the 4th century AD, when Constantine, who ruled from AD 324 to 337, converted to Christianity. His conversion came about just before the Battle of the Milvian Bridge in AD 311, when he had a vision of a flaming cross inscribed with the words "in this sign, conquer".

In AD 324, Constantine founded the city of Constantinople (the site of modern-day Istanbul), and within six years had made it the capital and Christian centre of the empire. Massive walls enclosed its seven hills, and the emperor ordered the construction of a hippodrome, forum and public baths. Coastal cities were plundered for works of art to adorn the new capital, and new settlers were enticed by offers of bread and land. Constantine was succeeded by Theodosius, after whose death the empire was divided into two halves ruled by his sons, Arcadius and Honorius. The division sowed the seeds of Rome's eventual decline.

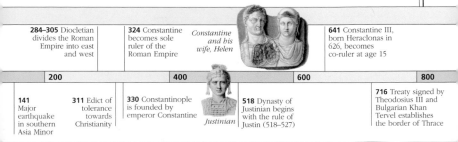

284–305 Diocletian divides the Roman Empire into east and west	324 Constantine becomes sole ruler of the Roman Empire	Constantine and his wife, Helen	641 Constantine III, born Heraclonas in 626, becomes co-ruler at age 15
200	400	600	800
141 Major earthquake in southern Asia Minor	311 Edict of tolerance towards Christianity	330 Constantinople is founded by emperor Constantine	518 Dynasty of Justinian begins with the rule of Justin (518–527) — Justinian	716 Treaty signed by Theodosius III and Bulgarian Khan Tervel establishes the border of Thrace

The Byzantine Empire

Greek cross

The Byzantine empire reached its height under Justinian (AD 527–65), who reconquered much of North Africa, Italy and southern Spain and initiated major building programmes, including the construction of the Haghia Sophia *(see pp82–5)*. Under his rule, Constantinople was endowed with beautiful palaces, churches and public buildings. In the 8th century, the empire became wracked by the iconoclastic dispute, which centred on the role of images in religious life, and its territory steadily shrank under pressure from Arab expansion and the influx of the Seljuk Turks.

THE BYZANTINE EMPIRE

☐ *Extent in AD 565*

CONSTANTINOPLE IN 1200

For almost a thousand years, Constantinople was the richest city in Christendom. At its core were the church of Haghia Sophia, the Hippodrome *(see p90)* and the Great Palace *(see pp92–3)*. In 1204 a Crusader army sacked the city and carried off many of its treasures.

Gate of St Romanus

Mocius Cistern

Church of St John of Studius

Walls of Constantine (now totally destroyed)

Forum of Arcadius

Harbour of Theodosius

BYZANTINE CHURCH ARCHITECTURE

Early Byzantine churches were either basilical (such as St John of Studius, *see p116*) or built to a centralized plan (as in SS Sergius and Bacchus, *see p92*). From the 9th century, churches were built around four corner piers, or columns. Exteriors consisted mostly of unadorned brickwork, but the interiors were lavishly decorated with golden mosaics. Although the Ottoman sultans converted Constantinople's churches into mosques after their conquest of the city, many original features are still clearly discernible today.

The narthex, a covered porch, forms the entrance to the church.

TYPICAL LATE BYZANTINE CHURCH

A central apse is flanked by two smaller side apses.

Four columns support the dome.

Brickwork may alternate with layers of stone.

Golden mosaics cover the ceilings and upper walls.

Walls of Theodosius
The land walls built by Theodosius II withstood many sieges until the Ottoman conquest in 1453.

"Greek Fire"
The Byzantines defended their shores using powerful ships called dromons, *oared vessels from which "Greek fire" (an early form of napalm) could be directed at enemy vessels.*

Blachernae
Palace

Aqueduct of Valens
Water from the Belgrade Forest and the mountains west of the city was brought into Constantinople on this double-tiered structure.

Forum of
Constantine
(see p91)

Basilica Cistern
(see p86)

Church of
SS Sergius
and Bacchus

Hippodrome
(see p90)

Great Palace
(see pp92–3)

Haghia Sophia
The great church (see pp82–5) blazed with mosaics, including this example showing Christ flanked by the Emperor Constantine IX and Empress Zoe.

**Justinian and Theodora, who ruled
the Byzantine Empire at its height**

ORIGINS OF THE TURKS

The Turkish people are descended from tribes of Central Asian nomads, known as the Turkmen. In the 10th century, some of these tribes moved into Russia, China and India, while others began raiding Byzantine-ruled Anatolia. The attacks increased as the century progressed, until one group, the Seljuks, broke away and gradually began to move eastward.

Around the middle of the 11th century, the Seljuk Turks crossed the Oxus River and invaded Persia. Baghdad fell in 1055, and it was here that Seljuk leader Tuğrul Bey, was crowned caliph – ruler of the Islamic world. Tuğrul Bey established the powerful Great Seljuk Sultanate, which ruled much of the Islamic world from 1055 until 1156.

Seljuk manuscript depicting Aristotle and disciples

THE SELJUK RUM SULTANATE

Alp Arslan, nephew of Tuğrul Bey, succeeded him as sultan in 1063, and went on to occupy Syria and Armenia, and to launch various raids into Anatolia. In 1071, the Byzantines tried to defeat the Seljuks, but their army was destroyed at the Battle of Manzikert (Malazgirt) on 26 August 1071, a disaster which saw the capture of the emperor, Romanus IV Diogenes.

Romanus IV Diogenes (left), vanquished at Manzikert

Although the victorious Seljuks did not actively seek to govern Anatolia, the vacuum left by the Byzantine defeat resulted in the formation of a series of Islamic-Turkish states. The most famous of these states was

the Seljuk Sultanate of Rum (1077–1308), initially based in Nicaea (modern-day İznik) *(see pp160–61)*. Other states established by the Seljuks were those of the Danışman at Sivas (1095–1175) and Saltuks (1080–1201) at Erzurum.

The period from the late 11th to late 12th century was one of turmoil in Anatolia. The arrival of the Crusaders, who seized Nicaea in 1097, and then Antioch (modern Antakya) the following year, altered the balance of power drastically. The Crusader influence was especially pronounced in southern Anatolia, where Crusader knights established the Principality of Antioch and the County of Edessa (centred on modern-day Şanlıurfa). The Seljuks moved their capital to Konya, and the Byzantines tried once more to repel the Seljuks, only to be soundly defeated at the Battle of Myriocephalon in 1176.

Under the rule of Kılıç Arslan II (1156–92), the Seljuk Sultanate of Rum became the most powerful state in Anatolia. The capture of Antalya

TIMELINE

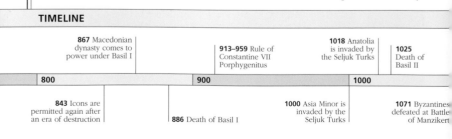

867 Macedonian dynasty comes to power under Basil I	**913–959** Rule of Constantine VII Porphygenitus	**1018** Anatolia is invaded by the Seljuk Turks	**1025** Death of Basil II
800	**900**	**1000**	
843 Icons are permitted again after an era of destruction	**886** Death of Basil I	**1000** Asia Minor is invaded by the Seljuk Turks	**1071** Byzantines defeated at Battle of Manzikert

Seljuk stone bridge near Aspendos

Under the Rum Seljuks, science and literature flourished, together with painting and sculpture. This cultural renaissance was partly caused by an influx of skilled and educated people fleeing the advance of the Mongols from the east.

(see pp218–19) in 1207 gave access to the Mediterranean, and Seljuk Anatolia prospered. The capture of Sinop in 1214 secured trade across the Black Sea, and the capture of Alanya *(see p226)* in 1221 provided an additional boost to maritime trade.

WEALTH AND PROSPERITY

To consolidate their power, the Seljuks forged trade relations with other states signing agreements with Byzantium, Cyprus, Provence, Pisa, Venice, Florence and Genoa between 1207 and 1253. They constructed bridges to facilitate overland trade and built *hans* and *caravanserais* *(see pp24–5)* to provide shelter for travelling merchants and their goods.

The Seljuk empire was at its height under Sultan Malik Şah (1072–92), who generously patronized the arts and sciences. Yet the hallmark of Seljuk civilization was their architecture, which reached a peak in the 13th century. The hospital complex at Divriği *(see p319)*, harbour fortifications at Alanya, the Sultanhanı near Aksaray *(see pp24–5)* and the Karatay theological college in Konya *(see pp250–51)* were all built during this efflorescence.

MONGOL DOMINATION

In 1243 Mongol forces defeated the Seljuk army at Kösedağ, and until 1308 the Seljuk sultans were reduced to the status of vassals under the Mongols. During the 13th and 14th centuries, many Christians converted to Islam, because the Mongols offered reduced taxation for Muslims.

The Mongols ruled Anatolia until 1335, when the first Beylik states were set up by rebel Turkmen. These included the Karamanids in the Taurus highlands and the Danişmandids in central Anatolia. However, it was the small emirate of Ertuğrul, based in Eskişehir, that triumphed. Ertuğrul's son, Osman, founded a dynasty known as the Ottomans, and created one of the greatest empires the world has known.

Mongol archers attacking Seljuk cavalry

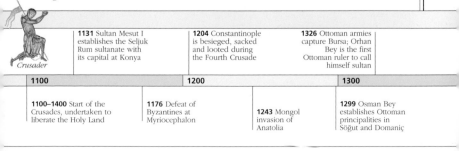

Crusader

1131 Sultan Mesut I establishes the Seljuk Rum sultanate with its capital at Konya

1204 Constantinople is besieged, sacked and looted during the Fourth Crusade

1326 Ottoman armies capture Bursa; Orhan Bey is the first Ottoman ruler to call himself sultan

| 1100 | 1200 | 1300 |

1100–1400 Start of the Crusades, undertaken to liberate the Holy Land

1176 Defeat of Byzantines at Myriocephalon

1243 Mongol invasion of Anatolia

1299 Osman Bey establishes Ottoman principalities in Söğüt and Domaniç

The Ottoman Empire

The expansion of the Ottoman lands accelerated during the late 13th century. A turning point was Mehmet II's capture of Constantinople in 1453. Constant wars advanced the imperial frontiers deep into the Balkans and the Middle East. Syria and Egypt fell in 1516–17, bringing the holy cities of Mecca and Medina under Ottoman control. By the mid-1500s the Ottoman sultan

Ottoman nargile was the central figure of the (Sunni) Muslim world. The Ottoman Empire, though often associated with excessive opulence, was characterized also by its efficient administration, religious tolerance and immense military power.

THE OTTOMAN EMPIRE
◼ *Maximum extent (1566)*

The elite Janissaries *(see p56)* were professional soldiers.

Foot soldiers were often poorly trained auxiliaries.

Cannons were used in large numbers by the Ottoman armies.

Osman I
The founder of the Ottoman dynasty ruled a small emirate on the frontiers of the declining Byzantine empire. Expansion of the Ottoman lands began under his son, Orhan.

The Fall of Constantinople
Constantinople, the last remnant of Byzantium, fell to the army of Mehmet II on 29 May 1453. This view shows the Turkish camp, and the bridge of boats built to cross the Golden Horn.

Mehmet II (The Conqueror)
The sultan safeguarded freedom of worship and successfully repopulated Constantinople.

Barbarossa
Regarded as a glorious Ottoman hero, and in 1543 admiral of the navy, to adversaries Barbarossa was a fearless corsair. Ottoman naval power was less invincible after his death.

Ottoman Cartography
In 1521, the Ottoman admiral and cartographer, Piri Reis, drew on the accounts of Spanish and Portuguese explorers and captured sailors to compile a remarkable map of the world on gazelle hide.

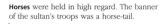

Horses were held in high regard. The banner of the sultan's troops was a horse-tail.

Ottoman soldiers were known for their skilful archery.

Sipahis fought on horseback.

Süleyman the Magnificent
One of the most enlightened sultans, Süleyman (1520–66) was a poet, lawmaker and patron of the arts. Art and architecture flourished during his prosperous rule.

THE BATTLE OF MOHACS

At Mohacs, on 28 August 1526, Süleyman the Magnificent led an army of 200,000 against the forces of Louis II, the 14-year-old king of Hungary. The Hungarian forces were out-manoeuvred by the Janissaries *(see p56)* and faltered under massed Ottoman artillery fire. Despite this great success, the expansion of the Ottoman empire into Europe came to an end after two unsuccessful sieges of Vienna in 1529 and 1532.

The Battle of Lepanto, 1571
Ottoman sea power was fatally weakened after the defeat by Don John of Austria, commanding the fleet of the Holy League in the waters of the Gulf of Patros.

THE EMPIRE OF SULEYMAN

The Ottoman Empire reached its zenith under the leadership of Sultan Süleyman the Magnificent (1520–66). It stretched from the borderlands of southern Hungary to Yemen, and from the Crimea to Morocco.

This advance was aided by well-organized administration, as well as military organization. A key practice was *devşirme*, which required rural Christian subjects to give one son to the service of the sultan. The boys converted to Islam and were educated to become civil servants or Janissaries (soldiers).

Janissaries were subject to strict discipline, including celibacy, but could gain high-ranking privileges that were previously reserved for bureaucrats. An ambitious *kul* (slave) could attain powerful status. In fact, many grand viziers (prime ministers) were products of the *devşirme* system.

By the 18th century, however, the former elite corps had become a corrupt political power and a serious threat to the sultanate. Whenever the Janissaries felt that their privileges were under threat, they rioted violently and no-one dared to intervene.

Members of the Janissary corps

Dolmabahçe Palace, a lavish display of opulence

DISPLAYS OF WEALTH

After Süleyman's death, the empire was ruled by a succession of mediocre sultans who concentrated on enjoying their riches rather than ruling their vast territories. Selim II (Selim the Sot) was known more for his fondness for wine than his interest in the affairs of state. Thus the empire became easy prey for the plotting and intrigue of the Janissaries, as well as the expansionist ambitions of other powers.

At the signing of the Treaty of Karlowitz in 1699, the empire lost half its European possessions. This marked the beginning of the empire's decline and opened the way for Russian advances in the Black Sea region. Long years of war followed, forcing the state to reorganize its finances.

Families that could afford to buy state land began to accumulate great personal wealth. In imitation of Sultan Ahmed III (1703–30), the elite built palaces on the Bosphorus, sported the latest European fashions and lived in luxury. Corruption and nepotism affected the entire empire, while its borders were constantly threatened. In 1730, an uprising in Istanbul overthrew Ahmed III. In short wars with Russia, Venice, Austria and Persia, the empire continued to lose territory.

REVIVAL AND DECLINE

A period of peace, from 1739 to 1768, produced an economic upswing and a brief artistic renaissance that saw the completion of the Nurosmaniye in 1755 – the first sultanic mosque complex built in Istanbul since that of

TIMELINE

1335 Beginning of the Beylik Period

1397 The first Ottoman siege of Constantinople

1513 Piri Reis creates a map of the world

1300	1400	1500	1600

1364 Sultan Orhan recaptures Edirne (Adrianople)

1453 Constantinople falls to Mehmet II, the Conqueror, and is renamed Istanbul

Mehmet the Conqueror

1533 Barbarossa becomes admiral of Ottoman fleet

1569 Great fire of Istanbul destroys much of the city

Ahmed I in 1617. This interlude was shattered when Russian troops mobilized by Catherine the Great invaded the feeble Ottoman empire. In two periods of war (1768–74 and 1788–91), the Russians gained access to the Black Sea and managed to annex the Crimean region. This was the first Muslim territory lost by the Ottomans and they were also forced to pay reparations to Russia.

Portrait of the hero Sultan Abdül Hamit II

on Western-style, secular ideals, was greeted with indignation.

TIMES OF WAR

In the 1870s, a reformist movement known as the Young Ottomans began to press for a constitutional monarchy. Sultan Abdül Hamit II enacted some liberal reforms, but dissolved the infant parliament in 1878 as the country entered a disastrous war with Russia.

In 1826, Mahmud II suppressed the Janissaries in a massacre known as the "Auspicious Event" and reorganized the bureaucracy in an effort to modernize the empire. Russia, meanwhile, encouraged Greece, Serbia, Moldavia and the Ottoman vassal state of Wallachia (in modern Romania) to demand self-rule. Mahmud II hoped that by passing the Tanzimat Reforms (1839 and 1856) he could ensure good government, equality for all and a stronger state. However, the edict of 1856, written under pressure from European powers after the disastrous Crimean War (1853–1856) and based

During the next few years, further debilitating wars took place, gradually ensuring the independence of the Balkan provinces. In 1908, a rebellious group of officers formed the Committee of Union and Progress, dubbed the Young Turks. When Abdül Hamit II refused to accept a constitution, he was replaced by the weak Mehmet V, and the CUP took control.

In 1912 and 1913, the empire lost most of its remaining European possessions in the Balkan Wars. Greatly weakened, it slid into World War I a year later on the side of Germany and Austria-Hungary. The cost of the war in economic and human terms was immeasurable. By 1918, only the heartland of Anatolia remained of the Ottoman Empire. Foreign troops occupied Istanbul, İzmir, Antakya and Antalya. Turkish nationalists reacted by setting up an assembly in Ankara, but the ensuing war for independence set the seal on a Turkey that determined its own destiny.

Russian troops fighting Turkish forces in the Caucasus in 1914

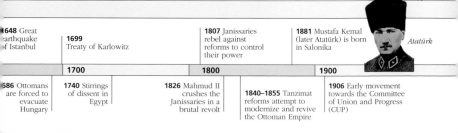

648 Great earthquake of Istanbul	**1699** Treaty of Karlowitz		**1807** Janissaries rebel against reforms to control their power	**1881** Mustafa Kemal (later Atatürk) is born in Salonika	Atatürk
	1700		**1800**	**1900**	
586 Ottomans are forced to evacuate Hungary	**1740** Stirrings of dissent in Egypt	**1826** Mahmud II crushes the Janissaries in a brutal revolt	**1840–1855** Tanzimat reforms attempt to modernize and revive the Ottoman Empire	**1906** Early movement towards the Committee of Union and Progress (CUP)	

THE TREATY OF LAUSANNE

The disastrous losses of World War I and the subsequent occupation of parts of Turkey by powers such as Britain, France and Italy, fuelled Turkish nationalism. When Greek troops occupied İzmir on 15 May 1919 and pushed eastwards to Ankara, the seeds for war were sown. Turkish efforts met with little success until Mustafa Kemal, an army officer respected for his heroism during the Gallipoli campaign of 1915–16, assumed the leadership. At Nationalist congresses in Erzurum and Sivas in 1919, his ideas for the establishment of a Turkish republic aroused unanimous support.

Signatories at Lausanne, with Mussolini among them

Atatürk, father of the Turkish Republic

Greek forces were routed by Nationalist forces in 1922 and Allied ambitions for power sharing in what remained of Ottoman territories faded. The Treaty of Lausanne (1923) recognized the borders and territories of the newly formed state and the Turkish Republic was proclaimed the same year, with Ankara as the new capital city.

As part of the peace settlement and to underpin the framework for a cohesive Turkish state, Greece and Turkey agreed to exchange their ethnic populations. Around 1.25 million Greeks returned to Greece, and 450,000 Muslims were repatriated to Turkey. The impact of resettling such considerable numbers delayed the recovery of both countries after the war.

ATATÜRK'S VISION

Mustafa Kemal's election as leader of the new state came as no surprise and he was, thereafter, known as Atatürk, father of the Turks. He greatly admired European lifestyles and culture and his forward-thinking ideas envisaged a modern, secular Turkish state. His aim was to establish a multi-party democracy with an opposition party. He instituted radical reforms and borrowed legal and social codes from other European countries. Ottoman scripts were replaced by the Latin alphabet and the new Turkish language. Dress codes changed and surnames were adopted. Schools and courts based on religious laws were abolished and, in 1928, a secular state underwritten by a

Atatürk demonstrating the Latin alphabet

TIMELINE

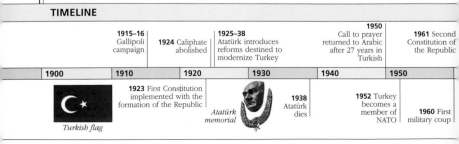

1915–16 Gallipoli campaign

1924 Caliphate abolished

1925–38 Atatürk introduces reforms destined to modernize Turkey

1950 Call to prayer returned to Arabic after 27 years in Turkish

1961 Second Constitution of the Republic

1900	1910	1920	1930	1940	1950

1923 First Constitution implemented with the formation of the Republic

Atatürk memorial

1938 Atatürk dies

1952 Turkey becomes a member of NATO

1960 First military coup

Turkish flag

civil constitution was recognized. Most Turks embraced democratic reform but some minorities, notably Kurds, who had been guaranteed land by Allied countries in World War I under the Treaty of Sèvres (1920), saw İslam and a chance for autonomy slipping away.

BUILDING THE STATE

Atatürk's founding doctrines gave Turks a distinct iden- tity and set the seal on the indivisibility of the Turkish state. When Atatürk died in 1938, Turkey had an im- pressive infrastructure and state-run enterprises which satisfied basic needs. During World War II, Turkey pursued peace- ful and friendly policies and remained neutral. The Truman Doctrine and Marshall Plan strengthened foreign policy and ties with the West. Turkey became a NATO member in 1952 and 5,500 Turkish troops fought in the Korean War (1950–54).

Veteran political leader Bülent Ecevit

GROWING PAINS

Turkey's military services, defenders of secularism and Atatürk's principles, intervened in 1960, 1971 and 1980 to restore law and order, with remote regions of Turkey remaining under martial law until the mid-1990s. During this period, civilian leaders such as Bülent Ecevit grappled with the challenges of political instability and economic modernization. The invasion of Cyprus by Turkey in 1974 left the island partitioned into Turkish and Greek sides. A Kurdish challenge for more self-expression slid into armed conflict that lasted until the capture of the Kurdish Workers' Party leader Abdullah Öcalan in 1999.

Balancing political stability and the demands of a modern economic state often undermined democratic goals. However, when Turgut Özal became Prime Minister in 1983 he spurred busi- nesses to realize their export poten- tial. Many factories today display his photograph and recall the exhilarating days of the "Great Transformation". Taxes like VAT were introduced to bolster state revenues. Tourism potential also began to be realized.

ECONOMIC MIRACLE

By 2001, however, Turkey's economy had drifted off course, inflation was over 100 per cent and the banking sys- tem had collapsed. In 2002 a religious- leaning party, the Justice and Devel- opment, or AK, Party was elected with a two-thirds majority. Prime Minister Recep Tayyip Erdoğan implemented unprecedented reforms with a commitment to steering Turkey into the European Union.

By 2004 inflation had reverted to sin- gle figures and sufficient reforms had been achieved for European leaders to agree to open membership talks with Turkey. Much has been achieved in recent years, although rapid change and high consumer prices have also brought financial burdens to many.

Folklore dancers in traditional dress

	NATO emblem	**1996** Turkey enters European customs union, bringing potential trade advantages	**1999** Earthquake shatters İzmit	**2009** Arrests of 56 people take place in connection with the Ergenekon plot to bring down the government	
1980 Military coup; third Constitution (1982)					
1970	**1980**	**1990**	**2000**	**2010**	**2020**
1971 Military coup	**1978** Kurdish Workers' Party formed	**1991** As NATO partner, Turkey provides support for the US during the Gulf War	**2006** The new Turkish Lira (TL) becomes the country's official currency		

INTRODUCING ISTANBUL

Istanbul at a Glance

Numerous interesting places to visit in Istanbul are
described in the *Area by Area* section of this book,
which covers the sights of central Istanbul as well as
those a short way out of the city centre. They range
from mosques, churches, palaces and museums to
bazaars, Turkish baths and parks. For a breathtaking
view across the city, climb Galata Tower *(see p110–11)*
or take a ferry ride *(see p409)* to the city's Asian shore.
If you are short of time, you will probably want to concentrate on only the most famous monuments, namely
Topkapı Palace, Haghia Sophia and the
Blue Mosque, which are located conveniently close to each other.

**The Church of St Saviour in
Chora** (see pp118–19)
*contains some of the
finest Byzantine
mosaics and frescoes.*

A boat trip along the Bosphorus
(see pp126–7) *is a wonderful way
of viewing sights such as the 14th-
century Genoese Castle (above the
village of Anadolu Kavağı).*

**THE BAZAAR
QUARTER**
(see pp94–105)

SULTANAHME
(see pp78–93)

**Süleymaniye
Mosque** (see
pp100–101) *was
built by the great
architect, Sinan,
in honour of his
patron, Süleyman
the Magnificent
(see pp54–5).*

The Grand Bazaar
(see pp104–105) *is a
maze of shops under
an intricately painted,
vaulted roof. Shop-
keepers are relentless,
and bargaining (see
p130) is a must.*

◁ View of Sülemaniye Mosque over the rooftops of Istanbul

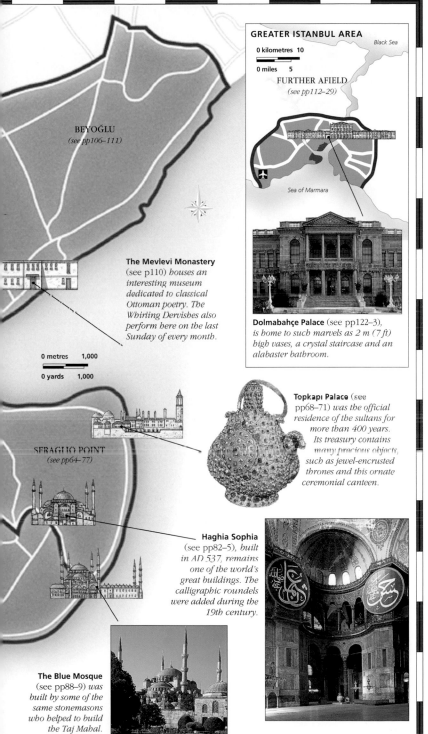

GREATER ISTANBUL AREA

0 kilometres 10

0 miles 5

Black Sea

FURTHER AFIELD
(see pp112–29)

Sea of Marmara

BEYOĞLU
(see pp106–111)

Dolmabahçe Palace (see pp122–3), *is home to such marvels as 2 m (7 ft) high vases, a crystal staircase and an alabaster bathroom.*

The Mevlevi Monastery (see p110) *houses an interesting museum dedicated to classical Ottoman poetry. The Whirling Dervishes also perform here on the last Sunday of every month.*

0 metres 1,000

0 yards 1,000

Topkapı Palace (see pp68–71) *was the official residence of the sultans for more than 400 years. Its treasury contains many precious objects, such as jewel-encrusted thrones and this ornate ceremonial canteen.*

SERAGLIO POINT
(see pp64–77)

Haghia Sophia (see pp82–5), *built in AD 537, remains one of the world's great buildings. The calligraphic roundels were added during the 19th century.*

The Blue Mosque (see pp88–9) *was built by some of the same stonemasons who helped to build the Taj Mahal.*

SERAGLİO POINT

The hilly, wooded promontory that marks the meeting point of the Golden Horn, the Sea of Marmara and the Bosphorus occupies a natural strategic position. In Byzantine times, monasteries and public buildings stood on this site. Today, it is dominated by the grandiose complex of buildings forming Topkapı Palace, the residence of the Ottoman sultans and the women of the Harem for 400 years.

Lion relief from the Ishtar Gate

The palace is open to the public as a rambling museum, with lavish apartments and glittering collections of jewels and other treasures. Originally, the palace covered almost the whole of the area with its gardens and pavilions. Part of the grounds have now been turned into a public park. Adjacent to it is the Archaeological Museum, a renowned collection of finds from Turkey and the Near East.

SIGHTS AT A GLANCE

Museums and Palaces
Archaeological Museum pp74–5 **2**
Topkapı Palace pp68–71 **1**

Churches
Haghia Eirene **4**

Historic Buildings and Monuments
Fountain of Ahmet III **5**
Imperial Mint **3**
Sirkeci Station **11**
Sublime Porte **9**

Streets and Courtyards
Cafer Ağa Courtyard **7**
Soğukçeşme Sokağı **6**

Parks
Gülhane Park **8**

Turkish Baths
Cağaloğlu Baths **10**

GETTING AROUND
With little traffic, this small area is easily explored on foot. Trams from the Grand Bazaar and the ferry piers at Eminönü stop outside Gülhane Park.

0 metres 400
0 yards 400

KEY

▧ Street-by-Street map *See pp66–7*

⛴ Ferry boarding point

🚉 Railway station

🚊 Tram stop

ℹ Tourist information

Ⓒ Mosque

— Walls

◁ **The Circumcision Pavilion in the third courtyard of Topkapı Palace**

Street-by-Street: The First Courtyard of Topkapı

The juxtaposition of Ottoman palace walls, intimately proportioned wooden houses and a soaring Byzantine church lends plenty of drama to the First Courtyard, the outer part of Topkapı Palace. This was once a service area, housing the former mint, a hospital, college and a bakery. It was also the mustering point of the Janissaries (see p56). Nowadays, the Cafer Ağa Courtyard and the Fatih Büfe, just outside the courtyard wall, offer unusual settings for refreshments. Gülhane Park, meanwhile, is one of the few shady open spaces in a city of monuments.

Gülhane Park
Once a rose garden in the outer grounds of Topkapı Palace, the wooded Gülhane Park provides welcome shade in which to escape from the heat of the city **⑧**

Soğukçeşme Sokağı
Traditional, painted wooden houses line this narrow street **⑥**

Museum of the Ancient Orient

Sublime Porte
A Rococo gate stands in place of the old Sublime Porte, once the entrance to (and symbol of) the Ottoman government **⑨**

Entrance to Gülhane Park

Alay Pavilion

0 metres	75
0 yards	75

ALEMDAR CAD

Gülhane tram stop

KEY

– – – Suggested route

Zeynep Sultan Mosque, resembling a Byzantine church, was built in 1769 by the daughter of Ahmet III, Princess Zeynep.

Fatih Büfe, a tiny ornate kiosk, sells drinks and snacks.

SOĞUKÇEŞME CAD

Otağ Music Shop sells traditional Turkish instruments.

Cafer Ağa Courtyard
The cells of this former college, arranged around a tranquil courtyard café, are now occupied by jewellers, calligraphers and other artisans selling their wares **⑦**

STAR SIGHTS

★ Archaeological Museum

★ Topkapı Palace

For hotels and restaurants in this region see pp326–330 and pp352–356

★ Archaeological Museum
Classical statues, dazzling carved sarcophagi, Turkish ceramics and other treasures from all over the former Ottoman Empire make this one of the world's great collections of antiquities ❷

LOCATOR MAP
See Street Finder map 5

Çinili Pavilion *(see p74)*

The Executioner's Fountain is so named because the executioner washed his hands and sword here after a public beheading.

★ Topkapı Palace
For 400 years the Ottoman sultans ruled their empire from this vast palace. Its fine art collections, opulent rooms and leafy courtyards are among the highlights of a visit to Istanbul ❶

Entrance to Topkapı Palace

Topkapı Palace ticket office

Imperial Mint
This museum houses exhibitions on the historical background to Istanbul ❸

Haghia Eirene
The Byzantine church of Haghia Eirene dates from the 6th century. Unusually, it has never been converted into a mosque ❹

Imperial Gate

Fountain of Ahmet III
Built in the early 18th century, the finest of Istanbul's Rococo fountains is inscribed with poetry likening it to the fountains of paradise ❺

Key to symbols *see back flap*

Topkapı Palace ●

Topkapı Sarayı

Süleyman I's *tuğra* over the main gate

Between 1459 and 1465, shortly after his conquest of Constantinople *(see p54)*, Mehmet II built Topkapı Palace as his principal residence. Rather than a single building, it was conceived as a series of pavilions contained by four enormous courtyards, a stone version of the tented encampments from which the nomadic Ottomans had emerged. Initially, the palace served as the seat of government and contained a school in which civil servants and soldiers were trained. In the 16th century, however, the government was moved to the Sublime Porte *(see p73)*. Sultan Abdül Mecid I abandoned Topkapı in 1853 in favour of Dolmabahçe Palace *(see pp122–3)*. In 1924 it was opened to the public as a museum.

★ Harem
The labyrinth of exquisite rooms where the sultan's wives and concubines lived can be visited on a guided tour (see p71).

Exhibition of arms and armour *(see p70)*

Entrance to Harem

Harem ticket office

Gate of Salutations: entrance to the palace

Divan
The viziers of the imperial council met in this chamber, sometimes watched covertly by the sultan.

Second courtyard

The Gate of Felicity is also called the Gate of the White Eunuchs.

The kitchens contain an exhibition of ceramics, glass and silverware *(see p70)*.

İftariye Pavilion

Standing between the Baghdad and Circumcision pavilions, this canopied balcony provides views down to the Golden Horn.

VISITORS' CHECKLIST

Babıhümayun Cad. **Map** 5 F3.
Tel (0212) 512 04 80.
Sultanahmet. 9am–
4:30pm Wed–Mon.
Harem 9am–4pm
Wed–Mon.

Baghdad Pavilion

In 1639 Murat IV built this pavilion to celebrate his capture of Baghdad. It has exquisite blue-and-white tilework.

Circumcision Pavilion

Pavilion of the Holy Mantle (see p71)

Exhibition of miniatures and manuscripts (see p71)

Konyalı Restaurant

The fourth courtyard is a series of gardens dotted with pavilions.

Third courtyard

Library of Ahmet III

Erected in 1719, the library is an elegant marble building. This ornamental fountain is set into the wall below its main entrance.

Exhibition of imperial costumes (see p70)

Throne Room

★ Treasury

This 17th-century jewel-encrusted jug is one of the precious objects exhibited in the former treasury (see pp70–71).

STAR FEATURES

★ Harem

★ Treasury

Exploring the Palace's Collections

During their 470-year reign, the Ottoman sultans amassed a glittering collection of treasures. After the foundation of the Turkish Republic in 1923 *(see p58)*, this was nationalized and the bulk of it put on display in Topkapı Palace. As well as diplomatic gifts and articles commissioned from the craftsmen of the palace workshops, many of the items in the collection were the booty from successful military campaigns. Many date from the massive expansion of the Ottoman Empire during the reign of Selim the Grim (1512–20), when Syria, Arabia and Egypt were conquered.

CERAMICS, GLASS AND SILVERWARE

The kitchens contain the palace's ceramics, glass and silverware collections. Turkish and European pieces are massively overshadowed by the vast display of Chinese (as well as Japanese) porcelain. This was brought to Turkey along the Silk Route, the overland trading link between the Far East and Europe. Topkapı's collection of Chinese porcelain is the world's second best, after China.

Japanese porcelain plate

The Chinese porcelain on display spans four dynasties: the Sung (10–13th centuries), followed by the Yüan (13–14th centuries), the Ming (14–17th centuries) and the Ching (17–20th centuries). Celadon, the earliest form of Chinese porcelain collected by the sultans, was made to look like jade, a stone believed by the Chinese to be lucky. The Ottomans prized it because it was said to neutralize poison in food. More delicate than these are a number of exquisite blue-and-white pieces, mostly of the Ming era.

Chinese aesthetics were an important influence on Ottoman craftsmen, particularly in the creation of designs for their fledgling ceramics industry at İznik *(see p161)*. Although there are no İznik pieces in the Topkapı collection, many of the tiles on the palace walls originated there. These clearly show the influence of designs used for Chinese blue-and-white porcelain, such as stylized flowers and cloud scrolls. Much of the later porcelain, particularly the Japanese Imari ware, was made for the export market. The most obvious examples of this are some plates decorated with quotations from the Koran. A part of the kitchens, the old confectioners' pantry, has been preserved as it would have been when in use. On display are huge cauldrons and other utensils wielded by the palace's chefs as they prepared to feed its 12,000 residents and guests.

ARMS AND ARMOUR

Taxes and tributes from all over the empire were once stored in this chamber, which was known as the Inner Treasury. Straight ahead as you enter are a series of horse-tail standards. Carried in processions or displayed outside tents, these proclaimed the rank of their owners. Viziers *(see p56–7)*, for example, merited three, and the grand vizier five, while the sultan's banner would flaunt nine.

The weaponry includes ornately embellished swords and several bows made by sultans themselves (Beyazıt II was a particularly fine craftsman). Seen next to these exquisite items, the huge iron swords used by European crusaders look crude by comparison.

Also on view are pieces of 15th-century Ottoman chain-mail and colourful shields. The shields have metal centres surrounded by closely woven straw painted with flowers.

IMPERIAL COSTUMES

A collection of imperial costumes is displayed in the Hall of the Campaign Pages, whose task was to look after the royal wardrobe. It was a palace tradition that on the death of a sultan his clothes were carefully folded and placed in sealed bags. As a result, it is possible to see a perfectly preserved kaftan once worn by Mehmet the Conqueror *(see p54)*. The reforms of Sultan Mahmut II included a revolution in the dress code. The end of an era came as plain grey serge replaced the earlier luxurious silken textiles.

Sumptuous silk kaftan once worn by Mehmet the Conqueror

TREASURY

Of all the exhibitions in the palace, the Treasury's collection is the easiest to appreciate, glittering as it does with thousands of precious and semi-precious stones. Possibly the only surprise is that there are so few women's jewels here. Whereas the treasures of the sultans and viziers were owned by the state, reverting to the palace on their deaths, those belonging to the women of the court did not.

In the first hall stands a diamond-encrusted suit of chainmail, designed for Mustafa III (1757–74) for ceremonial use. Diplomatic gifts include a fine pearl statuette of a prince seated beneath a canopy, which was sent to Sultan Abdül Aziz (1861–76) from India. The greatest pieces are to be seen in the second hall. Foremost among these is the Topkapı dagger (1741). This splendid object was commissioned by the sultan from his own jewellers. It was intended as a present for the Shah of Persia, but he died before it reached him. Among the exhibits are a selection of bejewelled *aigrettes* (plumes), which were used to add splendour to imperial turbans.

The Topkapı dagger

In the third hall is the 86-carat Spoonmaker's diamond, said to have been discovered in a rubbish heap in Istanbul in the 17th century, and bought from a scrap merchant for three spoons. The gold-plated Bayram throne was given to Murat III by the Governor of Egypt in 1574 and used for state ceremonies.

The throne in the fourth hall, a gift from the Shah of Persia, was acknowledged by the equally magnificent gift of the Topkapı dagger. In a cabinet near the throne is an unusual relic: a case containing bones said to be from the hand of St John the Baptist.

MINIATURES AND MANUSCRIPTS

It is possible to display only a tiny fraction of Topkapı's total collection of over 13,000 miniatures and manuscripts at any one time. Highlights include a series of depictions of warriors and fearsome creatures known as *Demons*

and Monsters in the Life of Nomads, which was painted by Mohammed Siyah Qalem, possibly as early as the 12th century. It is from this Eastern tradition of miniature painting, which was also prevalent in Mogul India and Persia, that the ebullient Ottoman style of miniatures (see p29) arose.

Also on show are some fine examples of calligraphy (see pp28–9), including copies of the Koran, manuscripts of poetry and several *firmans*, the imperial decrees by which the sultan ruled his empire.

CLOCKS

European clocks given as diplomatic gifts to, or bought by, various sultans form the majority of this collection, despite the fact that there were makers of clocks and watches in Istanbul from the 17th century. The clocks range from simple, weight-driven 16th-century examples to an exquisite 18th-century English mechanism encased in mother-of-pearl and featuring a German organ which played tunes every hour, on the hour. The only male European eyewitness accounts of life in the Harem were written by mechanics who serviced the clocks.

17th-century watch made of gold, enamel and precious stones

PAVILION OF THE HOLY MANTLE

Some of the holiest relics of Islam are displayed in these five domed rooms, which are a place of pilgrimage for Muslims. Most of the relics found their way to Istanbul as a result of the conquest by Sultan Selim the Grim of Egypt and Arabia, and his assumption of the caliphate (the leadership of Islam) in 1517.

The most sacred treasure is the mantle once worn by the Prophet Mohammed. Visitors cannot actually enter the room in which it is stored; instead they look into it from an antechamber through an open doorway. Night and day, holy men chant passages from the Koran over the gold chest in which the mantle is stored. A stand in front of the chest holds two of Mohammed's swords. Behind a glass cabinet in the anteroom are hairs from the beard of the Prophet, a tooth, a letter written by him and an impression of his footprint.

In other rooms are some of the ornate locks and keys for the Kaaba (Muslim shrine in Mecca), which were sent to Mecca by successive sultans.

LIFE IN THE HAREM

Apart from the sultan's mother, the most powerful woman in the Harem, and the sultan's daughters, the women of the Harem were slaves, gathered from the furthest corners of the Ottoman Empire and beyond. Their dream was to become a favourite of the sultan and bear him a son, which, on some occasions, led to marriage. Competition was stiff, however, for at its height the Harem contained over 1,000 concubines, many of whom never rose beyond the service of their fellow captives. The last women eventually left the Harem in 1909.

A Western view of life in the Harem, from a 19th-century engraving

Archaeological Museum ❷

See pp74–5.

Imperial Mint ❸
Darphane-i Amire

First courtyard of Topkapı Palace.
Map 5 E4. 🚇 *Gülhane or Sultanahmet.*

The Ottoman Mint opened here in 1727, but most of what can be seen today dates from the reign of Mahmut II (1808–39), when the complex was extended. In 1967, the mint moved to a new location. The buildings now house laboratories for the state restoration and conservation department, but visitors can look around the outside of the building during office hours.

Haghia Eirene ❹
Aya İrini Kilisesi

First courtyard of Topkapı Palace.
Map 5 E4. **Tel** (0212) 522 17 50.
🚇 *Gülhane or Sultanahmet.*
◯ *for concerts.*

Though the present church dates only from the 6th century, it is at least the third building to be erected on what is thought to be the oldest site of Christian worship in Istanbul. Within a decade of the Muslim conquest of the city in 1453 *(see pp54)* it had

One of the four elaborately decorated sides of the Fountain of Ahmet III

been incorporated within the Topkapı Palace complex and pressed into use as an arsenal. Today the building, which has good acoustics, is the setting for concerts during the Istanbul Music Festival *(see p35)*.

Inside are three fascinating features that have not survived in any other Byzantine church in the city. The *synthronon*, the five rows of built-in seats hugging the apse, were occupied by clergy officiating during services. Above this looms a simple black mosaic cross on a gold background, dating from the iconoclastic period in the 8th century, when figurative images were forbidden. At the back of the church is a cloister-like courtyard where deceased Byzantine emperors once lay in their porphyry sarcophagi. Most have been moved to the Archaeological Museum.

Fountain of Ahmet III ❺
Ahmet III Çeşmesi

Junction of İshak Paşa Cad & Babıhümayun Cad. **Map** 5 E4.
🚇 *Gülhane or Sultanahmet.*

Built in 1728, the most beautiful of Istanbul's countless fountains survived the violent deposition of Sultan Ahmet III two years later. Many other monuments constructed by the sultan during his reign, which has become known as the Tulip Period, were destroyed. The fountain is in the delicate Turkish Rococo style, with five small domes, mihrab-shaped niches and dizzying floral reliefs.

Ottoman "fountains" do not spout jets of water, but are more like ornate public taps. They sometimes incorporated a counter, or *sebil*, from which refreshments would be served.

In this case, each of the fountain's four walls is equipped with a tap, or *çeşme*, above a carved marble basin. Over each tap is an elaborate calligraphic inscription by the 18th-century poet Seyit Vehbi Efendi. The inscription, in gold on a blue-green background, is in honour of the fountain and its founder. At each of the four corners there is a *sebil* backed by three windows covered by ornate marble grilles. Instead of the customary iced water, passers-by at this fountain would have been offered sherbets and flavoured waters in silver goblets.

The apse of Haghia Eirene, with its imposing black-on-gold cross

Soğukçeşme Sokağı ❻

Map 5 E4. 🚇 *Gülhane.*

Charming old wooden houses line this narrow, sloping cobbled lane ("the street of the cold fountain"), which squeezes between the outer walls of Topkapı Palace and the towering minarets of Haghia Sophia. Traditional houses like these were built in the city from the late 18th century onwards.

The buildings in the lane were renovated by the Turkish Touring and Automobile Club (TTOK, *see p407*) in the 1980s. Some of them now form the Ayasofya Pansiyonları, a series of attractive pastel-painted guesthouses popular with tourists. Another building has been converted by the TTOK into a library of historical writings on Istanbul, and archive of engravings and photographs of the city. A Roman cistern towards the bottom of the lane has been converted into the attractive Sarnıç restaurant.

Traditional calligraphy on sale in Cafer Ağa Courtyard

Cafer Ağa Courtyard ❼

Cafer Ağa Medresesi

Caferiye Sok. **Map** 5 E3.
🚇 *Gülhane.* ⬜ 8:30am–8pm daily.

This peaceful courtyard at the end of an alley was built in 1559 by the architect Sinan *(see p101)* for the chief black eunuch as a *medrese* (theological college, *see p32*). Sinan's bust presides over the café tables in the courtyard. The former students' lodgings

Restored Ottoman house on Soğukçeşme Sokağı

are now used to display a variety of craft goods typically including jewellery, silk prints, ceramics and calligraphy.

Gülhane Park ❽

Gülhane Parkı

Alemdar Cad. **Map** 5 E3.
🚇 *Gülhane.* ⬜ *daily.* 🎫

Gülhane Park occupies what were the lower grounds of Topkapı Palace. Today it has a neglected air but it is still a shady place to stroll that also includes a couple of interesting landmarks.

The park no longer contains a zoo, but seek out the aquarium by the disused cascade on the right. It is housed in the cavernous vaults of a Roman water cistern. At the far end of the park is the Goths' Column, a well-preserved 3rd-century victory monument, surrounded by a cluster of clapboard teahouses. Its name comes from the Latin inscription on it which reads: "Fortune is restored to us because of victory over the Goths".

Across Kennedy Caddesi, the main road running along the northeast side of the park, there is a viewpoint over the busy waters where the Golden Horn meets the Bosphorus.

OTTOMAN HOUSES

The typical, smart town house of 19th-century Istanbul had a stone ground floor above which were one or two wooden storeys. The building invariably sported a *çıkma*, a section projecting out over the street. This developed from the traditional Turkish balcony, which was enclosed in the northern part of the country because of the colder climate. Wooden lattice covers, or *kafesler*, over the windows on the upper storeys ensured that the women of the house were able to watch life on the street below without being seen themselves. Few wooden houses have survived. Those that remain usually owe their existence to tourism and many have been restored as hotels. While the law forbids their demolition, it is very expensive to obtain insurance for them in a city that has experienced so many fires.

Sublime Porte ❾

Bab-ı Ali

Alemdar Cad. **Map** 5 E3.
🚇 *Gülhane.*

Foreign ambassadors to Ottoman Turkey were known as Ambassadors to the Sublime Porte, after this monumental gateway which once led into the offices and palace of the grand vizier. The institution of the Sublime Porte filled an important role in Ottoman society because it could often provide an effective counterbalance to the whims of sultans.

The Rococo gateway you see today was built in the 1840s. Its guarded entrance now shields the offices of Istanbul's provincial government.

Rococo decoration on the roof of the Sublime Porte

Archaeological Museum ❷
Arkeoloji Müzesi

Although this collection of antiquities was begun only in the mid-19th century, provincial governors were soon sending in objects from the length and breadth of the Ottoman Empire. Today the museum has one of the world's richest collections of classical artifacts, and also includes treasures from the pre-classical world. The main building was erected under the directorship of Osman Hamdi Bey (1881–1910), to house his finds. This archaeologist, painter and polymath discovered the exquisite sarcophagi in the royal necropolis at Sidon in present-day Lebanon. An additional wing, opened in 1991, contains a children's museum.

Roman statue of Apollo

★ Alexander Sarcophagus
This fabulously carved marble tomb from the late 4th century BC is thought to have been built for King Abdalonymos of Sidon. It is called the Alexander Sarcophagus because Alexander the Great is depicted on it winning a victory over the Persians.

Sarcophagus of the Mourning Women

KEY

- ☐ Classical Archaeology
- ☐ Children's Museum
- ☐ Thracian, Bithynian and Byzantine Collections
- ☐ Istanbul Through the Ages
- ☐ Anatolia and Troy
- ☐ Anatolia's Neighbouring Cultures
- ☐ Turkish Tiles and Ceramics
- ☐ Museum of the Ancient Orient
- ☐ Non-exhibition space

The porticoes of the museum take their design from the 4th-century BC Sarcophagus of the Mourning Women.

GALLERY GUIDE
The 20 galleries of the main building house the museum's important collection of classical antiquities. The additional wing has displays on the archaeology of Istanbul and nearby regions, and includes the Children's Museum. There are two other buildings within the grounds: the Çinili Pavilion, which houses Turkish tiles and ceramics, and the Museum of the Ancient Orient.

Çinili Pavilion

Outdoor café

STAR EXHIBITS

- ★ Alexander Sarcophagus
- ★ Karaman Mihrab
- ★ Treaty of Kadesh

★ Karaman Mihrab
This blue, richly tiled mihrab (see p32) comes from the city of Karaman in southeast Turkey, which was the capital of the Karamanid state from 1256–1483. It is the most important artistic relic of that culture.

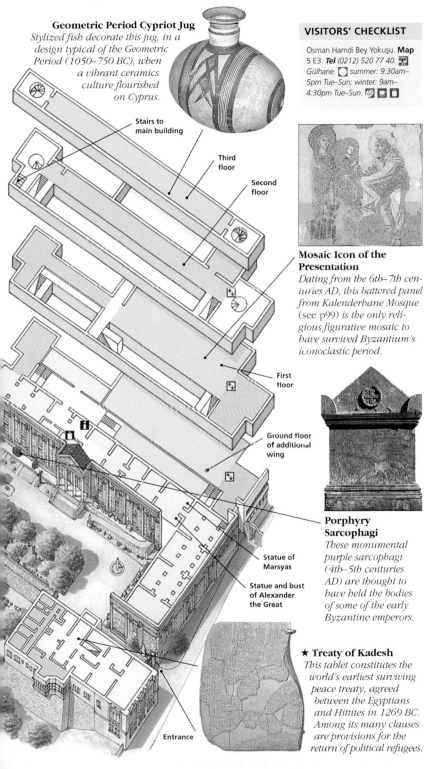

Geometric Period Cypriot Jug
Stylized fish decorate this jug, in a design typical of the Geometric Period (1050–750 BC), when a vibrant ceramics culture flourished on Cyprus.

Stairs to main building

Third floor

Second floor

First floor

Ground floor of additional wing

Statue of Marsyas

Statue and bust of Alexander the Great

Entrance

VISITORS' CHECKLIST

Osman Hamdi Bey Yokuşu. **Map** 5 E3. **Tel** (0212) 520 77 40. Gülhane. ☐ summer: 9:30am–5pm Tue–Sun; winter: 9am–4:30pm Tue–Sun.

Mosaic Icon of the Presentation
Dating from the 6th–7th centuries AD, this battered panel from Kalenderhane Mosque (see p99) is the only religious figurative mosaic to have survived Byzantium's iconoclastic period.

Porphyry Sarcophagi
These monumental purple sarcophagi (4th–5th centuries AD) are thought to have held the bodies of some of the early Byzantine emperors.

★ Treaty of Kadesh
This tablet constitutes the world's earliest surviving peace treaty, agreed between the Egyptians and Hittites in 1269 BC. Among its many clauses are provisions for the return of political refugees.

Cağaloğlu Baths ❿
Cağaloğlu Hamamı

Prof Kazım İsmail Gürkan Cad 34, Cağaloğlu. **Map** 3 E4 (5 D3). **Tel** (0212) 522 24 24. 🚇 Sultanahmet. ⏲ 8am–8pm daily (women), 8am–10pm daily (men). **www**.cagalogluhamami.com

Among the city's more sumptuous Turkish baths, the ones in Cağaloğlu were built by Sultan Mahmut I in 1741. The income from them was designated for the maintenance of Mahmut's library in Haghia Sophia (see pp82–5).

The city's smaller baths have different times at which men and women can use the same facilities. But in larger baths,

Corridor leading into the Cağaloğlu Baths, built by Mahmut I

such as this one, there are entirely separate sections. In the Cağaloğlu Baths the men's and women's sections are at right angles to one another and entered from different streets. Each consists of three parts: a camekan, a soğukluk and the main bath chamber or hararet, which centres on a massive octagonal massage slab.

The Cağaloğlu Baths are popular with foreign visitors because the staff are happy to explain the procedure. Even if you do not want to sweat it out, you can still take a look inside the entrance corridor and camekan of the men's section. Here you will find a small display of Ottoman bathing regalia, including precarious wooden clogs once worn by women on what would frequently be their only outing from the confines of the home. You can also sit and have a drink by the fountain in the peaceful camekan.

Sirkeci Station ⓫
Sirkeci Garı

Sirkeci İstasyon Cad, Sirkeci. **Map** 3 E3 (5 E1). **Tel** (0212) 520 65 75. 🚇 Sirkeci. ⏲ daily.

This magnificent railway station was built to receive the long-anticipated Orient Express from Europe. It was officially opened in 1890,

Sirkeci Station, final destination of the historic Orient Express

even though the luxurious train had been running into Istanbul for a year by then. The design, by the German architect Jasmund, successfully incorporates distinctive windows, arches and stonework that mirror Istanbul's diverse architectural traditions.

As part of a cultural enhancement project in the area, some of Topkapı Palace's entrepôt treasures will be displayed in the station concourse.

The station café is a good place to escape the bustle of the city for a while. Sirkeci serves the European part of Turkey and other Euro points west. Istanbul's other mainline railhead, Haydarpaşa (see p125), has lines to Asian Istanbul and Anatolia.

THE WORLD-FAMOUS ORIENT EXPRESS

The Orient Express made its first run from Paris to Istanbul in 1889, covering the 2,900-km (1,800-mile) journey in three days. Both Sirkeci Station and the Pera Palas Hotel (see p108, 110) in Istanbul were built especially to receive its passengers. The wealthy and often distinguished passengers of "The Train of Kings, the King of Trains" did indeed include kings among the many presidents, politicians, aristocrats and actresses. King Boris III of Bulgaria even made a habit of taking over from the driver of the train when he travelled on it through his own country.

A byword for exoticism and romance, the train was associated with the orientalist view of Istanbul as a treacherous melting pot of diplomats and arms dealers. It inspired no fewer than 19 books – Murder on the Orient Express by Agatha Christie and Stamboul Train by Graham Greene foremost among them – six films and one piece of music. During the Cold War standards of luxury crashed, though a service of sorts, without even a restaurant car, continued twice weekly to Istanbul until 1977.

A 1920s poster for the Orient Express, showing a romantic view of Istanbul

Turkish Baths

No trip to Istanbul is complete without an hour or two spent in a Turkish bath *(hamam)*, which will leave your whole body feeling rejuvenated. Turkish baths differ little from the baths of ancient Rome, from which they derive, except there is no pool of cold water to plunge into at the end.

A full service will entail a period of relaxation in the steam-filled hot room, punctuated by bouts of vigorous soaping and massaging. There is no time limit, but allow at least an hour and a half for a leisurely bath. Towels and soap will be provided, but you can take special toiletries with you. Two historic baths located in the old city, Çemberlitaş *(see p91)* and Cağaloğlu (illustrated below), are used to catering for foreign tourists. Some luxury hotels have their own baths *(see p322).*

Ornate wash basin

Choosing a Service
Services, detailed in a price list at the entrance, range from a self-service option to a luxury body scrub, shampoo and massage.

The *camekan* (entrance hall) is a peaceful internal courtyard near the entrance of the building. Bathers change clothes in cubicles surrounding it. The *camekan* is also the place to relax with a cup of tea after bathing.

Changing Clothes
Before changing you will be given a cloth (peştemal), *to wrap around you, and a pair of slippers for walking on the hot, wet floor.*

Corridor from street

Basin and tap for washing

Small, star-like windows piercing the domes

CAĞALOĞLU BATHS
The opulent, 18th-century Turkish baths at Cağaloğlu have separate, identical sections for men and women. The men's section is shown here.

The *soğukluk* (intermediate room) is a temperate passage between the changing room and the *hararet*. You will be given dry towels here on your way back to the *camekan*.

In the *hararet* (hot room), the main room of the Turkish bath, you are permitted to sit and sweat in the steam for as long as you like.

The Exfoliating Body Scrub
In between steaming, you (or the staff at the baths) scrub your body briskly with a coarse, soapy mitt (kese).

The Body Massage
A marble plinth (göbek taşı) *occupies the centre of the hot room. This is where you will have your pummelling full-body massage.*

SULTANAHMET

Two of the city's most significant monuments face each other across gardens, known as Sultanahmet Square. The Blue Mosque was built by Sultan Ahmet I, from whom this part of the city gets its name. Opposite is Haghia Sophia, an outstanding example of early Byzantine architecture, and still regarded as one of the world's most remarkable

Mosaic of Empress Irene in Haghia Sophia

churches. A square next to the Blue Mosque marks the site of the Hippodrome, a chariot-racing stadium built by the Romans in about AD 200. On the other side of the Blue Mosque, the city slopes down to the Sea of Marmara in a jumble of alleyways. Traditional-style Ottoman houses have been built over the remains of the Great Palace of the Byzantine emperors.

SIGHTS AT A GLANCE

Mosques and Churches
Blue Mosque pp88–9 **7**
Church of SS Sergius and
  Bacchus **14**
Haghia Sophia pp82–5 **1**
Sokollu Mehmet Paşa
  Mosque **13**

Museums
Mosaics Museum **6**
Museum of Turkish and
  Islamic Arts **8**
Vakıflar Carpet Museum **5**

Squares and Courtyards
Hippodrome **9**
Istanbul Crafts
  Centre **3**

Historic Buildings and Monuments
Basilica Cistern **2**
Baths of Roxelana **4**
Buçoleon Palace **15**
Cistern of 1001 Columns **10**
Constantine's Column **12**
Tomb of Sultan Mahmut II **11**

KEY

▨	Street-by-Street map See pp80–81
🚊	Tram stop
ℹ	Tourist information
☪	Mosque
—	Walls

GETTING AROUND
Trams from Eminönü and Beyazıt stop in Sultanahmet by the Firuz Ağa Mosque on Divanyolu Caddesi. From there, most of the sights are easily reached on foot.

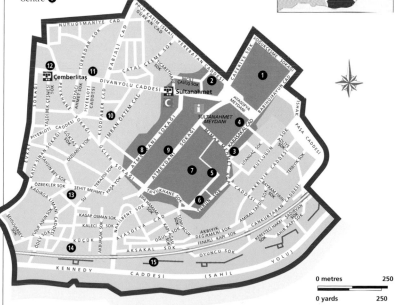

Street-by-Street: Sultanahmet Square

Two of Istanbul's most venerable monuments, the
Blue Mosque and Haghia Sophia, face each other
across a leafy square, informally known as
Sultanahmet Square (Sultanahmet Meydanı), next to
the Hippodrome of Byzantium. Also in this fascinating historic quarter are a handful of museums,
including the Mosaics Museum, built over part of
the old Byzantine Great Palace (see pp92–3), and
the Museum of Turkish and Islamic Arts. No less
diverting than the cultural sights are the cries of
the *simit* (bagel) hawkers and carpet sellers, and
the chatter of children selling postcards.

Tomb of Sultan Ahmet I
Stunning 17th-century İznik tiles
(see p161) adorn the inside of
this tomb, which is part of the
outer complex of the Blue Mosque.

★ **Blue Mosque**
Towering above
Sultanahmet Square
are the six beautiful
minarets of this world-
famous mosque. It was
built in the early 17th
century for Ahmet I **7**

Sultanahmet
tram stop

Firuz Ağa
Mosque

Fountain
of Kaiser
Wilhelm II

DİVA

Museum of Turkish
and Islamic Arts
Tents and rugs used by Turkey's
nomadic peoples are included in
this impressive collection **8**

Egyptian
Obelisk

AT MEYDANI SOK

ATMEYDANI SOK

KEY

– – – Suggested route

Serpentine
Column

Brazen
Column

TAVUKHANE SOK

Hippodrome
This stadium was the city's
focus for more than 1,000
years before it fell into ruin.
Only a few sections, such
as the central line of
monuments, remain **9**

Vakıflar
Carpet Museum
Part of the Blue
Mosque complex, this
museum displays fine
antique carpets **5**

Mosaics Museum
Hunting scenes are one of the
common subjects that can be
seen in some of the mosaics
from the Great Palace **6**

TORUN SOK

| 0 metres | 75 |
| 0 yards | 75 |

★ Basilica Cistern
This marble Medusa head is one of two classical column bases found in the Basilica Cistern. The cavernous cistern dates from the reign of Justinian I (see p49) in the 6th century ❷

A stone pilaster next to the remains of an Ottoman water tower is all that survives of the Milion, a triumphal gateway.

LOCATOR MAP
See Street Finder, maps 4 and 5

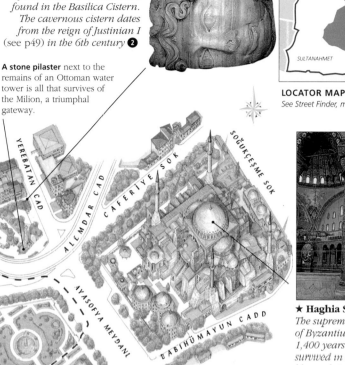

★ Haghia Sophia
The supreme church of Byzantium is over 1,400 years old but has survived in a remarkably good state. Inside it are several glorious figurative mosaics ❶

Baths of Roxelana
Sinan (see p101) designed these beautiful baths in the mid-16th century. They no longer serve their original function, however, having been converted into a state-run carpet shop ❹

Yeşil Ev Hotel
(see p325)

Istanbul Crafts Centre
Visitors have a rare opportunity here to observe Turkish craftsmen practising a range of skills ❸

Cavalry Bazaar
Eager salesmen will call you over to peruse their wares – mainly carpets and handicrafts – in this bazaar. With two long rows of shops on either side of a lane, the bazaar was once a stable yard.

STAR SIGHTS

★ Blue Mosque

★ Basilica Cistern

★ Haghia Sophia

Key to symbols *see back flap*

Haghia Sophia ❶
Aya Sofya

The "church of holy wisdom", Haghia Sophia is among the world's greatest architectural achievements. More than 1,400 years old, it stands as a testament to the sophistication of the 6th-century Byzantine capital and had a great influence on architecture in the following centuries. The vast edifice was built over two earlier churches and inaugurated by Emperor Justinian in 537. In the 15th century the Ottomans converted it into a mosque: the minarets, tombs, and fountains date from this period. To help support the structure's great weight, the exterior has been buttressed on numerous occasions, which has partly obscured its original shape.

Print of Haghia Sophia from the mid-19th century

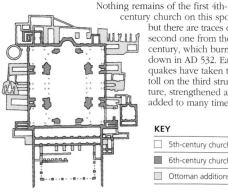

Seraphims adorn the pendentives at the base of the dome.

Calligraphic roundel

Kürsü *(see p33)*

Byzantine Frieze
Among the ruins of the monumental entrance to the earlier Haghia Sophia (dedicated in AD 415) is this frieze of sheep.

Buttress

Imperial Gate

Outer narthex

Inner narthex

Entrance

The galleries were originally used by women during services.

HISTORICAL PLAN OF HAGHIA SOPHIA

Nothing remains of the first 4th-century church on this spot, but there are traces of the second one from the 5th century, which burned down in AD 532. Earthquakes have taken their toll on the third structure, strengthened and added to many times.

KEY

☐ 5th-century church

■ 6th-century church

☐ Ottoman additions

STAR FEATURES

★ Nave

★ The Mosaics

★ Ablutions Fountain

★ Nave
Visitors cannot fail to be staggered by this vast space which is covered by a huge dome reaching to a height of 56 m (184 ft).

Brick minaret

★ The Mosaics
The church's splendid Byzantine mosaics include this one at the end of the south gallery. It depicts Christ flanked by Emperor Constantine IX and his wife, the Empress Zoe.

Sultan's loge

Müezzin mahfili *(see p32)*

The Coronation Square served for the crowning of emperors.

Mausoleum of Mehmet III

Library of Sultan Mahmut I

Mausoleum of Selim II
The oldest of the three mausoleums was completed in 1577 to the plans of Sinan (see p101). Its interior is entirely decorated with İznik tiles (see p161).

The mausoleum of Murat III was used for his burial in 1599. Murat had by that time sired 103 children.

Exit

The Baptistry, part of the 6th-century church, now serves as the tomb of two sultans.

★ Ablutions Fountain
Built around 1740, this fountain is an exquisite example of Turkish Rococo style. Its projecting roof is painted with floral reliefs.

Exploring Haghia Sophia

Calligraphic roundel

Designed as an earthly mirror of the heavens, the interior of Haghia Sophia succeeds in imparting a truly celestial feel. The artistic highlights are a number of glistening figurative mosaics – remains of the decoration that once covered the upper walls but which has otherwise mostly disappeared. The remarkable works of Byzantine art date from the 9th century or later, after the iconoclastic era. Some of the patterned mosaic ceilings, however, particularly those adorning the narthex and the neighbouring Vestibule of the Warriors, are part of the cathedral's original 6th-century decoration.

Interior as it looked after restoration in the 19th century

GROUND FLOOR

The first of the surviving Byzantine mosaics can be seen over the Imperial Gate. This is now the public entrance into the church, although previously only the emperor and his entourage were allowed to pass through it. The mosaic shows **Christ on a throne with an emperor kneeling beside him** ① and has been dated to between 886 and 912. The emperor is thought to be Leo VI, the Wise.

The most conspicuous features at ground level in the nave are those added by the Ottoman sultans after the conquest of Istanbul in 1453, when the church was converted into a mosque.

The **mihrab** ②, the niche indicating the direction of Mecca, was installed in the apse of the church directly opposite the entrance. The **sultan's loge** ③, on the left of the mihrab as you face it, was built by the Fossati brothers. These Italian-Swiss architects undertook a major restoration of Haghia Sophia for Sultan Abdül Mecit in 1847–9.

To the right of the mihrab is the **minber** ④, or pulpit, which was installed by Murat III (1574–95). He also erected four **müezzin mahfilis** ⑤, marble platforms for readers of the Koran *(see p32)*. The largest of these is adjacent to the **minber**. The patterned marble **coronation square** ⑥ next to it marks the supposed site of the Byzantine emperor's throne, or omphalos (centre of the world). Nearby, in the south aisle, is the **library of Mahmut I** ⑦, which was built in 1739 and is entered by a decorative bronze door.

Across the nave, between two columns, is the 17th-century marble **preacher's throne** ⑧, the contribution of Murat IV (1623–40). Behind it is one of several **maqsuras** ⑨. These low, fenced platforms were placed beside walls and pillars to provide places for elders to sit, listen and read the Koran.

In the northwestern and western corners of the church are two **marble urns** ⑩, thought to date from the Hellenistic or early Byzantine period. A rectangular pillar behind one of the urns, the **pillar of St Gregory the Miracle-Worker** ⑪, is believed to have healing powers.

As you leave the church you pass through the Vestibule of the Warriors, so called because the emperor's bodyguards would wait here for him when he came to worship. Look behind you as you enter it at the wonderful mosaic of the **Virgin with Constantine and Justinian** ⑫ above the door. It shows Mary seated

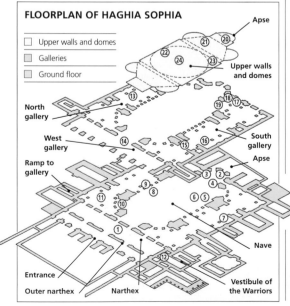

FLOORPLAN OF HAGHIA SOPHIA

☐ Upper walls and domes

☐ Galleries

☐ Ground floor

Apse

North gallery

West gallery

Ramp to gallery

Upper walls and domes

South gallery

Apse

Nave

Entrance

Outer narthex   Narthex

Vestibule of the Warriors

on a throne holding the infant Jesus and flanked by two of the greatest emperors of the city. Constantine, on her right, presents her with the city of Constantinople, while Justinian offers her Haghia Sophia. This was made long after either of these two emperors lived, probably in the 10th century, during the reign of Basil II *(see p52)*. Visitors exit the church by the door that was once reserved for the emperor, due to its proximity to the Great Palace *(see pp92–3)*.

Figure of Christ, detail from the Deësis Mosaic in the south gallery

GALLERIES

A ramp leads from the ground floor to the north gallery. Here, on the eastern side of the great northwest pier, you will find the 10th-century mosaic of **Emperor Alexander holding a skull ⑬**. On the west face of the same pier is a medieval drawing of a galleon in full sail. The only point of interest in the west gallery is a green marble disk marking the location of the Byzantine **Empress's throne ⑭**.

There is much more to see in the south gallery. You begin by passing through the so-called **Gates of Heaven and Hell ⑮**, a marble doorway of which little is known except that it predates the Ottoman conquest.

Around the corner to the right after passing through this doorway is the **Deësis Mosaic ⑯** showing the Virgin Mary and John the Baptist with Christ Pantocrator (the All-Powerful). Set into the floor opposite it is the tomb of Enrico Dandolo, the Doge of Venice responsible for the sacking of Constantinople in 1204 *(see p53)*.

In the last bay of the south gallery there are two more mosaics. The right-hand one of these is of the **Virgin holding Christ, flanked by Emperor John II Comnenus and Empress Irene ⑰**. The other shows **Christ with Emperor Constantine IX Monomachus and Empress Zoe ⑱**. The faces of the emperor and empress have been altered.

Eight **wooden plaques ⑲** bearing calligraphic inscriptions hang over the nave at the level of the gallery. An addition of the Fossati brothers, they bear the names of Allah, the Prophet Mohammed, the first four caliphs and Hasan and Hussein, two of the Prophet's grandsons who are revered as martyrs.

Mosaic depicting the archangel Gabriel, adorning the lower wall of the apse

UPPER WALLS AND DOMES

The apse is dominated by a large and striking mosaic showing the **Virgin with the infant Jesus on her lap ⑳**. Two other mosaics in the apse show the archangels **Gabriel ㉑** and, opposite him, Michael, but only fragments of the latter now remain. The unveiling of these mosaics on Easter Sunday 867 was a triumphal event celebrating victory over the iconoclasts.

Three mosaic portraits of **saints ㉒** adorn niches in the north tympanum and are visible from the south gallery and the nave. From left to right they depict: St Ignatius the Younger, St John Chrysostom and St Ignatius Theophorus.

In the four pendentives (the triangular, concave areas at the base of the dome) are mosaics of six-winged **seraphim ㉓**. The ones in the east pendentives date from 1346–55, but may be copies of much older ones. Those on the west side are 19th-century imitations that were added by the Fossati brothers.

The great **dome ㉔** itself is decorated with Koranic inscriptions. It was once covered in golden mosaic and the tinkling sound of pieces dropping to the ground was familiar to visitors until the building's 19th-century restoration.

Mosaic of the Virgin with Emperor John II Comnenus and Empress Irene

The cavernous interior of the Byzantine Basilica Cistern

Basilica Cistern ❷
Yerebatan Sarayı

13 Yerebatan Cad, Sultanahmet.
Map 5 E4. **Tel** (0212) 522 12 59.
Sultanahmet. ☐ 8:30am–5:30pm
daily (Oct–Apr 8:30am–4pm).

This vast underground
water cistern, a beautiful
piece of Byzantine engineering,
is the most unusual tourist
attraction in the city. Although
there may have been an earlier,
smaller cistern here, this
cavernous vault was laid out
under Justinian in 532, mainly
to satisfy the growing demands
of the Great Palace *(see
pp92–3)* on the other side of
the Hippodrome *(see p90)*. For
a century after the conquest
(see p54), the Ottomans did
not know of the cistern's
existence. It was rediscovered
after people were found to be
collecting water, and even fish,
by lowering buckets through
holes in their basements.

Visitors tread walkways, to
the mixed sounds of classical
music and dripping water.
The cistern's roof is held up
by 336 columns, each over
8 m (26 ft) high. Only about
two thirds of the original

structure is visible today, the
rest having been bricked up
in the 19th century.

In the far left-hand corner
two columns rest on Medusa
head bases. These bases are
evidence of plundering by the
Byzantines from earlier
monuments. They are thought
to mark a *nymphaeum*, a
shrine to the water nymphs.

Istanbul Crafts
Centre ❸
Mehmet Efendi Medresesi

Kabasakal Cad 5, Sultanahmet.
Map 5 E4. **Tel** (0212) 517 6780.
Adliye. ☐ 8:30am–5:15pm daily.

If you are interested in
Turkish craftwork, this former
Koranic college is worth a
visit. You can watch skilled
artisans at work: they may be
binding a book, executing an
elegant piece of calligraphy
or painting glaze onto ceramics. All the pieces that are
produced here are for sale.
Other good buys include
exquisite dolls, meerschaum
pipes and jewellery based on
Ottoman designs.

Next door is the Yeşil Ev
Hotel *(see p327)*, a restored
Ottoman building with a
pleasant café in its courtyard.

Baths of Roxelana ❹
Haseki Hürrem Hamamı

Ayasofya Meydanı, Sultanahmet.
Map 5 E4. **Tel** (0212) 638 00 35.
Sultanahmet. ☐ 8:30am–5:30pm
daily (to 6:30pm summer).

These baths were built for
Süleyman the Magnificent
(see pp54–5) by Sinan *(see
p101)*, and are named after
Roxelana, the sultan's devious
wife. They were designated

ROXELANA

Süleyman the Magnificent's
power-hungry wife Roxelana
(1500–58, Haseki Hürrem
in Turkish), rose from being
a concubine in the imperial
harem to become his chief
wife, or first *kadın (see p71)*.
Thought to be of Russian
origin, she was also the first
consort permitted to reside
within the walls of Topkapı
Palace *(see pp68–71)*.

Roxelana would stop at
nothing to get her own way.
When Süleyman's grand vizier and friend from youth,
İbrahim Paşa, became a threat to her position, she
persuaded the sultan to have him strangled. Much later,
Roxelana performed her *coup de grâce*. In 1553 she
persuaded Süleyman to have his handsome and popular
heir, Mustafa, murdered by deaf mutes to clear the way
for her own son, Selim, to inherit the throne.

The 16th-century Baths of Roxelana, now housing an exclusive carpet shop

for the use of the congregation of Haghia Sophia (see pp82–5) when it was used as a mosque. With the women's entrance at one end of the building and the men's at the other, their absolute symmetry makes them perhaps the most handsome baths in the city.

The building is now a government-run carpet shop, but the baths' original features are still clearly visible. A look around it is a must for those who have no intention of baring themselves in a public bath, but are curious about what the interior of a Turkish bath (see p77) is like.

Each end starts with a *camekan*, a massive domed hall which would originally have been centred on a fountain. Next is a small *soğukluk*, or intermediate room, which opens into a *hararet*, or steam room. The hexagonal massage slab in each *hararet*, the *göbek taşı*, is inlaid with coloured marbles, indicating that the baths are of imperial origin.

Vakıflar Carpet Museum **5**
Vakıflar Halı Müzesi

Imperial Pavilion, Blue Mosque, Sultanahmet. **Map** 5 E5. *Tel (0212) 518 13 30.* Sultanahmet. 9am–noon & 1–4pm Tue–Sat. public & religious hols.

A ramp to the left of the main doorway into the Blue Mosque (see pp88–9) leads up to the Vakıflar Carpet

Museum. It has been installed in what was formerly the mosque's imperial pavilion. This pavilion was built by Ahmet I and used on Fridays by him and his successors when they attended prayers.

The carpets (see pp378–9) are hidden from potentially destructive sunlight by stained glass windows. They date from the 16th to the 19th centuries and are mostly from the western Anatolian regions of Uşak, Bergama and Konya. For many years mosques have played a vital role in the preservation of early rugs: all the carpets in this museum once lay inside mosques.

Detail of a 5th-century mosaic in the Mosaics Museum

Mosaics Museum **6**
Mozaik Müzesi

Arasta Çarşısı, Sultanahmet. **Map** 5 E5. *Tel (0212) 518 12 05.* Sultanahmet. 9am–5pm Tue–Sun.

This museum was created simply by roofing over a part of the Great Palace of the Byzantine Emperors (see pp92–3) which was discovered in the 1930s. In its heyday the palace boasted hundreds of rooms, many of them glittering with gold mosaics.

The surviving mosaic floor shows a lively variety of wild and domestic beasts and includes some hunting and fighting scenes. It is thought to have adorned the colonnade leading from the royal apartments to the imperial enclosure beside the Hippodrome, and dates from the late 5th century AD.

Blue Mosque **7**

See pp88–9.

Museum of Turkish and Islamic Arts **8**
Türk ve İslam Eserleri Müzesi

Atmeydanı Sok, Sultanahmet. **Map** 5 D4. *Tel (0212) 518 18 05/06.* Sultanahmet. 9am–4:30pm Tue–Sun. www.tiem.org

Over 40,000 items are on display in the former palace of İbrahim Paşa (c.1493–1536), the most gifted of Süleyman's many grand viziers. The collection was begun in the 19th century and ranges from the earliest period of Islam, under the Omayyad caliphate (661–750), through to modern times.

Each room concentrates on a different chronological period or geographical area of the Islamic world, with detailed explanations in both Turkish and English. The museum is particularly renowned for its collection of rugs. These range from 13th-century Seljuk fragments to the palatial Persian silks that cover the walls from floor to ceiling in the palace's great hall.

On the ground floor, an ethnographic section focuses on the lifestyles of different Turkish peoples, particularly the nomads of central and eastern Anatolia. The exhibits include recreations of a round felt *yurt* (Turkic nomadic tent) and a traditional brown tent.

Recreated *yurt* interior, Museum of Turkish and Islamic Arts

Blue Mosque ❼
Sultan Ahmet Camii

The Blue Mosque, which takes its name from the mainly blue İznik tilework *(see p161)* decorating its interior, is one of the most famous religious buildings in the world. Serene at any time, it is at its most magical when floodlit at night, its minarets circled by keening seagulls. Sultan Ahmet I commissioned the mosque during a period of declining Ottoman fortunes, and it was built between 1609–16 by Mehmet Ağa, the imperial architect. The splendour of the plans provoked great hostility at the time, because a mosque with six minarets was considered a sacrilegious attempt to rival the architecture of Mecca.

A 19th-century engraving showing the Blue Mosque viewed from the Hippodrome *(see p90)*

Thick piers support the weight of the dome.

The loge *(see p33)* accommodated the sultan and his entourage during mosque services.

Mihrab

The Imperial Pavilion now houses the Vakıflar Carpet Museum *(see p87).*

Minbar
The 17th-century minbar is intricately carved in white marble. It is used by the imam during prayers on Friday (see p32).

Prayer hall

Exit for tourists

Müezzin mahfili *(see p32)*

Entrance to courtyard

★ İznik Tiles
No cost was spared in the decoration. The tiles were made at the peak of tile production in İznik (see p161).

STAR FEATURES

★ Inside of the Dome

★ İznik Tiles

★ View of the Domes

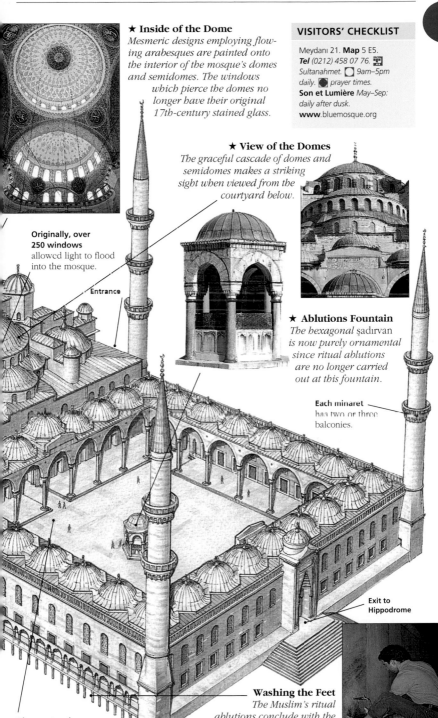

★ **Inside of the Dome**
Mesmeric designs employing flow-ing arabesques are painted onto the interior of the mosque's domes and semidomes. The windows which pierce the domes no longer have their original 17th-century stained glass.

★ **View of the Domes**
The graceful cascade of domes and semidomes makes a striking sight when viewed from the courtyard below.

Originally, over 250 windows allowed light to flood into the mosque.

Entrance

★ **Ablutions Fountain**
The hexagonal şadırvan is now purely ornamental since ritual ablutions are no longer carried out at this fountain.

Each minaret has two or three balconies.

Exit to Hippodrome

The courtyard covers an area the same size as the prayer hall, balancing the whole building.

Washing the Feet
The Muslim's ritual ablutions conclude with the washing of the feet (see p33). Taps outside the mosque are used by the faithful for this purpose.

Egyptian Obelisk and the Serpentine Column in the Hippodrome

Hippodrome ⑨

At Meydanı

Sultanahmet. **Map** 3 E4 (5 D4).
🚇 *Sultanahmet.*

Little is left of the gigantic
stadium which once stood at
the heart of the Byzantine city
of Constantinople *(see
pp50–1)*. It was originally laid
out by Emperor Septimus
Severus during his rebuilding
of the city in the 3rd century
AD. Emperor
Constantine I
(see p49) en-
larged the Hippo-
drome and
connected its
kathisma, or royal
box, to the near-
by Great Palace
(see pp92–3). It
is thought that
the stadium held
up to 100,000 people. The site
is now an elongated public
garden, At Meydanı, the Square
of the Horses. There are, however, enough remains of the
Hippodrome to get a sense of
its scale and importance.

The road running around the
square almost directly follows
the line of the chariot racing
track. You can also make out

**Relief carved on the base
of the Egyptian Obelisk**

some of the arches of the
sphendone (the curved end of
the Hippodrome) by walking
a few steps down İbret Sokağı.
Constantine adorned the
spina, the central line of the
stadium, with obelisks and
columns from Ancient Egypt
and Greece, importing a sense
of history to his new capital.
Conspicuous by its absence
is the column, which once
stood on the spot where the
tourist information office is
located. This was
topped by four
bronze horses
which were pil-
laged during the
Fourth Crusade
(see p52) and
taken to St Mark's
in Venice. Three
ancient monu-
ments remain,
however. The

Egyptian Obelisk, which
was built in 1500 BC, stood
outside Luxor until Constantine
had it brought to his city. This
beautifully carved monument
is broken and is probably only
one third of its original height.
It stands on a base, made in
the 4th century AD, showing
Theodosius I *(see p49)* and
his family in the *kathisma*

watching various events. The
four sides depict a chariot race;
Theodosius preparing to crown
the winner with a wreath of
laurel; prisoners paying hom-
age to the emperor; and the
erection of the obelisk itself.

Next to it is the **Serpentine
Column**, believed to date
from 479 BC, which was
shipped here from Delphi.
The heads of the serpents
were knocked off in the 18th
century by a drunken Polish
nobleman. One of them can
be seen in the Archaeological
Museum *(see pp74–5)*.

Another obelisk still standing, but of unknown date, is
usually referred to as the
**Column of Constantine
Porphyrogenitus**, after the
emperor who restored it in
the 10th century AD. It is also
sometimes called the Brazen
Column, because it is thought
to have once been sheathed
in a case of bronze. Its dilapi-
dated state owes much to the
fact that young Janissaries *(see
p56)* would routinely scale
it as a test of their bravery.

The only other structure in
the Hippodrome is a domed
fountain, which commemo-
rates the visit of Kaiser Wilhelm II to Istanbul in 1898.

The Hippodrome was the
scene of one of the bloodiest
events in Istanbul's history.
In 532 a brawl between rival
chariot-racing teams developed into the Nika Revolt,
during which much of the
city was destroyed. The end
of the revolt came when an
army of mercenaries, under
the command of Justinian's
general Belisarius, massacred
an estimated 30,000 people
trapped in the Hippodrome.

Cistern of 1,001 Columns ⑩

Binbirdirek Sarnıcı

Klodfarer Cad, Sultanahmet. **Map** 3
D4 (5 D4). 🚇 *Çemberlitaş.*

This cistern dates back to
around the 4th century
AD, and was second in size
only to the nearby Basilica
Cistern *(see p86)*. It was also
known as the Cistern of
Philoxenus and measured
64 m (210 ft) by 56 m (184 ft).

CEREMONIES IN THE HIPPODROME

Beginning with the inauguration of Constantinople on 11th May 330 *(see p49)*, the Hippodrome formed the stage for the city's greatest public events for the next 1,300 years. The Byzantines' most popular pastime was watching chariot racing in the stadium. Even after the Hippodrome fell into ruins following the Ottoman conquest of Istanbul *(see p54)*, it continued to be used for great public occasions. This 16th-century illustration depicts Murat III watching the 52-day-long festivities staged for the circumcision of his son Mehmet. All the guilds of Istanbul paraded before the Sultan displaying their crafts.

Sultan Murat III

Palace of İbrahim Paşa (Museum of Turkish and Islamic Arts, *see p163*)

Column of Constantine Porphyrogenitus

Serpentine Column

Egyptian Obelisk

It could hold enough water to supply a population of 360,000 for about 10 days.

The herring-bone brick roof vaults are supported by 264 marble columns – the 1,001 columns of its name is poetic exaggeration. Interestingly, due to its dampness, the cistern building proved to provide the ideal atmosphere for the silk weaving process and, for many decades, it was thus used by Istanbul's silk weavers as a workplace.

Tomb of Sultan Mahmut II ⓫

Mahmut II Türbesi

Divanyolu Cad, Çemberlitaş.
Map 3 D4 (4 C3). 🚋 *Çemberlitaş.*
⭕ *9:30am–4:30pm daily.*

This large octagonal mausoleum is in the Empire style (modelled on Roman architecture, made popular by Napoleon. It was built in 1838, the year before Sultan Mahmut II's death and is shared by sultans Mahmut II, Abdül Aziz and Abdül Hamit II *(see pp57)*. Within, Corinthian pilasters divide up walls which groan with symbols of prosperity and victory. The huge tomb dominates a cemetery that has beautiful headstones, a fountain and, at the far end, a good café.

Constantine's Column ⓬

Çemberlitaş

Yeniçeriler Cad, Çemberlitaş.
Map 3 D4 (4 C3). 🚋 *Çemberlitaş.*
Çemberlitaş Baths Vezirhanı Cad 8.
Tel (0212) 522 79 74. ⭕ *6am midnight daily.*

A survivor of both storm and fire, this 35-m (115 ft) high column was constructed in AD 330 as part of the celebrations to inaugurate the new Byzantine capital *(see p49)*. It once dominated the magnificent Forum of Constantine.

Made of porphyry brought from Heliopolis in Egypt, it was originally surmounted by a Corinthian capital bearing a statue of Emperor Constantine dressed as Apollo. This was brought down in a storm in 1106. Although what is left is relatively unimpressive, it has been carefully preserved. In the year 416 the 10 stone drums making up the column were reinforced with metal rings. These were renewed in 1701 by Sultan Mustafa III, and consequently the column

is known as Çemberlitaş (the Hooped Column) in Turkish. In English it is sometimes referred to as the Burnt Column because it was damaged by several fires, especially one in 1779 which decimated the Grand Bazaar *(see pp104–5)*.

A variety of fantastical holy relics were supposedly entombed in the base of the column, which has since been encased in stone to strengthen it. These included the axe which Noah used to build the ark, Mary Magdalen's flask of anointing oil, and remains of the loaves of bread with which Christ fed the multitude.

Next to Constantine's Column, on the corner of Divanyolu Caddesi, stand the Çemberlitaş Baths. This splendid *hamam* complex *(see p79)* was commissioned by Nur Banu, wife of Sultan Selim II, and built in 1584 to a plan by the great Sinan *(see p101)*. The original women's section no longer survives, but the baths still have separate facilities for men and women. The staff are used to foreign visitors, so this is a good place for your first experience of a Turkish bath.

Constantine's Column

Sokollu Mehmet Paşa Mosque ⑬
Sokollu Mehmet Paşa Camii

Şehit Çeşmesi Sok, Sultanahmet.
Map 5 D5. *Tel* (0212) 518 16 33.
🚋 *Çemberlitaş or Sultanahmet.*
⭕ *daily.* 📷 *donation.*

Built by the architect Sinan
(see p101) in 1571–2, this
mosque was commissioned by
Sokollu Mehmet Paşa, grand
vizier to Selim II. The simplicity of Sinan's design solution for the mosque's sloping
site has been widely admired.
A steep entrance stairway
leads up to the mosque courtyard from the street, passing
beneath the teaching hall of
its *medrese (see p32).* Only
the tiled lunettes above the
windows in the portico give a
hint of the jewelled mosque
interior to come.

Inside, the far wall around
the carved mihrab is entirely
covered in İznik tiles *(see
p161)* of a sumptuous green-
blue hue. This tile panel,
designed specifically for the
space, is complemented by
six stained-glass windows.
The "hat" of the *minbar* is
covered with the same tiles.
Most of the mosque's other
walls are of plain stone, but
they are enlivened by a few
more tile panels. Set into the
wall over the entrance there
is a small piece of greenish
stone, which is supposedly
from the Kaaba, the holy
stone at the centre of Mecca.

The Byzantine Church of SS Sergius and Bacchus, now a mosque

SS Sergius and Bacchus' Church ⑭
Küçük Ayasofya Camii

Küçük Ayasofya Cad. **Map** 5 D5.
🚋 *Çemberlitaş or Sultanahmet.*
⭕ *daily.* ♿

Commonly referred to as
"Little Haghia Sophia", this
church was built in 527, a few
years before its namesake *(see
pp82–5).* It too was founded
by Emperor Justinian *(see p51)*,
together with his empress,
Theodora, at the beginning of
his long reign. Ingenious and
highly decorative, the church
gives a somewhat higgledy-
piggledy impression both inside and out and is one of the
most charming of all the city's
architectural treasures.

Inside, an irregular octagon
of columns on two floors supports a broad central dome
composed of 16 vaults. The

Interior of the 16th-century Sokollu
Mehmet Paşa Mosque

RECONSTRUCTION OF THE GREAT PALACE

In Byzantine times, present-day
Sultanahmet was the site of the Great
Palace, which, in its heyday, had no
equal in Europe and dazzled medieval
visitors with its opulence. This great
complex of buildings – including royal
apartments, state rooms, churches,
courtyards and gardens – extended over
a sloping, terraced site from the
Hippodrome to the imperial harbour
on the shore of the Sea of Marmara.
The palace was built in stages, beginning under Constantine in the 4th
century. It was enlarged by Justinian
following the fire caused by the Nika
Revolt in 532. Later emperors, especially
the 9th-century Basil I, extended
it further. After several hundred
years of occupation, it was finally
abandoned in the second
half of the 13th century
in favour of
Blachernae Palace.

The Mese was a colon-
naded street lined with
shops and statuary.

Hippodrome
(see p90)

Hormisdas Palace

Church of SS Peter and Paul

Church of SS Sergius and Bacchus

mosaic decoration, which once adorned some of the walls, has long since crumbled away. However, the green and red marble columns, the delicate tracery of the capitals and the carved frieze above the columns are original features of the church.

The inscription on this frieze, in boldly carved Greek script, mentions the founders of the church and St Sergius, but not St Bacchus. The two saints were Roman centurions who converted to Christianity and were martyred. Justinian credited them with saving his life when, as a young man, he was implicated in a plot to kill his uncle, Justin I. The saints supposedly appeared to Justin in a dream and told him to release his nephew.

The Church of SS Sergius and Bacchus was built between two important edifices to which it was connected, the Palace of Hormisdas and the Church of SS Peter and Paul, but has outlived them both. After the conquest of Istanbul in 1453 (see p54) it was converted into a mosque.

Bucoleon Palace ⓳
Bukoleon Sarayı

Kennedy Cad, Sultanahmet.
Map 5 E5. 🚋 *Sultanahmet.*

Finding the site of what remains of the Great Palace of the Byzantine emperors requires precision. It is not advisable to visit the ruins alone as they are usually inhabited by tramps.

Take the path under the railway from the Church of SS Sergius and Bacchus, turn left and walk beside Kennedy Caddesi, the main road along the shore of the Sea of Marmara, for about 400 m (450 yards). This will bring you to a stretch of the ancient sea walls, constructed to protect the city from a naval assault. Within these walls you will find a creeper-clad section of stonework pierced by three vast windows framed in

marble. This is all that now survives of the Bucoleon Palace, a maritime residence that formed part of the sprawling Great Palace. The waters of a small private harbour lapped right up to the palace and a private flight of steps led down into the water, allowing the emperor to board imperial *caiques*. The ruined tower just east of the palace was a lighthouse, called the Pharos, in Byzantine times.

Wall of Bucoleon Palace, the only part of the Byzantine Great Palace still standing

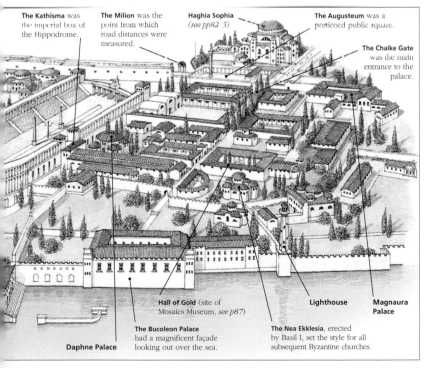

The **Kathisma** was the imperial box of the Hippodrome.

The **Milion** was the point from which road distances were measured.

Haghia Sophia (see pp82–5)

The **Augusteum** was a porticoed public square.

The **Chalke Gate** was the main entrance to the palace.

Hall of Gold (site of Mosaics Museum, see p87)

Lighthouse

Magnaura Palace

Daphne Palace

The **Bucoleon Palace** had a magnificent façade looking out over the sea.

The **Nea Ekklesia**, erected by Basil I, set the style for all subsequent Byzantine churches.

THE BAZAAR QUARTER

Trade has always been important in a city straddling the continents of Asia and Europe. Nowhere is this more evident than in the warren of streets lying between the Grand Bazaar and Galata Bridge. Everywhere, goods tumble out of shops onto the pavement. Look through any of the archways in between shops and you will discover courtyards or *hans (see pp24–5)* containing feverishly

Window from Nuruosmaniye Mosque

industrious workshops. With its seemingly limitless range of goods, the labyrinthine Grand Bazaar is at the centre of all this commercial activity. The Spice Bazaar is equally colourful but smaller and more manageable.

Up on the hill, next to the university, is Süleymaniye Mosque, a glorious expression of 16th-century Ottoman culture. It is just one of numerous beautiful mosques in this area.

SIGHTS AT A GLANCE

Mosques and Churches
Kalenderhane Mosque **7**
New Mosque **1**
Prince's Mosque **6**
Rüstem Paşa Mosque **3**
Sülemaniye Mosque pp100–101 **5**
Tulip Mosque **8**

Bazaars, Hans and Shops
Book Bazaar **11**
Grand Bazaar pp104–105 **13**
Spice Bazaar **2**
Valide Hanı **12**

Museums and Monuments
Forum of Theodosius **9**

Squares and Courtyards
Beyazıt Square **10**
Çorlulu Ali Paşa Courtyard **14**

Waterways
Golden Horn **4**

KEY

▢ Street-by-Street map
See pp96–97

⛴ Ferry boarding point

🚊 Tram stop

🚌 Main bus stop

C Mosque

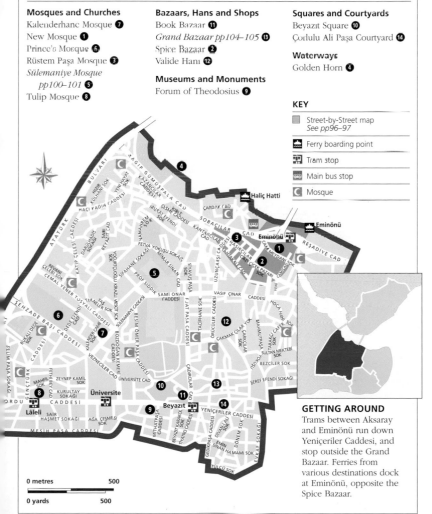

GETTING AROUND
Trams between Aksaray and Eminönü run down Yeniçeriler Caddesi, and stop outside the Grand Bazaar. Ferries from various destinations dock at Eminönü, opposite the Spice Bazaar.

0 metres   500
0 yards   500

◁ The inside of the Grand Bazaar, always thronging with bargain-hunters

Street-by-Street: Around the Spice Bazaar

The narrow streets around the Spice Bazaar encapsulate the spirit of old Istanbul. From here buses, taxis and trams head off across the Galata Bridge and into the interior of the city. The blast of ships' horns signals the departure of ferries from Eminönü to Asian Istanbul. It is the quarter's shops and markets, though, that are the focus of attention for the eager shoppers who crowd the Spice Bazaar and the streets around it, sometimes breaking for a leisurely tea beneath the trees in its courtyard. Across the way, and entirely aloof from the bustle, rise the domes of the New Mosque. On one of the commercial alleyways that radiate out from the mosque, an inconspicuous doorway leads up stairs to the terrace of the serene, tile-covered Rüstem Paşa Mosque.

Nargile on sale near the Spice Bazaar

★ **Rüstem Paşa Mosque**
The interior of this secluded mosque is a brilliant pattern-book made of İznik tiles (see p161) of the finest quality ❸

The *pastırma* shop at 11 Hasırcılar Caddesi sells thin slices of dried beef, spiced with fenugreek – a Turkish delicacy.

Bus station

Tahtakale Hamamı Çarşısı, now a bazaar, was formerly a Turkish bath.

KUTUCULAR CAD

UZUNÇARŞI CAD

BALKAPANI SOK

HASIRCILAR CAD

Kurukahveci Mehmet Efendi is one of Istanbul's oldest and most popular coffee shops. You can drink your coffee on the premises or buy a packet to take away with you.

TAHTAKALE CAD

SABUNCUHANI SOK

MARPUÇCUL

| 0 metres | 75 |
| 0 yards | 75 |

STAR SIGHTS

★ New Mosque

★ Rüstem Paşa Mosque

★ Spice Bazaar

Stall holders and street traders. such as this man selling garlic, ply their wares in Sabuncuhanı Sokağı and the narrow streets around the Spice Bazaar.

For hotels and restaurants in this region see pp326–330 and pp352–356

Eminönü is the port from which ferries depart to many destinations and also for trips along the Bosphorus (*see pp126–7*). It bustles with activity as traders compete to sell drinks and snacks.

LOCATOR MAP
See Street Finder maps 4 and 5

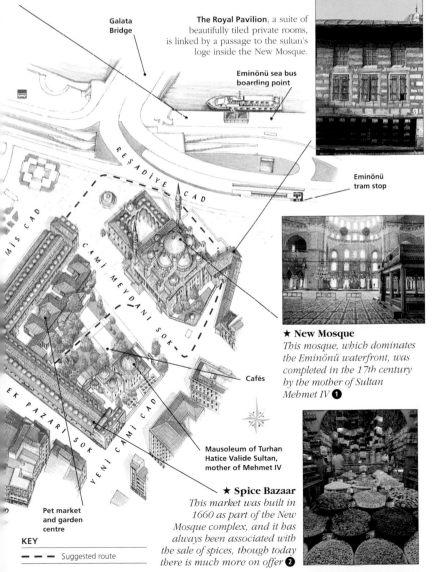

Galata Bridge

The Royal Pavilion, a suite of beautifully tiled private rooms, is linked by a passage to the sultan's loge inside the New Mosque.

Eminönü sea bus boarding point

Eminönü tram stop

Cafés

Mausoleum of Turhan Hatice Valide Sultan, mother of Mehmet IV

Pet market and garden centre

★ New Mosque
This mosque, which dominates the Eminönü waterfront, was completed in the 17th century by the mother of Sultan Mehmet IV ❶

★ Spice Bazaar
This market was built in 1660 as part of the New Mosque complex, and it has always been associated with the sale of spices, though today there is much more on offer ❷

KEY
■ ■ ■ Suggested route

Key to symbols *see back flap*

New Mosque ❶
Yeni Cami

Yeni Cami Meydanı, Eminönü.
Map 5 D2. 🚊 *Eminönü.* ◯ *daily.*

Situated at the southern end
of Galata Bridge, the New
Mosque is one of the most
prominent mosques in the city.
It dates from the time when a
few women from the harem
became powerful enough to
dictate the policies of the
Ottoman sultans.

The mosque was started in
1597 by Safiye, mother of
Mehmet III, but building was
suspended on the sultan's
death as his mother then lost
her position. It was not completed until 1663, after Turhan
Hatice, mother of Mehmet IV,
had taken up the project.

Though the mosque was
built after the classical period
of Ottoman architecture, it
shares many traits with earlier
imperial foundations, including a monumental courtyard.
The mosque once had a hospital, school and public baths.

The turquoise, blue and
white floral tiles decorating
the interior are from İznik
(see p161) and date from the
mid-17th century, though by
this time the quality of the
tiles produced there was already in decline. More striking
are the tiled lunettes and bold
Koranic frieze decorating the
porch between the courtyard
and the prayer hall.

At the far left-hand corner
of the upper gallery is the
sultan's loge *(see p33)*, which
is linked to his personal suite
of rooms.

A selection of nuts and seeds for sale in the Spice Bazaar

Spice Bazaar ❷
Mısır Çarşısı

Cami Meydanı Sok. **Map** 5 D2.
🚊 *Eminönü.* ◯ *8am–7pm Mon–Sat.*

This cavernous, L-shaped
market was built in the
early 17th century as an
extension of the New Mosque
complex. Its revenues once
helped maintain the mosque's
philanthropic institutions.

In Turkish the market is
named the Mısır Çarşısı – the
Egyptian Bazaar – because it
was built with money paid as
duty on Egyptian imports. In
English it is usually known as
the Spice Bazaar. From
medieval times spices were a
vital and expensive part of
cooking and they became the
market's main produce. The
bazaar came to specialize in
spices from the Orient, taking
advantage of Istanbul's site on
the trade route between the
East (where most spices were
grown) and Europe.

Stalls in the bazaar stock
spices, herbs and other foods
such as honey, nuts, sweetmeats and *pastırma* (dried
beef). Today's expensive
Eastern commodity,
caviar, is also available,
the best variety being
Iranian. Nowadays an
eclectic range of items

can be found in the Spice
Bazaar, from household
goods, toys and clothes to
exotic aphrodisiacs. The square
between the two arms of the
bazaar is full of commercial
activity, with cafés, and stalls
selling plants and pets.

Floral İznik tiles adorning the
interior of Rüstem Paşa Mosque

Rüstem Paşa
Mosque ❸
Rüstem Paşa Camii

Hasırcılar Cad, Eminönü.
Map 4 C2. 🚊 *Eminönü.* ◯ *daily.*

Raised above the busy
shops and warehouses
around the Spice Bazaar, this
mosque was built in 1561 by
the great architect Sinan *(see
p101)* for Rüstem Paşa, son-
in-law of and grand vizier to
Süleyman I *(see p55)*.

The staggering wealth of its
decoration says something
about the amount of money
that the corrupt Rüstem managed to salt away. Most of the
interior is covered in İznik
tiles of the highest quality.
The four piers are adorned
with tiles of one design, but
the rest of the prayer hall is a
riot of different patterns, from
abstract to floral. Some of the
finest tiles can be found on
the galleries, making it the
most magnificently tiled
mosque in the city.

The New Mosque, a prominent feature on the Eminönü waterfront

Golden Horn ❹
Haliç

Map 4 C1. 🚇 Eminönü.
🚌 55T, 99A.

Often described as the world's greatest natural harbour, the Golden Horn is a flooded river valley that flows southwest into the Bosphorus. The estuary attracted settlers to its shores in the 7th century BC and later enabled Constantinople to become a rich and powerful port. According to legend, the Byzantines threw so many valuables into it during the Ottoman conquest (see p54) that the waters glistened with gold. Today, numerous small boats can be seen plying the upper reaches of the estuary.

Spanning the mouth of the Horn is the Galata Bridge, which joins Eminönü to Galata. The bridge, built in 1992, opens in the middle to allow access for tall ships. It is a good place from which to appreciate the complex geography of the city and admire the minaret filled skyline. Fishermen's boats selling mackerel sandwiches are usually moored at each end.

The present Galata Bridge replaced a pontoon bridge with a busy lower level of restaurants. The old bridge has been reconstructed further up the Golden Horn, just south of the Rahmi Koç Museum.

Süleymaniye Mosque ❺

See pp100–101.

Prince's Mosque ❻
Şehzade Camii

70 Şehzade Başı Cad, Saraçhane.
Map 4 B3. 🚇 Laleli. ◯ daily.
Tombs ◯ 9am–5pm Tue–Sun.

This mosque complex was erected by Süleyman the Magnificent (see p55) in memory of his eldest son by Roxelana, Şehzade (Prince) Mehmet, who died of smallpox at the age of 21. The building was Sinan's (see p101)

Dome of the Prince's Mosque, Sinan's first imperial mosque

first major imperial commission and was completed in 1548. The architect used a delightful decorative style in this mosque before abandoning it in favour of the classical austerity of his later work. The mosque is approached through an elegant porticoed inner courtyard, while the other institutions making up the mosque complex, including a medrese (see p32), are enclosed within an outer courtyard. The mosque's interior is unusual and was something of an experiment: symmetrical, it has a semi-dome on all four sides.

The three tombs to the rear of the mosque, belonging to Şehzade Mehmet himself and grand viziers İbrahim Paşa and Rüstem Paşa, are the finest in the city. Each has beautiful İznik tiles (see p161) and original stained glass. That of Şehzade Mehmet also boasts the finest painted dome in Istanbul.

On Fridays you may notice a crowd of women flocking to another tomb within the complex, that of Helvacı Baba. This has been done traditionally for over 400 years. Helvacı Baba is said to miraculously cure crippled children, solve any fertility problems and find husbands or accommodation for those who beseech him.

Kalenderhane Mosque ❼
Kalenderhane Camii

16 Mart Şehitleri Cad, Saraçhane.
Map 4 B3. 🚇 Üniversite.
◯ prayer times only.

Sitting in the lee of the Valens Aqueduct, on the site where a Roman bath once stood, is this Byzantine church with a chequered history. Built and rebuilt several times between the 6th and 12th centuries, it was converted into a mosque shortly after the conquest in 1453 (see p54). The mosque is named after the Kalender brotherhood of dervishes, which used the church as its headquarters for some years after the conquest.

The building has the cruciform layout characteristic of Byzantine churches of the period. Some of the decoration remaining from its last incarnation, as the Church of Theotokos Kyriotissa (her Ladyship Mary, Mother of God), also survives in the prayer hall with its marble panelling and in the fragments of fresco in the narthex (entrance hall).

A shaft of light illuminates the interior of Kalenderhane Mosque

Süleymaniye Mosque ❺
Süleymaniye Camii

Istanbul's most important mosque is both a
tribute to its architect, the great Sinan, and
a fitting memorial to its founder, Süleyman the
Magnificent *(see p55)*. It was built above the
Golden Horn in the grounds of the old palace,
Eski Saray, between 1550 and 1557. Like the
city's other imperial mosques, the Süleymaniye
Mosque was not only a place of worship, but
also a charitable foundation, or *külliye (see p32)*.
The mosque is surrounded by its former hospital,
soup kitchen, schools, caravanserai and bath
house. This complex provided a welfare system
which fed over 1,000 of the city's poor – Muslims,
Christians and Jews alike – every day.

Courtyard
*The ancient columns that
surround the courtyard
are said to have come
originally from the
kathisma, the Byzantine
royal box in the Hippo-
drome (see p90).*

Muvakkithane Gateway
*The main courtyard
entrance (now closed)
contained the rooms of the
mosque astronomer, who
determined prayer times.*

Minaret

Tomb of Sinan

The caravanserai provided
lodging and food for travellers
and their animals.

**İmaret
Gate**

**Café in a
sunken
garden**

İmaret
*The kitchen – now a restaurant –
fed the city's poor as well as the mosque
staff and their families. The size of the
millstone in its courtyard gives some
idea of the amount of grain needed to
feed everyone.*

★ **Mosque Interior**
A sense of soaring space and calm strikes you as you enter the mosque. The effect is enhanced by the fact that the height of the dome from the floor is exactly double its diameter, which is 26 m (85 ft).

VISITORS' CHECKLIST

Prof Sıddık Sami Onar Cad, Vefa.
Map 4 C3. **Tel** (0212) 522 02 98.
⬚ Beyazıt or Eminönü.
◯ daily. ⬤ prayer times. Seek permission for photos/ access to minarets. ♿

The Tomb of Roxelana contains Süleyman's beloved Russian-born wife.

★ **Tomb of Süleyman**
Ceramic stars said to be set with emeralds sparkle above the coffins of Süleyman, his daughter Mihrimah and two of his successors, Süleyman II and Ahmet II.

Entrance

Graveyard

These marble **benches** were used to support coffins before burial.

"Addicts Alley" is so called because the cafés here once sold opium and hashish as well as coffee and tea.

The **medreses** to the south of the mosque house a library containing 110,000 manuscripts.

SINAN, THE IMPERIAL ARCHITECT

Like many of his eminent contemporaries, Koca Mimar Sinan (c.1491–1588) was brought from Anatolia to Istanbul in the *devşirme*, the annual roundup of talent Christian youths, and educated at one of the elite palace schools. He became a military engineer but won the eye of Süleyman made him chief imperial architect in With the far-sighted patronage of Sinan – the closest Turkey g Renaissance architect – cre masterpieces which demo master's status as the mos monarchs. Sinan died ag 131 mosques and 200 o

Bust of the great architect Sinan

Former hospital and asylum

STAR FEATURES

★ Mosque Interior

★ Tomb of Süleyman

Tulip Mosque ❽
Laleli Camii

Ordu Cad, Laleli. **Map** 4 B4.
🚇 Laleli. ⏰ prayer times only.

Built in 1759–63, this mosque complex is the city's best example of the Baroque style, of which its architect, Mehmet Tahir Ağa, was the greatest exponent. A variety of gaudy, coloured marble covers all of its surfaces. Underneath the body of the mosque is a great hall, supported on eight piers with a fountain in the middle, used as a market and packed with Eastern Europeans and Central Asians haggling over clothing.

The nearby Büyük Taş Hanı, or Big Stone Han, probably part of the mosque's original complex *(see pp32–3)*, now houses shops and a restaurant. To get to it, turn left outside the mosque into Fethi Bey Caddesi, and take the second left into Çukur Çeşme Sokağı. The main courtyard of the han is at the end of a long passage off this lane.

The Baroque Tulip Mosque, housing a marketplace in its basement

Forum of Theodosius ❾

Ordu Cad, Beyazıt. **Map** 4 C4.
🚇 Üniversite or Beyazıt.

The city of Constantinople *(see pp50–51)* was built around large public squares or forums, the largest of which stood on the site of Beyazıt Square. It was once known as the Forum Tauri (Forum of the Bull) because of the huge bronze bull in which sacrificial animals, and sometimes

column

criminals, were roasted. The huge columns, decorated with a motif reminiscent of a peacock's tail, are particularly striking. When the forum became derelict these columns were reused in the city, some in the Basilica Cistern *(see p86)*, and fragments from the forum were built into Beyazıt Hamamı, a Turkish bath *(see p77)* further west down Ordu Caddesi, now a bazaar.

Beyazıt Square ❿
Beyazıt Meydanı

Ordu Cad, Beyazıt. **Map** 4 C4.
🚇 Beyazıt.

Always filled with crowds of people and huge flocks of pigeons, Beyazıt Square is the most vibrant space in the old part of the city. During the week the square is the venue for a flea market, with carpets *(see pp378–9)*, silks and general bric-a-brac on sale and many cafés located beneath shady plane trees.

On the northern side of the square is the Moorish-style gateway leading into Istanbul University. Within the wooded grounds rises **Beyazıt**

Tower, a fire look-out point built in 1828. Two original timber towers were destroyed by fire. At one time you could climb to the top of the tower but it has been closed to the public since 1972.

On the square's eastern side is **Beyazıt Mosque**. Completed in 1506, it is the oldest surviving imperial mosque in the city. Behind the impressive outer portal is a harmonious courtyard with an elegant domed fountain at its centre. The layout of its interior is heavily inspired by the design of Haghia Sophia *(see pp82–5)*.

Beyazıt Tower, within the wooded grounds of Istanbul University

is region see pp326–330 and pp352–356

Book Bazaar ⓫
Sahaflar Çarşısı

Sahaflar Çarşısı Sok, Beyazıt.
Map 4 C4. 🚇 *Üniversite.*
◯ *8am–8pm daily.* ♿

Customers browsing in the Book Bazaar (Sahaflar Çarşısi)

This charming book-sellers' courtyard, on the site of the Byzantine book and paper market, can be entered either from Beyazıt Square or from inside the Grand Bazaar (*see pp104–105*). Early in the Ottoman period (*see pp54–5*), printed books were seen as a corrupting influence and were banned in Turkey, so the bazaar sold only manuscripts. On 31 January 1729 İbrahim Müteferrika (1674–1745) produced the first printed Turkish book, an Arabic dictionary, and today his bust stands in the centre of the market. Book prices are fixed and cannot be haggled over.

Valide Han ⓬
Valide Hanı

Junction of Çakmakçılar Yokuşu & Tarakçılar Cad, Beyazıt. **Map** 4 C3.
🚇 *Beyazıt, then 10 mins' walk.*
◯ *9:30am–5pm Mon–Sat.*

If the grand bazaar (*see pp104–105*) seems large, it is sobering to realize that it is only the covered part of a huge area of seething commercial activity which reaches all the way to the Golden Horn. Most of the manufacturing and trade takes place in *hans* (*see pp24–5*) hidden away from the street behind shaded gateways.

The largest han in Istanbul is Valide Han, built in 1651 by Kösem, the mother of Sultan Mehmet IV. You enter it from Çakmakçılar Yokuşu through a massive portal, pass through an irregularly shaped forecourt, and come out into a large courtyard centring on a Shiite mosque. This was built when the han became the centre of Persian trade in the city. The han now throbs to the rhythm of hundreds of weaving looms.

A short walk further down Çakmakçılar Yokuşu is Büyük

Yeni Han, hidden behind another impressive doorway. This 1764 Baroque han has three arcaded levels. In the labyrinth of streets around the hans, artisans are grouped according to their wares.

Grand Bazaar ⓭
See pp104–105

Çorlulu Ali Paşa Courtyard ⓮
Çorlulu Ali Paşa Külliyesi

Yeniçeriler Cad, Beyazıt. **Map** 4 C4.
🚇 *Beyazıt.* ◯ *daily.*

Like many others in the city, the *medrese* (*see p32*) of this mosque complex outside the Grand Bazaar has become the setting for a tranquil outdoor café. It was built for Çorlulu Ali Paşa, son-in-law

of Mustafa II, the grand vizier under Ahmet III.

The complex is entered from Yeniçeriler Caddesi by two alleyways. Several carpet shops now inhabit the *medrese* and rugs are hung and spread all around for prospective buyers. The carpet shops share the *medrese* with a *kahve*, a traditional café, which is popular with locals and university students. It advertises itself irresistibly as the "Traditional Mystic Water Pipe and Erenler Tea Garden" where you can sit, drink tea and perhaps smoke a *nargile* (bubble pipe), while deciding which carpet to buy (*see pp378–9*).

Situated across Bileyciler Sokak, an alleyway off Çorlulu Ali Paşa Courtyard, is the Koca Sinan Paşa tomb complex, the courtyard of which is another tea garden. The charming *medrese*, mausoleum and *sebil* (a fountain where water was handed out to passersby) were built in 1593 by Davut Ağa, who succeeded Sinan (*see p101*) as chief architect of the empire. The tomb of Koca Sinan Paşa, grand vizier under Murat III and Mehmet III, is a striking 16-sided structure.

Just off the other side of Yeniçeriler Caddesi is Gedik Paşa Hamamı, probably the city's oldest working Turkish baths (*see p77*), built around 1475 for Gedik Ahmet Paşa, grand vizier under Mehmet the Conqueror (*see p54*)

Carpet shops in Çorlulu Ali Paşa Courtyard

The Grand Bazaar ⑬
Kapalı Çarşı

Nothing can prepare you for the Grand Bazaar. This labyrinth of streets covered by painted vaults is lined with thousands of booth-like shops, whose wares spill out to tempt you and whose shopkeepers are relentless in their quest for a sale. The bazaar was established by Mehmet II shortly after his conquest of the city in 1453 *(see p54)*. It can be entered by several gateways, two of the most useful being Çarşıkapı Gate (from Beyazıt tram stop) and Nuruosmaniye Gate (from Nuruosmaniye Mosque). It is easy to get lost in the bazaar in spite of the signposting. Many of the bazaar's goods are made behind the scenes in secluded ateliers.

Muhlis Günbattı is a well-known textile and carpet shop *(see p131).*

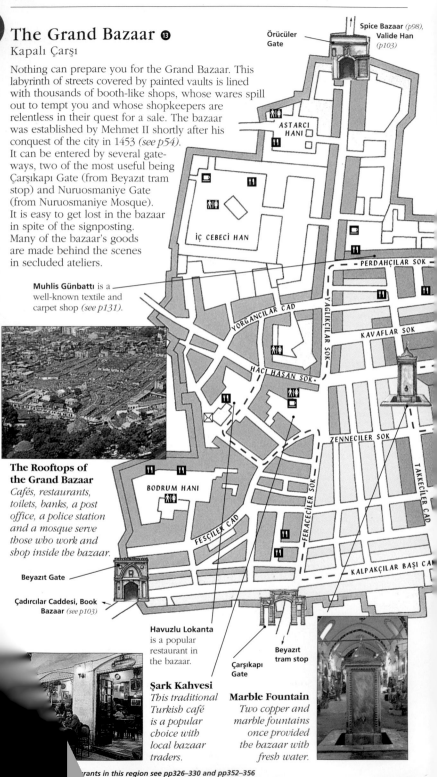

Örücüler Gate

Spice Bazaar *(p98),* **Valide Han** *(p103)*

ASTARCI HANI

İÇ CEBECİ HAN

PERDAHÇILAR SOK

YORGANCILAR CAD

YAĞLIKÇILAR SOK

KAVAFLAR SOK

HACI HASAN SOK

ZENNECİLER SOK

TAKKECİLER CAD

FERACECİLER SOK

The Rooftops of the Grand Bazaar
Cafés, restaurants, toilets, banks, a post office, a police station and a mosque serve those who work and shop inside the bazaar.

BODRUM HANI

FESÇİLER CAD

KALPAKÇILAR BAŞI CAD

Beyazıt Gate

Çadırcılar Caddesi, Book Bazaar *(see p103)*

Havuzlu Lokanta is a popular restaurant in the bazaar.

Beyazıt tram stop

Çarşıkapı Gate

Şark Kahvesi
This traditional Turkish café is a popular choice with local bazaar traders.

Marble Fountain
Two copper and marble fountains once provided the bazaar with fresh water.

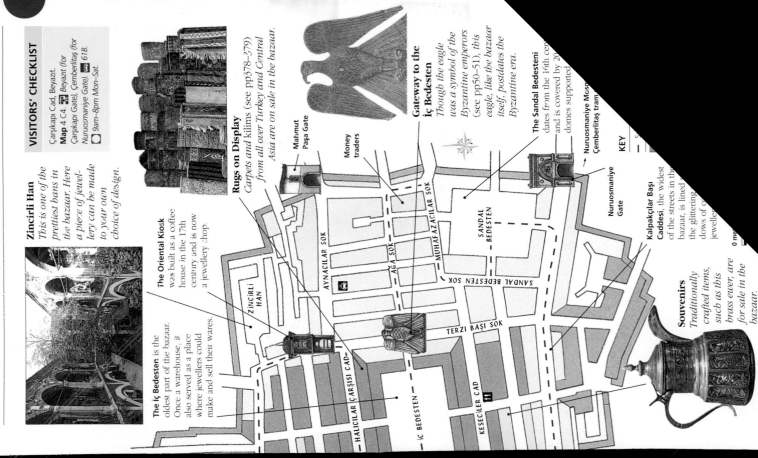

VISITORS' CHECKLIST

Çarşıkapı Cad, Beyazıt.
Map 4 C4. ☐ Beyazıt (for
Çarşıkapı Gate), Çemberlitaş (for
Nuruosmaniye Gate). ☐ 61B.
☐ 9am–8pm Mon–Sat.

Zincirli Han
*This is one of the
prettiest hans in
the bazaar. Here
a piece of jewel-
lery can be made
to your own
choice of design.*

The Oriental Kiosk
was built as a coffee
house in the 17th
century and is now
a jewellery shop.

The Iç Bedesten is the
oldest part of the bazaar.
Once a warehouse, it
also served as a place
where jewellers could
make and sell their wares.

Rugs on Display
*Carpets and kilims (see pp378–279)
from all over Turkey and Central
Asia are on sale in the bazaar.*

**Gateway to the
İç Bedesten**
*Though the eagle
was a symbol of the
Byzantine emperors
(see pp50–51), this
eagle, like the bazaar
itself, postdates the
Byzantine era.*

The Sandal Bedesteni
dates from the 16th cent
and is covered by 2
domes supported

Mahmut
Paşa Gate

Money
traders

Nuruosmaniye
Gate

**Kalpakçılar Başı
Caddesi,** the widest
of the streets in the
bazaar, is lined
the glittering
dows of c
jeweller

Souvenirs
*Traditionally
crafted items,
such as this
brass ewer, are
for sale in the
bazaar.*

Nuruosmaniye Mosqu
Çemberlitaş tram

KEY

AYNACILAR SOK
AĞA SOK
MUHAFAZACILAR SOK
SANDAL BEDESTEN
SANDAL BEDESTEN SOK
TERZI BAŞI SOK
KESECILER CAD
İÇ BEDESTEN
HALICILAR ÇARŞISI CAD
ZINCIRLI HAN

0 me

BEYOĞLU

For centuries Beyoğlu, a steep hill north of the Golden Horn, was home to the city's foreign residents. First to arrive here were the Genoese. As a reward for aiding the reconquest of the city from the crusader-backed Latin Empire in 1261, they were given the Galata area, which is now dominated by the Galata Tower. During the Ottoman period, Jews

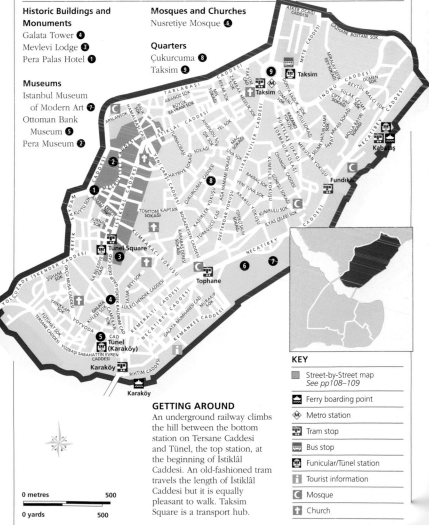

Monument of Independence, Taksim Square

from Spain, Arabs, Greeks and Armenians settled in communities here. From the 16th century the European powers established embassies in the area to further their interests within the lucrative territories of the Ottoman Empire. The district has not changed much in character over the centuries and is still a thriving commercial quarter today.

SIGHTS AT A GLANCE

Historic Buildings and Monuments
Galata Tower ❹
Mevlevi Lodge ❸
Pera Palas Hotel ❶

Museums
Istanbul Museum of Modern Art ❼
Ottoman Bank Museum ❺
Pera Museum ❷

Mosques and Churches
Nusretiye Mosque ❻

Quarters
Çukurcuma ❽
Taksim ❾

KEY

🟦 Street-by-Street map
See pp108–109

🛳 Ferry boarding point

Ⓜ Metro station

🚋 Tram stop

🚌 Bus stop

🚡 Funicular/Tünel station

ℹ Tourist information

Ⓒ Mosque

✛ Church

GETTING AROUND
An underground railway climbs the hill between the bottom station on Tersane Caddesi and Tünel, the top station, at the beginning of İstiklâl Caddesi. An old-fashioned tram travels the length of İstiklâl Caddesi but it is equally pleasant to walk. Taksim Square is a transport hub.

0 metres 500
0 yards 500

◁ The Galata Tower and backstreets of Beyoğlu, seen from the mouth of the Golden Horn

Street-by-Street: İstiklâl Caddesi

Crest on top of the Russian Consulate gate

The pedestrianized İstiklâl Caddesi is Beyoğlu's main street. Once known as the Grande Rue de Pera, it is lined by late 19th-century apartment blocks and European embassy buildings whose grandiose gates and façades belie their use as mere consulates since Ankara became the Turkish capital in 1923 *(see p58)*. Hidden from view stand the churches, which used to serve the foreign communities of Pera (as this area was formerly called), some still buzzing with worshippers, others just quiet echoes of a bygone era. Today, the once seedy backstreets of Beyoğlu, off İstiklâl Caddesi, are taking on a new lease of life, with trendy jazz bars opening and shops selling hand-crafted jewellery, furniture and the like. Crowds are also drawn by the area's cinemas and numerous stylish restaurants.

★ **Pera Palas Hotel**
This hotel is an atmospheric period piece. Many famous guests, like Agatha Christie, have stayed here since it opened in 1892. The hotel has been extensively restored to its original splendour ❶

St Mary Draperis
is a Franciscan church dating from 1789. This small statue of the Virgin stands above the entrance from the street. The vaulted interior of the church is colourfully decorated. An icon of the Virgin, said to perform miracles, hangs over the altar.

Tünel underground railway to Karaköy

Tünel Square

MEŞRU

ASMALI MESCİT SOK

İSTİKLÂL CAD

★ **Mevlevi Lodge**
A peaceful garden surrounds this small museum of the Mevlevi Sufi sect (see p255). On the last Sunday of every month visitors can see dervishes perform their famous swirling dance ❸

TÜNEL MEYDANI

Russian Consulate

Swedish Consulate

KEY

— — — Suggested route

| metres | 75 |
| yards | 75 |

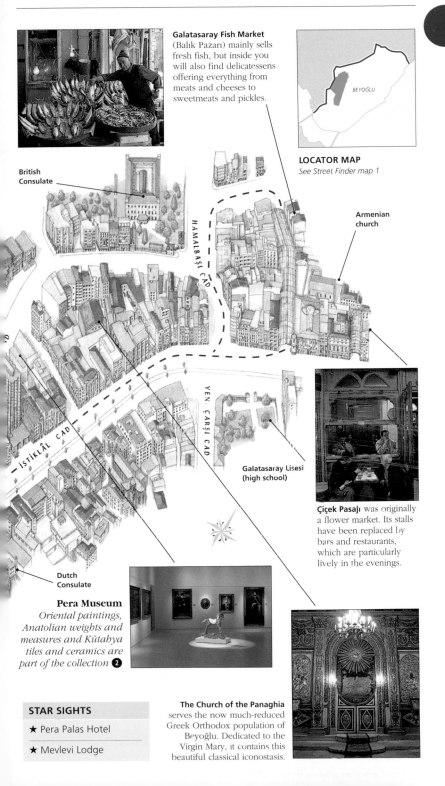

Galatasaray Fish Market (Balık Pazarı) mainly sells fresh fish, but inside you will also find delicatessens offering everything from meats and cheeses to sweetmeats and pickles.

LOCATOR MAP
See Street Finder map 1

BEYOĞLU

British Consulate

HAMALBAŞI CAD

Armenian church

YENİ ÇARŞI CAD

İSTİKLÂL CAD

Galatasaray Lisesi (high school)

Çiçek Pasajı was originally a flower market. Its stalls have been replaced by bars and restaurants, which are particularly lively in the evenings.

Dutch Consulate

Pera Museum
Oriental paintings, Anatolian weights and measures and Kütahya tiles and ceramics are part of the collection ❷

STAR SIGHTS

★ Pera Palas Hotel

★ Mevlevi Lodge

The Church of the Panaghia serves the now much-reduced Greek Orthodox population of Beyoğlu. Dedicated to the Virgin Mary, it contains this beautiful classical iconostasis.

The peaceful courtyard of the Mevlevi Lodge

Pera Palas Hotel ❶
Pera Palas Oteli

98–100 Meşrutiyet Cad, Tepebaşı.
Map 1 D3. **Tel** (0212) 251 45 60.
🚇 Tünel. ♿ by arrangement.
www.perapalas.com

Throughout the world
there are hotels that have
attained a legendary status.
One such hotel is the Pera
Palas, which opened in
1892 to cater for travellers on
the Orient Express (see p76).

After an extensive renovation, it still evokes images
of uniformed porters and
exotic destinations such as
Baghdad. The Grand Orient
bar serves cocktails beneath
its original chandeliers,
while the patisserie offers
irresistible cakes and a
genteel ambience. A room
used by the thriller writer
Agatha Christie can be
visited on request.

Pera Museum ❷
Pera Müzesi

Merutiyet Cad 141, Tepebaı.
Map 7 D4. **Tel** (0212) 334 99 00.
🚇 Tünel. 🚌 From Taksim Square
down Tarlabaı. 🕐 10am–7pm Tue–
Sat, noon–6pm Sun. ⬤ 1 Jan, first
day of Religious Holidays. ♿ 📷
(disabled visitors enter free). 🖥 📷
www.peramuzesi.org.tr

The Pera Museum was
opened in 2005 by the Suna
and İnan Kıraç Foundation.
Formerly the Hotel Bristol,
it has been transformed into
a fully equipped modern
museum. Notable collections
include Ottoman weights and
measures, over 400 examples
of 18th-century Kütahya tiles
and ceramics, and the Suna

and İnan Kıraç Foundation's
exhibition of Orientalist art.
This collection brings together
works by European artists
inspired by the Ottoman
world from the 17th century
to the early 19th century and
also covers the last two
centuries of the Ottoman
Empire.

Mevlevi Lodge ❸
Mevlevi Tekkesi

15 Galip Dede Cad, Beyoğlu. **Map** 1
D3. **Tel** (0212) 245 41 41. 🚇 Tünel.
🕐 9:30am–4:30pm Wed–Mon. 📷

Although Sufism was banned
by Atatürk in 1925, this
Dervish lodge has survived
as the Divan Edebiyatı Müzesi,
a museum of divan literature
(classical Ottoman poetry).
The lodge belonged to the
most famous Sufi sect, known
as the Whirling Dervishes (see
p255). The original dervishes
were disciples of the mystical
poet and great Sufi master

Celaleddin Rumi, known as
"Mevlâna" (Our Leader).

Tucked away off Galip
Dede, the focus of the 18th-
century lodge is a beautiful
octagonal wooden dance
floor where the sema (ritual
dance) is performed on the
last Sunday of every month.
There is also a small exhibition of artifacts belonging
to the sect.

Galata Tower ❹
Galata Kulesi

Büyük Hendek Sok, Şişhane.
Map 5 D1. **Tel** (0212) 293 81 80.
🚇 Tünel. 🕐 8am–7pm daily.
🍴 Restaurant & Nightclub.
🕐 8pm–midnight daily.
www.galatatower.net

The most recognizable feature on the Golden Horn,
the Galata Tower, is 60 m
(196 ft) high and topped by a
conical tower. Its origins date
from the 6th century when it
was used to monitor shipping.
After the conquest of Istanbul
in 1453, the Ottomans turned
it into a prison and naval
depot. Aviation pioneer,
Hezarifen Ahmet Çelebi
attached wings to his arms
and "flew" from the tower to
Üsküdar in the 1700s. The
building was subsequently
used as a fire watchtower.

It has been refurbished to
blend with local improvement
schemes and, in the evenings,
the 9th floor is a noteworthy
restaurant and nightclub with
authentic Turkish entertain-

The distinctive Galata Tower, as seen from across the Golden Horn

ment. The unmissable view from the top encompasses the Istanbul skyline and beyond to Princes' Islands *(see p158)*.

Ottoman Bank Museum 5
Osmanlı Bankası Müzesi

Voyvoda Cad 35–37, Karaköy.
Map 5 D1. *Tel (0212) 292 76 05.*
Tünel. 25E, 56. 10am–6pm daily.

The Ottoman Bank Museum has the most interesting collection of state archives in Turkey. From the official Ottoman state bank in 1856 to its incorporation into Garanti Bank in 2001, no other records mirror Turkey's recent social, political and economic events so authentically. Exhibits include Ottoman bank notes, promissory notes, photos of the Empire's ornately crafted bank branches and outstanding photos of employees throughout the bank's history.

Nusretiye Mosque

Nusretiye Mosque 6
Nusretiye Camii

Necatibey Cad, Tophane. **Map** 1 E3.
25E, 56. daily.

The Baroque "Mosque of Victory" was built in the 1820s by Kirkor Balian. A very ornate building, it is in fact more like a large palace pavilion than a typical mosque. It was commissioned by Mahmut II to

commemorate his abolition of the Janissary corps in 1826 *(see p57)*. The marble panel of calligraphy around the interior of the mosque is particularly fine.

Suzani textiles (see p130) on sale in Çukurcuma

Istanbul Museum of Modern Art 7
İstanbul Modern anat Müzesi

Meclis-i Mebusan Cad, Liman İşletmeleri Sahası, Antrepo 4, Karaköy. **Map** 1 B5.
Tel (0212) 334 73 00. Tophane. 56. 10am–6pm Tue–Sun. www.istanbulmodern.org

Perched on the Golden Horn, the Istanbul Modern opened in 2005 as the most upbeat and thoroughly European museum in Turkey. It houses both permanent collections and temporary exhibitions, providing a showcase for many of the eccentric and talented personalities who have shaped modern art in Turkey, and reflecting the main trends and themes of Turkish art from the early 20th century to the present day. Many of the paintings and drawings are from the private collection of the Ecacıbaşı family, who founded the museum.

The collection includes abstract art, landscapes, watercolours and the plastic arts as well as a sculpture garden and a stunning exhibition of black-and-white photography. Exhibitions by contemporary artists from abroad are held regularly, as the museum embraces "Modern Experiences".

Çukurcuma 8

Map 1 E4. Taksim.

This charming old quarter of Beyoğlu, radiating from a neighbourhood mosque on Çukurcuma Caddesi, has become an important centre for the furnishings and antiques trades. Old warehouses and homes have been converted into shops and showrooms, where modern

upholstery materials are piled up in marble basins and antique cabinets. Browsing can yield the likes of 19th-century Ottoman embroidery to 1950s biscuit boxes.

Taksim 9

Map 1 E3. Taksim. **Taksim Art Gallery** *Tel (0212) 245 20 68.* 11am–7pm Mon–Sat.

Centring on the vast, open Taksim Square (Taksim Meydanı), the Taksim area is the hub of activity in modern Beyoğlu. Taksim means "water distribution centre", and from the early 18th century it was from this site that water from the Belgrade Forest was distributed throughout the modern city. The original stone reservoir, built in 1732 by Mahmut I, still stands at the top of İstiklal Caddesi.

On Cumhuriyet Caddesi is the modern building of the **Taksim Art Gallery**, which shows temporary exhibitions as well as permanent displays of Istanbul landscapes by some of Turkey's most important 20th-century painters.

Opposite the Marmara hotel and the Metro entrance, an underground funicular descends to the Golden Horn at Kabataş and links with an east-west tram line.

An array of colourful flowers for sale at a stall in Taksim Square

FURTHER AFIELD

Away from Istanbul's city centre there are numerous sights worth visiting. Stretching from the Golden Horn to the Sea of Marmara, the Theodosian Walls are one of the city's most impressive monuments. Along the walls stand several ancient palaces and churches: particularly interesting is the Church of St Saviour in Chora, with its stunning Byzantine mosaics. If you follow the Bosphorus

Tiles depicting Mecca, Cezri Kasım Paşa Mosque, Eyüp

northwards it will bring you to Dolmabahçe Palace, an opulent fantasy not to be missed. Beyond it is peaceful Yıldız Park, with yet more beautiful palaces and pavilions. Not all visitors have time to see the Asian side of the city, but it is worth spending half a day here. Attractions include splendid mosques, an ornate railway station and a museum dedicated to Florence Nightingale.

SIGHTS AT A GLANCE

Mosques and Churches

Ahrida Synagogue ❶
Atik Valide Mosque ㉔
Church of the Pammakaristos ❸
Church of the Pantocrator ❼
Church of St John of Studius ❽
Church of St Saviour in Chora pp118–9 ⑭
Church of St Stephen of the Bulgars ❷
Eyüp Sultan Mosque ⑮
Fatih Mosque ❻
Greek Orthodox Patriarchate ❹

İskele Mosque ㉓
Kara Ahmet Paşa Mosque ⑫
Mosque of Selim I ❺
Şemsi Paşa Mosque ㉒

Historic Sights

Bosphorus Bridge ㉘
Fortress of Asia ㉚
Fortress of Europe ㉜
Fortress of Seven Towers ❾
Haydarpaşa Station ㉖
Leander's Tower ㉑
Military Museum ⑱
Ortaköy ㉗

Pierre Loti Café ⑰
Sakıp Sabancı Museum ㉛
Selimiye Barracks ㉕
Shrine of Zoodochus Pege ⑪
Theodosian Walls ⑩
Yıldız Park ⑳

Palaces

Beylerbeyi Palace ㉙
Complex of Valide Sultan Mihrişah ⑯
Dolmabahçe Palace pp122–3 ⑲
Palace of the Porphyrogenitus ⑬

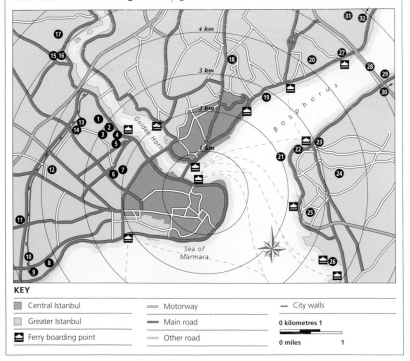

KEY

▪ Central Istanbul	▬ Motorway	▬ City walls
▫ Greater Istanbul	▬ Main road	0 kilometres 1
⚓ Ferry boarding point	▭ Other road	0 miles 1

◁ **Fountain in the grounds of the sumptuous Dolmabahçe Palace**

Ahrida Synagogue ❶
Ahrida Sinagogu

Gevgili Sok, Balat. 55T, 99A.
by appointment only. **Tel** *Karavan Travel, (0212) 523 47 29.*

The name of the oldest and most beautiful synagogue in Istanbul is a corruption of Ohrid, the name of a town in the former Yugoslavia from which its congregation came.

Founded before the Muslim conquest of Istanbul in 1453, it has been in constant use ever since. The painted walls and ceilings, dating from the late 17th century, have been restored to their Baroque glory. Pride of place, however, goes to the central Holy Ark, which is covered in rich tapestries.

Visits are possible by prior arrangement with one of various specialist tour operators, such as Karavan Travel.

Church of St Stephen of the Bulgars ❷
Bulgar Kilisesi

85 Mürsel Paşa Cad, Balat.
55T, 99A. Balat. *9am–4pm daily.*

Astonishingly, this entire church was cast in iron, even the internal columns and galleries. It was created in Vienna in 1871, shipped all the way to the Golden Horn *(see p99)* and assembled on

The Church of St Stephen of the Bulgars, wholly made of cast iron

its shore. The church was needed for the Bulgarian community who had broken away from the authority of the Greek Orthodox Patriarchate just up the hill. Today, it is still used by this community, who keep the marble tombs of the first Bulgarian patriarchs permanently decorated with flowers. The church stands in a pretty little park dotted with trees, and which runs down to the edge of the Golden Horn.

Church of the Pammakaristos ❸
Fethiye Camii

Fethiye Cad, Draman. 90, 90B.
prayer times only.

This Byzantine church is one of the hidden secrets of Istanbul. It is rarely visited despite the important role it

has played in the history of the city, and its breathtaking series of mosaics. For over 100 years after the Ottoman conquest it housed the Greek Orthodox Patriarchate, but was converted into a mosque in the late 16th century by Sultan Murat III.

The charming exterior is obviously Byzantine, with its alternating stone and brick courses and finely carved marble details. The main body of the building is the working mosque, while the extraordinary mosaics are in a side chapel. This now operates as a museum and officially you need to get permission in advance from Haghia Sophia *(see pp82–5)* to see it. However there is a chance that if the caretaker is around he may simply let you in.

Dating from the 14th century, the great Byzantine renaissance, the mosaics show holy figures isolated in a sea of gold, a reflection of the heavens. On either side are portraits of the Virgin Mary and John the Baptist beseeching Christ. They are overlooked by the four archangels, while the side apses are filled with other saintly figures.

Greek Orthodox Patriarchate ❹
Ortodoks Patrikhanesi

35 Sadrazam Ali Paşa Cad, Fener.
Tel *(0212) 521 19 21.* 55T, 99A.
9am–5pm daily.

This walled complex has been the seat of the patriarch of the Greek Orthodox Church since the early 17th century. Though nominally head of the whole church, the patriarch is now shepherd to a diminishing Istanbul flock.

The main door to the Patriarchate has been welded shut in memory of Patriarch Gregory V, hanged here for treason in 1821 after encouraging the Greeks to throw off Ottoman rule at the start of the Greek War of Independence (1821–32). Turkish–Greek antagonism worsened with the Greek occupation of parts

Byzantine façade of the Church of the Pammakaristos

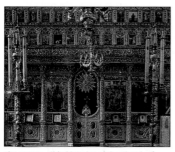

The ornate, gilded interior of the Church of St George in the Greek Orthodox Patriarchate

of Turkey in the 1920s *(see p58)*, anti-Greek riots in 1955, and the expulsion of Greek residents in the mid-1960s. Today the clergy at the Patriarchate is protected by a metal detector at the entrance.

The Patriarchate centres on the basilica-style Church of St George, dating back to 1720, yet the church contains much older relics and furniture. The patriarch's throne is thought to be Byzantine, while the pulpit is adorned with fine wooden inlay and icons.

Mosque of Selim I ❺
Selim I Camii

Yavuz Selim Cad, Fener. 🚌 *55T, 90, 90B, 99A.* ◯ *daily.*

This much-admired mosque is also known locally as Yavuz Sultan Mosque: Yavuz, "the Grim", being the nickname the infamous Selim acquired. It is idyllic in a rather off-beat way, which does seem at odds with Selim's barbaric reputation.

The mosque, built in 1522, sits alone on a hill beside what is now a vast sunken parking area, once the Byzantine Cistern of Aspar. Sadly, it is rarely visited and has an air of neglect, yet the mosque's intimate courtyard gives an

İznik tile panel in the Mosque of Selim I

insight into Islam's concept of paradise.

The windows set into the porticoes in the courtyard are capped by early İznik tiles *(see p161)* made by the *cuerda seca* technique – each colour is separated during the firing process, affording the patterns greater definition. Similar tiles lend decorative effect to the simple prayer hall, with its fine mosque furniture *(see pp32–3)* and original, carefully painted woodwork.

Fatih Mosque ❻
Fatih Camii

Macar Kardeşler Cad, Fatih. **Map** 4 A2. 🚌 *28, 87, 90, 91.* ◯ *daily.*

A spacious outer courtyard surrounds this vast Baroque mosque, the third major structure on this site. The first was the Church of the Holy Apostles, the burial place of most of the Byzantine emperors. Most of what you see today was the work of Mehmet Tahir Ağa, the chief imperial architect under Mustafa III. Many of the buildings he constructed around the prayer hall, including eight Koranic colleges *(medreses)* and a hospice, still stand. The only surviving parts of Mehmet the Conqueror's mosque are the three porticoes of the courtyard, the ablutions fountain, the main gate into the prayer hall and, inside, the mihrab. Two exquisite forms of 15th-century decoration can be seen over the windows in the porticoes: İznik tiles and lunettes adorned with calligraphic marble inlay. Stencilled patterns decorate the domes of the prayer hall, and parts of the walls are revetted with beautiful tiles.

The tomb of Mehmet the Conqueror stands behind the prayer hall, near that of his consort, Gülbahar. His sarcophagus and the turban decorating it are both appropriately large. It is a place of enormous gravity, always busy with supplicants.

If you pay a visit to the mosque on a Wednesday, you will also see the weekly market, which turns the streets around it into a circus of commerce. From tables piled high with fruit and vegetables to trucks loaded with unspun wool, this is a real spectacle.

Church of the Pantocrator, built by Empress Irene in the 12th century

Church of the Pantocrator ❼
Zeyrek Camii

İbadethane Sok, Küçükpazar. **Map** 4 B2. 🚌 *28, 61B, 87.* ◯ *prayer times daily.* ♿

Empress Irene, the wife of John II Comnenus, founded the Church of the Pantocrator ("Christ the Almighty") during the 12th century. This hulk of Byzantine masonry was once the centrepiece of one of Istanbul's most important religious foundations, the Monastery of the Pantocrator. The complex included an asylum, a hospice and a hospital. Now a mosque, it boasts a magnificent figurative marble floor and is composed of three interlinked chapels. A caretaker may let you in outside prayer times in the afternoon.

Church of St John of Studius ❽

İmrahor Camii

İmam Aşir Sok, Yedikule.
🚌 80, 80T. 🚇 Yedikule.

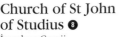

Istanbul's oldest surviving church, St John of Studius, is now merely a shell consisting of its outer walls, but you can still get an idea of the original beauty of what was once part of an important Byzantine institution.

The church was completed in AD 463 by Studius, a Roman patrician who served as consul during the reign of Emperor Marcian (450–57). Originally connected to the most powerful monastery in the Byzantine Empire and populated with ascetic monks, in the late 8th century it was a spiritual and intellectual centre under the rule of Abbot Theodore, who is now highly venerated in the Greek Orthodox Church as St Theodore. The most sacred relic housed in the church was the head of St John the Baptist, until its removal by the soldiers of the Fourth Crusade (see p50-51). The reigning emperor would visit the church each year for the Beheading of the Baptist feast on 29 August.

In the 15th century the church housed a university and was converted into a mosque. The building was abandoned in 1894 after it was damaged by an earthquake. The church is a perfect basilica, with a single apse at the east end, preceded by a narthex and a courtyard. It has a magnificent entrance portal, with carved Corinthian capitals and a sculpted architrave and cornice, but it is empty inside.

Battlements at Yedikule, an Ottoman addition to the fortress

Fortress of Seven Towers ❾

Yedikule

Kale Medanı 4, Yedikule İmrahor Mahallesi. **Tel** (0212) 585 89 33.
🚌 31, 80, 93T. ⏱ 9am–5pm daily.

Yedikule, the "Fortress of Seven Towers", was built in 1455 against the southern section of the Theodosian Walls. It displays both Byzantine and Ottoman features, being built in stages over a long period. Its seven towers are joined by thick walls to make a five-sided fortification. The two square marble towers built into the great land walls once flanked the Golden Gate (now blocked), which

Carving of the Byzantine eagle over Yedikule Gate

consisted of three magnificent golden portals. The gate was built by Emperor Theodosius I in AD 390 as the triumphal entrance into the thriving medieval city of Byzantium.

In the 15th century, Sultan Mehmet II (the Conqueror) completed Yedikule by adding three round towers and connecting curtain walls. After viewing the castle from the outside, you can enter through a doorway in the northeastern wall. The tower to your left as you enter is the *yazılı kule*, "the tower with inscriptions". It was used as a prison for foreign envoys and others who fell out of favour with the sultan. Its name is derived from the names and epitaphs which many of these doomed individuals carved into the walls. Some of these morbid inscriptions are still visible.

The northern of the two towers flanking the Golden Gate was a place of execution. Among those who met their end here was the 17-year-old Sultan Osman II, who was dragged off to Yedikule by his own Janissaries in 1622, after four years of misrule. The walkway around the ramparts is accessible via a steep flight of stone steps and offers good views of the land walls, the southern marble tower and market garden allotments.

Ruins of the Church of St John of Studius

Theodosian Walls ❿
Teodos II Surları

From Yedikule to Ayvansaray.
🚇 Ulubatlı. 🚋 Topkapı.

With its 11 fortified gates and 192 towers, this great chain of double walls sealed Constantinople's landward side against invasion for more than a thousand years. Extending for a distance of 6.5 km (4 miles) from the Sea of Marmara to the Golden Horn, the walls are built in layers of red tile alternating with limestone blocks. They can be reached by metro, tram or train, but to see their whole length you will need to take a taxi or dolmuş (see p408) along the main road that runs outside them.

The walls were built by Theodosius II in AD 412–22. They endured many sieges, and were only breached by Mehmet the Conqueror in May 1453 (see p54), when the Ottomans took Constantinople. Successive Ottoman sultans continued to maintain the walls until the end of the 17th century.

Many parts of the walls have been rebuilt, and the new sections give an idea of how the walls used to look. Some of the gateways are still in good repair, but a section of walls was demolished in the 1950s to make way for a road. The Charsius Gate (now called Edirnekapı), Silivrikapı, Yeni Mevlanakapı and other original gates still give access to the city. The Yedikule Gate (which stands beside the fortress of the same name) has an impressive imperial Byzantine eagle carved above its main archway.

Shrine of Zoodochus Pege ⓫
Balıklı Kilise

3 Seyit Nizam Cad, Silivrikapı.
Tel (0212) 582 30 81. 🚋 Seyitnizam.
🚌 93T. 🕐 8:30am–4pm daily.

The fountain of Zoodochus Pege ("Life-Giving Spring") is built over Istanbul's most famous sacred spring, which is believed to have miraculous

Silivrikapı, one of the gateways through the Theodosian Walls

powers. The fish in it are said to have arrived by miracle shortly before the fall of Constantinople (see p54). They are believed to have leapt into the water from a monk's frying pan on hearing him declare that a Turkish invasion of the fortified town was as likely as fish coming back to life. The spring was probably the site of an ancient sanctuary of Artemis.

Kara Ahmet Paşa Mosque ⓬
Kara Ahmet Paşa Camii

Undeğirmeni Sok, Fatma Sultan.
🕐 Prayer times only. 🚇 Ulubatlı.
🚋 Topkapı. 🚌 93T.

One of the most worthwhile detours along the city walls is the Kara Ahmet Paşa Mosque, which is also known as Gazi Ahmet Paşa. This lovely building, with its peaceful leafy courtyard and graceful proportions, is one of the imperial architect Sinan's (see p101) lesser known

achievements, which he built in 1554 for Kara Ahmet Paşa, a grand vizier of Süleyman the Magnificent (see p55).

The courtyard is surrounded by the cells of a *medrese* and a *dershane*, or main classroom. Attractive apple-green and yellow İznik tiles (see p161) dating from the mid-1500s grace the porch, with blue-and-white tiles on the east wall of the prayer hall. Outside the city walls is tiny Takkeci İbrahim Ağa Mosque, which dates from 1592 and has some particularly fine İznik tile panels.

Palace of the Porphyrogenitus ⓭
Tekfur Sarayı

Şişehane Cad, Edirnekapı. 🚌 87, 90, 126.

Only glimpses of the former grandeur of the Palace of the Porphyrogenitus (sovereign), during its years as an imperial residence, are discernible from the sketchy remains. Its one extant hall, now open to the elements, has an attractive three-storey façade in typically Byzantine style. It was most likely built in the late Byzantine era as an annexe of the Blachernae Palace. These palaces became the principal residences of the imperial sovereigns during the last two centuries before the fall of Constantinople to the Ottomans in 1453.

During the reign of Ahmet III (1703–30) the last remaining İznik potters (see p161) moved to the palace and it became a centre for tile production. Cezri Kasım Paşa Mosque in Eyüp has some very fine examples of these tiles.

Tilework over *medrese* doorway at Kara Ahmet Paşa Mosque

Church of St Saviour in Chora ⓮
Kariye Camii

Some of the very finest Byzantine mosaics and frescoes can be found in the Church of St Saviour in Chora. Little is known of the early history of the church, although its name "in Chora", which means "in the country", suggests that the church originally stood in a rural setting.

Scene from the Life of the Virgin

The present church dates from the 11th century. From 1315 to 1321 it was remodelled, and the mosaics and frescoes were added by Theodore Metochites, a theologian, philosopher and one of the elite Byzantine officials of his day.

View of St Saviour in Chora

THE GENEALOGY OF CHRIST

Theodore Metochites, who restored St Saviour, wrote that his mission was to relate how "the Lord himself became a mortal on our behalf". He takes the *Genealogy of Christ* as his starting point: the mosaics in the two domes of the inner narthex portray 66 of Christ's forebears.

The crown of the southern dome is occupied by a figure of Christ. In the dome's flutes are two rows of his ancestors: Adam to Jacob ranged above the 12 sons of Jacob. In the northern dome, there is a central image of the Virgin and Child with the kings of the House of David in the upper row and lesser ancestors of Christ in the lower row.

Mosaic showing Christ and his ancestors, in the southern dome of the inner narthex

THE LIFE OF THE VIRGIN

All but one of the 20 mosaics in the inner narthex depicting the *Life of the Virgin* are well preserved. This cycle is based mainly on the apocryphal Gospel of St James, written in the 2nd century, which gives an account of the Virgin's life. This was popular in the Middle Ages and was a rich source of material for ecclesiastical artists.

Among the events shown are the first seven steps of the Virgin, the Virgin entrusted to Joseph and the Virgin receiving bread from an angel.

THE INFANCY OF CHRIST

Scenes from the *Infancy of Christ*, based largely on the New Testament, occupy the semicircular panels of the outer narthex. They begin on

GUIDE TO THE MOSAICS AND FRESCOES

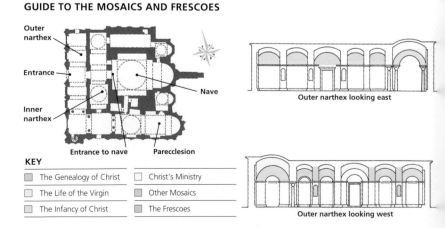

Outer narthex

Entrance

Nave

Inner narthex

Entrance to nave   Parecclesion

Outer narthex looking east

KEY

- The Genealogy of Christ
- The Life of the Virgin
- The Infancy of Christ
- Christ's Ministry
- Other Mosaics
- The Frescoes

Outer narthex looking west

the north wall of the outer narthex with a scene of Joseph being visited by an angel in a dream. Subsequent panels include Mary and Joseph's *Journey to Bethlehem*, their *Enrolment for Taxation*, the *Nativity of Christ* and, finally, Herod ordering the *Massacre of the Innocents.*

The *Enrolment for Taxation*

CHRIST'S MINISTRY

While many of the mosaics in this series are badly damaged, some beautiful panels remain. The cycle occupies the vaults of the seven bays of the outer narthex and some of the south bay of the inner narthex. The most striking mosaic is the portrayal of Christ's temptation in the wilderness, in the second bay of the outer narthex.

Theodore Metochites presents St Saviour in Chora to Christ

OTHER MOSAICS

There are three panels in the nave of the church, one of which, above the main door from the inner narthex, illustrates the *Dormition of the Virgin*. This mosaic, protected by a marble frame, is the best preserved in the church. The Virgin is depicted laid out on a bier, watched over by the Apostles, with Christ seated behind. Other devotional panels in the two narthexes include one, on the east wall of the south bay of the inner narthex, of the *Deësis*, depicting Christ with the Virgin Mary and, unusually, without St John. Another, in the inner narthex over the door into the nave, is of Theodore Metochites himself, shown wearing a large turban, and humbly presenting the restored church as an offering to Christ.

THE FRESCOES

The frescoes in the parecclesion are thought to have been painted just after the mosaics were completed, probably in around 1320. The

VISITORS' CHECKLIST

Kariye Camii Sok, Edirnekapı.
Tel (0212) 631 92 41. 28, 86 or 90 then 5 minutes' walk.
9am–4:30pm Thu–Tue (to 6pm summer).

most engaging of the frescoes – which reflect the purpose of the parecclesion as a place of burial – is the *Anastasis*, in the semidome above the apse. In it, the central figure of Christ, the vanquisher of death, is shown dragging Adam and Eve out of their tombs. Under Christ's feet are the gates of hell, while Satan lies before him. The fresco in the vault overhead depicts *The Last Judgment*, with the souls of the saved on the right and those of the damned to the left.

Figure of Christ from the *Anastasis* fresco in the parecclesion

Inner narthex looking east

Parecclesion and outer narthex looking south

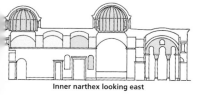

Inner narthex looking west

Parecclesion and outer narthex looking north

Visitors at the tomb of Eyüp Ensari, Mohammed's standard bearer

Eyüp Sultan Mosque **⑮**
Eyüp Sultan Camii

Cami-i Kebir Sok. **Tel** *(0212) 564 73 68.* 🚌 *39, 55T, 99A.* ⭕ *daily.*

Mehmet the Conqueror built the original mosque on this site in 1458, five years after his conquest of Istanbul, in honour of Eyüp Ensari. That building fell into ruins and the present mosque was completed in 1800, by Selim III.

The mosque's delightful inner courtyard features two huge plane trees on a platform. This was the setting for the Girding of the Sword of Osman, part of a sultan's inauguration in the days of Mehmet the Conqueror.

Opposite the mosque is the tomb of Eyüp Ensari himself, said to have been killed during the first Arab siege of Constantinople in the 7th century. The tomb dates from the same period as the mosque and its decoration is in the Ottoman Baroque style.

Complex of Valide Sultan Mihrişah **⑯**
Mihrişah Valide Sultan Külliyesi

Seyit Reşat Cad. 🚌 *39, 55T, 99A.* ⭕ *9:30am–4:30pm Tue–Sun.*

Most of the northern side of the street leading from Eyüp Mosque's northern gate is occupied by the largest

Baroque *külliye (see p32)* in Istanbul, although unusually it is not centred on a mosque. Built for Mihrişah, mother of Selim III, the *külliye* was completed in 1791.

The complex includes the ornate marble tomb of Mihrişah and a soup kitchen, which is still in use today. There is also a beautiful grilled fountain *(sebil)*, from which an attendant once served water and refreshing drinks of sweet sherbet to passersby.

Pierre Loti Café **⑰**
Piyer Loti Kahvesi

Gümüşsuyu Cad, Balmumku Sok 5, Eyüp. **Tel** *(0212) 616 23 44.* 🚌 *39, 55T, 99A.* ⭕ *8am–midnight daily.*

This famous café stands at the top of the hill in Eyüp Cemetery, a 20-minute walk up Karyağdı Sokağı from Eyüp Mosque. A funicular will also take you up and down the steep hill leading to the café. It is named after the French novelist, Julien Viaud, a French naval officer, popularly known as Pierre Loti, who frequented the café during his stay here in 1876. Loti defiantly fell in love with a married Turkish woman and wrote an autobiographical novel, *Aziyade*, about their affair. The café is prettily decked out with 19th-century furniture and the waiters wear period outfits. No alcohol.

Military Museum **⑱**
Askeri Müzesi

Vali Konağı Cad, Harbiye. **Map** 1 F1. **Tel** *(0212) 233 27 20.* 🚌 *46H.* ⭕ *9am–5pm Wed–Sun.* **Mehter Band performances** *3–4pm Wed–Sun.* 📷 📹

One of Istanbul's most impressive museums, the Military Museum traces the history of the country's conflicts from the conquest of Constantinople in 1453 *(see p54)* through to modern warfare. The building used to be the military academy where Atatürk studied from 1899 to 1905.

The museum is also the main location for performances by the Mehter Band *(see p383)*, formed in the 14th century during the reign of Osman I *(see p54)*. Until the 19th century the muscians were Janissaries, who accompanied the sultan into battle and performed songs about hero-ancestors and battle victories. The band had a wide influence and is thought to have provided some inspiration for Mozart and Beethoven.

Some of the most striking weapons on display on the ground floor are the curved daggers *(cembiyes)* carried at the waist by foot soldiers in the 15th century. These are ornamented with plant, flower and geometric motifs in relief and silver filigree. Other exhibits include 17th-century copper head armour for horses and Ottoman shields

Period interior of the Pierre Loti Café

An Ottoman curved dagger (cembiye) displayed in the Military Museum

made from cane and willow covered in silk thread.

A moving portrayal of trench warfare is included in the section concerned with the ANZAC landings of 1915 at Chunuk Bair on the Gallipoli peninsula *(see p168–9)*, and upstairs is a spectacular exhibit of the tents used by sultans on their campaigns.

From the nearby station on Taşkışla Caddesi you can take the cable car across Maçka Park to Abdi İpekçi Caddesi in Teşvikiye. Some of the best designer clothes, jewellery, furniture and art shops in the city are here *(see pp130–131)*.

Dolmabahçe Palace ⑲

See pp122–3.

Yıldız Park ⑳

Çırağan Cad, Beşiktaş. **Map** 3 D2. 🚌 *25E, 40.* ⭘ *dawn to dusk daily.* 🅿 *for vehicles.*

Yildiz Park was originally laid out as the garden of the first Çırağan Palace. It later formed the grounds of **Yıldız Palace**, an assortment of buildings from different eras now enclosed behind a wall and entered separately from Ihlamur-Yıldız Caddesi. The palace is a collection of pavilions and villas built in the 19th and 20th centuries. Many of them are the work of the eccentric Sultan Abdül Hamit II (1876–1909, *see p57*), who made it his principal residence as he feared a sea-borne attack on Dolmabahçe Palace *(see pp122–3)*. The main building in the entrance courtyard is the State Apartments (Büyük Mabeyn), dating from the reign of Sultan Selim III (1789–1807). Around the corner, the **City Museum** (Şehir Müzesi) has a

display of Yıldız porcelain. The Italianate building opposite is the former armoury, or Silahhane. Next door to the City Museum is the **Yıldız Palace Museum**, housed in what was the Marangozhane (Abdül Hamit's carpentry workshop), and containing a changing collection of the palace's art and objects.

Further on is Yıldız Palace Theatre (completed in 1889 by Abdül Hamit), now a museum. The theatre's restored interior is mainly blue and gold, and the stars on the domed ceiling refer to the palace's name: yıldız means "star" in Turkish. Backstage, the former dressing rooms contain theatre displays, including original costumes and playbills.

The lake in the grounds is shaped like Abdül Hamit's *tuğra (see p28)*. A menagerie was once kept on the lake's islands where some 30 keepers tended tigers, lions, giraffes and zebras.

Several other little pavilions dot Yıldız Park, which, with its many ancient trees and exotic shrubs, is a very popular spot for picnics. As the park is situated on a hill, and it is a fairly long climb to the top, you may prefer to take a taxi up to the Şale Köşkü (Chalet Villa) and walk back down past the other sights.

Şale Köşkü is one of the most impressive in the park and built by Abdül Hamit. Although its façade appears as a whole, it was in fact built in three stages.

The Malta and Çadır pavilions were built during the reign of Abdül Aziz who

ruled from 1861–76. Both of them formerly served as prisons but are open as cafés. Malta Pavilion, also a restaurant, is a favoured haunt of locals on Sundays.

Mitat Paşa, reformist and architect of the constitution, was among those imprisoned in Çadır Pavilion, for instigating the murder of Abdül Aziz. Meanwhile, Murat V and his mother were locked away in Malta Pavilion for 27 years after a brief incarceration in the Çırağan Palace.

In 1895 the Imperial Porcelain Factory began production here, to satisfy the demand of the upper classes for chic European-style ceramics. The unusual building was designed to look like a stylized medieval castle of Europe, complete with several turrets and portcullis windows. The original household items such as sugar bowls, vases and plates that were produced here usually depict idealized scenes of the Bosphorus and other local spots. Examples of these items can be seen today in various museums and palaces all over Istanbul.

🏛 **City Museum**
Tel (0212) 258 53 44.

🏛 **Yıldız Palace Museum**
Tel (0212) 258 30 80 (ext 280).

A bridge in the grounds of Yıldız Palace

Dolmabahçe Palace ⓳
Dolmabahçe Sarayı

Sultan Abdül Mecit built Dolmabahçe Palace in 1856. As its designers he employed Karabet Balyan and his son Nikoğos, members of the great family of Armenian architects who lined the Bosphorus (see pp126–7) with many of their creations during the 19th century. The extravagant opulence of the Dolmabahçe belies the fact that it was built at a time when the Ottoman Empire was in decline. The palace can be visited only on a guided tour, of which two are on offer. The best tour

Sèvres vase at the foot of the Crystal Staircase

takes you through the Selamlık (or Mabeyn-i Hümayun), the part of the palace that was reserved for men and which contains the state rooms and the enormous Ceremonial Hall. The other tour goes through the Harem, the living quarters of the sultan and his entourage. If you want to go only on one tour, visit the Selamlık.

★ **Crystal Staircase**
The apparent fragility of this glass staircase stunned observers when it was built. In the shape of a double horseshoe, it is made from Baccarat crystal and brass, and has a polished mahogany rail.

The Süfera Salon, where ambassadors waited for an audience with the sultan, is one of the most luxurious rooms in the palace.

Entrance

Imperial Gate of the Palace
Once used only by the sultan and his ministers, this gate is now the main entrance to the palace. The Mehter, or Janissary, Band (see pp383, 120) performs in front of the gate every Tuesday afternoon throughout the summer.

Swan Fountain
This fountain stands in the Imperial Garden. The original 16th-century garden here was created from recovered land, hence the palace's name, Dolmabahçe, meaning "Filled-in Garden".

Selamlık and Harem

The Red Room was used by the sultan to receive ambassadors.

★ **Ceremonial Hall**
This magnificent domed hall was designed to hold 2,500 people. Its chandelier, reputedly the heaviest in the world, was bought in England.

VISITORS' CHECKLIST

Dolmabahçe Cad, Beşiktaş.
Map 2 B4. *Tel (0212) 236 9000.*
25E, 40. 9am–4pm
(last adm) Tue, Wed & Fri–Sun
(Oct–Feb: last adm 3pm).

Blue Salon
On religious feast days the sultan's mother would receive his wives and favourites in the Harem's principal room.

The Zülvecheyn, or Panorama Room

Harem

The Rose-coloured salon was the assembly room of the Harem.

Reception room of the sultan's mother

Atatürk's Bedroom
Atatürk (see p58) died in this room at 9:05am on 10 November 1938. All the clocks in the palace, such as this one near the crystal staircase, are stopped at this time.

Main shore gate

Sultan Abdül Aziz's bedroom
had to accommodate a huge bed built especially for the 150 kg (330 lb) amateur wrestler.

★ **Main Bathroom**
The walls of this bathroom are revetted in finest Egyptian alabaster, while the taps are solid silver. The brass-framed bathroom windows afford stunning views across the Bosphorus.

STAR FEATURES

★ Ceremonial Hall

★ Crystal Staircase

★ Main Bathroom

Leander's Tower, on its own small island in the Bosphorus

Leander's Tower ㉑
Kız Kulesi

Üsküdar. **Map** 6 A3. 🚢 Üsküdar.
Tel (0216) 342 47 47.
www.kizkulesi.com.tr

Located on an islet offshore
from Üsküdar, the tiny,
white Leander's Tower is a
well-known Bosphorus landmark, dating from the 18th
century. The tower once
served as a quarantine centre
during a cholera outbreak, as
a lighthouse, a customs
control point and a maritime
toll gate. The tower is now
used as a restaurant and
pricey offshore disco.

In Turkish the tower is known
as the "Maiden's Tower" after
a legendary princess, confined
here after a prophet foretold
that she would die of a snake-
bite. The tower's English name
derives from the Greek myth
of Leander, who swam the
Hellespont (the modern-day
Dardanelles, *see pp168–9*) to
see his lover, priestess Hero.

Şemsi Paşa Mosque ㉒
Şemsi Paşa Camii

Sahil Yolu, Üsküdar. **Map** 6 A2.
🚢 Üsküdar. ◯ daily.

This is one of the smallest
mosques to be commis-
sioned by a grand vizier
(Ottoman prime minister).
Its miniature dimensions
combined with its picturesque
waterfront location make it
one of the most attractive
little mosques in the city. It
was built in 1580 by the

architect Sinan (*see p101*), at
the request of Şemsi Ahmet
Paşa, who succeeded Sokollu
Mehmet Paşa.

The mosque's garden, overlooking the Bosphorus, is
surrounded on two sides by
the theological college
or *medrese (see p32)*,
with the small
mosque on the
third side and
the sea wall on
the fourth. The
mosque itself is
also quite unusual
in that the tomb of
Şemsi Ahmet Paşa
is joined to the main
building, divided
from the interior by a grille.

**Dome in the entrance
to Atik Valide Mosque**

İskele Mosque ㉓
İskele Camii

Hakimiyeti Milliye Cad, Üsküdar.
Map 6 B2. 🚢 Üsküdar. ◯ daily.

One of Üsküdar's most
prominent landmarks, the
İskele Mosque (also known
as Mihrimah Sultan Mosque),

**Fountain set into the platform
below the İskele Mosque**

takes its name from the ferry
landing where it stands. A
massive structure on a raised
platform, it was built by Sinan
between 1547 and 1548 for
Mihriman Sultan, favourite
daughter of Süleyman the
Magnificent. Without space to
build a courtyard, Sinan constructed a large protruding
roof which extends to cover
the *şadırvan* (ablutions fountain) in front of the mosque.

Atik Valide Mosque ㉔
Atik Valide Camii

Çinili Camii Sok, Üsküdar. **Map** 6 C3.
🚌 12C (from Üsküdar). ◯ prayer
times only.

The Atik Valide mosque, set
on the hill above Üsküdar, was
one of the most extensive
mosque complexes in
the whole of
Istanbul. The name
translates as the
Old Mosque of the
Sultan's Mother, as
the mosque was
built for Nur Banu,
the wife of Selim II
("the Sot") and the
mother of Murat III.
She was the first of
the sultans' mothers to rule
the Ottoman Empire from the
Harem (*see p71*). Sinan
completed the mosque, which
was his last major work, in
1583. It has a wide shallow
dome which rests on five
semidomes, with a flat arch
over the entrance portal.

The interior is surrounded
on three sides by galleries, the
undersides of which retain
the rich stencilling typical of
the period. The mihrab apse is
almost completely covered
with panels of fine İznik tiles
(*see p161*), while the mihrab
itself and the *minbar* are both
made of sculpted marble. Side
aisles were added in the 17th
century, while the grilles and
architectural trompe l'oeil
paintings on the royal loge in
the western gallery date from
the 18th century.

Outside, a door in the north
wall of the courtyard leads
down a flight of stairs to the
medrese (theological college),
where the *dershane* (class-

room) projects out over the street below, supported by an arch. The *şifahane* (hospital), built around a central courtyard just east of the mosque, is also worth a visit.

Selimiye Barracks ㉕
Selimiye Kışlası

Çeşmei Kebir Cad, Selimiye.
Map 6 B5. 🚇 *Harem*, 🚌 *12*.

The Selimiye Barracks were originally made of wood and completed in 1799 under Selim III, who was sultan from 1789 to 1807. They were built to house the "New Army" that formed part of Selim's plan for reforming the Imperial command structure and replacing the powerful Janissaries *(see pp56–7)*. The plan backfired and Selim was deposed but the barracks were, nevertheless, a striking symbol of Constantinople's military might, perhaps becoming even more so when they were rebuilt in stone in 1829 by Mahmut II. The building still houses Istanbul's First Army Division and is off limits to the public.

The Florence Nightingale Museum is found within the Selimiye Barracks. It still contains some of the original

Haydarpaşa Station, terminus for trains arriving from Anatolia

furniture and the famous lamp which gave her the epitaph "Lady of the Lamp." Visits must be arranged in advance by faxing the Army Head-quarters, (0216) 333 10 09.

Nearby are two other sites worth seeing – the Selimiye Mosque and the British War Cemetery (also known as the Crimean Memorial Cemetery). The mosque was built in 1804 and is set in a lovely court-yard. The Cemetery, south on Burhan Felek Caddesi, contains the graves of men who died in the Crimean War, World War I battles at Gallipoli *(see pp168–9)* and during World War II in the Middle East.

Haydarpaşa Station ㉖
Haydarpaşa Garı

Haydarpaşa İstasyon Cad. **Tel** *(0216) 348 80 20.* 🚇 *Haydarpaşa or Kadıköy.* ⏲ *8am–6pm daily*

The waterfront location and grandeur of Haydarpaşa Station, together with the neighbouring tiled jetty, make it the most impressive point of arrival or departure in Istanbul. Built on land reclaimed from the sea, the station is surrounded by water on three sides – a unique feature.

The first Anatolian railway line, which was built in 1873, ran from here to İznik *(see p160)*. The extension of this railway was a major part of Abdül Hamit II's drive to modernize the Ottoman Empire. Lacking sufficient funds to continue the project, he applied for help to his German ally, Kaiser Wilhelm II. The Deutsche Bank agreed to invest in the construction and operation of the railway. In 1898 German engineers were contracted to build the new railway lines running across Anatolia and beyond into the far reaches of the Ottoman Empire. At the same time a number of stations were built.

Construction on Haydarpaşa, the grandest of these, started in 1906. Its two German archi-tects, Otto Ritter and Helmut Conu, chose to build on a grand scale, using a Neo-Classic German style. The station was completed in 1908.

FLORENCE NIGHTINGALE

The British nurse Florence Nightingale (1820–1910) was a tireless campaigner for hospital, military and social reform. During the Crimean War, in which Britain and France fought on the Ottoman side against the Russian Empire, she organ-ized a party of 38 British nurses. They took charge of medical services at the Selimiye Barracks in Scutari (Üsküdar) in 1854. By the time she returned to Britain in 1856, at the end of the war, the mortality rate in the barracks had decreased from 20 to 2 per cent, and the fundamental principles of modern nursing had been established. On her return home, Florence Nightingale opened a training school for nurses.

A 19th-century painting of Florence Nightingale in Selimiye Barracks

The Bosphorus Trip

Ceremonial gate, Çırağan Palace

One of the great pleasures of a visit to Istanbul is a cruise up the Bosphorus. It is relaxing and offers an excellent vantage point from which to view the city's famous landmarks. You can go on a pre-arranged guided tour or take one of the small boats that tout for passengers at Eminönü. But there is no better way to travel than on the official trip run by Turkish Maritime Lines *(TDI, see p405)*. Laden with sightseers, the TDİ ferry makes a round-trip to the upper Bosphorus once or twice daily, stopping at six piers along the way, including a leisurely stop at Anadolu Kavağı for lunch. You can return to Eminönü on the same boat or make your way back to the city by bus, dolmuş or taxi.

LOCATOR MAP

Sadberk Hanım Museum
Housed in two yalıs (see p31), this private museum contains ethnographic displays and a private archaeology collection.

Fortress of Europe
Situated at the narrowest point on the Bosphorus, this fortress was built by Mehmet II in 1452 as a prelude to his invasion of Constantinople.

Dolmabahçe Palace
This opulent 19th-century Baroque palace is a symbol of Ottoman grandeur.

Saıyer

Büyükder

Arnavutköy

Bosphorus Bridge

Cenge

Ortaköy

İnönü Stadium

Beşiktaş

İskele Mösque

Kabataş

Üsküdar

Karaköy

Eminönü

View of the City
As the ferry departs, you have a view of many of the old monuments of Istanbul, including Süleymaniye Mosque.

Leander's Tower

Harem

Rumeli Kavağı

Anadolu Kavağı

Anadolu Kavağı
The last stop on the trip brings you to this village and a ruined 14th-century Byzantine fortress, the Genoese Castle.

Huber Köşkü • Beykoz

Beykoz
Beykoz is the largest fishing village along the Asian shore. Situated in the village square is this fountain dating from 1746.

Yeniköy
Paşabahçe
İstinye • Çubuklu
Kanlıca
Fatih Sultan Mehmet Bridge
Fortress of Asia
dilli

Yeniköy
Handsome 19th-century yalıs line the waterfront of this ancient village. It was invaded by Cossacks who crossed the Black Sea in 1624.

Fortress of Asia
Fifty years older than the Fortress of Europe, this fortress was built by Sultan Beyazıt I just before the failed Ottoman siege of Constantinople in 1396–7.

| | 0 kilometres 2 |
| 0 miles 1 |

KEY
- Motorway
- Main road
- Other road
- Ferry boarding point
- --- Route of Bosphorus trip
- Viewpoint

The Bosphorus suspension bridge between Ortaköy and Beylerbeyi

Ortaköy ㉗

Map 3 F2. 🚌 *25E, 40, 41.*

Crouched at the foot of the Bosphorus Bridge, the suburb of Ortaköy has retained a village feel. Life centres on İskele Meydanı, the quayside square, which was once busy with fishermen unloading the day's catch. Nowadays, though, Ortaköy is better known for its lively Sunday market, which crowds out the square and surrounding streets, and its shops selling the wares of local artisans. It is also the location for a thriving bar and café scene, which in the summer is the hub of Istanbul's nightlife *(see pp132–3)*.

Mecidiye Mosque (better known as Ortaköy Cami), Ortaköy's most impressive landmarks, sits on the water-front. It was built in 1853 by Nikoğos Balyan, who was also responsible for Dolma-bahçe Palace *(see pp122–3)*.

Ortaköy's fashionable waterfront square and ferry landing

Bosphorus Bridge ㉘
Boğaziçi Köprüsü

Ortaköy and Beylerbeyi. **Map** 3 F2. 🚌 *200, 202 (double deckers from Taksim).*

Spanning the Bosphorus between the districts of Ortaköy and Beylerbeyi, this was the first bridge to be built across the straits that divide Istanbul and separate Europe from Asia. It was inaugurated on 29 October 1973, to coincide with the 50th anniversary of the founding of the Turkish Republic *(see p58)*. It is 1,074 m (3,524 ft) long, and is the world's ninth longest suspension bridge. It reaches 64 m (210 ft) above the water.

The Bosphorus is especially popular in summer, when cool breezes waft off the water.

Beylerbeyi Palace ㉙
Beylerbeyi Sarayı

Abdullah Ağa Cad, Beylerbeyi Mahallesi, Asian side. **Tel** (0216) 321 93 20. 🚌 *15 (from Üsküdar), 10 (from Beşiktaş).* 🚇 *from Üsküdar.* 🕐 *9:30am–6pm Tue–Wed & Fri–Sun.* 🎟🚫📷🚻🚾

Designed in the Baroque style of the late Ottoman period, Beylerbeyi Palace was built between 1861 and 1865 by members of the Balyan family under the orders of Sultan Abdül Aziz. A previous palace had stood here, and the gardens were already laid out by Murat IV in 1639. As the Ottoman empire withered, palaces proliferated in a flourish of grandeur and

showmanship. Abdül Aziz had Beylerbeyi built as a pleasure palace to entertain dignitaries and royalty. The Empress Eugénie of France (wife of Napoleon III) was a guest at the palace in 1869 on her way to the opening of the Suez Canal. The Duke and Duchess of Windsor also visited Beylerbeyi. The foun-tains, baths and colonnades were meant to impress, as were the lovely frescoes of Ottoman warships.

To keep himself distracted, Aziz also had a zoo built on the site and, apparently, delighted in the flocks of ostriches and several Bengal tigers. The zoo is no longer there, but parts of the palace have been refurbished and restored to some of their former elegance.

Third-but-last of the line of sultans, the autocratic Abdül Hamit II spent six years as a prisoner in an anteroom of the palace and died there, virtually forgotten, after being deposed in 1909.

There are superb views of the palace from the Bosphorus, from where the two promi-nent bathing pavilions – one for the Harem and the other for the *selamlık* (the men's quarters), can best be seen.

The most attractive room is the reception hall, which has a pool and fountain.

Ornate landing at the top of the stairs in Beylerbeyi Palace

Fortress of Asia ㉚
Anadolu Hisarı

Riyaziyeci Sokak (on the harbour front), Asian side. **Tel** (0212) 263 53 05.

The fortress of Asia was built around 1398 by Mehmet II's grandfather, Sultan Yildirim

The Fortress of Europe, built by Mehmet the Conqueror to enable him to capture Constantinople

Beyazıt I (1389–1402). It was the Sultan's trump card in his attempt to defend Constantinople from the haughty Venetians, who walked a tightrope between consolidating their territorial ambitions and trying to avoid conflicts that might threaten the riches of their lucrative Ottoman trade. In spite of the fortress as a deterrent, a low-level war took place, lasting from 1463 to 1497.

The Fortress of Asia is closed to the public, but the neighbourhood is one of Istanbul's most charming and least affected by modern life.

Sakıp Sabancı Museum ③¹
Sakıp Sabancı Müzesi

İstinye Cad 22, Emirgab 34467. *Tel* (0212) 277 22 00. 🚌 40, 41 from Taksim Sq; any bus to İstinye or Sarıyer. ☐ 10am–6pm Tue, Thu, Fri, Sun; 10am–10pm Wed, Sat. 📷 ♿ 🛗 🛍
www.muze.sabanciuniv.edu

With a superb view over the Bosphorus, the Sakıp Sabancı Museum, is also known as the Horse Mansion (Altı Kösk). exhibitions comprise over 400 years of Ottoman calligraphy and other Koranic and secular art treasures. The collection of paintings is exquisite, with works by Ottoman court painters and European artists enthralled with Turkey. A Picasso exhibition in 2005 made this museum the first in Turkey to host a major solo exhibition of a Western artist. This was followed by Rodin in 2006 and Dalí in 2008–2009.

Fortress of Europe ③²
Rumeli Hisarı

Yahya Kemal Cad 42, European side. *Tel* (0212) 263 53 05. 🚌 40 and 41 (from Taksim Square). ☐ 9am–5pm Thu–Tue. 📷

This fortress was built by Mehmet the Conqueror in 1452 as his first step in the conquest of Constantinople (*see p54*). Situated at the narrowest point of the Bosphorus, the fortress controlled a major Byzantine supply route. Across the straits is Anadolu Hisarı, the Fortress of Asia, which was built in the 14th century by Beyazıt I.

The Fortress of Europe's layout was planned by Mehmet himself. While his grand vizier (*see pp56–7*) and two other viziers were each responsible for the building of one of the three great towers, the sultan took charge of the walls. Local buildings were torn down to provide the stones and other building materials. One thousand masons laboured on the walls alone. It was completed in four months – a considerable feat, given the steep terrain.

The new fortress was garrisoned by a force of Janissaries (*see pp56–7*), whose troops trained their cannons on the straits to prevent the passage of foreign ships. After they had sunk a Venetian vessel, this approach to Constantinople was cut off. Following the conquest of the city, the fortress lost its importance as a military base and was used as a prison, particularly for out-of-favour foreign envoys and prisoners of war. The structure was restored only in 1953.

Today it is in excellent condition and is a pleasant place for an afternoon outing. Some open-air theatre performances are staged here during the Istanbul Festival of Arts and Culture (*see p35*).

BIRDS OF THE BOSPHORUS

In September and October, thousands of white storks and birds of prey fly over the Bosphorus on their way from their breeding grounds in eastern Europe to wintering regions in Africa. Large birds usually prefer to cross narrow straits like the Bosphorus rather than fly over an expanse of open water such as the Mediterranean. Among birds of prey on this route you can see the lesser spotted eagle and the honey buzzard. The birds also cross the straits in spring on their way to Europe but, before the breeding season, they are fewer in number.

The white stork, which migrates over the straits

SHOPPING IN ISTANBUL

Istanbul's shops and markets, crowded and noisy at most times of the day and year, sell a colourful mixture of goods from all over the world. The city's most famous shopping centre is the massive Grand Bazaar. Turkey is a centre of textile production, and Istanbul has a wealth of carpet and fashion shops. If you prefer to do all your

Contemporary glass vase

shopping under one roof, head for one of the city's modern shopping malls. Wherever you shop, be wary of imitations of famous brand products – even if they appear to be of a high standard and the salesman maintains that they are authentic. Be prepared to bargain where required: it is an important part of a shopping trip.

GENERAL INFORMATION

Most shops trade from 9am to 8pm Monday to Saturday, and markets open at 8am. Large shops and department stores open later in the morning. The Grand Bazaar and Spice Bazaar are open from 8:30am to 8pm. Malls are open from 10am to 10pm seven days a week. Details on payment, VAT exemption and buying antiques appear on pp374–5.

CARPETS AND KILIMS

In the Grand Bazaar *(see pp104–105)*, **Şişko Osman** has a good range of carpets, and **Galeri Şirvan** sells Anatolian tribal *kilims* (rugs). Award-

winning **Bereket Halicilik** is the most reliable seller of antique carpets. **Hazal Halı**, in Ortaköy, stocks a fine collection of kilims.

FABRICS

In addition to carpets and kilims, colourful fabrics in traditional designs from all over Turkey and Central Asia are widely sold. **Sivaslı Yazmacısı** sells village textiles, headscarves and embroidered cloths.

LEATHER

Turkish leatherwear, while not always of the best quality hides, is durable, of good

craftsmanship and reasonably priced. The Grand Bazaar is full of shops selling leather goods. **Meb Deri**, for example, offers a good range of fashion handbags and accessories, and **Desa** has an extensive range of both classic and fashionable designs.

JEWELLERY

The Grand Bazaar is the best place to find gold jewellery – it is sold by weight, with only a modest sum added for craftsmanship. The daily price of gold is displayed in the shop windows. Other shops in the same area sell silver jewellery, and pieces inlaid with precious stones. **Urart** stocks collections of unique gold and silver jewellery inspired by the designs of ancient civilizations. **Antikart** specializes in restored antique silver jewellery.

POTTERY, METAL AND GLASSWARE

Shops in the Grand Bazaar are stocked with traditional ceramics, including pieces

---

HOW TO BARGAIN

In up-market shops in Istanbul, bargaining is rare. However, in the Grand Bazaar and the shops located in or around the old city (Sultanahmet and Beyazıt) haggling is a must, otherwise you may be cheated. Bazaar shopkeepers, known for their abrasive insistence, expect you to bargain. Take your time and decide where to buy after visiting a few shops selling similar goods. The procedure is as follows:
• You will often be invited inside and offered a cup of tea. Feel free to accept, as this is the customary introduction to any kind of exchange and will not oblige you to buy.
• Do not feel pressurized if the shopkeeper turns the shop upside down to show you his stock – this is normal practice and most salesmen are proud of their goods.
• If you are seriously interested in any item, be brave enough to offer half the price you are asked.
• Take no notice if the shopkeeper looks offended and

refuses, but raise the price slightly, aiming to pay a little more than half the original offer. If that price is really unacceptable to the owner he will stop bargaining over the item and turn your attention to other merchandise in the shop.

Haggling over the price of a carpet

Brightly decorated candle lanterns in the Grand Bazaar

decorated with exquisite blue-and-white İznik designs *(see p161)*. Other types of pottery come from Kütahya, which makes use of a free style of decoration, and Çanakkale, which features more modern designs. For a modern piece of Kütahya ware, visit **Mudo Pera** which stocks pieces by master potter, Sıtkı Usta. Most museum shops also sell a good range of pottery.

The Grand Bazaar and the Cavalry Bazaar are centres of the copper and brass trade and offer a huge selection.

For glassware, **Paşabahçe**, the largest glass manufacturer in Turkey, offers the best range, and some exquisite, delicate pieces with gilded decoration.

HANDICRAFTS

Ideal gifts and souvenirs include embroidered hats, waistcoats and slippers, inlaid jewellery boxes, meerschaum pipes, prayer beads, alabaster ornaments, blue-eye charms

to ward off the evil eye and *nargiles* (bubble pipes). At the Istanbul Crafts Centre you can see calligraphers at work. **Rölyef** in Beyoğlu, the Book Bazaar and **Sofa** sell antique and reproduction calligraphy, as well as *ebru* (marbled paintings) and reproductions of Ottoman miniatures.

BOOKSHOPS

Books written in English on architecture, history, religion and travel, as well as popular and classic fiction, can be found at **Galeri Kayseri** in the heart of Sultanahmet and at **Robinson Crusoe** in Beyoğlu.

FOOD, DRINK, HERBS AND SPICES

The Spice Bazaar *(see p98)*, also known as the Egyptian Bazaar, is the place to buy nuts, dried fruits, herbs and spices, jams, various herbal teas, and even exotic delicacies such as caviar. The Galatasaray Fish Market is excellent.

International names alongside Turkish shops in Akmerkez

SHOPPING MALLS

Istanbul's modern shopping malls contain cinemas, "food courts", cafés and hundreds of shops. The most popular are **Akmerkez** in Etiler, **Galleria**, next to the yacht marina in Ataköy, and **Kanyon**, which features 160 local and global brands. Seasonal sales take place mainly in clothes shops, but also in department stores and some speciality shops.

DIRECTORY

CARPETS AND KILIMS

Berekct Halicilik
Peykhane Cad,
Sultanahmet.
Map 5 D4.
Tel (0212) 517 46 77.

Galeri Şirvan
52–54 Halıcılar Cad,
Grand Bazaar.
Map 4 C4.
Tel (0212) 520 62 24.

Hazal Halı
27–9 Mecidiye Köprüsü
Sok, Ortaköy.
Map 3 F3.
Tel (0212) 261 72 33.

Şişko Osman
49 Halıcılar Cad, Grand
Bazaar.
Map 4 C4.
Tel (0212) 528 35 48.

FABRICS

Sivaslı Yazmacısı
57 Yağlıkçılar Sok, Grand
Bazaar.
Map 4 C4.
Tel (0212) 526 77 48.

LEATHER

Desa
140 İstiklâl Cad, Beyoğlu.
Map 1 A4.
Tel (0212) 243 37 86.

Meb Deri
14/2 Abdi İspekci Cad,
Nişantası. **Map 1** C1.
Tel (0212) 576 26 10.

JEWELLERY

Antikart
209 İstiklâl Cad, 32 Atlas
Kuyumcular Çarşısı,
Beyoğlu. **Map 1** A4.
Tel (0212) 252 44 82.

Urart
18 Abdi İpekçi Cad,
Nişantaşı.
Map 1 C1.
Tel (0212) 246 71 94.

POTTERY, METAL AND GLASSWARE

Mudo Pera
401 İstiklâl Cad, Beyoğlu.
Map 1 A5.
Tel (0212) 251 86 82.

Paşabahçe
314 İstiklâl Cad, Beyoğlu.
Map 1 A5.
Tel (0212) 244 05 44.

HANDICRAFTS

Rölyef
16 Emir Nevruz Sok,
Beyoğlu. **Map 1** A4.
Tel (0212) 244 04 94.

Sofa
85 Nuruosmaniye Cad,
Cağaloğlu. **Map 5** D4.
Tel (0212) 520 28 50.

BOOKSHOPS

Galeri Kayseri
58 Divanyolu Cad,
Sultanahmet. **Map 5** D4.
Tel (0212) 512 04 56.

Pandora Bookshop
Büyükparmakkapi Sokak
3, off İstiklâl Cad, Beyoğlu.
Map 1 A5.
Tel (0212) 243 35 03.

Robinson Crusoe
389 İstiklâl Cad, Beyoğlu.
Map 1 A5.
Tel (0212) 293 69 68.

FOOD, DRINK, HERBS AND SPICES

Antre Gourmet
40A Akarsu Cad, Cihangir.
Map 5 D1.
Tel (0212) 292 89 72.

Kurukahveci Mehmet Efendi
66 Tahmis Cad, Eminönü.
Map 5 D1.
Tel (0212) 511 42 62.

Şekerci Hacı Bekir
83 Hamidiye Cad,
Eminönü. **Map 5** D3.
Tel (0212) 522 06 66.

SHOPPING MALLS

Akmerkez
Nispetiye Cad, Etiler.
Tel (0212) 282 01 70.

Galleria
Sahil Yolu, Ataköy.
Tel (0212) 559 95 60.

Kanyon
185 Büyükdere Cad,
Levent.
Tel (0212) 353 53 00.

ENTERTAINMENT IN ISTANBUL

Istanbul offers a great variety of leisure pursuits, ranging from arts festivals and folk music to belly dancing and nightclubs. The most important cultural event is the series of festivals organized by the Istanbul Foundation for Culture and the Arts between March and November. Throughout the year, traditional Turkish music, opera, ballet, Western classical music and plays are performed at the Atatürk Cultural Centre, Cemal Reşit Rey Concert Hall (CRR) and some other venues around the city. Beyoğlu

Belly dancer, Galata Tower

is the main centre for entertainment of all kinds. This area also has the highest concentration of cinemas in the city, and numerous lively bars and cafés. Though Konya *(see pp250–51)* is the home of the religious dervish order, productions of the mystical whirling dervish dance are staged at the Mevlevi Monastery in Beyoğlu once a month. Ortaköy, on the European shore of the Bosphorus, is another very popular venue for dining, music and dancing. For a trip to the beach on a hot day, the Princes' Islands *(see p158)* are best.

ENTERTAINMENT GUIDES

A bi-monthly magazine in English, *The Guide* lists cultural events and activities in the city. Entertainment information and contact numbers are available in the English *Turkish Daily News*, as well as Turkish Airlines' in-flight magazine and the Turkish daily newspaper *Hürriyet*.

Entertainment guides available in Istanbul

FESTIVALS

Five major annual festivals (theatre, film, music and dance, jazz, and a biennial fine arts exposition) are organized by the Istanbul Foundation for Culture and the Arts. All tickets can be obtained via telephone from the **Istanbul Festival Committee** or at the individual venues themselves.

Istanbul also hosts the Yapı Kredi Arts, Akbank Jazz, and Efes Pilsen Blues festivals in autumn each year.

During festivals a special bus service runs between show venues and the city centre.

CLASSICAL MUSIC AND DANCE

Each season the Istanbul State Opera and Ballet companies, State Symphony Orchestra and State Theatre perform a wide repertoire of classical and modern works in Taksim's purpose-

built, 900-seat **Atatürk Cultural Centre (AKM)**. These are very popular events and early booking is thus essential. The **Cemal Reşit Rey Concert Hall (CRR)** also stages Western classical music concerts and hosts music and dance groups. Concerts are also held at smaller venues in the city. Contact the Sultanahmet Tourist Office *(see p79)* for details.

BOOKING TICKETS

Most concert, theatre, arts and sports tickets can be booked by phone through Biletix (tel: 0216 556 98 00). You can also go to the website at www.biletix.com for more information about ticket availability; the website also shows point of sale outlets.

ROCK AND JAZZ

An increasing number of Istanbul's clubs and bars plays good live music. **Hayal Kahvesi** is a bar dedicated to jazz, rock and blues and has an outdoor summer venue in Çubuklu. The **Q Club**, in the grounds of the Çırağan Palace Hotel Kempinski, is an

exclusive jazz bar. The **Rock House Café** in Ortaköy has live bands on some weeknights. Other venues are **Babylon** and **Yeni Melek** (jazz and Turkish pop).

TRADITIONAL TURKISH MUSIC AND DANCE

Traditional turkish music performed at the CRR includes Ottoman classical, mystical Sufi and Turkish folk music. Summer recitals of Turkish music are organized in the Basilica Cistern *(see p86)*, which has wonderful acoustics. The Sultanahmet Tourist Office can provide more information.

Fasıl is a popular form of traditional music that is best enjoyed live in *meyhanes* (taverns) such as **Ece, Kallavi 20** and **Hasır**. It is performed on the *kanun* (zither), as well as *tambur* and *ud* (both similar to the lute). **Galata Tower** restaurant is an alternative venue for Turkish folk music and dance, while

Folk dancing at the Kervansaray venue

belly dancing is a nightclub attraction in Beyoğlu. Other places featuring top performers of traditional art are **Kervansaray, Orient House** and **Manzara**.

NIGHTCLUBS

A top nightclub is the **Sortie Bar Restaurant**, a bar-restaurant complex popular with celebrities and located in the centre of town. Its large outdoor space is a must for hot summer nights. Avoid seedy-looking clubs in the Beyoğlu district. These have been known to coerce clients into paying extortionate bills.

CINEMAS AND THEATRE

The latest foreign films are on circuit at the same time as in the rest of Europe, albeit with Turkish subtitles. **Alkazar, Emek** and **Beyoğlu** show

Classical concert in the church of Haghia Eirene *(see p72)*

mainly art-house films. The first show is half-price. Many cinemas offer half price tickets on Wednesdays, and students with a valid student card are entitled to discounts.

Theatres stage local and international plays, but only in Turkish. The theatre season runs from September to June.

SPORTS

Main five-star hotels have good swimming pools and welcome non-residents for a fee. Turks are fanatical about football: **Beşiktaş, Fenerbahçe** and **Galatasaray** are the league players.

Horse races take place at **Veli Efendi** racecourse on weekends and Wednesdays.

CHILDREN

Yıldız Park *(see p121)* has much to offer children, as does **Miniatürk**, with over 100 miniature replicas of Turkey's famous cultural landmarks.

LATE-NIGHT TRANSPORT

The last late-night buses and dolmuşes leave the Taksim area at midnight, but taxis are available all night. For more information *see pp408–11*.

DIRECTORY

ISTANBUL FESTIVAL COMMITTEE

Tel *(0216) 454 15 55.*
www.iksv.org

CLASSICAL MUSIC AND DANCE

AKM
Taksim Meydanı, Taksim.
Map 1 B3.
Tel *(0212) 251 56 00.*

CRR
Gümüş Sok, Harbiye.
Map 1 C1.
Tel *(0212) 232 98 30.*

ROCK AND JAZZ

Babylon
Sehbender Sok 3, Asmali-mescit, Tünel, Beyoğlu.
Tel *(0212) 292 73 68.*

Hayal Kahvesi (Beyoğlu)
Büyükparmak Kapı Sok 19, Beyoğlu.
Map 1 B4.
Tel *(0212) 244 25 28.*

Q Club
Çırağan Palace Hotel Kempinski, A Blok, Beşiktaş. **Map** 3 D3.
Tel *(0212) 236 24 89.*

Rock House Café
Dereboyu Cad 36–8, Ortaköy. **Map** 2 F3.
Tel *(0212) 227 60 10.*

Yeni Melek
Gazeteci Erol Dernek Sokak 13, Beyoğlu.
Tel *(0212) 244 97 00.*

TRADITIONAL TURKISH MUSIC AND DANCE

Ece
Tramvay Cad 104, Kuruçeşme. **Tel** *(0212) 265 96 00.*

Galata Tower
Büyükhendek Cad, Galata.
Map 1 A1.
Tel *(0212) 213 81 80.*

Hasır
Beykoz Korusu, Beykoz.
Tel *(0216) 322 29 01.*

Kallavi
Kallavi Sok 20, Beyoğlu.
Map 1 A4.
Tel *(0212) 251 10 10.*

Kervansaray
Cumhuriyet Cad 30, Harbiye. **Map** 1 C2.
Tel *(0212) 247 16 30.*

Manzara
Conrad Hotel, Yıldız Cad, Beşiktaş. **Map** 2 C3.
Tel *(0212) 227 30 00.*

Orient House
Tiyatro Cad 27, Beyazıt.
Map 4 C4.
Tel *(0212) 517 61 63.*

NIGHTCLUBS

Majesty
Muallim Naci Cad 10/2, Salhane Sok, Ortaköy.
Map 3 F3.
Tel *(0212) 236 57 57.*

Sortie Bar Restaurant
Muallim Naci Cad 54, Ortaköy. **Map** 3 F3.
Tel *(0212) 327 85 85.*

CINEMAS

Alkazar
İstiklal Cad 179, Beyoğlu.
Map 1 B4.
Tel *(0212) 293 24 66.*

Beyoğlu
İstiklal Cad 140, Halep-Pasajı, Beyoğlu. **Map** 1 B4.
Tel *(0212) 251 32 40.*

Emek
İstiklal Cad, Yeşil Çam Sok 5, Beyoğlu. **Map** 1 B4.
Tel *(0212) 240 50 97.*

SPORTS

Beşiktaş FC
Spor Cad 92, Beşiktaş.
Map 2 A4.
Tel *(0212) 227 87 80.*

Fenerbahçe FC
Kızıltoprak, Kadıköy.
Tel *(0216) 345 09 40.*

Galatasaray FC
Hasnun Galip Sok 7, Galatasaray. **Map** 1 B4.
Tel *(0212) 251 57 07.*

Veli Efendi Hipodromu
Osmaniye, Bakırköy.
Tel *(0212) 444 08 55.*

CHILDREN

Miniatürk
Imrahar Cad, Sütlüce.
Tel *(0212) 222 28 82.*

STREET FINDER

The map references that are given throughout this section refer to the maps on the following pages. Some small streets with references may not be named on the map. References are also given for hotels (*see pp326–330*), restaurants (*see pp352–357*), shops (*see pp130–31*) and entertainment venues (*see*

Commuters at a tram stop

pp132–3). The map provided below shows the area covered by the six maps, and the key lists the symbols that are used. The first figure of the reference tells you which map page to turn to; the letter and number indicate the grid reference. The map on the inside back cover shows public transport routes.

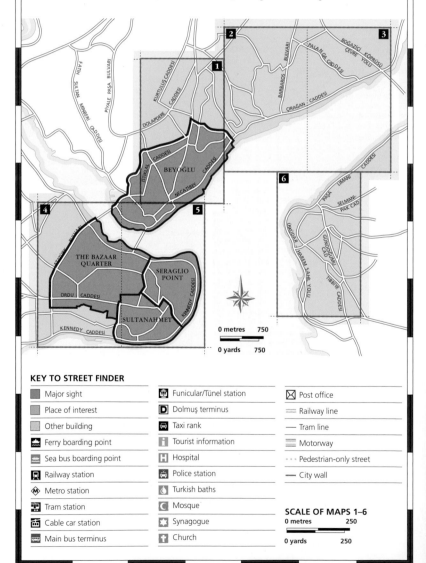

KEY TO STREET FINDER

▮ Major sight	
▮ Place of interest	
▯ Other building	
⛴ Ferry boarding point	
⛴ Sea bus boarding point	
▮ Railway station	
Ⓜ Metro station	
▮ Tram station	
▮ Cable car station	
▮ Main bus terminus	

▮ Funicular/Tünel station	
Ⓓ Dolmuş terminus	
▮ Taxi rank	
ℹ Tourist information	
🅷 Hospital	
▮ Police station	
▮ Turkish baths	
Ⓒ Mosque	
✡ Synagogue	
✝ Church	

⊠ Post office	
═ Railway line	
— Tram line	
▬ Motorway	
••• Pedestrian-only street	
— City wall	

SCALE OF MAPS 1–6

0 metres 250

0 yards 250

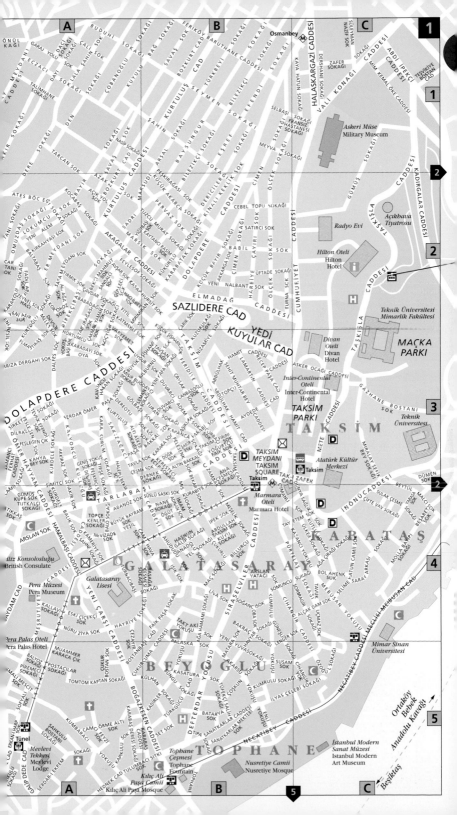

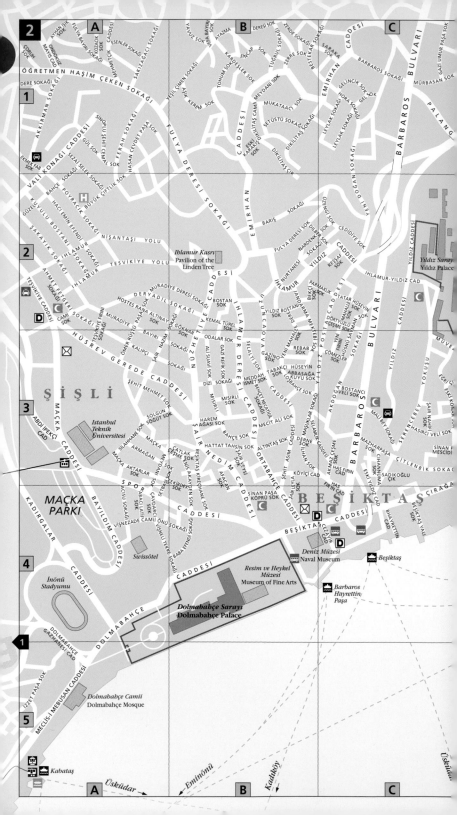

Street Finder Index

In Turkish, Ç, Ğ, İ, Ö, Ş and Ü are listed as separate letters in the alphabet, coming after C, G, I, O, S and U, respectively. In this book, however, Ç is treated as C for the purposes of alphabetization and so on with the other letters. Hence Çiçek follows Cibinlik as if both names began with C. Following standard Turkish practice we have abbreviated Sokak to Sok, Caddesi to Cad and Çıkmazı to Çık.

TURKEY REGION BY REGION

Turkey at a Glance

Turkey occupies the rugged Anatolian Plateau, an arid upland region that is encircled by the mighty Taurus and Pontic mountain systems. The country's unrivalled wealth of historic sights includes Istanbul – the capital of three empires, as well as the ruins of classical sites such as Ephesus, Hierapolis and Aphrodisias. In the interior of the country are the unique cave cities and churches of Cappadocia. The eastern provinces of Turkey are less frequently visited, but offer such spectacular attractions as Lake Van, Armenian churches and the enigmatic stone heads at the summit of Mount Nemrut.

Istanbul's skyline *is defined by the silhouettes of great mosques such as Süleymaniye Mosque (see pp100–101), built by the architect Sinan in the 16th century.*

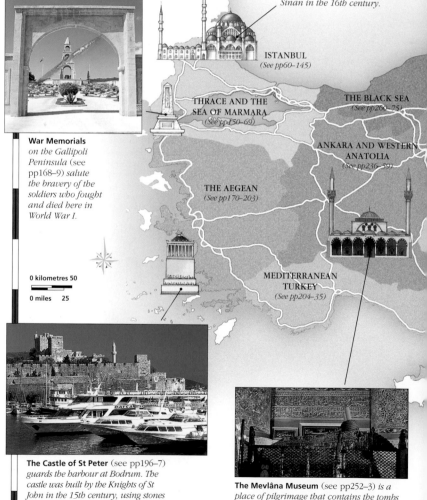

War Memorials *on the Gallipoli Peninsula (see pp168–9) salute the bravery of the soldiers who fought and died here in World War I.*

ISTANBUL
(See pp60–145)

THRACE AND THE SEA OF MARMARA
(See pp150–69)

THE BLACK SEA
(See pp260–75)

ANKARA AND WESTERN ANATOLIA
(See pp236–59)

THE AEGEAN
(See pp170–203)

MEDITERRANEAN TURKEY
(See pp204–35)

0 kilometres 50

0 miles   25

The Castle of St Peter (see pp196–7) *guards the harbour at Bodrum. The castle was built by the Knights of St John in the 15th century, using stones taken from the ruins of the celebrated Mausoleum of Halicarnassus.*

The Mevlâna Museum (see pp252–3) *is a place of pilgrimage that contains the tombs of important Mevlevi Dervish mystics. Nearby is the Selimiye Mosque, an emblem of Konya.*

◁ **The picturesque town of Mardin, near the Syrian border**

Haghia Sophia, *a Byzantine church in the historic port of Trabzon* (see pp270–71) *was rebuilt in the mid-13th century on the site of a Roman temple. The church, now a museum, was restored from 1957 to 1963, and features superb frescoes and mosaic floors.*

Mount Ağri (Ararat), *said to be where Noah's Ark came to rest after the biblical flood, looms over the eastern Anatolian town of Doğubeyazıt. İshak Paşa Sarayı* (see p315), *an 18th-century palace, lies outside the town.*

CAPPADOCIA AND CENTRAL ANATOLIA
(See pp276–99)

EASTERN ANATOLIA
(See pp300–319)

Sabancı Central Mosque *in Adana* (see pp230–31) *is one of the largest mosques in the Islamic world. The Ottoman-era clocktower is an older landmark of this fast-growing southern city.*

Cappadocia's *many churches, cave dwellings, monasteries and underground cities* (see p281) *were carved out of hardened volcanic ash deposited many thousands of years ago.*

THRACE AND THE SEA OF MARMARA

*S*tanding at a natural crossroads, Istanbul makes a good base for excursions into the neighbouring areas of Thrace and the Sea of Marmara. Whether you want to see great Islamic architecture, immerse yourself in a busy bazaar, relax on an island or catch a glimpse of Turkey's rich birdlife, you will find a choice of destinations within easy reach of the city.

On public holidays and at weekends nearby resorts are crowded with Istanbul residents taking a break from the noisy city. For longer breaks, they head for the Mediterranean or Aegean, so summer is a good, quiet time to explore the Thrace and Marmara regions.

The country around Istanbul varies immensely from lush forests to open plains and, beyond them, impressive mountains. The Princes' Islands, where pine forests and monasteries can be toured by a pleasant ride in a horse-drawn carriage, are also just a short boat trip away from the city. A little further away, the lakeside town of İznik is world famous for its ceramics. This art form, which reached its zenith in the 16th and 17th centuries, is one of the wonders of Ottoman art, and original pieces are highly prized.

To the northwest, near the Greek border, is Edirne, a former Ottoman capital. It is visited today for its mosques, especially the Selimiye. Edirne also stages Kırkpınar grease-wrestling matches every June when enthusiastic crowds flock to enjoy the contest and the accompanying folk festival.

South of the Sea of Marmara is the pretty spa town of Bursa. Originally a Greek city, it was founded in 183 BC. The first Ottoman capital, it has some fine architecture and also maintains the tradition of the Karagöz shadow puppet theatre. Near the mouth of the straits of the Dardanelles lie the ruins of the legendary city of Troy, dating from about 3600 BC. North of the Dardanelles are cemeteries commemorating the thousands of soldiers killed in the battles fought over the Gallipoli Peninsula during World War I.

Boats in Burgaz Harbour on the Princes' Islands, a short ferry ride from Istanbul

◁ The Green Tomb of Mehmet I in Bursa, one of the city's best-known landmarks

Exploring Thrace and the Sea of Marmara

Istanbul is the jewel of the Thrace and Marmara region, but places like Edirne and Bursa – and others within a radius of about 250 km (150 miles) – each have their own history and importance, with some fine museums and mosques. Şile, located on the Black Sea coast, is a day's outing from Istanbul, as is the quaint hamlet of Polonezköy. Bird parks, the superb tiles of İznik, along with the spas and ski slopes around Bursa give the Marmara area the edge for variety. A visit to the World War I battlefields and cemeteries of the Gallipoli Peninsula is a moving experience.

French war cemetery, Gallipoli Peninsula

Lalapaşa

Süloğlu Kırklareli

❶ EDİRNE
🏛🕌Ⓒ Hasköy

Havsa

Babaeski

Lüleburgaz

Uzunköprü

Hamidiye

Küplü 550

Paşayiğit

İpsala Malkara

Keşan İnecik

Karahisar Ballı

Enez

Mecidiye

Saros Körfezi

Bolayır

Gelibolu Karabiga

Lâpseki 555

Kabatepe Eceabat 200

GALLIPOLI ❾
PENINSULA
🏛⚔ Çanakkale

İğneada

Demirköy

Y ı l d ı z D a ğ l a r ı

Pınarhisar 020 Vize

Karacaoğlan Saray

Çerkezköy

Büyükkarıştıran 100

Hayrabolu Muratlı Çorlu

Banarlı Seymen

Tekirdağ Marmara
Ereğlis

Kumbağ

T e k i r D a ğ ı

Şarköy Marmara

M a r m a r a
A d a s ı

Erdek

Bandırm

BIRD PARADISE ❽
NATIONAL PARK

Biga

Gönen

SIGHTS AT A GLANCE

Bird Paradise National Park ❽
Bursa pp162–7 ❼
Edirne pp154–7 ❶
Gallipoli Peninsula pp168–9 ❾
İznik ❺
Polonezköy ❸
Princes' Islands ❷
Şile ❹
Uludağ National Park ❻

SEE ALSO

• **Where to Stay** pp330–332

• **Where to Eat** pp357–359

Bird Paradise National Park – an area rich in protected wildlife

GETTING AROUND

The Trans European Motorway (TEM) system means that a six-lane superhighway bypasses the hub of Istanbul using the Fatih Sultan Mehmet Bridge over the Bosphorus. On this toll road, the Istanbul to Ankara journey takes about 3 hours. Car ferries (no reservations required) commute frequently between Gebze and Yalova. A sea bus service (advance booking essential) does the Yenikapı (central Istanbul) to Bandırma run in a few hours. From Istanbul, local and intercity trains depart from Sirkeci Station on the European side and Haydarpaşa Station on the Asian side. Ferries depart from the Eminönü ferry piers in Istanbul to four of the Princes' Islands and from Kabataş, near the Dolmabahçe Palace, to the islands on the south coast of the Sea of Marmara, as well as from Bostanci on the Asian side.

Children walking up a picturesque street in an old quarter of Bursa

KEY

═══	Motorway
━━━	Major road
═══	Minor road
───	Scenic route
┄┄┄	Main railway
───	Minor railway
▬▬▬	International border

BLACK SEA

Sea of Marmara

Durusu Gölü

Ömerli Barajı

Kocaeli Yarımadası

İznik Gölü

Uluabat Gölü

Avdan Dağı

Dağları

Imralı Adası

ULUDAĞ NATIONAL PARK

Ankara

Eskişehir

ıköy
aracaköy
Şinekli
İvri
Büyük Çekmece
Küçük Çekmece
Çatalca
Bahçeköy
Durusu
Sarıyer
Beykoz
İSTANBUL
ŞİLE **4**
3 POLONEZKÖY
PRINCES' ISLANDS **2**
Gebze
Degirmendere
Gölcük
Kocaeli (İzmit)
Yalova
Armutlu
Gemlik
Sölöz
İZNIK **5**
Mudanya
Karacabey
BURSA **7**
6
İnegöl
Yenişehir
Bilecik
Orhaneli
Domaniç
Tavşanlı
alikesir
Sinat Çayı

0 kilometres	30
0 miles	15

Edirne ❶

Standing on the river Tunca near the border with Greece, Edirne is a provincial university town that is home to one of Turkey's star attractions, the Selimiye Mosque *(see pp156–7)*. As this huge monument attests, Edirne was historically of great importance. It dates back to AD 125, when the Emperor Hadrian joined two small towns to form Hadrianopolis, or Adrianople. For nearly a century, from 1361 when Murat I took the city until Constantinople was conquered in 1453 *(see p54)*, Edirne was the Ottoman capital. The town has one other claim to fame – the annual grease-wrestling championships in June.

Entrance arch, Mosque of the Three Balconies

Entrance to Beyazıt II Mosque viewed from its inner courtyard

⬛ Beyazıt II Mosque
Beyazıt II Külliyesi
Yeni Maharet Cad. ⬜ daily. **Health Museum Tel** *(0284) 212 09 22.*
⬜ *9:30am–5:30pm daily.*
📷 ♿

Beyazıt II Mosque stands in a peaceful location on the northern bank of the Tunca River, 1.5 km (1 mile) from the city centre. It was built in 1484–8, soon after Beyazıt II succeeded Mehmet the Conqueror *(see p54)* as sultan.

The mosque and its courtyards are open to the public. Of the surrounding buildings in the complex, the old hospital, which incorporated an asylum, has been converted into the **Health Museum**. Disturbed patients were treated in this asylum – a model facility for its time – with water, colour and flower therapies. The Turkish writer ...liya Çelebi (1611–84) ...orted that singers and ...rumentalists would play ...ing music here three ... a week. Overuse of

hashish was one of the most common afflictions. The colonnaded inner mosque courtyard, unlike most later examples, covers three times the area of the mosque itself. Inside, the weight of the impressive dome is supported on sweeping pendentives.

⬛ Mosque of the Three Balconies
Üç Şerefeli Camii
Hükümet Cad. ⬜ daily. 📷
Until the fall of Constantinople, this was the grandest building of the early Ottoman state. It was finished in 1447 and takes its name from the three balconies which adorn its southeastern minaret – at the time the tallest in existence. In an unusual touch, the other three minarets of the mosque are each of a different design and height. Unlike its predecessors in Bursa *(see pp162–7)*, the mosque has an open courtyard, a feature that set a precedent for the great imperial mosques of Istanbul. The interior plan was also innovative. With minimal obstructions, both the *mihrab* and *minbar* can be seen from almost every corner of the prayer hall.

⬛ Old Mosque
Eski Cami
Talat Paşa Asfaltı. ⬜ daily. 📷
The oldest of Edirne's major mosques, this is a smaller version of the Great Mosque in Bursa *(see p164)*. The eldest son of Beyazıt I, Süleyman, began the mosque in 1403, but it was his youngest son, Mehmet I, who completed it in 1414.

A perfect square, the mosque is divided by four massive piers into nine domed sections. On either side of the prayer hall entrance there are massive Arabic inscriptions proclaiming "Allah" and "Mohammed".

GREASE-WRESTLING

The Kırkpınar Grease-Wrestling Championships take place annually in June, on the island of Sarayiçi in the Tunca River. The event is famed throughout Turkey and accompanied by a week-long carnival. Before competing, the wrestlers don knee-length leather shorts *(kispet)* and grease themselves from head to foot in diluted olive oil. The master of ceremonies, the *cazgır*, then invites the competitors to take part in a high-stepping, arm-flinging parade across the field, accompanied by music played on a deep-toned drum *(davul)* and a single-reed oboe *(zurna)*. Wrestling bouts can last up to two hours and involve long periods of frozen, silent concentration interspersed by attempts to throw down the opponent.

Wrestlers performing a ceremonial ritual before the contest

🏛 Rüstem Paşa Caravanserai

Rüstem Paşa Kervansarayı
İki Kapılı Han Cad 57.
Tel (0284) 212 61 19.
Sinan *(see p101)* designed this caravanserai for Süleyman's most powerful grand vizier, Rüstem Paşa, in 1560–61. It was constructed in two distinct parts. The larger courtyard, or han *(see pp24–5)*, which is now the Rüstem Paşa Kervansaray Hotel, was built for the merchants of Edirne, while the smaller courtyard, now a student hostel, was an inn for other travellers.

A short walk away, on the other side of Saraçlar Caddesi, is the **Semiz Ali Paşa Bazaar**. This is also the work of Sinan, and dates from 1589. It consists of a long, narrow street of vaulted shops.

🏛 Museum of Turkish and Islamic Arts

Türk ve İslam Eserleri Müzesi
Kadir Paşa Mektep Sok. *Tel (0284) 225 11 20.* ◻ 8:30am–noon & 1:30–5:30pm Tue–Sun. 🎫
Edirne's small collection of Turkish and Islamic works of art is attractively located in the *medrese (see p32)* of the Selimiye Mosque.

The museum's first room is devoted to the local sport of grease-wrestling. It includes enlarged reproductions of miniatures depicting 600 years of the sport. These show the wrestling stars resplendent in their leather shorts, their skin glistening with olive oil.

Other objects on display include the original doors of the Beyazıt II Mosque. There are also military exhibits. Among them are some beautiful 18th-century Ottoman shields, with woven silk exteriors, and paintings of military subjects.

VISITORS' CHECKLIST

🗺 150,000. 🚌 Ayşekadın, (0284) 235 26 73. 🚍 E-5 exit at Highway Maintenance Depot, (0284) 226 00 20. 🛇 Rüstem Paşa Kervansaray Hotel. ℹ Hürriyet Meydanı 17, (0284) 213 92 08. 🛍 Mon, Wed, Sat. 🤼 Grease-Wrestling (Jun).

🟥 Muradiye Mosque

Muradiye Camii
Küçükpazar Cad. ◻ daily. 🗿
What is today a tranquil mosque was first built as a *zaviye* (dervish hospice) in 1421 by Murat II, who dreamed that the great dervish leader Celaleddin Rumi *(see p252, 255)* asked him to build a hospice in Edirne. Only later was it converted into a mosque. Its interior is notable for its massive inscriptions, similar to those in the Old Mosque, and for some fine early 15th-century İznik tiles *(see p161)*. It may be locked outside prayer times.

The tranquil 15th century Muradiye Mosque

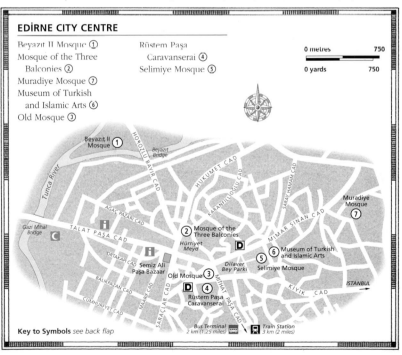

EDİRNE CITY CENTRE

Beyazıt II Mosque ①
Mosque of the Three Balconies ②
Muradiye Mosque ⑦
Museum of Turkish and Islamic Arts ⑥
Old Mosque ③
Rüstem Paşa Caravanserai ④
Selimiye Mosque ⑤

0 metres 750
0 yards 750

Key to Symbols *see back flap*

Bus Terminal 2 km (1.25 miles)
Train Station 3 km (2 miles)

Edirne: Selimiye Mosque
Selimiye Camii

The Selimiye is the greatest of all the Ottoman mosque complexes, the apogee of an art form and the culmination of a life's ambition for its architect, Sinan *(see p101)*. Built on a slight hill, the mosque is a prominent landmark. Its complex includes a *medrese (see p32)*, housing the Museum of Turkish and Islamic Arts, a school and the Kavaflar Arasta, a covered bazaar.

Selim II commissioned the mosque. It was begun in 1569 and completed in 1575, a year after his death. The dome was Sinan's proudest achievement. In his memoirs, he wrote: "With the help of Allah and the favour of Sultan Selim Khan, I have succeeded in building a cupola six cubits wider and four cubits deeper than that of Haghia Sophia." In fact, the dome is comparable in diameter and slightly shallower than the building Sinan had so longed to surpass.

★ Minarets
The mosque's four slender minarets tower to a height of 84 m (275 ft). Each one has three balconies. The two northern minarets contain three intertwining staircases, each one leading to a different balcony.

Ablutions Fountain
Intricate, pierced carving decorates the top of the 16-sided open şadırvan (ablutions fountain), which stands in the centre of the courtyard. The absence of a canopy helps to retain the uncluttered aspect.

STAR FEATURES
★ Minarets
★ Dome
★ Minbar

The columns supporting the arches of the courtyard are made of old marble, plundered from Byzantine architecture.

Courtyard Portals
Alternating red and honey-coloured slabs of stone were used to build the striking arches above the courtyard portals. This echoes the decoration of the magnificent arches running around the mosque courtyard itself.

★ Dome
The 43 m (141 ft) dome dominates the interior of the mosque. Not even the florid paintwork – the original 16th-century decoration underwent restoration in the 19th century – detracts from its effect.

VISITORS' CHECKLIST

Mimar Sinan Cad, Edirne.
Tel *(0284) 213 97 35.* ☐ *daily.*
● *prayer times.* 🖼 *donation.*

★ Minbar
Many experts claim that the Selimiye's minbar, with its conical tiled cap, is the finest in Turkey. Its lace-like side panels are exquisitely carved.

Mihrab, cut from
Marmara marble

The Interior
The mosque is the supreme achievement of Islamic architecture. Its octagonal plan allows for a reduction in the size of the buttresses supporting the dome. This permitted extra windows to be incorporated, making the interior exceptionally light.

The *müezzin mahfili*
still retains original, intricate 16th-century paintwork on its underside. Beneath it is a small fountain.

Entrance from
Kavaflar Arasta

Sultan's Loge
The imperial loge is supported on green marble columns. They are connected by pointed arches, whose surrounds are adorned with floral İznik tiles (see p161). Unusually, its ornately decorated mihrab contains a shuttered window, which opened on to countryside when the mosque was built.

Main
entrance

Burgazada, one of the relaxed and picturesque Princes' Islands

Princes' Islands ❷

Kızıl Adalar

🏛 17,200. 🚢 from Eminönü or sea bus from Kabataş (European side), sea bus from Kadıköy (Asian side) or from Bostanci (further Asian side). ℹ Town Hall, (0216) 382 70 71 and (0216) 382 78 56.

The pine-forested Princes' Islands provide a welcome break from the bustle of the city and are just a short ferry ride southeast of Istanbul. Most ferries call in turn at the four largest of the nine islands: **Kınalıada, Burgazada, Heybeliada** and **Büyükada**.

Easily visited on a day trip, the islands take their name from a royal palace built by Justin II on Büyükada, then known as Prinkipo (Island of the Prince) in 569. In Byzantine times the islands became infamous as a place of exile, and also as the site of several monasteries.

In the latter half of the 19th century, with the inauguration of a regular steamboat service from Istanbul, many wealthy

Visitors strolling along a street in the village of Büyükada

foreigners settled on the islands. One who found the tolerant attitude to foreigners and generous morality attractive was Leon Trotsky, who lived in one of Büyükada's finest mansions from 1929 to 1933. Zia Gökalp (*see p310*), a key figure in the rise of Turkish nationalism, lived here during the waning years of the Ottoman era.

Büyükada is the largest of the Princes' Islands, and it attracts many visitors because of its lovely sandy beaches, outdoor summer culture and the Art Nouveau style of the wooden dwellings that have given the island much of its lingering Ottoman atmosphere. Büyükada and Heybeliada shun any form of motorized transport in favour of horse-drawn carriages or donkeys. At the top of Büyükada's wooded southern hill stands the Monastery of St George, built on Byzantine foundations.

Heybeliada, the second largest island, houses the imposing former Naval High School (Deniz Harp Okulu), built in 1942. Less touristy than Büyükada, this island offers quieter pleasures such as lovely, tiny beaches and walks in pine groves. The island's northern hill is the stunning location of the Greek Orthodox School of Theology, which was built in 1841. Its library, famous

Door to the Monastery of St George, Büyükada

among Orthodox scholars, is open and worth a visit.

The smaller islands of Kınalıada and Burgazada are less developed and therefore more peaceful.

Polonezköy ❸

🏛 800. 🚌 221 from Taksim or 101 from Beşiktaş to Beykoz, then dolmuş. 🎉 Cherry festival (first two weeks of Jun).

Polonezköy still reflects clear signs of the Polish roots of its founders, who came here in 1842 fleeing Russian oppression. United by politics, Poles fought in Abdül Mecid I's army against Russia in the Crimean War (1853–56). Exempted from taxes for their efforts in the war, they settled in their namesake village.

Unlike many people who came to Istanbul principally for trade, Poles came here in search of freedom and some of them converted to Islam. Polonezköy's old-world charm and culinary traditions are still there, but it has become very popular for a day's outing or a weekend break. Turks make up most of its current population.

There are excellent walks in the surrounding countryside and, even though villas and spas have sprung up, there are still several authentic restaurants serving Polish specialities, including the wild boar for which the town was once well known.

The surrounding beech forest, which also offers pleasant walks, has become a conservation area protected from further development.

Şile ❹

🏛 5,000. 🚌 from Üsküdar.

The quintessential Black Sea holiday village, Şile has several fine, sandy beaches and a large, black-and-white striped lighthouse high on a clifftop. In ancient times, the village, then known as Kalpe, was a port used by ships sailing eastward from the Bosphorus. Şile's lighthouse, the largest in Turkey, was built by the French for Sultan Abdül Aziz in 1858–9. Visiting it after dusk on a warm evening makes a pleasant outing. Apart from tourism, Şile is known for producing cotton, as well as a cool, loose-weave cotton cloth, known as *şile bezi*, which is sold in local shops.

İznik ❺

See pp160–61.

Uludağ National Park ❻
Uludağ Milli Parkı

Tel (0224) 283 21 97. 🚌 City bus marked "Teleferik" from Koza Park, then cable car to look-out point at Sarıalan. 🚍 to Sarıalan, then dolmuş ⬜ daily. 🅿 only for vehicles.

One of a number of Turkish mountains to claim the title of Mount Olympus, Uludağ, at 2,540 m (8,340 ft), was believed by the Bithynians (of northwestern Asia Minor) to be the abode of the gods. In the Byzantine era, it was home to several monastic orders. After the Ottoman conquest of Bursa, Muslim dervishes *(p255)* moved into the abandoned monas-

teries. Nowadays, however, no traces of Uludağ's former religious communities remain.

Spring and summer are the best times for visiting Uludağ National Park, as its alpine heights remain relatively cool, offering a welcome escape from the heat of the lower areas. Visitors will find plenty of good opportunities for peaceful walking and picnicking.

The park includes about 670 sq km (258 sq miles) of woodland. As you ascend, the deciduous beech, oak and hazel gradually give way to juniper and aspen, and finally to dwarf junipers. In springtime, the slopes are blanketed with hyacinths and crocuses.

The main tourist season in Uludağ starts in November, when it becomes Turkey's most fashionable and accessible ski resort, with a reliable cable-car service and a good selection of hotels.

Osman Gazi *(see p54)* is supposed to have founded seven villages for his seven sons and their brides here. **Cumalıkızık**, on the lower slopes of Uludağ, is the most perfectly preserved of the five surviving villages and it is registered as a national monument. Among its houses are many 750-year-old half-timbered buildings.

Bursa ❼

See pp162–7.

Spoonbill wading in the lake at Bird Paradise National Park

Bird Paradise National Park ❽
Kuşcenneti Milli Parkı

Tel (0266) 735 54 22. 🅳 from the old bus station in Bandırma. ⬜ sunrise to sunset daily. 🅿 🅲

An estimated 255 species of birds visit Bird Paradise National Park at the edge of Kuş Gölü, the lake formerly known as Manyas Gölü. Located on the great migratory paths between Europe and Asia, the park is a happy combination of plant cover, reed beds and a lake that supports at least 20 species of fish. The park will delight amateur and professional birdwatchers alike, and a good field guide and some mosquito repellent will enhance the experience.

At the entrance to the park, there is a small museum with displays about various birds. Binoculars are provided at the desk and visitors make their way to an observation tower.

Two main groups of birds visit the lake: those that come here to breed (March–July), and those that pass by during migration, either heading south (November) or north (April–May). Among the birds that breed around the lake are the endangered Dalmatian pelican, the great crested grebe, cormorants, herons, bitterns and spoonbills. Over 3 million birds fly across the area on the great migratory routes – storks, cranes, pelicans and birds of prey like sparrowhawks and spotted eagles. April and May are the best months to enjoy this area. Close to the main park area, there is a restaurant that serves fresh trout, and it is a good spot to break for lunch.

Uludağ National Park, a popular ski resort in winter

İznik ❺

🏠 20,122. 🚌 Yeni Mahalle, Yakup Sok. (0224) 757 25 83. ℹ️ Belediye Hizmet Binası, Kılıçaslan Cad 97, (0224) 757 19 33, (0224) 757 14 54. 🏛️ Wed. 🎭 İznik Flower and Summer Festival (1st or 2nd week of May); Liberation Day (28 Nov).

A charming lakeside town, İznik gives little clue now of its former glory as a capital of the Byzantine Empire. Its most important legacy, however, dates from the 16th century, when its kilns produced the finest ceramics ever made in the Ottoman world.

The town first reached prominence in AD 325, when it was known as Nicaea. In that year Emperor Constantine (see p49) chose it as the location of the first Ecumenical Council of the Christian Church. The meeting produced the Nicene Creed, a statement of doctrine on the nature of Christ in relation to God.

The Seljuks (see p52) took Nicaea in 1081 and renamed it İznik. It was recaptured in 1097, during the First Crusade, on behalf of Emperor Alexius I Comnenus. After the Crusader capture of Constantinople in 1204 (see p53), the city served as the capital of the "Empire of Nicaea" for 50 years. In 1331, Orhan Gazi captured İznik and incorporated it into the Ottoman empire. İznik still retains

Grand domed portico fronting the Archaeological Museum

its original layout. Surrounded by the town walls, its two main streets are in the form of a cross, with minor streets running out from them on a grid plan. The walls still more or less delineate the town's boundaries. They were built in 300 BC by the Greek Lysimachus, then ruler of the town, but were frequently repaired by the Byzantines and, later, the Ottomans. Extending for some 3 km (2 miles), the walls are punctuated by huge gateways. The main one, Istanbul Gate (İstanbul Kapısı), marks İznik's northern limit. It is decorated with a carved relief of fighting horsemen and is flanked by Byzantine towers.

Istanbul Gate from within the town walls

One of the town's oldest surviving monuments, the ruined church of **Haghia Sophia**, stands at the intersection of the main streets, Atatürk Caddesi and Kılıçaslan Caddesi. An earlier version of the church was

the principal place of worship in Byzantine Nicaea. The current building was erected after an earthquake in 1065. The remains of a fine mosaic floor, and also of a Deësis (a fresco depicting Christ, the Virgin and John the Baptist), are protected from damage behind glass screens. Just off the eastern end of Kılıçaslan Caddesi, the 14th-century **Green Mosque** (Yeşil Camii) is named after the tiles covering its minaret. Unfortunately, the original tiles have been replaced by modern copies of inferior quality. Opposite the mosque, the Kitchen of Lady Nilüfer (Nilüfer Hatun İmareti), one of İznik's loveliest buildings, now houses the town's **Archaeological Museum**. This *imaret* was set up in 1388 by Nilüfer Hatun, wife of Orhan Gazi, and served as a hospice for wandering dervishes. Entered through a spacious five-domed portico, the central domed area is flanked by two more domed rooms. The museum has displays of Roman antiquities and glass, as well as some recently discovered examples of Seljuk and Ottoman tiles.

🏛 **Haghia Sophia**
Atatürk Cad. **Tel** (0224) 757 10 27.
🕐 9am–noon & 1–5:30pm daily. 🎟

🇨 **Green Mosque**
Müze Sok. 🕐 daily (except prayer times).

🏛 **Archaeological Museum**
Müze Sok. **Tel** (0224) 757 10 27.
🕐 9am–noon & 1–5:30pm daily. 🎟

Green Mosque, named after the green tiles adorning its minaret

İznik Ceramics

İznik was one of two major centres (the other being Kütahya) where fine, painted and glazed pottery was fashioned during the Ottoman period. Pottery vessels, plates, and flat and shaped tiles were produced at İznik from the 15th to the 17th century. The last major commission was for 21,043 tiles of some 50 different designs for the Sultanahmet Mosque in Istanbul, completed in 1616. Early İznik pottery

16th-century İznik mosque lamp

is brilliant blue and white. The potteries reached their peak in the 16th century when the famous "tomato red" colour was fully developed. Today visitors can see it sparkle on the superb tilework of the 1561 Rüstem Paşa Mosque *(see p98)* in Istanbul. This period of İznik greatness in ceramic art coincided with the great period of design at the Nakkaşhane design studio in the Topkapı Palace *(see pp68–71)*.

Chinese porcelain, *which was imported into Turkey from the 14th century and of which there is a large collection in Topkapı Palace, often inspired the designs used for İznik pottery.*

During the 16th century, İznik potters produced imitations of pieces of Chinese porcelain, such as this copy of a Ming dish.

Cobalt blue and white *was the striking combination of colours used in early İznik pottery (produced between c.1470–1520). The designs used were a mixture of Chinese and Arabesque, as seen on this tiled panel on the wall of the Circumcision Chamber in Topkapı Palace. Floral patterns and animal motifs were both popular at this time.*

Rock and wave border pattern

Damascus ware *was the name erroneously given to ceramics produced at İznik during the first half of the 16th century. They had fantastic floral designs in the new colours of turquoise, sage green and manganese. When such tiles were discovered at Damascus, the similar İznik pots were wrongly assumed to have been made there.*

Armenian bole, *an iron-rich red colour, began to be used around 1550, as seen in this 16th-century tankard. New, realistic tulip and other floral designs were also introduced, and İznik ware enjoyed its heyday, which lasted until around 1630.*

Miniature depicting potters

Wall tiles *were not made in any quantity until the reign of Süleyman the Magnificent (1520–66). Süleyman used İznik tiles to refurbish the Dome of the Rock in Jerusalem.*
Some of the best examples are seen in Istanbul's mosques, notably in the Süleymaniye (see pp100–101), Rüstem Paşa Mosque and, here, in this example from the Blue Mosque (pp88–9).

Bursa ❼

Basin, Museum of Turkish and Islamic Arts

The city of Bursa – known to Turks as *yeşil Bursa* ("green Bursa") – has tranquil parks and leafy suburbs set on the lower slopes of Mount Uludağ (*see p159*). This disguises the vibrant commercial heart of the city, which is today made prosperous by automobiles, food and textiles, as it was by the silk trade in the 15th and 16th centuries. The Romans developed the potential of Bursa's mineral springs, and there are estimated to be about 3,000 thermal baths in the city today. In 1326 Bursa became the first capital of the Ottoman Empire after it succumbed to Osman (*see p54*).

View over the rooftops of the city of Bursa

Bursa has been a provincial capital since 1841 and, despite its commercial centre, it has retained its pious dignity. No city in Turkey has more mosques and tombs. Paradoxically, it is also the home of the satirical shadow-puppet genre known as Karagöz (*see p26*).

⬛ Yıldırım Beyazıt Mosque
Yıldırım Beyazıt Camii
Yıldırım Cad. ⬭ *daily (except prayer times).*
This mosque is named after Beyazıt I, whose nickname was "Yıldırım", meaning "thunderbolt". This referred to the speed with which he reacted to his enemies. Built in 1389, just after Beyazıt became sultan, the mosque at first doubled as a lodge for Sufi dervishes (*see p255*). It has a lovely portico with five domed bays.

Inside, the prayer hall and interior court (a covered "courtyard" in Bursa mosques, which prefigures the open ones preferred by later Ottoman architects) are divided by an impressive arch. This rises from two *mihrab*-like niches. The walls of the prayer hall itself are adorned with several attractive pieces of calligraphic design (*see pp28–9*).

⬛ Green Tomb
Yeşil Türbe
Yeşil Cad. ⬭ *daily.* 🖼 *donation.*
The tomb of Mehmet I, which stands elevated among tall cypress trees, is one of the city's most prominent landmarks. It was built between 1414 and 1421.

The tomb is much closer to the Seljuk style of architecture than classical Ottoman. Its exterior is covered in green tiles – mainly 19th-century replacements for the original faïence. A few older tiles survive around the entrance portal. The interior, entered through a pair of superbly carved wooden doors, is simply dazzling. The space is small and the ornamentation, covering a relatively large surface area, is breathtaking in its depth of colour and detail. The *mihrab* has especially intricate tile panels, including a representation of a mosque lamp hanging from a gold chain between two candles.

The sultan's magnificent sarcophagus is covered in exquisite tiles and adorned by a long Koranic inscription. Nearby sarcophagi contain the remains of his sons, daughters and nursemaid.

⬛ Green Mosque
Yeşil Camii
Yeşil Cad. ⬭ *daily (except prayer times).*
Bursa's most famous monument was commissioned by Mehmet I in 1412, but it remained unfinished at his death in 1421 and still lacks a portico. Nevertheless, it is the finest Ottoman mosque built prior to the conquest of Constantinople (*see p54*).

The main portal is tall and elegant, with an intricately carved canopy. It opens into the entrance hall. Beyond this is an interior court with a carved fountain at its centre. A flight of three steps leads up from here into the prayer hall. On either side of the steps are niches for worshippers to leave their shoes. Above the entrance to the court is the sultan's loge (*see p33*), resplendent in richly patterned tiles created using the *cuerda seca* technique. They are in beautiful greens, blues and

The distinctive and prominent Green Tomb of Sultan Mehmet I

yellows, with threads of gold that were added after firing. The tiling of the prayer hall was carried out by Ali Ibn İlyas Ali, who learned his art in Samarkand. This was the first time that tiles were used extensively in an Ottoman mosque, and it set a precedent for the later widespread use of İznik tiles (see p161). The tiles covering the walls of the prayer hall, which is well lit by floor-level windows, are simple, green and hexagonal. Against this plain backdrop, the effect of the *mihrab* is especially

glorious. Predominantly turquoise, deep blue and white, with touches of gold, the *mihrab*'s tiles depict flowers, leaves, arabesques and geometric patterns. The mosque's exterior was also once clad in tiles, but these have disappeared over time.

🏛 Museum of Turkish and Islamic Arts

Türk ve İslam Eserleri Müzesi Yeşil Cad. **Tel** (0224) 327 76 79. ◻ 8am–noon, 1–5pm Mon–Fri. This interesting museum is housed in a fine Ottoman-era building, once the *medrese* (see p32) associated with the Green Mosque. The façade of the building is quite striking. A colonnade surrounds its courtyard on three sides. The cells leading off from this courtyard are now exhibition galleries. Exhibits date from the 12th to the 20th centuries, and include Seljuk and

Façade of the Museum of Turkish and Islamic Arts

Ottoman ceramics, elaborately decorated Korans and beautiful ceremonial costumes.

🏛 Bursa City Museum

Bursa Kent Müzesi Atatürk Cad 8. **Tel** (0224) 220 26 26. ◻ 9:30am–5:30pm Tue–Sun. ♿ The former Justice courts have been restored as a lively museum that traces local life over many years. Displays show how culinary skills, handicrafts, costumes, archaeological artifacts and city planning moulded urban spirit. Bursa city fathers, Atatürk and the local *commedia dell arte* puppet genre of Karagöz (see p26) have first-rate exhibits.

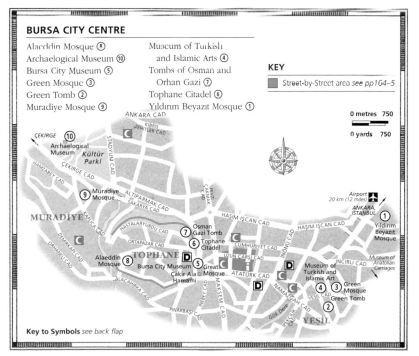

BURSA CITY CENTRE

Alaeddin Mosque ⑧
Archaeological Museum ⑩
Bursa City Museum ⑤
Green Mosque ③
Green Tomb ②
Muradiye Mosque ⑨
Museum of Turkish and Islamic Arts ④
Tombs of Osman and Orhan Gazi ⑦
Tophane Citadel ⑥
Yıldırım Beyazıt Mosque ①

KEY

▨ Street-by-Street area see pp164–5

0 metres   750
0 yards   750

ÇEKİRGE ⑩ Archaeological Museum   *Kültür Parkı*

Muradiye Mosque ⑨

MURADİYE

Alaeddin Mosque ⑧   TOPHANE   Bursa City Museum ⑤   Çakır Ağa Hamamı

Osman Gazi Tomb ⑦   Tophane Citadel ⑥

Great Mosque

Airport 20 km (12 miles) ✈   ANKARA, İSTANBUL

Yıldırım Beyazıt Mosque ①

Museum of Anatolian Carriages

Museum of Turkish and Islamic Art ④

Green Mosque ③
Green Tomb ②

YEŞİL

Key to Symbols see back flap

Bursa: The Market Area

Bursa's central market area is a warren of streets and Ottoman *hans* (warehouses). The area emphasizes the more colourful and traditional aspects of this busy industrial city and is a good place to experience the bustle of inner-city life. Here too you can buy the local fabrics for which the city is famous, particularly hand-made lace, towelling and silk. The silkworm was introduced to the Byzantine empire in the 6th century and, until recently, there was still a brisk trade in silk cocoons in Koza Han in June and July. Here you can also find hand-made, camelskin Karagöz puppets *(see p26)*.

★ Covered Bazaar
The great bazaar, built by Mehmet I in the 15th century, consists of a long hall with domed bays, with an adjoining high, vaulted hall. The Bedesten is home to jewellers' shops.

★ Great Mosque (Ulu Camii)
A three-tiered ablutions fountain stands beneath the central dome of this monumental mosque, which was erected in 1396–9.

Şengül Hamamı Turkish baths

FEVZI ÇAKMAK CAD

Bey Han (also called Emir Han) was built as part of the Orhan Gazi Mosque complex, to provide revenue for the mosque's upkeep.

Cafés

KOZA PARKI

ATATÜRK CAD

Umur Bey Hamamı, built by Murat II (1421–51), is one of the world's oldest Turkish baths. It now houses workshops.

Koza Park
The gardens in front of Koza Han, with their fountains, benches and shaded café tables, are a popular meeting place for locals and visitors throughout the day.

★ Koza Han
This is the most attractive and fascinating building in the market area. Since it was built in 1491 by Beyazıt II, it has been central to the silk trade.

Flower Market
The numerous bunches of flowers for sale in the streets around the town hall make a picturesque sight in the midst of Bursa's bustling market area.

Geyve Han is also known as İvaz Paşa Han.

Fidan Han dates from around 1470, when it was built by a grand vizier of Mehmet the Conqueror.

İçkoza Han

BORSA SOK

UZUN ÇARŞI CAD

ÇÖMLEK SOK

0 metres		40
0 yards		40

STAR SIGHTS

★ Great Mosque

★ Covered Bazaar

★ Koza Han

The Belediye, Bursa's town hall, is a Swiss chalet-style, half-timbered building that forms a surprising landmark in the centre of the city.

BELEDIYE CAD

ⓘ
Tourist information

KEY

– – – Suggested route

Orhan Gazi Mosque
Built in 1339, just 13 years after the Ottoman conquest of Bursa, this mosque is the oldest of the city's imperial mosques.

Exploring Bursa

The clocktower in Tophane

Tophane, the most ancient part of Bursa, is distinguished by its clock-tower, which stands on top of a hill. This area was formerly the site of the citadel and is bounded by what remains of the original Byzantine walls. It is also known as Hisar, which means "fortress" in Turkish. If you continue westwards for 2 km (1 mile), crossing the Cılımboz River, you come to the historic district of Muradiye. Çekirge (or "cricket") is Bursa's most westerly area. The origin of this name is not known, but the cool, leafy character of this suburb gives Bursa the tag of *yeşil*, or "green", by which it is known in Turkey.

Tophane

Tophane's northern limit is marked by the best-preserved section of the citadel walls, built on an outcrop of rock. At the top is a pleasant park, filled with cafés, which also contains the imposing clock-tower and the tombs of Osman and Orhan Gazi, the founders of the Ottoman dynasty.

delineated the entire circumference of the ancient city. How-ever, Orhan en-couraged Bursa's expansion and developed the present-day com-mercial heart of the city further to the east.

⚏ Tophane Citadel

Hisar
Osman Gazi Cad. ◯ *daily.* ♿
The Citadel walls can be viewed from a set of steps leading uphill from the inter-section of Cemal Nadir Caddesi and Atatürk Caddesi. These steps end at the tea gardens above. The citadel fell into Ottoman hands when Orhan Gazi's troops broke through its walls. Later, he built a wooden palace inside the citadel and had the old Byzantine ramparts re-fortified. Until this era the walls had

⚏ Tombs of Osman and Orhan Gazi

Osman & Orhan Gazi Türbeleri
Ulu Cami Cad. ◯ *daily.* 📷 *donation.*
Osman Gazi began the process of Ottoman expansion in the 13th century *(see p52)* and attempted to capture Bursa. But it was his son, Orhan, who took the city just before Osman Gazi died. Orhan brought his father's body to be buried in the bap-tistry of a converted church and he himself was later buried in the nave. The tombs that can be seen today date from 1868.

Tomb of Osman Gazi, the first great Ottoman leader

⚏ Alaeddin Mosque

Alaeddin Camii
Alaeddin Mahallesi. ◯ *daily.* ∅
The Alaeddin Mosque is the oldest in Bursa: it was built in 1335, only nine years after the city was conquered in 1326. It is in the form of a simple domed square, fronted by a portico of four Byzantine columns with capitals. The mosque was commissioned by Alaeddin Bey, brother of and vizier to Orhan Gazi.

Muradiye

Muradiye is a leafy, residential district of Bursa. Close to the Muradiye Mosque, the Hüsnü Züber House is a fine example of a traditional Turkish home. It is no longer open to the public but the fine architec-ture can be seen from the outside. To the north is a park; among the attractions are a boating lake and the Archaeological Museum.

⚏ Muradiye Mosque

Muradiye Külliyesi
Murat II Cad. ◯ *daily.* 📷 *donation.*
This mosque complex was built by Murat II, the father of Mehmet the Conqueror *(see p54)*, in 1447. The mosque itself is preceded by a graceful domed portico. Its wooden door is finely carved and the interior decorated with early İznik tiles *(see p161)*. The *medrese (see p32)*, next to the mosque, now serves as a dispensary. It is a perfectly square building, with cells surrounding a central garden courtyard. Its *dershane*, or main classroom, is richly tiled and adorned with an ornate brick façade.

The mosque garden, with its cypresses, well-tended flower beds and fountains, is one of Bursa's most tranquil retreats. Murat II was the last of the Ottoman sultans to be buried in Bursa and his mausoleum stands in the garden beside the mosque. The other 11 tombs in the garden are a reminder of the Ottoman code of succession,

Popular café in the park above the ancient citadel walls in Tophane

Interior of Muradiye Mosque, showing the decorative *mihrab*

which recognized a future sultan as the strongest (or most cunning) male relative, even if not always the most suitable to rule. Competing male relatives could expect to be put to death or spend most of their lives in enforced solitary confinement, known as "the cage". This did not, however, prevent the ruling offspring from having an emotive memorial built for a deposed brother. Selim II ("the Sot"), for example, had an elaborate octagonal mausoleum built in Bursa for his older brother, Mustafa.

🏛 Archaeological Museum
Arkeoloji Müzesi
Reşat Oyal, Kültür Parkı. *Tel (0224) 234 49 18.* ◻ *8am–noon & 1–5pm Tue–Sun.*

Finds dating from the 3rd millennium BC up to the Ottoman conquest of Bursa in 1326 are collected in this museum. The ceremonial armour accessories are the most interesting items, with the Roman glass a close second. There are a number of Roman statues and bronzes, as well as Byzantine religious objects and coins. The labelling of objects has been improved.

🏛 Bursa Museum of Anatolian Carriages
Bursa Anadolu Arabaları Müzesi
Umurbey Mah, Kapıcı Cad, Yıldırım. *Tel (0224) 329 39 41.* ◻ *10am–5pm Tue–Sun.* ◻ &. *(the musem is mostly on one floor).*
The discovery of a 2,600-year-old carriage made of iron and wood stimulated interest in the

city's non-motorized transport heritage. This museum traces the wheeled history of *kupa* (war chariots), ox carts, gun mountings, hay ricks, pleasure carriages and horse-drawn railway rolling stock. Artistic motifs painted on carriages were a craftsman's early trademark.

The museum skilfully highlights carriage-making as a precision engineering trade. Bursa is modern Turkey's "motown" and a local automotive producer sponsored the research and reconstruction, applying modern spare-parts cataloguing techniques to latter-day wagons. Housed in a former silk-making factory, the museum is enhanced by beautiful gardens and mature trees. A bookshop sells mainly books and posters of the various wagons.

The art of carriage-making, Bursa Museum of Anatolian Carriages

Çekirge
The Çekirge neighbourhood offers some of the most prominent and best developed natural mineral springs *(kaplıca)* in Turkey. In the 6th century, Emperor Justinian *(see p49)* built a bath house here; his wife, Theodora, arrived later with a retinue of about 4,000 to take the waters.

Today, Çekirge is the city's most attractive residential area, still known for its therapeutic hot springs and having excellent spa accommodation. Located above the city, there are wonderful alpine vistas and cool breezes.

🔷 New Spa
Yeni Kaplıca-Karamustafa Kaynarca Termal Otel and Baths, Kükürtlü Mah, Osmangazi. *Tel (0224) 236 69 68.* ◻ *5am–11pm daily (separate spas for men and women).*
Contrarily, the New Spa baths have a substantial pedigree and were rebuilt in 1522 by Rüstem Paşa, grand vizier to Süleyman the Magnificent. Two steamy thermal water sources, Kaynarca and Karamustafa, feed the therapeutic pools and treatment centres, all set in expansive tropical gardens.

Karamustafa has been restored as an aqua culture residential complex. Kaynarca is only for women, with professional spa staff, private baths and social facilities. Visitors unfamiliar with Turkey's spa heritage will be warmly welcomed here.

🛏 Çelik Palas Hotel
Çelik Palas Otel
Çekirge Cad 79. *Tel (0224) 233 38 00.*
This five-star hotel is a famous local icon. Built in 1933, it is the city's oldest and most prestigious spa hotel. Atatürk *(see p58)* frequented its baths, which are open to both sexes.

🔷 Old Spa
Eski Kaplıca
Kervansaray Termal Oteli, Çekirge Meydanı *Tel (0224) 233 93 00.* ◻ *8am–10:30pm daily.*
The Old Spa baths were established by Sultan Murat I in the late 14th century and renovated in 1512 during the reign of Beyazıt II. The spa contains radium and is for men only. The women's section focuses more on cosmetic, not thermal, treatments.

Attractive, tranquil interior of the Old Spa baths

Gallipoli Peninsula 9
Gelibolu Yarımadası

Shell cases at Alçitepe

Washed by the Aegean Sea to the west, the Gallipoli Peninsula is bordered to the east by the Dardanelles, a strategic waterway giving access to the Sea of Marmara, the Bosphorus and the Black Sea. In ancient times, this deep channel was called the Hellespont. Today, the peninsula is an unspoiled area of farmland and pine forest, with some lovely stretches of sandy beach.

However, it was also the scene of one of the bloodiest campaigns of World War I, in which more than 500,000 Allied (Australian, British, French, Indian and New Zealand) and Turkish soldiers laid down their lives. The region has three museums, and is dotted with cemeteries and monuments. In 1973, the Gallipoli National Historic Park was created in recognition of the area's great historical significance.

Suvla Bay
On 7 August 1915, British troops landed here in an attempt to break the stalemate further south.

★ Kabatepe Information Centre
The centre is also a museum, with letters, photographs, shrapnel and other memorabilia relating to the Gallipoli campaign.

At Y Beach, ambiguous signals led to an unauthorized withdrawal on both sides.

The Çanakkale Şehitleri Abidesi commemorates Turkish soldiers.

0 kilometres	
0 miles	2

French Cemetery
A sombre obelisk and rows of striking black crosses honour the French troops who fell during the Anglo-French landing at Cape Helles on 25 April 1915.

Reconstructed Trenches

At some points, the Allied and Turkish trenches were no more than a few metres apart.

★ **Chunuk Bair**
Various monuments honour the 28,000 men who died here on 6–9 August 1915.

Kumköy
üyükanafarta
Yalova
iallipoli ttlefields E87
Rigalı
Ataturk Statue
Chunuk Bair
hmetcik emorial Kilye Bay
Eceabat (Maidos)
tatürk luseum
Çanakkale
Kilitibahir The Narrows
Kepez

KEY
— Major road
— Other road
— Minor road
— River, lake or dam

★ **Mehmetcik Memorial**
This memorial was unveiled in 1985. Atatürk's eulogy unites the fallen sons of Turkey (Mehmetcik) with the Allied dead ("Johnnies").

THE GALLIPOLI CAMPAIGN 1915–16

After the start of World War I, Allied leaders developed a plan to seize the Dardanelles. This would give them control of Constantinople and diminish the threat of Russia gaining control of the strategic waterway. A naval assault was repulsed by Turkish shore batteries and minefields, so the order was given to land troops to secure the straits. At dawn on 25 April 1915 British and French troops landed at the tip of the Gallipoli Peninsula. Further north, a large force of ANZACs (Australia and New Zealand Army Corps) came ashore but met dogged opposition from the Turkish defenders. A second landing at Suvla Bay failed to win any new ground. Many soldiers died from disease, drowning or the appalling conditions of trench warfare. After nine months, the Allied force withdrew.

British troops landing under fire at Cape Helles

STAR SIGHTS

★ Chunuk Bair

★ Kabatepe Information Centre

★ Mehmetcik Memorial

THE AEGEAN

iscovering the Aegean region of Turkey takes visitors on a panoramic, classical journey, from Çanakkale on the Dardanelles (the ancient Hellespont) to the finger of land off Marmaris known as the Datça Peninsula. Together, the coast and hinterland tell a story spanning some 5,000 years of Greek and Roman history. This is where Homer's myths and heroes come to life.

Here, it is easy to imagine the sculpture classes at Aphrodisias, the busy streets of ancient Ephesus or a medical lecture at the famous Asclepium at Pergamum (Bergama).

Most of modern-day Turkey was once part of the eastern Roman empire, known as Asia Minor. Many of the remote classical sites in the Aegean region formed part of ancient Caria, an independent kingdom whose boundaries roughly corresponded to the Turkish province of Muğla. Caria's origins are disputed but its resistance to Hellenization is well documented. The Carians prospered under Roman rule but retained some autonomy, with their sanctuary at Labranda, and Zeus as their deity. The Carian symbol, a double-headed axe, was inscribed on many buildings as a defiant trademark. The Mausoleum at Halicarnassus (modern-day Bodrum), built as the tomb of the Carian king Mausolus, was one of the Seven Wonders of the Ancient World.

The Aegean region contains many Christian sights. The Seven Churches of the Apocalypse, mentioned in the Book of Revelation, surround İzmir; the last resting place of the Virgin Mary is just outside Ephesus; St John's Basilica is in Selçuk and the castle of the Knights of St John still guards the harbour at Bodrum.

The Aegean's original tourist resorts, such as Kuşadası, Marmaris and Bodrum, have now matured, and offer superb facilities and sophisticated nightlife. Bodrum's Halikarnas disco has an international reputation, and Kuşadası is known for its shopping.

Roman arched gateway at the ruined city of Hierapolis, near Denizli

◁ The inviting yacht harbour at Marmaris

Exploring the Aegean

Around 26 million people – roughly a third of Turkey's population – inhabit the Aegean region. Here, incomes are generally higher and the lifestyle more westernized than elsewhere in the country. Tourists are attracted to this area for its beaches, nightlife and yachting, but there are many other worthwhile sights from the green and fertile Menderes River Valley to the Roman city of Ephesus near Selçuk. Visitors can explore the countryside in day-trips from Marmaris to Knidos on the scenic Datça Peninsula.

SIGHTS AT A GLANCE

Altınkum **21**
Aphrodisias pp188–9 **15**
Aydın **12**
Ayvalık **4**
Behram Kale (Assos) **3**
Bergama (Pergamum) pp176–7 **5**
Bodrum pp194–7 **25**
Çanakkale **1**
Çeşme **8**
Denizli **16**
Didyma **19**
Ephesus pp182–3 **10**
Foça **6**
Güllük **24**
Hierapolis pp186–7 **14**
İzmir pp178–9 **7**
Kuşadası **11**
Labranda **22**
Lake Bafa **20**
Marmaris pp200–201 **27**
Menderes River Valley **13**
Milas (Mylasa) **23**
Miletus **18**
Priene **17**
Selçuk **9**
Troy **2**

Tours

Bodrum Peninsula Tour pp198–9 **26**
Datça Peninsula Tour pp202–203

Temple of Trajan, Bergama (Pergamum)

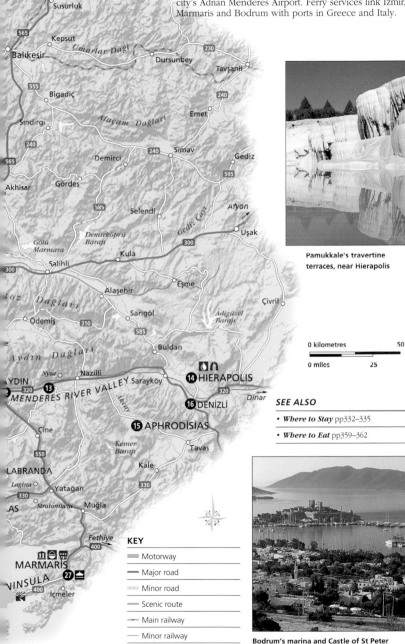

GETTING AROUND
The Aegean region is well served by good roads and public transport. Dolmuşes ply the routes to the smaller towns and villages. İzmir and Bodrum both have airports with frequent connections to Istanbul. İzmir is also served by rail, with connections to the city's Adnan Menderes Airport. Ferry services link İzmir, Marmaris and Bodrum with ports in Greece and Italy.

Pamukkale's travertine terraces, near Hierapolis

0 kilometres 50

0 miles 25

SEE ALSO

• **Where to Stay** pp332–335

• **Where to Eat** pp359–362

KEY

▬▬	Motorway
▬	Major road
═	Minor road
	Scenic route
▬•▬	Main railway
—	Minor railway

Bodrum's marina and Castle of St Peter

Çanakkale, a historic crossing point between Asia and Europe

Çanakkale ❶

🏛 81,000. 🚢 from Eceabat or Kilitbahir. 🚌 Atatürk Cad. ℹ İskele Meydanı 67, (0286) 217 11 87. 🛳 Fri. 🎭 Navy Days (13–18 Mar), ANZAC Days (24–25 Apr), Sardine Festival (30–31 Jun – Gelibolu)).

Çanakkale occupies the narrowest point of the straits called the Dardanelles, which are 1,200 m (3,937 ft) wide at this point. In 450 BC, the Persian King Xerxes built a bridge of boats here to land his troops in Thrace, and the final battles of the Peloponnesian War took place in these waters around 400 BC.

During his campaign to take Constantinople in 1453, Mehmet II (the Conqueror) built two fortresses to secure the straits: Kilitbahir (on the European side) and Çimenlik (in Çanakkale harbour).

Today, ferry services link Çanakkale with Kilitbahir and Eceabat on the other side. Çanakkale makes the most convenient base for tours of the Gallipoli battlefields (see pp168–9) across the straits.

The town has an attractive harbour, a naval museum and the landmark clock in the main square. Çanakkale means "pottery castle" and the town was once a centre for the production of high-quality kaolin for a flourishing ceramics industry. Today this type of clay is imported, but the vitreous enamel ware (see p376) made in Çanakkale remains one of Turkey's top export earners.

Environs

A few kilometres south of the town is the **Archaeological Museum**, which should not be missed.

🏛 Archaeological Museum

Arkeoloji Müzesi
Barbaros Mahallesi, Yüzüncü Yıl Cad. **Tel** (0286) 217 67 40. ⏰ 8am– noon, 1–5pm Tue–Sun. 📷

Troy ❷

ℹ İskele Meydanı 67, Çanakkale, (0286) 217 11 87. 🚗 from Çanakkale, then taxi. 🎭 Troy Festival (based in Çanakkale but includes Troy and environs, 10–18 Aug).

Few areas of Turkey have been as thoroughly excavated as Troy (Truva in Turkish). Nine different strata have yielded pieces of a history that runs from around 4000 BC until about AD 300. Troy was the pivot of Homer's *Iliad* and was where the decade-long Trojan War (13th century BC) was fought.

The site is known as **Hisarlık**, or "castle kingdom" in Turkish. The stonework and walls are impressive. Visible today are a defence wall, two sanctuaries (probably dating from the 8th century BC), houses from various periods and a Roman theatre. The site called the Pillar House at the southern gate may have been the palace of King Priam.

The site is well marked with 12 information points and some ongoing excavations. The most visible attraction is a large wooden Trojan Horse, a reconstruction of the device used by the Greeks to deceive and ultimately vanquish the Trojans, and a universal symbol of treachery today. In August each year, Turkish schoolchildren release a white dove from the Trojan Horse to celebrate peace.

Reconstruction of the Trojan Horse

🏠 Hisarlık

5 km (3 miles) from main E87 road. 🚗 from Çanakkale every 30/40 minutes. ⏰ 8am–7:30pm (5pm in winter) daily. 📷 📷 📷

SCHLIEMANN'S SEARCH FOR ANCIENT TROY

The German-born Heinrich Schliemann – regarded by many as an unscrupulous plunderer and by others as an archaeological pioneer – nurtured a lifelong ambition to discover Homer's Troy. In 1873, three years after starting excavations at Hisarlık, he stumbled upon what he claimed to be King Priam's hoard of gold and silver jewellery. The over-eager explorer damaged the site, but his valuable find demonstrated that Greek civilization started 1,000 years earlier than previously believed. Part of the hoard, which was on display in a Berlin museum, vanished after World War II. It reappeared in the Pushkin Museum in Russia in 1996. Its return, authenticity and origins are still controversial.

Heinrich Schliemann's wife, wearing "Priam's" jewellery

Humpbacked Ottoman bridge on the outskirts of Behram Kale

Behram Kale ❸ (Assos)

🏠 3,000. 🚌 to Ayvacık, 19 km (12 miles) N, then dolmuş. 🅓 from Edremit or Çanakkale.

Nestled on the shores of the Gulf of Edremit and sheltered by the Greek island of Lesbos, 10 km (6 miles) offshore, it is easy to see why Assos enjoyed the reputation of the most beautiful place in Asia Minor. Ancient Assos reached the pinnacle of its glory when Plato's protégé, Aristotle, founded a school of philosophy here in 340 BC. In the 2nd century BC, the town included not only the present citadel, with the remaining Doric columns of the Temple of Athena (built in the 6th century BC), but also the village of Behram Kale, 238 m (781 ft) below.

St Paul is reputed to have passed through Assos on his third biblical journey, and the town is referred to in the Acts of the Apostles. After the fall of the Byzantine empire, the town's commercial fortunes declined, but today this charming and cultured retreat attracts many artists and scholars, who leave the bustle of the city and find a source of inspiration here.

As you come into the town, note the fine Ottoman bridge dating from the 14th century. There is also a mosque and a fort from this time, all built by Sultan Murat I. Residents of Assos favour houses with archways and overhanging balconies, and there is bougainvillea everywhere.

Ayvalık ❹

🏠 30,000. 🚌 1.5 km (1 mile) N of town centre. ℹ Opposite the yacht harbour, (0266) 312 21 22. 🛒 Thu. 🚢 🏠

Ayvalık takes its name from *ayva*, the Turkish word for quince, but the fruit is only available in season (January and February). Of the many villages along the Aegean coast peopled by Greeks until 1923 *(see p58)*, Ayvalık is the one that has most retained the flavour of a bygone age. There are many stone houses, and the town's mosques betray their Greek Orthodox origins. A Greek church and a few Greek-speakers remain.

Ayvalık's appeal stems from its cobbled streets and leisurely lifestyle. The beach at Sarımsaklı and peninsula of Alibey (also known by its Greek name of Cunda) are within reach by road, but the ferry journey is more restful.

Bergama (Pergamum) ❺

See pp176–7.

Foça ❻

🏠 14,000. ℹ Atatürk Bulvarı 1 (entrance to Foça), (0232) 812 55 34. 🚌 from İzmir to Foça turnoff on main E87. 🅓 from junction of E87. 🎭 Tourism & Culture Festival (Aug–Sep).

Phocaea, ancient Foça, was probably settled around 1000 BC and was part of the Ionian League *(see p190)*. Around 500 BC the Phocaeans were famed as mariners, sending vessels powered by 50 oarsmen into the Aegean, Mediterranean and Black Sea. There is a small theatre dating from antiquity at the entrance to the town. Near the centre of town, you will find a stone tomb known as **Taş Küle**. There is also a restored Genoese **fortress**. But apart from a few *hamams* (Turkish baths), this is the extent of Old Foça.

Environs
23 km (14 miles) up the coast is the town of Yenifoça (New Foça), with good campsites and beaches. The military presence in the area may have helped keep it off the tourist trail. Apart from summer weekends and holidays, it is an ideal place to escape the crowds. The area is known for its monk seal conservation programme, but they are seldom seen.

Boats, old houses and up-market cafés in Foça's harbour

Bergama (Pergamum) ⑤

★ **Temple of Trajan**
Built of white marble, it was completed during Hadrian II's reign (AD 125–138).

Perched on a hilltop above the modern town of Bergama, the great acropolis of Pergamum is one of the most dramatic sights in Turkey. Originally settled by the Aeolian Greeks in the 8th century BC, it was ruled for a time by one of Alexander the Great's generals. The city prospered under the Pergamene dynasty founded by Eumenes I, who ruled from 263 to 241 BC, when this was one of the ancient world's main centres of learning. The last ruler of this dynasty, Attalus III, bequeathed the kingdom to Rome in 133 BC, and Pergamum became capital of the Roman province of Asia. The great physician Galen was born here in AD 129, and established a famous medical centre, the Asclepieum.

Statue of Hadrian, Bergama Museum

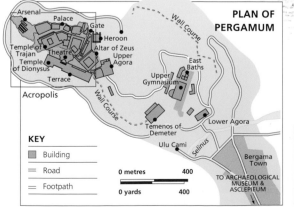

King's Palace

Arsenal

City Walls
Eumenes II (197–159 BC) extended the city walls until they reached a length of about 4 km (3 miles), enclosing the entire hilltop.

Temple of Dionysus

PLAN OF PERGAMUM

Arsenal — Palace — Gate — Heroon — Altar of Zeus — Temple of Trajan — Theatre — Temple of Dionysus — Terrace — Upper Agora — Acropolis — Wall Course — Upper Gymnasium — East Baths — Temenos of Demeter — Lower Agora — Ulu Cami — Selinus — Bergama Town

0 metres 500
0 yards 500

KEY

■ Building
= Road
= Footpath

0 metres 400
0 yards 400

TO ARCHAEOLOGICAL MUSEUM & ASCLEPIEUM

STAR SIGHTS

★ Altar of Zeus

★ Temple of Trajan

★ Theatre

Library Ruins
Reputedly containing 200,000 parchment scrolls, many works from Pergamum went to its rival library in Alexandria as part of Mark Anthony's wedding gift to Cleopatra in 41 BC.

Temple of Athena

The Heroon was a shrine built to honour the kings of Pergamum.

★ Altar of Zeus
One of Pergamum's largest temples, the first stone reliefs of the building were found in the 1870s. The altar was rebuilt in Berlin's Pergamum Museum.

Upper Agora
The agora (marketplace) lay immediately below the Altar of Zeus. From here, a ramp led up to the main city gate.

Theatre Terrace

★ Theatre
Constructed in the 3rd century BC, the theatre has 80 rows of seats and an estimated capacity of 10,000. The seats were constructed of andesite, and the royal box in the lower section of marble.

İzmir ❼

The most western-leaning of Turkish cities, İzmir's position at the head of the Gulf of İzmir (İzmir Körfezi) has given it a trading edge that has lasted from the 3rd century AD to today. For centuries, it was known as Smyrna, a name possibly derived from the myrrh trees that grow here. The city's origins are believed to date back to 3000 BC, based on finds from the Bayraklı Mound. Until 1922, the city had a large Christian population, including thousands of Greek Orthodox, most of whom fled during the turmoil of the War of Independence (see p58). As Turkey's third largest city and the regional headquarters of NATO, İzmir has a multicultural sophistication.

Konak Clock Tower

The Governor's Palace, in the centre of the city

Exploring İzmir

İzmir's broad boulevards are balanced by leafy pedestrian precincts. Buses, ferries and a Metro make it easy to get around, or horse-drawn carriages will do for the more sedate tourist. Be sure to explore the old wharf area (İzkele), now restored as a stylish shipping pier.

🏛 Archaeology Museum

Halil Paşa Cad, Bahri Baba Park İçi. **Tel** (0232) 445 73 90. ◯ 8:30am–6pm (5pm in winter) Tue–Sun. 🎫 📷 with permission.
The main displays consist of artifacts from the Bayraklı Mound, which was settled from about 3000 to 300 BC. The Byzantine glassware is especially eye-catching, but the highlight is the Treasury (Hazine). It is kept locked and the guard may need to be summoned, but the gold jewellery dating from the 6th–3rd centuries BC offers ample proof of ancient artistic talent. The Roman and Byzantine imperial silver and gold coins are well displayed.

🏛 Ethnographic Museum

Next to the Archaeology Museum. **Tel** (0232) 489 07 96. ◯ 8:30am–noon & 1–5:30pm (5pm in winter) Tue–Sun. 🎫
Housed in a former French hospital, built in 1831, the museum highlights local crafts and skills – from quilting and felt-making to weapons and woodblock printing. Bridal costumes, glassware, an oven used to fire blue beads (mavi boncuk) and a replica of İzmir's first apothecary shop.

🕌 Konak Clock Tower

Saat Kulesi
Konak Square. 🚌 any bus marked "Konak".
Built in 1901, the clock tower is the symbol of İzmir. It was one of 58 built in Ottoman times to encourage Turks to adopt European timekeeping habits. İzmir's is one of the finest of these monuments. Its ornate

The Konak mosque, adorned with ceramic tiles from Kütahya

decorative style offers a strong contrast to the exquisite simplicity of the tiny Konak Mosque (Konak Camii) that nestles beside it.

🏪 Kızlarağası Han

Look for signs off the N end of Fevzi Paşa Cad. ◯ 8am–9pm daily.
This typical Ottoman trading complex (see pp24–5) has been restored, with the courtyard turned into a café. There are craft and furniture restoration workshops on the upper floor. This is a good place to purchase handicrafts and copper.

✝ St Polycarp Church

Necatibey Sok 2.
Tel (0232) 484 84 36. ◯ 9am–noon, 3–5pm daily.
The patron saint of İzmir, St Polycarp was a Christian martyr who gave us the adage, "The spirit indeed is willing, but the flesh is weak." This is the oldest Roman Catholic church in İzmir and the seat of the Catholic archbishop. Permission to build a chapel to St Polycarp was granted in 1620 by Süleyman the Magnificent (see p56). To the right of the altarpiece is a self-portrait of Raymond Peré, designer of the Konak Clock Tower.

Corinthian columns in the Agora, the city market in Roman times

VISITORS' CHECKLIST

🏙 3,500,000. 🚢 Alsancak.
🚉 Basmane, Eyül Meydanı 9;
Alsancak, Ziya Gökalp Bulvarı,
(0232) 464 77 95. ✈ Adnan
Menderes, 12 km (8 miles) SE of
city centre, (0232) 274 26 26.
🚌 8 km (5 miles) NE of city
centre, (0232) 472 10 10.
ℹ Akdeniz Mah 1344 Sok 2,
Pasaport, (0232) 445 73 90.
🎭 Liberation Day (9 Sep), International Arts Festival (10 Jun–
10 Jul). www.izmirturizm.gov.tr

0 metres 400

0 yards 400

Alsancak terminal
600 metres (650 yards)

Kulturparki

Airport
20km (12 miles)
Bus terminal
8km (5 miles)

ANKAYA
FEVZİPAŞA BUL
AKINCİ
ANAFARTALAR CAD
Basmane
Train Station
GAZİLER CAD

6 Agora

7 Velvet Castle

Agora

🕐 8:30am–noon & 1–5:30pm
Tue–Sun.

The present remains of the
Agora, the central market of
the Roman city of Smyrna,
date from about the 2nd century AD, when it was rebuilt
by the Emperor Marcus
Aurelius following an earthquake in AD 178. There are
several Corinthian columns
with well-preserved capitols
still standing, and enough
arches, as well as part of a
basilica (city hall), to give
the flavour of a Roman
town. It was used until
the Byzantine period.

Velvet Castle
Kadifekale

🚌 from Konak Clock Tower
marked "Kale", then on foot.

Also known as Mount
Pagos, the Velvet Castle
was built on Hellenistic
foundations. Originally it
had 40 towers, with num-
erous additions made by
the Romans, Genoese and
Ottomans over the cen-
turies. The castle is a
good spot for an after-
noon's outing, and
offers unsurpassed
vistas over İzmir Bay.

Dario Moreno Street, with the
Asansör in the background

Asansör

🕐 7am–late. tel (0232) 261 26 26
(restaurant).

The Asansör is a working
19th-century elevator in the
Karataş district. From its rooftop restaurant, there are fine
views over the city.

Leafy Dario Moreno Street
(Dario Moreno Sokaği) lies
in a restored section of İzmir's
old Jewish quarter. The street
is named after a 1960s singer
who was fond of the city.

Key to Symbols see back flap

SIGHTS AT A GLANCE

The Velvet Castle (Kadifekale), İzmir's ancient citadel

Çeşme 8

🏛 *21,120.* 🚢 *from Brindisi, Bari, Venice and Chios.* 🚌 *1 km (0.5 mile) S of ferry dock.* 🅿 *for local sights.* 🛈 *İskele Meydanı 8, (0232) 712 66 53.* 🍽 *Wed and Sun; Sat (Alaçatı).* 🎭 *İzmir International Arts Festival (10 Jun–10 Jul).*

The town's main feature is the 14th-century Genoese Castle of St Peter, a powerful symbol of Italian Renaissance mercantilism. Sultan Beyazıt II (1481–1512) fortified the castle to counter attacks by both pirates and the Knights of St John, who operated from bases on the island of Rhodes and at Bodrum *(see pp196–7)*. The castle contains a **museum** with nautical exhibits. The hotel next to the harbour was formerly a caravanserai *(see pp24–5)*.

Unlike other more popular resorts, Çeşme is dedicated to promenading, yachting and the simpler pleasures of life. There are several fine restaurants, and the cosmopolitan, tolerant atmosphere attracts world-class performers, who come here for the month-long İzmir International Arts Festival.

The long peninsula around Çeşme is serviced by a fast, six-lane highway from İzmir. However, you can still take the old road, stopping at beaches in Ilıca or spending an afternoon at Alaçatı, the windsurfing capital of Turkey, where wind energy supplies a quarter of the town's power requirements.

🏛 **Museum**
Çeşme Castle. 🕐 *9am–noon & 1–5:30pm Tue–Sun.* 🎫

Çeşme waterfront, with the Castle of St Peter above the town

Selçuk 9

🏛 *25,000.* 🚆 *from İzmir or Denizli.* 🚌 *Atatürk Cad.* 🛈 *Agora Çarşısı 35 (0232) 892 69 45.*
www.selcuk.gov.tr.
🍽 *Sat.* 🎭 *Camel Wrestling (3rd and 4th week in Jan).*

Visitors often bypass Selçuk on their way to Ephesus, but it deserves a stopover. The town is dominated by a 6th-century Byzantine citadel (Ayasoluk Hill) with 15 well-preserved towers. Nearby are the remains of a Byzantine church and a Seljuk mosque. You enter the citadel through a Byzantine gate. At the foot of the hill is the Basilica of St John, built by the Emperor Justinian *(see p50)* in the 6th century on the site of an earlier shrine. It is believed to contain the tomb of St John the Evangelist, who spent his later years at Ephesus during the 1st century. Restoration has brought back some of the basilica's former glory, and there are some fine frescoes in the chapel.

The **Ephesus Museum** is one of Turkey's best. Marble and bronze statues and frescoes are beautifully displayed, and exhibits include a sculpture of Artemis, jewels and numerous artifacts thought to have come from the nearby Artemision, the ancient Temple of Artemis (one of the Seven Wonders of the Ancient World). Today, the ruins of the Artemision are waterlogged.

The İsa Bey Mosque (also known as the Selim Mosque), an ornate 14th-century Seljuk mosque, is located near the museum. It is not always open to visitors but the exterior calligraphy and inlaid tilework are worth a visit.

🏛 **Ephesus Museum**
Behind Tourism Information Office. **Tel** *(0232) 892 60 10.* 🕐 *8:30am–noon & 12:30–5pm daily.* 🎫

Environs
The former Greek village of Şirince, 8 km (5 miles) east of Selçuk, has a peaceful air that is welcoming after the bustle of Ephesus.

At Çamlik is the **Open-Air Steam Train Exhibition**, a museum run by Turkish State Railways. There are more than 24 steam locomotives and other railway vehicles on display at the site.

🏛 **Open-Air Steam Train Exhibition**
Çamlik, 12 km (7 miles) S of Selçuk on the E87. 🎫

Byzantine gateway in Selçuk, at the foot of Ayasoluk Hill

Ephesus 10

See pp182–3.

Kuşadası ⓫

🏛 50,000. 🛳 from Samos (Apr–Oct). 🚌 from Selçuk, Söke and İzmir. 🚐 1 km (0.5 mile) S of town centre on Söke road. 🅸 Liman Cad 13, (0256) 614 11 03. 🛍 Wed.

Kuşadası is a frequent port of call for luxury cruise liners. Only Bodrum and Istanbul can match it for fast-paced, hedonistic nightlife.

The town's name, meaning "bird island", is taken from an islet, known as Pigeon Island, tacked onto the mainland by a causeway. A 14th-century Genoese fort reveals the town's commercial origins.

Environs
Dilek Peninsula National Park protects the last of Turkey's wild horses and rare Anatolian cheetahs. The military presence has ensured that the area has been left undisturbed. Hike to the summit of Samsun Dağı (ancient Mount Mycale) for fine views of the peninsula.

🦌 Dilek Peninsula National Park
Dilek Yarımadası Milli Parkı 18 km (11 miles) W of Söke. 🅳 from Kuşadası or Söke. *Tel* (0256) 646 10 79. ⏰ 8am–6pm daily. 🎫 extra for vehicles.

Camel wrestling, a popular event in Aydın

Aydın ⓬

🏛 150,000. 🚐 700 m (0.5 mile) S of town centre 🚉 from İzmir and Denizli. 🅸 Adnan Menderes Mah-Denizli Bul 2, (0256) 211 28 42. 🛍 Tue. 🐫 Camel Wrestling (Sep–Mar), Fig Festival (1st week in Sep), Chestnut Festival (Dec).

Known in Roman times as Tralles, Aydın's tranquil appearance stems from long periods of prosperity. It was known variously as Caesarea and Güzelhisar before falling under Ottoman rule in the late 14th century. Frequent earthquakes have meant that there are few ruins to be seen, and the region is still subject to tremors.

The region is famous for its figs (*incir*), black olives, cereals, and cotton, and Aydın is a leading exporter of snails

and salmon. In the 1920s, Atatürk (*see p58*) targeted the region as the focus of a new state-owned cotton industry. Today, raw cotton and ready-to-wear clothing remain Turkey's biggest export commodities.

Suffering badly in the War of Independence (*see p58*), nowadays Aydın is more peaceful, with a **museum** and several distinctive mosques.

🏛 Museum
W of gardens. *Tel* (0256) 225 22 59. ⏰ 9am–noon, 1:30–5pm Tue–Sun. 🎫 📷 📹

Menderes River Valley ⓭

One of Turkey's main grain-growing regions, and a major producer of fruit and cotton, the Menderes Valley is made up of the Büyük Menderes (Great Meander) and Küçük Menderes (Lesser Meander) rivers, with a wide alluvial plain in between. The S-shaped bends formed by the slow-moving Büyük Menderes below Aydın have given us the word "meander".

Nysa, a Seleucid foundation dating from around 280 BC, presents a lovely sight as you approach from Sultanhisar (just to the south). There is a theatre overlooking a tributary of the Büyük Menderes, and a a gymnasium, library, agora and council house. The whole city is built in and over a ravine (although the bridge is in poor condition). Its claim to fame was as a sanctuary to Pluto, god of the underworld.

At **Tire**, north of Aydın, lie the remains of a number of caravanserais (*see pp24–5*) dating from the 14th and 15th centuries. In the wake of the capture of Constantinople in 1453, Mehmet II (*see p54*) ordered the removal of the inhabitants of Tire, as part of the effort to repopulate the capital. There is a dramatic domed bazaar building here and a lively bazaar is still held each week on Tuesdays.

The yacht marina at Kuşadası, one of the largest on the Aegean coast

Ephesus ⑩

Ephesus is one of the greatest ruined cities in the western world. A Greek city was first built here in about 1000 BC and it soon rose to fame as a centre for the worship of Cybele, the Anatolian Mother Goddess. The city we see today was founded in the 4th century BC by Alexander the Great's successor, Lysinachus. But it was under the Romans that Ephesus became the chief port on the Aegean. Most of the surviving structures date from this period. As the harbour silted up the city declined, but played an important role in the spread of Christianity. Two

Statue of Artemis

great Councils of the early Church were held here in AD 431 and 449. It is said that the Virgin Mary spent her last days nearby and that St John the Evangelist came from the island of Patmos to look after her.

Restored Mural
Murals in the houses opposite the Temple of Hadrian indicate that these were the homes of wealthy people.

★ Library of Celsus
Built in AD 114–117 by Consul Gaius Julius Aquila for his father, the library was damaged first by the Goths and then by an earthquake in 1000. The statues occupying the niches in front are Sophia (wisdom), Arete (virtue), Ennoia (intellect) and Episteme (knowledge).

The Commercial Agora was the main marketplace of the city.

The brothel was adorned with a statue of Priapus, the Greek god of ferility.

Private houses featured murals and mosaics.

Temple of Domitian

| 0 metres | 200 |
| 0 yards | 200 |

THE HOUSE OF MARY

According to the Bible, the crucified Jesus asked St John the Evangelist to look after his mother, Mary. John brought Mary with him to Ephesus in AD 37, and she spent the last years of her life here in a modest stone house. The house

The house of the Blessed Virgin

of the Blessed Virgin is located at Meryemana, 8 km (5 miles) from the centre of Ephesus. The shrine, known as the Meryemana Kultur Parkı, is revered by both Christians and Muslims, and pilgrims of both faiths visit the shrine, especially on 15 August every year.

STAR SIGHTS

★ Library of Celsus

★ Temple of Hadrian

★ Theatre

For hotels and restaurants in this region see pp332–335 and pp359–362

★ Theatre
Carved into the flank of Mt Pion during the Hellenistic period, the theatre was later renovated by the Romans.

VISITORS' CHECKLIST

3 km (2 miles) W of Selçuk, on Efes Müzesi Uğur Mumcu Sevgi Yolu. **Tel** (0232) 892 60 10 (museum). 🚏 Selçuk tourist office, (0232) 892 69 45. 🄳 from Selçuk. ☐ 8:30am–4:30pm (to 7pm summer) daily. 🅰 🅱 🅲

The *skene*
(stage building) featured elaborate ornamentation.

Marble Street
was paved with blocks of marble.

★ Temple of Hadrian
Built to honour a visit by Hadrian in AD 123, the relief marble work on the facade portrays mythical gods and goddesses.

Gate of Hercules

The gate at the entrance to Curetes Street takes its name from two reliefs showing Hercules draped in a lion skin. Originally a two-storey structure, and believed to date from the 4th century AD, it had a large central arch with winged victories on the upper corners of the archway. Curetes Street was lined by statues of civic notables.

The Odeon (meeting hall) was built in AD 150.

Baths of Varius

Colonnaded Street

Lined with Ionic and Corinthian columns, the street runs from the Baths of Varius to the Temple of Domitian.

The impressive two-storey façade of the Library of Celsus ▷

Hierapolis ⓮

Necropolis tomb doorzway

In Hellenistic times, the thermal springs at Hierapolis made the city a popular spa. Today, the ruins of Hierapolis still draw visitors, who come to swim in its mineral-rich pools and to see the startling white travertine terraces of nearby Pamukkale.

Founded by Eumenes II, king of Pergamum *(see pp176–7)*, the city was noted for its textiles, particularly wool. Hierapolis was ceded to Rome in 133 BC along with the rest of the Pergamene kingdom. The city was destroyed by an earthquake in AD 60, and was rebuilt and reached its peak in AD 196–215. Hierapolis fell into decline in the 6th century, and the site became partially submerged by water and deposits of travertine.

Necropolis

Site of early theatre

Baths and church

Agora

★ Arch of Domitian
The main thoroughfare of Hierapolis was a wide, colonnaded street called the Plateia, which ran from the Arch of Domitian to the south gate.

Pool
The popular bathing pool, littered with fragments of marble columns, may be the remains of a sacred pool associated with the Temple of Apollo.

Church

Nymphaeum

Site museum in Roman baths

PAMUKKALE

The spectacular white travertine terraces at Pamukkale, next to Hierapolis, have long been one of Turkey's most popular (and photographed) sights. The terraces form when water from the hot springs loses carbon dioxide as it flows down the slopes, leaving deposits of limestone. The layers of white calcium carbonate, built up in steps on the plateau, have earned the name of Pamukkale (cotton castle). To protect them from damage, the terraces are now off-limits to visitors.

Travertine terraces, Pamukkale

6th-century basilica

VISITORS' CHECKLIST

19 km (12 miles) N of Denizli
Tel (0258) 272 20 77. 🚌 from
İzmir, get off at Denizli. 🚪 from
Denizli. ⬜ 8am–5pm (7pm in
summer) daily. 🅿 additional fee
for parking. 🎭 Pamukkale
Festival (music and folklore per-
formances, late May/early Jun).

Necropolis

*The largest ancient graveyard in Anatolia, with more than
1,200 tombs, the necropolis (one of two at Hierapolis)
contains tumuli, sarcophagi and house-shaped tombs
from the Roman, Hellenistic and early Christian periods.*

★ Martyrium of St Philip
*Built in the 5th century AD,
on the site where the apostle was
crucified and stoned in
AD 80, the building measures
20 m (65 ft) per side. The side
arcades were used as
accommodation.*

The octagonal rotunda was paved
in marble.

The crypt is believed to
have contained the
body of St Philip.

Eight-sided chambers
were separated by eight
polygonal spaces.

Entrance chambers
were paved with limestone.

★ Theatre

*The well-preserved theatre,
built in 200 BC, could seat
20,000. However only
30 rows of seats have
survived. Shown here is the
skene, or stage building.*

STAR SIGHTS

★ Arch of Domitian

★ Martyrium of
St Philip

★ Theatre

0 metres   125

0 yards   125

Aphrodisias ⑮

Marble frieze in the museum

The site of Aphrodisias was a shrine as early as 5800 BC, when Neolithic farmers came here to worship the Mother Goddess of fertility and crops. At some point, the site was dedicated to Aphrodite, goddess of love, and was given the name Aphrodisias during the 2nd century BC.

For centuries it remained little more than a shrine, but when the Romans defeated the Pontic ruler Mithridates *(see p48)* in 74 BC, Aphrodisias was rewarded for its loyalty and prospered as a cultural and artistic hub known for its exquisite marble sculptures. During the Byzantine era, the Temple of Aphrodite became a Christian basilica. Gradually, the city faded into obscurity, later becoming the Turkish village of Geyre.

★ Stadium
The stadium is one of the best preserved structures of its kind from the classical era.

Gable ends were surmounted by statues, called *akroteria.*

★ Temple of Aphrodite
Fourteen columns of the temple have been re-erected. The lateral colonnades shown here became the nave of the Christian basilica.

The stepped platform was built on a stone foundation.

The west cella was used as a treasury.

PLAN OF APHRODISIAS

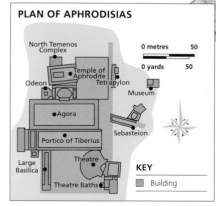

North Temenos Complex
Temple of Aphrodite
Odeon
Tetrapylon
Museum
Agora
Sebasteion
Portico of Tiberius
Large Basilica
Theatre
Theatre Baths

0 metres 50
0 yards 50

KEY
■ Building

STAR SIGHTS

★ Stadium

★ Temple of Aphrodite

★ Tetrapylon

★ **Tetrapylon**
*One of the jewels of Aphrodisias,
this 2nd-century gateway was
reconstructed with four groups
of Corinthian columns.*

VISITORS' CHECKLIST

Between Aydın and Denizli,
40 km (24 miles) S of E87
highway to Geyre. **Tel** (0256)
448 80 86 (museum). ◯
9am–6pm daily.

Sculptures
*Works produced by
the city's famous
school of sculpture
were exported as far
afield as North
Africa and Rome.
Some are exhibited
in the museum.*

Fluted columns
were constructed
from marble
drums that were
quarried nearby.

★ **Temple of Aphrodite**
*Completed in the 1st century AD, the
temple was the heart of Aphrodisias.
It was later converted for Christian
worship, with walls and colonnades
dismantled and reused to enlarge
and modify the building.*

The cult statue
of Aphrodite stood
in the cella.

Theatre
*Completed in 27 BC, structural changes were made in
AD 200 to make it suitable for gladiatorial spectacles.*

The Atatürk Ethnography Museum
in Denizli

Denizli ⑯

🏠 275,000. **ℹ** 554/1 Sokak 5,
(0258) 264 39 71.

Denizli is often thought of
as a tourist backwater,
but the town has little need
to pander to visitors. It is a
thriving agricultural centre, a
centre for carpet production
and one of Turkey's major
textile towns, continuing a
prosperous trade begun as far
back as Roman times. Today,
Aegean cotton fibres fetch
more on world markets than
many other spun cottons.

Denizli, literally translated as
"with sea", takes its name from
the many springs that feed the
River Lycus. In pre-Roman
times, another city linked with
water, Hydrela, was located
here. Denizli is a good base
for touring the ancient sites of
Hierapolis and Pamukkale
(*see pp186–7*), the latter being
about 22 km (16 miles) away.

The town was conquered
by the Seljuks in the 11th century and came under Ottoman
rule in 1428. At some point in
between, when Denizli was
known as Ladik, it seems that
the inhabitants of nearby
Laodiceia moved here after
their own city was ravaged by
one of the many earthquakes
that have marked this region.

The **Atatürk Ethnography
Museum** has some interesting
local folk art and decorative
artifacts on display. Denizli's
Great Mosque (Ulu Camii) is
also worth a visit.

🏛 **Atatürk Ethnography
Museum**
Kayalık Cad, Saraylar Mah 459
Sok 10. **Tel** (0258) 262 00 66.
◯ 8am–5pm Tue–Sun (to 7pm
summer).

The Temple of Athena at Priene, a superb example of Ionian architecture

Priene ⑰

D *from Söke or Milas to Güllübahçe.*
🕐 *8am–7pm (5pm in winter) daily.*

The ancient city of Priene has a breathtaking setting between the Büyük Menderes River and Mount Mykale. Like Miletus and Ephesus *(see pp182–3)*, it was a member of the Ionian League, a group of 12 city-states believed to have been settled by Greek colonists before 1000 BC.

Laid out by the architect Hippodamos of Miletus in about 450 BC, Priene is in a good state of preservation. The Temple of Athena, built in the 4th century BC in honour of the city's patron goddess, is considered one of the great achievements of Ionian architecture. The work was supervised and financed by Alexander the Great *(see pp46–7)* when he occupied the city. Because of Priene's strong Greek ties, it was not viewed with favour by the Romans. Its importance declined and by Byzantine times it had been abandoned. This neglect has meant that Priene is one of the most intact Hellenistic settlements to be seen. The theatre, dating from the 3rd century BC, could seat 5,000

people. The bou leuterion (council chamber) could hold 640 delegates. There is also a stadium, complete with starting blocks for athletes, and sanctuaries to Demeter and Kore. The lower gymnasium walls are adorned with schoolboy graffiti from 2,000 years ago!

Miletus ⑱

D *from Söke or Milas.* 🚌 *take the road that descends to Didyma, turn W at the village of Akköy, 7km (4 miles) from the main road.*

Although less impressive than Priene, Miletus was more renowned for its art, politics and trade than many other Greek cities. Known as Milet today, it was once the principal port of the Ionian League, and flourished as a

İlyas Bey Mosque, built in the 15th century at Miletus

centre for art and industry. In Roman times it supplied wool and textile dyes to the wool trade in Ankara *(see p240)*. One of its sons, the scientist and mathematician Thales – known as one of the Seven Sages of Antiquity – correctly forecast a total eclipse of the sun in 580 BC.

The Persians took control of the Ionian cities in the mid-6th century BC. Miletus led a revolt against Persian rule in 500–494 BC, but in 479 BC succumbed to the tyrannical Persian king, Darius. It was rebuilt by the Romans.

Of the surviving buildings, the finest is the 15,000-seat theatre, dating from AD 100. Over the centuries, Greeks, Romans and Byzantines all made alterations to the structure. The bouleuterion (council chamber) was built in 175–164 BC during the reign of the Seleucid king, Antiochus IV Ephiphanes. The well-preserved Baths of Faustina date from AD 43, and were named for the wife of Emperor Marcus Aurelius. The complex includes a palaestra (gymnasium), and there is a stadium nearby. The Baths of Faustina was a model for the development of the Turkish bath, or *hamam (see p77)*. It is also worth strolling around the stadium, nymphaeum (reservoir) and shrine of Apollo Delphinius (built in 500 BC).

Incongruously, a mosque reposes amid the ruins of ancient Miletus. The İlyas Bey (or Balat) Mosque was built in 1403 by İlyas Bey, emir (ruler) of the Beylik of Menteşe. It celebrated his return from exile at the court of the Mongol ruler Timur, also known as Tamerlane *(see p53)*, after Timur's invasion of Anatolia in 1402. The mosque is built of brick and both white and coloured marble that was taken from Roman Miletus. There is splendidly detailed carving on the marble window grilles, screen and prayer niche *(mihrab)*, and the use of coloured marble on the façade is impressive. The dome measures 14 m (45 ft) in diameter and was the largest built during the Beylik period *(see p53)*. İlyas Bey died the year after the mosque was completed and is buried in the adjacent tomb (dated 1404). The mosque is a beautiful early forerunner of the Ottoman *külliye (see p32)*, a building style that flourished during the 16th century. The *külliye* combined social welfare and residential functions with facilities for Islamic worship.

The Temple of Apollo in Didyma, with its ornate carved columns

Didyma ⑲

🚌 from Söke or Milas to Yenihisar.
🚌 from Bodrum twice a week in summer (check first). 🛈 Kaymakamlık Binası, (0256) 811 37 25. ◯ 9am–7pm (5pm in winter) daily. 📷

The prime reason to visit Didyma (modern Didim) is for the Temple of Apollo, built in the 7th century BC to honour the god of prophecy and oracles. By 500 BC, the shrine at Didyma was one of the leading oracles of the Greek world. It even had a sacred spring. Branchid priests, who were reputedly connected to the great oracle at Delphi, were in charge of the shrine. Marble from nearby Lake Bafa *(see p192)* was used to build the temple.

Head of Medusa, Didyma

A carved relief of the head of Medusa, with its serpentine curls, has become almost synonymous with Didyma.

The well below the Medusa head was the place where arriving pilgrims would purify themselves before approaching the oracle. It is now roped off to prevent accidents.

In its heyday, the Temple of Apollo featured 108 Ionic columns. Only three are still intact. However, the surviving stumps are still impressive.

The Temple of Apollo was destroyed by Persians in the mid-6th century BC, but was restored around 350 BC by Alexander the Great. With the coming of Christianity, the temple was converted into a church and Didyma became a bishopric. In 1493, an earthquake destroyed the temple and Didyma was abandoned. The Ottomans renamed it Yenihisar (new castle) in the 18th century.

The impressive theatre at Miletus, capable of seating 15,000 in Roman times

Lake Bafa ⑳

25 km (16 miles) W of Söke. 🚉 via Söke or Milas. 🍴 ▢ ♨ 🛒 Ⓓ 🚶

Considered one of the most picturesque landscapes in Turkey, the Lake Bafa area is the setting for several classical gems, with the peaks of Mount Latmos as a backdrop. Rising to 1,500 m (4,915 ft), the mountain is aptly known as Beş Parmak (five fingers).

In ancient times, Lake Bafa was an arm of the sea. When silt eventually closed the gulf, the port of **Herakleia**, near the eastern shore of the lake, was left landlocked. The same process was responsible for the decline of Miletus and Priene *(see pp190–91)*. Lake Bafa is brackish and supports many species of fish.

Herakleia, also known as Herakleia-under-Latmos, occupies a dramatic setting at the lakeside. Its fortifications, towers and well-preserved Temple of Athena are tangible vestiges of its former status. In such settings, legends are fostered: a young shepherd, unrequited love and eternal sleep are part of local lore. A shrine to the shepherd-hero, Endymion, can be visited near the lake. There are some difficult-to-reach monasteries high up the mountain.

Herakleia
10 km (6 miles) from Camiçi (by car on track). 🚤 from Lake Bafa.

Environs
Euromos, located to the southeast of Lake Bafa, wholly deserves its reputation as having one of the best preserved temples in Turkey.

Lake Bafa, an arm of the Aegean in ancient times

Euromos was, in fact, an amalgamation of several cities, including Herakleia, owing allegiance to Milas *(see p193)*. In time, rivalries emerged between them, and Euromos (meaning "strong" in Greek), turned out to be politically fickle. Like many cities of ancient Caria, it opted to ally itself with Rome and Rhodes, not Greece.

🏛 Euromos
12 km (7 miles) NW of Milas. Ⓓ from Selimiya to Milas. ◯ 8am–7pm (5pm in winter).

Altınkum ㉑

4 km (3 miles) S of Didyma. 🚌 2,300. Ⓓ via Priene and Miletus.

The protected sandy bay of Altınkum offers a relaxing spot to unwind, especially after a day spent tramping around classical ruins. Most day trips to Priene, Miletus and Didyma *(see pp190–91)* end up here. In fact, locals generally refer to the area as Didyma, or Didim (on bus

schedules, for example). Like many idyllic retreats that have experienced rapid growth, Didyma's success has spilled over to nearby towns. Charter groups and tours flock to Altınkum and it can be very busy in summer. This was one of Turkey's original camping venues. As it grew, pensions opened, and Turkish families began to flock here for sun and sand. There is not much else here – for anything more, you will have to go to Yenihisar (ancient Didyma). Few people know how to enjoy themselves as much as Turks, and Altınkum finds them in full holiday mode.

Labranda ㉒

15 km (9 miles) N of Milas on unsurfaced track (by car, taxi, or on foot from Milas). ◯ 8am–7:30pm (5pm in winter).

Getting to Labranda is certainly worth the effort for those who persevere. This Carian sanctuary nestles high on the mountains above Milas, at an impressive elevation of 610 m (2,000 ft), giving good views of the surrounding area. From early times, it fell under the jurisdiction of Milas (Mylasa). The remains of the sacred way leading there are one of the sights to note.

Despite being damaged by several fires and earthquakes, the remains of a stadium have been uncovered by Swedish archaeologists. Baths and a fountain house (which may have been a water storage

The popular beach at Altınkum

depot) date from about the 1st century BC and the area still boasts an abundant source of spring water. The most interesting buildings are three androns (banqueting halls), the second built by Mausolus (see p194), who ruled from nearby Milas.

The chamber tombs and sarcophagi, although pillaged, are unusual and reveal much about ancient burial practices.

Milas (Mylasa) ㉓

🏛 42,000. ✈ 13 km (8 miles) SW of town, (0252) 523 01 01. 🚌 Intercity buses to Bodrum. ℹ at airport, (0252) 523 00 66. 🏪 Tue.

The origins of Milas are uncertain and the many theories are largely unsubstantiated. What is clear is that its most noteworthy and prosperous period was when it was capital of Caria and the administrative seat for the Persian satrap (subordinate ruler), Mausolus. Like most Carian cities, Milas was ruled in turn by the Persians, Alexander the Great, the Romans and the Byzantines before finally falling under Ottoman control in 1425.

Local carpet in Milas

The remains of the ancient city lie within the present town centre. The first thing you notice is the two-storey **Gümüşkesen** (silver money-bag) **Mausoleum**, a structure of uncertain age. The lower floor is the actual tomb, with an aperture in the roof to provide sustenance to the deceased. The town's most intact monument is the handsome Baltılı (Axe) Gate.

As an administrative seat, Milas issued regulatory decrees, notably concerning money. Inscriptions dating from the 3rd century AD list detailed regulations that ban illegal conversions from imperial (Roman) to local money and black-market money dealings.

Save some time for modern Milas, which has some charming timber houses with

The Gümüşkesen Mausoleum, a Carian monument in Milas

lattice-work shutters. The town is justly famed for its carpets, characterized by soft neutral and beige tones.

Environs

Yatağan, site of a thermal power station and known for its environmental pollution, has little to offer, but two interesting sights are located in the area. **Stratonikeia** was founded in 295 BC. It was apparently named after the wife of Seleucas I, king of Syria. The ruins to be seen – an agora (market-place), a rather unkempt Hellenistic theatre with seating for 10,000 and the Temple of Sarapis – are in the village of Eskihisar on the 330 road, south of the city.

The town's small museum houses mainly Roman finds but includes a Mycenaean mug from about 1000 BC.

Lagina is located northwest of Yatağan and is best known for its association with the cult of Hecate, the Greek

goddess of darkness and sorcery. The gate of the temple precinct dates from between 125 and 80 BC. The Temple of Hecate would have stood here but the site has not yielded major finds.

🏛 **Stratonikeia**
20 km (12 miles) W of Milas. 🚗 Own transport. 🅳 on main Yatağan–Milas road. 📷

🏛 **Lagina**
15 km (9 miles) N of Yatağan. 🚗 Own transport essential.

Güllük ㉔

🏛 5,600. 🅳 from Milas, 28 km (17 miles) SE of Güllük, then 8 km (5 miles) to town

This is a lovely bay and harbour with a genuine nautical atmosphere and lots of accommodation. The real reason for coming to Güllük is to see the site of ancient **Iasus**, with its elaborate wall, 810 m (2,658 ft) long, built during the 5th century AD.

The fortunes of Iasus were tied to fishing. Bronze Age finds from here bear detailed inscriptions that have shed new light on the lifestyles of the ancients. Legends of boys frolicking with dolphins also originated here.

Almost opposite Güllük on the main 330 road is the site of Cindya. To the south is the ancient Barbylia (modern Varvil Bay), a town that grew wealthy by trading in salt.

🏛 **Iasus**
🚢 by boat from Güllük to Kıyıkışlacık. 🚗 18 km (11 miles) from main Milas road.

The large ruined theatre at Stratonikeia

Bodrum ㉕

Bodrum is the modern name for the ancient Dorian city of Halicarnassus, location of the famous Mausoleum built by Mausolus (375–53 BC), ruler of ancient Caria, who made the city his capital. The city walls, also built by Mausolus, were almost destroyed during Alexander the Great's siege in the 4th century BC. Herodotus, the father of written history, was born here in 484 BC, as was Dionysius, the great rhetoric teacher of the 1st century BC. Modern Bodrum was the first Turkish town to experience a tourist boom, its major sight being the 15th-century Castle of St Peter *(see pp196–7)*, now a museum of nautical archaeology.

Carian statue in the castle

The busy harbour, attracting cruising yachts of all sizes

Exploring Bodrum

Bodrum is subtly divided by the Castle of St Peter into a bustling, vehicle-free eastern sector with beaches and a quieter western hub which borders the yacht harbour. Dolmuşes make transport easy. Those marked "Şehir İçi" (inner city) stop at all major points. Boat trips to nearby beaches are also available from the harbour.

♫ Halikarnas Disco
Cumhuriyet Cad, No 178.
◯ *Apr–Sep.* **Tel** *(0252) 316 80 00.*
www.halikarnas.com.tr.
Located at the water's edge with a view of the Castle of St Peter, open-air Halikarnas is one of the most famous nightclubs in Turkey and an an emblem of hedonistic nightlife. With a capacity of 5,000, Halikarnas offers a spectacular laser light show and the best DJs. The open-air cabaret, revue and musical acts feature top performers. Smart dress is required.

🏛 Zeki Müren Museum
Zeki Müren Sanat Müzesi
Zeki Müren Cad 11. **Tel** *(0252) 313 19 39.* ◯ *Tue–Sun.* ▣
Zeki Müren (1931-1986) was one of Turkey's most accomplished and beloved singers and composers, with a career that spanned 45 years. He was fondly known as "The Sun of Art" and, although considered the Turkish Liberace, only the glitzy attire was comparable. Müren was a professional musician, actor and his unpretentious home is preserved as a delightful

The superb and renowned Turkish bath

museum. His extravagant costumes are in the limelight along with record albums, radiograms and other musical and personal memorabilia.

Rooms and furnishings seem to be anticipating his arrival, for example the 1950s' Cadillac reposing on the front lawn.

The museum is an inspiring memory to an outstanding Turkish cultural idol, who died in 1996 during a live performance. Thousands attended his funeral.

♨ Bodrum Hamam
Cevat Şakir Cad, Fabrika Sok (opposite the bus station). ◯ *6am–midnight daily.* **Tel** *(0252) 313 41 29.* **www**.hamam.com. ▣
Linked to the Çemberlitaş Baths in Istanbul, the Bodrum Hamam is housed in a lovely old stone building. Service is highly professional, emphasizing cleanliness and an authentic Turkish bath experience. Masseurs are well-trained and you are bound to feel like a "new penny" when you exit. The owners claim a 500-year lineage. The hamam runs a shuttle that will collect and return you, suitably pampered.

🏛 Old Dockyard (Tersane) and Arsenal Point
W of the marina entrance at the end of Neyzen Tevfik Cad.
◯ *dawn to dusk.* ▣
The ancient dockyard on the end of Arsenal Point is part of the effort to restore Bodrum's walls. Its position, opposite the Castle of St Peter, overlooks the main harbour. The dockyard was built in the 18th century, when the Ottoman sultans made an attempt to revive the empire's naval strength.

Attractions include a cistern, an Ottoman Tower on the west side of the harbour, a graveyard, fortification to protect the shipyard and a grand tomb built in 1729 to commemorate Cafer Paşa, who was a naval hero and prominent city patron.

The scant remains of the great Mausoleum

Mausoleum

Turgut Reis Cad (corner of Hamam Sok). ◯ 8am–noon & 1:30–5pm Tue–Sun.

The colossal Mausoleum of Halicarnassus was one of the Seven Wonders of the Ancient World. Named for Mausolus, ruler of Caria, and intended as his tomb, work on the structure began in 355 BC and was completed by his widow, Artemisia, the only woman to rule Caria. It measured 41 m (134 ft) in height, with a podium, a colonnade of 36 columns and a pyramid, resplendently topped by a horse-drawn chariot statue.

The tomb stood for about 1,500 years but had fallen into ruin by 1402, when the

Knights of St John arrived and conveniently used many of the stones for constructing the Castle of St Peter.

As you enter, don't miss the authentic reconstruction models to the left.

Antique Theatre

Kıbrıs Şehitler Cad (N of the Mausoleum). ◯ dawn to dusk. Little remains of the ancient city of Halicarnassus, but the theatre on the south slopes of the Göktepe district is one of the more intact sites. Excavations began here in 1973 and restoration still goes on. Dating from the 4th century BC, the theatre

The Myndos Gate, the western portal of the city in ancient times

consists of a stage building, an orchestra and rows of seating. It was probably used more for gladiatorial fights than for theatrical performances. The unusual balustrades in the orchestra may have been put there to protect spectators!

Myndos Gate

Cafer Paşa Cad. ◯ dawn to dusk. The Myndos Gate was the western exit from ancient Halicarnassus and originally featured two monumental towers made of andesite blocks. The gate and most of the city walls were demolished by Alexander the Great in 334 BC. The structure was restored in 1998,

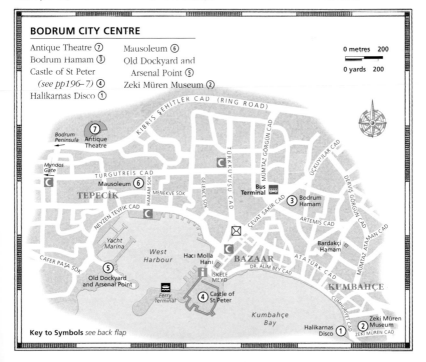

BODRUM CITY CENTRE

Antique Theatre ⑦
Bodrum Hamam ③
Castle of St Peter (see pp196–7) ④
Halikarnas Disco ①
Mausoleum ⑥
Old Dockyard and Arsenal Point ⑤
Zeki Müren Museum ②

Castle of St Peter

Bodrum's most distinctive landmark is its castle, begun in 1406 by the Knights of St John *(see p227)*. Its five towers represented the nationalities of its formidable inhabitants. When Süleyman the Magnificent conquered Rhodes in 1523, both Bodrum and Rhodes came under Ottoman rule and the knights left for Malta. Neglected for centuries, the castle became a prison in 1895 and was damaged by shells from a French warship during World War I. In the early 1960s, it was used to store artifacts found by local sponge divers. This led to a fruitful Turkish-American partnership to restore the castle and put on display the spectacular undersea treasures found around Turkey. The innovative reconstructions of ancient shipwrecks and their cargoes have brought the museum international acclaim.

Heraldic relief carving

German Tower
This is one of two towers that are open to the public.

Gatineau Tower

Spanish (or Snake) Tower

Glass Hall
The Mycenaean beads and Damascus glass date from between 15 BC and AD 11. Syrian glass ingots, used in the production of various glass items, date from the 14th century BC.

Land-facing battlements

★ Glass Shipwreck Hall
A steel frame supports the original timbers of a Fatimid-Byzantine ship thought to have sunk in 1025. The glass shards and ingots, among other finds, make this a time capsule of the era.

Outer entrance

Castle moat

STAR FEATURES

★ Amphora Exhibit

★ Glass Shipwreck Hall

★ Late Bronze-Age Shipwrecks

★ Amphora Exhibit
Earthenware jars and pots were used to transport oil, wine and dry foods in ancient times. Pointed bases allowed for upright storage in layers.

View of the Castle Across the Harbour
Medieval engineers ensured that the castle was virtually immune to attack. It even had secure water supplies.

VISITORS' CHECKLIST

In Bodrum harbour. *Tel* (0252) 316 25 16. ◯ 9am–noon & 2–7pm. Allow a minimum of 2–3 hours. ⬤ Mon (also Sat & Sun for Glass Shipwreck Hall and Carian Princess Hall). 🎟 several exhibits charge an additional entry fee. ▣ ▢
www.bodrum-museum.com

French Tower

Italian Tower

5th-century BC shipwreck

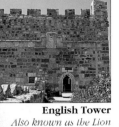

English Tower
Also known as the Lion Tower, it was one of England's first foreign projects funded by taxpayers.

Carian Princess Hall

Chapel and Eastern Roman Shipwreck

★ Late Bronze-Age Shipwrecks
Ancient nautical life and trade are captured in this life-size replica of a ship that sank off Kaş (see p214) in the 14th century BC.

he Commander's Tower
orms the inner entrance to he castle and details some Vorld War I history.

Diver recovering amphorae from the floor of the Mediterranean

DIVING FOR TREASURE

Many underwater treasures were located accidentally by sponge divers who risked their health and endurance working at depths of 40–50 m (131–164 ft). Some of the museum's priceless displays are the result of more than 20,000 dives and painstaking scientific research by experts and restorers. The partnership between the museum and the Institute of Nautical Archaeology has made Bodrum a showpiece of historical treasures beautifully preserved in their last port of call.

Bodrum Peninsula Tour ㉖

Friendship statue, Turgut Reis

The Bodrum Peninsula was originally peopled by the Lelegians, migrants from mainland Greece who maintained historic ties to the Carians. There were eight Lelegian cities, dating from as early as the 4th or 5th century BC. Myndos was the most prominent, but Pedasa offers the most to see.

Today, the Bodrum Peninsula is renowned as a holiday paradise. Its secluded bays are ideal for yachting, watersports and getting away from it all. The windmills to be seen on the hills were once used to grind grain. The terrain varies from lush coniferous forests to rocky cliffs and sandy coasts. The coastline claimed many ancient ships and some of their treasures are displayed in Bodrum's Castle of St Peter *(see pp196–7).*

Yalıkavak ⑥
Formerly an important sponge-fishing port, Yalıkavak is an ideal spot for a meal. Local delicacies include sea beans and stuffed marrow flowers.

AEGEAN SEA

Bahçe

Yaka

Gürece

Akçaalan

Bağla

Akyarlar

Çiftlik Ca

Gümüşlük (Myndos) ⑤
Gümüşlük occupies the site of ancient Myndos, founded by King Mausolus *(see pp194–5)* in about 350 BC. The remains of a sunken city lie offshore.

Kadıkalesi ④
The town takes its name from *kadı*, (Arabic for "judge"), after a former resident. The old Greek church (now a private residence) on the hill is probably the most intact Greek building in the area. Tangerine groves are a beautiful sight, either in blossom or bearing fruit, and there are superb views of the nearby islets.

Turgut Reis ③
The town is named after a famous Ottoman admiral and naval hero. The rich alluvial soil is perfect for growing figs, which abound in this area.

KEY

- ■ Tour route
- ═ Other road
- ☀ Viewpoint

Göl Türkbükü ⑦
Two neighbouring towns,
Gölköy and Türkbükü,
amalgamated their names in
1999. Watersports are a
speciality here. The area is a
hideaway for celebrities.

Küçük Tavşan Island

Gölköy

*Yuk.
Gölköy*

•Torba

*Mustafa
Paşa
Tower*

Bodrum•

Gümbet

İç Island

Karaada Island

Pedasa ①
Though difficult to reach,
Pedasa is worth the journey.
The ruins cover about
2.5 sq km (1 sq mile), and
show a typical Lelegian
town. Extensive research
and restoration is being
done on the site, which
includes the remains of a
citadel, main gate, rampart
walls and castle keep.

0 kilometres	5
0 miles	2.5

Ortakent ②
This inland village boasts
the imposing 17th-century
Mustafa Paşa Tower, a rare
example of local architecture.
It is one of the easiest sights
to reach on the peninsula,
and has abundant water
and lovely orchards.

TIPS FOR DRIVERS

Tour length: 100–120 km
(63–75 miles), with paved roads
and two-way traffic most of the
way. The tour can be done by
dolmuş, but it is then more
difficult to see the ancient sites.
🛈 *Turgut Reis, (0252) 382 39
33. Turgut Reis is the only major
town, with a number of petrol
stations and amenities.*
When to go: Any time of year.

Marmaris 🚗

Waterside statue of Atatürk

Like most of the resorts along the Aegean coast, it is difficult to envisage Marmaris as the quaint fishing village it used to be. The stretch of beach, now lined with hotels, extended to the main street until the 1990s. Marmaris was extensively damaged by an earthquake in 1957, which destroyed most of the old town. Today the rebuilt (and greatly expanded) town is a top holiday destination.

Ancient inscriptions indicate that Marmaris was once the Dorian city of Physcus, attached to the city of Lindos and part of the island state of Rhodes. Süleyman the Magnificent *(see pp56–7)* assembled a mighty fleet here in 1522 to prepare for his conquest of Rhodes, at which time he regained possession of the Datça Peninsula *(see pp202–203)* and had Marmaris Castle rebuilt.

Exploring Marmaris

Few places can compete with Marmaris' exclusive setting in a sheltered bay rimmed with oleanders, liquidambar trees and pine forests. All major attractions are located within a few metres of the seafront and can be reached on foot. The harbour and quay extend along a beach walkway that runs the length of the town.

Netsel Marina

Tel *(0252) 412 27 08 and 412 14 39.*
Fax *(0252) 412 53 51.*
www.netselmarina.com

Turkey's largest and most luxurious marina has it all – parking, top-class restaurants, entertainment, bars, excellent shops and plenty of service facilities such as banks, ATMs and travel agents. All major currencies and credit cards are accepted for mooring, refuelling and other marina

services. Among several yacht brokerage firms here, **Gino Marine** will organize luxury charter cruises for a view of Marmaris from the water. There is berthing for over 750 yachts up to 40 m (130 ft) in length.

The Netsel call sign on VHF channel 06 is "Port Marmaris". Marmaris is a safe anchorage, with no underwater currents, sandbanks or rocks, and can be approached night and day in most weather conditions.

Gino Marine

Tel *(0252) 412 06 70 / 80.*
Fax *(0252) 412 53 51.*

🍸 Bar Street

Hacı Mustafa Sokağı
Most tourist towns have their bars and pubs concentrated on a couple of streets. Those in Marmaris occupy much of Hacı Mustafa Sokağı. Despite the noise, it is always worth

strolling along the street to observe those who want to be observed. Some of the bars have been nicely done up and, decibels aside, this is not an unattractive area. There are also a number of hotels and pensions in the area, but visitors in search of rest and relaxation would do better to look elsewhere.

Restored Greek houses in the Old Quarter near the harbour

🏛 Greek Revival Houses in Old Quarter

Tepe Mahallesi.
The Old Quarter around the Castle is by far the most charming part of Marmaris. Many houses that were either abandoned or derelict have been restored to their original appearance. Most belong to professional people who seem to be accustomed to strangers peeking into a shady courtyard or admiring a handsome brass knocker. Karaca Restaurant, just outside the entrance to the Castle, has a well-preserved interior. From the top terrace of the restaurant, you will get a wonderful view of the town and its numerous delightful "barbecue" chimneys. See if you can spot the one and only remaining original Greek chimney from here. As you wander the cool and shady lanes above the bustle of the harbour, you could find yourself wishing that some of Turkey's other coastal resorts had retained the same quaint neighbourhood appeal as this corner of Marmaris.

Netsel Marina, offering a complete service to touring yachts

For hotels and restaurants in this region see pp332–335 and pp359–362

The Castle, incorporating a nautical museum

VISITORS' CHECKLIST

🏛 35,000. ⛴ from Rhodes.
✈ Dalaman, 120 km (75 miles)
E of town, (0252) 792 52 91.
🚌 NE of town centre on Muğla
road. ℹ iskele Meydanı (central
harbour), (0252) 412 10 35.
📅 Thu. ⛵ Yacht Race Week
(Apr 2008, then every three years).

🏛 Castle and Museum

Tel (0252) 412 14 59. 🕐 8am–noon
& 1–5:30pm Tue-Sun. 🈂

The original castle was rebuilt
by Süleyman the Magnificent
in 1522 after his successful
campaign against Rhodes.
Today, the restored structure
is a museum housing a small
collection of nautical items.
There are also inscriptions
and sculptures displayed in
the courtyard. More engaging
for most visitors, however,
will be the panoramic view of
the harbour and old
renovated Greek houses.

🏪 Bazaar

Entrance from Kordon Caddesi and
the street beside the tourist office.

You may find a unique
item among the tourist
bric a brac offered
up for sale in the
bazaar, among the
leather goods,
jewellery, herbs,
spices and teas.
A delicious local
speciality is Marmaris honey,
which is produced along
the scenic Datça Peninsula
(see pp202–203). Both pine
(çam) or flower (çiçek)

Marmaris honey

honey are fragrant, thick and
dark. By the end of October
the last of the honey and
fresh summer produce will
have been sold.

Environs

A number of large holiday
villages are located in **İçmeler**,
about 6 km (4 miles) around
the bay from Marmaris.
Transport to and from
Marmaris is easy, as
dolmuşes make
the trip on a
regular basis.
İçmeler lacks the
quaint atmosphere
of an old Turkish
town, as do many
parts of Marmaris, but many
visitors (particularly families
with children) prefer the
more up-to-date facilities and
much cleaner beaches here.

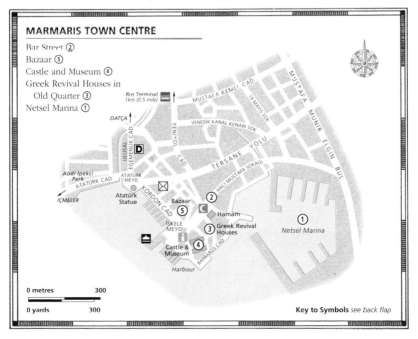

MARMARIS TOWN CENTRE

Bus Terminal
1km (0.5 mile)

MUSTAFA KEMEL CAD
DATÇA
VENEDİK KANAL KENARI SOK
YENİYOL CAD
ULUSAL EGEMENLİK CAD
TERSANE YOLU
19 MAYIS SOK
MUSTAFA MUNIR ELGIN BUL
HACI MUSTAFA SOKAGI

Abdi İpekci
Park
ATATÜRK CAD
ATATÜRK
MEYD
İÇMELER
Atatürk
Statue
KORDON CAD
Bazaar ⑤
Hamam
②
Greek Revival
Houses ③
① Netsel Marina
İSKELE
MEYD
Castle &
Museum ④
BARBAROS CAD
Harbour

0 metres 300
0 yards 300

Key to Symbols see back flap

Datça Peninsula Tour ⊛

Restored window in Eski Datça

The narrow finger of the Datça Peninsula, pointing westward from Marmaris, lies at the place where the Mediterranean and the Aegean meet. Locals claim that the air is rich in oxygen, thanks to the prevailing wind *(meltem)* and the mixing of salinity levels and current patterns in the sea.

The route along the peninsula follows narrow and twisting roads, affording glimpses of the sea though pine-clad gullies. At the western tip, about 35 km (21 miles) west of Datça, lie the ruins of Knidos, one of the most prosperous port cities of antiquity. In its heyday it was home to an eminent medical school. Here, you can lunch on seafood, and swim in the sheltered bay.

Knidos ⑤

This port was the site of a shrine of Aphrodite, dating from about 360 BC. The remains of a theatre, agora, houses and a round temple are visible today.

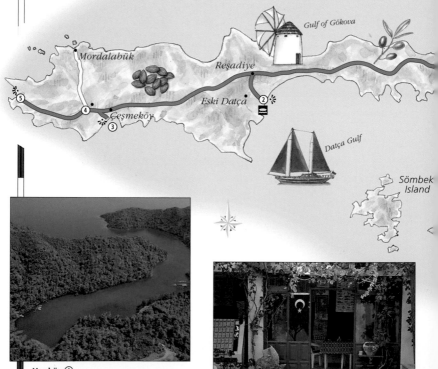

Yazıköy ④

The western half of the peninsula consists of rugged, pine-clad mountains dotted with olive and almond groves. The village of Yazıköy, at the end of the paved portion of the road, lies deep in the olive-growing region.

Palamut Bükü ③

This bay can also be reached by boat from Datça, and offers a long, tranquil pebble beach lapped by brisk, clear water. Palamut Bükü is a good spot for lunch, with several simple but good fish restaurants.

Orhaniye/Keçibükü ⑥
On the way back to Marmaris, take the Bozburun road to Orhaniye (turn right just after Değirmenyanı), and continue on for about 7 km (4 miles) to Keçibükü. Lovely sea views make the little town an idyllic place to stop.

Bençik ①
This, the narrowest point of the peninsula, is a mere 800 m (2,600 ft) wide. Locals used to call it *Balıkaşıran* (the place where the fish pass over).

Marmaris

Kamerye Island

Bozburun

0 kilometres   5

0 miles   2.5

TIPS FOR DRIVERS

Tour length: *Day trip (or 2 hours' drive) from Marmaris, west on the main road, about 62 km (39 miles) from Marmaris to Datça, and 21 km (13 miles) from Datça to Knidos. Sections of the road to Knidos are in poor condition – care is advised. Boat tours run from Marmaris to Knidos, with various stops.*
When to go: *Spring, when the almond trees are in blossom*
Where to stay: *Campsites are available at Çubucak Forest Campsite and İnbükü Camping Ground. ⬜ Both sites are open May–Oct.*

KEY

▬ Tour route

= Other road

⛴ Boat trips

❀ Viewpoint

Datça ②
The small town of Datça has a busy yacht harbour, and many shops and restaurants. A few kilometres inland is the old town, Eski Datça, with many lovely stone houses.

MEDITERRANEAN TURKEY

*T*urkey's Mediterranean coast is synonymous with turquoise
seas, sun and blue skies, and has a wealth of ancient remains.
Originally colonized by the Greeks and later ruled by the
Romans, the region is littered with well-preserved classical sites.
However, Hittites, Seljuks, Ottomans, Armenians and even the
Crusaders have all left their distinctive imprints upon these shores.

The highlands of Lycia, between Fethiye and Antalya, were the seat of an impressive civilization whose distinctive stone tombs – both free standing and cliff-hewn – still dot the landscape. At ruined cities such as Pınara, Myra and Xanthos, it is possible to glimpse the achievements and scale of the Lycian civilization.

The city of Antalya, an important gateway to the Mediterranean region, boasts a spectacular cliff-top setting and quaint walled quarter. It is also a good base for visits to the romantic mountain-top ruins of the Pisidian capital of Termessos and the monumental Roman remains at Perge and Aspendos. Bustling Side, with its temples of Apollo and Athena, is renowned for stunning sunsets.

The Cave of St Peter in Antakya and St Paul's well in Tarsus – birthplace of the Apostle – are reminders of the role of Christianity in fostering the area's cultural and religious diversity.

The short French protectorate era (1918–39) in the Hatay, in the far southeast, left a European colonial legacy in urban planning and local architecture. This corner of the Mediterranean region contains the multicultural cities of İskenderun and Antakya (ancient Antioch on the Orontes), where the Arab-Syrian influence is clearly visible. Antakya is also renowned for its Roman mosaics.

An ancient Lycian tomb rising above the placid waters of a coastal inlet

◁ Mamure Castle near Anamur, a well-preserved crusader castle

Exploring the Western Mediterranean Coast

Separated from the dry Anatolian plateau by the Taurus Mountains, the Mediterranean coast of Turkey is dominated by plunging cliffs and headlands interspersed with fertile alluvial flood plains, and fringed in places with fine sandy beaches. Throughout the region, the many civilizations that have shaped Turkey left their mark on cities, harbours, roads and rivers. To leave your own footprints, venture along the Lycian Way from Fethiye to Antalya, now rated as one of the world's top treks, or take the "Blue Voyage" on a traditional *gület* (wooden yacht).

Butterfly Valley, near Ölü Deniz

Hiking in Saklıkent Gorge

GETTING AROUND

Antalya's Bayındır International Airport is gradually opening up direct access to European destinations. From here, fast main roads run east and west, parallel to the coast. In many places, two-lane roads snake around steep, rocky gorges. Views are dramatic but care is required. With only a few exceptions, all the main sights and attractions are easily accessible by bus and dolmuş.

The Vespasian Monument, a Roman fountain in Side

SIGHTS AT A GLANCE

Alanya ㉒
Anamur and Anemurium ㉓
Antalya pp218–19 ⑯
Aspendos p221 ⑳
Caunos ②
Dalyan ③
Demre (Myra) ⑬
Fethiye ⑤
Finike ⑭
Göcek ④
Kalkan ⑩
Kaş ⑪
Kayaköy ⑥
Köyceğiz ①
Ölü Deniz ⑦
Perge ⑱
Phaselis ⑮
Pınara ⑨
Saklıkent Gorge ⑧
Side pp224–5 ㉑
Selge ⑲
Termessos ⑰
Uçağız, Simena and
    Kekova Island ⑫

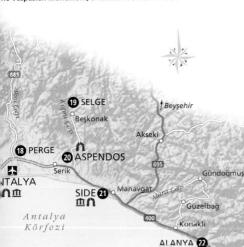

⑲ SELGE
Beşkonak
Beyşehir
Akseki
⑱ PERGE
⑳ ASPENDOS
Serik
NTALYA
SIDE ㉑
Manavgat
Hadım
Taşkent
Gündoğmuş
Antalya Körfezi
Güzelbağ
Sulugöl Tepesi 2579m
Ermenek
Konaklı
ALANYA ㉒
Çamyolu
Kazancı
Kızıl Dağ 2257m
MEDITERRANEAN SEA
Gazipaşa
Uçarı
ANAMUR & ANEMURIUM ㉓
Silifke

KEY

— Motorway
— Major road
═ Minor road
— Scenic route
△ Summit

SEE ALSO

The picturesque yacht harbour at Antalya

Exploring the Eastern Mediterranean Coast

The Mediterranean coastline east of Alanya is much less populous (and visited) than the western portion, but offers sights every bit as diverse. These include the bird-watcher's paradise of the Göksu Delta, several Armenian and Crusader castles, and the important Hittite site of Karatepe. The region also has a decidedly Middle Eastern flavour: the further east you go, the more lively and colourful the bazaars become and the foods tingle with stronger spices. This influence is most apparent in the southeast, around İskenderun and Antakya. Turkey's fourth largest city, Adana, is the main centre in the area. It has a subtropical climate, which receives rainfall mainly during the autumn and winter months.

Remnants of the Temple of Zeus, Silifke

SEE ALSO

- *Where to Stay* pp335–338
- *Where to Eat* pp362–365

Castle on an island off Kızkalesi (ancient Korykos)

KEY

▬▬	Motorway
▬▬	Major road
▬▬	Minor road
▬	Scenic route
▬▬	Main railway
▬	Minor railway
▬▬	International border
△	Summit

For additional map symbols *see back flap*

SIGHTS AT A GLANCE

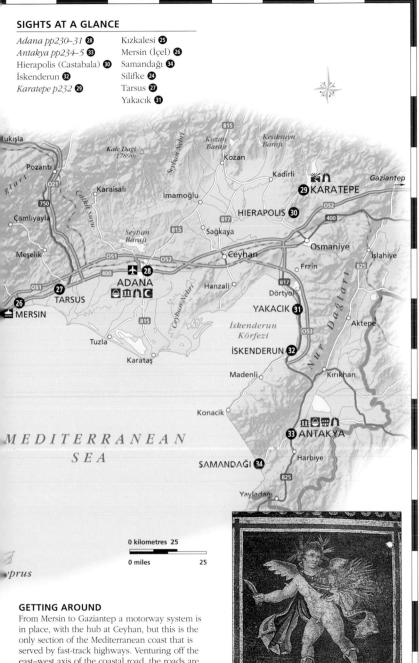

GETTING AROUND

From Mersin to Gaziantep a motorway system is in place, with the hub at Ceyhan, but this is the only section of the Mediterranean coast that is served by fast-track highways. Venturing off the east–west axis of the coastal road, the roads are picturesque and generally passable, but winding and narrow. The Taurus mountain range runs the length of the coast; respect the mountains and remember that, in winter, minor roads may be blocked by snow and tyre chains are essential if you plan to drive over the mountain passes.

Mosaic in the Antakya Archaeological Museum

Lake Köyceğiz, a haven for water birds

Köyceğiz ❶

30 km (19 miles) N of Dalyan.
🏠 8,600. 📞 (0252) 262 47 03.

Independent Menteşe clans governed this area even after the beginning of Ottoman rule in 1424. By the late 1830s, when the English archaeologist Charles Fellows visited the area, the power of the family had declined, however. The family *konak* (manor house) has been restored. Another manor, once the centre of a cotton estate belonging to the *khedive* (viceroy) of Egypt, is now the Dalaman state farm. Many people in Köyceğiz village are distant descendants of African slaves brought here to work on cotton plantations. A plantation of *liquidambar orientalis*, the tree used to produce church incense, survives as a reminder of a once-important local industry.

The reed-fringed lake of Köyceğiz, 10 m (33 ft) deep in places, is home to many water birds, including the rare Smyrna kingfisher.

Caunos ❷

6 km (4 miles) from Dalyan.
***Tel** (0252) 284 20 44.* ☐ *Apr–Sep.*
🎫 *included in price of boat tour.*

The ancient city of Caunos bordered the kingdoms of Lycia and Caria. Although a Carian foundation, its culture shared aspects of both states. The local tombs are Lycian *(see p215)* in style, but were in fact carved by the Carians. Like Xanthos, capital of Lycia, Caunos resisted the Persian

general, Harpagus, during the 6th century BC, for which many citizens of Caunos were slaughtered in a final sally. The city was re-established and Hellenized, especially by the Carian ruler, Mausolus *(see pp194–5)*. Caunos welcomed Alexander the Great, but after his death came under the rule of Rhodes. It won independence from Rome, but after supporting Mithridates against the Romans, the city was punished by return to Rhodian rule. Caunos was known both for its figs and malarial mosquitoes. It was a major seaport until the harbour silted up.

Turtle Statue in Dalyan

At the site are defensive walls built in the 4th century BC, a theatre dating from the 2nd century BC, a temple to Apollo and a Roman bath. There is a Doric temple and an agora (marketplace) with a nymphaeum (fountain) thought to have been built to honour Emperor Vespasian.

Dalyan ❸

13 km (8 miles) from the main D400 road. 🏠 8,250. ✈ Daliaman, 25 km (16 miles) E of Dalyan, (0252) 792 52 91. 🚌 Ortaca, 13 km (8 miles) NE of Dalyan. 🅳 entry road to Dalyan, (0252) 284 24 58. 🛈 (0252) 284 42 35. 🎭 Caretta (turtle) Festival (end Aug–early Sep). 🛒 Sat.

This bustling resort takes its name from the Dalyan River (Dalyan Çayı), meaning "fishing weir", which flows through the town. Although the town is a fast-growing tourist centre, fishing has long been the mainstay of the local economy. Over the years, the town replaced ancient Caunos as a fishery when the latter's harbour became choked by silt. A weir built on the river, together with a fish-processing plant, means that you can enjoy the delicious local red roe caviar, which comes in a pot sealed with beeswax. Local fish is available at waterside eateries.

The threatened loggerhead turtle *(see p211)* has become a symbol of Dalyan, drawing increasing numbers of visitors to the area. This came about in 1986, when conservationists managed to persuade civic authorities to protect the turtles' breeding ground from development. Since then, local people have adopted the loggerhead turtle as a motif for the town. The Turtle Statue (Kaplumbağa Heykeli) on Cumhuriyet Meydanı is a

The resort town of Dalyan, by the tranquil Dalyan River

tangible symbol of Dalyan's new passion for conservation.

On the eastern bank of the Dalyan River are two rows of tombs cut into the cliffs. Constructed for the citizens of Caunos, the tombs are mainly of the house type and date from the 4th century BC, *(see p215)*, with Ionic columns and triangular pediments. Most have a small chamber with three stone benches to accommodate the dead. The surviving inscriptions are mainly in Latin, for the tombs were reused during Roman times. They are fenced off and must be viewed from some distance away. The rock tombs can be reached by river-boat tours, which depart from the Dalyan Sea Co-operative.

Environs

A short distance upriver from Dalyan (about 10 minutes by boat) lie the **mud baths** of Ilica. With a constant temperature of 40°C (104°F), they are reputed to be beneficial for rheumatism and gynaecological disorders, and are certainly relaxing. Beyond Ilica, at Sultaniye Kaplıcaları, on the shores of Lake Köyceğiz, a domed building lined with marble surrounds a natural pool where water wells up at 39–41°C (102–106°F). Locals report that, after the Adana earthquake of 1998, the water at the bathhouse gave off a plume of sulphur gas and that the water changed colour and appeared gassy.

Turtle Beach (ıztuzu Plajı), which partly bars the mouth of the Dalyan River, has for centuries been a refuge for

Yachts moored in Gocek's harbour

breeding loggerhead turtles and is now a protected area. Until recently, the significance of this endangered species was poorly understood. The beach is now closed to tourists at night so that the young turtles are not attracted by the bright lights, which would lead them away from the life-giving sea.

Staying on the beach after dark is forbidden, so you are unlikely to catch a glimpse of the turtles, but you may see blue crabs. The best way to get to the beach is to take a boat from the river bank near the centre of Dalyan. There are full-day tours to the beach that take in both Caunos and the mud baths at Ilica.

◻ Mud Baths
Çamurlu Kaplıcası
Tel (0252) 284 20 35. ◻ daily.
▨ ▢

✕ Turtle Beach
İztuzu Plajı
12 km (7.5 miles) from town centre.
▨ from Dalyan (40 min): depart before 10:30am, return between 3pm and sunset. ▨ for car park only.

Göcek ❹

23 km (14 miles) E of Dalaman.
▨ 1 km (0.5 mile) from town centre.
🛈 Club Marina (private yacht club), (0252) 645 18 00; municipal yacht club, (0252) 645 19 38.

Near the pass of the same name, and just south of the main D400 road, Göcek is now a major yachting centre. Popularized by Prince Charles and former Turkish president, Turgut Özal, the town has a remarkable concentration of up-market facilities, including a luxury hotel and several striking waterside housing developments. The public marinas have berths for about 350 boats, with a further 200 berths available in a secluded private marina. Near the tip of the peninsula can be seen the ruins of the Roman town of Lydae, with two mausolea and a fort.

LOGGERHEAD TURTLES

The loggerhead turtle *(Caretta caretta)* has become closely associated with Dalyan, where soft sand and a tranquil south-facing beach provide an ideal nesting ground.

Loggerhead turtles can mate several times in a season. Between May and September, the females arrive *en masse* to drag themselves up onto the beaches where they themselves hatched. There they laboriously dig a pit and lay their eggs above the tide line. The sand keeps the eggs at an even temperature until they are ready to hatch.

Loggerhead turtle *(Caretta caretta)*

Kayaköy, once the prosperous Greek community of Levissi but abandoned in 1923

Fethiye ❺

🏛 62,000. ✈ Dalaman, 50 km (31 miles) NW of town. 🚌 2 km (1 mile) E of town centre. ⛴ from Rhodes (summer only). 🛈 İskele Karşısı, No. 1, (0252) 614 15 27 and 612 19 75. 🏛 Tue.

A medium-sized market town and agricultural centre, Fethiye fringes a sheltered bay with a large harbour, making it a good place for scuba diving and boating. In addition to having many upscale holiday resorts, Fethiye has a splendid farmers' market every Friday that attracts crowds of locals as well as visitors.

Modern Fethiye stands on the ruins of the Lycian city of Telmessus. Earthquakes in

1856 and 1957 levelled most of the ancient edifices, which included a temple of Apollo, but a Roman theatre near the harbour survives. Cut into the cliffs above the town's market are several Lycian temple tombs (see p215), some from the 4th century BC. Charles Texier, a 19th-century French explorer, carved his initials on one of these tombs.

Fethiye Museum displays artifacts from the half-flooded ruins of Letoön (see p214), including stelae, which scholars used in their efforts to decode the Lycian language.

🏛 **Fethiye Museum**
Fethiye Müzesi
Off Atatürk Cad.
Tel (0252) 614 11 50. ◯ 8:30am–5pm Tue–Sun. 📷

Kayaköy ❻

10 km (6 miles) SW of Fethiye.
Ⓓ from Fethiye or Ölü Deniz.

Derelict Kayaköy, formerly known as Karmylassos, then Levissi, was a thriving Greek town until it was abandoned in the exchange of populations that took place in 1923 (see p58). About 400 roofless houses stand on the hillside overlooking a fertile plain. The Orthodox church of Panayia Pyrgiotissa has been restored and is the main focus of movement for peace and international reconciliation.

After being designated a UNESCO World Heritage site, Kayaköy and its ruins will be preserved as an historic settlement. The town inspired the novel *Birds Without Wings*, which focuses on the rise of Turkish patriotism after the disintegration of the Ottoman Empire.

Ölü Deniz ❼

20 km (12 miles) S of Fethiye.
🏛 1,200. Ⓓ from Fethiye.
🛈 Tourism Co-operative, (0252) 617 04 38, (0252) 617 01 45.

Made famous in the 1970s by visitors from Britain, the inviting beach and lagoon at Ölü Deniz (which means dead sea – because of the

Lycian tombs cut into the cliffs above Fethiye

calm water) now adorn many posters promoting Turkish travel. The land behind the restaurant-fringed beach has been appropriated for hotels, pensions and camp sites. The adjoining mountain, Baba Dağı, is the jump-off point for paragliders, who soar over the lagoon. Ölü Deniz also marks the start of the Lycian Way, Turkey's first long-distance walking route, which ends just short of Antalya.

Saklıkent Gorge ❽

30 km (18 miles) E of Fethiye.
from Fethiye and then on foot.
summer only.

Saklıkent Gorge cuts into the rugged flank of the 3,016 m (9,895 ft) Gömbe Akdağı, and delivers a rushing stream of pure limestone-filtered water. From the restaurants at the base of the gorge, which specialize in trout from local trout farms, you can walk for a few hundred metres into the gorge on platforms built over the torrent. Bougainville Travel of Kaş *(see p387)* organizes abseiling trips into the gorge. These involve scrambling over rocks to cross the waterfalls that tumble down the walls.

If you enter by road and footpath, along the flank of Akdağı, there is quite a steep descent, but this brings you to the trout farms. At Saklıkent, 7 km (4.5 miles) from the main D400 road, consider a meal at one of the trout restaurants, which have low tables placed over the water. Enjoy the cool air before you return to sea level – when the temperature is 40°C (104°F) at the coast, Saklıkent is very refreshing.

Also in the area is the ruined city of Tlos, one of the oldest and most important Lycian cities. Hittite records from the 14th century BC refer to a settlement called Tlawa, which was probably Tlos. Built on a hill, with a commanding view over the valley of the Eşen River (Eşen Çayı) – known in ancient times as the Xanthos – the main Lycian/Roman remains consist of tombs hewn from rock, as well as a stadium, gymnasium and palaestra, and baths. In Byzantine times, Tlos was a bishopric, and the churches at the site were most probably former temples. The acropolis was used until the 19th century, when it was the stronghold of a pirate known as Kanlı Ali Ağa (Bloody Ali).

Agencies in Fethiye and Kaş offer tours of both Saklıkent Gorge and Tlos.

Catwalk built over the water in Saklıkent Gorge

The beautiful lagoon and beach at Ölü Deniz

BUTTERFLY VALLEY

Euplagia quadripunctaria

From Ölü Deniz, it is a short boat ride to Butterfly Valley (Kelebek Vadisi), a flat-bottomed valley enclosed by towering cliffs. The valley was named for the migratory *Euplagia quadripunctaria*, commonly known as the Jersey Tiger, a spectacular red, black and white tiger moth that colonizes the valley by the thousand during the summer. Other species are present year-round, with some unique to the area. A 20-minute trek leads to a waterfall from the mill stream at Faralya, which cascades into the valley, providing damp conditions for the butterflies and supporting a variety of plants. No permanent buildings are allowed on or behind the beach, but a wooden bar-restaurant supplies beer and food to those wishing to camp. Alternative access is by steep path from Faralya, the village perched 600 m (1,968 ft) above, but this route is not recommended since the path is dangerous.

Tombs cut into the rock at Pınara

Pınara ❾

50 km (31 miles) E of Fethiye.
⬤ 9am–5:30pm Tue–Sun.

One of the most important cities of ancient Lycia, Pınara, whose name means "round", is situated on and around a huge circular plug of rock above the village of Minare, some 5 km (3 miles) west of the main D400 road. The entrance is about 3 km (2 miles) along an unpaved track that is passable by car.

The rock face is honey-combed with tombs, mainly square holes, which must have been sealed after use. The acropolis is approached by steps carved into the rock. A well-preserved theatre is cut into the hillside below, with baths nearby. The agora (marketplace) lies just above the ticket office.

Visitors strolling through the picturesque streets of Kalkan

Kalkan ❿

🏠 9,000. 🚌 at junction with main coast road. ☀ Thu.

The village of Kalkan has been permanently inhabited only since the eradication of malaria-bearing mosquitoes in the 1950s. In earlier times, the local people avoided the pests by migrating in summer to the *yayla* (summer pasture) of Bezirgan, above the village. The core of stone, Greek-style houses built around the harbour has now been augmented by modern colour-washed villas on the hills. Good accom-modation and a choice of restaurants make it an ideal base for the ancient Lycian cities of Xanthos, Letoön and Patara.

Xanthos (now Kınık), the ancient capital of the Lycian League *(see p215)*, is 30 min-utes by bus west of Kalkan, just before the bridge span-ning the Eşen River. The site is extensive and spectacular, and includes superb examples of Lycian tombs. A bilingual Greek-Lycian pillar found at the site helped researchers to decipher the Lycian language.

Letoön, site of the temples of Leto, Artemis and Apollo, was a cult centre favoured by Alexander the Great. Letoön and Xanthos are both UNESCO World Heritage sites and reflect the way Hellenistic and Lycian cultures influenced each other.

Patara was once the major port of the Lycian League. Damaged by earth-quakes in AD 141 and AD 240, its harbour silted up.

Kaş ⓫

🏠 8,500. ✈ Dalaman, 155 km (96 miles) NW of town, or Bayındır Intl Airport (Antalya), (0242) 330 36 00, 210 km (130 miles) NE of town. 🚌 Atatürk Cad. 🛈 5 Cumhuriyet Meydanı, (0242) 836 12 38. ☀ Fri. 🎭 Kaş/Lycia Festival (Sep).

Kaş was built adjoining a long, narrow peninsula, over the ancient port city of Antiphellos (port of Phellos), and was noted for its cork oaks. In 1839, it was so tiny and impoverished that the English archaeologist Charles Fellows (who excavated the nearby Lycian site of Xanthos) had to cross to the island of Castellorizo to buy chickens to eat. Today, the situation is reversed: the islanders buy their chickens at Kaş market on Fridays. The harbours are filled with scuba-diving boats and yachts making trips to the Blue Cave and the sunken city at Kekova *(see p216)*, with hotels and pensions along the waterfront. Uzun Çarşı, the shopping street, has many

"Hand of Fatma" door knocker, Kaş

unusual and original handicraft and antique shops. A 5th-century BC Lycian sarcoph-agus is at the top of the street.

The tourism information office in the main square can provide information on the annual Kaş/Lycia Festival, which makes good use of the tiny Hellenistic theatre located on the peninsula road just west of the town.

Fishing boats and touring yachts in the harbour at Kaş

Lycian Tombs

Ancient Lycia, a federation of 19 independent cities, lay in the mountainous area between modern Fethiye and Antalya.

Burials must have had an important role in the beliefs of the Lycians, for they cut hundreds of tombs into cliff faces and crags that can be seen throughout the area. They were probably copies of domestic architecture, intended as houses for the dead. Most have carved doors, beam ends, pitched roofs and prominent lintels – typical of construction in wood.

During the 4th century BC, the rulers of Xanthos (modern Kınık) produced some of the most remarkable tombs, combining Greek and Persian styles. One of the most famous of these, the Nereid Monument, is now in the British Museum in London.

Tomb relief

The doorway of a house tomb often featured a sliding slab.

The house tomb *of one to three storeys, shown here at Tlos, was carved into solid rock. A sliding slab door opened into an inner chamber. Some tombs had exterior porticoes with carvings.*

House tombs at Myra, *near Demre, feature richly carved façades. The elaborate reliefs on some of the tombs still bear traces of paint applied by the original builders.*

Rock cut away to make a roof space

Sarcophagus placed atop the pillar base

Partly hollow base topped by a stepped lid

The freestanding temple tomb *had a temple façade and a portico, from which a door led to a grave chamber with benches for the dead.*

Pillar tombs *(on a stepped base or built directly on rock) are the oldest Lycian tombs. These are found only at Xanthos, the chief city of Lycia, and Apollonia. This example is from Xanthos.*

Prominent lid ridge

"Beam ends" used to open the lid of the sarcophagus

Stepped base

Sarcophagus tombs *had a stepped base, a lower grave chamber (called a hyposorion), a flat plate for the coffin and a lid. The pitched, rounded lid symbolized a house roof, and had a prominent ridge. From 500 BC to AD 300, elaborate "saddlebacked" sarcophagus tombs were produced.*

Varnished charter vessels and quaint fishing boats share the little harbour at Üçağız

Üçağız, Simena and Kekova Island ⑫

38 km (24 miles) E of Kaş.
🏛 2,800. 🚤 from Demre or Kaş.

The picturesque waterfront village of Üçağız ("Three Mouths") is a 19 km (12 mile) drive south of the D400, just east of Kaş. Dolmuşes will drop you at the main road, but no scheduled transport leads directly to the village.

Built on the site of (and using stones from) the Lycian town of Teimiussa, houses, restaurants and pensions front a sheltered bay with three openings to the sea. There are some signs of subsidence, probably as a result of an earthquake that took place in about AD 530. Submerged saddleback tombs (see p215)

can be seen at the Lycian site of Aperlae and the village of Kale (ancient Simena) nearby, where a castle built in around 1440 surrounds a tiny theatre cut into the rock. A pleasant stroll along the coast via the marked Lycian Way leads to its rarely visited twin.

Above Demre, an asphalt road provides a shortcut to Üçağız. Daily boat tours call in to the pretty bay enclosed by Kekova Island (Kekova Adası).

Demre (Myra) ⑬

🏛 19,200. 🚤 100 m (100 yards) from main square. 🛈

The ancient city of Myra and the port of Andriake, 3 km (2 miles) southwest of Demre, date from around the 5th century BC, and grew rich

on coastal trade, supplying incense (derived from the *liquidamber orientalis* tree) to Egypt and Constantinople. The modern town of Demre, which is also known as Kale, is 3 km (2 miles) from the ruins of Myra.

The most popular parts of Myra are the theatre and two cliffs carved with spectacular house tombs. When Charles Fellows visited the site in 1840, the paint on the tombs was still visible and letters of the inscriptions were picked out in red and blue. The oldest part of Myra was on the acropolis hill, with a 5th-century BC defensive wall. Myra's water supply ran in channels cut into the wall of the Demre gorge and the frigid sulphur springs at Andriake provided therapeutic baths and healing drinking waters.

St Nicholas legends originated in Mediterranean Patara (his birthplace) but the Church of St Nicholas is the most charming reason to linger in Demre. This petite Byzantine church is spiritually and architecturally heavenly and some long-concealed frescoes are being brushed back into life.

THE REAL SANTA CLAUS

Nicholas, the 4th-century Bishop of Myra, was famed for his unfailing generosity and piety. He was beatified, and legend established him as the patron of fishermen and children, and the town as a place of pilgrimage. (He is also the patron saint of bakers, brewers and brides.) There are two statues of St Nicholas (Noel Baba in Turkish) in Demre: one is a gift from the Russian Orthodox Church, and is mounted on a revolving pedestal. The saint's myrrh-impregnated bones were buried on his church's premises. Although this church was destroyed by the Arabs in 809, the bones survived and were moved to Bari, Italy, in 1087. The church at Demre was rebuilt by a Russian prince in the 19th century. Demre is also the headquarters of the St Nicholas Foundation.

Statue of St Nicholas in Demre

Carved mask relief from the theatre at Myra

Finike

🏠 25,000. 🛈 Halk Kütüphane, (0242) 855 39 92. 🚌 off D400 highway. 🚢 Sat.

Finike is a market town located at the foot of the Gülmez Dağları, a long spur of the Taurus Mountains, and on the banks of the Karasu (Black Water) River.

In ancient times, Finike was known as Phoenicus. The original harbour, once noted for its export of the timber that was used in building the Ottoman fleet, is now buried under silt, and a modern yacht harbour has replaced it. In Byzantine times, the surrounding mountains were a source of cedar of Lebanon (used in shipbuilding), but the tree is rarely found in these parts today.

Finike has since prospered through the export of citrus fruit and other produce. Its fertile orchards brim with orange and lemon trees, and the town's logo is an orange.

To the north lie the ruins of Limyra, with a theatre, many tombs and a monument to Gaius Caesar, adopted son of the Emperor Augustus, who died here on his way back from Armenia in 44BC.

Not much is known about the early history of **Olympos**, although it was an influential member of the Lycian League. The site is reached by a dirt track through a narrow gorge with a seasonally dry river bed. The ruined city occupies a charming setting adjoining a 4-km-long (3-mile) beach. To the south is an extensive necropolis, including unique square tombs with sliding doors. A theatre, baths and landing stages also occupy the south bank. The northern side has an acropolis, more tombs, a temple dating from the time of Emperor Marcus Aurelius and a Byzantine bathhouse. The whole site is starred with anemones in spring; kingfishers whirr over the stream and ducks nest in the reeds.

At the northern end of the beach, past Çıralı and at an altitude of 300 m (984 ft), are two outcrops of volcanic

Escaping natural gas burning near Olympos

rock, where escaping natural gas is permanently alight. The flame is known as Yanartaş (burning stone). In ancient times, the fire was guided upwards to light a beacon to warn ships of impending danger. There is also a Byzantine church here, probably once a temple of Vulcan.

According to myth, this mountain is where the hero Bellerophon, mounted on the winged horse, Pegasus, killed the three-headed Chimaera by pouring molten lead into the monster's mouth.

Olympos

11 km (7 miles) E of main D400 road 🅳 from café on D400, or taxi. 🛥

Phaselis

40 km (24 miles) SW of Antalya. ⭕ daily. 📷 🖂

Decked with flowers in spring, the ruined city of Phaselis is a popular stopping place for cruise yachts.

The Lycian port city was sold to Greek settlers from Rhodes by a local shepherd in the 7th century BC. They built an extensive town with three harbours around an acropolis on a headland. The canny Phaselians, noted for their skill in trade and commerce, invited Alexander the Great to winter here in 333 BC, even presenting him with a golden crown in return for valuable protection. Phaselis became a pirate stronghold before it was absorbed into the Roman province of Lycia-Pamphylia in AD 43. It survived Arab raiding, only to be eclipsed by Antalya in Seljuk times.

Most of the ruins date from the Roman era. They include a theatre, two sets of baths, an agora, an aqueduct leading from Mount Olympos and a marble gateway erected in honour of Emperor Hadrian.

The north harbour at Phaselis, with Mt Olympos in the background

Antalya ⑯

Mask carved in relief

Antalya's population has increased rapidly since the tourism boom began in the late 1980s. Mountains, beaches and the seaside setting are the obvious magnets, and the city is now one of Turkey's premier resort areas. Antalya (ancient Attaleia) was founded by Attalus II, a king of Pergamum, in 159 BC. The city prospered during the Roman, Byzantine and Seljuk eras before coming under Ottoman rule in 1390. The most important remains are the Roman city walls and the imposing Hadrian's Gate.

Roman marble sculpture from the Antalya Archaeological Museum

The attractive old harbour, showing remnants of the city walls

Exploring Antalya

Antalya's broad, palm-lined boulevards and interesting Old Town (Kaleiçi) make it a pleasant place to explore. The beaches, parks, excellent shops and lively cultural scene make it a focal point of the Mediterranean coast.

Antalya has one speciality not found anywhere else in Turkey – *hibeş*, a hot, spicy sesame-oil dip.

Minicity Antalya

Arapsu Mahallesi, Konyaaltı.
Tel (0242) 229 45 45. ◯ May–Oct: 9am–11pm daily; Nov–Apr: 9am–7pm daily. 🎦 ▢ ▢ 🛍 ♿

A Mediterranean theme pervades here, with diminutive beaches and sail boats as well as miniature replicas of many of Turkey's historic sights. Replicas of the Gallipoli graves are particularly moving.

Pyramid Congress Centre

Yeni Yüzyıl Bulvarı.
Tel (0242) 243 76 40 (during conferences only).

The Pyramid Congress Centre (also known as AKM), a copy of I M Pei's Louvre extension

in Paris, was built in 1996 as a venue for a four-yearly World Forestry Congress. It can hold 3,000 delegates, and is home to a variety of congresses, trade fairs and concerts. The centre is often confused with the Culture Centre, which lies 200 m (650 ft) away, towards the Sheraton Hotel.

🏛 Antalya Archaeological Museum

Kenan Evren Bulvarı, Konyaaltı
Tel (0242) 238 56 88. ◯ 9am–6:30pm Tue–Sun. 🎦 ▢ ▢ 🛍
📷 with prior permission.

The museum, perched on the cliffs 2 km (1.25 miles) west of the city centre, is the true jewel of Antalya. It houses a unique collection of Roman marble sculptures dating from the 2nd century AD, many of them from nearby Perge (see p220). The statues and friezes are displayed in the new green-marble Perge gallery.

Displays also include Bronze-Age urn burials, silver found in Phrygian

tumulus burials, relics of St Nicholas (see p216) and a collection of early Byzantine church silver. There is also an ethnography section. If your time in Antalya is limited, save it for this – one of the handful of Turkish museums that is truly outstanding. The Sarcophagi Hall and Gallery of the Gods are also recommended viewing. Don't miss the sarcophagus dog called Sephanos.

Yacht Harbour

Yat Limanı
Yeşil Cad. **Tel** (0224) 327 76 79.
◯ 8am–5pm Tue–Sun. 🎦

In the 1990s, Antalya built a new harbour 10 km (6 miles) west of the city to replace its historic old harbour, which had become overcrowded due to the surge in tourism. The new harbour is also the site of Antalya's fish market. The picturesque old harbour is now used mainly for gulet (see p206) tours to Rat Island or the waterfalls at Lara. The waterfront is lined with restaurants and is a pleasant place to stroll or people-watch. Antalya's harbour won an award some years ago for its attractive setting, plan and use of resources.

⋂ Fluted Minaret

Yivli Minare
A 13th-century minaret dating from the reign of Seljuk Sultan Alaeddin Keykubad (see p250), this has become the symbol of Antalya. The red bricks were once decorated with turquoise tiles. The adjoining mosque is still used, and just above is the Fine Arts Gallery, built over a former mosque.

The Fluted Minaret

Hadrian's Gate, with the deep wheel ruts clearly visible

⋔ Clock Tower
Saat Kulesi
Cumhuriyet Cad
This local landmark was built in 1244 and marked the upper limit of the Old Town. Its sombre appearance indicates that the tower was once part of the city's defensive system.

⋔ Hadrian's Gate
Hadrian'in Kapısı
Atatürk Cad.
Built to honour the visit of Emperor Hadrian in AD 130,

Hadrian's Gate consists of three arched gateways fronted by four Corinthian columns. For years, the structure was encased in the Seljuk city wall and was uncovered only in the 1950s. Restoration work has been carried out and the pavement between the arches stripped back to the Roman level, showing clearly the wheel ruts cut into the stone.

⋔ Truncated Minaret
Kesik Minare
Hesapçı Sok.
The Truncated Minaret is the landmark decapitated tower next to the ruins of what has been, variously, a Greek temple, the Church of St Peter and a mosque. The tower was badly damaged by fire in 1851. Various architectural styles, especially on the capitals, give clues to its past. You cannot go inside, as railings surround the site, but it is worth a look.

⚘ Karaalioğlu Park and Hıdırlık Tower
Located on the southeastern side of the harbour, the park has a variety of mature exotic trees in which wild ring-necked parakeets nest. It also has tea gardens with fabulous views over the Gulf of

Tea garden beside a reflecting pool in Karaalioğlu Park

Antalya, Mount Tahtalı and the distant Beydağları Mountains.

The circular Hıdırlık tower dates from the 2nd century BC, and was a lighthouse in Roman times. Locals linger here to watch the setting sun.

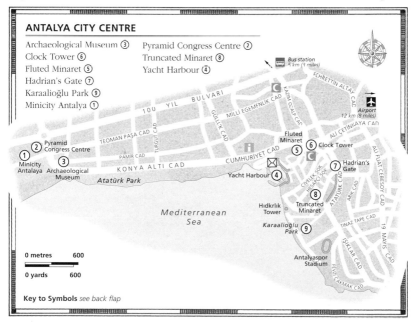

ANTALYA CITY CENTRE

Archaeological Museum ③
Clock Tower ⑥
Fluted Minaret ⑤
Hadrian's Gate ⑦
Karaalioğlu Park ⑨
Minicity Antalya ①

Pyramid Congress Centre ②
Truncated Minaret ⑧
Yacht Harbour ④

Bus station 5 km (3 miles)

Airport 12 km (8 miles)

100 YIL BULVARI

EHRETTIN ALTAY CAD

KAZIM ÖZALP CAD

MILLI EGEMENLIK CAD

GÜLLÜK CAD

ALI ÇETINKAYA CAD

TEOMAN PAŞA CAD

TURGUT CAD

Fluted Minaret ⑤

⑥ Clock Tower

ALI FUAT CEBESOY CAD

② Pyramid Congress Centre

PAMIR CAD

CUMHURIYET CAD

⑦ Hadrian's Gate

① Minicity Antalya

③ Archaeological Museum

KONYA ALTI CAD

Yacht Harbour ④

⑧

ATATÜRK CAD

ARIK CAD

Atatürk Park

CIVELEK SOK

HESAPÇI SOK

Mediterranean Sea

Hıdırlık Tower

Truncated Minaret

TINAZ TEPE CAD

Karaalioğlu Park ⑨

IŞIKLAR CAD

19 MAYIS CAD

0 metres 600

0 yards 600

Antalyaspor Stadium

FEYZI ÇAKMAK CAD

Key to Symbols *see back flap*

Termessos ⑰

35 km (22 miles) NW of Antalya;
9 km (6 miles) off the main road.
◯ 7:30am–7:30pm daily. 📷

Termessos was built by the
Solymians in a strategic
position on the shipping route
to the Aegean. The Greek
historian Arrian (around AD
95–180) said of the location
that "the two cliffs make a sort
of natural gateway so that
quite a small force can, by
holding the high ground,
prevent an enemy from getting
through". The city's formidable
natural defences convinced
Alexander the Great not to
attempt to take the city during
the 4th century BC.

The main buildings visible
today are a theatre, the defensive walls below the gymnasium, the gymnasium itself, the
temples of Hadrian and Zeus,
an odeon (for musical performances), cisterns in the agora,
the stoas (covered walk) of
Attalos and Osbaras, and the
temple of Artemis. A large
necropolis extends upwards
as far as a modern fire-watch
tower on the hill. You can
walk from the gymnasium
down to sea level along the
old road, ending in a gorge.

Termessos lies in Güllük
Dağ National Park, which
includes an area for breeding
wild goats and deer, and may
be the last refuge of the
Anatolian lynx. The area is
also known for its butterflies.

The remains of the Hellenistic Gate at Perge

Perge ⑱

18 km (11 miles) NE of Antalya.
◯ 9am–7:30pm daily. 📷

Located on the Kestros River
(modern-day Aksu), Perge
was once a wealthy city. It
declined in Byzantine times,
and was abandoned in the
7th century. However, it still
presents an impressive sight.
The theatre is one of the most
impressive remnants: its
frieze of Neptune with sea
creatures can be seen in the
Archaeological Museum in
Antalya (see p218). The huge
stadium is largely intact. The
isolated site is best visited as
part of a group.

A pair of Hellenistic towers
marks the entry to the city.
The towers front a courtyard
with a fountain. On the left,
baths with hypocaust (under-
floor heating) systems face a
colonnaded agora. A water

channel leads from a second
fountain on the acropolis hill
into a channel down the main
street, which cooled the air in
summer. Plancia Magna, the
city's benefactress, was buried
outside the walls; a marble
statue of her is in the Antalya
Archaeological Museum.

Selge ⑲

92 km (57 miles) NE of Antalya.
◯ daily. 📷

The village now occupying
the site gives no idea of the
former importance of Selge.
Founded by Calchas of Argos
(who also founded Perge), it
was the first Pisidian city to
mint coins, in the 5th century
BC. Coins from Selge were
used until the 5th century AD.
The classical geographer
Strabo cites olives, wine and
medicinal plants as sources of
revenue. Selge seldom features
in classical histories, but we
know from the Greek historian
Polybius that, in 218 BC, when
Selge was at war with the city
of Pednelissos, it was able to
field an army of 20,000 men.
Selge was defeated in this war
and had to pay tribute to its
enemy. However, it regained
prosperity and independence
and flourished, especially in
the 2nd century AD.

Visible today are a theatre,
a stadium, a large temple to
Zeus, a smaller one to
Artemis, and a cistern. The
site, with its spectacular
mountain surroundings and
cool air, is now part of the
Köprülü Çayı National Park.

The theatre at Termessos, with seating for more than 4,000 people

Aspendos ⑳

Carving on theatre seat

Aspendos, located on the Euromedion River (now the Köprülü River), was once the easternmost city of the kingdom of Pergamum (see pp176–7). In Roman times it became an important trading centre. Today, its main attraction is a beautifully preserved Roman amphitheatre, built around AD 162 by the architect Zeno. The structure is enclosed by a stage building that once had a timber canopy. The theatre hosts the annual Aspendos Opera and Ballet Festival (mid-June–early July). Aspendos also has a remarkable aqueduct, and numerous remains.

VISITORS' CHECKLIST

50 km (31 miles) E of Antalya.
⏰ 8am–7pm (summer); 8:30am–5pm (winter) daily.
🎭 early closing (4pm) for festival performances (Jun). 📷
🅿 in Belkis village.
♿ ground level only.

Arched Gallery
Running right round the top of the theatre, the restored gallery provided patrons with an all-weather vantage point.

★ Amphitheatre
The amphitheatre, which can seat 12,000, was maintained by the Seljuks and traces of 13th-century paint still adorn the stage building.

Roof over the stage building

Granite bedrock

Dressing rooms

Covered passageway

Forty rows of marble seats divided into sections by staircases

Stage Building
The stage building features carved niches intended to hold statues. Originally, the niches were separated by columns.

Public entrance, used for festival performances today

★ Aqueduct
The aqueduct, built in around AD 100 by the architect Tiberius Claudius Italicus, incorporated a 1 km (0.5 mile) siphon system.

STAR SIGHTS

★ Aqueduct

★ Amphitheatre

Side ㉑

The classical geographer Strabo tells us that Side (whose name means pomegranate) was settled by Greek colonists from Aeolia, near Smyrna (modern İzmir), in the 7th century BC. In the 2nd century BC, Side became a centre for pirates, who made large profits from slave trading. Under the Romans, it remained an important slave market. Excavations have shown that the city was burned by Arab raiders in the 7th century, but it revived under the Seljuks. During the 1920s, Side was resettled by Muslims returning from Crete.

Statue of Hercules

The partially reconstructed Temple of Apollo

⋔ Temples of Apollo and Athena

At sunset, the marble columns and re-erected pediments of the temples of Apollo and Athena frame superb views of the Gulf of Antalya. Around the temples is a basilica, built later in a contrasting rough aggregate stone. The Medusa heads of the friezes date from the 2nd century AD.

⋔ Theatre

◯ 9am–10pm daily (later in summer).
▨ at theatre, grants entrance to the whole site, reduction after 5pm.

Almost entirely freestanding, Side's large theatre was built on arches over Hellenistic foundations during the 2nd century AD. The lower seats are partially supported by the hillside, but the upper seats rest entirely on huge arches.

This was the largest theatre in Pamphylia, and could hold 17,000 spectators. There are 29 rows of seats above and 29 below the main lateral aisle. Changes to the structure of

The tranquil harbour, cradled by the remains of ancient breakwaters

Exploring Side

The busy resort of Side is an ideal place to take in ancient ruins, beaches and shopping without venturing too far afield. It is a haven for shoppers, with its leather, jewellery and souvenir stores and many bars and eateries in summer. Pedestrianization, the small pensions and quaint, family-run facilities have enabled the town to retain its "village" charm. Its monuments lend discipline and historic value to the narrow streets.

▦ Harbour

Side occupies a peninsula that terminates in a small harbour. The remains of moles built in antiquity are visible in places offshore. From here, you can take a luxurious boat trip up the Manavgat River (Melas in ancient times), see a waterfall and a stop for some lunch at a trout restaurant.

Waterfall on the Manavgat River, upstream from the town

GOLFING IN BELEK

Between Side and Antalya lies the purpose-built golfing resort of Belek. Here, there are four 18-hole courses, all beautifully landscaped through mature pine forests and offering considerable contrast, ranging from a links course to one set amid lakes and huge trees. The Belek courses operate in close partnership with excellent five-star hotels and have golf professionals who speak a variety of languages. The Mediterranean region's mild winter and early spring make this the most attractive time to visit. Several tournaments are held here each year.

Typical landscaped golf course

◁ Ölü Deniz, with its curving beach and a gulet (wooden yacht) in the foreground

The large Roman theatre, built on Hellenistic foundations

the building permitted the orchestra pit to be flooded in order to enact naval dramas. The stage building had two storeys, decorated, as at Perge (*see p220*), with friezes of the story of Dionysus. These are currently being displayed in the nearby agora or museum garden while restoration work is carried out on them.

⏛ Vespasian Monument, Arch and Colonnaded Street

The arched gateway that marks the entrance to Side from its neighbour, Manavgat, blocks most vehicular traffic. Next to the arch is a fountain adorned with carved basins, dedicated to the Emperor Vespasian. From here runs a colonnaded street lined with plain granite columns and the

remains of Roman shops leading to the main street. A local tractor pulls an open bus, saving visitors the walk from the bus station.

⏛ Museum in Roman Bathhouse

Tel *(0242) 753 10 06.* 🕐 *9am– 12pm & 1:30–6:30pm (5pm in winter) daily.* 🖼

The museum occupies a charming setting – the largest of Side's baths – and includes a number of superb marble sarcophagi, a trio of statues known as the Three Graces and another statue showing Hercules holding the golden apples of the Hesperides. There are also elegant portrait heads and tiny carvings that include a house complete with dog peering around the door. The garden features a cupola with maze decoration and many friezes.

The Vespasian Monument, with a carved pediment and inscription

The Three Graces, Museum in Roman Bathhouse

⏛ Aqueduct, Nymphaeum and City Walls

The Romans installed an impressive water-supply system. Outside the main gate was a nymphaeum (ornamental fountain), which was fed by a two-storey aqueduct running on arches for 30 km (19 miles) from the Melas (now the Manavgat) River. Clay pipes were used to distribute water to homes from the city cisterns.

Outside the massive Roman city walls are necropoli, with examples of temple tombs.

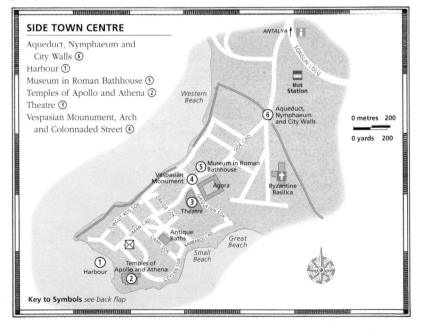

SIDE TOWN CENTRE

Aqueduct, Nymphaeum and
    City Walls ⑥
Harbour ①
Museum in Roman Bathhouse ⑤
Temples of Apollo and Athena ②
Theatre ③
Vespasian Mounument, Arch
    and Colonnaded Street ④

ANTALYA

Western Beach

Bus Station

⑥ Aqueduct, Nymphaeum and City Walls

0 metres   200
0 yards   200

⑤ Museum in Roman Bathhouse
Vespasian Monument ④
Agora
Byzantine Basilica
③ Theatre
Antique Baths
Great Beach
Small Beach
① Harbour
Temples of Apollo and Athena ②

SORGUN YOLU
SIDE CAD
GAZI LAYAN SOK
BARBAROS CAD
CAMİ SOK
CEYLAN SOK
LIMAN CAD
TURGUT REIS SOK
OKLU DE SOK

Key to Symbols *see back flap*

The Red Tower, dominating the harbour at Alanya

Alanya ㉒

🏠 110,000. 🚇 3 km (2 miles) W of city centre. 🚌 Damlataş Cad 1 (near the cave), (0242) 513 12 40. 🎫 Wed & Fri. 🎪 International Triathlon (Sep). www.sunsearch.info

The promontory and castle of Alanya are visible for miles and offer superb views of beaches and mountains. Now a large modern resort, in Roman times Alanya was called Coracesium, and was a stronghold of the pirates who menaced the grain fleets on their passage to Rome. After the defeat of the pirates in 65 BC, Coracesium became a thriving city. The Seljuk ruler, Alaeddin I Keykubad, made Alanya his winter residence and fortified it heavily.

A double line of defensive walls mount the promontory to enclose the Citadel (Kale), inside which is a Byzantine church. Punctuated by towers and gates, the walls are still in good condition. It takes about an hour to walk to the top, but there is an hourly bus service.

The harbour is commanded by the 35 m-high (115 ft) Red Tower (Kızılkule), a hexagonal structure built by Alaeddin Keykubad I in 1226 and now restored. The Red Tower protected Alanya's strategic dockyard, or *tersane*, which could accommodate five ships under construction at once. In Seljuk times, the plentiful local forests provided ample timber for shipbuilding and even for export.

The garden of the museum has a collection of farming tools as well as items from Pamphylian sites in the area. A Phoenician inscription from the 6th century BC shows the development of lettering from its cuneiform origins.

Atatürk visited Alanya for a few days in 1935. The owner of the house where he stayed turned it into a museum. The ground floor has photographs and Atatürk memorabilia, and the upper floor displays the furniture of a typical Alanya house in Republican times.

There are several caves around the base of the cliffs, including a phosphorus cave, a pirate cave and a lovers' cave. The best known is the stalactite-hung **Damlataş Cave**, said to provide relief from asthma. The internal temperature registers a steady 23°C (73°F). Access is from the western beach, behind the Damlataş restaurant.

🏛 Museum
Hilmi Balcı Cad, Damlataş Cad.
Tel (0242) 513 12 28 and 513 71 16.
🕐 9am–noon & 1:30–6:30pm. 🎫

🏛 Damlataş Cave
Damlataş Mağarası
🕐 6–10am for spa patients & 10am–7pm for the public. 🎫

Environs
Near Ehmedek, a village where local women sell silk and lace handicrafts, is a *bedesten* (trading hall) converted into a hotel, with high-arched rooms around a courtyard. There is a pool, a vaulted hall and cisterns below. Nearby is the restored 16th-century Süleymaniye Mosque and a 13th-century *türbe* (tomb).

Anamur and Anemurium ㉓

110 km (68 miles) SE of Alanya. 🚌 on the coast road. 🚍 at the bus station, (0324) 814 35 29.

The town of Anamur is bisected by the D400 coastal road, with the town centre to the north and the harbour to the south. There are good beaches and important turtle nesting sites here, and more to see at ancient Anemurium, located on a coastal headland – the southernmost tip of Turkey – west of the modern town.

Anemurim ("Place of the Winds"), first noted by the classical geographer Strabo (63 BC–AD 23), was founded in the 1st century AD, and thrived under the Byzantines. It was battered by an earthquake in around 580, and after the Arabs took Cyprus in 649, the city became vulnerable and was abandoned. It was never resettled, so many of the old Roman and Byzantine houses and tombs remain in good condition, particularly the mosaics and frescoes.

Environs
On the coast road 2 km (1 mile) east of Anamur lies **Mamure Castle**. Built over a Byzantine fort, the castle was occupied by the Crusaders. Rebuilt by Alaeddin Keykubad I, it was used by the Karamanoğlu dynasty and garrisoned by the Ottomans. Today, the fortress is often used as a film set.

🏰 Mamure Castle
Mamure Kalesi **Tel** (0324) 814 16 77. 🕐 9am–5:30pm daily. 🎫

The large baths complex at Anemurium

The Crusades in Turkey

Mediterranean Turkey is closely associated with the impact of the Crusades – the military campaigns mounted from the late 11th century onwards, in order to wrest the Holy Land from Muslim control.

The crusader armies marched through Anatolia to reach the Holy Land, capturing cities such as Edessa (Şanlıurfa) and Antioch (Antakya). The period reached its nadir with the sack of Constantinople by a crusader army in 1204 *(see p50)*.

The military orders – the Knights Templar, Hospitaller Knights of St John and the Teutonic Order – were active all along the coast. The most prominent symbol of their presence is the Castle of St Peter at Bodrum *(see p196–7)*.

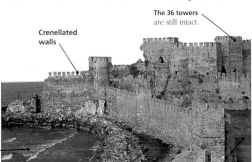

A crusader knight

COASTAL FORTRESSES

Mamure Castle, near Anamur, is one of the best-preserved crusader castles on the southern coast of Turkey. The Ottomans expanded the castle and used it until 1921.

Crenellated walls

The 36 towers are still intact.

The castle is surrounded on three sides by the sea.

Shallow moat

Great Court

Death of Friedrich II
The Holy Roman Emperor drowned near Silifke in 1290. Silifke itself was held by the Knights of St John in 1211–66.

The Siege of Antioch 1095
Captured from the Seljuks during the First Crusade after a seven-month siege, Antioch (Antakya) became the seat of the Principality of Antioch, one of the three main Crusader kingdoms. It fell to the Mamelukes in 1284.

Insignia of the Templar order

The Capture of Rhodes
After taking Rhodes in 1310, the Knights of St John moved operations to Smyrna (now İzmir) in 1344. When Smyrna was lost to the Mongols, the knights moved down the coast to Bodrum.

The Knights Templar
The order was active in the Amanus Mountains and around Antioch (Antakya). The knights safeguarded the route into Syria.

The Knights of St John
The crests of English, French and German crusaders are carved into the walls of the Castle of St Peter at Bodrum.

Grand Master of the Teutonic Knights
The Teutonic Order held castles in Cilicia, in the Crusader-aligned Kingdom of Lesser Armenia (1198–1375).

Corinthian columns of the Temple of Zeus Olbia at Uzuncaburç

Silifke 🄬

🏛 *105,000.* 🚌 *İnönü Cad.*
ℹ *Göksu Mahallesi, Gürten*
Bozbey Cad 6, (0324) 714 11 51.
⚫ *weekends.* 🎭 *Folklore and*
Culture Festival (3rd week in May).

Founded as Seleucia by one of Alexander the Great's generals, Silifke lies on an important route to Konya and the interior by way of the Göksu River valley. A temple of Jupiter, with its surviving columns topped by stork's nests, a Byzantine cistern and a Roman bridge can still be seen today. St Paul passed through here, and Thecla, his disciple, founded an underground church about 5 km (3 miles) east of Silifke. This is currently being restored. A Byzantine castle is accessible

from the Konya road and, 9 km (6 miles) to the north, is a monument that points to where the Holy Roman Emperor Frederick Barbarossa drowned on 10 June 1190 while attempting to ford the deep Göksu River during the Third Crusade.

Silifke Museum, 1 km (0.5 mile) west of the town, houses the Gülnür hoard, a superb collection of 5,200 silver and gold coins dating from the reign of Alexander the Great.

🏛 **Silifke Museum**
Taşucu Cad. **Tel** *(0324) 714 10 19.*
⚫ *8am–noon & 1:30–5pm*
Tue–Sun. 🎫

Environs
At **Uzuncaburç**, about 28 km (17 miles) north of Silifke, lie

the remains of an impressive Roman city. Inhabited from Hittite times, the city was called Olba by the Greeks and Diocaesarea by the Romans.

Beside the road are several temple tombs, complete with sarcophagi, which are worth a look. The centrepiece is the Temple of Zeus, with about 30 massive peristyle columns. However, the walls of the cella (which would have enclosed the statue of Zeus) were removed when the building was converted into a church. Other sights include a charming Greek theatre and two city gates. Also worth exploring are a Hellenistic tower, the necropolis and a pyramid-roofed mausoleum. Apple orchards and fig trees surround the ruins today.

🏛 **Uzuncaburç**
⚫ *9am–6pm daily.* 🎫 🏛 🍴

The romantic sea castle, off the coast near Kızkalesi

Kızkalesi 🄭

Kızkalesi is situated where the narrow coastal strip opens out onto the Çukurova plain. Its chief landmarks are two castles, one on the shore, and its sister, 200 m (656 ft) out to sea. Local fishermen will ferry you over to explore the ruins. The 12th-century castle on the shore was built on the ancient site of Korykos from the stones of Greek and Roman buildings preceding it.

In the early 19th century, a lighthouse marked the end of a mole leading from the sea castle, which lay on an island. Legend has it that a jealous father confined his daughter to this sea-bound castle, but

BIRDS OF THE GÖKSU DELTA

South of the main coast road near Silifke, where the Göksu River reaches the sea, 145 sq km (56 sq miles) have been designated as a region of outstanding environmental importance. The two lagoons are home to migrating and permanently residing water birds, including Dalmatian pelicans, pygmy cormorants, marbled and white-headed

Nesting storks, Göksu Delta

ducks, ospreys and terns. The marshlands provide food for wagtails, egrets, spoonbills and squacco, grey and purple heron. The best times to see the birds are at dawn and dusk in spring and autumn. Bird-watchers need their own transport to tour the delta, which is also an important nesting area for loggerhead and green turtles.

the fortress was more likely built for protection from the Mediterranean's fierce pirates.

Three km (2 miles) east of Kızkalesi are the ruins of **Elaiussa Sebaste**, bisected by the main road. The area around the theatre is under excavation by an Italian team. There is a Byzantine church and harbour buildings to the south of the road. The town must have been important in classical times, for no less than three aqueducts and numerous reservoirs were built to supply it with water. Four km (3 miles) further along the coast is Kanlıdivane ("Place of Blood"), a huge chasm 60 m (197 ft) deep, into which prisoners were thrown to their deaths. There are several churches and a Hellenistic tower around the the chasm, which features carvings in niches in the side, and has become a haven for local wildlife. From this point onwards, the coast abounds in ancient ruins, although the population is sparse until you reach the holiday villages associated with Mersin.

The spectacular Selale Waterfall on the Tarsus River, outside Tarsus

🏛 **Elaiussa Sebaste**
🕘 9am–6pm daily. 💳

Mersin (İçel) 🟡

🏙 750,000. 🚌 NE of city centre (service buses from train station). 🚆 İstiklal Cad NE of city centre, (0324) 238 16 48. ⛴ Near tourist office in the harbour area. 🛈 İsmet İnönü Bul 5, (0324) 238 32 71. 🎭 Mersin Arts Festival (Sep).

Mersin is a harbour city with relatively few tourist attractions. The main reason to stay here is to catch a ferry to Northern Cyprus. Accommodation is plentiful and restaurants varied, with good fish and fast food. Mersin's **museum** contains local archaeological remains such as glass, earthenware and bronze items.

Mersin means "myrtle" in Turkish, referring to the shrub found all along the coast. The city's official name is İçel (the name of the province of which it is the capital).

Compared to other Turkish cities, Mersin is fairly young,

and was first incorporated in 1852, with a cosmopolitan population of Turks, Greeks and Armenians. The Turkish government had plans to turn Mersin into a strategic port, but this never happened.

In 1989, the government initiated a housing scheme here for nomads displaced by ethnic fighting in the eastern provinces. But the transition to city life has been hard for these people, and many remain jobless. Mersin has the transient feel of a port, which many believe stems from the city not having enjoyed the benefits of a structured Ottoman administration.

About 12 km (8 miles) west of Mersin lie the ruins of Pompeiopolis, where the remains of a harbour and a column-lined street that date from the 2nd century AD survive. In 1812, Captain Francis Beaufort described this street, the city gates, a substantial theatre and a "beautiful harbour with parallel sides and circular ends" as being on the whole so imposing that even "the most illiterate seaman in the ship could not behold it without emotion".

🏛 **Mersin Museum**
Republic Square, Halkevi Binası.
Tel (0324) 231 96 18. 🕘 9am–noon & 1:30–4:30pm Tue–Sun. 💳

Tarsus 🟡

🏙 21,300. 🚌 Drop-off point at Cleopatra's Gate. 🚆 from Adana.

Although St Paul is referred to in the Bible as "the man from Tarsus", this does not mean that there is a lot to see in the town. The museum has moved to a cultural centre, near an excavated portion of the old city. Here, a section of Roman street, complete with stoas (covered walk-ways), has been exposed to a depth of 2–3 m (6.5–10 ft) below today's street level. In the back streets of the town is a covered well, named after St Paul, which is still a place of pilgrimage.

St Paul's well, Tarsus

Tarsus once controlled the Cilician Gates, a strategic pass through the Taurus Mountains into the Anatolian interior. The route is now bypassed by a motorway carrying oil tankers and other truck traffic to Ankara and beyond.

Adana ㉘

Adana is an important manufacturing centre, with its origins rooted in commerce and trade. The city lies on the Seyhan River, which is spanned by a Roman bridge. This bridge marks the lowest possible ford over the river, which bisected a crucial extension of the Silk Route through the Cilician Gates. The pass linked the coast with the interior of Anatolia. Adana was ruled by the Arabs, Seljuks, Armenians and Mamelukes until it came under Ottoman sovereignty in 1516. From 1918 until 1922 France held sway over Adana.

Shield from the Ethnography Museum

The Archaeological Museum, with local finds displayed outside

Exploring Adana

Adana's old quarter includes metal workshops, an 18th-century church and a clock tower. The Roman Stone Bridge, restful park and stunning Central Mosque are all worth visiting, and the city makes a comfortable base if you are travelling further east.

Be sure to sample Adana's speciality kebab, which is made of highly spiced minced meat pressed onto a skewer and grilled. This is served with *şalgam*, a cooling blood-red drink made from carrot and turnip juice, or *aşlama*, a liquorice drink.

Colourful traditional *kilim* (rug) in the Ethnography Museum

🏛 Ethnography Museum

Etnografya Müzesi
İnönü Cad (off Ziyapaşa Bulvarı).
Tel (0322) 363 37 17. ◻ 8:30am–noon & 1:30–5pm Tue–Sun. 🖼
The museum is housed in a former church situated to the west of the old town, and

includes a reconstruction of an old Adana house. There is a collection of ceremonial weaponry and firearms, while the displays of copper kitchenware illustrate a prominent local trade. Tents, carpets and textiles complete the display.

🏛 Archaeological Museum

Adana Müzesi
Fuzuli Sok 10. **Tel** (0322) 454 38 55.
◻ 8:30am–noon & 1:30–5pm (5:30pm in summer) Tue–Sun.
🖼 👬
The museum contains objects from excavations of local late-Hittite sites, as well as Hellenistic and Roman remains from in and around the city. A highlight is the natural crystal figure of a Hittite god, Tarhunda, clad in a pointed hat, together with Eastern Anatolian Urartian belts from around 600 BC.

There is also a gold and silver ram-headed bracelet and a gold ring bearing the head of a woman. The fine Achilleus marble sarcophagus, from the 2nd century AD, has lively battle scenes; another sarcophagus is adorned with standing draped women. A Roman mosaic shows animals listening to lyre music.

🅲 Sabancı Central Mosque

Merkez Camii
Fuzuli Cad (near the Roman Stone Bridge). ◻ daily (except during prayer times). 🖼 donation.
Completed in 1998, this is Turkey's largest mosque and rivals most in the Middle East for sheer size. The principal dome is 54 m (177 ft) high. The architectural style of the mosque follows that of the Blue Mosque (see p88) in Istanbul and Edirne's Selimiye Mosque (see p154). Only the Sabancı and Blue mosques feature the hallowed six minarets. All work on the mosque, down to state-of-the-art wireless acoustics, was carried out by Turkey's most prestigious craftsmen.

The massive Sabancı Central Mosque, with its six minarets

For hotels and restaurants in this region see pp335–338 and pp362–365

The Roman Stone Bridge, still in use after more than 18 centuries

Roman Stone Bridge

Taş Köprü

The graceful, 14-arch Roman Stone Bridge over the Seyhan River is 319 m (1,056 ft) long. Built in the 2nd century AD, during the reign of Emperor Hadrian, the bridge may be one of the oldest still used by vehicular traffic. It originally had 21 arches, but only 14 of these are visible and in use today. The bridge has been restored several times, first by Emperor Justinian in the 6th century and later under the Ottomans.

Great Mosque

Ulu Camii

Abidinpaşa Cad daily (except during prayer times). donation.
The Great Mosque was begun in 1507 by Halil Ramazanoğlu, scion of a powerful dynastic clan; however, it was not completed until 1541. Its octagonal minaret is a particularly striking feature. The bands of black and white stone used for the mosque are a typical feature of Syrian religious architecture. The

The Great Mosque, decorated with black and white marble

impressive tomb of the Ramazanoğlu family, located inside the mosque, is finished in beautiful tiles. A *medrese* (Koranic seminary) is located in the east wing of the building.

Covered Bazaar

Near the clock tower on Ali Münif Cad. dawn to dusk, daily.
Adana's medieval-looking clock tower was built in late Ottoman times. It overlooks the Covered Bazaar, where handicrafts, trinkets and food items are sold. Near the Covered Bazaar is the Çarşı Hamamı, a beautiful, domed Turkish bath with an exquisite marble interior. The baths are open to all.

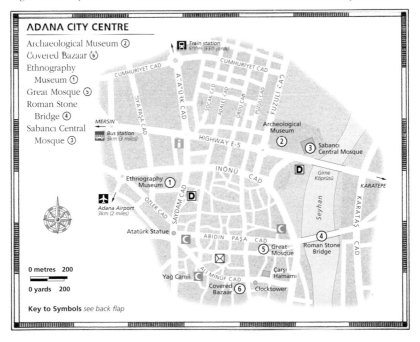

ADANA CITY CENTRE

Archaeological Museum ②
Covered Bazaar ⑥
Ethnography Museum ①
Great Mosque ⑤
Roman Stone Bridge ④
Sabancı Central Mosque ③

0 metres 200
0 yards 200

Key to Symbols *see back flap*

Karatepe 29

Karatepe is a late Hittite fortress dating from the 9th century BC built on a hill beside the Seyhan River. It was discovered by the German archaeologist H T Bossert in 1946. When Bossert's team excavated the site, they found two entrances. Each was lined with relief carvings and featured an inscription in both ancient Phoenician and Hieroglyphic Hittite. As the

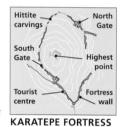

Monumental stone lion

Phoenician language had already been deciphered, this turned out to be a vital clue to the interpretation of the hieroglyphic form of the Hittite language, which was found to be close to Luwian, another ancient Anatolian language.

The pleasant hilltop site, next to a man-made lake, has several picnic areas and is well worth the 70 km (44 mile) drive from Adana.

Karatepe Hill *juts into the waters of a lake created by the construction of the Aslantaş Dam. Water from the lake irrigates the fertile farmlands around Adana.*

Hittite carvings   North Gate
South Gate   Highest point
Tourist centre   Fortress wall

KARATEPE FORTRESS

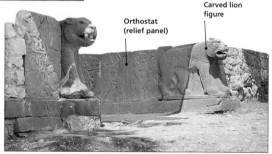

The Karatepe site *is believed to have been the fortified residence of the Hittite king of Adana, Azatiwatas. Entry was through formal gateways, one of which is shown at right. Each was lined with orthostats (carved relief panels). The gateways are now roofed to protect the ancient stonework.*

Orthostat (relief panel)

Carved lion figure

The orthostats *consist of carvings of sacrificial, hunting and feasting scenes. There are numerous figures of gods and sphinxes, interspersed with scenes of ordinary people, all done in a cheerful cartoon style.*

Warrior figure

Relief carvings *at Karatepe show influences from a number of cultures, including Assyria and ancient Egypt. Because of this, archaeologists believe the carvings were executed by foreign craftsmen recruited by King Azatiwatas to work on the site.*

The remains of the theatre at Hierapolis (Castabala)

Hierapolis (Castabala) 30

22 km (14 miles) N of Osmaniye.
🚪 8am–noon & 2–5pm daily. 🎫

On the road leading to the Hittite site of Karatepe, take some time to see the ancient Roman city of Hierapolis (Castabala) – not to be confused with the other Hierapolis (see pp186–7), near Denizli. Hierapolis (Castabala) was mentioned by the elder Pliny (AD 23–79) around AD 70. There is a colonnaded street, theatre, baths and a hill fortress.

Yakacık 31

22 km (14 miles) N of İskenderun.
🛈 in the town hall. 🚪 8am–5pm daily. 🎫 P 🚻

Yakacık (Ancient Payas) is the site of the Sokollu Mehmet Paşa complex. This is not well known, even though the local municipality, which runs the site with great enthusiasm, claims that many thousands of visitors come here each year. The complex features all the amenities beloved by Ottoman travellers – mosque, baths, caravanserai and theological college. The caravanserai was built in 1574 for Muslims making the *haj*

(pilgrimage to Mecca). It was the brainchild of Sokollu Mehmet Paşa, one of the most enlightened grand viziers ever to serve the Ottoman state. A Serb who rose to power from humble beginnings, Sokollu Mehmet Paşa served under three sultans between 1564 and 1579. It was under his initiative that Sultan Selim II (1524–74) seized Cyprus from the Venetians in 1571. However, Selim's fondness for the island's wine earned him the nickname of "the Sot" and proved to be his undoing, as

he allegedly slipped in the bath while inebriated and never regained consciousness.

İskenderun 32

🏙 166,000. 🚌 Atatürk Cad, (0326) 616 36 31. 🚉 İstasyon Cad, (0326) 614 00 49. 🚢 İskele Cad, (0326) 613 54 00. 🛈 Atatürk Bulvarı 49/B, (0326) 614 16 20. 🎭 İskenderun Culture and Fine Arts Week (1st week in Jul).

The city of İskenderun, (formerly Alexandretta), was originally founded to commemorate Alexander the Great's victory over Persian emperor Darius at the Battle of Issus in 332 BC (see pp46–7). It was a major trading centre in Roman times, and is still an important port. The people of İskenderun are proud of their multicultural city and of its remaining Christian and Jewish communities. The surviving Armenian, Catholic, and Orthodox churches are hidden in the backstreets, along with mosques. None are particularly old, but all will welcome visitors on Sundays. The promenade, with its attractive French colonial architecture, is a favourite place for an evening stroll.

Massive Atatürk memorial statue on the promenade at İskenderun

Antakya ㉝

Mosaic in the Archaeological Museum

Antakya was founded (as Antioch) by the Seleucids in 300 BC, and was their capital. Later, it became the third-largest city of the Roman Empire, and an important Christian centre. Antioch was devastated by earthquakes in the 6th century and fell into Arab hands in 628. Although recaptured by the Byzantines, its role was gradually displaced by the rise of Constantinople. In 1098, Antakya was captured by the Crusaders after a seven-month siege, and became capital of the Principality of Antioch. It passed to the Mamelukes in 1268 and the Ottomans in 1516, and eventually slipped into decline.

Exploring Antakya

Antakya is located on the Asi (Orontes) River. After World War I, it was part of French-ruled Syria until a plebiscite in 1939 (*see p59*) returned it to Turkey, together with the rest of the Hatay Province. The city's mixed population, Arab cultural influence and vestiges of French colonial rule give Antakya a distinct character. You are likely to hear Arabic spoken, and many local dishes, such as *şam oruğu*, a wheaten ball filled with minced meat and walnuts, have Arabic origins.

The Grotto where St Peter preached to the early Christians

🕳 St Peter's Grotto

🕐 *9am–noon & 1:30–6:30pm (flexible for group tours) Tue–Sun.*

This cave church is thought to have been founded by St Luke. It is named, however, after Peter, who was in the forefront of the early church movement from his head-quarters in Antioch. Rebuilt by the Crusaders, it is partially floored with mosaic, and the remains of frescoes can be seen. A tiny spring in the church was used for baptisms. The church was repaired in the 19th century by Capuchin monks, who are now its custodians. A festival is held here annually on 29 June.

Near the church is a relief portrait carved into the hillside. This is thought by some to be a representation of Charon, the boatman who conveyed the dead to Hades. However, the image is more likely to be that of a member of the Seleucid dynasty, founders of the city.

Two other churches are still functioning in the city. One is a Capuchin chapel on Kurtuluş Caddesi, the other a Greek Orthodox church near the Rana Bridge.

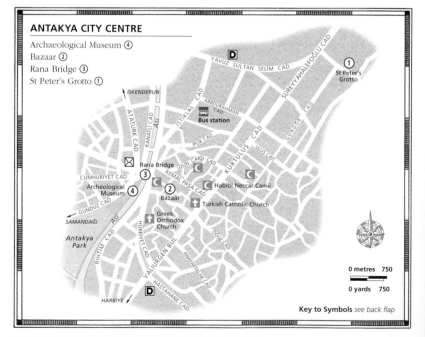

ANTAKYA CITY CENTRE

Archaeological Museum ④
Bazaar ②
Rana Bridge ③
St Peter's Grotto ①

ISKENDERUN

YAVUZ SULTAN SELIM CAD

SÜREYYAHALEFOĞLU CAD

①
St Peter's Grotto

ATATÜRK CAD

KANATLI CAD

ISTIKLAL CAD

ABBDURAHMAN CAD

GÜNGÖR CAD

Bus station

IPLIK CAD

ULUS CAD

KURTULUŞ CAD

UZUN CARŞI CAD

Rana Bridge ③

CUMHURIYET CAD

KEMAL PAŞA CAD

C

C

Habibi Neccar Camii

Archeological Museum ④

Bazaar ②

Turkish Catholic Church

GÜNDÜZ CAD

SAMANDAĞI

ASI

HÜRRIYET CAD

Greek Orthodox Church

OĞUZ CAD

Antakya Park

RIHTIM CAD

VALIURGEN BUL

ANAFARLAR CAD

HARBIYE

HASTAHANE CAD

D

0 metres   750

0 yards   750

Key to Symbols *see back flap*

A cobbler at his work bench in the Bazaar

Bazaar

🕐 9am–9/10pm Mon–Sat.

A warren of streets to the east of the Rana Bridge houses Antakya's bazaar. Here, you can see *hans* (warehouses) dating from Ottoman times, in which skilled metalworkers are hard at work. Donkeys are a common sight in the streets around the bazaar, and the aroma of exotic foods fills the air. The shops facing the Rana Bridge sell *künefe*, a pudding made of cream cheese and spun wheat, baked in a sweet sauce and served warm. This is only one of the local specialities to be savoured in the city. Many restaurants are in the bazaar.

Habibi Neccar Camii is a mosque converted from a Byzantine church, which itself succeeded a classical temple. The minaret was added in the 17th century. It is a place of pilgrimage in honour of a local saint, whose head is reputedly buried beneath it.

Rana Bridge

Antakya is bisected by the Asi River (known as the Orontes in ancient times, when it was a major focus of settlement). The two halves of the city are joined by the Rana Bridge, built by the Romans during the 3rd century AD. Near this landmark lies the site of the Golden Oratory church, built by Emperor Constantine I (in around AD 280–337).

VISITORS' CHECKLIST

🏛 150,000. 🚌 Abdürrahman Melek Cad, NE of town centre, (0326) 214 91 97. 🚉 Şehit Mustafa Sevgi Cas 8/A, (0326) 216 60 98. 🎫 St Peter's Catholic Church Festival (29 Jun). 🚇 Mon–Sat.

🏛 Archaeological Museum

Gündüz Cad 1. **Tel** (0326) 214 61 68. 🕐 8.30am–noon & 1:30–5pm (8am–noon & 1:30–6pm in winter) Tue–Sun.

This museum was originally built by the French to store finds unearthed by foreign excavations when the Hatay Province was part of the French protectorate of Syria.

Today, the museum houses an impressive collection of Roman mosaics, surpassed only by the finds at Gaziantep recovered from Zeugma *(see p308)*. The Antakya mosaics were found all over the province, though many come from the ancient pleasure gardens of Daphne (modern-day Harbiye). Executed in a lively, libertine style, the mosaics portray the deeds of Thetis, Orpheus, Dionysus, Hercules and other mythical figures. The museum also has a coin collection, displays of palaeolithic objects and Hittite sculptures from Carchemish and other sites in northern Syria. The nearby park is a peaceful refuge from the city.

Statue in the Archaeological Museum

Environs

South of Antakya lies **Harbiye**, famed for its forests of cypress and laurel, and for its waterfalls and trout streams. In antiquity, the valley was known as Daphne, after the mythical "queen of the nymphs" pursued by Apollo, and was a popular resort. However, the ruins of the temple to Apollo and the ancient pleasure gardens have all disappeared. Reachable by dolmuş from Antakya, there are several good restaurants here, and local gift shops sell the popular laurel soap.

Samandağı 🟤

25 km (15 miles) SW of Antakya.
🚐 local dolmuş from Antakya.

Southwest of Antakya lies Samandağı, a modest, largely Arabic-speaking resort town near the border, where you will feel that you have already entered Syria. There are a couple of hotels and seaside restaurants along the somewhat scruffy beach.

North of the town is the site of Seleucia ad Piera (modern-day Çevlik), founded as the port of Antioch in around 300 BC. This was the site of an important temple to Zeus, which still stands above the coast and affords grand views over the sea.

Because ancient Antioch lay at the junction of important trading routes, Seleucia ad Piera became a major port, but the danger posed by the region's periodic but devastating floods led Emperor Vespasian to commission a tunnel to divert floodwaters from the town. The **Titus Tunnel** (Titus ve Vespasianyus Tüneli), completed by Vespasian's son, Titus, is an impressive cutting running 1,300 m (4,265 ft) through solid rock. The tunnel is 7 m (23 ft) high and 6 m (20 ft) wide.

🟤 Titus Tunnel

25 km (16 miles) SE of Antakya.
🕐 daily. 📷 Only in summer.

The Titus Tunnel, a flood-control project built by the Romans

ANKARA AND WESTERN ANATOLIA

*A*nkara, the bustling capital of Turkey, can appear rather soulless and cold in its modernity as it rises from the plains of Western Anatolia. When Atatürk chose it as his capital in the 1920s, his determination to westernize led him to commission the German architect, Hermann Jansen, to build a thoroughly new city. Today, most tourists visit Ankara for its outstanding museums.

No doubt the most fascinating sight in Ankara is the superb Museum of Anatolian Civilizations, housing the greatest collection of Hittite antiquities in the world. The Hittite civilization flourished in central Anatolia during the second millennium BC, and for some time their empire almost rivalled that of ancient Egypt. The exquisite relief carvings and statues conjure up an intriguing picture of a civilization about which relatively little is known. Also worthy of a visit is the impressive Atatürk Mausoleum, the great leader's enduring symbol of immortality.

The western approach to Ankara winds over monochrome, flat, steppe country. Near Polatlı – the easternmost point reached by Greek forces in 1922 during the War of Independence – lies Gordion, capital of the ancient kingdom of Phrygia and seat of the legendary King Midas. The more picturesque route runs northwest from Ankara through the forests and mineral springs of Kızılcahamam National Park.

Much of the area encompassed by Eskişehir and Afyon is inhospitable and forbidding. By comparison, the Lake District forms a welcome oasis with an abundance of birds attracted by its reeds and marshlands. Lake Eğirdir is an unspoiled resort area.

Kütahya owes its existence to an illustrious tile making tradition on which the town still relies today.

Konya is the cultural gem of Western Anatolia. Its Seljuk architecture and the impressive Mevlâna Museum, home of the whirling dervish sect, make it one of the country's most visited sights. Konya's Karatay Museum houses an important tile collection.

Sunflowers thrive on the rolling Anatolian plain

◁ Anıtkabir, Atatürk's colossal Mausoleum in Ankara

Exploring Ankara and Western Anatolia

Western Anatolia may seem somewhat bleak and inhospitable, yet the vast steppes, remote towns and salt lakes have much to offer the visitor. This is also where Turkey's administrative heart beats. Ankara, the efficient modern capital, has excellent transport links to the rest of the country and is a good starting point for tours of the region. Southeast of the pious city of Konya, former capital of the Seljuk Sultanate of Rum, lies the Bronze-Age site of Çatalhöyük, widely regarded as the world's earliest urban settlement.

Houses painted in pastel shades, Afyon

SIGHTS AT A GLANCE

Afyon **6**
Ankara pp240–47 **1**
Beyşehir **4**
Çatalhöyük **3**
Çavdarhisar **11**
Eğirdir **5**
Eskişehir **9**
Konya pp250–253 **2**
Kütahya pp258–9 **10**
Şehitgazi Valley **8**
Sivrihisar **7**

KEY

══ Motorway
━ Major road
═ Minor road
─ Scenic route
┄ Main railway
── Minor railway
△ Summit

Sunset at tranquil Lake Eğirdir

0 kilometres

0 miles 25

For additional map symbols *see back flap*

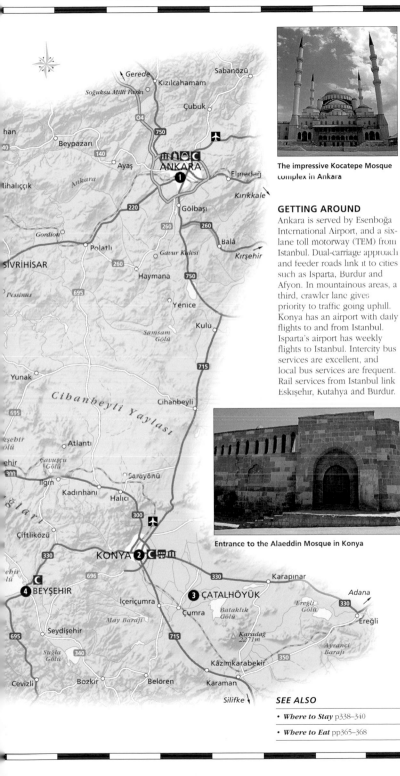

The impressive Kocatepe Mosque complex in Ankara

GETTING AROUND

Ankara is served by Esenboğa International Airport, and a six-lane toll motorway (TEM) from Istanbul. Dual-carriage approach and feeder roads link it to cities such as Isparta, Burdur and Afyon. In mountainous areas, a third, crawler lane gives priority to traffic going uphill. Konya has an airport with daily flights to and from Istanbul. Isparta's airport has weekly flights to Istanbul. Intercity bus services are excellent, and local bus services are frequent. Rail services from Istanbul link Eskişehir, Kutahya and Burdur.

Entrance to the Alaeddin Mosque in Konya

SEE ALSO

- **Where to Stay** p338–340
- **Where to Eat** pp365–368

Ankara ❶

Ankara, the modern capital of the Turkish Republic, occupies a strategic location on the east–west route across the Anatolian steppe. Believed to have been the site of a Hittite city, there is evidence of Phrygian settlement here in 1200 BC, when it was known as Ancyra. The city was occupied by the Lydians and Persians before its absorption into the Roman Empire in 24 BC. Annexed by the Seljuks in 1073, the city played a military and commercial role until Byzantine times. At this time, wool from the Angora (Ankara) goat became a major export. When Atatürk chose Ankara as the new capital in 1923, land values boomed and developments spread out across the surrounding hills.

Hittite bronze deer

A typical shop selling old carpets in the Hisar area

View of Ankara, a modern capital with attractive, wide boulevards

Exploring Ankara

A new metro, state theatres and good museums combine with lush parks and good shopping in the Ulus/Hisar district to ensure a pleasant visit. Buses and dolmuşes cover the main routes in the city.

🏛 Roman Baths

Hamamları
Çankırı Cad, Ulus. **Tel** (0312) 310 72 80. 🚌 Ulus. ◯ 8:30am–5pm daily. 🏷

Very little remains to be seen of these 3rd-century Roman baths. With the trademark features of *frigidarium* (cold room), *tepidarium* (warm room) and *caldarium* (hot room), these baths were built to honour Asclepius, the Greek god of medicine.

🏛 Temple of Augustus and Rome

Augustus Tapınağı
Ulus. 🚌 Ulus. ◯ daily.
This temple was built in about 20 BC by King Pylamenes of Galatia to honour a visit by

the great Roman emperor, Augustus. The inscription on the outer walls is one of the few surviving testaments to authenticate Augustus's accomplishments. The temple became a Byzantine church in the 4th century AD.

Adjoining the temple are the mosque (dating from 1425) and tomb of **Hacı Bayram Veli** (1352–1429), founder of the Bayrami religious sect. The fine Seljuk wooden interior, in particular, is worth seeing. Some renovation work was done in the 17th century by the famous architect Mimar Sinan (see p101).

Nearby is the **Column of Julian**, reaching 15 m (49 ft) and dating from AD 362. The column commemorates a visit by this Roman emperor.

🏛 Hacı Bayram Veli

🚌 Ulus. ◯ daily (except during prayer times). 🏷 donation appreciated.

🏛 Column of Julian

Jülyanüs Direği. 🚌 Ulus.

🏛 Museum of the War of Independence

Kurtuluş Savaşı Müzesi
Cumhuriyet Bulvarı, Ulus. **Tel** (0312) 310 71 40. 🚌 Ulus. ◯ 9am–noon & 1–5pm Tue–Sun. 🏷 (students, soldiers and teachers free).

ANKARA CITY CENTRE

The attractive museum building once served as the Grand National Assembly. A collection of photographs, ephemera and documents records the events that led up to the founding of the Republic (1919–23). Although captions are in Turkish, the exhibits are self-explanatory.

🏛 Republic Museum
Cumhuriyet Müzesi
Cumhuriyet Meydanı.
Tel (0312) 310 53 61. 🚌 Ulus.
Ⓜ Ulus. 🕙 9am–noon & 1–5pm Tue–Sun. 🎫 (students, soldiers and teachers free.)
The displays in the museum celebrate the advances and achievements that the Turkish Republic has made since its inception in 1923. Most of the labels are in Turkish.

Bazaars and Markets
🚌 Ulus. 🕙 9:30am–5:30pm daily.
The most interesting and "authentic" shopping districts are in the Ulus/Hisar area. The streets to look for are Salman Sokak, Konya Sokak and Çıkrıkçılar Sokak. Markets cater to tourists and sell a wide range of jewellery, carpets, herbal remedies, spices, iron and copper trinkets, as well as various textiles. Also look out for the Bakırçılar Çarşısı (Copper-workers' Bazaar) on Salman Sokak.
Local flea markets and produce markets are held in most districts at least once a week. One of the best takes place on Saturdays on Konya Sokak in the Ulus area.

🏛 Ethnography Museum
Etnoğrafik Müzesi
Talat Paşa Bulvarı. **Tel** (0312) 311 95 56. 🚌 Ulus. 🕙 8:30am–12:30pm & 1:30–5:30pm Tue–Sun. 🎫 🚻
Set in a pretty, white marble kiosk (summerhouse), with beautiful Ottoman interiors, and carpets and mosque woodwork dating from Seljuk

times onwards, the museum offers a charming record of Turkish costume and handi-crafts through the years.

🏛 Çengelhan Rahmi M. Koç Museum
Çengelhan Rahmi M. Koç Müzesi
Sutepe Mah, Depo Sokak 1, Altındağ, Ankara. **Tel** (0312) 309 68 00. 🕙 10am–5pm Tue–Thu, 10am–7pm Sat & Sun. 🎫 🅿 🚻 ♿
www.rmk-museum.org.tr
A sister museum to the Rahmi Koç Industrial Museum in Istanbul, the Ankara site is opposite the entrance to Ankara Castle in a restored 16th century caravanserai. Eclectic exhibits range from toys, bicycles, prams and scientific instruments to air, rail and sea transport. Early motor cars include a 1918 Model T Ford. A replica of the Nile river boat from the film "African Queen" is amongst the 1,200 items on display. The museum café is pleasant but try the Brasserie on the ground floor for gourmet fare.

🏛 Turkish Grand National Assembly
T.B.M.M. (Türkiye Büyük Millet Meclisi)
Ismet Inönü Bul. **Tel** (0312) 420 67 42. 🚌 Bakanlıklar. ⚫ Closed to the public.
This impressive complex, housing the legislature, is of a pre-World War II, German design. The public are no longer allowed into the buildings or grounds. Many foreign embassies and con-sulates are located in the area.

Triangular fountain outside the Turkish Grand National Assembly

Roman Baths ①
🅿 Airport 30 km (20 miles)
CANKIRI CAD
Ⓒ Hacı Bayram Veli
US ② Temple of Augustus and Rome
③ Museum of the War of Independence
Inönü Park
HISAR PARKI CAD
BENDERESI CAD
ULUS MEYDANI
⑤
⑨ Citadel
ublic eum
Bazaars ⑦ ⑧ Çengelhan Rahmi M Koç Museum
us
✉
HISAR
ANAFARTALAR CAD
Museum of Anatolian Civilizations
ULUCANLAR CAD
HASIRCILAR CAD
TALAT PAŞA CAD
⑥ Ethnography Museum
Ⓒ Yeni Ankara Hamamı
UL SIHHIYE MEYD
CEMAL GÜRSEL CAD
Ⓜ Kurtuluş
hhiye Ⓜ
Abdi İpekçi Park
Kurtuluş Park
KURTULUŞ
ZIYA GÖKALP CAD
MITHAT PAŞA CAD
Ⓜ Kızılay
Ⓜ Kolej
✉
MESRUTIYET CAD
LIBYA CAD
⑭ ⑬ Kocatepe Mosque
KOCATEPE
ATATÜRK BULVARI
AKAY CAD
⑯ kish Grand nal Assembly
ESAT CAD
TUNUS CAD
YER BUL DERESI CAD
Küçükesat Hamamı
PARIS CAD
TUNALI HILMI CAD
NENEHATUN CAD
BULVARI
GÜVENLİK CAD
CINNAH CAD
Kuğulu Park Ⓒ Karum
⑮ Kavaklidere
Çankaya, Presidential Palace
Atakule, Botanical Gardens

0 metres   200
0 yards   200

Key to Symbols see back flap

Museum of Anatolian Civilizations
Anadolu Medeniyetleri Müzesi

Turkey's most outstanding museum occupies two renovated Ottoman-era buildings and is situated in the Atpazarı (horse market) district of the city, below the citadel. The museum displays the achievements of Anatolia's many diverse cultures. Exhibits range from simple Paleolithic stone tools to clay tablets inscribed in Assyrian cuneiform and exquisite Hellenistic and Roman sculptures. The displays are laid out in chronological order, and include a statuette of the Mother Goddess from Çatalhöyük *(see p254)*, Bronze-Age treasures from the royal tombs at Alacahöyük *(see p294)* and superb Hittite sculptures and orthostat reliefs.

★ Serving Table
*Found at Gordion (see p247),
this 8th-century BC folding
wooden table is an
outstanding example
of Phrygian
craftsmanship.*

Lecture
theatre

Urartian Lion Statuette
*Unearthed at Kayalıdere,
this small bronze lion
shows the skill of the
Urartian craftsmen.*

Museum Entrance
*The main displays are housed in the
Mahmut Paşa Bedesten, a bazaar
warehouse built in the 15th century.*

Terracotta Cooking Pot
*Neolithic peoples favoured
the use of terracotta. This
small pot and stand,
found at Çatalhöyük
(see p254), dates from
approximately the
6th millennium BC.*

STAR EXHIBITS

- ★ Roman Head
- ★ Serving Table
- ★ Sphinx Relief

★ Sphinx Relief
This well-preserved Neo-Hittite stone relief, dating from the 9th century BC, was found at Carchemish.

VISITORS' CHECKLIST

Saraçlar Sokak (below the Citadel). **Tel** *(0312) 324 31 60.*
🚌 🚇 *Ulus.* ⏰ *9am–5pm daily.* ♿ 📷 🚫 📹

Ground floor

Interior
The uncluttered layout of the interior provides the perfect setting for the vast range of historic collections.

Golden Bowl with Studs
This early Bronze-Age bowl from Alacahöyük dates from the 3rd millennium BC.

★ Roman Head
The spread of classical Greek and Roman civilization gave rise to more realistic works of art, such as this marble head.

Lower floor

KEY

☐	Urartian Period
☐	Phrygian Period
☐	Hittite Period
☐	Assyrian Colonies
☐	Early Bronze Age
☐	Chalcolithic and Neolithic
☐	Paleolithic
☐	Classical Period

Artifacts displayed in the museum gardens

Exploring Ankara

Visitors to Ankara will notice the striking contrasts between the modern city centre and the old town. Wide, tree-lined boulevards, green parks, smart embassies, government buildings and universities make up the new administrative centre, while parts of the old town – particularly certain streets around the citadel – appear to be remarkably simple and traditional. Atatürk's mausoleum dominates the modern part of Ankara, symbolizing a fusion of ancient and modern concepts.

Boating on the pleasant lake in Youth Park

♠ Citadel
Hisar

Hisarparkı Cad. 🚌 *Hisar.* ◯ *daily.*
The Hisar, or Byzantine citadel, dominates the northern
end of Ankara. The walls
enclose a ramshackle collection of wooden houses, with
some passable restaurants,
several carpet shops and
junkyards filled with antiques
and collectables. Salman
Sokak, or "Copper Alley",
lives up to its nickname, with
plenty of old and new copper
pieces on offer. You will find
bargains and bric-à-brac here,
but few real treasures.

Youth Park
Gençlik Parkı

Atatürk Bulvarı. 🚇 *Opera or Ulus.*
🚇 *Ulus.* ◯ *dawn to dusk daily.*
The Youth Park just south
of Ulus is Ankara's liveliest
and most popular area for
urban recreation. It has an
artificial lake, where small
boats can be hired. There
are also a few pleasant cafés,
where tea is served in a
samovar (double-tiered pot)

at tables overlooking the lake.
And, of course, there is a
funfair *(luna park)*, a sports
stadium, tennis courts and a
swimming pool.

The lovely Korean Garden,
on the other side of Cumhuriyet
Bulvarı, commemorates the oft-
forgotten combat role played
by Turkish soldiers during the
Korean War (1950–54). The
45 m-high (148 ft) Parachute
Tower here was once
popular with daredevils
willing to pay for leaping
from its heights.

🏛 Turkish Railways Open-Air Steam Locomotive Museum
Açık Hava Buharlı Müzesi

Ankara Gar Sahası, Celâl Bayar
Bulvarı üzeri.
Tel *(0312) 309 05 15.*
◯ *9am–6pm daily.* 🖼
This open-air museum
close to the Ankara
Railway Station is
bound to appeal to a
broad audience, and not
simply those visitors
interested in steam traction. It

should not be confused with
the Turkish Railways (TCDD)
Museum inside the station.
Atatürk's personal railway carriage, a gift from Adolf Hitler,
can be seen adjacent to the
main station concourse. The
open-air collection of steam-
driven giants, located across
the railway tracks to the left,
includes several old German
models used during the
invasion of Russia in World
War II.

In the event that
you find the museum
closed, ask the railway
personnel in the station
building to arrange for
someone to open it for
you.

Guard at the Atatürk Mausoleum

⚰ Atatürk Mausoleum
Anitkabir

Anıt Cad, Anıttepe.
Tel *(0312) 231 79 75.* 🚌
Anıttepe. 🚇 *Tandoğan.*
◯ *Jun–Sep: 9am–5pm daily;*
Oct–May: 9am–4pm daily.
Sound and light show (summer). 📷
Ankara's most imposing site
commands a hill to the west of
the city. Construction of this
monument, begun in 1944,
was completed in 1953. To
one side of the central courtyard, bronze doors open into
the marble-lined hall and
cenotaph, where visiting heads
of state and vast numbers of
ordinary Turks still come to
pay their respects to Turkey's
supreme leader. İsmet İnönü,
second President of the
Republic, is entombed
opposite. A hall nearby houses
some splendid vintage cars
used by Atatürk, and visitors
can also admire a display of
personal possessions and gifts
presented to Atatürk by fellow
heads of state over the years.

Vintage steam engine at the Open-Air Steam Locomotive Museum

For hotels and restaurants in this region see pp338–40 and pp365–368

C Kocatepe Mosque

Kocatepe Camii
Olgunlar Sok. 🚌 Kocatepe.
Ⓜ Kızılay. ◯ daily (except during
prayer times). 💰 donations
appreciated.

Kocatepe Mosque is a landmark in Ankara. One of the
world's largest mosques, it is
a four-minaret replica of the
Blue Mosque (see pp88–9) in
Istanbul. Underneath it is a
western-style shopping centre
called Beğendik, as well as a
large car park.

Chandelier inside the Kocatepe Mosque

Atatürk Boulevard

Atatürk Bulvarı
Ankara's premier boulevard
links the old city with the
Presidential Palace and the
official government buildings.
Along the way is the original
home of the Red Crescent
(Kızılay), the Islamic equiva-
lent of the Red Cross, as well
as Turkey's first department
store, Gima.

🛍 Kavaklıdere and Çankaya

Ankara's up-market shopping
areas cater for the diplomatic
corps and government elite.
The best can be found south
of Kızılay in the suburbs of
Kavaklıdere and Çankaya,
where many foreign
embassies are located. Going
south on Tunalı Hilmi
Caddesi, parallel to Atatürk
Bulvarı, you reach Kuğulu
Park and Cinnah Caddesi
Both streets are studded with
designer boutiques. Karum,
opposite the park, is an
exclusive shopping centre. Do
not expect bargains here.

🛍 Atakule

Atatürk Bulvarı terminates in
Çankaya Caddesi. A short

stroll down this lively street
will take you to the impressive
Atakule tower and shopping
complex. In good weather,
the restaurant at the top of
the 125-m high (410 ft) tower
affords excellent views over
the city.

🏛 Presidential Palace

Cumhurbaşkanlığı Köşku
Çankaya Cad. **Tel** (0312) 440 72 10.
🚌 Çankaya. ◯ 1–5pm Sun only.
💰 no entrance fee, but passport or
identity card required. 📷

Set in a formal garden, the
residence is not open to the
public, but visitors can
view Atatürk's house,
which is now a
museum, within the
grounds. The father
of the Turkish
republic moved here in
1921 and this is where
he planned the direc
tion his country would
take in years to come.
The house has a slightly
sombre atmosphere.
The ground floor is decorated
in a classic Ottoman fashion,
while upstairs provides visitors
with a glimpse of Atatürk's
lifestyle and personal tastes.

**Sign at
Atatürk Farm**

🐾 Atatürk Farm and Zoo

Atatürk Orman Çiftliği
Çiftlik Cad. **Tel** (0312) 211 01 70.
📷 Gazi. ◯ 9am–5pm Tue–Thu &
Sat–Sun.

Ankara's many parks were
established in the early years
of the republic, since Atatürk
believed that parks and natural recreation areas were part
of his country's heritage.
His farm on the outskirts of
Ankara is one such peaceful
retreat and is a good destination for those with children.
Apart from a replica
of Atatürk's boyhood
home in Salonika
(modern Thessa-
loniki), there are large
leafy grounds and
orchards to explore
and enjoy.
Much of the produce
that can be sampled at
the farm, such as ice
cream, yoghurt, and
meat rolls, are made
on site. There is also a
beer brewery.
The farm grounds adjoin the
railway line. It is most convenient to take the suburban
train to Gazi Station and
make your way from there.

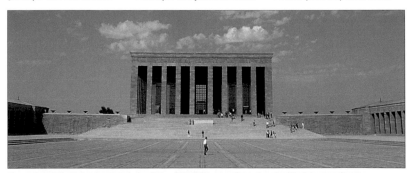

The vast central courtyard and stark simplicity of Atatürk's mausoleum, housing his plain sarcophagus

Ankara: Further Afield

Life in the Turkish capital is enhanced by a number of green belts situated around the outskirts of the city. Here, the focus is on outdoor and leisure activities. These are made possible by the proximity of forests, ski centres, thermal spas and some attractive picnic areas. Most forest areas and parks are open from dawn to dusk; a guardian or ranger is generally in attendance and a small fee will be charged for

Basin used at spa baths

vehicles. Taking your own vehicle is recommended for maximum enjoyment; the centres are clearly marked off the main roads. Note that camping is restricted to designated areas only. Most of the attractions listed here are day outings from Ankara, but if you want to "take the waters" at a spa, plan to spend a few days.

A pleasant outdoor swimming pool at Kızılcahamam

these is **Kızılcahamam**. Of all the thermal spas scattered around Ankara, it is also the most suited to tourists. There are comfortable hotels and other facilities for visitors who want to stay for a few days. Some treatments involve not only bathing in, but also drinking, the mineral-rich waters, which contain bicarbonate, chloride, sodium and carbon dioxide.

The town of Kızılcahamam, with the blue spa building on the left

🗻 Bolu
137 km (85 miles) NE of Ankara. Take toll motorway (E89) from Ankara to Istanbul, or highway (no toll) E80.
📱 (0374) 212 22 54.
The Bolu area is known for its deciduous forests and a steep mountain pass, which affords splendid views. It also produces a delicious ewe's milk cheese. At Kartalkaya, 42 km (26 miles) east of the town of Bolu, there is a pleasant ski centre open from December to March.

🗻 Diamond Head
Elma Dağı
23 km (14 miles) E of Ankara on the Sivas road.
Located at an altitude of 1,855 m (6,085 ft), this is the nearest ski centre to Ankara. On snowy weekends the slopes are crowded with locals skiing, skating and tobogganing. Although the season here is limited and the runs short and busy, Diamond Head makes a good place to practise before heading eastwards to try the more challenging runs at Palandöken (see p319).

975 m (3,200 ft), has picnic places and well-marked hiking trails, and offers a relaxing retreat from the city.

The region's many natural hot mineral springs have been developed to create spa resorts. One of the best of

Shady forest footpath in the Soğuksu National Park

🗻 Soğuksu National Park
Soğuksu Milli Parkı
82 km (51 miles) N of Ankara.
Tel (0312) 736 11 15 (national park office).
If you like walking and trekking in a beautiful and safe forest area, this is the ideal place to go. The forest park, situated at an altitude of

🗻 Gölbaşı Lake and Çubuk Dam
25 km (16 miles) S of Ankara along the E90 towards Konya.
If you enjoy picnicking, these areas make a pleasant weekend trip. Both Gölbaşı and the Çubuk Dam are popular with Turkish families for day outings, weekend picnics and informal waterside lunches. There are also some excellent lakeside restaurants.

🗻 Haymana Hot Springs
Haymana Kaplıca
60 km (38 miles) S of Ankara.
Tel contact hotels directly for bookings. 🗻 Hot Springs Festival (3rd week in Jun).
Haymana is one of six thermal spas within easy reach of Ankara, and its history extends as far back as Roman times.

Municipal water fountain in the centre of Haymana

It is worth coming here for the relaxing atmosphere and to experience the feeling of physical well-being after a good soak. At Haymana, the waters emerge at 45°C (113°F) and you can smell the calcium, magnesium, sodium and bi-carbonate. There are several good hotels here, providing a wide range of facilities.

♪ Infidel's Castle
42 km (26 miles) NE of Haymana
☐ daily.
A sight worth visiting in this region is the **Infidel's Castle** (Gavur Kalesi). Strategically perched on a sheer cliff, it consists of an underground cult tomb with two adjoining tomb chambers, and was dis-covered in 1930. Although this is thought to be a Hittite site, there is doubt about the dating of the stone relief figures of gods and goddesses on the walls, since these do not have the characteristic conical headgear shown in other Hittite relief carving.

Polatlı and Gordion
70 km (43 miles) W of Ankara.
🚌 intercity bus between Ankara and Afyon, getting off at Polatı. Take a taxi or one of the infrequent dolmuşes from there.
The village of Yassıhöyük stands on the site of Gordion, the capital of ancient Phrygia, dating from around the 8th century BC. There are several sights worth seeing here, and you can easily tour the site in the course of a day trip from Ankara. If you wish to stay over, however, the nearby town of **Polatlı**, some 18 km (11 miles) to the southeast is

well supplied with hotels and some good restaurants.

Gordion was famous as the seat of the legendary King Midas, whose touch was said to have turned everything to gold. Legend has it that this power turned on Midas when he touched his daughter, as well as his food and drink. The problem was solved only when the god Dionysus took pity on him and granted him a cure. It is thought that Midas took his own life in 695 BC after a crushing military defeat.

Phrygia reached its zenith in the middle of the 8th century BC, but Gordion was made famous again by Alexander the Great (see pp46–7). In 333 BC, after wintering in Lycia, Alexander led his army northward from Sagalassos to Gordion. Here, he came upon and cut the Gordion knot (see p47), fulfilling a prophecy that whoever loosed the bond would become the ruler of the known world.

Today, little remains of the palace, but about 80 burial mounds of Phygian kings have been excavated in the Gordion area over the past 40 years. The most interesting of these is the **Midas Tomb** (Midas Tümülüsü), which lies within the grounds of the **Gordion Museum** (Gordion Müzesi). The large mound is thought to cover the chamber in which the king was buried,

Phrygian mosaic, Gordion Museum

and is 50 m (164 ft) in height. When archaeologists opened the tomb they found the skeleton of a man of around 60 years of age, who is now believed to be another king from the same dynasty.

The acropolis has also been excavated, and shows layers of civilization from the Bronze Age to Greek and Roman times. Although the acropolis gives an idea of the size and extent of the historic settlements in the region, most of the mosaics found there have been moved and are now kept in the museum. In other places, simple roof structures have been erected to protect excavated mosaics from the elements.

The Gordion Museum was established in 1963, and has been nominated for several awards over the years. It displays Bronze Age, Hittite, Hellenistic, Greek and Roman finds, but its displays concen-trate on the Phrygian period, and feature many superbly crafted artifacts. The exhibits include ceramics, woodwork and several bronze vessels found in the Midas Tomb, as well as musical instruments and more.

♪ Midas Tomb
☐ 8am–5pm daily. 🎫

⛩ Gordion Museum
9 km (5 miles) N of the town.
Tel (0312) 638 21 88. ☐ 8am–5pm Tue–Sun. 🎫

Entrance to the burial mound said to house the tomb of King Midas

The distinctive green-tiled dome of the Mevlâna Museum in Konya ▷

Street-by-Street: Konya ②

Konya is set on a high, bleak plain in the middle of the Anatolian steppe. Known throughout Turkey for its pious inhabitants and strong Islamic leanings, this ancient city has an increasingly modern and prosperous appearance.

Samovar for sale in the park

Konya has been inhabited since Hittite times. It was known as Iconium to the Romans and Byzantines. The city's heyday was in the 12th century, when it was the capital of the Seljuk Sultanate of Rum.

At the heart of the city lies the circular Alaeddin Park (Alaeddin Parkı), a low hill dominated by the Alaeddin Mosque, Konya's largest. It was finished in 1220 by Alaeddin Keykubad I (1219–36), the greatest and most prolific builder of the Seljuk sultans.

Villa of Sultan Kılıç Arslan
A concrete arch covers the remains of this Seljuk landmark. Nearby are tea gardens.

★ Konya Fairground
Fairs are now held elsewhere, so the shady gardens are a cool, restful retreat.

ALAEDDIN BULVARI

The Seminary of the Slender
Minaret, now housing the Museum of Wood and Stone Carving, is named for its elegant tiled minaret.

| 0 metres | 80 |
| 0 yards | 80 |

Ottoman House
Gracious three-storey houses with projecting balconies are typical of middle-class homes built during the late Ottoman period.

STAR SIGHTS

★ Alaeddin Mosque

★ Karatay Museum

★ Konya Fairground

For hotels and restaurants in this region see pp338–340 and pp365–368

★ Karatay Museum
Housed in the Great Karatay Seminary, a 13th-century Seljuk theological school, the Karatay Museum has a superb collection of ceramics and tiles.

VISITORS' CHECKLIST

🏙 1,000,000. 🚌 25 km (15 miles) NW of city centre, (0332) 265 02 45. ✈ 20 km (12 miles) N of city centre, (0332) 444 08 49. 🚉 Ferit Paşa Cad, (0332) 332 36 70. 🛈 Mevlâna Cad 65, (0332) 351 10 74, 353 4020. 🎭 Mevlâna Festival (10–17 Dec). 🔓 daily.

★ Alacddin Mosque
The mosque is set in beautiful wooded surroundings on a site that has been used since prehistoric times.

Tiled mihrab
The mihrab in the Alaeddin Mosque is adorned with some of the finest Seljuk tilework.

ANKARA CAD

ALAEDDIN BULVARI

Car Park

KEY

— — — Suggested route

Mevlâna Museum
Mevlâna Müzesi

The city of Konya has close links with the life and work of Celaleddin Rumi, or Mevlâna, the 13th-century founder of the Mevlevi dervish sect – better known as the "whirling" dervishes *(see p255)*. Rumi developed a philosophy of spiritual union and universal love, and is regarded as one of the Islamic world's greatest mystics. He settled in Seljuk-ruled Konya and is believed to have died here in 1273.

The museum is an enlargement of the original dervish lodge *(tekke)*. It contains the tomb of Rumi, the ceremonial hall *(semahane)*, and displays of memorabilia and manuscripts. There are also galleries for spectators and musicians.

The entrance to the museum, with the famous green-tiled dome

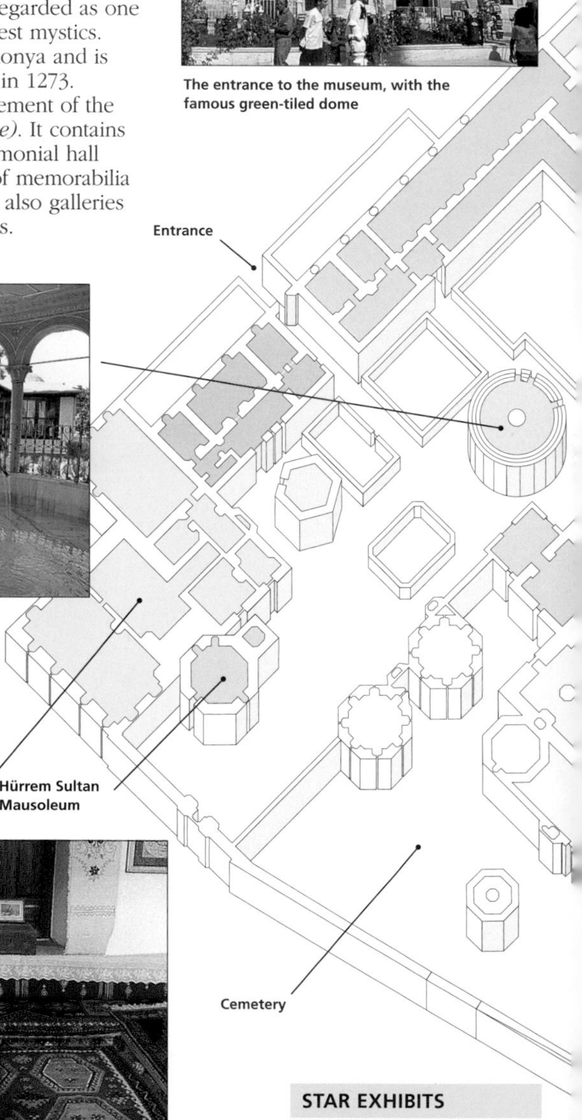

Entrance

★ Ablutions Fountain
Used in the dervish cleansing ritual, the ablutions fountain (şadırvan) *is pleasantly cooling on hot days.*

Hürrem Sultan
Mausoleum

Cemetery

Dervish Life
Life-like mannequins clad in authentic dress illustrate the spiritual aspects of the daily life of an initiate in the lodge.

STAR EXHIBITS

★ Ablutions Fountain

★ Mevlâna's Tomb

★ Semahane

Mother-of-Pearl Case
This finely worked case is said to contain the beard of Mevlâna.

Prominent **female** members of the Mevlâna order are buried in this graveyard.

Verandah

★ Semahane (Ceremonial Hall)
Once the setting for the whirling ceremony, the Semahane now houses museum displays.

Musical Instruments
Instruments used by the dervishes include this ud, finely worked in ivory with a mother-of-pearl fretboard.

★ Mevlâna's Tomb
Gilded calligraphy adorns the walls around the sarcophagus. The tombs of Rumi's father and other dervish leaders are nearby.

KEY

☐	Dervish Lodge
☐	Administrative Offices
☐	Dervish Assembly Chamber
☐	Monumental Fountain
☐	Recitation Room
☐	Mescid-Chapel Mosque
☐	Semahane (Ceremonial Hall)
☐	Tombs of Çelebi

Çatalhöyük ❸

60 km (36 miles) S of Konya. Own transport or taxi recommended. Turn left to Çumra, from the Karaman/ Mersin road. **www**.catalhoyuk.com

Dating from as early as 7000 BC, Çatalhöyük is one of the world's earliest urban settlements. It was originally discovered and excavated by James Mellaart in 1958. Research resumed in 1997, after a 30-year interval.

It is thought that roughly 10,000 people lived here in flat-roofed square houses with rooftop entrances and high windows. The city was the focus of a culture that produced an array of mural decoration, decorative textiles and pottery.

Visitors can enter the site only when accompanied by an official museum guide. The **Çatalhöyük Museum** displays the latest finds, and there are "virtual reality" exhibits in houses and shrines. Artifacts displayed in the museum are reproductions; the originals are either in museums in Konya or the superb Museum of Anatolian Civilizations *(see pp242–3)* in Ankara.

Bronze bowl found at Çatalhöyük

🏛 **Çatalhöyük Museum**
Tel *(0332) 452 57 20.* ◯ *8am–5pm daily.* 🖼

Eğirdir Lake, a tranquil haven for naturalists

Beyşehir ❹

🏠 *67,872.* 🚌 *frequent buses from Konya, or intercity buses to Burdur.*

Beyşehir is the largest of the fresh-water lakes in what is known as Turkey's Lake District, and the third largest in the country. Its shallow waters contain carp, perch and pike. The town of the same name, at the southeastern corner of the lake, features an unusual combined weir and bridge.

One of the main reasons for coming to Beyşehir is to see the **Eşrefoğlu Mosque** (Eşrefoğlu Camii), dating from 1297. The wooden interior, with its 48 wooden columns and *mihrab* (prayer niche) decorated with cut tiles, is among the finest

examples of this type of architecture remaining from the Beylik period *(see p53)*.

🟩 **Eşrefoğlu Mosque**
Beside the bus station, NW after crossing the weir-bridge. ◯ *prayer times, but a guardian will let visitors in at other times.* 🖼 *donation.*

Eğirdir ❺

🏠 *40,817.* 🚆 *daily to Istanbul via Afyon, (0246) 311 46 94.* 🚌 *(0246) 311 40 36.* 🛈 *2 Sahil Yolu, (0246) 311 43 88.* 🛍 *Thu.* 🎉 *Apple Festival (Sep).*

Ringed by mountains rising to 3,000 m (9,842 ft), Eğirdir Lake makes a good base for walkers, birders and flower enthusiasts. When the snow melts in May, the hills display many flowering bulbs, orchids and become a stop-over for migrating birds. Eğirdir makes an ideal base for exploring the St Paul trail, Turkey's second longest long-distance walk.

Environs
Antiocheia-in-Pisidia is famous as the place where St Paul first preached to the Gentiles. The ruins of the city include the basilica of St Paul, a synagogue, Roman theatre, baths and a superb aqueduct.
Davraz Ski Centre is opera-tional from December to April. There is also a 50-bed ski lodge at Çobanisa, 27 km (17 miles) from Isparta, with a chairlift to the north face of the mountains.

Davraz Ski Centre
🎿 *(0246) 218 44 38, for the most up-to-date information.*

The unusual wooden interior of the Eşrefoğlu Mosque

The Whirling Dervishes

The Mevlevi order, better known as the Whirling Dervishes, was founded by the Sufi mystic, Celaleddin Rumi, also called Mevlâna. He believed that music and dance represented a means to induce an ecstatic state of universal love and offered a way to liberate the individual from the anxiety and pain of daily life. His greatest work, the six-volume *Mesnevi*, consists of 25,000 poems that were read in the *tekkes* (lodges) of the order.

Celaleddin Rumi

Central to the practice of the dervishes is the *sema*, or whirling ceremony. This consists of several parts, each with its own meaning. Love is the central theme of the mystical cycle of the *sema*, which symbolizes the sharing of God's love among earthly beings. For man, the dance is a spiritual ascent to divine love. The *sema* combines both spiritual and intellectual elements, emphasizing self-realization and the ultimate goal, which is perfect union with God.

Conical headdress

Black cloak

Clothing
Clothing worn for the sema *has symbolic meaning. The headdress, for example, stands for the tomb of the ego.*

Ud Duvar Cymbals

Ney

Musical accompaniment *is highly symbolic: the ney (reed flute) represents the breath of God.*

THE SEMA RITUAL

The *sema* consists of five parts, the first three of which are prayers, greetings, and musical improvizations. The ritual then moves into four salutes *(selams)*: truth through knowledge, the splendour of creation, total submission before God and coming to terms with destiny.

Whirling *is the climax of the sema. Its selams (salutes) represent stages during the rapture of submission to God.*

The wide white skirt symbolizes the ego's shroud.

The movement concludes *with a bow, signifying the return to a state of subservience.*

The dervishes greet one another *and salute the soul, which is "enslaved" by shapes and bodies.*

The dervishes extend their arms, *to allow divine energy to enter the right palm, move through the body, and pass out through the left palm into the earth.*

Verses from the Koran *are read after the dance, including a prayer for the peace of all souls.*

Cobbled street in the old quarter of Afyon

Afyon ❻

🏠 820,000. 🚌 İsmet İnönü Cad, (0272) 212 09 63. 🚉 (0272) 213 00 22. 🛈 Valilik Binası, Kat 3, Suite 333, (0272) 213 54 47.

The word Afyon means "opium", and it is difficult not to miss the fields of white and dark purple opium poppies if you visit the area in May. Opiates are extracted for medicinal purposes at a factory in nearby Bolvadın, using the special poppy straw method. The town museum has exhibits detailing various methods of opiate extraction.

Other local products are a white, soft marble, which is found in huge slabs along the roadsides and is used for everything from gravestones to kitchen basins. Afyon Kaymağı, a rich clotted cream, is typically served on small metal trays and eaten with honey for breakfast.

Towering over the town is a 225 m (738 ft) crag that can be reached by climbing 700 steps. The Hittites and Byzantines may have used its commanding position for a fortress, but exact dates are speculative.

The Seljuks left the greatest mark on Afyon's history. The major Seljuk building is the **Great Mosque** (Ulu Camii), completed in 1272. It features a geometric ceiling and 40 wooden columns, some with traces of paint on the capitals.

The **Archaeological Museum** contains a collection of largely Roman artifacts, which were excavated from around Isparta, Uşak, Burdur and Kütahya.

Afyon was Atatürk's headquarters for the final stages of Turkey's War of Independence (see p58), which reached a climax with the victory over the advancing Greek army at Dumlupınar on 26 August 1922. The **Victory Museum** (Zafer Müzesi), known more for its classical Anatolian architecture than for its contents, recalls the heady days of national liberation. Most of the top Republican commanders stayed in this building during the campaign. There is also a war memorial at nearby Dumlupınar.

🄲 Great Mosque
Ulu Camii
⬜ during prayer, or ask the guardian on duty to let you in. 🗃 donation.

🏛 Afyon Archaeological Museum
Kurtuluş Cad 96. **Tel** (0272) 215 11 91. ⬜ 8am–noon & 1–5:30pm Tue–Sun. 🗃

🏛 Victory Museum
Zafer Müzesi
In front of the Governor's Building. **Tel** (0272) 212 09 16. ⬜ 9am–noon & 1–5pm Tue–Sun.

Sivrihisar ❼

🏠 32,600. 🚌 along the E90 from Polatlı, then dolmuş to the town.

Sivrihisar is the ancient town of Justinianopolis, built by Emperor Justinian (see p49) to guard the western route to Ancyra (ancient Ankara). The modern town is spread out at the foot of a crag, on which lie the remains of the original Byzantine fortress. The Great Mosque (Ulu Camii), built in 1247, is an excellent example of a Seljuk mosque. Some of its 67 wooden pillars have intricately carved and painted capitals. A warren of pretty Ottoman houses surrounds the mosque, and the Sivrihisar area is famous for fine hand-woven kilims.

Environs
14 km (9 miles) to the south of Sivrihisar lie the ancient ruins of **Pessinus**, near the modern village of Ballıhisar (honey castle). During the 3rd century BC, Pessinus was an important Phrygian cult centre but was abandoned in around AD 500 or 600. Sights include the scant remains of a temple of Cybele, the Anatolian mother goddess. However, nothing is left of the stadium and theatre. At one time, it is believed that there were over 360 springs here, and the remains of hydraulic works can still be seen. The site is open to the public and access is free, if not easy.

The "forest of columns" in the Great Mosque in Sivrihisar

The Tomb of King Midas (left), cut from solid rock

Şehitgazi Valley ❽

🏠 *32,600.* **D** *or on foot.*

The village of Şehitgazı is named after Şehit Battal Gazi, an Arab commander and martyr (*şehit*), and "warrior of the faith", who died during the siege of Afyon in about AD 750. His large tomb, and that of the Byzantine princess who fell in love with him, are housed in a beautiful *tekke* (monastery complex), built by Hacı Bektaş Veli (*see p293*) about 10 km (6 miles) to the northwest of the town centre.

The main attraction of the valley is the monumental tomb (5th or 6th century BC) of King Midas at Midasşehir, or Yazılıkaya. The tomb lies 65 km (40 miles) south of Eskişehir in a marvellous, open-air setting. The site is open from dawn to dusk and you can wander freely here and in the small museum.

Aslantaş, 35 km (22 miles) north of Afyon, was a major Phrygian cult centre. There are other Phrygian sites at Kümbet and Aslankaya, but the roads here are unpaved and there are few visitors.

Eskişehir ❾

🏠 *872,650.* 🚆 *from Istanbul and Ankara, (0222) 231 13 65.* 🚌 *(0222) 225 80 94.* ℹ️ *Valilik Binası, ground floor, (0222) 230 17 52.* 🎭 *International Yunus Emre Culture and Fine Arts Week (6–10 May), Meerschaum Festival (3rd week Sep).* 🍽️ *most days.*

Commanding the main road from Istanbul to Ankara, Eskişehir (ancient Dorylaeum)

has prospered from trade for centuries, but has also been ravaged by passing armies. It was badly damaged during the War of Independence and has few historical monuments. Today, it is a major railway junction, as well as the home base of the Turkish air force.

Eskişehir is also a mining centre, with supplies of borax, chrome and manganese, as well as meerschaum (or "sea foam"), a soft, porous, heat-resistant, light white clay used to make elaborate carved tobacco pipes (*see p376*), which are popular among visitors to Turkey. The **Meerschaum Museum** (Lületaşı Müzesi) has displays of historic pipes and old photos of the mines. You can watch carvers at work on Sakarya Caddesi, and purchase pipes and other decorative items made from meerschaum.

Meerschaum pipe

🏛️ **Meerschaum Museum**
Lületaşı Müzesi
İki Eylül Cad. **Tel** *(0222) 233 05 82.*
⏰ *10am–5pm daily.* 🎫

Kütahya ❿

See pp258–9.

Çavdarhisar (Aezani) ⓫

60 km (37 miles) SW of Kütahya.
D *infrequent dolmuş to and from Kütahya.* ⏰ *9am–noon & 1–5pm daily.* 🎫

The Phrygian site at Aezani (today's Çavdarhisar) does not feature on most tourists' itineraries, but a visit here will be highly rewarding.

Aezani reached its zenith in the 2nd century AD, when it was transformed from a minor Phrygian settlement into a large, thriving city and sanctuary of Zeus, ruler of the gods. At this time, the legend of Zeus's birth in the nearby cave at Steunos reinforced the belief in pagan culture, even though such cult worship was at that time being challenged elsewhere by early Christian communities. Today, the cave can be reached only with a four-wheel-drive vehicle.

The most impressive remains are of the Temple of Zeus, built during the reign of Emperor Hadrian (AD 117–138). There is a crypt underneath the temple that is believed to have been the seat of the cult of Cybele, the mother goddess of Anatolia.

The scattered remains of a theatre, municipal gymnasium and stadium are visible today. These were envisaged on a scale that would rival cities like Ephesus or Pergamum. However, Aezani's influence had begun to wane by the 3rd century AD. In 1970, an earthquake demolished much of the site. Some fine mosaics of Phrygian gods can be seen in the ruins of the bathhouse and gymnasium.

Remains of the well-preserved Temple of Zeus at Aezani

Kütahya ⑩

Tilework at the main
water fountain

Kütahya's earliest inhabitants were the Phrygians in the 7th century BC. Alexander the Great called the city Kotaeon and used it as his headquarters as he advanced on Gordion (see p247) in 332 BC. The Byzantines later occupied the fortress on the acropolis hill until it fell to the Seljuks. Kütahya's golden age was under Sultan Selim I (the Grim; 1512–20), when ceramic craftsmen from Persia were settled here. In 1833, the breakaway ruler of Egypt, Paşa Muhammad Ali, occupied Kütahya. In 1922, Greek forces were routed near here, marking a turning point in the War of Independence (see p58). Today, this is a peaceful and devout town and most shops shut during prayer times on Fridays. The numerous splendid period houses hint at untapped tourist potential.

The Dumlupınar monument,
honouring Turkish war dead

Exploring Kütahya

Almost all of the town's sites can be seen on foot. Allow at least an afternoon to see the scores of mansions and townhouses.

Between the 15th and the 17th centuries, Kütahya was the rival of İznik (see pp160–61) in the painting and glazing of tiles and ceramics. By the early 20th century, the local ceramic industry had all but vanished. Now, Kütahya is again the focus of a revival of this skilled art. The town is acclaimed for beautiful hand-painted ceramic items, and workshops are found in many of the back streets.

The Dumlupınar monument, 50 km (31 miles) south of the town, is also worth visiting. It commemorates the soldiers who fell in the decisive battle of the War of Independence.

⌂ Kossuth House Museum

Kossuth Evi Müzesi
Macar Sokak (off Gediz Cad).
Tel (0274) 223 62 14. ◯ 8am–noon & 1–6pm Tue–Sun. 🖼 🖸

This house/museum complex was the home of Hungarian freedom fighter, Lajos Kossuth (1802–94), who sought refuge in Turkey after leading an unsuccessful revolt to free his homeland from the rule of the Hapsburgs in 1848. Kossuth and his family stayed here as the guests of the Ottoman government in 1850–51, and the 19th-century stone-and-wood house where they lived has changed remarkably little since that time.

The statue of Kossuth in the rose garden was erected in 1982, and Hungarians renew friendship ties here annually on 5 April. The house is also referred to as "the House of the Hungarian Patriot".

The double-walled fortress, built by the Ottomans

♣ Fortress

Kale
Proceed up Gediz Cad from the Kossuth House Museum.

The ruined fortress resembles many other Ottoman-period citadels. Not much is known about its history, but the Kütahya-born historian and traveller, Evliya Çelebi (1811–82), wrote that it had 70 towers. One of the few remaining ones has been extensively restored. Most people come here for the delightful revolving restaurant, **Döner Gazino**, at the top.

Döner Gazino

◯ dawn to dusk daily.

🏛 Kütahya Tile Museum

Kütahya Çini Müzesi
Gediz Cad. **Tel** (0274) 223 69 90.
◯ 8am–noon & 1:30pm–5:30pm Tue–Sun. 🖼 ⚹

Since 1999, the Tile Museum has been housed in a restored 15th-century soup kitchen (imaret) located behind the Great Mosque (Ulu Camii). This is one of Turkey's most attractive small museums. The displays focus on tiles, vases, ewers and decorative porcelainware produced in the town from the 14th century to the present, and are arranged around a typical ornamental pool (şadırvan).

Restored mosque soup kitchen, now housing the Kütahya Tile Museum

C Great Mosque

Ulu Camii
End of Cumhuriyet Cad, Börekciler
Mahallesi. ○ daily, except at prayer
times. 🎫 donation.

This is the biggest mosque in
Kütahya, but not the oldest.
Building started under Sultan
Yıldırım Beyazıt early in the
15th century, but it was not
finished until the time of
Mehmet II (1451–81). Many
of the marble columns come
from Aezani (see p257). The
Sakahanesi (watersellers'
square) near the mosque is a
popular local gathering place.

🏛 Bazaars

○ 9am–6pm Mon–Sat.

Kütayha's bazaars occupy two
buildings. The Grand Market
(Büyük Bedesten) was built in
the 14th century and stands
on Çemberciler Caddesi. The
15th-century Small Market
(Küçük Bedesten) is just next

Spices and pulses for sale outside the
Grand Market

Interior of the Great Mosque
showing the women's balcony

to it on Kavafiye Sokak (Shoe-
maker's Street). Don't miss the
vaulted ceilings. Today, the
bazaars sell chiefly vegetables
and second-hand goods. More
specialized traders overflow
into the surrounding streets.

🏛 Kütahya Archaeology Museum

Kütahya Arkeoloji Müzesi
Gediz Cad, Börekciler Mahallesi.
Tel (0274) 224 07 85. ○ 9am–1pm
& 1:30–5:30pm Tue–Sun. 🎫

Adjoining the Great Mosque,
the museum is housed in the
mosque's former seminary,
the Vacidiye Medresesi, built
in 1314 by a local ruling clan.
The museum was restored in

1999, and its centrepiece is a
stunningly beautiful Amazon
tomb dating from the 2nd
century AD, found at Aezani
in 1990. The displays also
include fossils, Phrygian
terracotta toys, Roman glass
and sculptures and delicate
earthenware figurines.

🏛 Historic Kütahya Manor Houses

Tarihi Kütahya Konakları
The town's spacious period
houses date mainly from the
18th and 19th centuries. All
are derelict and so only the
exteriors can be seen. They
usually have three storeys,
projecting balconies and front
and back entrances. Look
near the Ulu Camii on Ahi
Erbasan Sokak (in Gazi Kemal
Mahallesi) and Germiyan
Sokak for typical examples.

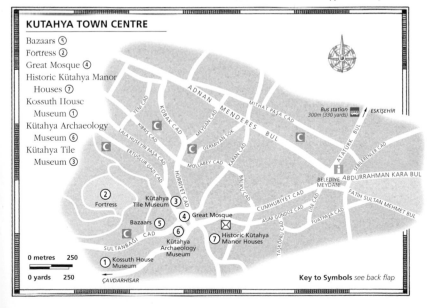

KUTAHYA TOWN CENTRE

Bazaars ⑤
Fortress ②
Great Mosque ④
Historic Kütahya Manor
   Houses ⑦
Kossuth House
   Museum ①
Kütahya Archaeology
   Museum ⑥
Kütahya Tile
   Museum ③

0 metres 250
0 yards 250

Bus station
300m (330 yards) / ESKİŞEHİR

Key to Symbols see back flap

THE BLACK SEA

Although it is the least visited part of Turkey, the Black Sea region is one of the loveliest, most scenic and culturally authentic areas of the country. Take some time to explore the hidden treasures of this diverse region, which include the beautiful ports of Amasra and Sinop, the historic coastal city of Trabzon, and Safranbolu, a gem of Ottoman architecture and a UNESCO World Heritage Site.

Until the 1920s, the Black Sea coast was strongly influenced by Greek culture. Its major city, Trabzon, was once capital of a Byzantine state ruled by the Comnene family. The Genoese and Venetians were also active along the coast, as can be seen from the many ruined castles.

For travellers with an interest in religion and history, the region has many Christian sites to explore. Chief among these are Trabzon's church of Haghia Sophia and the Sumela Monastery, as well as the Georgian churches and monasteries in the Artvin area.

This is Turkey's wettest region, and the climate is moist and moderate even in summer. From the coastal highway, the coastal plain rises to lush tea and hazelnut plantations, virgin forests and the Pontic mountain ranges, which form an almost unbroken barrier. The peaks around Çamlıhemşin attract trekkers and mountaineers from all over the world.

The local people are down-to-earth and industrious. Smallholdings are common, and many of the owners have retained their Caucasian origins and traditions. Temel and İdris are popular Black Sea boys' names. Temel is Turkey's archetypal slow learner, and is often the butt of jokes.

A Black Sea sardine known as *hamsi* is the symbol of the region and the nickname for its people.

The centre of Trabzon, around the historic castle

◁ Mosque on the shore of Uzungöl, a glacial lake in the foothills of the Pontic Mountains

Exploring the Black Sea

With its mild, damp climate, the Black Sea region is suitable to visit all year round. The best time to go is in springtime, when the mountain valleys are carpeted with wild flowers. The high peaks of the coastal mountains are known for their luxuriant pine forests, alpine lakes and racing rivers which descend to the coastal plain. In the extreme northeast, the Kaçkar range is the highest of the Pontic mountain chain, which defines the region. These mountainous areas receive heavy snowfalls in winter.

Safranbolu and Sumela Monastery are the outstanding sights of the region. There are many villages where locals still practise Ottoman-era crafts: Devrek, for example, is renowned for its decorative wooden canes.

Picturesque Amasra, built on a rocky promontory

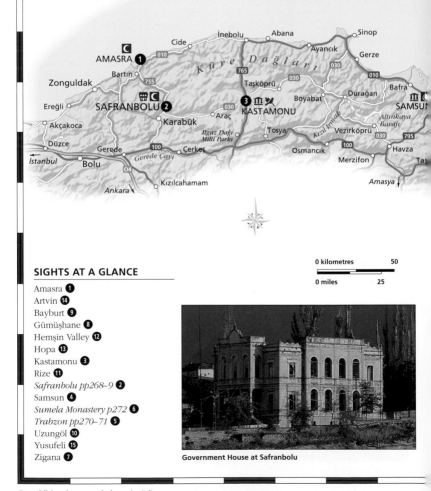

SIGHTS AT A GLANCE

Amasra ❶
Artvin ⑭
Bayburt ❾
Gümüşhane ❽
Hemşin Valley ⑫
Hopa ⑬
Kastamonu ❸
Rize ⑪
Safranbolu pp268–9 ❷
Samsun ❹
Sumela Monastery p272 ❻
Trabzon pp270–71 ❺
Uzungöl ⑩
Yusufeli ⑮
Zigana ❼

0 kilometres   50

0 miles   25

Government House at Safranbolu

GETTING AROUND

Renting a car, or even a four-wheel-drive vehicle, is probably the best way to see the Black Sea coast. This option offers the flexibility to explore minor roads and lanes. Take the central highway only when necessary, or risk missing much of what the region has to offer.

Samsun and Trabzon are both served by non-stop flights from Istanbul and Ankara. Intercity buses run daily, or more frequently, to the major centres. Otherwise, visitors must rely on local minibuses, erratic dolmuşes or foot. Take walking shoes and rain gear in any season. Don't expect to find the same sophisticated, scheduled transport as in other parts of Turkey. But if you are adventurous and flexible, a Black Sea journey will be highly rewarding.

Breathtaking Sumela Monastery

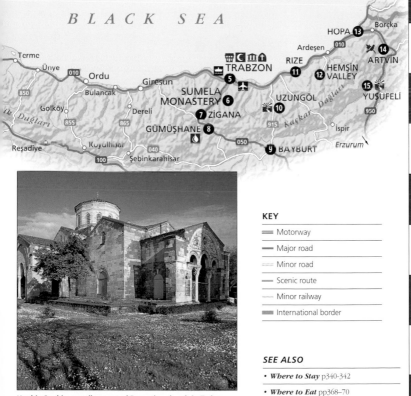

BLACK SEA

HOPA **13**
Borçka
Ardeşen **14**
010
ARTVİN
RİZE **11**
TRABZON
5
HEMŞİN **12** VALLEY
15
YUSUFELİ
Terme
Ünye
010
Ordu
Giresun
Bulancak
SUMELA MONASTERY **6**
UZUNGÖL
10
950
850
Gölköy
Dereli
7 ZİGANA
915
Kaçkar Dağları
Dağları
855
865
GÜMÜŞHANE **8**
İspir
Reşadiye
Koyulhisar
040
050
9 BAYBURT
Erzurum
100
Şebinkarahisar

Haghia Sophia, a well preserved Byzantine church in Trabzon

KEY

▬▬ Motorway

▬▬ Major road

═══ Minor road

─── Scenic route

──── Minor railway

▬▬ International border

SEE ALSO

- *Where to Stay* p340–342
- *Where to Eat* pp368–70

The small harbour at Amasra, with its Roman bridge and watch tower

Amasra **❶**

🏛 8,200. 🚌 Atatürk Meydanı. ℹ️
Büyük Liman Cad, (0378) 315 12 19.

The picturesque and tranquil
town of Amasra is located
about 15 km (9 miles) from
Bartın. In the 6th century BC,
Amasra was called Sesamus,
and its inhabitants were
known as Megara. By the
9th century, Amasra was of
sufficient importance to be
designated a bishopric. It was
destroyed by Arab raiders,
and then rebuilt in the 12th
century by the Genoese.
They recognized the trading
advantages that Amasra could
give them and rented the
castle and harbour from the
Byzantines. The two fortresses
built by the Genoese during
the 14th century can still be
seen today. One
overlooks the
main harbour
and the other
– no more than
the remains of a
small tower – sits
at the harbour
mouth. Amasra
came under Otto-
man rule in 1460.

   Interesting places
to see in the town include the
Fatih Mosque, a former
Byzantine church, and the
19th-century **İskele Mosque**.
Some portions of the
Byzantine city walls are still
standing, as is a Roman
bridge in the harbour.

**Carved wooden
implements, Amasra**

🏛 **Fatih Mosque**
In the town centre. ◯ daily (except
during prayer times).

🏛 **İskele Mosque**
On the harbour. ◯ daily (except
during prayer times).

Safranbolu **❷**

See pp268–9.

Kastamonu **❸**

🏛 60,000. 🚌 10 min walk N of
town centre. ℹ️ Nasrullah Meydanı,
(0366) 212 01 62. 🔄 Wed & Sat.
🎭 Atatürk Hat Festival (23–30 Aug),
Garlic Festival (1st week Sep).
🔴 near Daday at Çömlekciler.

Kastamonu is well known for
outdoor activities as well as
for crafts. The
pastures of
nearby
Daday offer
some of the
very finest
trail riding in
all of Turkey.
The local women
are famed for hand-
printed tablecloths
and upholstery
fabrics made from cotton and
flax. Other specialities of the
area include colourful knitted
wool socks and fruit jams.

   During the 11th century,
Kastamonu was controlled
by the powerful Comnene
family, rulers of Trabzon (see
pp270–71). Indeed, the
town's name probably comes
from Castra Comneni (Latin
for "camp of the Comnenes").

   The town fell under Ottoman
rule in 1459. During this era,
the region around Kastamonu
produced rice, iron, cotton
fabrics and mohair, mostly for
export. Kastamonu Castle was
built by the Byzantines in the
12th century and was kept in
good repair by the Seljuks
and Ottomans. Today, its
remains serve as a fire tower
and lookout point.

   Displays at the Kastamonu
Ethnographic Museum
include Byzantine and Greek
mementos and 17th-century
agricultural tools. There is a
library on the first floor and
a coin display. The building
itself is of historic importance,
for it was here on 25 August
1925 that Atatürk delivered a
famous speech forbidding the
wearing of the fez (the old-
fashioned conical felt hat).

   The **Archaeology Museum**
displays finds from Byzantine
and Ottoman times, and has a
room that commemorates
Atatürk's 1925 visit to the town.

   The town's main mosques
are the Atabey Mosque
(uphill, behind the Aşir Efendi
Han shopping centre), with
its 40 wooden pillars and
stone door, and the İbni
Meccar Mosque, built in 1353
by the Çandaroğulları family.
This lovely mosque in stone
and wood is also known as
Eli güzel ("beautiful hand").

Mahmut Bey Mosque, containing a beautiful wooden interior

🏛 Ethnographic Museum
Hepkebirler Mah, Sakarya Cad. **Tel** (0366) 214 01 49. ⬤ 9am–noon & 1pm–5:30pm Tue–Sun. ♿

🏛 Archaeology Museum
İsfendiyarbey Mahallesi, Cumhuriyet Cad 6. **Tel** (0366) 214 10 70. ⬤ 9am–noon & 1pm–5:30pm Tue–Sun. ♿

Environs
The Mahmut Bey Mosque is located some 17 km (10 miles) northwest of Kastamonu in the village of Kasaba. For a small donation, the local *imam* (Muslim priest) will open the mosque. Inside the well-preserved building are some beautiful paintings and fine calligraphy.

Cide, Abana and İnebolu are all easy day trips from Kastamonu. Cide is a pretty, unspoiled fishing village, and Abana is renowned for its fish restaurants and good, clean swimming. İnebolu has some well-preserved houses.

About 63 km (39 miles) south of Kastamonu is **Ilgaz Mountain National Park**, reachable by dolmuş or your own transport. Visitors to the park can see bears, foxes and deer. There is also a deer breeding and research station. This area offers excellent skiing from November until March. A culinary speciality here is whole lamb, cooked *tandır* style (in a wood-fired clay oven) for four to five hours until the meat falls off the bone. The dish is tradition-ally eaten with the fingers.

🦌 Ilgaz Mountain National Park
Tel (0336) 212 58 71. ⬤ all year. ♿ for vehicles.

Samsun ❹

🏯 355,000. 🚉 Yaşar Doğu Spor Salonu, (0362) 431 12 28. 🚌 from Ankara to Atatürk Bulvarı, (0362) 445 15 82. 🚌 Yeni Garajlar 1, (0362) 238 11 70. ✈ direct from Ankara or Istanbul; 8 km (5 miles) from Samsun on the Amasya road. 🚢 from Istanbul (30 hrs). 🎉 Samsun Fair (Jul), Akdağı Annual Summer Migration Festival "Hıdrellez" (Jun or Jul depending on weather). 🛒 Sat.

Apart from producing a popular cigarette brand, Samsun also holds a proud place in Turkish hearts as the place where Atatürk came after his escape from Istanbul on 19 May 1919, to draw up plans for a Turkish republic. Today, this anniversary is celebrated as a national holiday, Youth and Sports Day.

Samsun has two good museums devoted to the revered memory of Atatürk and his legacy. The **Gazi Museum** occupies a former hotel where he stayed in 1919 and the **Atatürk Museum** has displays of his clothing, various personal items and a collection of photographs.

The **Archaeological and Ethnographic Museum** is a treasure-trove of antiquities from the surrounding villages. It has Bronze-Age artifacts as well as ceramics, bronze and brass implements, glass and mosaics dating from the Hittite, Hellenic, Roman and Byzantine eras. There is also

some beautiful gold and silver jewellery, as well as several fine, hand-written books and hand-woven kilims.

About 80 km (50 miles) southwest of Samsun in the **Havza** district are a number of thermal springs *(kaplıca)* that are very popular.

🏛 Gazi Museum
Tel (0362) 431 75 35. ⬤ 9am–noon & 1pm–5:30pm Tue–Sun. ♿

🏛 Atatürk Museum
Tel (0362) 435 75 35. ⬤ 9am–noon & 1pm–5:30pm. ♿

🏛 Archaeological and Ethnographic Museum
Cumhuriyet Meydanı. **Tel** (0362) 431 68 28. ⬤ 9am–noon & 1–5:30pm Tue–Sun. ♿

Atatürk and aides, Atatürk Museum

Environs
Near Bafra, about 40 km (25 miles) northwest of Samsun, excavations at a site called İkiztepe (twin hills) have revealed early Hittite bronze finds. The bronze items have been removed, but the site is open and there is no entrance fee. Hittite copper and bronze artifacts have also been uncovered at Dündartepe, 3 km (2 miles) outside Samsun, where excavations continue.

Men's section at a thermal spring in the Havza area

Traditional Ottoman architecture in Safranbolu ▷

Street-by-Street: Safranbolu ❷

Finely carved fountain (çeşme)

Safranbolu's market area, a warren of narrow streets and merchant shops, has many restored Ottoman dwellings *(see p31)*. Because of its important architectural heritage, Safranbolu has been declared a World Heritage Site.

In Ottoman times, the town lay on a major trade route. Its many handsome three-storey stone-and-timber *konaks* (mansions) were erected by wealthy merchants and craftsmen. In summer they lived in the cool Bağlar district, and in winter they moved down to the more sheltered Çarşı (bazaar) quarter around the Kazdağı Mosque.

Köprülü Mehmet Paşa Mosque
The mosque, located near the massive Cinci Hanı, opened for worship in 1661.

★ Cinci Hanı
The 350-year-old Cinci Hanı, a refuge for travelling merchants and now a hotel, gives a good idea of the scale of commerce centuries ago.

Kastamonu

CİNCİ HANI

ŞEKERCİLER SOKAK

YUKARI ÇARŞI SOKAK

ARA

The Covered Way
was formerly used by cobblers and shoemakers.

Cinci Hamamı
is a 17th-century Turkish bath still in use today.

★ Kazdağı Mosque
Located in the main square, the mosque was built in 1779.

Kiranköy

STAR SIGHTS

★ Cebeciler Konak

★ Cinci Hanı

★ Kazdağı Mosque

KEY

- - - Suggested route

Sundial
An interesting sundial occupies the shady courtyard of the Köprülü Mehmet Paşa Mosque.

VISITORS' CHECKLIST

🏠 23,500. ✈ 10 km (6 miles) SW of town centre in Karabük. 🚆 in Karabük. ℹ Arasta Çarşısı 7, (0370) 712 38 63. 🛍 Sat. www.safranbolu.gov.tr

Shoemakers' Street
The name of this street recalls a local craft. During World War I the town made boots for the Ottoman army.

Grain Market

KUNDURACILAR SOKAK

ESKİ HAMAM SOKAK

ÇEBİCİ SOKAK

ARASTA SOKAK

MÜTFÜSÖSÖKAK

★ Cebeciler Konak
The upper storey of the Cebeciler Konak shows typical wooden shutters and stencilled wall decorations made with natural dyes.

The Tourism Information Office is in the *Arasta* (market) area.

Market Street
Restored konaks line the narrow Arasta Sokak (Market Street). Some of these old houses have been turned into atmospheric guest houses, complete with authentic decor and furniture.

0 metres 40
0 yards 40

Trabzon ❺

The earliest evidence of civilization in Trabzon dates from 7000 BC. Established as a Greek colony (with Amasra and Sinop), the town benefited from its position on the busy trade route between the Black Sea and the Mediterranean. It grew quickly and was a focal point for the Pontic kings.

Fresco, Gülbahar Mosque and Tomb

At the beginning of the 13th century, the Comnene dynasty established a Byzantine state with its capital at Trabzon. During the Comnene era, the city gained a reputation as a beautiful, sophisticated cultural centre. The Genoese and the Venetians came here to trade, as Trabzon was the terminus of a northern branch of the Silk Route. In 1461, Trabzon fell under Ottoman rule.

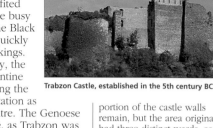

Trabzon Castle, established in the 5th century BC

🏛 Church and Museum of Haghia Sophia
Aya Sophia Müzesi
Follow İnönü Cad. *Tel (0462) 223 30 43.* ◯ *8am–noon & 1–5:30pm Tue–Sun (8:30am–noon & 1–5:30pm Tue–Sun in winter).* 🏷 📷 📱
This restored 13th-century Byzantine church situated just a few kilometres from the city centre, is by far the most impressive sight in Trabzon. It was originally built by the Comnene emperor, Manuel VII Palaeologus. In 1577, it reverted to a mosque and, after serving as an ammunition depot and as a hospital, became a museum in 1957. The interior frescoes depicting scenes from the Old Testament are among the finest in Turkey. The patterned mosaics date from Byzantine times, and you can still see the original coloured marble covering of the floor. Restoration work on the old frescoes is intermittent.

🏛 St Anne's Church
Küçük Ayvasıl Kilisesi
Kahraman Maraş Cad.
An Armenian church built in the 9th century, St Anne's has a beautiful exterior and the entrance is adorned with crucifixes and angels. With advance notice to the Tourism office, groups are allowed inside to view the interior. Another Armenian church, St Basil's (Büyük Ayvasil), is also located nearby.

🏯 Trabzon Castle
Trabzon Kalesi
İç Kale Sok.
The castle is located on the flat-topped hill (*trapezus* in Greek) that gave Trabzon its name. Today, only a small portion of the castle walls remain, but the area originally had three distinct wards, each with its own mosque. The only one still standing is the Fatih Camii in the Ortahisar (middle castle) section. Before it became a mosque, this was the principal church of the Comnene dynasty and its dome was topped with gold. Sadly, the gold, like the mosaics and frescoes inside, is long gone.

🏯 Zağnos Bridge and Tower
Zağnos Köprüsü ve Kale Kule
Zağnos Cad.
Built in 1467, the Zağnos Bridge crosses the Kuzgun ravine. In Ottoman times, the bridge provided access to charitable institutions. The Zağnos Tower was formerly a much-feared prison. Today, there is little reminder of its grim past, and visitors can tour the site and enjoy a meal at the tower restaurant.

🅲 Gülbahar Mosque and Tomb
Gülbahar Hatun Camii
Tanjant Yolu. ◯ *except during prayer times.*
Built in 1514 by Sultan Selim the Grim in memory of his mother, Gülbahar, this is one of the few mosques in the city that was not originally a church. Gülbahar was noted for her charity work, and the mosque was built as part of an *imaret*, an Ottoman social welfare institution consisting of a soup kitchen and hostel for students and the poor. The main place of worship was the black-and-white stone section, with its five cupolas. The mosque is all that remains of

Fresco in Haghia Sophia, showing the Last Supper

St Eugenius Church, turned into a mosque in 1461

the complex. Just to the east is Gülbahar's octagonal tomb.

🏠 St Eugenius Church

Yeni Cuma Camii
Follow signs from Fatih Hamami on Kasım Sok. ◯ 9am–5pm.
In the 14th century, this was the Church of St Eugenius, named for the martyred 5th-century archbishop of Carthage. In Ottoman times, the church became a mosque.

🏛 Trabzon Museum

Uzun Sok, Zeytinlik Cad 10.
Tel (0462) 322 38 22. ◯ 9am–noon & 1–5:30pm Tue–Sun. 🍽
Trabzon Museum occupies a mansion built in the late 19th century for a Greek banker. The finely restored house is decorated in Baroque style and contains displays of local archaeology and ethnography.

Environs

A few kilometres outside the centre of the city is **Atatürk's Villa**, an ornate three-storey mansion where Atatürk stayed several times after 1924. It was here that he made his will in 1937, the year before his death. The house was built in 1903, and is a typical example of upper-class Crimean architecture. The city of Trabzon presented it to Atatürk, and he left it to his sister, Makbule Atakan, at his death. The interior has been left almost undisturbed.

🏠 Atatürk's Villa

Atatürkün Köşkü
Soğuksu Cad, 4 km (2.4 miles) SW of city centre. **Tel** (0462) 231 00 28. ◯ 8:30am–4:30pm daily. 📷 on inquiry at the entrance. 🍽

Atatürk's Villa, a handsome early 20th-century mansion

TRABZON CITY CENTRE

Church and Museum of Haghia Sophia ①
Gülbahar Mosque and Tomb ⑤
St Anne's Church ②
St Eugenius Church ⑥

Trabzon Castle ③
Trabzon Museum ⑦
Zağnos Bridge and Tower ④

Key to Symbols see back flap

Sumela Monastery 6
Sümela Manastırı

Monastery entrance

Sumela Monastery sits high up on the cliffs of Mt Mela, southeast of Trabzon. It was founded in the 4th century by two Greek monks, Barnabas and Sophronius, who were guided to the site by an icon of a "black" image of the Virgin, allegedly painted by St Luke. After their deaths, Sumela became a place of pilgrimage. It was decorated with frescoes, and its treasures included priceless manuscripts and silver plates. The monastery was rebuilt several times – the ruins seen by today's visitors date largely from the 19th century.

In the Ottoman era, Sumela enjoyed the protection of the sultans, but it was abandoned and badly damaged during the War of Independence. Extensive restoration work has been carried out to preserve the monastery.

VISITORS' CHECKLIST

55 km (34 miles) SE of Trabzon in
Altındere National Park.
Tel (0462) 230 19 66 (lower
entrance) and (0462) 531 10 64
(upper entrance). ☐ May–Oct:
8am–6pm daily; Nov–Apr: 9am–
3pm daily. ▨ ▢ ▯

★ Frescoes
*Though badly
damaged by
vandals, lovely
fresco panels
cover the walls
of the church.*

Restoration
*A fire in the 1920s left
many of the monastery
buildings roofless and
exposed to the elements.
Restoration work involves
rebuilding the roof trusses
and adding tiles.*

★ Living Quarters
*The cells used by the
Greek Orthodox
monks are ranged
along the five-storey
outside building
overlooking the
Altındere valley.*

Forest Path
*A 1 km (0.5 mile)
path winds through
pine forest to the
often mist-shrouded
monastery. It takes
30 minutes to make
the ascent.*

STAR FEATURES

★ Frescoes

★ Living Quarters

Zigana ❼

🎭 *Kadırga Festival: migration to high pastures and nomadic origins (usually held in spring and summer).*

After visiting the Sumela Monastery, travellers can return to Trabzon or continue further southwest to reach the spectacular alpine area known as Zigana and situated in the Kalkanlı Mountains. There is some skiing here, but only day trips are possible as there are no hotels.

Fog and snow cover the Zigana area for about seven months of the year, and it is usually damp here. Heavy winter snowfalls make access difficult and even dangerous.

To get to Zigana, you can drive through the 1,500 m (4,291 ft) mountain tunnel, the longest in Turkey.

A more challenging, but much more scenic route runs parallel to the main 885 road through Hamsiköy village. It is worth stopping here to sample the excellent local cuisine. The speciality is a nourishing, creamy rice pudding.

Gümüşhane ❽

🏛 37,500. ℹ *Valilik Binası, Kat 4, (0456) 213 10 07.*

Gümüşhane (silver works) takes its name from the rich deposits of silver ore found here. In the late 16th century, silver was more valuable than gold. However, by the late 19th century, the silver industry had declined.

Before World War I, the area was a focus of conflict between the Russians and the

A ruined Byzantine church in the old section of Gümüşhane

The Çoruh River, running through the fortress town of Bayburt

Ottomans, for Gümüşhane occupied a strategic position on the trade route between Anatolia and Persia (Iran).

Here, visitors can explore the surrounding castles, and several mosques. The most interesting of these is the Süleymaniye (or Küçük) Camii. There are also eight *hamams* (Turkish baths), which cater for men and women.

Gümüşhane is renowned for its rosehip *(kuşburun)* syrup and sweet cherry jam *(kiraz reçeli)*.

Wild poppy near Bayburt

Bayburt ❾

🏛 38,000. ℹ *Hükümet Binası, Kat 4, (0458) 211 44 29.* 🏛 Mon. 🎭 *Dedekorkut Cultural Festival (2nd week in Jul).*

Situated on the Çoruh River, Bayburt is the capital of the smallest of Turkey's 78 provinces. Bayburt Castle was probably built in Byzantine times, but there is evidence of an older fortress on the site.

The castle has a violent history. It had to be rebuilt by the Byzantine Emperor Justinian and was repaired by both Seljuks and Ottomans

following various attacks. At its peak, there were 300 houses within the complex. Provision for daily needs included a bakery and flour mill. The community even produced its own paint.

Today, visitors can see a theological school, a mosque, *hamams* and kitchens, as well as a dervish lodge. The eastern corner contains the remains of a church built between the 8th and 14th centuries.

On the hills at the southern edge of the city stand the twin mausoleums of Şehit (martyr) Osman and his sister. Osman Park, beside the river, is a good place to relax and enjoy a glass of tea.

About 20 km (12 miles) northwest of Bayburt are the remains of underground cities dating from Byzantine times. These are usually open to visitors. For details, inquire at the tea garden at the entrance or at the tourism office in the town centre.

Outside Bayburt, on the way to Aşkale and Erzurum, travellers must negotiate a spectacular mountain pass which rises to the dizzying height of 2,302 m (7,552 ft).

Village on the shores of Uzungöl (Long Lake)

Uzungöl ❿

🚌 *tour bus from Trabzon or dolmuş from Of (90 min); dolmuşes are less frequent in the winter months.*

For mountain scenery, few places in Turkey compare with this alpine lake, which was carved out during the Ice Ages. At an altitude of over 1,000 m (3,280 ft), Uzungöl (Long Lake) is a hidden gem surrounded by lush greenery and remote meadows.

At weekends, Uzungöl is popular with local people, who journey here by dolmuş from the coastal village, Of, but there is not much to do besides camping, hiking in the nearby hills, fishing and relaxing. The village has a few basic hotels, and the local lake trout is excellent.

Rize ⓫

🏙 *72,000.* 🚉 *0.8 km (0.5 mile) west of town.* ℹ️ *Valilik Binası, A Blok, Kat 5, (0464) 213 04 07.* 🅿️ *Russian bazaar daily.* 🎪 *Tea Festival (3rd week Jun).*

In ancient times, Rize was ruled by the Pontic kings *(see p298)* and was known as Rhizus. The name means rice, although the town is now better known for its tea.

Rize was strongly fortified by the Byzantines in the 6th century and later became part of the Comnene empire. Like Trabzon, it came under Ottoman control in 1461.

In Ottoman times, many people left Rize to seek work in Russia. There they learned the art of bread- and pastry-

making, which they brought back with them when they returned. Today, many of Turkey's master pastry chefs and bakers come from Rize.

Visitors will notice many locals clad in the versatile *Rize bezi*, a light cloth made of silk, cotton or wool, in black and purple. It is mainly used as a head covering for women, but also doubles as a useful rain bonnet and a handy receptacle when the local women go out to gather tea leaves.

The small **Rize Museum** is not outstanding, but has some displays of local life and lore.

🏛 **Rize Museum**
Piri Çelebi Mahellesi, PTT Arkası.
Tel (0464) 214 02 35. ⏰ *9am–noon & 1–5:30pm Tue–Sun.* 📷

Corn bread, Hemşin Valley

Hemşin Valley ⓬

42 km (26 miles) E of Rize.

East of Rize, the road turns off to the Hemşin Valley. About 20 km (12 miles) further east a second turning goes to Çamlıhemşin. The road rises steeply and the air is filled with the smell of boxwood trees. This area lies deep within the Kaçkar Mountains (Kaçkar Dağları), at an altitude of 3,932 m (12,900 ft).

Continue on the same road signposted to Ayder, famous for its hot springs. The local inhabitants, the Hemşin, were once Christian Armenians who converted to Islam. They delight in their seasonal festivals, folklore traditions, and distinctive ethnic costumes.

A staple food of the valley is *mıhlama* (corn bread), that is served hot from the baking pan. Sometimes, *lor* (white, unsalted cheese) is served alongside *mıhlama* as a breakfast dish.

There are two castles near Çamlıhemşin. One is Kale-i Bala, above the village of Hisarcık Köyü, dating from 200 BC. Further up the valley is the lonely Zilkalesi (Bell Castle) with eight ramparts overlooking the valley of the Storm River (Fırtına Çayı).

TURKISH TEA

Turkey's first tea plants were brought from Japan in 1878, but the industry did not take off until the 1930s. The moist climate of the Black Sea coast provides superb growing conditions. Rize is the centre of the Turkish tea industry, and the home of the country's Tea Institute (Çay Enstitüsü). To sample the best tea, look for *tomurcuk* (the flowering bud of the tea bush). Leaves from other parts of the plant are not as flavourful. Turks prefer the black tea sold in local markets; green tea is exported. Specialized fragrant teas are also produced, again mostly for export. Glasses, spoons, sugar and some good company are all part of enjoying Turkish tea, which is brewed in a double boiler. The leaves are scalded before brewing to impart an earthy, smoky flavour.

Turkish tea served in a typical "tulip" glass

Roads and driving in general are a challenge in the Hemşin Valley's short summer season. A four-wheel-drive vehicle is recommended, as local dolmuş transport can be daily, not hourly.

Because of the vertical valleys, local people have devised an ingenious transport solution: the *vargel*, a cable car on a pulley system. It is powered by electricity (or people power, if no electricity is available). It is a quaint solution, which offers a bird's eye view of the isolated gorges.

Bulls fighting at the Kafkasör Festival in Artvin

Russian dolls for sale in Hopa, near the Georgian border

Hopa ⓭

on W bank of river

Hopa is the last main town before the frontier with Georgia. It is a garrison town, and there is a strong military presence. Hopa was a major port in ancient times, and is still the main seaport (after Trabzon) on the eastern Black Sea coast. Today, the town is dominated by the boat-building industry and a large thermal power station.

Artvin ⓮

25,000. Katliotopark Binası, Kat 3, (0466) 212 30 71. Kafkasör Festival (Jun). www.artvin.gov.tr

Artvin receives more rain than any other place in Turkey, so everything grows wonderfully here. The people of Artvin are known for their many festivals, which feature traditional dancing, games, music, food and costumes. The major annual celebration is the Kafkasör (Caucasian) Festival in June, featuring the spectacle of fighting bulls.

Around Artvin are a number of beautiful villages. Şavşat, about 55 km (34 miles) to the east on the road to Ardahan, is a lovely alpine hamlet. The road goes on to Veliköy and, 19 km (11 miles) further on, reaches the **Karagöl-Sahara National Park**, which has extensive forests and lakes.

Environs
The natural beauty of the north-eastern reaches of the Çoruh Valley around Artvin had once only been visited by more adventurous travellers. Conservation groups, like TEMA Tours, offer visitors rustic accommodation and ecological tours that support the dwindling lifestyles of the region. For more details see www.biyotematur.com

🦌 Karagöl-Sahara National Park
Tel (0466) 531 21 37. ◯ May–Oct daily. 🚗 for cars only. 🏕

Yusufeli ⓯

68 km (42 miles) S of Artvin or 150 km (93 miles) NE of Bayburt (difficult route). 4,000.

Yusufeli is a nature-lover's paradise, with some of the most rugged scenery in Turkey. As it is a designated conservation area, hunting is strictly controlled and many wild species are protected.

Yusufeli is becoming well known for whitewater rafting *(see p384)* on the challenging Çoruh River. The best time to go is in spring when the wild flowers are in bloom. There are outstanding opportunities for photography, particularly around the deep, icy lakes.

Around Yusufeli, there are many Georgian and Armenian churches and out-of-the-way castles. Dört Kilise (Four Churches) is a few kilometres southwest of the town, while İşhan is a superb 11th-century church in the mountains east of Yusufeli off the main road (signposted to Olur). A track leads to the church.

The churning waters of the spectacular Çoruh River

CAPPADOCIA AND CENTRAL ANATOLIA

entral Anatolia is one of Turkey's few completely landlocked regions. The ancient cities of Boğazkale and Alacahöyük reveal the Hittite presence in this area during the 1st and 2nd millennia BC. Most of the artifacts from these places are now housed in museums, but visitors can imagine the impact and extent of the impressive civilization that once flourished in the region.

In the ancient Persian language, Cappadocia meant "land of beautiful horses", and in Roman times, brood mares from Cappadocia were so highly prized that a special tax was imposed on their sale.

Trying to describe Cappadocia in physical terms simply does not do justice to the air of mystery that pervades the area. Remarkable conical rock outcrops, called peri bacaları (fairy chimneys), are the region's most famous and characteristic feature. Carved into the rock are scores of hidden chapels adorned with exquisite frescoes – ample proof of the strength of the Christian faith that was established here by the 4th century AD.

Over the centuries, Central Anatolia has nurtured vast armies and great empires, and its history and prosperity have always been linked to the land and agriculture. Today, tourism has become the mainstay of the local economy, but the region still produces many of Turkey's cereal crops as well as grapes, vegetable oils and sugar beets. The diary of a 4th-century saint even records wine as a local product.

Kayseri, the major city, is known as much for its many varieties of cured beef (pastırma) as for its industrious but conservative inhabitants. A gentler side of the region is to be found near Amasya along the picturesque Yeşilırmak River.

Konaks (mansion houses) along the bank of the Yeşilırmak River

◁ **"Fairy chimneys" with caps, in the vicinity of Ürgüp**

Exploring Cappadocia and Central Anatolia

The majestic jewel of Central Anatolia is the Cappadocia region, a bewitching landscape of spectacularly eroded tuff (hardened volcanic ash). Mount Erciyes (Erciyes Dağı), an extinct volcano, looms over this haunting panorama. Volcanic deposits have made this a fertile area for agriculture, with grapes, apricots, cherries, sugar beets and chickpeas grown locally.

The main Hittite sites in Asia Minor are found at Boğazkale and Alacahöyük. Often neglected, Kayseri is a treasure-trove of Seljuk history and should not be missed. The Pontic kings (see p48) once ruled in Amasya, an unspoiled town in the valley of the Yeşilırmak River. The region's varied sights complement the country crafts, such as carpet weaving and the beautiful decorative pottery produced around Avanos.

Uçhisar village, overlooked by cave dwellings

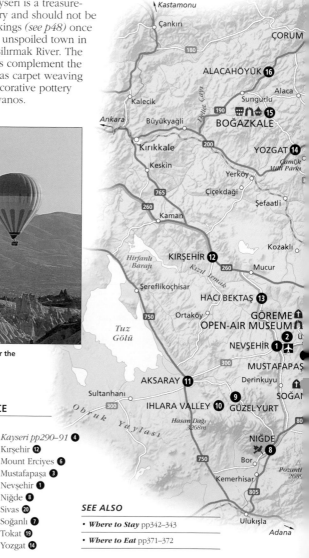

Hot-air balloon drifting over the eroded tuff landscape

SIGHTS AT A GLANCE

SEE ALSO

• **Where to Stay** pp342–343
• **Where to Eat** pp371–372

The King's Gate at Boğazkale, in Hattuşaş National Park

KEY

— Major road

═══ Minor road

— Scenic route

▪▪▪ Main railway

— Minor railway

△ Summit

GETTING AROUND

Kayseri and Nevşehir are both served by intercity buses, as well as regular flights to and from Istanbul. Most of the main sights are a 40–60-minute drive on good paved roads from these centres. Minibuses and dolmuşes run frequently between major tourist attractions, but renting your own vehicle will give you the greatest flexibility. Some sights (even the underground cities) involve quite a bit of walking. Coach tours from centres throughout Turkey serve the region.

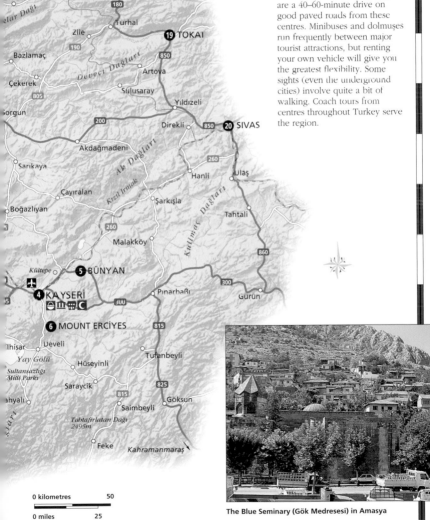

The Blue Seminary (Gök Medresesi) in Amasya

0 kilometres 50

0 miles 25

Rock Formations of Cappadocia

The landscape of Cappadocia was created around 30 million years ago, when erupting volcanoes blanketed the region with ash. The ash solidified into an easily eroded material called tuff, overlain in places by layers of hard volcanic rock. Over time, the tuff was worn away, creating distinctive formations, including the capped-cone "fairy chimneys" near Ürgüp.

Cappadocia covers a relatively small area – around 300 sq km (116 sq miles). It has become a popular area for tourists, and the area around Nevşehir, together with nearby Ürgüp and Göreme *(see pp282–5)*, offer the best opportunities to see the bewitching natural formations for which the region is celebrated.

LOCATOR MAP

☐ *Tuff formations*

Mushroom Shape
This "mushroom" rock, an unusual example of erosion, is located near Gülşehir.

EROSION AND WEATHERING

Cappadocia's extraordinary landscape is partly the result of erosion by water, wind and changes in temperature. Rainfall and rivers wear down the tuff and, like the wind, carry away loose material. In winter, extreme temperature changes cause the rocks to expand and contract and eventually to disintegrate.

Cavities below the hard layer are turned into dwellings.

FAIRY CHIMNEYS

The extraordinary formations pictured below are called "fairy chimneys" because early inhabitants of Cappadocia believed that they were the chimneys of fairies, who lived under the ground. Some of them reach heights of up to 40 m (130 ft).

Complete erosion wears away the protective caps and creates the conical shapes found in the Göreme Valley.

Elongated Shape
These columns are capped with layers of slightly harder material.

Pedestal Shape
Created when a lump of basalt rests atop a tuff column.

Cone Shape
Erosion thins tuff beneath the basalt cap, which then falls off.

Eroded Tuff Field
In the triangle defined by Nevşehir, Ürgüp and Avanos, the tuff layer was originally up to 100 m (328 ft) thick. As the older tuff continues to erode, younger cones are formed. This process has been taking place for around 10 million years.

Lava flows harden into a protective layer over the tuff.

Erosion widens cracks and fissures, separating sections from the main body and allowing for the development of strange shapes.

Underground cities

Cracks in the tuff layers allowed people to hollow out dwellings and churches.

Protective caps give a tubular shape to the eroded formation.

VOLCANOES OF ANATOLIA

Snowcapped Mount Erciyes, 20 km (13 miles) southwest of Kayseri

Volcanic activity in Central Anatolia is a product of the region's position *(see pp18–19)* at the boundaries of two of the tectonic plates that make up the Earth's crust. Mount Erciyes is the largest in a chain of extinct volcanoes created by the collision of the heavy Arabian with the lighter Anatolian Plate. The collision pushed magma to the surface, building up immense pressure and eventually causing Mounts Erciyes, Hasan and others to erupt, spewing forth enormous amounts of rock and lava that greatly altered the landscape of Central Anatolia. The Hittites *(see pp44–5)* worshipped snow-covered Mount Erciyes. They called it "Harkassos" (White Mountain).

Underground Cities
The softness of the tuff made it easy to excavate in order to create dwellings. In some places, as at Derinkuyu (above), whole cities were constructed underground. These settlements had living quarters, stables, wells, ventilation systems, churches and storage rooms.

Nevşehir ❶

Sunflower from the Nevşehir area

As the capital of Cappadocia, Nevşehir makes a very good starting point for touring the region. Known as Nyssa in antiquity, the town has the Kurşunlu Mosque and *medrese (see p32)*, dating from 1725, as well as a castle and a good museum. The surrounding tuff formations and troglodyte (underground) cities are the most popular attractions, but visitors are likely to leave the Nevşehir area with strong memories of sunflowers, chickpeas, donkeys and sugar beets, as well as apricots drying on rooftops. A striking feature of the Nevşehir area is its strong Christian leaning. As early as the 4th century, monks and hermits inhabited Cappadocia.

Passageway in Derinkuyu, showing "millstone" door

Zelve

10 km (6.2 miles) NE of Nevşehir.
⬜ May–Oct: 8:30am–7pm daily;
Nov–Apr: 8:30am–5:30pm daily. 🖼️
A secluded monastic retreat, Zelve lies in a series of deep valleys and is dotted with rooms and caves on many levels. Metal walkways and stairs lead to less accessible chapels and hideaways which hold a few frescoes. In 1950 an earthquake shook the Çavuşin/Zelve area, and the cave dwellings remain somewhat unkempt today. The nature of the site will appeal to the fit and adventurous. Many of the caves and rooms are only accessed by clambering through dark holes and tunnels, so bring a torch and spare batteries.

Two small churches lie on the valley floor: the üzümlü Kilise (Grape Church) and the Balık Kilise (Fish Church), both featuring ornate carvings. The latter is an Ottoman mosque, but with a stone steeple.

Derinkuyu

30 km (18.6 miles) S of Nevşehir.
⬜ May–Oct: 9am–7pm daily;
Nov–Apr: 9am–5pm daily. 🖼️
There are believed to be about 36 underground cities in this region, but only a few have been excavated. Of these, Derinkuyu (deep well) is the biggest, most popular and best lit. It is thought to have been home to around 20,000 people. The eight-level complex is 60 m (197 ft) deep. A long "transit" tunnel

was supposed to have linked Derinkuyu with a similar "ant hill" settlement at Kaymaklı, about 10 km (6 miles) away. At peak times (11am–3pm) the tunnels can get somewhat uncomfortably crowded – anyone who tries to backtrack will be very unpopular.

The first levels include a stable, wine-press and a large vault. Deeper down, there are living quarters, a kitchen and a church.

The heavy millstones recessed into the walls were, in fact, doors that could be rolled into place to seal off strategic areas of the settlement. Huge ventilation shafts still function, but damp is a problem. Living here for any extended period of time could not have been easy.

Spread over three valleys and with many fairy chimneys, Zelve was inhabited until 1952

For hotels and restaurants in this region see pp342–343 and pp371–372

House in Ürgüp dating from the period of Greek habitation

Ürgüp

12km (7 miles) E of Nevşehir.
15,000. Parkı İçi, (0384) 341 40 59. Wine/grape Festival (end Sep, early Oct).

Ürgüp is now so synonymous with the troglodyte cities built during Byzantine times that it is easy to overlook the town's Roman and Seljuk history. Ürgüp's ancient name was Assiana, and it was known as Başhisar under the Seljuks. Seljuk influence can be seen in the 13th-century remains of the Kadıkalesi (castle) and the Altıkapı Tomb. Near the Nükrettin Mausoleum is a library named after Tasinağa, a 19th-century town squire. Until 1923, when Turkey became a republic, the town had a large Greek population.

Ürgüp's **museum** contains ceramics and statues from pre-historic to Byzantine times, as well as displays of textiles, costumes, weapons and books.

Ürgüp is a convenient base to tour Cappadocia. There are plenty of pensions and hotels, yet the town has retained its village charm. This area has always been well known for its farm produce, particularly for grapes. ürgüp-labelled wine is refreshing and light. In general, the white wines are more authentic and interesting than the reds.

Several local spots offer impromptu entertainment in the evenings.

🏛 Museum

Next to tourist office, at park entrance. **Tel** (0384) 341 40 82. 8am–noon & 1–5pm Tue–Sun.

Avanos

16 km (10 miles) NE of Nevşehir.
14,500. Atatürk Cad, (0384) 511 43 60.

Watered by the Kızılırmak (Red River), Avanos is a pretty, leafy town noted for its pottery and ceramics. Carpet-weaving and tapestry-making are equally important local skills.

In Roman times, Avanos was called Venessa. It fell under Ottoman suzerainty in 1466 along with Nevşehir. Today it is a typical country town, albeit with a lack of grand mosques or *medreses*. In the town centre is the Yeraltı (Ulu) Mosque, dating from the 15th century, and the Alaeddin Mosque, built by the Seljuks.

Ceramics and wine are the town's lifeblood. Visitors can purchase many serviceable pottery items, while exquisite porcelain designs are the stock in trade of places like Kaya Seramik Evi. These pieces are thrown by hand, then painted and glazed. The intricate designs are pains-takingly reproduced from the İznik originals *(see p161)*, and even manage to capture the typical milky, opaque porcelain background.

Display of local wine from the Ürgüp area

About 5 km (3 miles) east of Avanos is Sarıhan, a Seljuk *han* or caravanserai *(see p24)* built in 1238 on the classic square plan. The repaired *han* gives a good idea of the accommodation facilities, as well as stables and a small mosque, available to traders making the long trek along the Silk Route *(see pp24–5)*.

Shaping a jug in a pottery workshop in Avanos

Kaymaklı

20 km (12 miles) S of Nevşehir.
May–Oct: 9am–7pm daily; Nov–Apr: 9am–5pm daily.

Discovered in 1964, Kaymaklı is the second most important underground city in the region. It is believed to have housed thousands of people from the 6th to 9th centuries. Although five levels are open to visitors, experts believe Kaymaklı has eight levels. It is unclear when the first floor was originally excavated. The underground area is thought to cover an area of about 2.5 sq km (1 sq mile).

Being smaller and less crowded than many of the region's other underground cities, the rooms and their various functions seem more convincing. To appreciate the area as it was centuries ago, try to get there early.

Göreme Open-Air Museum ②

The Göreme Valley holds the greatest concentration of rock-cut chapels and monasteries in Cappadocia. Dating largely from the 9th century onwards, the valley's 30 or more churches were built out of the soft volcanic tuff. Many of the churches feature superb Byzantine frescoes depicting scenes from the Old and New Testaments, and particularly the life of Christ and deeds of the saints. The cultural importance of the valley has been recognized by the Turkish government and they have restored and preserved the many caves to create the Göreme Open-Air Museum. UNESCO has declared the Göreme Valley a World Heritage Site. A 2006 excavation of tombs uncovered human skeletons.

Tokalı Church
The Tokalı Church, located near the entrance to the museum, contains some of the most beautiful frescoes in the Göreme Valley.

The walking route starts at the car park near the entrance.

★ Kızlar Monastery
Monks lived and worked in this hollowed-out formation. Ladders or scaffolding were probably used to reach the upper levels.

STAR SIGHTS

- ★ Karanlık Church
- ★ Elmalı Church
- ★ Kızlar Monastery

Camel Tours
Portions of the Göreme Valley and surrounding area can be viewed from atop a camel on guided tours.

★ Karanlık Church
A pillared church, built around a small courtyard, the Karanlık Church contains frescoes depicting the ascension of Christ.

Katherina Church

Çarıklı Church

Dining Hall

Yılanlı Church
The barrel-vaulted church has painted panels devoted to a number of saints.

Entrances to Monks' Cells
The southern end of the valley is honeycombed with the tiny cells once occupied by monks.

★ Elmalı Church
Noted for the sophistication of its frescoes, the church dates from the 11th century.

Barbara Church
The church takes its name from a fresco on the west wall, which is thought to depict St Barbara. A seated figure of Christ occupies the central apse. Saints Georgius and Theodorus are depicted killing the dragon.

The Church of Constantine and Helen, in Mustafapaşa

Mustafapaşa ❸

6 km (4 miles) S of Ürgüp.
🏠 *3,800.*

Formerly known as Sinasos, Mustafapaşa is a perfectly preserved Greek village, whose inhabitants left during the exchange of populations between Greece and Turkey in 1923. The houses have a wealth of carved stonework, wall paintings and reminders of the former inhabitants' lifestyles. Although some houses are neglected, the balconies and sculptured windows are sure to delight. Sadly, the 19th-century Church of Constantine and Helen in the town centre

is in a particularly bad state. Of note are the monastery of St Nicholas and the Church of St Basil, the latter located outside the village.

Several pensions and a few hotels have been restored to their former Greek appearance.

Kayseri ❹

See pp290–91.

Bünyan ❺

35 km (22 miles) E of Kayseri.
🏠 *5,780.* 🎪 *Yoghurt Festival (18 May).*

Bünyan lies east of Kayseri, off the main highway to Sivas. This is a good place for a relaxed outing for a few hours or an afternoon, and often features on sightseeing tours to the region.

The economic mainstay of the town is handicrafts, mainly the carpets handwoven by the women. You can see them at work on the looms and learn about the designs and the amount of work involved. A particular feature of carpets from Bünyan is the use of thin, high-tensile mercerized cotton to make bedspreads, floor rugs, and prayer mats. This ensures that the finished carpet always lies flat.

Mount Erciyes ❻
Erciyes Dağı

Mount Erciyes, at a height of 3,916 m (12,848 ft), is Cappadocia's dominant natural landmark. Locals regard this extinct volcano with respect because of its role in shaping the landscape when it buried the area in volcanic dust and ash millions of years ago. The residual tuff – fine-grained, compressed volcanic ash – is the area's major geological feature *(see pp280–81).* The calcium in the tuff enriches the soil, encouraging the growth of trees and vines.

Between the two peaks (Greater and Lesser Erciyes) are two lovely moraine lakes, Cora and Sarı. Mount Erciyes is also a ski centre *(see p384)* with a chairlift and a lodge. The season runs from November to May. Hiking is possible in summer, but you will need a guide and proper gear.

Soğanlı ❼

38 km (24 miles) S of Ürgüp.
🏠 *4,650.* ⏰ *8:30am–5:30pm daily.* 🎟

The main attraction of the Soğanlı Valley is that it is quiet and undisturbed. It is possible, even, to think of this valley as a microcosm of

Pigeon coops cut into the rocks at Soğanlı, marked with white rings to attract the birds

◁ **Troglodyte dwellings in the rock above the village of Uçhisar**

the whole Göreme Valley. There are six interesting churches to visit here, though it is thought that more than 100 flourished at one time. All six are in good condition and can be seen on foot during the course of a day trip.

The delicate, pastel tones of Soğanlı's frescoes differ from the harsher hues to be seen in the churches at Göreme, where ongoing restoration has produced stronger colours.

The distinctive, colourful cloth dolls sold throughout Cappadocia are produced by Soğanlı's handicraft industry.

Niğde ❽

🏘 72,000. 🚌 Emin Eşirgil Cad, 1 km (0.5 mile) from town centre. 🚉 end of İstasyon Cad, 1 km (0.5 mile) from town centre, (0388) 232 35 41. 🛈 Belediye Sarayı, (0388) 232 33 93. 🛍 Women's Handicraft Market (Sat) 🎭 Tepecuması Folklore and Country Festival (27 May).

Known in Hittite times as Nahita, Niğde survived 10th-century Arab raids better than its neighbours. Its position on a major trade route to the Mediterranean appealed to the enterprising Seljuks, and so Niğde flourished as a regional capital until the time of the Mongol invasions (see p53).

White-headed duck

The Seljuks filled the town with fine architecture, notably the Alaeddin Mosque (1223), distinguished by its superb stonework, ornate portal and typical squat minaret, and the Great Mosque (Ulu Camii), which was built around 1335. There is also a Seljuk tomb, the Hüdavend Hatun Türbe, featuring the octagonal forms typical of Seljuk architecture.

Niğde's bazaar (bedesten), with its fine clock tower, is a vestige of the town's heyday. The museum has sections on ethnography and Asian civilizations, and displays the mummified remains of a nun from the Ihlara Valley (see p292).

Do try and taste Niğde's deliciously creamy ewe's milk cheese, which comes "packaged" in a woolly sheepskin. Such local cheeses are called *tulum peynırı*.

Environs
There are several interesting places near Niğde. The best are **Bor**, a carpet-weaving centre that lies 15 km (9 miles) to the southwest, and **Kemerhisar**, which is 20 km (12 miles) to the south. This Hittite site dates from about 1200 BC. At the site, you can see the arches of an aqueduct and a mineral spring.

The Byzantine monastery church at **Eski Gümüş**, about 9 km (6 miles) northeast of Niğde, was restored in the early 1990s and is one of the best-kept secrets in Turkey. The frescoes here are outstanding by any standards.

If you are a mountaineer, the **Aladağlar Mountains** offer some excellent climbing and include Demirkazık, the highest peak in the region. To reach the summit, the best starting point is the village of the same name, which lies 65 km (40 miles) east of Niğde.

To the north-east of Niğde is **Sultansazlığı Bird Sanctuary**, which is considered to be Turkey's most important bird sanctuary after Lake Manyas (Kuşcenneti; see p157). With a

A narrow gorge in the spectacular Aladağlar Mountains, near Niğde

total area of 172 sq km (66 sq miles), the marshes are regarded as some of the largest and most important wetlands in Europe and the Middle East. Since 1993, the area has been protected under the terms of the Ramsar Convention, an agreement signed in Iran in 1971 to conserve wetlands and their resources. The reserve is a haven for around 300 species of bird, including ducks, flamingoes, terns, cranes, egrets and plovers. Partridges, swordbeaks, whimbrels and pelicans all come here to breed. The best bird-watching spot is the lookout at Ovaçiftlik, where there is also a museum.

🦆 Sultansazlığı Bird Sanctuary
70 km (44 miles) SW of Kayseri.
Tel (0352) 658 55 49.
🕐 5am–midnight daily. 🈂

The Sultansazlığı Bird Sanctuary, a bird-watcher's paradise

Kayseri ④

Seljuk stone carving

Dominated by Mount Erciyes, Kayseri has been fought over by Persians, Arabs, Mongols and Ottomans. Its most prosperous era was undoubtedly under the Romans – when it was known as Eusebeia/Mazaka and then Caesarea – but it also flourished under the Seljuks. At the junction of five roads, the city was a key point on the Roman road system, and the Romans established an imperial munitions factory here. By the 4th century Kayseri was a focal point of Christian life and faith. Its most famous cleric (and bishop) was St Basil the Great (around AD 329–379), who defended church doctrine against heretical movements.

Exploring Kayseri

Kayseri was once a prominent centre of education, and has many religious institutions, tombs and mosques to visit. Nowadays, textiles and sugar beet are the main industries, but the city is also known for fine carpets. In addition, the best *sucuk* (salami) in Turkey comes from here and the 20 varieties of *pastırma* (cured beef) are a regional speciality.

C Twin-Turreted Theology Complex

Çifte Medresesi
Sinan Park. **Tel** (0352) 231 35 65.
⏱ 8am–5pm Wed–Sun.
The complex consists of two adjoining theological centres, the Gıyasiye Medresesi and the Şifahiye Medresesi. The Seljuks placed great emphasis on learning – this extended to anatomy and medicine. This was the first Seljuk academy of medicine and is now called the Gevher Nesibe Medical History Museum. Here you can learn more

about Seljuk medical practices. There is an operating theatre, consultant's offices and accommodation for psychiatric patients.

The architectural scheme incorporates arches, vaulted antechambers *(eyvan)* and an open courtyard.

🏛 Three Bazaars

Behind the Ulu Camii. ⬤ *Sun.*
Kayseri's three bazaars offer a contrast to the city's wealth of tombs and mausoleums. The Covered Bazaar (Kapılı Çarşı) dates from 1859, but the other two, the Bedesten and Vizir Han, date from the 15th and 16th centuries respectively.

There are few places that capture the keen spirit of age-old trading better than the bazaars of Kayseri. All three are still patronized by local people and traders, who barter and haggle in a lively atmosphere. Many of the local specialities, such as textiles and carpets, can be bought in the bazaars.

Entrance to the Twin-Turreted Theology Complex

♜ Citadel

Kale
The north wall and ramparts of the Citadel were built by the Emperor Justinian in the 6th century. However, little of the outer fortifications can be seen today. The black basalt structure originally had 195 bastions, and it is still an imposing sight – albeit as a shopping centre today.

🏛 Güpgüpoğlu Stately Home

Güpgüpoğlu Konağı
Tennuri Sok, Cumhuriyet Mahallesi.
Tel (0352) 222 95 16. ⏱ 8:30am–noon & 1:30–5pm Tue–Sun. 📷
A family home built between 1417 and 1419, the house has been carefully preserved and restored to its former glory, with each room highlighting specific aspects of Ottoman life. There are guest rooms, a bridal chamber, meeting areas for family gatherings and men's and women's quarters. Notable features are the built-in cupboards *(yüklük)* for storing mattresses, and the kitchen area, which consists of a pantry and a large main kitchen *(tokana)*.

C Huand Hatun Mosque Complex

Huand Hatun Camii ve Medresesi
Behind tourism information office.
⏱ 9am–5:30pm daily.
This *külliye* (religious and educational institution adjoining a mosque) was one of the first mosque precincts the Seljuks built in Anatolia, although the minaret was erected in 1726.

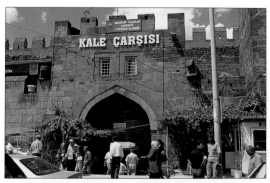

The 13th-century Citadel, now a busy shopping centre

For hotels and restaurants in this region see pp342–343 and pp371–372

Owner of a typical *pastırma* (cured beef) shop in Kayseri

The complex has a mosque, training centre and *hamam* (Turkish bath) for men and women, and also includes the substantial mausoleum of Mahperi Huand Hatun, wife of Alaeddin I Keykubad (see p250). Her inscription on the east door dates back to 1238.

⋔ Octagonal Tomb
Döner Kümbet
Talas Cad.
There are many grand tombs to be found all around Anatolia, but the elegance and pure simplicity of the Döner Kümbet makes it one of the most impressive. The tomb was constructed around 1250 as the final resting

The Octagonal Tomb

place of Şah Cihan Hatun, who was a Seljuk princess.

⏛ Archaeology Museum
Arkeoloji Müzesi
Gültepe Mah. Kışla Cad 2.
Tel (0352) 222 21 49 and 232 48 12. ☐ 8am–noon & 1–5pm Tue–Sun.
The museum consists of two large halls and a pleasant garden. The displays run in chronological sequence from the Bronze Age to the Byzantine period. By far the most valuable and interesting items to be seen are the series of cuneiform tablets documenting the commercial transactions of the

Assyrian trading colony which flourished here during the late Hittite era (see pp24–5).

Environs
Kültepe, formerly known as Kanesh or Kanış, and now Karum, is one of the most important Bronze-Age sites in Turkey. In the second millennium BC, Kültepe was the foremost Assyrian trading colony. Most of the objects found here can now be seen in the museum in Kayseri or in the Museum of Anatolian Civilizations in Ankara (see pp242–3).

Kültepe
21 km (13 miles) NE of Kayseri on the Sivas highway. **Tel** (0352) 289 32 32 (summer only). ☐ 8am–5pm daily.

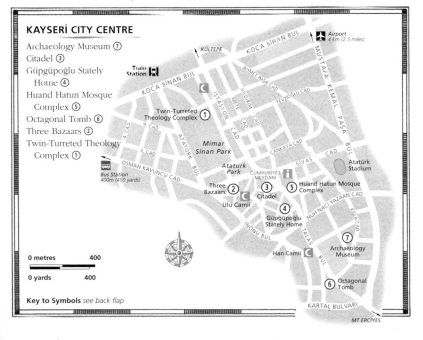

KAYSERİ CITY CENTRE

Archaeology Museum ⑦
Citadel ③
Güpgüpoğlu Stately Home ④
Huand Hatun Mosque Complex ⑤
Octagonal Tomb ⑥
Three Bazaars ②
Twin-Turreted Theology Complex ①

0 metres   400
0 yards   400

Key to Symbols see back flap

Güzelyurt ⑨

28 km (17 miles) SE of Aksaray.
🏠 4,380. 🚌 infrequent from
Aksaray or Ihlara Valley.

Güzelyurt means "beautiful country" and is an apt description of this charming and friendly town, which is surrounded by citrus groves. This is a popular area for horseback riding and mountain biking. The latter is a restful alternative to driving.

It is estimated that there were over 50 Greek Orthodox churches here once, though only a few endure today. The church of St Gregory of Nazianzus, one of the four founders of the Greek Orthodox church, has been converted into a mosque. It was first built in AD 385, but the current church dates from 1896.

A government protection order is in force in Güzelyurt, so all restoration and construction work must conform to official guidelines. Local stone must be used and the buildings must be appropriate to the town.

The valley 4 km (2 miles) to the northeast of the town, also known as the Monastery Valley, has an abundance of rock-carved churches.

Ihlara Valley ⑩

To many people, the Ihlara Valley is more compelling than the rock churches and dwellings in the region. The setting is dramatic, with the Melindiz River winding along the canyon floor.

The main part of the valley lies between the village of Selime to the north and the town of Ihlara to the south. You could spend an entire day exploring the 15 km-long (9 mile) canyon.

Of the 60 or so original churches in the valley, which was known as Peristrema in Greek times, only about 10 can be seen and some of the interior frescoes are in less than pristine condition.

Most of the churches in the valley date from the 11th century. Their unusual names signify their use or a peculiar feature: Hyacinth, Black Deer, Crooked Stone and Dovecote. Many of the interior frescoes depict scenes from the lives of the saints, the lives of the ascetic monks, or punishments for wrongdoing.

It was once thought that a medical school, where the art of mummification was taught and practised, was located between the villages of Belisırma and Yaprakhisar.

The Eğri (Leaning) Minaret, built by the Seljuks in the 13th century

Aksaray ⑪

🏠 153,000. 🚌 0.5 km (0.3 mile) from main square. 🛈 Taşpazar Mahallesi, Kadıoğlu Sok 1, (0382) 213 24 74 and 212 46 88.

In Roman times, Aksaray was known as Archelais, after Archelaus II, the last king of Cappadocia. By 20 BC, the kingdom had been reduced to a virtual protectorate of Rome and the king enjoyed only token status.

From the south, Aksaray is overlooked by the twin peaks of Mount Hasan (Hasan Dağı), an extinct volcano known as "little sister" to Mount Erciyes.

The spectacular Ihlara Valley, one of Central Anatolia's best hiking areas

For hotels and restaurants in this region see pp342–343 and pp371–372

Aksaray is close to the eastern end of the Tuz Gölü (Salt Lake). In Ottoman times, the lake brought prosperity to Aksaray as it was the main source of salt for almost the whole of Anatolia.

Aksaray might appear to be a sleepy base for tourists, but spare some time to view the fine Seljuk building styles and architecture, with vestiges of the original ochre-coloured sandstone. Worth seeing are the Great Mosque (1314), with its beautifully carved *minbar* (pulpit), and the **Zinciriye Medresesi**, a 14th-century Koranic school, that now serves as the museum.

Aksaray has its own leaning tower, the Eğri (Leaning) Minaret, on Nevşehir Caddesi. The minaret is part of the Kızıl (Red) Minare Mosque, which was built in 1236 during the reign of the great Seljuk Sultan Alaeddin I Keykubat *(see p250)*. The mosque was built on sand, which has shifted over time, causing the minaret to lean.

🏛 **Zinciriye Medresesi**
Muhsin Çelebi Sokak. *Tel (0382) 213 16 67.* ◯ *8am–noon & 1–5pm daily.* 🈁

Kırşehir ⓬

160 km (100 miles) SE of Ankara.
🏠 83,450. 🚹 *Terme Cad, Ulucan I Apartman, Kat 1, (0386) 213 14 16.*

In Byzantine times, Kırşehir was known as Mokyssos. It prospered under the Seljuks, who renamed it Gülşehir, or Rose Town. One of the finest of the city's Seljuk buildings is the Cacabey Mosque, built in 1272 as an astrological observatory and theological college. The Alaeddin Mosque, built in 1230, and the Ahi Evran Mosque are also located in Kırşehir. The latter contains the tomb of Ahi Evran, founder of a *tarikât* (religious brotherhood) whose members helped to spread the message of Islam to the Christian communities of Anatolia.

Various artifacts from Kalehöyük, an important Hittite archaeological site 55 km (34 miles) to the north-west of Kırşehir, are on display in the excellent **Archaeology Museum**. Kalehöyük is one of the many Hittite centres that are being excavated in the area. The museum has more than 3,300 artifacts on display, including coins, ethnographic items and archaeological materials.

Another prime reason for visiting the area is a Japanese arboretum, the **Mikasonmiya Memorial Garden** (Mikasonmiya Anı Bahçesi). One of the largest and most pleasant parks in Turkey, it is planted with some 16,500 trees, made up of 33 different species.

Doorway into the tomb of Hacı Bektaş, in the third courtyard

🏛 **Archaeology Museum**
Ankara Cad (in the Culture Centre). *Tel (0386) 213 33 91.* ◯ *9am–noon & 1–5pm daily.* 🈁

🌿 **Mikasonmiya Memorial Garden**
🚹 *Contact the Kırşehir tourist office, (0386) 213 1416, for opening hours.*

Hacı Bektaş ⓭

🏠 9,348. 🚹 *Opposite the Museum, (0384) 441 30 87.* 🈁 🈁 *Hacı Bektaş Veli Commemoration Festival (16–18 Aug).*

Gravestone at Hacı Bektaş

The mystic and spiritual philosopher Hacı Bektaş arrived in this area from Iran, via Mecca, in the late 13th century, and founded a centre of learning. His ideas were an offshoot of the Shi'ite sect of Islam, and rested on a belief in natural harmony that was bolstered by mysticism and divine love. The teachings of Hacı Bektaş offered an approachable and compassionate alternative to the main current of Islam. The Bektaşi doctrine, as set out in his book the *Malakat*, is based on both Islamic and Christian principles. This made it a popular belief. He attracted many

devotees, most notably among the Janissaries, who were the elite fighting force of the Ottoman sultans *(see p56)*.

The **Hacı Bektaş Museum** (Pirevi, or "founder's house") is the chief attraction, along with the stunning wood carvings of the archaeological museum. Be sure you allow sufficient time to see the whole complex: there are tombs, courtyards, initiation cells, pools and a refectory (dining room) with authentic kitchen cauldrons. The tomb of Hacı Bektaş, in the third courtyard, has seven doors, and is particularly striking. Some of the inscriptions were done with natural dyes from the madder root, and later restored with oil-based paint. Atatürk came through here in 1919 on his way from Sivas to Ankara; his visit is marked on 22 and 23 December each year. Admiration for the order did not prevent him banning all mystical sects and dervish lodges in 1925, because they were contrary to Turkey's secular state dogma.

The symbol of the order is the rose and blond onyx that is found in the area. It is known as Hacı Bektaş stone.

🏛 **Hacı Bektaş Museum**
Nevşehir Cad. *Tel (0384) 441 30 22.* ◯ *8:30am–12:30pm & 1:30–5:30pm Tue–Sun.* 🈁

The 19th-century clock tower in the main square in Yozgat

Yozgat ⑭

🏠 80,000. 🏛 İl Özel İdare Hizmet Binası, Kat 3, (0354) 212 64 23. 🚌 (0354) 212 41 15. 🎪 Tue. 🎭 Summer Folklore and Culture Festival (10–15 Jun).

Research shows that there were settlements here as early as 3,000 BC. However, the tides of history barely affected Yozgat until it fell to the Ottomans in 1408 and the influential Çapanoğlu dynasty made the town their seat. The Çapanoğlus built or repaired many fine mosques, including the Ulu (Çapanoğlu) Camii. The **Yozgat Ethnographic Museum** is housed in a 19th-century *konak* (mansion), the Nizamoğulu Konağı.

In the centre of the town there is an interesting, though garish, clock tower built in 1897 by Ahmet Tevfikzade, the mayor of the town. Ask to see the mechanism if you are interested in timepieces.

🏛 **Yozgat Ethnographic Museum**
Emniyet Cad. *Tel (0354) 212 27 73.* 🕐 8am–noon & 1–5pm Tue-Sun.

Environs
Çamlık National Park, located about 5 km (3 miles) south of Yozgat, covers 8 sq km (3 sq miles) of woodland, and has abundant fauna and flora, picnic areas and mineral springs.

🎿 **Çamlık National Park**
Tel (0354) 212 10 84. 🕐 daily

Boğazkale ⑮

See pp296–7.

Alacahöyük ⑯

30 km (19 miles) SE of Çorum.

Located between Sungurlu and Çorum, Alacahöyük is the third and most important site (after Boğazkale and Yazılıkaya) in the Hattuşaş complex of Hittite sites in this region. Most of the artifacts found at the site are displayed in museums in Ankara *(see pp242–3)* and Çorum.

Excavations at Alacahöyük have yielded items ranging from the Chalcolithic period (5500 BC–3000 BC) up to the Phrygian period (750 BC–300 BC) – a staggering time span that makes the site one of Turkey's most important archaeological centres.

At the site itself, the Sphinx Gate is an imposing reminder of cult power, its half-man, half-animal statues displaying striking Egyptian influences.

The royal tombs can also be seen. The **Alacahöyük Museum** displays some of the earthenware pots that were used for burial rites.

🏛 **Alacahöyük Museum**
Tel (0364) 422 70 11. 🕐 8am–noon & 1–5pm Tue-Sun.

One of the carved sphinxes that guard the gate at Alacahöyük

Çorum ⑰

🏛 Yeni Hükümet Binası, A Blok, Kat 4, (0364) 213 85 02. 🎭 Hittite Festival (mid-Jun).

The town of Çorum dates from Roman times, when it was known as Niconia. The surrounding area is rich in Hittite history, making it likely that the site was inhabited as early as 1400 BC. Throughout Turkey, the name of Çorum is associated with roasted chickpeas *(leblebi)*, one of the many nuts that Turks munch compulsively. A particularly delicious local cheese is

Shop in Çorum specializing in the famous local produce, chickpeas

For hotels and restaurants in this region see pp342–343 and pp371–372

Kargi, made from cow's milk. Çorum makes a good base from which to tour two major Hittite sights, Boğazkale *(see pp296–7)* and Alacahöyük. Both are located to the southwest of the town.

The **Çorum Museum** sprawls over several buildings. It is a serious and informative place with many artifacts and ethnographic displays, among them very good Hittite objects, as well as local *kilims* (rugs).

Çorum Museum
Town centre. *Tel (0364) 213 15 68.*
☐ 8:30am–noon & 1–5:30pm
Tue–Sun. ▨

Amasya ⑱

See pp298–9.

Tokat ⑲

▨ 121,000. ▯ Valilik Binası, Kat. 3, (0356) 214 37 53. ▦ 2 km (1 mile) from main square, (0356) 214 22 20. ▨ Pinecone Festival (mid-Sep).

Tokat deserves a place on visitors' itineraries because there is a lot more to see here than ankle-high ruins. The Seljuks left the most to see, but the town is also known for resisting Ottoman rule. In protest at Ottoman authority, Turcoman tribesmen took to wearing red headgear, thus earning the name of Kızılbaşı (redheads), which became a term for "rebels".

The town flourished after Sultan Beyazıt I won control of trade routes to Erzincan. Trade caravans then began to use the Amasya–Tokat route, skirting Trabzon (Trebizond), to reach Bursa *(see pp162–7)*, the commercial jewel of the 15th and 16th centuries.

The Seljuks and Ottomans endowed Tokat with many fine buildings, especially the Blue Seminary (Gök Medrese) and two restored 19th-century Ottoman *konaks* (mansions): the Madımağın Celal'ın House and the Latifoğlu House. If time is limited, Tokat's interesting **Archaeological Museum** is the place to go.

Tokat has a proud 300-year tradition of hand-printed

The Heavenly Seminary in Sivas, showing filigree stonework

textiles *(yazmacılık)*. The craft still thrives in the Gazi Emir Han near the business hub of Sulu Sokak. The town is also renowned for copper-working and ceramics in bold primary colours.

Specialities include *pekmez*, a delicious drink made from concentrated grape juice, and the full-bodied, fruity Karaman red wine.

Archaeological Museum
Gaziosmanpaşa Bulvarı 143.
Tel (0356) 214 15 09. ☐ 8:30am–noon & 1–5pm Tue–Sun.

Environs

The ruined city of Sebastopolis is located 68 km (42 miles) southwest of Tokat. The modern name, Sulusaray (watery palace), comes from the thermal springs, which bubble water at 50°C. Interesting finds here include a city wall, bath chambers and a temple.

Shop selling hand-printed textiles in Tokat

Sivas ⑳

▨ 251,000. ▯ Atatürk Kültür Merkezi, (0346) 223 92 99. ▯ İstasyon Cad, (0346) 221 10 91 ▦ 3 km (2 miles) SE of main square, (0346) 226 15 90. ▨ Nevruz (21 Mar). www.sivas.gov.tr

Situated at an altitude of 1,275 m (4,183 ft), Sivas is the highest city in Central Anatolia. Known as Sebasteia in Roman times, its position on a caravan route made it an important trade centre.

Sivas boasts the cream of Seljuk architecture, with tiles, intricately etched stonework, star mosaics, honeycombed decorative motifs and bold blue hues all in evidence. The Heavenly Seminary (Gök Medresesi), built in the 1200s, and Twin Minaret Seminary (Çifte Minareli Medresesi), with its outstanding carved details, should not be missed. The Darüşşifası (Medical Hospice) housed a hospital. The Bürüciye Medresesi (1271) has a quiet courtyard and some excellent tilework.

The Sivas Congress (to consolidate Atatürk's plans to free Turkey from foreign domination) was held in a schoolroom here in 1919. The room is preserved in the **Ethnography Museum**. Local artisans are known for long-stemmed wooden pipes, penknives and bone-handled knives.

Ethnography Museum
Istasyon Cad. *Tel (0346) 221 04 46.*
☐ 8:30am–noon & 1–5:30pm
Tue–Sun. ▨

Boğazkale ⑮
Hattuşaş National Park

Boğazkale is the modern name for the ancient Hittite capital city of Hattuşaş, built around 1600 BC on a strategic site occupied since the third millennium BC by a people known as the Hatti. An Assyrian trading colony was also active here early in the second millennium BC. It is one of the most important ancient sites to be found in Anatolia. The many thousands of clay and bronze tablets discovered here have provided scholars with a wealth of information about the ancient Hittite civilization.

The city occupies an extensive site bordered on three sides by steep ravines. Sections of the walls, including the impressive Lion's and King's gates, are still standing. The builders adapted the fortifications in masterly fashion to take advantage of topographical features.

Bronze Plaque
This plaque found at Boğazkale records a treaty between the Hittite king, Tudhaliyas IV, and another ruler.

Modern village of Boğazköy

Entry to excavation site

Yenice Citadel

★ Lion's Gate (Aslanlıkapı)
The Lion's Gate takes its name from the two lion statues that guarded the city over 3,000 years ago. The lions here are only replicas – the originals are now in the Museum of Anatolian Civilizations in Ankara (see pp242–3).

HITTITE CIVILIZATION

A people of Indo-European origin, the Hittites arrived in Anatolia from the Caucasus region around 2000 BC. Over the next few centuries, they built up a powerful state, with a capital at Hattuşaş (now known as Boğazkale). At its height, the Hittite kingdom controlled much of Anatolia, rivalling both Egypt and Babylon. Hittite art reached its peak between 1450 and 1200 BC, and Hittite artisans were renowned as superb carvers and metalworkers.

One of the twelve gods in stone relief at Yazılıkaya, near Boğazkale

0 metres   55
0 yards   550

The Sphinx Gate (Yerkapı) is built into an artificial hill, and incorporates a tunnel 70 m (230 ft) in length.

★ Great Temple (Büyük Mabet)
One of the best preserved Hittite temples, the Great Temple was built around 1400 BC, and was dedicated to the storm god, Teshub. The temple complex contains ritual chambers, administrative areas and storage rooms.

The Citadel (Büyükkale)
The walled citadel was the seat of government at Hattuşaş. A monumental staircase led up to three courts, one of which contained the living quarters of the royal household.

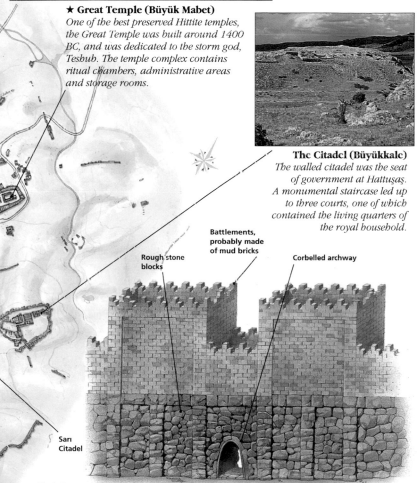

Battlements, probably made of mud bricks

Rough stone blocks

Corbelled archway

Sarı Citadel

King's Gate

★ RECONSTRUCTION OF THE KING'S GATE
The King's Gate (Kral Kapı) was named after the regal-looking Hittite war god on the stone relief guarding the entrance. The city wall is built with huge, roughly worked stone blocks, and totals about 7 km (5 miles) in length. The height of the stone portion was about 6 m (20 ft). Like the other structures in the city, this would have been overlaid with sun-dried brick.

STAR FEATURES

★ Great Temple

★ King's Gate

★ Lion's Gate

Amasya ⑱

Lying in a secluded valley of the Yeşilırmak River, Amasya has seen the passage of nine civilizations, from the Hittites to Ottomans. Its most prosperous era was as royal capital of the Roman kingdom of Pontus, when it was called Amaseia; the tombs cut into the cliffs above the town contain the graves of the Pontic kings. However, a glance at Amasya's many fine Ottoman buildings will confirm that the four centuries of Ottoman rule were equally illustrious. In the 15th century, Amasya was second only to Bursa in cultural and trading importance. By the 1800s, the city excelled as the empire's leading centre for Islamic education.

Bust in the Archaeology Museum

The carved portal of the Teaching Hospital Complex

Exploring Amasya

Its dramatic location and air of tranquillity aside, Amasya is known for the tasty apples grown on the surrounding farms and for colourful hand-knitted socks. All main sights are conveniently accessible on foot. The citadel is the only exception, but it can be reached by car.

The Citadel, perched dramatically on a hilltop

🅲 Large-Doored Seminary

Büyük Ağa Medresesi
Zubediye Hanım Sok. ⬤ *during lessons.*
The wonderful airy symmetry and octagonal plan of this complex, also known as the Kapıağası, are its outstanding features. It was built in 1488 by Hüseyin Agha, a private consort of Sultan Beyazıt II. The vaulted porticoes and domed rooms are now used by Koranic students, who adhere to exactly the same rigorous discipline as their predecessors did two or three centuries ago.

⚜ Citadel

Kale
Can be reached by 2-hour climb from the front, or by a road from behind.
The original Hittite fortress was reinforced by the Pontic king, Mithradates *(see p48)*. He built eight layers of walls, with 41 towers, to protect a self-sustaining complex with a palace, cisterns, storage areas, powder magazine and cemetery. From the Citadel there are stupendous views of the nearby Rock Tombs.

🪦 Rock Tombs

Kral Kaya Mezarları
Entrance under the railway line off Hazeranlar Sok. *Tel (0358) 218 96 34.* ⬤ *8am–5pm (7pm in summer).* 🖼
The tombs of the Pontic kings date from 333 BC to 44 BC, covering the Hellenistic and Roman periods. The Mirror Cave (Aynalı Mağrası), about 1 km (0.5 mile) from the main tombs, has a coloured painting showing the Virgin Mary and the Apostles.

🏥 Teaching Hospital Complex

Daruşşifa/Bimarhane Medresesi
Atatürk Cad. ⬤ *9am–6pm daily.*
The outer walls of the original asylum date from 1308. The complex served as a medical research centre, a school for interns and a hospice for mental patients. Music and speech therapy were used to calm disturbed patients. The carved front portal is wonderfully detailed and represents a rare architectural remnant of the Ilhanid Persian empire of the 13th century. The building houses a café and the offices of the local Music and Fine Arts Directorate.

🏥 Hazeranlar Mansion

Hazeranlar Konağı
Hattuniye Mahallesi. *Tel (0358) 218 40 18.* ⬤ *8am–5pm (7pm in summer).* 🖼 🚻 📷
This restored mansion dates from 1865. It was built by a local treasury officer, Hasan Talat Efendi, in memory of his sister, Hazeran Hanım (Lady Hazeran). The layout, typical of the time, features separate areas for men and women. The carpets, from the late Ottoman period, are particularly fine.

The tombs of the Pontic kings, carved into the limestone cliffs

For hotels and restaurants in this region see pp342–343 and pp371–372

Konaks (mansion houses) along the Yeşilırmak River

C Sultan Beyazıt Mosque and Theological College

Sultan Beyazıt II Külliyesi
Mustafa Kemal Paşa Cad. ● *during prayer times* ● *donation.*
This was Amasya's primary theological complex, eclipsing all other places of religious learning. It was a product of the prosperity and social stability that prevailed under Sultan Beyazıt II (1481–1512). In that era, Muslim principles and obedience to the state were instilled at an early age. The wonderful domes and portals are inspirational in themselves, and the oak trees in the garden are said to be as old as the mosque itself.

🏛 Archaeology and Ethnography Museum

Arkeoloji ve Etnografik Müzesi
Mustafa Kemal Paşa Cad 91.
Tel (0358) 218 45 13. ● 9am–noon & 1:30–5:30pm Tue–Sun. ●
The museum has been improved and modernized, and so the concept of space is much enhanced. Notable among its exhibits is the bronze statue of the Hittite storm god, as well as a collection of Roman coins minted in the town.

The museum is best known for its collection of mummies, which were found in Anatolia and date from the Ilhanid period (around the 14th century). Previously housed in a dank tomb adjacent to the museum, these now have much more prominence in their display cases.

The Sultan Beyazıt Mosque, completed in 1486, with its famous rose garden

VISITORS' CHECKLIST

🏠 265,230. ✈ 2 km (1 mile) W of town centre, (0358) 218 12 39. 🚌 2 km (1 mile) NE of town centre, (0358) 218 80 12. 🛈 Atatürk Cad, Pirinç Mah (opposite Bimarhane), (0358) 218 50 02.

C Blue Seminary

Gök Medresesi
Mustafa Kemal Paşa Cad (Torumtay Sok). ● *contact a guardian to let you in.* ● *during prayer time.* ● *donation.*
A theological complex dating from 1267, the Blue Seminary is typical of 13th-century Seljuk architecture. It was formerly used as a mosque and Koranic school, and takes its name from the turquoise/blue tiles and glazed bricks used in its construction. The elaborately carved wooden doors contrasted with the austere interior and are now housed in the Archaeology and Ethnographic Museum.

Adjoining the complex is the Torumtay Türbe, a square tomb built in 1279 in memory of the Emir Torumtay, Seljuk governor of the province and founder of the seminary.

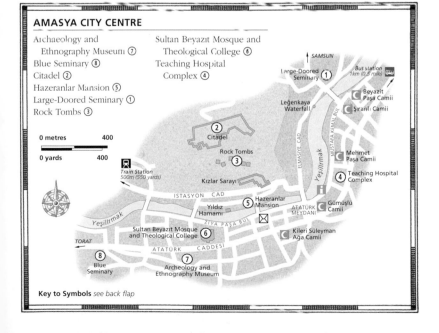

AMASYA CITY CENTRE

Archaeology and
  Ethnography Museum ⑦
Blue Seminary ⑧
Citadel ②
Hazeranlar Mansion ⑤
Large-Doored Seminary ①
Rock Tombs ③

Sultan Beyazıt Mosque and
  Theological College ⑥
Teaching Hospital
  Complex ④

SAMSUN

Large-Doored Seminary ①
Bus station 1km (0.5 mile)

Leğenkaya Waterfall

Beyazıt Paşa Camii
Şıranlı Camii

Citadel ②

Rock Tombs ③

0 metres 400
0 yards 400

Train Station 500m (550 yards)

Kızlar Sarayı

ELMASİYE CAD

Yeşilırmak

MUSTAFA KEMAL BUL

Mehmet Paşa Camii

Teaching Hospital ④ Complex

ISTASYON CAD

Hazeranlar ⑤ Mansion
Yıldız Hamamı

ZİYA PAŞA BUL

ATATÜRK MEYDANI

Gümüşlü Camii

Yeşilırmak

TORAT

Sultan Beyazıt Mosque and Theological College ⑥

ATATÜRK CADDESİ

Kileri Süleyman Ağa Camii

⑧ Blue Seminary

⑦ Archeology and Ethnography Museum

Key to Symbols *see back flap*

EASTERN ANATOLIA

he vast, high plateau of eastern Turkey is dominated by the extinct volcano of Mount Ağrı (Ararat), which soars to a height of 5,165 m (16,945 ft). The surface of Lake Van reflects the summits of the surrounding peaks. Trapped by the mountains, the lake has no outflow. In the south, the eastern extension of the Taurus range crumbles suddenly into the sun-baked Mesopotamian plain.

The region is drained by two great rivers – the Euphrates (Fırat) and Tigris (Dicle) – as well as their tributaries. For centuries, the Euphrates demarcated the eastern frontier of the Roman and Byzantine empires. Today, the rivers have been harnessed by the Southeast Anatolian Project (GAP) to supply the southeastern part of the country with irrigation water and hydro-electric power.

This border zone has always been a cultural melting pot – Monophysite Christian Armenians and Syrians lived alongside Orthodox Greeks and later Arabs and Turks, while Kurds have long occupied the highlands.

Modern, bustling Gaziantep is the gateway from the southeast, leading to the golden apricot orchards of Malatya, the huge stone heads on the summit of Mount Nemrut (Nemrut Dağı), and Abraham's legendary birthplace at Şanlıurfa. Diyarbakır's austere basalt walls loom dramatically over the Tigris, guarding the road north to the interior plateau. Van was once the seat of the sophisticated Urartian kingdom. The rough frontier town of Doğubeyazıt was home to fiercely independent Kurdish princes. Kars, 10th-century capital of Armenia and access point for Ani, has been fought over many times by Russians and Turks. During World War I, Russian forces reached as far west as Erzurum, a Seljuk city with imposing medieval tombs and religious buildings, which guards the strategic highway into central Anatolia.

Snowcapped Mount Ağrı (Ararat), legendary resting place of Noah's Ark

◁ The remains of a 12th-century bridge over the Tigris River at Hasankeyif

Exploring Eastern Anatolia

From the baking plains of Upper Mesopotamia to the icy heights of Mount Ağrı (Ararat), this vast region of Turkey is relatively undeveloped and unspoiled, making it a natural target for the more adventurous traveller. It is a land of frontiers, from cold and lonely Kars – a short step away from Armenia – through the Turkish-Iranian border town of Doğubeyazıt, to the bustling bazaar city of Şanlıurfa close to Syria. Many peoples have lived in and fought over this land. Visitors can see Armenian churches and Kurdish castles, Arab houses, Syrian Orthodox monasteries and both Seljuk and Ottoman mosques vying with ruins from the Urartian and Roman eras. Late spring and early autumn are the best seasons to visit.

The citadel at Şanlıurfa

Stone head on Mount Nemrut

SIGHTS AT A GLANCE

Ağrı ⑪
Ani pp316–17 ⑬
Divriği ⑯
Diyarbakır pp310–311 ⑧
Doğubeyazıt ⑩
Erzincan ⑮
Erzurum pp318–19 ⑭
Gaziantep Archaelogical Museum pp308–9 ⑤
Kahramanmaraş ④
Kâhta ①
Kars ⑫
Lake Van ⑨
Malatya ③
Mardin ⑦
Mount Nemrut p306 ②
Şanlıurfa ⑥

SEE ALSO

• **Where to Stay** pp344–345

• **Where to Eat** pp372–373

0 kilometres   80

0 miles   40

For additional map symbols see back flap

KEY

- ▬▬ Motorway
- ▬ Major road
- ═══ Minor road
- ▬ Scenic route
- ╌╌ Main railway
- ── Minor railway
- ▬▬ International border
- △ Summit

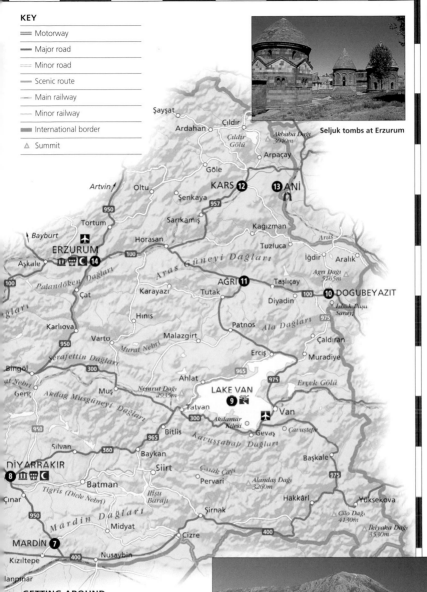

Seljuk tombs at Erzurum

Şayşat
Ardahan
Çıldır
Çıldır Gölü
Akbaba Dağı 3040m
Arpaçay
Göle
Artvin
Oltu
KARS **12**
13 ANİ
Şenkaya
957
Tortum
950
Sarıkamış
Kağızman
Aras
Baybur
Horasan
Tuzluca
İğdir
Aralık
ERZURUM
100
Aras Güneyi Dağları
Aşkale
Palandöken Dağları
Çat
Karayazı
Tutak
AGRI **11**
Taşlıçay
Ağrı Dağı 5165m
Diyadin
100
10 DOGUBEYAZIT
Ishak Paşa Sarayı
975
Hınıs
Patnos
Ala Dağları
Karlıova
Varto
Malazgirt
Çaldıran
950
Murat Nehri
Erciş
Muradiye
Bingöl
Şerafettin Dağları
300
Ahlat
965
Erçek Gölü
Genç
Akdağ Musguneyi Dağları
Muş
Nemrut Dağı 2935m
LAKE VAN **9**
975
Talvan
Van
Bitlis
300
Akdamar Kilesi
Gevaş
Çavuştepe
965
Silvan
560
Kavuşşabap Dağları
Baykan
DİYARBAKIR **8**
Siirt
Başkale
Çatak Çayı
Pervari
Alandaş Dağı 3260m
975
Batman
Tigris (Dicle Nehri)
Hasu Barajı
Hakkâri
Yüksekova
Çınar
950
Şırnak
Cilo Dağı 4130m
Mardin Dağları
Midyat
İkiyaka Dağı 3530m
MARDİN **7**
Cizre
400
Kızıltepe
Nusaybin
400
lanpınar

GETTING AROUND

Comfortable intercity coaches connect all the major cities in the region, and are reasonably priced. For rural areas or out-of-the-way sites, the best option is a locally hired taxi. Rental cars are not widely available and driving conditions can be difficult, with bad, potholed roads and heavy truck traffic in many areas. Non-stop flights from Istanbul and Ankara serve Erzurum, Malatya, Gaziantep, Diyarbakır and Van. Rail travel between Erzurum and Kars, and Malatya and Tatvan, on Lake Van, is slow but scenically rewarding.

The island of Akdamar, in Lake Van

The Atatürk Dam, centrepiece of the GAP (Southeast Anatolian Project)

Kâhta ❶

43 km (27 miles) E of Adıyaman.
🅸 *Kâhta Kaymakamlik, (0416) 725
50 05 (all year); (0416) 725 50 07
(summer only).* 🎭 *International Kâhta
Kommagene Festival (last week in Jun).*

Locals like to claim that dusty
Kâhta has become a seaside
town now that the lake
created by the **Atatürk Dam**
(Atatürk Barajı) – the fourth
largest in the world when it
was completed in 1990 – laps
at the town's eastern edge.
Apart from a few hotels,
Kâhta's main attraction is its
proximity to Mount Nemrut
(Nemrut Dağı), located 70 km
(44 miles) to the northeast.

Environs
The Atatürk Dam, part of the
GAP project, has intruded into
the Euphrates basin's ancient
past. Building of this and other
dams has flooded important
historic treasures and sites.
   The town of **Adıyaman** is
slightly further away from
Mount Nemrut (about a half-
hour drive west of Kâhta), and
makes an alternative base.

Adıyaman
🅸 *Atatürk Bul 184, (0416) 216 10 08.*

Mount Nemrut ❷
Nemrut Dağı

See p306.

Malatya ❸

🏠 *500,000.* ✈ *4 km (2.5 miles) W
of city centre, off Turgut Özal Bul,
(0422) 238 47 68.* 🚉 *2 km (1 mile)
W of city centre, (0422) 212 40 40.*
🚌 *23 km (14 miles) W of city centre.*
🅸 *Valilik Binası, (0422) 323 30 25 / 29
42.* **Culture Centre** *İstasyon Virajı No
35, (0422) 324 76 12.* 🎭 *daily.*
🎭 *Cherry Festival (18 Jun); Apricot
Festival (3rd week Jul).*

Malatya is famous for its
apricots, grown in the vast
surrounding orchards.
It was also the birthplace of
two Turkish presidents: İsmet
İnönü, Atatürk's right-hand
man during the War of
Independence; and Turgut
Özal, an economist who
served first as Prime Minister,
and then President, from the
mid-1980s *(see p59).*

**Apricot vendor in Malatya's Apricot
Bazaar**

Malatya is a pleasant and fairly
prosperous town with a university and a military base,
but makes a less convenient
base than Kâhta for trips to
Mount Nemrut.
   The town's most interesting
sights are its bazaars. The
Apricot Bazaar specializes in
locally grown and dried
apricots. Trading takes place
after the harvest, and during
the Apricot Festival in July.
Around the central mosque is
the **Copper Bazaar**, a group of
copper-beating workshops
where you can buy hand-
made trays, pots and vases.
   The **Archaeological Museum**
features finds from Aslantepe,
a Hittite site located 4 km
(3 miles) northeast of Malatya,
which was flooded as a result
of the GAP project. Items
including Hittite stone god
statues, cuneiform seals, bone
idols and early bronze swords
were transferred to the
museum. There are over
15,500 items spanning most
historic periods. The Neolithic
sculptures from 8000 BC are
particularly impressive, as are
the obsidian knives.
   Local carpets and *kilims*
(rugs) have distinctive features,
such as the rectangular "tower
bastion" motif. The *yedi dağ
çiçeği* (seven-point flower)
motif can be found on *kilims*.
Carpets generally have
simpler designs in strong,
primary colours, with borders

featuring stylized flowers, rams, medallions or dragons. Small hand-loomed carpets and goat-hair rugs are also found in and around Malatya.

Apricot Bazaar
New Malatya Quarter. ☐ Mon–Sat.

Copper Bazaar
New Malatya Quarter. Adjoining the Apricot Bazaar. ☐ Mon–Sat.

🏛 Archaeological Museum
Dernek Mahallesi, Kanal Boyu.
Tel (0422) 321 30 06. ☐
May–Oct: daily. 🎫

Environs
Eski Malatya, the old part of town, lies about 12 km (7.5 miles) north of the modern centre. A little village of 2,000 inhabitants has developed inside these walls, once an important Roman and then Byzantine stronghold. The 17th-century Silahtar Mustafa Paşa Caravanserai had been restored, but is now sadly neglected and visitors have to wander around among chickens and donkeys.

The much-restored **Great Mosque** (Ulu Camii) is built around a tiny courtyard, its graceful interior divided into separate summer and winter areas. The winter area is supported by massive pillars and enclosed by thick walls, while the summer section has a beautifully carved wooden pulpit, and amazing herringbone brick vaulting decorated with scattered turquoise tiles.

C Great Mosque
Ulu Camii
Opposite the bus station. ☐ daily (except during prayer times).

Kahramanmaraş ❹

🏠 326,000. 🚌 W of main highway on Azerbaycan Bulvarı, (0344) 235 30 06. 🚆 Cumhuriyet Cad, (0344) 235 00 75. 🛈 Valilik Bahçesi, (0344) 223 03 55.

Like many other towns in Turkey, Kahramanmaraş has a deceptive air of calm and tranquillity that conceals a turbulent past. The first part of its name (meaning "heroic") was added by Atatürk in recognition of the town's successful expulsion of French and British troops in 1920.

It is, however, often just called "Maraş", after its particularly famous product, Maraş Dondurması – a delicious type of ice cream containing gum arabic that is pounded or whipped into

Copper tea pot from Malatya

glutinous form. It is sold all over Turkey by costumed vendors. Locally, it is sold by the metre and cut with a knife. You can also buy it served in a cone.

As early as the 1940s, Kahramanmaraş was an important centre for shoe- and bootmaking. However, due to increased irrigation from the GAP project, this area now

The pleasant park below the citadel at Kahramanmaraş

produces more cotton than Turkey's Aegean region.

The town's citadel, probably used as defence against Arab raiders in the 7th century, is now a popular tea garden and park. Two mosques, the Great Mosque and the Hatuniye Camii, date from the 15th- and 16th century Beylik period. Their interiors feature fine wooden carvings.

The local **Archaeological and Ethnographic Museum** displays Hittite statues, ceremonial costumes, *kilims* and textile items from various eras.

🏛 Archaeological and Ethnographic Museum
Azerbaycan Bul.
Tel (0344) 223 44 88.
☐ 9am–noon & 1–5:30pm Tue–Sun. 🎫

The 17th-century Silahtar Mustafa Paşa Caravanserai in Eski Malatya

Mount Nemrut ❷
Nemrut Dağı

The huge stone heads on the summit of Mount Nemrut (Nemrut Dağı) were built by King Antiochus I Theos, who ruled the Commagene kingdom between 64 and 38 BC. To glorify his rule, the king had three enormous terraces (east, west and north) cut into the mountaintop. Colossal statues of himself and the major gods (both Greek and Persian) of the kingdom were placed on the terraces, and the summit became a sanctuary where the king was worshipped. Today's visitors can still see the remains of the east and west terraces (not much is left of the north terrace), which also feature large, detailed stone reliefs.

Stone head of Zeus

The enigmatic site was discovered in 1881 by a German engineer, Karl Sester, but was not fully documented until the 1990s.

VISITORS' CHECKLIST

70 km (44 miles) from Kâhta,
84 km (52 miles) from Adıyaman
in Nemrut Dağı National Park.
Tel *(0416) 725 50 07.*
◻ *May–Oct: 8am–8pm daily.*
⬤ *Nov–Apr.* 🏷

★ **East Terrace**
The site affords superb views of the surrounding region. Behind the sanctuary rises a 50 m (165 ft) high mound rumoured to contain the tumulus of King Antiochus.

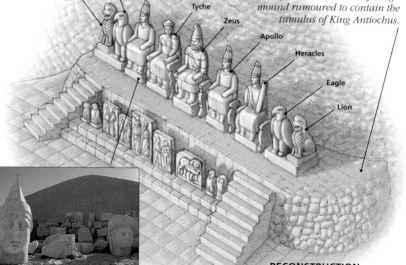

Eagle
Lion
Tyche
Zeus
Apollo
Heracles
Eagle
Lion

Head of Antiochus
The re erected head of King Antiochus stands near the tumbled one of Tyche, Commagene goddess of fortune.

RECONSTRUCTION
This artists' impression depicts the East Terrace as it probably looked in the 1st century BC. The limestone figures were 8–10 m (26–33 ft) in height.

★ **Stone Reliefs**
This life-size relief carving of a lion surrounded by stars and a crescent moon is considered to be one of the oldest horoscope representations in the world.

STAR FEATURES

★ East Terrace

★ Stone Reliefs

Gaziantep Archaelogical Museum ❺

See pp308–9

Şanlıurfa ❻

🏛 *650,000.* 🚍 *1 km (0.5 mile) W of city centre.* ✈ *6 km (4 miles) S of city centre, (0414) 247 03 43.* 🛈 *Atatürk Bul, Vilayet Binası, Kat 3, (0414) 312 53 32.*

The city of Şanlıurfa offers visitors to this region the most to see and should not be missed. First settled by the Hurri peoples around 3,500 years ago, it was occupied by a succession of peoples, such as the Hittites, Assyrians, Greeks and Romans.

Alexander the Great named it Edessa, and the Ottomans renamed it Urfa. The city acquired the prefix *şanlı* (glorious) through the role it played in resistance to the French in 1920.

During Şanlıurfa's long Christian history it was used as a centre of the Nestorian movement, and later became the capital of a crusader state (1097–1144). Churches, now mosques, in the old town include the Selahattin Eyubi Camii, once the church of St John. Many Armenians lived in Urfa until 1920.

Most visitors, however, come here to see the Gölbaşı (lakeside) area at the foot of the citadel. This pleasantly landscaped garden contains the Pool of Abraham, said to be the site where the biblical prophet was saved from the

The Pool of Abraham in Şanlıurfa

vengeful Assyrian king, Nimrod (Nemrut). A small cave nearby is said to be the birthplace of Abraham.

The stone covered bazaar, or Kapalı Çarşı, is an Ottoman structure, with designated rows of streets devoted to particular trades. Traditional crafts and skills predominate, and it is a good place to shop for locally produced cloth.

Be sure to sample the local specialities: *çiğ köfte* (raw meatballs), once believed to be a dish prepared for Hittite kings; and *lahmacun* (a flat, pizza-like bread topped with spicy meat).

Mardin ❼

🏛 *122,000.* 🛈 *Valilik Binası, (0482) 212 18 52, (0482) 212 37 76.* 🎏 *Kite Festival (third week Jun).* **www**.*mardin.gov.tr*

A dramatic location on Anatolian and Mesopotamian trading routes has endowed

Mardin with turbulent history and poetic architecture. The city was captured by Muslims in about 640 AD and ruled by various Arab and Kurdish states until the 11th century. Some exceptional theological buildings, like the Zinciriye Medresesi and the Kasımiye Medresesi, date from the 14th and 15th centuries respectively.

The unusual terrace-style dwellings and narrow, labyrinth-like streets invoke the style and form of their Arab heritage. A city landmark is the **Mardin Museum**, whose archaeological section displays works from 4000 BC until the 7th century BC.

The Ulu Camii, a 12th-century Syrian-style mosque, built by an Artukid chieftain, is another city symbol. It rises in stately contrast to the animated, ethnic bazaar that surrounds it. In the bazaar, look for the artisanal silver *tekari* (jewellery), for which Mardin is famous.

Environs
Mor Gabriel Monastery, 18 km (11 miles) west of Midyat, was founded by two monks in 397 AD and is one of the world's oldest functioning monasteries.

🏛 **Mardin Museum**
Cumhuriyet Meydanı, Latifiye Mah, Mardin. **Tel** *(0482) 212 77 97.* 🕐 *9am–6pm Tue–Sun.*

🕌 **Mor Gabriel Monastery**
Midyat, Mardin.
Tel *(0482) 462 14 25.* 🕐 *9:30am–11:30am, 1–4:30pm daily.* 🚫 *Guided tours only.*

Mardin museum, which was formerly the Syrian Catholic Patriarchate

Gaziantep Archaeological Museum ❺

A bulla, or clay seal.

Gaziantep's Archaeological Museum showcases outstanding classical mosaics dating from the 2nd and 3rd centuries AD. These once adorned the villas of prosperous citizens in Zeugma, a Roman garrison town. State-of-the- art technology helped recover and relocate the mosaics, which were displaced by an irrigation project *(see p21)*. Restoration and conservation work was supported by the Packard Humanities Institute.

Hittite Stele
This carved stone panel dating from the 9th century BC is of the Storm God Teshub.

Ground Floor

★ Gypsy Girl Mosaic
Compared to the Mona Lisa due to her charismatic expression, the Gypsy Girl mosaic is a regional idol and symbol of the Zeugma excavations. She was once part of a larger mosaic.

Euphrates Salon

★ Statue of Mars
The virile and sensuous bronze statue of the God of War was discovered with broken pithos and amphoras.

Clay seals

Achilles Salon

Aphrodite Salon

Oceanos and Tethys
This mosaic of the river god Oceanos and his wife Tethys encircled by sea creatures is the most complete mosaic recovered.

Oceanos Salon

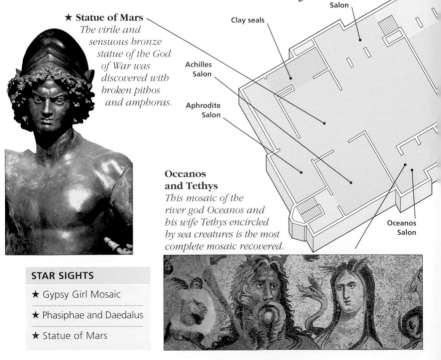

STAR SIGHTS

★ Gypsy Girl Mosaic

★ Phasiphae and Daedalus

★ Statue of Mars

First Floor

VISITORS' CHECKLIST

İstasyon Caddesi 2, Gaziantep.
Tel (0324) 324 88 09. ⏰ 9am–
7pm Tue–Sun. 🌐 🖥 📷 ♿
www.gaziantepmuzesi.gov.tr

Gaziantep

🏢 1,400,000. 🚌 İstasyon Cad,
(0342) 323 31 96. ✈ Sazgan, 18 km
(11 miles) from city centre, (0342) 582
11 11. 🚆 5 km (3 mile) North of city
centre, (0342) 230 99 60. ℹ Yüzyıl
Atatürk Kültür Parkı, (0342) 230 59 69.
🎪 Pistachio Festival (1st week in Sep).

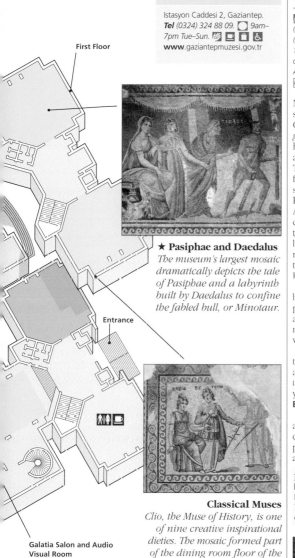

★ **Pasiphae and Daedalus**
*The museum's largest mosaic
dramatically depicts the tale
of Pasiphae and a labyrinth
built by Daedalus to confine
the fabled bull, or Minotaur.*

Entrance

Classical Muses
*Clio, the Muse of History, is one
of nine creative inspirational
dieties. The mosaic formed part
of the dining room floor of the
Euphrates Villa.*

**Galatia Salon and Audio
Visual Room**

KEY

- ☐ Mosaic floors
- ☐ Artifacts and excavated materials
- ☐ Wall mosaics
- ☐ Restored villa with mosaic floor
- ☐ Clay seals
- ☐ Sarcophogus
- ☐ Non-exhibition space

Named Ayntap, or pure
spring, by the Byzantines,
Gaziantep's modern prefix of
gazi (war hero) derives from
heroic resistance to French
and English invaders in 1920.
The site has been occupied
for 8,000 years and was a
strategic defence hub in
Hittite times (1200–700BC).
An impressive fortress and
citadel stand as reminders of
the city's past. The town has
boomed throughout the years,
mainly due to its proximity to
the Southeast Anatolian
Project *(see p19)*.

Just below the citadel is a
bazaar, where craftsmen
produce and sell copperware
and furniture inlaid with
mother-of-pearl, a craft for
which the town is famous.

Stroll around the old town
to see traditional architecture
adapted for regional life, like
the *hayat*, or summer courtyard, seen in the **Hasan Süzer
Ethnographic Museum**.

Gaziantep is an important
agricultural and industrial
centre, and olives, grapes and
pistachio nuts are grown
around the city.

🏛 **Hasan Süzer
Ethnography Museum**
Eyüboğlu Mah, Hanifioğlu Sok 64.
Tel (0342) 230 47 21. ⏰ 9am–12pm
& 1:30–4:30pm Tue–Sun. 🌐

GALLERY GUIDE

*Entry is via the museum
where wall and floor mosaics
and reconstructed villas are
exhibited over two floors. A
ramp leads to the original
museum where exhibits are
arranged chronologically. The
garden has Roman tombstones,
featuring figures and eagles,
as well as late Hittite steles
depicting funeral banquets.*

**Gaziantep's bazaars, colourful and
brimming with local goods.**

Diyarbakır ⑧

Frieze, Great Mosque

Southeastern Turkey's liveliest city, Diyarbakır is situated on the edge of a high bank dropping down to the Tigris River. Its 6 km (4 miles) of black basalt walls encircle an old centre of cobbled streets and alleys, mosques, churches and mansions.

As the unofficial capital of Turkey's Kurdish-dominated southeast, political feelings can run high here. However, the inhabitants are generally warm and open to visitors, and justly proud of their atmospheric but economically deprived home city.

Diyarbakır is renowned for the gigantic watermelons sold in its markets. Watered by the Tigris River and fertilized with pigeon droppings, these can reach weights of up to 50 kg (112 lbs).

Vendor offering one of the region's famous watermelons

Exploring Diyarbakır

Most of the city's sights are concentrated in the central area and can be seen on foot. Walking alone around the walls is not recommended.

🏛 Archaeology Museum

Arkeoloji Müzesi
Elazığ Cad. **Tel** (0412) 224 67 40, 221 27 55. ◻ 9am–noon & 1–5:30pm Tue–Sun. 🖼
The most interesting section of this Archaeology Museum (situated outside the city walls, not far from the Harput Gate) is devoted to the Akkoyun and Karakoyun (White and Black Sheep). These Turcoman tribal groups ruled the region in the period between the decline of the Seljuks and the rise of the Ottomans.

🏨 Hasan Paşa Hanı

Gazi Cad. ◻ daily. ● Sun.
Located opposite the Great Mosque (Ulu Camii), and built by governor Verizade Hasan Paşa, the 16th-century *han* (see pp24–5) is still used by traders, and has some decent jewellery, carpet and antique outlets. The black basalt façade is dignified by a bold white limestone frieze.

◻ Great Mosque

Ulu Camii
Gazi Cad. ◻ daily. ● during prayer times.
A fairly plain building with a basilica-plan style, the Great Mosque is the most significant building in Diyarbakır, and is regarded as one of the holiest places in the Islamic world.

The Great Mosque, originally built by the Arabs in the 7th century

It was built on the site of a church around AD 639 after the Arabs captured the city. In 1091–92, the Seljuk ruler Malik Şah remodelled the building, using the revered Great Ummayad Mosque in Damascus as a model.

The interior is spacious and austere, while the courtyard buildings are built from black basalt with bands of white limestone, faced with blind arches supported by Roman columns interspersed with Seljuk friezes. The mosque faces a Roman *stoa* (portico), topped by a library.

🏛 Ziya Gökalp Museum

Ziya Gökalp Müzesi
Ziya Gökalp Bul. **Tel** (0412) 221 24 75. ◻ 8:30am–noon & 1–5pm Tue–Sun. 🖼
Ziya Gökalp, one of the chief ideologues of Turkish nationalism during the period of the Young Turks (see p57), was born in Diyarbakır. His house is now a museum.

◻ Kasım Padişah Mosque

Dört Ayaklı Camii
Yeni Kapı Cad. ◻ daily. ● during prayer times. 🖼 donation.
This was the last of the great mosques built under the reign of the Akkoyun (White Sheep) Turkomans. It is unusual for its free-standing minaret supported by four 2 m (6.5 ft) high basalt pillars carved from a single block of stone, known as the Dört Ayaklı Minare (four-legged minaret). It is said that your wish will be granted if you walk seven times around its pillars.

◻ Behram Paşa Mosque

Behram Paşa Camii
Melik Ahmet Cad. ◻ daily. ● during prayer times. 🖼 donation.
Built in 1572 on the orders of the governor, Behram Paşa, this centrally located mosque is the city's largest. The black basalt exterior is enlivened by white stone banding, and the interior is light and graceful. The central ceiling has a calligraphic frieze of inlaid mother-of-pearl.

Black-and-white banding on the Behram Paşa Camii

The impressive walls surrounding the old city

VISITORS' CHECKLIST

1,000,000. ✈ Kaplaner, 3 km (2 miles) SW of city centre.
🚆 1 km (0.5 mile) W of city centre, (0412) 221 87 87/87 86.
🚌 2 km (1 mile) NW of city centre, Ziya Gökalp Bulvarı.
ℹ Dağıkapı Burçu Giriş Bölümü, (0412) 228 17 06. 🎭
Watermelon Festival (Sep); Nevruz (21 Mar); Hıdrellez Festival celebrating spring migration (6 May, depending on weather).

🏰 City Walls

Diyarbakır'ın Kalesi

The black walls encircling the city – said to be visible from space – were originally built by the Romans (who captured Diyarbakır from the Sassanids in the 3rd century AD), since the city lacked natural defences. The Byzantines added to the structure, but what can be seen today is mainly the work of Seljuks, who captured the city in 1088.

Constructed from blocks of black basalt, the walls are pierced by four major gates (Harput, Yenikapi, Mardin and Urfa) and studded with 72 towers. The walls are 12 m (39 ft) high and more than 5 km (3 miles) in length. It is possible to walk along the top for much of the way.

The most impressive views are from the southern walls, looking down over the Tigris River winding its way towards Iraq. The Tower of the Seven Brothers (Yedi Kardeş Burçu), located between the Mardin and Urfa gates and built in 1208, provides a particularly good vantage point.

Environs

The **Atatürk Villa** was given to the founder of the Turkish Republic in 1937 by the citizens of Diyarbakır. On display are period photographs and personal effects. It is situated a few kilometres south of the city, off the road to Mardin, and has expansive views of the Tigris and the Dicle Köprüsü (Tigris Bridge). Built in 1065 on the site of an older structure, the bridge spans the river in 10 arches.

🏛 Atatürk Villa

Atatürk Köşkü

Tel (412) 223 30 70. ⏰ 8:30am–noon & 1:30–5pm daily. 🎫

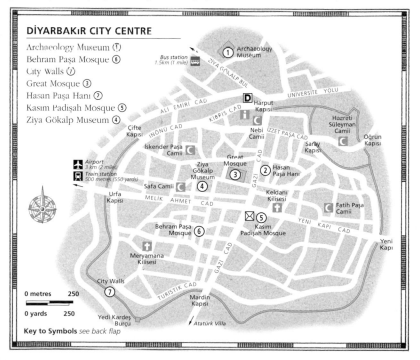

DİYARBAKıR CITY CENTRE

Archaeology Museum ①
Behram Paşa Mosque ⑥
City Walls ⑦
Great Mosque ③
Hasan Paşa Hanı ②
Kasım Padişah Mosque ⑤
Ziya Gökalp Museum ④

Bus station 1.5km (1 mile)

ZİYA GÖKALP BUL

Archaeology Museum ①

UNIVERSITE YOLU

UNIVERSITE YOLU

ALI EMIRI CAD

KIBRIS CAD

D Harput Kapısı

Çifte Kapısı

İNÖNÜ CAD

İskender Paşa Camii C

Nebi Camii

İZZET PAŞA CAD

Hazreti Süleyman Camii

Saray Kapısı

Oğrun Kapısı

Airport 3 km (2 miles)
Train station 500 metres (550 yards)

Ziya Gökalp Museum ④

Great Mosque ③

Hasan Paşa Hanı ②

GAZİ CAD

Urfa Kapısı

Safa Camii C

MELIK AHMET CAD

Keldani Kilisesi

Fatih Paşa Camii C

Behram Paşa Mosque ⑥

Kasım Padişah Mosque ⑤

YENI KAPI CAD

Yeni Kapı

Meryamana Kilisesi

GAZİ CAD

City Walls ⑦

0 metres 250
0 yards 250

TURİSTİK CAD

Mardin Kapısı

Yedi Kardeş Burçu

Atatürk Villa

Key to Symbols see back flap

Lake Van ❾

🏠 *250,000.* ✈ *6 km (4 miles) S of city centre, (0432) 216 10 19.* 🚌 *Ipek Yolu, NW of town centre.* 🚆 *to Tatvan, (0432) 223 41 38.* ⛴ *5 km (3 miles) from town centre.* ℹ *Cumhuriyet Cad 105, (0432) 216 25 30.*

The startlingly blue waters of Lake Van (Van Gölü) mirror the surrounding peaks, the highest of which soars to a dizzying 4,058 m (13,313 ft). The lake is seven times larger than Lake Geneva and may be up to 400 m (1,312 ft) deep. The lake has a salinity level well above that of sea water. It is so alkaline that locals need not use soap for washing. It is lovely for swimming.

The Van basin was once the centre of the Urartian civilization (contemporaries and foes of the Assyrians). The remnants of their fortified capital straddle the imposing Rock of Van, located close to the eastern shore of the lake. A few kilometres away is the modern town of Van. The small **Van Museum** contains many Urartian artifacts, including some fine gold jewellery. There is an ethnographic section on the first floor. The region is proud of its local champion breed of cat, with one blue eye and one amber. Out of character for a cat, this breed enjoys water.

🏛 **Van Museum**
Hacıosman Sok, Serefiye Mahallesi. **Tel** *(0432) 216 11 39.* ⏱ *9am–noon & 1–5:30pm Tue–Sun.* 📷

The Rock of Van, with an ancient Urartian citadel at the summit

Environs
Çavuştepe, 35 km (22 miles) southeast of Van, is another Urartian site, with a palace, sacrificial altar and inscriptions. It is best visited en route to the stark and hauntingly beautiful 17th-century castle at Hoşap, 60 km (37 miles) from Van on the same road.

The high point of a visit to the Lake Van area is the exquisite 10th-century Armenian **Church of the Holy Cross** (Akdamar Kilise), on a small island a few kilometres from the southern shore of the lake. The exterior boasts a remarkable series of bas-relief carvings and friezes showing biblical scenes. Cruciform in plan, and just 15 x 12 m (49 x 39 ft) in size, the church is topped by a conical roof. Its classical beauty makes this church one of the most photographed buildings in eastern Anatolia. The frescoes that adorn the interior walls and cupola are unique in their artistic merit. After a spectacular renovation, new life has been breathed into the 1,100-year-old church. Turkish officials have christened it a museum and are reticent on the subject of reconsecration.

On the lake's north-western shore is the crescent-shaped crater lake on Nemrut Dağı (not the mountain with the statues near Kâhta) and the Seljuk cemetery and *kümbet* (domed tombs) at Ahlat. Both are worth a visit and can be accessed from Tatvan.

The local cheese, *otlu peynir*, is a real delicacy. A whole-milk cheese flecked with nutritious and flavoursome mountain herbs, it is now rarely found outside the Van area.

ℹ **Church of the Holy Cross**
40 km (25 miles) SW of Van. ⛴ *from Gevaş.*

Doğubeyazıt ❿

🏠 *42,873.* 🚌 *Belediye Cad, W of town centre.*

Situated on the main road between Turkey and Iran, Doğubeyazıt is a half-hour drive from the border. Mount Ağrı (Ararat), Turkey's highest mountain, rises 5,165 m (16,945 ft) above the landscape. Although said to be the resting place of Noah's Ark, little evidence has ever been found to support this

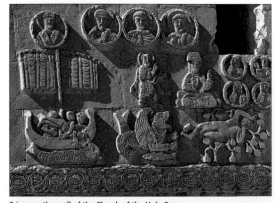
Frieze on the wall of the Church of the Holy Cross

◁ **Celme Hatun Mausoleum, Seljuk Cemetery, Lake Van.**

claim. Access is difficult and prospective climbers need to obtain permission from the Ministry of Culture and Tourism in Ankara *(see p387)* in advance.

The impressive **İshak Paşa Sarayı** lies 8 km (5 miles) southeast of Doğubeyazıt. The fortress-like palace was constructed from honey-coloured sandstone by an Ottoman governor in the late 18th century, although the variety of building styles (Ottoman, Persian, Armenian/Georgian and Seljuk) makes it difficult to attach an exact date. In Ottoman times, the palace lay on an important caravan route, explaining why such an opulent structure was erected in this lonely and remote part of the country.

The lavish arrangement of 366 rooms includes a harem with 14 bedrooms, *selamlık* (men's quarters) and a small but beautiful mosque whose interior has been badly damaged over the years. Ottoman and Russian troops occupied **İshak Paşa Sarayı** at various times and showed little regard for its historic importance.

Nearby attractions, best visited on a dolmuş tour from Doğubeyazıt, are the sulphur springs at Diyadin, and the Meteor Çukuru (meteor crater), just before the Iranian border.

🏛 İshak Paşa Sarayı
Tel (0472) 312 69 09. ⬜ 9am–noon & 1–5:30pm Tue–Sun.

Ağrı ⑪

🏘 92,500. 🚌 W side of town. ✈ (0472) 216 04 02. 🛈 Özel İdare Binası, Kat 4/11, (0472) 216 04 50/215 32 16.

The little town of Ağrı (the name means "pain" in Turkish) is located 1,640 m (5,380 ft) above sea level. The importance of the town stems from its position on the main road to Iran. Although unremarkable, Ağrı has accommodation and makes a convenient staging post for Doğubeyazıt to the east, Erzurum to the west and Van to the south.

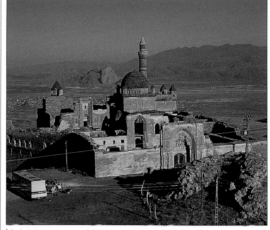
İshak Paşa Sarayı, on a hillside southeast of Doğubeyazıt

Kars ⑫

🏘 105,000. 🚌 2 km (1 mile) SE of town centre, (0474) 223 14 45. 🚆 off Cumhuriyet Cad, (0474) 223 43 99/43 98. ✈ (0474) 223 06 74. 🛈 Cumhuriyet Mah, Lise Sokak 15, (0474) 212 68 17.

Remote but strategically very important, Kars is set on a grassy plain that is backed by distant peaks. The word *kar* means "snow" in Turkish and winters here are long and cold, while the spring and autumn rains turn streets to mud. The brief summer season is hot, dry and dusty.

Founded in the 10th century by the Armenian King Abas I, Kars was once a metropolis of around 100,000 inhabitants. In 1064, it was captured by the Seljuks, and subsequently came under Georgian and Ottoman rule. It was held by the Russians from 1878 to 1919, and the grid plan and numerous run-down Neo-Classical houses are significant reminders of their presence here.

The citadel (Kars Kalesi) was built by the Ottomans, as was the 15th-century Taş Köprü (stone bridge) over the River Kars. The 10th-century Armenian Church of the Apostles now houses the Havariler Museum.

The small **Archaeological Museum**, just east of the town centre, is surprisingly good, particularly its displays of

kilims (rugs) and carpets.

Kars is known for its huge wheels of Kaşar, a classic cow's milk cheese. One of the city's gourmet secrets is its Gruyère that is produced by one cheese-maker using authentic Swiss techniques.

Environs
Many visitors visit Kars to see Ani *(see pp316–17)*, a visually dramatic, ruined 11th-century Armenian city 43 km (27 miles) away to the east, on the border with Armenia.

🏛 Archaeological Museum
Cumhuriyet Cad 365.
Tel (0474) 212 14 30.
⬜ 9am–noon & 1–5:30pm Tue–Sun.

The citadel at Kars, overlooking a Turkish bath

Ani ⑬

The ruined city of Ani, on the border with Armenia, is one of the most evocative historical sites in Turkey. Set on a windswept, grassy plateau along the Barley River (Arpa Çayı), the site contains important remnants of Armenian architecture, including the city walls protecting its northern border, parts of which are still intact.

Slit window, Ani Cathedral

In 961, Ani became the capital of the Bagratid kings of Armenia. It reached its apogee under King Gagik I (990–1020), when it was known as "the city of a thousand and one churches". Sacked by the Turks in 1064, Ani eventually recovered, only to be razed by an earthquake in 1319.

Tickets to the site are available from the Archaeological Museum in Kars, as well as at the entrance to the site itself.

Church of St Gregory (of Gagik)

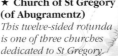

★ **Church of St Gregory (of Abugramentz)**
This twelve-sided rotunda is one of three churches dedicated to St Gregory.

View from Menücehr Mosque
This bridge, now ruined, spanned the Barley River (Arpa Çayı) in a single arch 30 m (32 yards) in length. The river demarcates the border between Turkey and Armenia.

City Walls

Maiden's Ca

Citadel
The Citadel is the oldest part of Ani and housed most of its residents until 961, when the Bagratids moved their capital here from Kars. It contains the ruined palace of the Bagratid kings.

STAR SIGHTS

★ Ani Cathedral

★ City Walls

★ Church of St Gregory

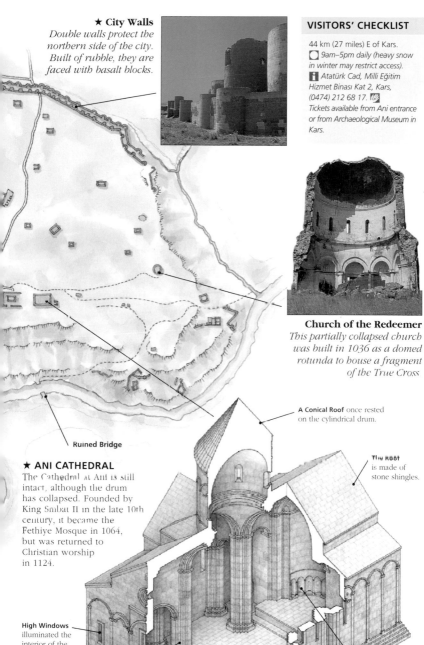

★ **City Walls**
Double walls protect the northern side of the city. Built of rubble, they are faced with basalt blocks.

VISITORS' CHECKLIST

44 km (27 miles) E of Kars.
🗓 *9am–5pm daily (heavy snow in winter may restrict access).*
ℹ️ *Atatürk Cad, Milli Eğitim Hizmet Binası Kat 2, Kars,* (0474) 212 68 17. 🎫
Tickets available from Ani entrance or from Archaeological Museum in Kars.

Church of the Redeemer
This partially collapsed church was built in 1036 as a domed rotunda to house a fragment of the True Cross

A Conical Roof once rested on the cylindrical drum.

Ruined Bridge

The Roof is made of stone shingles.

★ **ANI CATHEDRAL**
The Cathedral at Ani is still intact, although the drum has collapsed. Founded by King Smbat II in the late 10th century, it became the Fethiye Mosque in 1064, but was returned to Christian worship in 1124.

High Windows illuminated the interior of the cathedral.

Four Columns supported the drum.

The West Entrance was used by the citizens of Ani.

The Apse is lined with semicircular niches.

The South Entrance, reserved for the king, was one of three entrances.

Erzurum

Sandals formerly used in the Turkish Baths

Sprawling across a vast plain at an altitude of almost 2,000 m (6,560 ft) and ringed by mountains, Erzurum is one of Turkey's coldest cities. It is also by far the most developed city in the region. Because it was located astride the main caravan route from India to Europe, and controlled the passage between the Caucasus and Anatolia, Erzurum was fought over and ruled by many peoples – Byzantines, Sassanids, Arabs, Armenians, Seljuk Turks, Mongols and Ottomans. Its most famous sights date from Seljuk times. Like Kars, the city was in Russian hands for over 40 years. In 1919, Atatürk's Nationalists met here to map out the frontiers of modern Turkey.

The ornate entrance portal of the Yakut Seminary

Exploring Erzurum
Erzurum has a university and a large garrison population. It also hosts a rough-and-ready horseback competition (*cirit*), which involves throwing a spear at a target.

🏛 Archaeological Museum
Arkeoloji Müzesi
Paşalar Cad 11. **Tel** (0442) 233 04 14. ◻ *8am–5pm daily.* 🎟
Exhibits here range from Urartian metalwork and pottery to the jewellery and glassware of the Hellenistic and Roman eras.

🇨 Lala Mustafa Paşa Mosque
Lala Mustafa Paşa Camii.
Cumhuriyet Caddesi. ◻ *daily.* 🎟
This charming Ottoman mosque, built in 1562, conforms to a typical square-plan design, with columns and cupolas around a courtyard with a fountain. Original tile work adorns the interior.

🇨 Yakut Seminary
Yakutiye Medrese
Cumhuriyet Cad. ◻ *8:30am–noon & 1:30–5pm Tue–Sun.* 🎟
Built in 1310 by Hoca Yakut, governor of the İlhan Mongols,

this ornate Koranic school is widely regarded as the city's most beautiful building. The carved stonework around the entrance is very appealing and the short minaret has an elaborate lattice of brick and turquoise tiles.

🏰 Citadel
Kale
N of Çifte Minareli Medresesi.
◻ *8:30am–noon & 1:30–5:30pm daily (7pm in summer).* 🎟
The citadel was built in the 5th century, during the reign of Byzantine Emperor Theodosius. It was restored in 1555 by Sultan Süleyman I (the Magnificent) and served as the eastern base of the Janissaries (*see p56*). Inside is a ruined

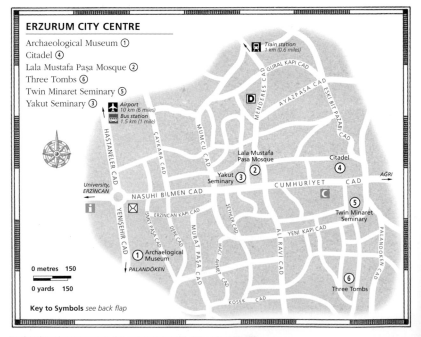

ERZURUM CITY CENTRE

Archaeological Museum ①
Citadel ④
Lala Mustafa Paşa Mosque ②
Three Tombs ⑥
Twin Minaret Seminary ⑤
Yakut Seminary ③

0 metres   150
0 yards   150

Key to Symbols *see back flap*

VISITORS' CHECKLIST

🏔 250,500. ✈ 10 km (6 miles) NE of city centre, (0442) 218 19 04. 🚌 1 km (0.5 mile) NE of city centre. 🚊 1 km (0.5 mile) N of city centre. 🛈 Cemal Gürsel Caddesi 9, (0442) 233 71 99 and 235 09 25. 🎭 Atatürk Congress and Festival (23 Jul). 📅 most days.

clocktower and also a mosque. There are fine views over the city from the walls.

🅒 Twin Minaret Seminary

Çifte Minareli Medresesi
Cumhuriyet Cad. ☐ 8am–5pm daily. 🆓

The two minarets that flank the soaring portal of the Çifte Minareli Medresesi have become the symbols of Erzurum. They are thought to have been built in 1253 on the authority of Huant Hatun, daughter of Seljuk Sultan Alaeddin Keykubad II. At the rear of the complex is the 12-sided cylinder tomb that contains her remains.

Twin Minaret Seminary

🏛 Three Tombs

Üç Kümbet
S of Twin Minaret Seminary. ☐ daily.
Built by the Seljuks, the oldest of these conical mausoleums dates from the early 12th century. It is distinguished by the use of contrasting light and dark stone and by its truncated cone.

Environs

Erzurum has a reliable ski season that runs from November to May. Palandöken Ski Centre (see p384), situated 8 km (5 miles) southwest of the city centre, has two hotels and six ski lifts serving 30 km (19 miles) of piste.

The gorge of the Euphrates (Firat) near Kemaliye

Erzincan ⑮

🏔 280,118 🛈 Atatürk Mah, Barış Manço Parkı içi, Kültür Sitesi, (0446) 214 30 79 or 223 06 71.

Erzincan's history has been marked by earthquakes, notably in 1939 and 1992. It was once considered one of Turkey's most impressive cities, but rebuilding work over the years has left it with few historic attractions.

Erzincan's specialities include decorative copperware and *tulum peynir*, a cheese made from raw milk, and sold encased in a sheep skin.

Environs

Altıntepe (Golden Hill), a Urartian site 27 km (17 miles) east of Erzincan, dates from around 700 BC. Many of the objects found here are now on display in Ankara's Museum of Anatolian Civilizations (see p242–3). One of the best of these is a bronze cauldron with handles in the shape of bulls' heads.

The little town of **Kemaliye** (formerly known as Eğin) lies in the Munzur Mountains not far from Erzincan. Founded in the 11th century, Kemaliye's pebbled streets, wild streams and trim wooden buildings offer a charming snapshot of life in Ottoman times.

Carving detail, Divriği

The Village Life Museum in Ocakköyü, near Kemaliye, is the only private ethnographic museum in Turkey.

🏛 Village Life Museum

Köy Müzesi
Ocakköyü. **Tel** (0446) 754 40 65.
☐ 9am–noon & 1–5pm Tue–Sun.

Divriği ⑯

🏔 18,000. 🚌 S of town centre, on road to Elazığ. 🚊 from Sivas, Erzincan or Malatya.

After the Seljuk victory at Manzikert (Malazgirt) in 1071 (see p52), Divriği became the seat of the Mengüçek state and was ruled by the Mengüç family from 1142 to 1252. Among many fine buildings they left behind is the *külliye* (mosque-hospital complex), the best example of 13th-century Seljuk stonecarving in Turkey, and now a UNESCO World Heritage Site. The ornate portals of the **Süleyman Şah** or Kale mosque (built around 1229) and the adjoining *daruşşifa* (hospital) – easy to spot as you come into town – display exceptionally rich decoration.

🅒 Süleyman Şah

Şehir district. ☐ 9am–5pm Mon–Fri. 🔴 weekends.

TRAVELLERS' NEEDS

WHERE TO STAY

Whether you wish to stay in an Ottoman sultan's opulent palace, a quaint *yalı* (traditional wooden summer house) on the Bosphorus, or a comfortable, cosy family home, you can find the accommodation of your choice in Turkey. Camping has become popular, and the new interest in trekking holidays means that you can sleep under the stars. Turkey's hotels and guesthouses cater for a wide range of budgets and, in general, are found clustered around the main sightseeing areas: in

Doorman at Hilton Hotel

Sultanahmet and Aksaray in Istanbul for instance. Some of the old towns, notably Safranbolu *(see pp268–9)*, offer accommodation in restored mansions and family homes around the historic town centre. The choice of hotels in Turkey's eastern provinces is more restricted. However, tourism potential here is now on an upward curve and accommodation in all price ranges is steadily improving. You can use the hotel listings provided on pp326–45 to find a place to stay that will suit your needs and price range.

CHOOSING A HOTEL

Many hotels in Turkey are rated by the Ministry of Tourism according to a star system, from one to five, with five stars being the most luxurious. Municipalities also use stars to rate their local accommodation, which can be confusing. Try not to base your choice exclusively on star ratings. Reputable hotels will allow you to see a room before you decide to stay. Hotel staff will often come to meet arriving buses and try to convince you to stay at their establishment.

Most hotels can be easily reached by public transport from the airport, bus or train station. With advance notice, most hotels will ferry guests to and from the airport. Many hotels in resort areas close from the end of October until March or April. Ask about this when you book, or look it up on the Internet. Most of the

major hotels have websites. Some hotels even advertise that they have a generator, ensuring that their services are not affected by Turkey's regular power cuts.

In southern coastal areas and inland plains, summer is hot and humid, so paying extra for an air-conditioned room can make a difference. Water shortages are a fact of life, so ask the smaller hotels if they have sufficient water. It also worth asking if the hotel has sufficient hot water.

Special License Hotels *(see p323)* are usually considered to be luxury establishments. Even if the listing says it is a *pansiyon* (pension), the comfort and décor will be first-rate, as well as the food. It is essential to book well in advance at these establishments and it is rare to find discounts here.

Lounge of the Ceylan Inter-Continental Hotel in Beyoğlu *(see p329)*

LUXURY HOTELS

Most of the up-market international hotel chains are represented in Istanbul, Ankara and İzmir, as well as the other larger cities around Turkey. Almost all five-star hotels offer fine views over a city skyline, the Bosphorus, a dreamy coastal vista or some picturesque harbour scene.

Luxury hotels typically have swimming pools, fitness and health facilities, *hamams* (Turkish baths), saunas and conference facilities. Resort hotels and holiday villages, in particular, feature extensive nightly entertainment. Most hotels will gladly arrange city or boating tours, as well as day trips, to local attractions. You can, of course, also organize these trips yourself at a lower cost.

Many hotels have set aside non-smoking areas. Many also make provision for disabled guests.

The cosy Konak Melsa Hotel in Dalyan, on the Mediterranean *(see p336)*

◁ Ottoman-style slippers for sale in the Grand Bazaar in Istanbul *(see pp104–105)*

Club Lykia World holiday village, nestling in a cove near Ölü Deniz

HOLIDAY VILLAGES

The coastal areas of Turkey have numerous holiday villages, self-contained resort complexes that offer a full range of holiday options for visitors, with access to their private stretch of beach. These may be more like mini-towns, but the lure of a holiday with all the frills and none of the concomitant worries continues to attract customers. Staying in a holiday village can be very economical, especially for families with children, as a great number of activities are included in the price of the holiday.

All the holiday villages offer programmes for children, as well as babysitting services and nightly entertainment programmes. Some, like the MIA Belpark Village near Belek *(see p336)* and Club Lykia World *(see p338)* near Ölü Deniz, cater for foreign diplomats and destination-management companies.

CHEAPER HOTELS

There is a wide choice of cheaper accommodation in Turkey, ranging from hotels and motels to family-run *pansiyons* (pensions). Some of the cheaper one-star hotels are not rated by the Ministry of Tourism, but by the local municipality, whose standards depend on the region. Therefore, when choosing one of the cheaper

hotels, take care not to base your decision on what you see in the newly renovated lobby; it is always best to see if the carpet runs past the first stairs. Most one-star hotels provide only minimal services, which could mean communal washing facilities. The safest bet would be to try to find a room in a *pansiyon*. Older ones are more like private houses with rooms to rent, but many of the newer ones are much like hotels in terms of services offered.

Hotel doorway, Selçuk

SPECIAL LICENSE HOTELS

Special license hotels are usually historic buildings that have been restored and transformed into quaint hotels. These do not fall under the auspices of the Turkish Ministry of Tourism and their facilities vary from grand luxury to the very basic. Most are found in the older quarters of Istanbul, and give guests a feeling for the lifestyle of the late Ottoman era. Many Special License Hotels are run by the **Turkish Touring and Automobile Club**, or TTOK *(see p407)*, which campaigns for the historic value of these buildings.

WHAT TO EXPECT

All hotels listed in this book were chosen because they provide comfortable, welcoming and secure accommodation. In the popular regions, front desk staff can be expected to speak English, but this is less likely in more remote areas. Hotel rooms cater for couples, with twin beds or a double bed and enough space to add a third if necessary.

Most multistorey hotels will have lifts but this will not be the case in older buildings converted into Special License Hotels. Facilities for wheelchair users are also found mainly in the more expensive hotels. Noise can be quite a problem in cities, even in the luxury hotels, so ask for a quiet room. It is perfectly in order to request hotel staff to put you in another room for any reason.

The price of the room will usually include breakfast. This will be either a set Turkish breakfast of fresh bread, butter, jam, soft white cheese, tomatoes, cucumbers and black olives, or a self-service buffet. In recent years, many hotels have begun to offer half board, with an evening meal thrown in. If you want to be independent, make this clear when you arrive. The evening meal may well turn out to be yet another buffet.

Yeşil Ev, a Special License Hotel *(see p327)*

The restored Sumengen and Historia hotels in Istanbul

PRICES AND DISCOUNTS

Hotel prices are quoted per room (not per person) in US dollars, Euros or Turkish lira. Bargaining is perfectly acceptable, and discounts are often available if you pay in hard currency. Even luxury hotels will offer a discount to business travellers. Ask for the corporate rate. In general, your success in bargaining will depend on how busy the hotel is. If it is empty, as is often the case in winter, then you have some leeway for negotiation. You can expect to pay premium prices during religious or national holidays, however, when virtually all accommodation is booked.

BOOKING A ROOM

It is always a good idea to book, especially in Istanbul or other large cities, and in the summer season between May and October. Telephone, fax and e-mail bookings are all accepted but, for peace of mind, try to confirm all your reservations and travel needs by fax. If you are travelling

Luxurious double room at the Bosphorus Palace Hotel in Istanbul *(see p330)*

with an organized tour, your agent should handle all the arrangements for you. Arriving in Turkey with a confirmed, written booking is always a good idea.

If you haven't pre-booked accommodation, or if you have changed your itinerary to get off the beaten track, visit any of the local tourist information offices to inquire about available accommodation. They will give you a list of local hotels, but leave it to you to make your choice and booking. Tourist offices can also give advice on approximate prices.

Don't be shy about looking around, seeing rooms and comparing prices.

CHECKING OUT AND PAYING

All guests are expected to check out by noon, but on special request most hotels will agree to hold luggage for collection later.

Except for the very remote or most economical establishments, most hotels listed in this guide accept major international credit cards. Fewer will accept travellers' cheques, and may even charge a commission to cash them.

Value-added tax (VAT) is known as KDV in Turkish *(see p397)* and is generally included in the price of a room. When you register at a hotel, you will often be

asked for your credit card, which will then be swiped through an authorization machine. You will be asked to sign the form and the card must then be resubmitted for payment when your account is finally settled.

As with most hotels, tips for the staff are always very much appreciated and remembered. A few dollars is adequate for junior personnel, while a little more is called for if the front desk has done something special for you.

Remember that phone calls and minibar drinks are additional charges that increase your bill substantially.

Hotel guests relaxing by the pool

CHILDREN

In most hotels, children up to the age of six years can stay in their parents' room at no extra charge. Many hotels also offer up to 50 per cent discount rates for 12–15-year-olds sharing a room with their parents. Cots for babies are willingly provided even by mid-range hotels. Children's menus are usually available in family resort areas and holiday villages. In Turkey, children generally are expected to eat when their parents do and they also tend to stay up late, particularly in the hot summer months.

HOSTELS AND STUDENT LODGINGS

Turkey has many youth hostels, student lodgings and even a state-sponsored youth travel scheme for those who are travelling on a limited budget, such as university students and backpackers. The state-sponsored scheme was initiated in 2000 for students between the ages of 18 and 26, and requires the travellers concerned to be able to identify themselves with an International Student Identity or Youth Hostel Association card. Students have half-price access to selected hotels all over Turkey, as well as camp sites and university dormitories. The dormitories, however, are only available during university holidays. Entry to all Culture Ministry museums and sites is half the posted price. Full details are available from the **Student Travel Association General Directorate**, or Yurtkur, in Ankara, and the **Interyouth Hostel** in Istanbul.

CAMPING AND CARAVANNING

Caravanning and camping holidays are becoming increasingly popular and many new areas are being developed into well-equipped, highly organized camping grounds that provide ample space for tents or trailers, as well as ablution facilities.

In parts of the country, cosy, furnished bungalows may be available for self-catered forest holidays.

However, please note that camping is only allowed in designated areas, so be sure to check with the **Turkish Camping and Caravanning Association**, who will be able to provide you with a list of approved sites.

Parking a caravan or pitching a tent on any deserted beach, or simply pulling over to the side of the road in a caravan is discouraged.

A quaint, old-fashioned pension in the back streets of Selçuk

GUESTHOUSES

This is a little-known type of accommodation in Turkey. The **Association for the Development of Tourist Guesthouses**, which is run by volunteers, gets requests for accommodation in all price ranges from all over the world. Even if municipalities or tourist information bureaux do not keep a list, patience is often rewarded, and excellent accommodation can nearly always be found.

SELF-CATERING

Most cities and towns in Turkey have apartment hotels for short-term rental. Pensions, too, often include cooking facilities, but these are usually shared with other guests. For tax reasons, not many self-catering apartments advertise openly, and word of mouth is the best way to locate these places. Some travel agents have lists of apartments, which they own and maintain, available for self-catering holidays.

Camping in the remote Kaçkar Mountains

DIRECTORY

HOTELS

Turkish Hotel Operators Union
Cumhuriyet Cad, Pak Apartman, Kat 6, Daire 12, Harbiye, Istanbul.
Tel (0212) 296 08 80 and 296 24 64.
Fax (0212) 343 84 36.
www.turob.org.tr

SPECIAL LICENSE HOTELS

Turkish Touring and Auomobile Club (TTOK)
(Turk Tur ve Otomobil Kulübü)
Oto Sanayi Sitesi Yanı 1, Seyrantepe Yolu, IV Levent, Istanbul.
Tel (0212) 282 81 40.
Fax (212) 282 80 42.
www.turing.org.tr

STUDENT TRAVEL

Student Travel Association General Directorate
Yurtkur (Ministry of Tourism for Student Travel), Ankara.
Tel (0312) 430 17 80.
www.kyk.gov.tr

CAMPING

Turkish Camping and Caravanning Association
Bestekar Sok 62/12, Kavaklıdere, Ankara.
Tel (0312) 466 19 97.
Fax (0312) 426 85 83.

Filiz Sok 52, Kartaltepe, Bakırköy, Istanbul.
Tel (0212) 571 42 44.
www.campcaravan.org

Bursa branch, Mudanya Cad, Ertürk Sok, Ermek Sitesi, F-Block, Sirameseler.
Tel (0224) 236 06 06.
Fax (0224) 256 88 26.

GUESTHOUSES

Association for the Development of Tourist Guesthouses
Cumhuriyet Bul, Elbir İşhanı 84/404, Alsancak, İzmir.
Tel (0232) 421 42 95.

Choosing a Hotel

The hotels in this guide have been selected across a wide range for their good value, facilities and location. For wheelchair access, please phone ahead. All the entries are alphabetical within each price category and map references refer to the Istanbul Street Finder maps on pp134–40.

PRICE CATEGORIES
For a standard double room per night, inclusive of breakfast, service charges and any additional taxes.

€ Under €50
€€ €50–75
€€€ €75–€100
€€€€ €100–€150
€€€€€ Over €150

ISTANBUL

SERAGLİO POINT Ararat
€€   Map 5 E5

Torun Sokak 3, Sultanahmet, 34400 **Tel** *(0212) 516 04 11* **Fax** *(0212) 518 5241* **Rooms** *11*

An unusual and highly individualistic family-run hotel that offers a variety of rooms, each with its own theme and one-of-a-kind décor. Ararat is located close to the Blue Mosque, and has splendid views across the Sea of Marmara, especially from the top-floor terrace. The owner is very helpul and knowledgeable about the area. **www.ararathotel.com**

SERAGLİO POINT Spectra Hotel
€€   Map 5 D3

Şehit Mehmetpaşa Yok 2, Sultanahmet, 34400 **Tel** *(0212) 516 35 46* **Rooms** *19*

One of the assets of this hotel is the owner, a retired archaeologist, who is a source of wisdom on many aspects of local life. Rooms are comfortable and well-appointed, and breakfast is served on the terrace with grand views of the Blue Mosque. Guests have free Internet access. Good location for all central sights. **www.hotelspectra.com**

SERAGLİO POINT Kybele Hotel
€€€   Map 5 E4

İncili Çavus Sok 37/3, Alemdar Mah, 34410 **Tel** *(0212) 511 77 66* **Fax** *(0212) 513 43 93* **Rooms** *16*

This tiny, multi-storied hotel is located in the heart of the tourist area, and with an array of antiques and craft items on display, Kybele has a homely, friendly atmosphere. A wonderful breakfast is served in the garden in summer, and in one of the ornate rooms in winter. A firm favourite with visitors. **www.kybelehotel.com**

SERAGLİO POINT Ayasofya Evleri
€€€€   Map 5 E4

Soğukçeşme Sokak, Sultanahmet, 34122 **Tel** *(0212) 513 36 60* **Fax** *(0212) 513 36 69* **Rooms** *64*

Nine restored wooden houses comprise this charming accommodation on the cobbled street behind Haghia Sophia. With beautiful names such as Jasmine, Honeysuckle and Rose, the houses are appropriately painted in pastel colours. Rooms are elegant and decorated with antiques. Booking is essential. **www.ayasofyapensions.com**

SERAGLİO POINT Mavi Ev
€€€€   Map 5 E5

Dalbastı Sokak 14, Sultanahmet, 34400 **Tel** *(0212) 638 90 10* **Fax** *(0212) 638 90 17* **Rooms** *27*

With the same polished management as the Pudding Shop, Mavi Ev is a distinctive Wedgwood blue *konak* (wooden mansion) restored in period style in the heart of Sultanahmet. It is peaceful and has a leafy garden and acclaimed rooftop restaurant. The views over the Sea of Marmara are magnificent. **www.bluehouse.com.tr**

SERAGLİO POINT Seven Hills
€€€€   Map 5 E5

Tevkifhane Sokak 8/A, Sultanahmet, 34400 **Tel** *(0212) 516 94 97/98/99* **Rooms** *14*

This is a hotel that goes out of its way to ensure its guests' stay exceeds expectations. Rooms are beautifully decorated and suites are spacious with private Jacuzzis and fitness facilities in each room. Incredible views, along with a first-class restaurant, are found on the terrace. **www.hotelsevenhills.com**

SULTANAHMET Dersaadet
€€   Map 5 E5

Küçük Ayasofya Cad, Kapıağası Sokak 5, 34400 **Tel** *(0212) 458 07 60/61* **Rooms** *17*

An impeccable hotel that features authentically designed and furnished rooms by traditional artisans. Small details abound in Dersaadet, including the Sultan's Penthouse suite. The owner is always around to ensure your stay is memorable. **www.hoteldersaadet.com**

SULTANAHMET Empress Zoe
€€   Map 5 E4

Akbıyık Cad, Adliye Sokak 4, 34400 **Tel** *(0212) 517 70 67* **Rooms** *22*

The two buildings that make up this hotel have been restored to an exceptionally high standard of design and come with an abundance of spacious suites. It is claimed that Empress Zoe actually lived here. The garden is idyllic and contains the remains of a bath house built in 1483. There are some no-smoking rooms available. **www.emzoe.com**

SULTANAHMET Hotel Alp Guest House
€€   Map 5 E4

Akbıyık Cad, Adliye Sokak 4, 34400 **Tel** *(0212) 517 70 67* **Rooms** *14*

There are wonderful views from the roof terrace of this hotel, hidden away behind the Blue Mosque. It is known as a friendly place to stay with excellent service and is designed to a high standard, with traditional furnishings in the bedrooms. **www.alpguesthouse.com**

Key to Symbols *see back cover flap*

SULTANAHMET Hotel Nena

Binbirdirek Mahallesi, Klodfarer Cad 8–10, 34400 **Tel** *(0212) 516 52 64* **Rooms** *29*   **Map** *5 D4*

Hotel Nena has a Byzantine atmosphere and is richly decorated and very comfortable. Some rooms have balconies with lovely sea and mosque vistas. The beautiful conservatory basks in the sun and has wrought-iron and glass furniture as well as flourishing tropical greenery. **www.nenahotel.com**

SULTANAHMET Nomade

Divanyolu Cad, Ticarethane Sok 15, 34410 **Tel** *(0212) 513 81 72* **Fax** *(0212) 513 24 04* **Rooms** *16*   **Map** *5 E4*

One of the oldest houses in this area, the Nomade has wonderful rooms. The owners have added appealing designer touches to the individually designed bedrooms and bathrooms. Meals and afternoon drinks are served on the rooftop terrace. **www.hotelnomade.com**

SULTANAHMET Sari Konak

Mimar Mehmet Ağa Cad 42–46, Sultanahmet, 34400 **Tel** *(0212) 638 62 58* **Rooms** *17*   **Map** *5 E5*

Sarı means "yellow" in Turkish, and this delightful wooden house is easily identifiable by its distinctive hue. The hotel has a charming patio, marble fountain and latticed balconies, and the rooms are tastefully decorated. The suites have high-speed Internet access. **www.istanbulhotelsarikonak.com**

SULTANAHMET Side Hotel and Pension

Utangaç Sokak 20, Sultanahmet, 34400 **Tel** *(0212) 458 58 70/517 22 82* **Fax** *(0212) 638 10 56* **Rooms** *36*

This family-run establishment offers a pension for budget-conscious guests as well as a ritzier hotel. Pension prices are cheaper and facilities fewer, with no air conditioning in rooms. The hotel is comfortable and some rooms have private Jacuzzis available as an extra. **www.sidehotel.com**

SULTANAHMET Alzer

At Meydanı 72, Sultanahmet, 34400 **Tel** *(0212) 516 62 62/63* **Fax** *(0212) 516 00 00* **Rooms** *21*   **Map** *5 D4*

This town house with beautifully furnished rooms has plenty of definitive touches. In the summer, tables are laid out at street level, but the greatest attraction is the roof restaurant. A cheerful bijou hotel with attentive service. **www.alzerhotel.com**

SULTANAHMET Avicenna

Amiral Tafdil Sokak 31–33, 34400 **Tel** *(0212) 517 05 50/54* **Fax** *(0212) 516 65 55* **Rooms** *49*   **Map** *5 E5*

Occupying two handsome Ottoman buildings, this conveniently located mid-range hotel has luxurious interior furnishings, including rich textiles, carpets and traditional wooden floors. Try to reserve rooms on the attic floors for panoramic sea views. **www.avicenna.com.tr**

SULTANAHMET Citadel

Kennedy Cad, Sahil Yolu 32, Ahırkapı,, 34400 **Tel** *(0212) 516 23 13* **Rooms** *31*   **Map** *5 E5*

Part of the Best Western group, this dusty pink Citadel hotel occupies a large stone building under the city walls. Rooms are small but pleasantly furnished with all the essentials. No-smoking rooms are available and some rooms look directly on to the sea. **office@citadelhotel.com**

SULTANAHMET İbrahim Paşa

Terzihane Sokak 5, Sultanahmet, 34400 **Tel** *(0212) 518 03 94* **Fax** *(0212) 518 44 57* **Rooms** *16*   **Map** *5 D4*

This charming stone-built hotel is located opposite the Museum of Turkish and Islamic Arts. Rooms are individually furnished and, along with the rooftop terrace, are stylish and unique. The decor successfully blends Art Deco with traditional Turkish influences. **www.ibrahimpasha.com**

SULTANAHMET Pierre Loti

Piyerloti Cad 5, Çemberlitaş, 34400 **Tel** *(0212) 518 57 00* **Fax** *(0212) 516 18 86* **Rooms** *36*   **Map** *5 D4*

Named after a Romantic novelist who lived in Istanbul, this was one of the first hotels in the area to be renovated to a high standard. The hotel is in the thick of things on the main road, but the summer garden and glass café give a fine view of the world going by. Rooms are small but wonderfully comfortable. **www.pierrelotihotel.com**

SULTANAHMET Valide Sultan Konağı

Kutlugün Sokak 1, Sultanahmet, 34400 **Tel** *(0212) 638 06 00* **Fax** *(0212) 638 07 05* **Rooms** *17*   **Map** *5 D4*

A long-term favourite with visitors to Istanbul, especially because of its proximity to the Topkapı Palace. The hotel rooms have been individually decorated and, although small, are comfortable. There is a glorious summer terrace with good views. **www.hotelvalidesultan.com**

SULTANAHMET Sultanahmet Palace

Torun Sokak 19, Sultanahmet, 34400 **Tel** *(0212) 458 04 60* **Fax** *(0212) 518 62 24* **Rooms** *36*   **Map** *5 D5*

This is the ideal place to spoil yourself. Less authentically refurbished than some other establishments, it is, nevertheless, a refined hotel that deserves its palace title. The garden is perfect, and the service is subtle and polished. The domes of the Blue Mosque rise right beside the hotel. **www.sultanahmetpalace.com**

SULTANAHMET Yeşil Ev

Kabasakal Sokak 5, Sultanahmet, 34400 **Tel** *(0212) 517 67 85* **Rooms** *19*   **Map** *5 E4*

Yeşil Ev (Green House) is a local landmark that typifies the spirit of Ottoman luxury. Rooms are furnished with antiques, one even has its own Turkish bath, and the service is impeccable. The secluded garden is beautiful and the restaurant outstanding. **www.istanbulyesilev.com**

SULTANAHMET Four Seasons 🍽 🛗 📋 €€€€€

Tevkifhane Sokak 1, Sultanahmet, 34110 **Tel** *(0212) 638 82 00* **Fax** *(0212) 638 85 30* **Rooms** *65* **Map** *5 E4*

Built as a prison for dissident writers in 1917, the Four Seasons has been restored to a Neo-Classical haven of luxury. Every room has a theme that blends Turkish traditions with contemporary comfort. It is ideally situated a short distance from the main Sultanahmet sights. **www.fourseasonshotel.com/Istanbul**

SULTANAHMET Kalyon 🍽 🛗 📋 🅿 €€€€€

Sahil Yolu 34, Cankurtaran, 34122 **Tel** *(0212) 517 44 00* **Fax** *(0212) 638 11 11* **Rooms** *112* **Map** *5 E5*

The Kalyon's position away from the centre of Sultanahmet means that it is quiet and faces directly on to the Sea of Marmara, attracting tourists, business customers and locals alike. Rooms are beautifully furnished to a superb standard, and the restaurant is one of the most underrated in the city. **www.kalyon.com**

THE BAZAAR QUARTER Aspen 🛗 📋 🅿 €

Aksaray Cad 25, Aksaray, 34470 **Tel** *(0212) 518 53 61* **Fax** *(0212) 518 53 91* **Rooms** *63* **Map** *4 A2*

Although there are no glorious views or extra luxuries, Aspen is an excellent hotel for those on a budget who do not want to sacrifice a central location. The hotel is near all the main sights with good public transport links in the busy Aksaray area. Service is cheerful. **www.aspenhotel.com.tr**

THE BAZAAR QUARTER Bulvar Palas 🍽 🛗 📋 🅿 €€

Atatürk Bul 152, Aksaray, 34470 **Tel** *(0212) 528 58 81* **Fax** *(0212) 528 60 81* **Rooms** *80* **Map** *4 A3*

This cheerful hotel has a pleasant atmosphere and comes equipped with a beauty treatment and fitness centre as well as a hairdressing salon and Turkish bath. The decor is traditional, and the large restaurant serves good Turkish dishes. An excellent hotel at a fair price. **www.hotelbulvarpalas.com**

THE BAZAAR QUARTER Royal Hotel 🍽 🛗 📋 €€

Aksaray Cad 16, Laleli, 34480 **Tel** *(0212) 518 51 51* **Fax** *(0212) 518 51 60* **Rooms** *128* **Map** *4 A4*

Within walking distance of all the main sights and transport facilities, the Royal Hotel is a popular place. While it is very good value for the money, the hotel still provides good services, including a satellite TV and a minibar in each room. Comfortable, well furnished and meticulously maintained. **www.royalhotelistanbul.com**

THE BAZAAR QUARTER President 🍽 🛗 📋 €€€

Tiyatro Cad 25, Beyazıt, 34126 **Tel** *(0212) 516 69 80* **Fax** *(0212) 516 69 98* **Rooms** *204* **Map** *4 C4*

The first hotel in Istanbul to have an English pub, the President has an excellent reputation. It is located in the heart of the city with well-appointed rooms and good service. Wireless Internet is available in the the reception area and in many rooms. The Turkish nights and belly-dancing evenings are legendary. **www.thepresidenthotel.com**

THE BAZAAR QUARTER Antik Hotel 🍽 🛗 📋 €€€€

Ordu Cad, Sekbanbaşı Sokak 10, Beyazıt, 34134 **Tel** *(0212) 638 58 58* **Rooms** *96* **Map** *4 B4*

This comfortable hotel, built around a 1,500-year-old water cistern, offers fine views over the Sea of Marmara. It also has an acclaimed pub, wine bar and unusual restaurant. The cistern itself has been converted into a subterranean night club. The Antik is a lively hotel that makes all ages feel at home. **www.antik-hotel.com**

BEYOĞLU Hotel La Villa 🛗 📋 🅿 €€

Topçu Cad 28, Taksim, 34437 **Tel** *(0212) 256 56 26/27* **Fax** *(0212) 297 53 28* **Rooms** *28* **Map** *1 B3*

La Villa is a small, low-cost but attractive hotel in the shadow of many prestigious, high-rise neighbours. It has all the things one would expect from a modern hotel, including Internet access, no-smoking rooms and 24-hour room service. The hotel arranges day trips and Turkish evenings for guests. **www.hotellavilla.net**

BEYOĞLU Aygün 🍽 🛗 📋 €€€

Lamartin Cad 53–55, Taksim, 80090 **Tel** *(0216) 338 48 38* **Fax** *(0212) 235 47 47* **Rooms** *28* **Map** *1 B3*

Tucked away in a tranquil corner of Taksim, the Aygün is well equipped as a home away from home. Rooms are beautifully designed and there is a Turkish bath and fitness centre, along with restaurants and a Vitamin Bar. A homely, extremely comfortable hotel. **www.aygunhotels.com**

BEYOĞLU Hotel Residence 🛗 📋 €€€

İstiklâl Cad, Sadri Alışık Sokak 19, Taksim, 80090 **Tel** *(0212) 252 76 85/87* **Rooms** *46* **Map** *1 B4*

From the slick reception area to the beautifully furnished rooms, Residence Hotel offers outstanding value given its location in the middle of the city. The rooms have an upmarket feel to them, and there is a fine restaurant with some inspired touches. **www.hotelresidence.com.tr**

BEYOĞLU Gezi Hotel 🛗 📋 €€€€

Mete Cad 42, Taksim, 80090 **Tel** *(0212) 251 74 30* **Fax** *(0212) 251 74 73* **Rooms** *46* **Map** *1 C3*

The Gezi has been upgraded, and offers well-equipped rooms. Some have spectacular views of the Bosphorus bridge, while others look out over Taksim Park. There is an excellent restaurant with a formal atmosphere and beautifully presented classic dishes. **www.hotelgezi.com**

BEYOĞLU Green Park 🍽 🛗 📋 €€€€

Abdülhak Hamit Cad 50, Taksim, 34173 **Tel** *(0212) 238 05 05* **Fax** *(0212) 237 76 46* **Rooms** *179* **Map** *1 B3*

One of the first modern hotels to open in Taksim, the Green Park has comfortable, well-decorated rooms. The restaurant is spacious and serves up good food and a wonderful open buffet breakfast. The staff can arrange tours of the city, as wells as car hire and Bosphorus cruises. **www.thegreenpark.com**

Key to Price Guide *see p326* **Key to Symbols** *see back cover flap*

BEYOĞLU Lamartine

Lamartin Cad 25, Taksim, 80090 **Tel** *(0212) 254 62 70* **Fax** *(0212) 256 27 76* **Rooms** *67*

Map *1 B3*

Named after the French poet who once visited Istanbul, Lamartine has a great location and is only a stone's throw away from Taksim's many sights, as well as the shopping outlets. The hotel itself is comfortable and room prices affordable. It is a short walk to the lively cultural district of Beyoğlu. **www.lamartinehotel.com**

BEYOĞLU Taxim Hill

Sıraselviler Cad 5, Taksim, 80090 **Tel** *(0212) 334 85 00* **Fax** *(0212) 334 85 98* **Rooms** *58*

Map *1 B4*

A distinctive landmark on the corner of Taksim's main square, Taxim Hill is a great place to stay with excellent business facilities, Jacuzzis and a well-equipped health club. Rooms are attractively decorated and comfortable, and some offer views over the Bosphorus. **www.taximhill.com**

BEYOĞLU Central Palace

Lamartin Cad 18, Taksim, 34437 **Tel** *(0212) 313 40 40* **Fax** *(0212) 313 40 39* **Rooms** *107*

Map *1 B3*

At this eminent hotel, late Ottoman style is combined with modern luxuries to great success. The rooms are luxurious and supremely comfortable, and there is an excellent health food restaurant. No alcohol is sold or served in the hotel but guests are permitted to drink in their rooms, if desired. **www.thecentralpalace.com**

BEYOĞLU Ceylan Intercontinental

Asker Ocağı Cad 1, Taksim, 34435 **Tel** *(0212) 368 44 44* **Fax** *(0212) 368 44 99* **Rooms** *382*

Map *1 C3*

This is one of the top hotels in Istanbul with first-class facilities, and is a favourite with stars and celebrities. The tea lounge is something of an afternoon tradition at the hotel, and the live harp music played here adds to the air of sophistication. The lively City Lights bar with its innovative design is a popular choice. **www.interconti.com.tr**

BEYOĞLU Divan

Cumhuriyet Cad 2, Elmadağ, 80090 **Tel** *(0212) 315 55 00* **Fax** *(0212) 315 55 15* **Rooms** *175*

Map *1 C3*

The Divan has long been one of the city's top hotels, offering superb service, excellent attention to detail and tastefully decorated rooms. It reopens in 2010 following a large renovation project so check the website for the latest information. The attached pub serves terrific food, as does the sushi restaurant. **www.divan.com.tr**

BEYOĞLU Hyatt Regency

Taşkışla Cad 1, Taksim, 34437 **Tel** *(0212) 368 12 34* **Fax** *(0212) 368 10 00* **Rooms** *360*

Map *1 C3*

The Hyatt Regency offers everything a guest could wish for, including three excellent restaurants (one of which is the best Japanese restaurants in town), lounge bars, a fitness centre, spa facilities and an indoor tennis court. All the rooms are richly furnished and decorated, and many have good views. **www.istanbul.hyatt.com**

BEYOĞLU Marmara Pera

Meşrutiyet Cad, Tepebaşı, 34437 **Tel** *(0212) 251 46 46* **Fax** *(0212) 249 80 33* **Rooms** *203*

Map *1 A5*

Marmara Pera provides every service a guest could ever need, and offers 360-degree views of the city. The hotel is particularly popular with business travellers, as wireless Internet access is available in every room.
www.themarmarahotels.com

BEYOĞLU Marmara Taksim

Taksim Meydanı, Tak-ı Zafer Cad, Taksim, 34430 **Tel** *(212) 251 46 96* **Rooms** *377*

Map *1 B4*

The rooms here are extremely comfortable and beautifully decorated. The Panorama restaurant on the hotel roof is a presitigious eating spot, while the trendy cafe on the ground floor is one of Istanbul's favourite meeting places. The hotel staff are friendly and helpful. **www.themarmarahotels.com**

BEYOĞLU Ritz Carlton

Süzer Plaza, Elmadağ, Şişli, 34367 **Tel** *(0212) 334 44 44* **Fax** *(0212) 334 44 55* **Rooms** *244*

Map *1 C3*

The Ritz Carlton stands out from the crowd with its classy, contemporary style and practised elegance. Every amenity is on offer here; even costumed Ottoman staff are on hand to help. The highly recommended restaurants serve the best of Turkish food, and the spa is one of the best in the city. **www.ritzcarlton.com**

BEYOĞLU Taksim Select

Topçu Cad 19, Taksim, 34437 **Tel** *(0212) 235 10 00* **Fax** *(0212) 254 75 95* **Rooms** *61*

Map *1 C3*

This is one of the friendliest mid-range hotels in the crowded hotel quarter bordering Taksim Square. Expect well-appointed rooms with good amenities and a fantastic breakfast that is served with great coffee. Good transport links for shopping in Nişantaşı and Beyoğlu. **www.taksimselect.com**

FURTHER AFIELD Kariye

Kariye Camii Sokak 18, Edirnekapı, 34240 **Tel** *(0212) 635 79 97/534 84 14* **Rooms** *27*

Situated close to the Church of St Saviour in Chora, the Kariye is a wooden *konak* (mansion) renovated in the style of the early 1900s. The rooms feature polished wooden floors and latticed windows, and the Asitane restaurant is famous for its rare Ottoman recipes. **www.kariyeotel.com**

FURTHER AFIELD Village Park Country Resort

Ayazma Mahallesi 19, Ishaklı Köyü, Beykoz, Asian Side, 81680 **Tel** *(0216) 434 59 31* **Rooms** *32*

This is a haven of peace and tranquility for those who prefer a rural setting. Weekend packages are available as well as country pursuits, such as horse riding and spa facilities. A restaurant, several bars and a popular picnic area make this a sought-after retreat. Dogs are welcome and kennels are provided. **www.villagepark.com.tr**

FURTHER AFIELD Bebek

Cevdetpaşa Cad 34, Bebek, Bosphorus 80810 **Tel** *(0212) 358 20 00* **Fax** *(0212) 263 26 36* **Rooms** *42*

Bebek is the ultimate in sumptuous living, as well as dining and clubbing. The bar at Bebek has been legendary for several decades, and the hotel has roomy, designer rooms. The restaurant is first rate and the setting, overlooking a bay, is particularly fine. **www.bebekhotel.com.tr**

FURTHER AFIELD Çınar

Şevketiye Mahallesi, Fener Mevkii, Yeşilköy **Tel** *(0212) 663 29 00* **Fax** *(0212) 663 29 21* **Rooms** *224*

The Çınar borders the Sea of Marmara, so rooms facing the sea are particularly sought after. The hotel has quality restaurants and bars, and the outdoor pool area and terrace can be enjoyed during the summer months. Easily reached from the airport (about a five-minute drive). **www.cinarhotel.com.tr**

FURTHER AFIELD Taşhan

Taşhan Cad 57, Bakırköy, 34142 **Tel** *(0212) 543 65 75* **Fax** *(0212) 561 09 8* **Rooms** *40*

Since being taken over by the Best Western hotel group, the Taşhan is greatly improved and is a friendly, efficient hotel. Snuggled in a leafy residential area, it is refreshingly remote from city lights, and is a short walk from Ataköy Marina, the Galleria shopping centre, and a ten-minute journey to the airport. **www.tashanhotel.com.tr**

FURTHER AFIELD Bentley Hotel

Halaskargazi Cad 75, Harbiye, 34367 **Tel** *(0212) 291 77 30* **Fax** *(0212) 291 77 40* **Rooms** *50*   **Map** *1 C1*

The Bentley symbolizes luxury and style, and has a great location in the heart of the city. Beautifully furnished suites are available, and the guest list of the glamorous and famous is impressive. The fusion cuisine restaurant and stylish bar are highly reputed. **www.bentley-hotel.com**

FURTHER AFIELD Bosphorus Palace

Yalıboyu Cad 64, Beylerbeyi, Bosphorus, 34676 **Tel** *(0216) 422 00 03* **Fax** *(0216) 422 00 12* **Rooms** *14*

A meticulously restored summer house on the Bosphorus waterfront, this is one of Istanbul's "super" hotels. High ceilings, gilded furniture and fabulous chandeliers set the imperial tone and is more European than Ottoman in style. A private boat commutes to central Istanbul. **www.bosphoruspalace.com**

FURTHER AFIELD Çırağan Palace Kempinski

Çırağan Cad 32, Beşiktaş, Bosphorus 34349 **Tel** *(0212) 326 46 46* **Rooms** *315*   **Map** *3 D3*

Designed to make guests feel like a sultan, the Çırağan is one of the city's leading hotels. A restored residence of the last Ottoman sultans, it retains its glory and oozes five-star opulence. It has a glorious summer terrace with the Bosphorus below. **www.ciragan-palace.com**

FURTHER AFIELD Istanbul International Airport Hotel

Atatürk Airport International Terminal, Yeşilköy, 34831 **Tel** *(0212) 465 40 30* **Rooms** *85*

The first of the hotels to be opened within Atatürk Airport, it is conveniently accessible by foot from the baggage claim area. The hotel has everything you are likely to want, but at a cost. Nevertheless, the bars, food and excellent service exceed anything available elsewhere in the airport. **www.airporthotelistanbul.com**

FURTHER AFIELD Swissotel The Bosphorus

Bayıldım Cad 2, Maçka, 34104 **Tel** *(0212) 326 11 00* **Fax** *(0212) 326 11 22* **Rooms** *600*   **Map** *2 A4*

Run by the Raffles Group, Swissotel is a popular choice with the jet set when in Istanbul. Set within 65 acres (26 ha) of grounds, and with Bosphorus vistas, it has ten restaurants and bars, a spa and wellness centre, and tennis courts. The glamorous shopping arcade will entice serious shoppers. **www.swissotel.com**

FURTHER AFIELD W Istanbul

Süleyman Seba Cad 22, Beşiktaş, 34357 **Tel** *(0212) 381 21 21* **Fax** *(0212) 381 21 85* **Rooms** *134*   **Map** *2 B4*

Located close to Akaretler Row, one of Istanbul's coolest neighbourhoods, the W offers rooms with opulent decor inspired by a mix of Ottoman harem and Zen. Many of the 134 rooms have a private garden. Dine on fusion food in the excellent Spice Market restaurant or enjoy cocktails in one of two relaxed lounge bars. **www.wistanbul.com.tr**

THRACE AND THE SEA OF MARMARA

BANDIRMA Eken Prestige Hotel

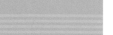

Uğur Mumcu Cad 9, 10230 **Tel** *(0266) 714 78 00* **Fax** *(0266) 712 53 55* **Rooms** *90*

Eken Prestige Hotel is a beautiful hotel overlooking the harbour of Bandirma. The hotel offers pleasant rooms, friendly service and wonderful dining. The town can get noisy with car traffic due to the ferry service that lands here, but still remains quaint. **www.ekenhotels.com**

BURSA Kent Hotel

Ataturk Cad 69, 16010 **Tel** *(0224) 223 54 20* **Fax** *(0224) 224 40 15* **Rooms** *54*

Kent Otel is conveniently located near all the sites of Bursa, as well as the shopping district and fashionable restaurants and bars. The rooms are pleasantly furnished; however, the bathrooms have only showers. There are two restaurants and a bar on the premises. Kent Otel has been a Bursa institution since 1968. **www.kentotel.com**

Key to Price Guide *see p326* **Key to Symbols** *see back cover flap*

BURSA Safran Hotel
Orta Pazar Cad, Arka Sok 4, Tophane, 16040 **Tel** *(0224) 224 72 16* **Fax** *(0224) 224 72 19* **Rooms** *9*

Safran is a small, boutique hotel located in a restored Ottoman house in Tophane's historical area. It is a short walk from the bazaar and the Osmangazi and Orhangazi tombs. The basement restaurant serves classic Turkish fare accompanied by live traditional music on weekends.

BURSA Central Hotel
Ulubatli Hasan Bulvari 55, 16240 **Tel** *(0224) 273 55 00* **Fax** *(0224) 273 52 70* **Rooms** *53*

Although Allstar Cental Hotel caters more to business travellers, its location is ideal for holidaymakers, too. It is close to the beaches on the shore of the Sea of Marmara, the historical sites of Bursa and Iznik, and Uludag Mountain. The bar is a popular Bursa watering hole. **www.centralotel.com.tr**

BURSA Holiday Inn Bursa
Uludag Universitesi, Gorukle Kampusu, 16240 **Tel** *(0224) 442 85 40* **Fax** *(0224) 442 87 96* **Rooms** *131*

Holiday Inn Bursa has everything that one might expect from a large hotel chain. A pool, health and fitness centre, fine dining and a nightclub are but a few of the amenities available. The hotel is located just outside the city of Bursa, allowing a peaceful stay while remaining close to all that the city has to offer. **www.holidayinnbursa.com**

BURSA Kervansaray Termal Hotel
Çekirge Meydanı, 16080 **Tel** *(0224) 233 93 00* **Fax** *(0224) 233 93 24* **Rooms** *211*

The stylish Kervansaray Termal has all the amenities of a modern large hotel, as well as the 700-year-old *hamam* (Turkish Bath), which is the central feature of the hotel. There are two swimming pools, one of which has an indoor and outdoor section. **www.kervansarayhotels.com**

BURSA Almira Hotel
Ulubatlı Hasan Bulvari, 5, 16200 **Tel** *(0224) 250 20 40* **Fax** *(0224) 250 20 39* **Rooms** *235*

The Almira Hotel is a modern five-star hotel located in the centre of Bursa. It has five restaurants, three bars, a pool, billiard tables and much more. The hotel also offers the Ottoman Square, which has 17 duplex villas, and provides a glimpse into Ottoman culture. **www.almira.com.tr**

BURSA The Celik Palas
Cekirge Cad 79, 16070 **Tel** *(0224) 233 38 00* **Fax** *(0224) 236 19 10* **Rooms** *156*

Founded in 1935 at the request of Mustafa Kemal Ataturk, Çelik Palas Otel is one of the oldest and most famous spa hotels in Turkey. From healing thermal spring waters to immaculate dining at the Marmara Restaurant, this hotel offers high-class luxury. **www.celikpalas.com**

BURSA/ULUDAĞ Ergün Hotel
Oteller Bölgesi, 16355 **Tel** *(0224) 285 21 00* **Fax** *(0224) 285 21 02* **Rooms** *31*

Ergün is a lovely hotel, right in the middle of Uludağ's ski resorts. The hotel has a charming atmosphere and is equipped with two restaurants, three bars, a sauna and much more. The amenities of a large luxury hotel can be enjoyed at this small hotel, but without the crowds. **www.uludaghotels.com/ergunhotel_uludag.html**

BURSA/ULUDAĞ Agaoglu My Resort Uludağ
Oteller Bölgesi, 16355 **Tel** *(0224) 285 20 01* **Fax** *(0224) 285 22 21* **Rooms** *184*

Agaoglu My Resort Uludağ has just about everything there is to offer. An all-around hotel, it caters mostly to skiers, and snowboards and skis are available to rent. There is a restaurant, two bars, a nightclub, an arcade, game room and children's club. Closed 1 Apr–1 Dec. **www.agaoglumyresort.com.tr**

BURSA/ULUDAĞ, Beceren Hotel
Oteller Bölgesi, 16355 **Tel** *(0224) 285 21 11* **Fax** *(0224) 285 21 19* **Rooms** *75*

Beceren Hotel is a classic Uludağ Mountain ski resort. Founded in 1947, the hotel boasts several activity areas and a fantastic Ottoman restaurant as well as warm, comfortable rooms. The hotel is open year-round, offering a multitude of winter sports during the winter months and health retreats during the summer. **www.beceren.com.tr**

ÇANAKKALE Anzac Hotel
Saat Kulesi Meydani 8, 17100 **Tel** *(0286) 217 77 77* **Fax** *(0286) 217 20 18* **Rooms** *27*

This boutique hotel is located near the famous clock tower in the centre of Çanakkale and is two minutes' walk from the harbour. Its amenities surpass its three-star rating. It has a restaurant with 24-hour room service and two bars. **www.anzachotel.com**

ÇANAKKALE Akol Hotel
Kordon Boyu, 17100 **Tel** *(0286) 217 94 56* **Fax** *(0286) 217 28 97* **Rooms** *136*

Akol Hotel is the only four-star hotel in Çanakkale. It is situated in the town centre, on the sea front and a few minutes away from the ferry landing. The rooftop restaurant and garden offers spectacular views and good food and there is a swimming pool. **www.hotelakol.com.tr**

ÇANAKKALE Tusan Hotel
Güzelyali, 17100 **Tel** *(0286) 232 87 47* **Fax** *(0286) 232 82 26*

Tusan Hotel offers the best of both worlds: it is close to all the historical sites in the area and also has the luxury of a private beach, hidden away in a pine forest. The hotel also has two wonderful restaurants and a good English pub. **www.tusanhotel.com**

EDİRNE Park Hotel

Maarif Cad 2 **Tel** (0284) 225 46 10 **Fax** (0284) 225 46 35 **Rooms** 60

Park Hotel is the perfect place for a short stay in Edirne. The rooms are basic but comfortable, the restaurant boasts the best kebabs in town and the lobby bar is said to be one of the oldest in the area. What Park Hotel lacks in luxury, it more than makes up for in character. **www.parkotel.com**

İZMİT Allstar Altinnal Hotel

Alemdar Street 7, 41040 **Tel** (0262) 321 54 72 **Fax** (0262) 322 05 33 **Rooms** 80

With beautiful views of the Gulf of İzmit from the restaurant, Allstar Altinnal Hotel is conveniently located in the centre of the city. The hotel offers comfortable rooms and a relaxed atmosphere with friendly staff. The restaurant offers both Turkish and French cuisine. **www.otelaltinnal.com**

ULUDAĞ Grand Yazici Hotel

Gelişim Bölgesi 1, 16355 **Tel** (0224) 285 20 50 **Fax** (0224) 285 20 48 **Rooms** 260

This hotel is one of the larger hotels in Uludağ. It opened its doors in 1983 and has been satisfying its guests ever since. The Grand Yazici is very well known and is frequented by many Turkish celebrities. The Grand Yazici Chalet is a separate building on-site, with 25 rooms in a traditional chalet style. **www.grandyazici.com**

THE AEGEAN

AYVALıK Kelebek Pension

Maresal Cakmak, Cad 108 **Tel** (0266) 312 39 08 **Fax** (0266) 312 39 08 **Rooms** 7

Kelebek Pension is a small pension, located within the historical city centre of Ayvalık, and is run by the Kiray family (he is Turkish and she is Dutch), who do everything possible to make their guests feel at home. The hotel is close to everything in Ayvalık, and the Kirays even offer specially designed tours of the area. **www.kelebek-pension.com**

BODRUM Yalı Han Hotel

Sah Cad 14, 48410 **Tel** (0252) 363 77 72 **Fax** (0252) 363 81 84 **Rooms** 16

Situated directly on the seafront, Yalı Han Hotel is only a few steps away from the beach. There is a pool and bar-café that is open all day, a Turkish-style buffet breakfast on offer and traditional tea and cakes served in the afternoon. Airport transfers are available on request. **www.yalihanotel.com**

BODRUM Aegean Holiday Village TMT

Ataturk Cad 134 (PK 63), 48400 **Tel** (0252) 316 12 08 **Fax** (0252) 316 26 47 **Rooms** 175

The TMT Aegean Holiday Village has 175 rooms plus 34 villas. There are superb gardens, friendly staff, and the rooms, although basic, are very clean. The location is ideal too, just outside of Bodrum – a leisurely stroll along the cliff path to the harbour will take about ten minutes. **www.bodrum-hotels.com/tmt/index.htm**

BODRUM Hotel L`Ambiance

Büyük Iskender Yolu Myndos Kapısı Pk: 422, 48400 **Tel** (0252) 313 83 30 **Fax** (0252) 313 82 00 **Rooms** 162

L'Ambiance is resort hotel located in the historic area near Myndos Gate. Although it does not have direct access to the beach, its guests are entitled to use the facilities at the Xuna Beach Club in Yalıkavak (30 mins away, with free transfers). The hotel has a beautiful pool and garden and offers fine dining. **www.lambiance.com**

BODRUM Azka Hotel, Bodrum

Bardakçı Cove, 48400 **Tel** (0252) 316 89 92 **Fax** (0252) 316 82 14 **Rooms** 200

This is a lovely, well maintained hotel with fantastic facilities although it is situated at the bottom of a steep hill. The beach is lovely and guests have free use of the canoes, which make it easy to explore the bay. Guests are not allowed to bring food or water from outside the hotel complex. **www.azkaotel.com**

BODRUM Club Flipper

Tilkicik Mevkii, Yalikavak, 48400 **Tel** (0252) 385 33 33 **Fax** (0252) 385 33 65 **Rooms** 50

Club Flipper, located 30 minutes by bus from Bodrum, is a large, well-regarded resort with its own private beach, swimming pools and excellent dining. The resort offers self-catering apartments and hotel rooms and the full list of facilities. **www.clubflipper.com.tr**

BODRUM Majesty Marina Vista Hotel Bodrum

Neyzen Teyfik Cad. 226, Marina Karsisi, 48400 **Tel** (0252) 313 03 56 **Fax** (0252) 316 23 47 **Rooms** 84

Located directly across from the marina, this hotel has wonderful views and is in walking distance to the centre of Bodrum. The decor is lovely, and in the tranquil inner courtyard is a large swimming pool with a separate children's pool and a snack bar. Dinner on the roof is a must. **www.majesty.com.tr**

BODRUM Myrina Hotel

Kücükbük Mevki, Gündoğan, 48400 **Tel** (0252) 387 83 31 **Fax** (0252) 387 83 34 **Rooms** 40

This is a good option for a family holiday in a small, quiet town on the Bodrum peninsula. Rooms are in two-story buildings that surround a large swimming pool and are set in lovingly tended gardens. The beach is a four-minute walk. **www.hotelmyrina.com**

Key to Price Guide see p326 **Key to Symbols** see back cover flap

BODRUM Antique Theatre, Bodrum

Kibris Sehitleri Cad 243, 48400 **Tel** *(0252) 316 60 53* **Fax** *(0252) 316 08 25* **Rooms** *20*

Named after the ancient theatre across the street, this hotel offers rooms that are simple but come with small marble bathrooms. All of the rooms offer spectacular views as does the pool and the bar. The Antique Theatre is set back from the marina and harbour. **www.antiquetheatrehotel.com**

BODRUM Barcelo Rexene Resort

Asarlık Mevkii Gümbet, 48400 **Tel** *(0252) 317 25 68* **Fax** *(0252) 317 25 77* **Rooms** *166*

The Rexene Resort is located close to the centre of Bodrum and is made up of 24 apartments, all of which are air conditioned and have a balcony or terrace. Each apartment offers an attractive view of the outdoor swimming pool and on-site facilities include a bar, restaurant, and children's playground. **www.rexeneresort.com**

BODRUM Lavanta Hotel

Papatya Sokak 32, Yalikavak, 48400 **Tel** *(0252) 385 21 67* **Fax** *(0252) 385 22 90* **Rooms** *8*

This boutique hotel with a large pool offers a luxurious retreat in a peaceful hillside location above the seaside town of Yalıkavak. Eight individually styled rooms are furnished with antiques and local carpets. There is great attention to detail throughout, from the warm welcome provided by the owners to the delicious cuisine. **www.lavanta.com**

BODRUM Maki Hotel

Mimoza Sokak 10, Türkbükü, 48400 **Tel** *(0252) 377 61 05* **Fax** *(0252) 377 60 56* **Rooms** *60*

Located on the seafront with direct access to the sea, the Maki offers comfortable, spacious rooms with either sea or garden views. A sea plane taxies guests in from Istanbul and excursions by yacht are available. There's a pool with a smaller children's pool attached to it and a restaurant serving excellent Italian cuisine. **www.makihotel.com.tr**

BODRUM Fuga Fine Times

Asarlık Mevkii, 48400 **Tel** *(0252) 317 23 60* **Fax** *(0252) 317 23 63* **Rooms** *213*

Fuga Fine Times is a contemporary, laid back hotel with a private beach, spectacular views, well-rated food and comfortable lounging and sunbathing areas. The hotel is on a steep incline, and courtesy electric buggies and a cable car offer transport to the beach and restaurant if your room is further away. **www.fuga.com.tr**

BODRUM Hapimag Resort Sea Garden

Yaliciftlik 3, 48400 **Tel** *(0252) 368 90 10* **Fax** *(0252) 368 90 56* **Rooms** *285*

Hapimag Resort Sea Garden is a large, beautiful resort about half an hour away from Bodrum and located within a pine forest. The grounds are magnificent and there are three private beaches, two quiet and one which offers water sports. All amenities available. **www.hapimag-seagarden.com**

BODRUM Kempinski Hotel Barbaros Bay Bodrum

Kizilagac Koyu, 48400 **Tel** *(0252) 311 03 03* **Fax** *(0252) 311 03 00* **Rooms** *148*

Located on a cliff overlooking Barbaros Bay, this hotel is famed for its Six Senses Spa, and is one of the most luxurious hotels in Bodrum. Some of the amenities include a private beach, a huge swimming pool, free Wi-Fi, a helicopter pad and a marina dock. It also boasts the only Vietnamese restaurant in Turkey. **www.kempinski-bodrum.com**

BODRUM Kervansaray Bodrum Village

Zeytinlikhahve Mevkii Torba, 48400 **Tel** *(0252) 337 14 00* **Fax** *(0252) 337 14 30* **Rooms** *468*

Kervansaray Resort Bodrum is an all-inclusive resort just outside of Bodrum and probably has the most stunning garden of any Bodrum hotel. The rooms are comfortable and clean, the food is excellent and the pool and beach are breathtaking. For a large hotel, there is surprising attention to detail. **www.kervansarayhotels.com**

BODRUM The Marmara Bodrum

Yokusbasi Mah. Suluhasan Cad 18, 48400 **Tel** *(0252) 313 81 30* **Fax** *(0252) 313 81 31* **Rooms** *100*

The Marmara Bodrum is a small luxury hotel and the stylish, Japanese-influenced rooms all have balconies. There is a rooftop restaurant, swimming pool and splendid garden. The Party Animal Suite is available for private parties, complete with butler. **www.themarmarahotels.com**

DATCA Olive Garden

Musediye Bay, Ovabuku, Datca, 48900 **Tel** *(0252) 728 00 56* **Fax** *(0532) 615 41 06* **Rooms** *14*

The Olive Garden offers a good selection of rooms with balconies and sea views. The hotel has a charming garden and a swimming pool. The restaurant is superb with a wonderful assortment of main courses and snacks available all day. **www.olivegardenhotel.com**

GÜLLÜK Ikont

Yeni Mah 22, Mailbox 18, 48670 **Tel** *(0252) 522 28 21* **Fax** *(0252) 522 24 26* **Rooms** *36*

This hotel is just outside of Bodrum, away from the crowds, and has its own private beach as well as two public beaches nearby. Also available is table tennis and a tennis court, and mountain bikes to rent. For nightlife, the hotel has a restaurant and three bars. **www.ikonthotel.com**

GÜLLÜK Corinthia Labranda Hotel

Güllük, 48670 **Tel** *(0252 522 29 11* **Fax** *90 252 522 20 09* **Rooms** *140*

The hotel overlooks the fishing village of Güllük and offers breathtaking views of Mandalya Bay. It is in a quiet location yet offers the facilities of an exciting beach resort. It should be noted that Bodrum is 30 minutes away and its beach is not spectacular. **www.corinthiahotels.com**

İZMİR Crowne Plaza Hotel İzmir

 €€€

İnciraltı Cad 67, 35340 **Tel** *(0232) 292 13 00* **Fax** *(0232) 292 13 13* **Rooms** *219*

Situated twenty minutes from İzmir's centre, this very modern hotel has spacious, luxurious rooms and a bar with panoramic views. The hotel is conveniently near a large shopping centre and guests have free use of the spa, which has two pools, a Turkish bath, jacuzzi, sauna and a hydropool. Prices are lower at weekends. **www.cpizmir.com**

İZMİR Kaya Prestige

€€€

Şair Eşref Bulvari 1371 Sok 7, 35280 **Tel** *(0232) 483 03 23* **Fax** *(0232) 489 22 99* **Rooms** *142*

Kaya Prestige has medium-sized rooms that are well decorated with good quality furniture. The decoration is modern and mainly in pastel shades. Although this is an average standard hotel, it is in an ideal location in the heart of the city and close to the main shopping and sightseeing attractions. **www.kayaprestige.com.tr**

İZMİR Anemon Hotel İzmir

€€€€

Mürselpaşa Bul. 40, 35280 **Tel** *(0232) 446 36 56* **Fax** *(0232) 446 36 55* **Rooms** *101*

Anemon Hotel İzmir is situated in the centre of İzmir near the International Fair Grounds. It is a traditionally decorated hotel and offers non-smoking floors. The lobby and restaurant are decorated with unique samples of oriental design. **www.anemonizmir.com**

İZMİR İzmir Princess Hotel – Balçova

 €€€€

Ilica Mah. Zeytin Sk. 112, 35330 **Tel** *(0232) 238 51 51* **Fax** *(0232) 239 09 39* **Rooms** *300*

This hotel is located in an area surrounded by lovely greenery. The rooms have good views over the Gulf of İzmir and the forest, and have thermal water in the bathrooms. The wellness section is good for massage and beauty treatments, and the food has a good reputation. **www.izmirprincess.com.tr**

İZMİR Hilton İzmir

€€€€€

Gazi Osmanpaşa Bulvari 7, 35210 **Tel** *(0232) 497 60 60* **Fax** *(0232) 497 60 00* **Rooms** *381*

The İzmir Hilton is the tallest building in İzmir, giving the rooms some magnificent views. Expect an excellent breakfast, and there is an amazing restaurant on the 31st floor. A city hotel that comes equipped with a pool and fitness centre. **www.izmir.hilton.com**

KUŞADASı Anzak Golden Bed Boutique Pension

€

Aslanlar Cad., Ugurlu 1 Cikmazi 4, 09400 **Tel** *(0256) 614 87 08* **Fax** *(0256) 614 87 08* **Rooms** *15*

This is an authentic Turkish bed and breakfast, situated in the old quarter of Kuşadası. The hotel is minutes from the shopping area, port and beaches. All rooms have private bathrooms and some have balconies with a view of the sea. There is a spectacular view from the restaurant on the garden roof top. **www.kusadasihotels.com/goldenbed**

KUŞADASı Eke Apart Hotel

€

Birlik Yapi Koop Amber Sokak 23, 09400 **Tel** *(0256) 618 16 97* **Fax** *(0256) 618 26 95* **Rooms** *51*

The Eke is a friendly, family-run hotel that makes guests feel right at home. The rooms are clean and the hotel is spotless throughout. The hotel is about ten minutes walk up a hill from the city centre and in a quiet residential area. There is a pool and disco and very friendly staff. Children are welcome. **www.ekehotel.com**

KUŞADASı Grand Özçelik

 €

Yavansu Mevkii, 09400 **Tel** *(0256) 622 18 18* **Fax** *(0256) 622 03 65* **Rooms** *116*

Positioned right on the beach, Grand Özçelik is a beach lovers dream. This hotel is a bit out of town, but taxis are easily available for transport to Kuşadası. The wonderful views of the sun setting from the hotel is reason enough to stay here, and there are lots of fun activities for kids. **www.ozcelikhotels.com**

KUŞADASı Sözer Hotel

€

Yat Limanı Karşısı Atatürk Bulvarı 68, 09400 **Tel** *(0256) 614 89 36* **Fax** *(0256) 614 89 40* **Rooms** *90*

Sözer Hotel is probably one of the best value accomodations in Kuşadası. The rooms are clean and the staff are very courteous. The hotel is situated directly across from the marina, so the views are spectacular from the front rooms. It is very centrally located so everything is within walking distance. **www.hotelsozer.com**

KUŞADASı Tuntaş Apart Hotel

€

Boyalik Cad 2 No 36, 09400 **Tel** *(0256) 613 36 55* **Fax** *(0256) 613 36 58* **Rooms** *70*

Tuntas Apart Hotel has seventy individual apartments, each accomodating four people and with kitchens. There is a pool party on Wednesdays and a Turkish night on Fridays with a buffet and belly dancers. Can be noisy but a lot of fun, if you don't mind being thrown into the pool. **www.tuntashotels.com**

KUŞADASı Grand Önder Hotel

€€

Ataturk Bulvari, 09400 **Tel** *(0256) 618 16 90* **Fax** *(0256) 618 16 89* **Rooms** *80*

Just minutes from the centre of Kuşadası, the Grand Önder, although not a modern hotel, is one of the most dependable in Kuşadası. The sea views from many of the rooms are amazing, and the staff are very friendly and go out of their way to make their guests' stay a pleasant one. **www.onderotel.com**

KUŞADASı Hotel Grand Blue Sky

 €€

Kadinlar Denizi, 09401 **Tel** *(0256) 612 77 50* **Fax** *(0256) 612 42 25* **Rooms** *325*

A Kuşadası legend, The Grand Blue Sky is a beautiful hotel with large and comfortable rooms and friendly, hospitable staff. All food and drink is included as well as many activities. The beach is down 90 steps, making the hotel not suitable for anyone with walking difficulties. **www.grandbluesky.com**

Key to Price Guide *see p326* **Key to Symbols** *see back cover flap*

KUŞADASı Polat Beach Hotel

Söke Yolu, Yavansu Mevkii, 09400 **Tel** *(0256) 622 09 09* **Fax** *(0256) 622 10 04* **Rooms** *65*

Polat Beach Hotel is about ten minutes' taxi ride from Kuşadası. It has an indoor and an outdoor swimming pool, sauna and massage room. Table tennis, beach volley ball, jet-ski, canoe rentals and water skiing are some of the available activities. The hotel is right on the beach. **www.polatbeach.com**

KUŞADASı Tusan Beach Resort, Kusadası

Tusan Beach Resort, 09400 **Tel** *(0256) 618 15 15* **Fax** *(0256) 618 15 55* **Rooms** *366*

This all-inclusive hotel has many good features, but perhaps its best is its location – it is far enough away from the town to feel secluded but close enough to be in town in five minutes. A huge number of activities are available; however, this hotel is not recommended for people with walking difficulties. **www.tusan.com.tr**

KUŞADASı Fantasia Hotel de Luxe

Yavansu Mevkii, 09400 **Tel** *(0256) 622 05 50* **Fax** *(0256) 622 07 65* **Rooms** *331*

Fantasia Hotel is an all-inclusive resort right on the beach, with dolmus connections to Kuşadası and beyond. The staff are friendly and efficient and there is plenty to entertain both children and adults alike. The private beach is too deep for children to swim in, so good for those wanting quiet. **www.fantasia.com.tr**

KUŞADASı Hotel Kismet

Gazi Begendi Bulvari 1, 09400 **Tel** *(0256) 618 12 90* **Fax** *(0256) 618 12 95* **Rooms** *107*

Hotel Kismet is Kuşadası royalty. It was founded by the Late Princess Hümeyra Özbaş, and her elegant touches can be seen throughout the hotel. The hotel is conveniently located and has beautiful views and gardens.Even if you don't stay here, it is worth visiting for afternoon tea in the garden. **www.kismet.com.tr**

KUŞADASı Imbat Hotel

Kadinlar Denizi, 09401 **Tel** *(0256) 614 20 00* **Fax** *(0256) 614 49 61* **Rooms** *313*

The rooms at Imbat Hotel are spacious and clean, and it has a lovely pool and sandy beach. There is entertainment by the pool during the day, fun for both children and adults. Drinks and food are in abundance throughout the day, and in the evening the buffet provides a good selection of dishes. **www.imbat.com.tr**

KUŞADASı Korumar Hotel

Gazi Beğendi Mevki P.K.18, 09400 **Tel** *(0256) 618 15 30* **Fax** *(0256) 618 11 10* **Rooms** *272*

Korumar Hotel is one of Kuşadası's finest hotels. Its location is amazing and the views are spectacular. It deserves the five-star rating it has been awarded, having all the normal trappings of a five-star hotel, but offers good value for the luxury provided. **www.korumar.com.tr**

KUŞADASı Aqua Fantasy Holiday Village

Ephesus Beach (Pamucak) Selçuk, 09400 **Tel** *(0232) 893 11 11* **Fax** *(0232) 893 14 10* **Rooms** *868*

Aqua Fantasy Holiday Village is one of the best rated hotels in Kuşadası. Connected to the Aqua Fantasy Water Park, it attracts more children than other resorts, but for adults there are a number of restaurants and bars to entertain and an amazing spa. **www.aquafantasy.com**

KUŞADASı Hotel Ephesus Princess

Pamucak/Selçuk, 35920 **Tel** *(0232) 893 10 11* **Fax** *(0232) 893 10 38* **Rooms** *352*

The Hotel Ephesus Princess is a large all-inclusive resort located on the outskirts of Kuşadası (there are frequent buses to town). The rooms are basic but clean and there is a choice of hotel rooms or villas. There is a private beach, swimming pools and fantastic entertainment for both adults and children **www.princess.com.tr**

MEDITERRANEAN TURKEY

ALANYA Saray Beach Hotel

Sarah Mah Atatürk Cad 151, 07400 **Tel** *(0242) 512 60 80* **Fax** *(0242) 519 08 51* **Rooms** *69*

Saray Beach Hotel is located on the famous Cleopatra Beach in Alanya. Although not overly luxurious, Saray Beach goes out of its way to make its guests' holiday memorable, and provides friendly Turkish hospitality. The hotel has a private beach and pool, and at night there's live music and a beach party. **www.saraybeach.com**

ANTALYA Sealife Resort Hotel & Spa

Konyaalti Sahil Şeridi, 07590 **Tel** *(0242) 229 28 00* **Fax** *(0242) 229 19 93* **Rooms** *126*

Situated in Konyaalti, Antalya, Sealife hotel is located in a modern building. As it right opposite the beach and near town it is in a convenient location but can get noisy and rooms can get hot during the day. The resort does not have its own private beach and water cannot be brought in from outside. **www.sealifehotel.com**

ANTALYA Alp Paşa Boutique Hotel

Barbaros Mah Hesapci Sok 30, 07100 **Tel** *(0242) 247 56 76* **Fax** *(0242) 248 50 74* **Rooms** *72*

Alp Paşa Hotel is an authentic antique Ottoman home that has been transformed into a hotel. The hotel is exquisite; they offer a whirlpool filled with milk and rose petals, but it is expensive and decent beaches are a bus or taxi ride away. The hotel is half-board, so no water can be brought in from outside. **www.alppasa.com**

ANTALYA Marina Residence Hotel   🍴 ▤   €€

Mermerli Sok 15, Kaleici, 07980 **Tel** *(0242) 247 54 90* **Fax** *(0242) 241 17 65* **Rooms** *41*

Built from three Ottoman mansions, Marina Residence Hotel has a charm all its own. This is a special class hotel but would have five stars if it was larger. The rooms are extremely comfortable with fantastic views of the marina, and there is a pool surrounded by a lovely garden and an excellent restaurant. **www.marinaresidence.net.tr**

ANTALYA Riviera Suite Hotel   🍴 🧍 ▤ P   €€€

Akdeniz Bulvari, 07070 **Tel** *(0242) 229 01 93* **Rooms** *36*

Located on Konyaalti beach, Riviera Suite Hotel is a comfortable hotel with a great view. The hotel comes equipped with a swimming pool, children's pool, an outdoor and an indoor restaurant, a snack bar, a pool bar, laundry service, rent-a-car service, water sports and live music. **www.rivierasuitehotel.net**

ANTALYA Dedeman Antalya Resort and Convention Centre   🍴 🧍 ▤ P   €€€€

Lara Yolu, 07100 **Tel** *(0242) 316 20 20* **Fax** *(0242) 316 20 30* **Rooms** *482*

Dedeman Antalya is a large hotel situated just outside the old town area, in a sublime location. The rooms are quite large and comfortable and there is an open-air terrace restaurant. There is a noisy disco on the beach until 3am every night so enquire about a quiet room if this would bother you. **www.dedemanhotels.com**

ANTALYA Divan Antalya Talya Hotel   🍴 🧍 ▤ P   €€€€

Fevzi Çakmak Cad 30, 07100 **Tel** *(0242) 248 68 00* **Fax** *(0242) 241 54 00* **Rooms** *204*

Antalya's oldest hotel is situated near the old town and harbour and is thus a short walk to everything central. It has its own ocean swimming area (with elevator access) and views over Antalya Bay. The restaurant serves fantastic food –the Sunday garden brunch is recommended–and the open buffet is huge. **www.divan.com.tr**

ANTALYA Sheraton Voyager Antalya Hotel, Resort & Spa   🍴 🧍 ▤ P   €€€€

100 Yil Bulvari, Konyaaltı Sahili, 07050 **Tel** *(0242) 238 55 55* **Fax** *(0242) 238 55 70* **Rooms** *400*

The Sheraton Voyager is one of the first five-star hotels in Antalya. The rooms are spacious and very clean, the food is top notch, and there is also a wonderful spa onsite. The staff and management will do all they can to ensure their guests' stay is an enjoyable one. **www.sheraton.com/antalya**

BELEK MIA Belpark Village   🧍 ▤ P   €€

Belek Turizm Merkezi, İskele Mevkii, 07980 **Tel** *(0242) 715 13 00* **Fax** *0242) 715 13 17* **Rooms** *320*

One of an international chain of resorts, the MIA Belpark Village offers a great range of activities for children as well as nightly entertainment. There is a doctor on call, baby-sitting service, indoor football, volleyball, water sports, boutique and car rental.

BELEK Gloria Verde Resort & Spa   🍴 🧍 ▤ P   €€€€

Ileribası Mev. Belek, 07500 **Tel** *(0242) 710 05 00* **Fax** *(0242) 715 24 19* **Rooms** *292*

Gloria Verde Resort & Spa is the sister resort of the larger Gloria Golf Resort. Guests at either resort can use all the services of each and there is a shuttle between the two. There is plentiful entertainment for both children and adults and a DJ or live music on most nights. **www.gloria.com.tr**

BELEK Cornelia De Luxe Resort   🍴 🧍 ▤ P   €€€€€

Ileribasi Mevkii, Belek, 07980 **Tel** *(0242) 710 15 00* **Fax** *(0242) 715 25 05* **Rooms** *291*

The Cornelia is the all-inclusive of all-inclusives. If possible, stay at the villas, which are connected to the pools via special bridges, providing the opportunity to swim when desired. The resort has all the amenities and activities of other all-inclusives, but the Cornelia just does it better. **www.corneliaresort.com**

BELEK Xanadu Resort Hotel   🍴 🧍 ▤ P   €€€€€

Acısu Mevkii PK 49, Belek, 07500 **Tel** *(0242) 710 00 00* **Fax** *(0242) 715 24 81* **Rooms** *420*

Xanadu Resort Hotel is one of the best hotels in Turkey, providing amazing service, food, activities and rooms, and everything is immaculately clean and well cared for. There is an antique-style amphitheatre and columns that surround the pools. **www.xanaduresort.com.tr**

CALKAYA WOW Kremlin Palace   🍴 🧍 ▤ P   €€€€€

Kundu Village, Calkaya, 07110 **Tel** *(0242) 431 24 00* **Fax** *(0242) 431 24 16* **Rooms** *837*

WOW Kremlin Palace is part of the WOW chain and is designed after the Kremlin, and actually is very impressive. As with all WOW Hotels, this is an all-inclusive hotel and has all the same amenities. The Kremlin's rooms, and staff, however, are the best of them all. **www.wowhotels.com**

CALKAYA WOW Topkapi Palace   🍴 🧍 ▤ P   €€€€€

Kundu Köyü, Calkaya, 07110 **Tel** *(0242) 431 23 23* **Fax** *(0242) 431 23 22* **Rooms** *908*

World of Wonders Topkapi Palace is something of a design marvel – the resort is a replica of the famous Topkapi Palace in Istanbul. It has all the same amenities and activities that other WOW Hotels have but with an added palatial charm. The resort is beautiful and the rooms sumptuous. **www.wowhotels.com**

DALYAN Konak Melsa   🍴 ▤ P   €

Köyceğiz Cad, Çavuşlar Mah **Tel** *(0252) 284 51 04/51 05* **Fax** *(0252) 284 39 13* **Rooms** *25*

The highly professional Dutch-Turkish owners have done up this lovely little hotel in caravanserai style using local stone and carved wood. The rooms are on the small side but it is in a quiet location and has a pool, bar, restaurant and an Internet café. **www.konakmelsa.com**

Key to Price Guide *see p326* **Key to Symbols** *see back cover flap*

GÖCEK Hotel Forest Gate

Cumhuriyet Mah No:13 Yeşilvadi, 48310 **Tel** (0252) 645 26 29 **Fax** (0252) 645 24 32 **Rooms** 24

The idyllic Hotel Forest Gate is surrounded by a beautiful pine forest and comes equipped with a pool, restaurant and bar. The rooms are very nicely decorated and, although the hotel is in a forest, the hotel is still close to the sea and is walking distance from town. **www.hotelforestgate.com**

GÖCEK Swissôtel Göcek Marina Resort

Cumhuriyet Mahallesi, Göcek, 48310 **Tel** (0252) 645 27 60 **Fax** (0252) 645 27 67 **Rooms** 57

This small, luxury hotel is quiet and tranquil and only 20 minutes from Dalaman airport. The hotel's pebbly beach is the only beach in the area and is ten minutes walk or five minutes by the hotel's golf buggy. There are good restaurants and a few shops within walking distance making a car unnecessary. **www.gocek.swissotel.com**

KALKAN Hidden Garden

İslamlar Yolu Üzeri - Akbel, 07690 **Tel** (0242) 844 10 41 **Fax** (0242) 844 10 42 **Rooms** 20

Why stay in a hotel when there is the opportunity to stay in a cedar wood bungalow set in a wonderful garden. This is a side of Turkish life that other tourists miss out on. Enjoy the peace and quiet of being away from the masses without being too isolated and relax in the beautiful gardens.

KALKAN Hotel Pirat

Kalkan Marina, 07960 **Tel** (0242) 844 31 78 **Fax** (0242) 844 31 83 **Rooms** 136

Hotel Pirat is located in the Kalkan Marina. The two good sized swimming pools have great views and there is an à la Carte restaurant, roof-top terrace, café bar and disco. The hotel is close to Kalkan's only beach and there are plenty of restaurants nearby. Ask to stay in the reception block if you do not want to walk up stairs. **www.hotelpirat.net**

KALKAN Club Xanthos Hotel Antalya

Kalamar Köyü, Kalkan, 07960 **Tel** (0242) 844 23 88 **Fax** (0242) 844 23 55 **Rooms** 70

A great hotel overlooking the sea and with an amazing view. Staff are friendly and the food is good. Note that Kalkan is a good half hour walk and taxis are expensive; however, the hotel does offer one-way courtesy shuttles. The hotel is half board and drinks are expensive. No special children's entertainment. **www.clubxanthos.com**

KAŞ Hideaway Hotel

Anfitiyatro Sok 7, Yeni Camii Mah **Tel** (0242) 836 18 87 **Fax** (0242) 836 34 52 **Rooms** 20

Located in a quiet, centrally located residential area, and with dazzling sea vistas (the top floor has the best views) this charming and tasteful family-run hotel comes highly recommended. The hotel offers home cooked Turkish food on its rooftop restaurant and the staff are extremely helpful. **hideaway@superpostra.com**

KAŞ Hotel Kayahan

Koza Sokak 9, 07580 **Tel** (0242) 836 13 13 **Fax** (0242) 836 20 01 **Rooms** 33

Hotel Kayahan is centrally located in the lively town of Kaş and is close to the beach. The rooms are basic but air conditioned and comfortable. Breakfast and dinner are open-buffet and are served on the terrace, which has a wonderful view. There is a small pool; however, it is not suitable for small children. **www.hotelkayahan.com**

KAŞ Aquapark Hotel Antalya

Cukurbag Yarimadasi, 07580 **Tel** (0242) 836 19 01 **Fax** (0242) 836 19 92 **Rooms** 123

This hotel has a stunning sea view and every room has a balcony to admire it from. There are excellent children's facilities including a children's pool, two water slides, playground, garden and daily scheduled activities. For adults, there are shops, bars and a disco. **www.aquapark.org**

KAŞ Gardenia Hotel

Hükümet Cad 47 Küçükçakıl Mevkii, 07580 **Tel** (0242) 836 23 68 **Fax** (0242) 836 28 91 **Rooms** 11

When guests step into one of the rooms at Gardenia, they can relax. All the rooms are charming, comfortable, clean and elegantly furnished and with magnificent views. Dinner is recommended and the owners have great attention to detail. The hotel has many returning guests. **www.gardeniahotel-kas.com**

KAŞ Kaş Hotel Club Barbarossa

Cukurbag Peninsula P.Box 13, 07580 **Tel** (0242) 836 40 71 **Fax** (0242) 836 40 84 **Rooms** 21

This hotel, situated about six km outside of Kaş on the peninsula, is only open during the summer months. The hotel provides a number of excursions (extra) and is ideal for independent holiday makers. They have a restaurant with a fine menu. **www.hotelbarbarossa.com**

KEMER Rosarium Hotel

Atatürk Cad 4, 07980 **Tel** (0242) 814 50 36 **Fax** (0242) 814 50 40 **Rooms** 42

Rosarium Hotel is a family-run all-inclusive hotel in Kemer with basic but clean rooms. The architecture of the hotel is very beautiful as is the pool. The hotel has a private, blue flag beach nearby with free use of sun loungers and umbrellas. **www.rosariumhotel.com**

KEMER Alatimya Village Hotel Antalya

Ataturk Cad 20, Kemer, 07980 **Tel** (0242) 814 69 00 **Fax** (0242) 814 69 10 **Rooms** 336

Alatimya Village is a resort built directly on the beach. The guests are mainly Turkish and German, but that is not a problem as most of the staff speak English. This is a great place for kids as the hotel has a tremendous amount of activities for children. As an all-inclusive, everything is free. **www.alatimya.com.tr**

KEMER The Maxim Resort Hotel   🍴 🏊 📋 🅿   €€€

Atatürk Bulvarı, 07980 **Tel** *(0242) 814 70 00* **Fax** *(0242) 814 70 70* **Rooms** *304*

The Maxim is an all-inclusive resort hotel with a private beach nearby and is in walking distance of Kemer. Expect luxury, but without the hefty price tag. Children are well catered for with many facilities and activities, and there are excellent spa facilities. **www.themaximhotels.com**

KEMER Orange County Resort Hotel   🍴 🏊 📋 🅿   €€€€

Atatürk Bulvarı Yeni Mah, 07980 **Tel** *(0242) 814 72 00* **Fax** *(0242) 814 72 33* **Rooms** *513*

Orange County Resort Hotel have created a miniature Holland in Turkey with this resort. The hotel offers a reasonable all-inclusive package but with over 500 rooms, be warned it does get busy! The majority of guests are German and there are no demarcated no-smoking areas. **www.orangecounty.nl**

KEMER WOW World Palace   🍴 🏊 📋 🅿   €€€€

Kiriş Mevkii, Kemer, 07980 **Tel** *(0242) 824 69 50* **Fax** *(0242) 824 69 70* **Rooms** *815*

World of Wonders World Palace Hotel is another all-inclusive WOW hotel in Kemer and is well-run and friendly. A large range of activities for both adults and children are on offer. The private beach is stony but there are swimming pools. There are beautiful gardens and shops. **www.wowhotels.com**

KEMER WOW Kiris Resort   🍴 🏊 📋 🅿   €€€€€

Kiriş Mevkii, Kemer, 07985 **Tel** *(0242) 824 70 50* **Fax** *(0242 824 70 60* **Rooms** *773*

World of Wonders Kiris Resort is an all-inclusive hotel with large rooms and a distinctly Polynesian feel. Situated right on the beach, the hotel offers a full range of activities for adults and kids alike and a wide range of dining facilities. **www.wowhotels.com**

MARMARIS Grand Cettia Hotel   🍴 🏊 📋 🅿   €€

Şehit Ahmet Benler Cad 97, 48700 **Tel** *(0252) 417 40 00* **Fax** *(0252) 417 40 07* **Rooms** *244*

This modern all-inclusive hotel has large rooms and a full range of activities, although the food selection is not always exciting. Be warned that it is situated on a slope so not suitable for anyone with walking difficulties. It is closed in winter. **www.cettia.com**

ÖLÜ DENİZ Club Lykia World   🏊 📋 🅿   €€€

PO Box 102 **Tel** *(0252) 617 02 00* **Fax** *(0252) 617 03 70* **Rooms** *824*

Popular with holidaymakers with young families, this is a large holiday resort right on the beach with large rooms, a busy programme of activities, adult (quiet) areas and a disco.The location is hilly but there are wheelchair walkways and buggies for transport. **www.lykiaworld.com**

SIDE Lotus Motel   🍴 📋 🅿   €

1003 Sok No: 6 Yali Mah, 07331 **Tel** *(0242) 753 53 83* **Fax** *(0242) 753 53 82* **Rooms** *27*

Lotus Motel is an adorable little motel with the beach nearby, and they will ferry you between here and the hotel. They have a delightful little restaurant that serves freshly home-made Turkish dishes. Have a drink by the poolside bar and relax the day away. **www.lotus-motel.com**

SIDE Sertkaya Hotel   🍴 🏊 📋 🅿   €

Yali Mah Çigdem Sk No:18, 07331 **Tel** *(0242) 753 52 22* **Fax** *(0242) 753 26 89* **Rooms** *105*

The rooms at Sertkaya Hotel are basic but clean, as are the pools and fitness areas. This is an all-inclusive hotel that won't break the budget. The hotel also has a beach, where chairs and umbrellas are free of charge. At night, there are a variety of shows. **www.sertkayahotel.com**

TEKİROVA Rixos Hotel Tekirova   🍴 🏊 📋 🅿   €€€€€

Tekirova Beldesi PK 137, 07995 **Tel** *(0242) 821 40 32* **Fax** *(0242) 821 40 44* **Rooms** *600*

Rixos Tekirova is a beautiful, all-inclusive hotel with its own bay. The rooms are not overly large but they are clean and nicely decorated. There is an evening dress code, the food is excellent and the staff very helpful. The hotel feels spacious and comfortable and the activities team is very good. **www.rixos.com/tekirova**

ANKARA AND WESTERN ANATOLIA

ANKARA Alfin Hotel   🍴 📋 🅿   €

Menekşe 1 Sok No:11, 06440 **Tel** *(0312) 417 84 25* **Fax** *(0312) 418 62 07* **Rooms** *40*

Alfin is a nicely decorated small hotel and has very friendly members of staff who provide a high standard of customer care. The hotel is great for families and is centrally located and close to all the sights. The restaurant is quite good and their prices are very reasonable. **www.alfin.com.tr**

ANKARA Almer Hotel   🍴 📋 🅿   €

Cankiri Cad 17, 06300 **Tel** *(0312) 309 04 35* **Fax** *(0312) 311 56 77* **Rooms** *72*

Hotel Almer is ideally situated in the centre of Ankara, only a few minutes from the Ulus square and close to the bus depot. The rooms are pleasant and clean. There is an à la carte restaurant in the evenings and an open-buffet continental breakfast in the morning. **www.almer.com.tr**

Key to Price Guide *see p326* **Key to Symbols** *see back cover flap*

ANKARA Atalay Hotel

Çankırı Cad 20, Ulus, 06300 **Tel** *(0312) 309 15 15* **Fax** *(0312) 309 27 57* **Rooms** *90*

The Atalay Hotel is located in the centre of Ankara. The rooms are nicely furnished, although basic, and well equipped. There's a large meeting room for conferences, a nice restaurant and bar, and for families there is a good reliable babysitting service. There is a Turkish breakfast buffet and international cuisine throughout the day. **www.atalayhotel.com**

ANKARA Capital Hotel Ankara

Çankırı Cad 21, Ulus 06300 **Tel** *(0312) 310 45 75* **Fax** *(0312) 310 45 80* **Rooms** *58*

Capital Hotel Ankara is located conveniently in the middle of the historical and business centres. All rooms are air conditioned and furnished with fully orthopaedic beds. The hotel offers good value for money, helpful staff and excellent food. **www.hotelcapital.com.tr**

ANKARA Hotel Oğultürk

Rüzgarlı Cd. Eşdost Sok 6, 06030 **Tel** *(0312) 309 29 00* **Fax** *(0312) 311 83 21* **Rooms** *68*

Hotel Oğultürk is a pleasant small hotel in the centre of Ankara, and the management go out of their way to make guests feel at home. This hotel is the closest to sights such as Ankara Castle, Museum of Anatolian Civilization and Ethnographic Museum and the Roman Baths. The hotel also has a superb restaurant. **www.ogulturk.com**

ANKARA Şahinbey

Hisarpark Cad Alataş Sok 5, 06300 **Tel** *(0312) 310 49 55* **Fax** *(0312) 310 78 77* **Rooms** *25*

Although it has a rather bland exterior, Şahinbey Hotel offers outstanding value for money in the centre of the city, close to many historical sights as well as a multitude of bars and restaurants. Twenty minutes drive from Ankara airport and with 24 hour room service and mini-bar. **www.sahinbeyhotel.com**

ANKARA Turist Hotel

Çankırı Cad 37, 06300 **Tel** *(0312) 310 39 80* **Fax** *(0312) 311 83 45* **Rooms** *120*

The modern guestrooms of Turist Hotel are decorated in white with colourful touches. The hotel is a short walk from Ulus Square, and each room has its own balcony. Facilities include a restaurant, bar, conference facilities and fitness centre. **www.turisthotel.com.tr**

ANKARA Best Western Ikibin (2000)

Bestekar Sok 29, Kavaklidere 06680 **Tel** *(0312) 419 90 01* **Fax** *(0312) 419 90 16* **Rooms** *61*

Best Western Hotel Ikibin (2000) caters more for stop-over or business travellers. There are a wide range of amenities as expected from a respected chain, such as sauna and Jacuzzi, but this is generally not an extended stay hotel. A benefit of a Best Western hotel is that guests know what to expect. **www.hotel2000.com**

ANKARA Hotel Dedeman Ankara

Akay Cad, Büklüm Sok 1, 06660 **Tel** *(0312) 417 62 00* **Fax** *(0312) 417 62 14* **Rooms** *299*

At Dedeman Ankara the rooms are small and basic, but comfortable. Request a quiet room as some can be noisy from traffic outside. Amenities include swimming pools, sauna, fitness centre and high-speed wireless internet connection in public areas (free). The hotel also has three restaurants. **www.dedemanhotels.com/ankara**

ANKARA Radisson SAS Hotel

İstiklal Cad 20, 06030 **Tel** *(0312) 310 48 48* **Fax** *(0312) 309 36 90* **Rooms** *202*

The Radisson Ankara is another splendid hotel by Radisson SAS. Comfort is assured and there is a fitness centre and business facilities. The hotel has two lovely restaurants, and at one you will find the finest Mexican cuisine in Ankara. The hotel has views over a park and is conveniently situated next to a subway. **www.radissonsas.com**

ANKARA Neva Palas

Küçükesat Cad 32, 06700 **Tel** *(0312) 419 58 88* **Fax** *(0312) 419 58 25* **Rooms** *60*

The Neva Palas is centrally located in the fashionable Çankaya district and a few minutes walk from the city centre. The rooms are elegantly decorated as is the lobby and reception. They offer fine dining in a choice of three restaurants, which offer Turkish, international and vegetarian cuisine. **www.nevapalas.com/tr**

ANKARA Ramada

Tunali Hilmi Cad 66, Kavaklidere 06680 **Tel** *(0312) 428 20 000* **Fax** *(0312) 428 47 27* **Rooms** *72*

This is not your run of the mill Ramada; this hotel has pulled out all the stops to make their guests feel as relaxed and entertained as possible. From the plasma TVs to the elegant colour schemes, this hotel is quite special. Located in the centre of Ankara and near all attractions. **www.ramadaankara.com**

ANKARA Sürmeli Ankara

Cihan Sok 6, 06430 **Tel** *(0312) 231 76 60* **Fax** *(0312) 229 51 76* **Rooms** *205*

Sürmeli Ankara is centrally located and offers good value for money. It has very large rooms, two restaurants and a bar and nightclub. There is an outdoor pool, Turkish bath, sauna, and fitness club. Largely discounted rates can be found online. **www.surmelihotels.com**

ANKARA Houston

Guniz Sok 26, 06700 **Tel** *(0312) 466 16 80* **Fax** *(0312) 466 16 74* **Rooms** *59*

Hotel Houston is an immaculately decorated hotel. The rooms are large and attractive with very nice bathrooms. There is a sauna and fitness room and massage is also available. The hotel aims to allow their guests to relax and rid themselves of the stresses of the day. The management and staff are very attentive. **www.hotelhouston.com.tr**

ANKARA Ankara Hilton SA
🍴 🏃 ▤ 🅿 €€€€

Tahran Cad 12, Kavaklidere 06700 **Tel** *(0312) 455 00 00* **Fax** *(0312) 455 00 55* **Rooms** *315*

Ankara Hilton is similar to all other Hilton hotels, offering a wide range of services and luxurious, well-appointed rooms. Located in a quiet residential area, near a shopping mall and district but further from the airport than some more centrally located hotels. The restaurant is good and the staff friendly. **www.hilton.co.uk**

ANKARA Bilkent Hotel and Conference Centre
🍴 🏃 ▤ 🅿 €€€€

Bilkent 1 Cad, 06700 **Tel** *(0312) 266 46 86* **Fax** *(0312) 266 46 79* **Rooms** *114*

Although primarily known as a business hotel, Bilkent Hotel is a quality hotel and offers classically styled rooms, a 24-hour room service menu, an outstanding Sunday brunch in other words, the full range of amenities. The Ashram Spa is heavenly and well worth a visit. **www.bilkentotel.com.tr**

ANKARA Mega Residence Hotel Ankara
🍴 🏃 ▤ 🅿 €€€€

Tahran Cad 5, 06700 **Tel** *(0312) 468 54 00* **Fax** *(0312) 468 54 15* **Rooms** *29*

Mega Residence Ankara is a high-class hotel. The rooms are beautiful and extremely comfortable – this hotel is all about comfort. The standard of the cuisine at the Schnitzel Restaurant is excellent and a relaxing drink or an Italian snack can be enjoyed at the Gusto Bar. **www.megaresidence.com**

ANKARA Swissôtel Ankara
🍴 🏃 ▤ 🅿 €€€€

Yildizevler Mah, Jose Marti Cad 2, Çankaya, 06550 **Tel** *(0312) 409 3000* **Fax** *(0312) 409 33 99* **Rooms** *150*

Located in Çankaya, Swissotel Ankara is a neighbour to most embassies and the Presidential Palace. This hotel has taken luxury to a new level – amenities such as rainforest showers, espresso machines and LCD TVs are just some of the delights. There is also a pool, spa and fitness centre, two world-class restaurants and a great bar. **www.ankara.swissotel.com**

ANKARA Sheraton Hotel & Convention Centre
🍴 🏃 ▤ 🅿 €€€€€

Noktali Sokak, 06700 **Tel** *(0312) 457 60 00* **Fax** *(0312) 457 61 00* **Rooms** *414*

The Sheraton Ankara is perhaps the best-rated hotel in Ankara. When considering the quality of the rooms, the selection of restaurants, its perfect location, its own shopping mall and its amazing health club, it's not hard to see why. This is truly an amazing hotel. **www.sheraton.com/ankara**

ESKIŞEHIR Yimpas Hotel Eskişehir
🍴 ▤ 🅿 €€€€€€

Sivrihisar Cad 155, 26100 **Tel** *(0222) 220 35 75* **Rooms** *79*

Yimpas Hotel is one of the best hotels in Eskişehir and is situated close to the city centre. The hotel has plenty of amenities; all rooms have private bathrooms, satellite TVs, air conditioning, mini bars, balconies and 24-hour room service.

THE BLACK SEA

AKÇAKOCA / DÜZCE Diapolis Hotel
🍴 🏃 ▤ 🅿 €€€

Baklikçi Baranaği Mevkii Yali Mah, Inönü Cad 34 **Tel** *(0380) 611 37 41* **Fax** *(0380) 611 37 90* **Rooms** *60*

A lovely hotel on the shores of the Black Sea, the rooms are large and comfortable, and there are several restaurants on site. Activities and facilities include an indoor and outdoor swimming pool, fitness centre, children's playground, paintball and a cinema. **www.diapolishotel.com**

AMASYA Apple Palace Hotel
🍴 🏃 ▤ 🅿 €€€

Cakallar Mah Vermis Sok 7, **Tel** *(0358) 219 00 19* **Fax** *(0358) 219 00 15* **Rooms** *60*

The Apple Palace, located high up in the mountains overlooking the town of Amasya, is a beautiful hotel perfect for a relaxing stay in the Black Sea region. Amasya is famous for its namesake apple so there is a distinct apple theme. The rooms are rather basic but clean. The view from the pool is reason enough to stay here. **www.theapplepalace.com.tr**

ARTVIN Cihan Hotel
🍴 🏃 ▤ 🅿 €

Turgay Ciner Cad **Tel** *(0466) 351 23 33* **Fax** *(0466) 351 48 98* **Rooms** *43*

Hotel Cihan is a cute little hotel by the sea. The rooms are basic but clean, and the hotel has all the required amenities to ensure a comfortable stay. The restaurant has a 21-choice breakfast buffet and two bars, while the roof terrace restaurant provides local cuisine and wonderful views. **www.hotelcihan.com**

BOLU Bolu Thermal Hotel
🍴 🏃 🅿 €€

Karacasu Mevkii, 14020 **Tel** *(0374) 262 84 72* **Fax** *(0374) 262 83 07* **Rooms** *77*

This thermal spring spa, is relatively unknown by outsiders. The thermal spring water, good for bathing and drinking, especially good for conditions such as rheumatism, skin problems, blood circulation, bone and arthritis problems, and heart diseases related with the metabolism and diet. **www.bolutermalotel.com**

BOLU Dorukkaya Greenpark Gerede
🍴 🏃 ▤ 🅿 €€€

Cankurtaran, Tesisleri Karisi, Pk 51, Gerede 14020 **Tel** *0 90 374 325 10 61* **Fax** *0 90 374 325 10 69* **Rooms** *44*

At this hotel there are two sand-ground tennis courts, two football fields and a field for goal keeper training. Whether an avid outdoors person or just wanting to relax, this is one of the most peaceful places in the country. The rooms are large and clean. **www.kayatourism.com.tr**

Key to Price Guide *see p326* **Key to Symbols** *see back cover flap*

BOLU Koru Hotel

Yesilkoy Bakirli Mev 10 **Tel** *(0374) 225 22 90* **Fax** *(0374) 225 28 12* **Rooms** *128*

Koru Hotel is a charming, modern hotel half way between Istanbul and Ankara and with a mountain view. Rooms are basically furnished but comfortable. There are four restaurants, an indoor pool, fitness centre, sauna, Turkish bath, massage, football pitch, tennis court and a disco. **www.koruhotel.com.tr**

BOLU Dorukkaya Ski & Mountain Resort

Alkaya Mevkii Pk 51, Kartalkaya, 14020 **Tel** *(0374) 234 50 26* **Fax** *(0374) 234 50 25* **Rooms** *259*

Dorukkaya Ski & Mountain Resort is an all-inclusive offering both skiing and snowboarding in an Austrian-designed 'snowpark', the only in Turkey. The large hotel offers a full range of facilities and après-ski events in winter. There are special facilities and skiing lessons available for children. **www.kayatourism.com.tr**

GIRESUN Başar Hotel

Atatürk Bulvari, Liman Mev, 28100 **Tel** *(0454) 212 99 20* **Fax** *(0454) 212 99 29* **Rooms** *54*

Located right on the coast in Giresun, Hotel Başar has more than just spectacular views. The rooms are somewhat basic but still pleasant. It is the restaurant, however, that makes this hotel: the menu consists mainly of local dishes, such as *mücver* (fried fritter) and sardine pasty. **www.hotelbasar.com.tr**

GIRESUN Kit-Tur Hotel

Arifbey Cad 2, 28000 **Tel** *(0454) 212 02 45* **Fax** *(0454) 212 30 34* **Rooms** *50*

Kit-Tur Hotel may not be luxurious but it has true charm. The rooms are attractively decorated and the restaurant serves fine food and has a wonderful view. There is also a roof bar, small fitness room and sauna. Most interesting is the Giresun Room where tea is served in a room decorated in typical Giresun fashion. **www.otelkittur.com**

ORDU Balıktaşı Otel

Güzelyali Mah Sahil Cad 36, 52100 **Tel** *(0452) 223 06 11* **Fax** *(0452) 223 06 15* **Rooms** *48*

This is an adorable little hotel right on the water in Ordu. Recommended is the restaurant, which serves fine Black Sea cuisine. Recreational activities available include an outdoor swimming pool with a children's section, a gymnasium hall and a fitness centre.

ORDU Belde Hotel

Kiraz Limanı Mev, 52100 **Tel** *(0452) 214 39 87* **Fax** *(0452) 214 93 98* **Rooms** *64*

Located on the shore in Ordu, Belde Hotel has one of the best locations on the Black Sea. The rooms are very large, though plainly decorated, and there is an outdoor pool, jacuzzi, Turkish bath and sauna. There are also four restaurants on the premises. This hotel is relatively unknown to English-speaking travellers. **www.beldeotel.net**

RİZE Dedeman Hotel-Rize

Merkez Alipaşa Köyü, 53100 **Tel** *(0464) 223 44 44* **Fax** *(0464) 223 53 48* **Rooms** *82*

Dedeman Rize is the perfect place to stay to enjoy the natural beauty of Rize. The hotel lives up to the Dedeman standard, with clean comfortable rooms, excellent dining and extras such as an indoor swimming pool, private beach, fitness and health club, sauna, massage facilities and solarium. **www.dedemanhotels.com/**

SAFRANBOLU Çelikpalas Hotel Safranbolu

Baris Mah Araphaci Sok 1 **Tel** *(0370) 712 71 72* **Fax** *(0370) 712 28 00* **Rooms** *26*

This hotel was first opened 74 years ago, only to later be used as a courthouse. It is a very attractive building with interesting rooms, and there is a fantastic restaurant which serves a great variety of Turkish fare including many local dishes. **www.safranbolucelikpalas.com**

SAFRANBOLU Cinci Han Hotel

Eski Çarşi Çeşme Sok Cinci Han **Tel** *(0370) 712 06 80* **Fax** *(0370) 712 06 54* **Rooms** *25*

Ever imagined having a holiday in a hotel that has been used as an inn for over 300 years? This can be made a reality by staying at Cincihan Hotel. The hotel, built in 1645 and used as an inn, has been renovated and turned into a marvellous holiday experience. There is fine dining and a bar. **www.cincihan.com**

SAMSUN Hatice Hanim Konağı

Baba Sultan Mah Naip Tarla Sok 4 **Tel** *(0370) 712 75 45* **Fax** *(0370) 712 60 63* **Rooms** *50*

Hatice Hanim Konağı is a 17th-century Ottoman home that has been transformed in to a special-class hotel. The décor is traditional Turkish and very authentic. There is a delightful restaurant and bar, and the family that run the hotel are very friendly. **www.hotelhaticehanim.com**

SAMSUN Omtel Hotel Samsun

Kurupelit Kampüsü 2, **Tel** *(0362) 457 54 81* **Fax** *(0362) 457 63 02* **Rooms** *44*

Omtel Hotel is a good budget hotel and offers plenty to keep guests busy, such as the beach, volleyball, billiards, table tennis or just relaxing in their garden. There is a children's playground for the kids and for adults there is a restaurant and bar as well as the barbeque, which guests are allowed to use.

SİNOP Zinos Country Hotel Guest

Enver Bahadir Yolu 71 **Tel** *(0368) 260 56 00* **Fax** *(0386) 260 56 03* **Rooms** *14*

Zinos Country Hotel is a cute little hotel on a hill above Sinop. There are delightful large rooms decorated in old Ottoman style and a great restaurant and bar. At the beach, the hotel provides snacks and sandwiches and aperitif drinks. The hotel sponsors an annual sailing regatta that is a Sinop tradition. **www.zinoshotel.com**

TRABZON Zorlu Grand Hotel

Maras Cad 9, 61100 **Tel** *(0462) 326 84 00* **Fax** *(0462) 326 84 58* **Rooms** *157*

Zorlu Grand Hotel is one of the only five-star hotels in the Black Sea region. The rooms are very large, and there is a great selection of dining and drinking establishments as well as a health club and pool. It is a very comfortable hotel to use as a base to explore Trabzon and its environs. **www.zorlugrand.com**

CAPPADOCIA AND CENTRAL ANATOLIA

AFYON Korel Thermal Resort

Kütahya Karayolu, 03040 **Tel** *(0272) 252 22 22* **Fax** *(0272) 252 22 52* **Rooms** *329*

Located in Central Anatolia, 13 km (8 miles) from Afyon city centre, is the five-star Korel Thermal Resort. Luxury facilities include Turkish baths, Finnish baths and a spa offering a wide range of treatments. There are indoor and outdoor pools, and children are well catered for with activities and entertainment. **www.korelthermal.com.tr**

AVANOS Grand Avanos Hotel

Kapadokya Cad 46 Avanos, 50200 **Tel** *(0384) 511 35 77* **Fax** *(0384) 511 48 63* **Rooms** *60*

The Grand Avanos is a modern hotel in the town of Avanos. It is a good alternative to the cave hotels of the area as it has all the amenities that a modern hotel should have. The rooms are comfortable and clean, although a bit dated. There is a pool and an excellent restaurant. **www.buyukavanos.com**

GÖREME Göreme Ottoman House Hotel

Orta Mah Uzundere Sok 25, 50180 **Tel** *(0384) 271 26 16* **Fax** *(0384) 271 26 19* **Rooms** *32*

The Ottoman House Hotel may lack the charm of the cave hotels, but offers a good level of comfort in exchange. It is decorated with carpets from around the region, as well as ceramics, costumes and folk crafts. The staff are very friendly and helpful. **www.ottomanhouse.com.tr**

GÖREME Sato Cave Hotel and Pension

Orta Mah, Konak Sok 7, Goreme, 50180 **Tel** *(0384) 271 26 22* **Fax** *(0384) 271 24 12* **Rooms** *9*

Located just on the edge of the town of Göreme, Sato Cave Hotel is a very small hotel with only nine cave rooms. The rooms are very comfortable and relaxing. A wonderful breakfast is served and dinner is also available at the hotel. There is a magnificent view of the town. **www.satocavehotel.com**

GÖREME Travellers Cave Pension

Gaferli Mah 28, 50180 **Tel** *(0384) 271 27 07* **Fax** *(0384) 271 26 24* **Rooms** *14*

If on a budget and needing a place to stay in Cappadocia, Travellers Cave Pension is definitely the place to be. Guests are welcomed with unbelievable hospitality, and the rooms are clean and comfortable, though not all have private baths. There is also an outstanding restaurant. **www.travellerscave.com**

GÖREME Elif Star Hotel

Göreme, 50180 **Tel** *90 384 271 24 79* **Fax** *n/a* **Rooms** *7*

Carved out of the cliffs, this hotel is close to the centre of the village, yet just steps from the trail to complete isolation, with great views of the fairy chimneys. The rooms are quite nice with some lovely Turkish touches. Sizes vary considerably, from very large triples and quads to snug doubles. Children are welcome. **www.elifstar.com**

GÖREME Kelebek Hotel and Pension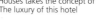

Aydınlı Mah, 50180 **Tel** *(0384) 271 25 31* **Fax** *(0384) 271 27 63* **Rooms** *19*

Kelebek offers rooms and suites, some built into caves and others in traditional arched rooms, in two different cave hotels, Kelebek Boutique Hotel and Kelebek Pension. A look at the rooms on their website shows that comfort, décor and activities are first-rate here. **www.kelebekhotel.com**

GÖREME Anatolian Houses

Gaferli Mah, 50180 **Tel** *(0384) 271 24 63* **Fax** *(0384) 271 22 29* **Rooms** *19*

The hotel is gorgeous, centrally located and the rooms are large and beautiful. Antolian Houses takes the concept of cave hotels to a new level: a true luxury hotel with all the charm that cave rooms offers. The luxury of this hotel could rival any large five-star city hotel. **www.anatolianhouses.com**

NEVŞEHIR Peri Tower Hotel

Otel Cad, Adnan Mendres Bul 13, 50200 **Tel** *(0384) 212 88 16* **Fax** *(0384) 213 90 28* **Rooms** *126*

This is an interesting hotel that was constructed to resemble the caves of Cappadocia. The hotel has a pool, sauna and Turkish bath, and the rooms are large and clean. Food at the hotel is very good. The only real detraction for this hotel is that it is rather a distance from any sights or shopping. **www.peritower.com**

UCHISAR Museum Hotel

Tekeli Mahallesi 1, 50240 **Tel** *(0384) 219 22 20* **Fax** *(0384) 219 24 44* **Rooms** *26*

The Museum Hotel is a cave hotel with all the amenities of a five-star hotel. The staff are very friendly and helpful, and provide excellent service and advice. The kitchen specializes in a form of Ottoman cuisine that is disappearing from modern Turkey. The restaurant and pool are exquisite. **www.museum-hotel.com**

Key to Price Guide *see p326* **Key to Symbols** *see back cover flap*

ÜRGÜP Cappadocia Palace Hotel

Dua Yeri Mah Mektep Sok 2, 50400 **Tel** *(0384) 341 25 10* **Fax** *(0384) 341 53 14* **Rooms** *18*

Cappadocia Palace offers a peaceful balance between modern comfort and tradition. With its convenient location in the centre of Ürgüp, it is the perfect base for daily excursions within Cappadocia. Breakfast is served in an open courtyard in summer and indoors in winter. **www.cappadocciapalace.com**

ÜRGÜP Hotel Surban

Yunak Mah PK 55, 50400 **Tel** *(0384) 341 46 03* **Fax** *(0384) 341 32 23* **Rooms** *31*

Hotel Surban is located in the centre of the town of Ürgüp, very close to all the sights of the area. The rooms are Cappadocia rooms, carved out of volcanic rock. The hotel is run by a French/Turkish couple and has all modern conveniences. There is a great restaurant serving Turkish cuisine. **www.hotelsurban.com.tr**

ÜRGÜP Kayadam Cave House

Esbelli Sok 6 **Tel** *(0384) 341 66 23* **Fax** *(0384) 341 59 82* **Rooms** *9*

This is a simple cave house B&B. Dwellings date from the 4th to 6th centuries AD, and historic touches remain, such as an oven dug into the floor and stone rings used for tethering animals. Furniture is simple but attractive, the gardens are beautiful and the patio has incredible views. **www.kayadam.com**

ÜRGÜP Urgup Inn Cave Hotel

Temenli Mah Sagir Mescit Sok 20, 50400 **Tel** *(0384) 341 41 47* **Rooms** *6*

Ürgüp Inn Cave Hotel is a comfortable, superbly furnished family-run hotel that enjoys a prime position in the heart of the city centre of Ürgüp, yet near to the ruins of Kayakapi and the Temenni wish hill. All rooms have a private bathroom, central heating, Internet access, TV and breakfast any time desired. **www.urgupinncavehotel.com**

ÜRGÜP Alfina Hotel

Istiklal Cad 89, 50400 **Tel** *(0384) 341 4822* **Fax** *(0384) 341 24 24* **Rooms** *38*

At the Alfina, the rooms are very large and all have central heating; air conditioning is not necessary due to the nature of the stone which keeps the rooms cool throughout the summer months. Guests can dine in the restaurant or on one the many terraces that have amazing views of the area. There is also a bar. **www.hotelalfina.com**

ÜRGÜP Elkep Evi

Club Ürgüparkasi Ayvalı Köyü 26, 50400 **Tel** *(0384) 341 60 00* **Fax** *(0384) 341 80 89* **Rooms** *21*

The hotel is located at the top of Mount Esbelli and gives great views over the valleys surrounding Ürgüp; at night guests can watch the sunset from the Hilltop terrace. The food from the traditional Turkish kitchen is recommended, especially for dinner, which comes accompanied with good live music. **www.elkepevi.com**

ÜRGÜP Selcuklu Evi

Yunak Mahallesi PK 55, 50400 **Tel** *(0384) 341 74 60* **Fax** *(0384) 341 74 63* **Rooms** *20*

The hotel consists of five Seljuk houses, which are connected via stone staircases around a secluded central courtyard. The rooms in the hotel are lovely and have been carefully restored by local craftsmen using original materials. Dinner at the hotel is recommended. **www.selcukluevi.com.tr**

ÜRGÜP Temenni Evi

Temenni Tepesi, 50400 **Tel** *(0384) 341 47 10* **Fax** *(0384) 341 70 82* **Rooms** *14*

Temenni Evi (which means 'House of Wishes' in Turkish) is a boutique hotel with each of its rooms decorated in a different, tasteful style. The best surprise of this hotel is its underground tunnels, which lead to the most spectacular of views. **www.temennievi.com**

ÜRGÜP Dedeman Cappadocia

Ürgüp Yolu Üzeri 2 km, 50200 **Tel** *(0384) 213 99 00* **Fax** *(0384) 213 21 58* **Rooms** *349*

Dedeman Cappadocia is a large modern hotel, and the only five-star hotel in the area, with all the amenities expected of such a hotel, including big outdoor and indoor pools and excellent food. The enormous buffets offer almost any Turkish dish imaginable, for both breakfast and dinner. **www.dedeman.com**

ÜRGÜP Dinler Hotel Ürgüp

Mehmet Dinler Bulvari 7, Ürgüp, 50400 **Tel** *(0384) 341 30 30* **Fax** *(0384) 341 48 96* **Rooms** *172*

Dinler Hotel Ürgüp is a pleasant modern hotel in a good location and with large and clean rooms. It offers many services and activities, such as outdoor and indoor restaurants, bars, disco, a swimming pool, children's swimming pool, soccer field, and fitness centre. The hotel also offers buffet breakfast, lunch and dinner. **www.dinler.com**

ÜRGÜP Esbelli Evi

Esbelli Sokak, 8 (PK 2), 50400 **Tel** *(0384) 341 33 95* **Fax** *(0384) 341 88 48* **Rooms** *13*

This hotel is tastefully decorated, the rooms are clean, large and comfortable and the bathrooms are large and modern. A wonderful breakfast is served on the lovely patio that overlooks the town of Ürgüp. The views are breathtaking. Perhaps the best feature of this hotel is its hospitality. **www.esbelli.com.tr**

ÜRGÜP Yunak Evleri Ürgüp

Yunak Mah, 50400 **Tel** *(0384) 341 69 20* **Fax** *(0384) 341 69 24* **Rooms** *30*

Yunak Evleri is a fantastic cave hotel in Ürgüp, converted from six 5th century cave dwellings and a 19th century Greek mansion. The rooms are spacious and some have arched stone ceilings. The bathrooms are luxurious marble, and breakfast and dinner are recommended. There is no pool. **www.yunak.com**

EASTERN ANATOLIA

ADANA Boutique Hotel Princess Maya

Turhan Cemal Beriker Bul 16, 01220 **Tel** *(0322) 459 09 66* **Fax** *(0322) 459 77 10* **Rooms** *32*

This small boutique hotel is in a period building with character in a central location. The hotel offers Cable TV, wireless Internet connection, 24-hour room service, laundry and dry cleaning services. Located close to airport. **princessmaya@ttnet.net.tr**

ADANA Hilton SA Adana

Sinanpasa Mah 1, Yuregır / Adanan, 01220 **Tel** *(0322) 355 50 00* **Fax** *(0322) 355 50 50* **Rooms** *308*

This luxury, river-view hotel offers everything one expects from five-star accommodation: indoor and outdoor pools, disabled and non-smoking rooms, Cable TV, internet connection, a sauna, Jacuzzi, hairdresser, child facilities, solarium, Turkish bath, fitness facilities including two lit tennis courts and a jogging track. **www.hilton.co.uk**

ADIYAMAN Zeus Otel

Mustafa Kemal Cad 20, 02000 **Tel** *(0416) 725 56 95* **Fax** *(0416) 725 56 96* **Rooms** *66*

Situated around a garden and outdoor pool, the hotel offers all the expected amenities of a four-star, such as a fitness club, Jacuzzi, children's facilities, TV room and facilities for the disabled. Located close to the airport, it is centrally located. It has four restaurants serving international and local cuisine. **www.zeusotel.com**

ADIYAMAN Grand İsias Hotel

Atatürk Bulvarı 180, 02100 **Tel** *(0416) 214 88 00* **Fax** *(0416) 214 97 33* **Rooms** *67*

Centrally located in Khata, this hotel has basic rooms that offer all the comforts of a 4-star, such as digital TV, 24-hour room service, hairdryer, safety deposit and mini bar. The hotel also has a TV room, Turkish bath, sauna, fitness centre, jacuzzi and a night club. Pets are welcome. Convenient for a trip to Nemrut Daği. **www.grandisias.com**

ANTAKYA Narin Otel

Atatürk Cad 11, Cebrail Mah, 31030 **Tel** *(0326) 216 75 00* **Fax** *(0326) 216 75 09* **Rooms** *59*

This basic hotel is centrally located and offers guests tea and coffee machines, a mini bar, room service and wireless Internet connection in rooms. It has a Turkish bath, sauna, massage facilities and a TV room. There are two restaurants, a café and a bar offering international cuisine. Dry cleaning and laundry services are available. **www.narinotel.com**

ANTAKYA Büyük Antakya Oteli

Ataturk Cad 8, 31040 **Tel** *(0326) 213 58 58* **Fax** *(0326) 213 58 69* **Rooms** *72*

A modern hotel with a swimming pool that offers all the amenities of a luxury hotel, such as Internet connection, 24-hour room service, digital and satellite TV, and laundry services as well as a night club, bar and restaurant that serves Turkish, Italian and French cuisine as well as vegetarian dishes. **www.buyukantakyaoteli.com**

DIYARBAKIR Class Hotel

Gazi Cad 101, 21400 **Tel** *(0412) 229 50 00* **Fax** *(0412) 229 25 99* **Rooms** *114*

All the luxury facilities of a five-star establishment are available in this centrally located hotel. The hotel complex has a range of shops, and further shopping and banking facilities are very close by. Rooms are large and comfortable and the staff professional and helpful. **www.diyarbakirclasshotel.com**

DIYARBAKIR Hotel Dedeman Diyarbakir

Elaziğ Cad Büyükşehir Belideye Yani, 21400 **Tel** *(0412) 229 00 00* **Fax** *(0412) 224 73 53* **Rooms** *98*

Situated in gardens,and in a central location near the old city, this modern hotel offers rooms that are equipped with cable TV, Internet connection and direct telephones. The hotel has four restaurants and various bars offering local and international cuisine and staff speak excellent English. **www.dedeman.com**

ELAZIĞ Akgün Otel Elazığ

Universite Mah Sehit Korgen, Hulusi Sayin Cad 20, 23270 **Tel** *(0424) 248 20 00* **Fax** *(0424) 248 20 19* **Rooms** *142*

This modern conference hotel offers all the luxuries of a major chain and offers plenty of activities and services for holiday makers, such as a pool, sauna, cinema, and two restaurants serving international cuisine, as well as many bars and cafes. **www.akgunelazighotel.com**

ERZINCAN Büyük Erzincan Otel

Erzurum Karayolu Üzeri Tedaş Karşisi, 24000 **Tel** *(0446) 226 09 10/12* **Fax** *(0446) 226 09 09* **Rooms** *88*

This hotel is centrally located and rooms are equipped with satellite TV, mini bar and hairdryer. Amenities include tennis courts, an outdoor pool, disabled and child facilities, a doctor on site, a market and a hairdressers. Pets are welcome. **www.buyukerzincanoteli.com.tr**

ERZURUM Dilaver Otel

Mumcu Cad Pelit Meydani, 59, 25100 **Tel** *(0442) 235 00 68* **Fax** *(0442) 233 52 00* **Rooms** *75*

This centrally located hotel is basic but clean. Amenities that are available in rooms include direct phone lines, TV, mini bar and room service. The hotel also has internet connection and offers laundry and ironing services. There are three bars as well as a meeting hall. The airport is within easy reach. **www.dilaverhotel.com**

Key to Price Guide *see p326* **Key to Symbols** *see back cover flap*

ERZURUM Palan Hotel
P. Box 47 Palandoken, 24000 **Tel** *(0332) 317 07 07* **Fax** *(0442) 317 07 00* **Rooms** *160*

Located on the ski mountain, this hotel has rooms fitted with all the amenities of a luxury hotel. There are many shops in the arcade, ski rental, a nightclub and a skating rink. There is also a fitness centre, massage room, sauna and a Turkish bath. Ski facilities include a ski tube and a baby lift. **www.palanotel.com**

ERZURUM Renaissance Polat Erzurum
Ibrahim Polat Cad Telefirik Önü Palandöken, 25010 **Tel** *(0442) 232 00 10* **Fax** *(0442) 232 00 99* **Rooms** *234*

This large ski hotel is situated on the mountain overlooking the city and is part of the Palandöken Ski Resort. It has spacious rooms, all amenties, is close to the city centre and within easy reach of the airport (the hotel offers a courtesy shuttle service for guests). **www.polatrenaissance.com**

GAZIANTEP Grand Hotel Gaziantep
Ali Fuat Cebesoy Bulvari Cad 32, 27090 **Tel** *(0342) 325 65 65* **Fax** *(0342) 325 65 66* **Rooms** *93*

This hotel is very central and modern, and offers a variety of restaurants, including a rooftop one, and has a smart a nightclub. The website offers full details, including a wide selection of photographs, which could help visitors gets a feel for the place before they decide to book. **www.gaziantepgrandhotel.com**

GAZIANTEP Tuğcan Otel
Ataurk Bulvari 34, 27010 **Tel** *(0342) 220 43 23* **Fax** *(0342) 220 32 42* **Rooms** *141*

Rooms offer a mini bar, shower and bath, 24-hour room service and cable TV. The hotel has four restaurants, offering Turkish and international cuisine, bars, a beer house and a disco. There is an indoor pool, massage room, Jacuzzi and fitness facilities. Table tennis and billiards tables are also available. **www.tugcanhotel.com.tr**

GAZIANTEP Hotel Ravanda
İnönü Cad 178, 27010 **Tel** *(0342) 230 57 57* **Fax** *(0342) 230 67 67* **Rooms** *86*

This is a modern hotel, which takes its name from the Ravanda Castle, in the nearby Belenozun village. The hotel is well-appointed, with friendly, professional staff, Turkish cuisine in a choice of restaurants and bars and live music in the evenings. **www.ravanadaotel.com**

KARS Çamkar Hotel
Cıbıltepe Kayak Tesisleri 36500 **Tel** *(0474) 413 52 59* **Fax** *(0474) 413 62 42* **Rooms** *55*

Çamkar Hotel is a cute little hotel close to Sarıçam with excellent skiing facilities. Aside from skiing the hotel offers an open buffet and à la carte restaurant, a winter garden, children's game centre, lobby bar, disco, sauna, Jacuzzi, massage rooms and fitness centre. This hotel is developing rapidly, to meet the skiing demand. **www.camkar.com**

ŞANLIURFA Edessa Hotel
Balıklıgol Mev, 63200 **Tel** *(0414) 215 99 11* **Fax** *(0414) 215 50 30* **Rooms** *64*

Edessa is the old name for the city. This hotel, located in the old town centre, in front of the Mosque Halilul Rahman and so called "Lake of Fishes" is a charming period building. The hotel is rated as the best hotel in town, although it is not very luxurious. **www.hoteledessa.com**

ŞANLIURFA Harran Hotel
Atatürk Bulvarı, 63200 **Tel** *(0414) 313 28 60* **Fax** *(0414) 313 49 18* **Rooms** *118*

The Harran hotel is close to all sights and is the only place in Sanluirfa that serves alcoholic drinks in its bar. It also has comprehensive amenities, such as a fitness centre, sauna and indoor and outdoor swimming pools. The hotel will help arrange guided tours and car hire. **www.hotelharran.com**

SIVAS Sultan Otel
Eski Belediye Sok 18, **Tel** *(0346) 221 29 86* **Fax** *(0346) 225 21 00* **Rooms** *27*

This is a small and very central hotel within easy reach of Sivas airport. The rooftop restaurant is a popular place to go and serves excellent Turkish fare as well as alcohol. There is also live music most nights, with a band playing traditional and modern folk. The breakfast room is kitted out like a 1950s American diner. **www.sultanotel.com**

VAN Akdamar Hotel
Kazim Karabekir Ca., 65100 **Tel** *(0432) 214 99 23* **Fax** *(0432) 212 08 68* **Rooms** *72*

Though the building holds no special charms, this hotel is central and the rooms are basic but clean. Each room has a TV, satellite connection, hairdryer and central heating. There is a hairdressers and a games room on the grounds as well as a public TV room. Internet connection, dry cleaning and laundry services are available. **www.hotelakdamar.com**

VAN Büyük Urartu Otel
Cumhuriyet Cad 32, 65100 **Tel** *(0432) 212 06 60* **Fax** *(0432) 212 16 10* **Rooms** *75*

This centrally located hotel offers clean rooms and many facilities, such as an indoor pool, sauna, doctor on site and squash court. All rooms are equipped with a hairdryer, safety deposit, digital TV and wireless Internet connection. It has two restaurants, a snack bar and three bars. **www.buyukurartuotel.com**

VAN Merit Sahmaran Hotel
Edremit Rd 12 km, 65170 **Tel** *(0432) 312 30 60* **Fax** *(0432) 312 22 95* **Rooms** *90*

The lakeside location of this hotel is its most outstanding feature, while remaining close to city centre. There is an indoor pool, a beach, a sauna, Turkish bath and facilities for the disabled as well as two restaurants, a café, bar and patisserie. Heating is centrally controlled, so there is no need for air conditioning. **www.merithotels.com**

WHERE TO EAT

Restaurants in Turkey range from the informal *lokanta* and kebab house, found on almost every street corner, to the gourmet restaurants of large luxury-class hotels. There are international restaurants in most major tourist centres. In Istanbul, restaurants purvey a wide variety of almost every style of cuisine, from French to Korean. Restaurants on the Mediterranean and Aegean coasts specialize in seafood dishes, and Cappadocia is famous for its grapes and wines. Interesting local dishes can be found along the Black Sea coast and in the interior of Anatolia. Each region has its own culinary specialities: you can sample thick, clotted cream in Afyon, spicy meatballs in Tekirdağ, chewy ice cream in Kahramanmaraş and whole-milk yoghurt in distant Erzurum. As you move further away from Istanbul, vegetarian restaurants become somewhat scarce. Excellent light meals and snacks are often sold by street vendors, and most cafés and bars have a menu with light refreshments.

Dried grapes in Safranbolu

WHERE TO LOOK

Generally, the smartest and most expensive restaurants are to be found in the five-star international hotel chains all over Turkey. They always serve both Western and Turkish food.

The main roads and central business districts of most towns have a selection of fast-food eateries, cafés and inexpensive restaurants where the locals go to eat. Coastal resorts cater for all ages and tastes and offer dishes from all over the world. In the interior, most restaurants serve good, cheap regional food and cater for locals as much as tourists. Most towns have a number of cafés, patisseries and pudding shops. The latter specialize in *muhallebici* (traditional sweet milk puddings).

Slicing meat from a revolving grill for a döner kebab

The sumptuous Beyti Restaurant in Florya, Istanbul *(see p356)*

TYPES OF RESTAURANT

The most common type of restaurant in Turkey is the traditional *lokanta*. These establishments offer a variety of dishes, often listed on a board near the entrance. They serve *hazır yemek* (prepared food), usually consisting of hot meat and vegetable dishes that are displayed in a *bain marie*, or steam table. Other dishes on the menu may be *sulu yemek* (broth or stew) and *et* (meat – meaning grilled meat and kebabs).

Equally popular is the *kebap* or *ocakbaşı* (kebab house). In addition to grilled meats, most kebab houses serve the popular *lahmacun*, a thin dough base topped with fried onions, minced meat and tomato sauce. This dish is the Turkish version of pizza. Some also serve *pide*, a flatbread base served with various toppings such as eggs, cheese and salami.

If you have had too much to drink you may need a bowl of *işkembe* (tripe soup), the traditional Turkish cure for a hangover, before going to bed. *İşkembe* restaurants stay open until the early hours of the morning.

Fish restaurants are often concentrated along the same street, creating a lively atmosphere and making the street seem like one large restaurant. The meal typically consists of a selection of *mezes* (appetizers) *(see p350)*, followed by the catch of the day, which might include *palamut* (bonito), *sardalya* (fresh sardines) and *levrek* (sea bass). Also popular are Black Sea *hamsi* (a kind of anchovy), *istavrit* (bluefin) and *mezgit* (whiting). However, as fish is becoming scarcer and more expensive, farmed fish has become more widely accepted, particularly *alabalık* (trout) and a type of bream known as *çipura*. Fish is

A trout restaurant on the river at Saklıkent

served grilled or fried, and is usually accompanied by salad and *rakı (see p351)*, an anise-flavoured spirit.

International culinary influences are encouraging local chefs to be adventurous and innovative. Many restaurants are known for superb, original food in a beautiful ambience. Turks frequent the many foreign restaurants found all over Istanbul, while global icons like Starbucks and Gloria Jean's are part of everyday life. A *meyhane* is more like a tavern, serving alcohol and *mezes*. These are cheap and convivial places, and often have live music.

OPENING HOURS

For government employees, lunch hour is from noon to 1pm, and many restaurants cater for them. But you will not find many set lunch hours throughout Turkey. Turks eat when they are hungry, without looking at the clock, and will simply drop in at the most convenient place they can find. Restaurants and kebab houses open at about

11am and stay open for business until the last customer leaves in the evening.

During Ramadan (Ramazan), Muslims fast from sunrise to sunset. As a result, many restaurants are closed during the day, or they may serve only a special *iftar* (fast-breaking) menu in the evening. More and more foreign restaurants are now appearing on the scene, and some of these close on Sundays, as they would in their native country. However, there are no firm guidelines on opening hours for such eating establishments, and most of them stay open longer than their counterparts in other countries. Seasonal restaurants are a different matter and many of Turkey's popular tourist resorts simply grind to a halt after 29 October to reopen around March or April, as soon as the weather improves. Some places open just for New Year's Eve *(see p37)*, which is always festive.

Drying chillis, Bodrum

WHAT TO EXPECT

Food and eating are among life's finest pleasures, and nowhere more so than in Turkey. A meal is always an occasion and, for special meals, it is best to book. In large centres vegetarians can enjoy variety, and designer vegetarian restaurants seem to be

enjoying much interest. They do, however, become scarcer the further east you travel.

While most restaurants try to cater for non-smokers, there are no hard and fast rules on smoking in eating establishments, and so it is usually left up to the individual restaurant owner. It is, however, becoming increasingly common for restaurants to offer a smoke-free dining area.

Lower inflation has not decreased prices; meals in Turkey can be significantly more expensive than in other countries. When choosing a place to eat, remember that many of the cheaper restaurants and kebab houses do not serve alcohol. Also, many places will have a separate section for men only and another for families or women. These are designated by a sign with the words *aile salonu* (family room), where single men do not enter. Turks are proud of their hospitality and service. Good service is always found in the up-market restaurants that can afford well-trained, professional waiters and kitchen staff. You may find that the same standards do not apply in cheaper places. It is natural for Turks to call a waiter by saying, "bakar mısınız" (service, please). The cheerfulness and enthusiasm of restaurant staff generally compensates for minor shortcomings.

SERVICE AND PAYING

The major credit cards are widely accepted, except in the cheaper restaurants, kebab houses, local *bufes* (snack kiosks) and some *lokantas*. Restaurants usually display the credit card sign or symbol on the entrance if they accept this form of payment. Value-added tax (KDV in Turkish) is always included in the bill, but the policy on service varies. Some places add 10 per cent or more to round up the bill while others leave it to the customer's discretion. Feel free to ask if you are unsure.

Waterside restaurant on Bird Island, near the Aegean resort of Kuşadası

The Flavours of Turkey

The wide range of climatic zones across Turkey make it one of the few countries that can grow all its own food. Tea is cultivated in the mountains by the Black Sea and bananas in the sultry south. The Anatolian plain in between is criss-crossed by wheat fields and rich grasslands on which cattle graze, providing top quality meat and dairy produce. Fruit and vegetables flourish everywhere and fish abound in the salty seas that lap the nation's shores. Freshness is the hallmark of this varied cuisine, drawn from the many cultures that were subject to nearly five centuries of Ottoman rule.

Pomegranates

A stall in the Spice Bazaar, one of Istanbul's oldest markets

quick and easy to prepare. Turkey's most famous culinary staples - yogurt, flat bread and the kebab - originate in this region. The common use of fruits, such as pomegranates, figs and apricots, in Turkish savoury dishes stems from Persian influences, filtering down with the tribes that came from the north of the steppe. From the Middle East, further south, nomads

introduced the occasional fiery blast of chilli. Its use was once an essential aid to preserving meat in the searing desert heat.

OTTOMAN CUISINE

It was in the vast, steamy kitchens of the Topkapı Palace in Istanbul that a repertoire of mouth-watering dishes to rival the celebrated cuisines of

THE ANATOLIAN STEPPE

The steppe stretching from Central Asia to Anatolia is one of the oldest inhabited regions of the world. Dishes from this vast area are as varied as the different ethnic groups that live here, but are mainly traditional and simple. To fit in with a mainly nomadic way of life, food generally needed to be

Lamb şiş kebab
Chicken şiş kebab
Stuffed aubergine (eggplant)
Chilli sauce
Prawn (shrimp) kebab
Lamb cutlet
Doner kebab
A selection of typical Turkish kebabs

LOCAL DISHES AND SPECIALITIES

Fish has been caught and consumed in abundance in Turkey since Ottoman times and is usually prepared very simply. Since ancient times the Bosphorus has been known for its excellent fishing and in the winter months especially, there is a bounty of oil-rich fish, such as bluefish, bream, bonito tuna, sea bass, mullet and mackerel, waiting to be reeled in. The Black Sea in the North is also provided with a steady supply of juicy mussels and *hamsi*, a type of anchovy. Sweets are also popular and eaten throughout the day, not just after a meal. They are sold in shops, on stalls and by street vendors. Istanbul is renowned for its *baklava*, sweet pastries coated with syrup and often filled with nuts.

Turkish Delight

Midye dolması *Mussels are stuffed with a spiced rice mixture, steamed and served with a squirt of lemon juice.*

A splendid array of fruit, vegetables and dried goods in the Spice Bazaar

BAZAAR CULTURE

A visit to the food markets in Turkey, especially Istanbul's Spice Bazaar (see p98) is a must. A cornucopia of fine ingredients is brought here daily from farms that surround the city. Apricots, watermelons, cherries and figs sit alongside staple vegetables, such as peppers, onions, aubergines and tomatoes. Fine cuts of lamb and beef, cheeses, pickles, herbs, spices and honey-drenched pastries and puddings are also on offer.

France and China grew up. At the height of the Ottoman Empire, in the 16th and 17th centuries, legions of kitchen staff slaved away on the Sultan's behalf. Court cooks usually specialized in particular dishes. Some prepared soups, while others just grilled meats or fish, or dreamed up combinations of vegetables, or baked breads, or made puddings and sherbets. As Ottoman rule expanded to North Africa, the Balkans and parts of southern Russia, influences from these far-flung places crept into the Turkish imperial kitchens. Complex dishes of finely seasoned stuffed meats and vegetables, often with such fanciful names as "lady's lips", "Vizier's fingers" and the "fainting Imam", appeared. This imperial tradition lives on in many of Turkey's

restaurants, where dishes such as *karniyarik* (halved aubergines (eggplant) stuffed with minced lamb, pine nuts and dried fruit) and *hünkar begendili köfte* (meatballs served with a smooth purée of smoked aubergine and cheese) grace the menu.

Fresh catch from the Bosphorus on a fish stall in Karaköy

KNOW YOUR FISH

The profusion of different species in the waters around Turkey makes the country a paradise for fish lovers:

Barbun Red mullet

Çupra Sea bream

Dilbaligi Sole

Hamsi Anchovy

Kalamar Squid

Kalkan Turbot

Kefal Grey mullet

Kiliç Swordfish

Levrek Sea bass

Lüfer Bluefish

Midye Mussels

Palamut Bonito tuna

Uskumru Mackerel

İmam bayildi *Aubergines, stuffed with tomatoes, garlic and onions, are baked in the oven until meltingly soft.*

Levrek pilakisi *This stew is made by simmering sea bass fillets with potatoes, carrots, tomatoes, onions and garlic.*

Kadayif *Rounds of vermicelli are stuffed with nuts and doused with honey to make a sumptuous dessert.*

Mezes

As in many southern European countries, a Turkish meal begins with a selection of appetizing starters known as *mezes*, which are placed in the middle of the table for sharing. In a basic *meyhane* restaurant, you may be offered olives, cheese and slices of melon, but in a grander establishment the choice will be enormous. Mainly consisting of cold vegetables and salads of various kinds, *mezes* can also include a number of hot dishes, such as *börek* (cheese pastries), fried mussels and squid. *Mezes* are eaten with bread and traditionally washed down with *rakı* (a clear, anise-flavoured spirit).

Humus with *pide* bread

Zeytinyağli enginar
(artichokes cooked in olive oil)

Coban salatasi
(tomato, red onion and cucumber salad)

Ayse fasulye
(green beans with tomato sauce)

Melon with beyaz peynir
(melon with a creamy, feta-like cheese)

Yalaci yaprak dolmasi
(stuffed vine leaves)

Tarama (a dip made with cod's roe, garlic and olive oil)

TURKISH BREADS

Bread is the cornerstone of every meal in Turkey and comes in a wide range of shapes and styles. Besides *ekmek* (crusty white loaves) the other most common types of Turkish bread are *yufka* and *pide*. *Yufka*, the typical bread of nomadic communities, is made from thinly rolled sheets of dough which are cooked on a griddle, and dried to help preserve them. They can then be heated up and served to accompany any main meal as required. *Pide* is the type of flat bread that is usually served with *mezes* and kebabs in restaurants. It consists of a flattened circle or oval of dough, sometimes brushed with beaten egg and sprinkled with sesame seeds or black cumin, that is baked in an oven. It is a staple during many religious festivals. In the month of Ramadan, no meal is considered complete without *pide*. Another popular bread is *simit*, a crisp, ring-shaped savoury loaf that comes covered in sesame seeds.

A delivery of freshly baked *simit* loaves

What to Drink in Turkey

The most common drink in Turkey is tea (*çay*), which is normally served black in small, tulip-shaped glasses. It will be offered to you wherever you go: in shops and bazaars, and even in banks and offices. Breakfast is usually accompanied by tea, whereas small cups of strong Turkish coffee (*kahve*) are drunk mid-morning and also at the end of meals. Cold drinks include a variety of fresh fruit juices, such as orange and cherry, and refreshing syrup-based sherbets. Although Turkey does produce its own wine and beer, the most popular alcoholic drink is rakı, which is usually served to accompany mezes.

Soft drinkseller

SOFT DRINKS

Bottled mineral water (*su*) is sold in corner shops and served in restaurants everywhere. If you're feeling adventurous, you might like to try a

vişne suyu   **Ayran**

glass of *ayran*, salty liquid yoghurt. *Boza* is made from bulgur wheat and is another local drink to sample. There is always a variety of refreshing, cold fruit and vegetable juices available. They include cherry juice (*vişne suyu*), turnip juice (*şalgam suyu*) and şıra, a juice made from fermented grapes.

COFFEE AND TEA

Turkish coffee is very dark, strong and served in tiny cups. It is ordered according to the amount of sugar required: *az* (little), *orta* (medium), *çok şekerli* (a lot). Insist on Turkish coffee, or the waiter may assume you want Nescafé. The ubiquitous daily drink is tea (*çay*), which is served with sugar, but without milk and comes in a small, tulip-shaped glass.

Most popular is the apple (*elma*) flavour, but there are also rosehip (*kuşburnu*) and a delicious mint (*nane*) variety.

Traditional samovar for tea

Apple tea   **Limeflower tea**

ALCOHOLIC DRINKS

Turkey's national alcoholic drink is rakı, a clear, anise-flavoured spirit that turns cloudy when water is added and is drunk with fish and mezes. The Turkish wine industry has yet to realize its full potential. Kavaklıdere and Doluca, the best-known brands, are overpriced for table wines. Villa Doluca is preferable. Sevilen offers several interesting wines, such as Majestic, and an outstanding Merlot. All alcohol attracts a tax at over 400 per cent, making simple table wine a luxury. The locally brewed Efes Pilsen beer, also widely available on draught, is excellent but note that alcohol may not be served in some cheaper restaurants and kebab houses.

Rakı   **Beer**   **Red wine**   **White wine**

Turkish coffee is a very strong drink and an acquired taste for most people.

Sahlep is a winter drink made from orchid root.

Choosing a Restaurant

These restaurants have been selected across a wide price range for their exceptional food, good value and location. Please note that unless stated, alcohol is not served in many restaurants, particularly in Eastern Anatolia. Map references refer to the Istanbul Street Finder maps on pp134–40.

PRICE CATEGORIES
Price categories include a three-course meal for one (excluding alcohol) and all unavoidable extras including service and tax.
€ Under €10
€€ €10–€15
€€€ €15–€20
€€€€ €20–€25
€€€€€ Over €25

ISTANBUL

SERAGLİO POINT Backpackers Restaurant €
Yeni Akbıyık Cad 14/1, Sultanahmet, 34400 **Tel** *(0212) 638 55 86* **Map** *5 D5*

Simple, upbeat snacks are served here with the accent more on wines and beer than food. This is very much a cheerful and informal budget gathering place. People congregate to drink, eat hearty snacks, swap travel stories and plan their next journey.

SERAGLİO POINT Doy-Doy €
Şifa Hamamı Sok 13, Sultanahmet, 34110 **Tel** *(0212) 517 15 88* **Map** *5 D5*

An impressive selection of soups, kebabs, *pide* (flat bread) in abundance, colourful salads, vegetarian dishes and rich desserts are on offer here. Everything is prepared very authentically. Doy-Doy is a cheerful venue with great prices, but alcohol is not served. The rooftop terrace is perfect in summer.

SERAGLİO POINT Group Restaurant €
Şehit Mehmet Paşa Yokuşu 4, Sultanahmet, 34110 **Tel** *(0212) 517 47 00* **Map** *5 D5*

Part gift shop, part café and restaurant, this is a magnet for tourists and is always bustling. The coffee and sticky pastries are popular but more substantial fare is also served. Grills, salads and stews are on the menu and served in generous portions at reasonable prices. Alcohol is available.

SERAGLİO POINT Ahırkapı Lokanta €€€
Armada Hotel, Ahır Kapı Sok, Sultanahmet, 34110 **Tel** *(0212) 455 44 55* **Map** *5 F3*

This restaurant has the atmosphere of a 1930s Turkish tavern and live *fasıl* music. In keeping with the decor, the cuisine is typically Turkish with a variety of delicious mezes and main dishes, such as *yoğurtlu yaprak dolması* (minced meat in vine leaves with yoghurt). The rooftop terrace boasts views over Sultanahmet.

SERGLİO POINT Konyalı €€€€
Topkapı Palace, Sultanahmet, 34110 **Tel** *(0212) 513 96 96* **Map** *5 F3*

This gastronomic landmark has been in business for four decades, serving appetizing mezes, meats, salads and fish. There is an award-winning à la carte menu. Located within the Topkapı Palace, it has commanding views of the Bosphorus. Try the elegant "afternoon tea" menu.

SERGLİO POINT Sarnıç €€€€
Soğukçeşme Sok, Sultanahmet, 34110 **Tel** *(0212) 512 42 91* **Map** *5 E4*

Converted from a Byzantine cistern with lofty columns and a domed ceiling, Sarnıç is dimly lit by wrought-iron chandeliers and candles, and has an impressive fireplace. Piano music is often played in the evenings. The menu has variety but diners come here more for the atmosphere than the top cuisine.

SERAGLİO POINT Seven Hills Restaurant €€€€€
Tevkifhane Sok 8, Sultanahmet, 34110 **Tel** *(0212) 516 94 97* **Map** *5 E4*

The chef here is from Bolu, a region that nurtures Turkey's most creative chefs. The food is outstanding and the choice is sumptuous – try the fresh fish, lobster and seafood, or the star dish, the Sultan's Lamb. Top it off with well-chosen wines and a view over Haghia Sophia. This restaurant is part of the Seven Hills Hotel.

SULTANAHMET Café Camille €
Bab-i Ali Cad 8, Cağaloğlu, 34110 **Tel** *(0212) 527 81 77* **Map** *5 D4*

This small café, with its industrious, bustling kitchen, is the place to grab a cup of coffee or a foaming cappuccino and home-made cakes. Simple lunches with quiche, omelettes and salads are popular. They serve delicious fresh fruit juices and milk shakes. The service is brisk and friendly.

SULTANAHMET Cafe Müze €
Divanyolu Cad 84, Çemberlitaş, 34110 **Tel** *(0212) 512 00 80* **Map** *4 C4*

Lacking any pretensions, this is a small café adjacent to the old printing presses at the Press Museum. Omelettes, hot and cold snacks, sandwiches and a few salads are on offer, and the coffee is good. They also serve draft beer. It is a relief to come here to escape the bustle of the busy street outside.

Key to Symbols *see back cover flap*

SULTANAHMET The Cure

Divanyolu Cad, Ticarethane Sokak 35, Sultanahmet, 34110 **Tel** *(0212) 528 19 22*   **Map** *5 E4*

There is a staggering selection of international dishes to sample here. Liver with an onion and spinach sauce is popular, the *fajitas* are delicious and so is the hot corn soup. The service is enthusiastic. Prices for exotic cocktails are high and light jazz is played on occasion.

SULTANAHMET The Pudding Shop

Divanyolu Cad 6, Sultanahmet, 34110 **Tel** *(0212) 522 29 70*   **Map** *5 E4*

In the 1950s, nowhere else in Istanbul provided food and tourist information to backpackers. They serve wonderfully cooked Turkish fare. There is an excellent choice of soups, grilled meats, salads, stews and sautéed dishes and, of course, rich puddings. Former customers frequently return.

SULTANAHMET Valide Sultan Konak

Kutlugün Sokak 1, Sultanahmet, 34110 **Tel** *(0212) 638 06 00*   **Map** *5 E4*

The semicircular rooftop restaurant of the Valide Sultan Konağı Hotel commands stunning views of the sea and historic surrounding area. Menus are well balanced with meat, vegetables, *meze*, kebabs and stews. The stuffed vegetables are particularly creative and taste as good as they look. They also serve seafood and pizzas.

SULTANAHMET Adonin Cafe/ Restaurant

Divanyolu Cad, Ticarethane Sok 27/31, 34110 **Tel** *(0212) 514 00 29*   **Map** *5 E4*

A few minutes walk from the Blue Mosque, Adonin has a lively, enjoyable atmosphere and a great Ottoman/ Anatolian menu. A magazine corner offers a spot for quiet reading and wireless laptops are also available for use outside peak periods.

SULTANAHMET Rumeli Café

Ticarethane Sok 8, Sultanahmet, 34110 **Tel** *(0212) 512 00 08*   **Map** *5 E4*

This is an atmospheric restaurant just off the busy Divanyolu. Housed in an old printing factory, the Rumeli has a strong Greek flavour to it as well as Mediterranean aromas. Vegetarian dishes are popular and specialities include grilled lamb with various sauces. Tomatoes, herbs and yoghurt feature in many dishes.

SULTANAHMET Balıkcı Sabahattin

Seyt Hasankuyu Sok 1, Sultanahmet, 34110 **Tel** *(0212) 458 23 02*   **Map** *5 E3*

Everything works well at this delightful fish restaurant. They have a delicious menu, and have been in business since 1927. The fish and seafood are mouthwatering and other dishes include spicy squash with yoghurt. Recommended for smart service and consistently good food. There is a no-smoking section.

THE BAZAAR QUARTER Subaşi

Nuruosmaniye Caddesi, Kılıçcilar Sokak 48, Çarşıkapı, 36420 **Tel** *(0212) 522 47 62*   **Map** *5 D4*

Located near the Nuruosmaniye Gate of the Grand Bazaar, Subaşi is an uncomplicated traditional eatery serving up freshly cooked dishes every day. This is mainly a lunch place and diners will find the food at its freshest and tastiest at this time. You can select various stews, meats and baked dishes before you are seated.

THE BAZAAR QUARTER Borsa Lokanta

Yalı Köşkü Cad, Yalı Köşkü Han 60, Sirkeci, 36420 **Tel** *(0212) 511 80 79*   **Map** *5 D2*

There are two eateries here, a fast-food, self-service one on the ground floor and a more formal one on the level above. Borsa Lokanta has many branches in Istanbul. One of their trademark recipes is *beğendili kebabı* (meat with a creamy aubergine sauce). The service is extremely competent. Alcohol is served.

THE BAZAAR QUARTER Havuzlu

Gani Çelebi Sok 3, Grand Bazaar, Beyazıt, 36420 **Tel** *(0212) 527 33 46*   **Map** *4 C4*

Havuzlu is a small restaurant serving honest local food. Everything is freshly cooked. The soups, *dolma* (stuffed vine leaves) and different kinds of kebabs and grills are great snacks. Havuzlu means "with pool" and is named after the burbling fountain found inside.

THE BAZAAR QUARTER İskender Saray

Atatürk Bulvarı 116, Aksaray, 36420 **Tel** *(0212) 520 34 04*   **Map** *4 A3*

This classic restaurant serves döner kebabs, and signature dishes include *İskender kebab* (döner meat on bread with a rich sauce) and *saç kavurma* (lamb and vegetables flambéed at the table). The white table cloths and cheerful, friendly staff lend a professional touch. They do a handy takeaway service, too. No alcohol is served.

THE BAZAAR QUARTER Karaca

Gazi Sinan Paşa Sok, Vezir Han 1/A, Nuruosmaniye, 36420 **Tel** *(0212) 512 90 94*   **Map** *5 D4*

This large restaurant is part of an authentic Ottoman *caravanserai*. Diners eat very well here and dishes such as *pazı dolması* (stuffed chard) and *islim kebabı* (lamb with aubergine) are hearty and filling. Save room for the calorific *kabak tatlısı* (pumpkin pudding). The clientele includes shopkeepers from the Grand Bazaar.

THE BAZAAR QUARTER Dârüzziyafe

Şifahane Cad 6, Süleymaniye, 36420 **Tel** *(0212) 511 84 14*   **Map** *4 B2*

The former kitchens of the Süleymaniye Mosque house this excellent restaurant, serving unusual Ottoman dishes. The nourishing house soup is made with spinach, vegetables and meat. Mezes are available. For dessert, try *keşkül* (milk pudding with pistachios and almonds). It is best to reserve. No alcohol served.

THE BAZAAR QUARTER Pandelli
Mısır Çarşı 1, Eminönü, 36420 **Tel** *(0212) 527 39 09* **Map** *5 D2*

Pandeli is ideally located in the middle of the Spice Bazaar; so this restaurant is always crowded and lively.
Locals come for the *patlıcan böreği* (aubergine pastry) and *kağıtta levrek* (sea bass steamed in wax paper). It is
advisable to reserve.

BEYOĞLU Nature and Peace
Büyükparmakkapı Sokak 15, Beyoğlu, 34430 **Tel** *(0212) 252 86 09* **Map** *1 B4*

Nature and Peace was one of Istanbul's first vegetarian restaurants and it has stayed in the forefront when it comes
to providing wholesome, healthy foods. Vegan dishes are also served. Chicken and fish are on the menu but red
meat is not on offer. Desserts, tea-time and fresh fruit juices are available all day. Highly recommended.

BEYOĞLU Hacı Baba
İstiklâl Cad 49, 34430 **Tel** *(0212) 244 18 86* **Map** *1 B4*

This busy and popular restaurant on two floors turns out the most amazing variety of tasty, colourful dishes – over
40 different hot main meals, mezes and 25 different desserts. Try the star dish, *kuzu tandır* (slow-baked lamb). The
service is polished and professional, however, the decor is somewhat drab.

BEYOĞLU İmroz
Nevizade Sokak 24 **Tel** *(0212) 249 90 73* **Map** *1 B4*

An historic Greek *meyhane,* or taverna, and one of the oldest on the busy Nevizade Sokak near the fish market,
İmroz is a favourite with locals. On the menu you'll find high-quality fish and meat dishes. Wooden tables and faded
photographs contribute to the cozy, relaxed mood. In summer you can dine at tables set out on the street.

BEYOĞLU Natural Grill House
Şehit Muhtar Cad 38/A, Taksim, 34430 **Tel** *(0212) 238 33 61* **Map** *1 B3*

Rustic tables and talented cooking are the appeal here. Fresh salads, grilled meats and baked vegetarian dishes are
well cooked and presented. Mexican steak is one of the house specialities. The Grill House is popular with locals and
also guests from the nearby hotels. Several different beers are served.

BEYOĞLU Zencefil Restaurant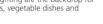
Kurabiye Sokak 8–10, Beyoğlu, 34430 **Tel** *(0212) 243 82 34* **Map** *1 B4*

This gem of a restaurant with a small, attractive garden is hidden away from the crowds, behind Istiklal Caddesi. The
mainly vegetarian menu includes soups, salads and main courses, all served with home-made bread and olive oil.
There's also a daily specials board. Try the famous mushroom balls. It's a good place for coffee and cake too.

BEYOĞLU Asir Rest
Kalyoncu Kulluk Cad 94, Beyoğlu, 34430 **Tel** *(0212) 297 05 57* **Map** *1 A4*

Asir is a friendly, convivial place. The staff are friendly and attentive, and the food is outstandingly good and
economical. Over 50 varieties of mezes are offered and many innovative dishes with fish, chicken and chick peas.
Typical of *meyhane* (wine bar) culture, there is live *fasıl* music in the evenings.

BEYOĞLU Chez Vous
Firuzağa Mah, Cezayir Sok 21, Galatasaray, Beyoğlu, 34430 **Tel** *(0212) 245 95 32* **Map** *1 A4*

Part of the rebirth and design revolution sweeping most of Beyoğlu, this small café (part of a restored period
mansion) clings to the steep steps of trend-setting French Street. Light snacks and salads are served. The service is
rushed and the table wines are expensive, but trendy Chez Vous is great fun.

BEYOĞLU Leb-i-Derya
İstiklâl Cad, Kumbaracı Yokuşu, Kumbaracı Han 57/7, 34430 **Tel** *(0212) 293 49 89* **Map** *1 A5*

It is hard to beat this restaurant's marvellous view over Istanbul. Glass, wood and soft lighting are the backdrop for
the abundance of appetizers and well-cooked Mediterranean-style healthy main courses, vegetable dishes and
salads. There is a lively bar that attracts a dedicated happy-hour crowd.

BEYOĞLU Otto Sofyali
Asmalı Mescit 22/A, Tünel–Beyoğlu, 34430 **Tel** *(0212) 252 65 88* **Map** *1 A5*

With four branches across Istanbul, Otto is a firm favourite with both locals and tourists alike, who come for the
tasty food and energetic club atmosphere. Quality Turkish and Mediterranean dishes are served, including authentic
pizzas, and there's a good range of drinks available – try the delicious nut vodka. DJs keep things jumping until late.

BEYOĞLU Fisher
İnönü Cad 40/A, Taksim, 34430 **Tel** *(0212) 245 25 76* **Map** *1 C4*

Fisher was one of the first middle-European restaurants in Istanbul. The clientele has stayed loyal after decades and
dishes such as *borscht, schnitzel, pirogies* and *strudel* are still popular today. It is a little drab, even austere, but the
owners seem reluctant to renovate or change too much of a good thing.

BEYOĞLU Flamm
Sofyali Sok 12/1, Asmalımescit, 34430 **Tel** *(02120 245 76 04/05* **Map** *1 A5*

Flamm is small and intimate with a casual, friendly cocktail bar. The owner came to Istanbul from Bodrum, and
imported some dishes from sunny Med-side kitchens, including ingenious ways with pasta and rice. Diners usually
want to return for the excellent honest cooking and convivial ambience.

Key to Price Guide see p352 **Key to Symbols** see back cover flap

BEYOĞLU Gitane

*Firuzağa Mah, Cezayir Sok 3 (French St), Galatasaray, 34430 **Tel** (0212) 245 92 63* **Map** 1 A4

Gitane is owned by one of Turkey's most renowned fashion designers. The extensive menu has choices for breakfast, brunch, lunch and festive dinners, and there is excellent local wine on offer. The cheese platter highlights the interest in Anatolian cheeses.

BEYOĞLU Refik

Sofyalı Sok 10–12, Tünel, 34430 Tel (0212) 243 28 34 Map 1 A5

Refik is an icon of Bohemian Beyoğlu. The restaurant retains its faded plastic tablecloths and bygone era ambience. Intellectuals and media types frequent here every evening. It is an authentic meyhane (wine bar) that favours Black Sea dishes. The mezes here are large enough for a main meal. Alcohol is served here.

BEYOĞLU Asmalimescit Balikçisi

*Asmalımescit Mah, Sofyalı Sok 5/A Tünel, 34430 **Tel** (0212) 251 39 39* **Map** 1 A5

The pulse of Beyoğlu beats at this popular fish-only restaurant. Linen, silver service and candles add class to the stone walls and cheerful, chic atmosphere. Every kind of fresh daily catch in Istanbul is served here. Desserts are good and there is a reasonable wine list. There are monthly art exhibitions that adorn the walls.

BEYOĞLU Mikla

*Marmara Pera Hotel, Meşrutiyet Cad 167/185, Tepebaşı, 34430 **Tel** (0212) 293 56 56* **Map** 1 A5

Mikla provides a magnificent dining experience – if you can get a reservation. It offers a predominantly seafood menu but unusual culinary influences mingle and the results are exquisite. The decor is subtle and the mood dignified. There are stunning vistas from the bar at the top of the Marmara Pera Hotel.

THE BOSPHORUS Çınaraltı

*İskele Meydanı 48, Ortaköy, European Side **Tel** (0212) 261 46 16* **Map** 3 F3

This is one of the restaurants on the waterfront in Ortaköy. Freshly prepared, colourful mezes, salads, meat and fish dishes are all smartly served. The tables are close together and they pack in trendy customers at peak times, particularly at weekends.

THE BOSPHORUS Pafuli

*Kuruçeşme Cad 116, Kuruçeşme, European Side **Tel** (0212) 263 66 38*

In business for over two decades, Pafuli has indoor and outdoor tables. Fish and seafood, such as shrimp and squid, are freshly cooked and the superb Black Sea dishes are first rate. Mıhlama (corn bread), hamsi (anchovy) and cheese dishes are legendary. There is an extensive menu and wine list.

THE BOSPHORUS Hidiv Kasrı

*Hidiv Yolu 32, Çubuklu, Asian side **Tel** (0216) 425 06 03*

Perched high on a hill with sweeping vistas of the straits, this former palace stands in the midst of a beautiful park. There is a large, formal restaurant that keeps up Turkish culinary traditions, while the terrace is open for buffet brunches on weekends. Come here for the view and sea breezes. No alcohol is served.

THE BOSPHORUS Konak

*Istinye Cad, 23–25, Emigan, European Side **Tel** (0121) 32 36 00/01*

This restored wooden mansion house is set on three floors on the water's edge. There is a wide selection of meat, salad and international favourites, but the fish is the dish of choice. There is alfresco dining under umbrellas, on the terrace in summer.

THE BOSPHORUS Kız Kulesi

*Leander's Tower, off Üsküdar ferry pier, Asian Side **Tel** (0216) 342 47 47* **Map** 6 A3

Located just offshore from Üsküdar on its own little islet in the Bosphorus, this old building is a self-service cafeteria during the day, and it rebounds spectacularly at night with a full-service restaurant, gourmet food and live music. Bookings for the restaurant and ferry service are advised.

THE BOSPHORUS Kordon

*Kuleli Cad 51, Çengelköy, Asian Side **Tel** (0216) 321 04 73*

This romantic restaurant is located in a smart and cleverly modernized warehouse. Seafood dishes are artistically presented and there is a fine selection of fresh fish daily. People come for the tempting food as much as for the stunning views of Istanbul's European shores. There is outdoor dining in summer.

THE BOSPHORUS Poseidon

*Cevdetpaşa Cad 58, Bebek, European Side **Tel** (0212) 263 38 23*

Poseidon boasts a dream location on a wooden terrace jutting out over the Bosphorus with geraniums and charming tables. There is an extensive Turkish and international menu but the staff encourage diners to order fish dishes. The fish chowder is sublime but can come with a large price tag, so beware.

FURTHER AFIELD à la Turka

*Hazine Sokak 8, Ortaköy, 34349 **Tel** (0212) 258 79 24* **Map** 3 E2

Tucked away on a side street near Ortaköy mosque, à la Turka is a modest but attractive restaurant. It serves mostly classic Turkish dishes done to perfection. Particularly good are the dolma (stuffed vine leaves), and the chef uses herbs very creatively. It is recommended as a reliable favourite.

FURTHER AFIELD Beyti   €€
Orman Sokak 8, Florya, 34710 **Tel** *(0212) 663 29 92*

Beyti is a 60-year-old Istanbul institution and award-winning legend when it comes to meat and kebabs. There is a vast dining area, with 12 dining rooms and secluded nooks. It is crowded here for lunch and dinner and the good service matches the unerringly excellent food. Beyti kebab is a speciality. There is a good wine selection.

FURTHER AFIELD ıl Piccolo   €€
Bağdat Caddesi, Ogün Sokak 2, Caddebostan, 95230 **Tel** *(0216) 369 64 43*

An established favourite that has been serving well-cooked dishes for many years and keeping up with the trends. Located in an energetic shopping district on the Asian Side, meals are served outdoors in Summer and a live band plays on weekends. They have simple pizzas and pasta dishes with great sauces, plus good wines and Italian cheese.

FURTHER AFIELD Zeyrekhane   €€
Sinanağa Mah, ıbadethane Arkası Sok 10, Zeyrek, Fatih, 35600 **Tel** *(0212) 532 27 78*   **Map** *1 C3*

This café in a restored Ottoman building, is best for light meals and snacks. The cool, leafy outdoor courtyard is used in summer. The main restaurant succeeds spectacularly with traditional Ottoman recipes. Alcohol is served. It is best to make a booking for an evening meal.

FURTHER AFIELD Develi   €€€
Gümüşyüzük Sok 7, Samatya, Kocamustafapaşa, 35420 **Tel** *(0212) 632 79 82*

It is no exaggeration to say that you have not really eaten a kebab until you have tucked into a Develi one. Kebabs here are prepared in unusual ways and the quality keeps getting better. The service is slick and all the touches that make dining a great experience are found here. Develi easily tops the kebab charts.

FURTHER AFIELD Hünkar   €€€
Akdeniz Cad 21, Fatih, 35600 **Tel** *(0212) 525 77 18*

This family-run restaurant has an admirable record for serving tasty Turkish food, including delightful and little known Ottoman dishes. The walls are decorated with jars of bright pickled fruits and a small fountain sits in the midst of diners. *Böreks* (stuffed pastry parcels), *köfte* (meatballs), *pilavs* (rice dishes) and salads are well prepared.

FURTHER AFIELD Picante   €€€
Iskele Caddesi, Salhane Sok 2, Ortaköy, 34349 **Tel** *(0212) 236 17 35*   **Map** *6 B4*

This hip, chic eatery serves an array of Latin American, Tex-Mex and Colombian dishes. It is particularly renowned for its delicious fajitas and potent margaritas. The original Picante opened in Bodrum in 1993; this Ortaköy branch is located in one of the neighbourhood's most beautiful buildings and offers splendid views over the Bosphorus.

FURTHER AFIELD Denizkızı   €€€€
Çakmaktaşı Sok 3/5, Kumkapı, 28601 **Tel** *(0212) 518 86 59*   **Map** *4 C5*

The cobbled streets of the old fishing neighbourhood of Kumkapı are dense with fish restaurants and *meyhanes* (traditional taverns). Denizkızı (which means mermaid) is one of these in a lively district. Diners select fish from the tank and the chef will fry, grill or steam it for you with vegetables.

FURTHER AFIELD House Café   €€€€
Salhane Sok 1, Ortaköy, 34349 **Tel** *(0212) 227-26 99*   **Map** *3 F3*

There are no restaurants that epitomize Istanbul's dynamic revival quite like this one. The colourful salads, snacks and main courses are excellent and the funky decor is amazing, especially the ornately carved bar and octopus chandeliers. It is a magnet for celebrities and is always busy.

FURTHER AFIELD Doğa Balık   €€€€€
Akarsu Cad 46, Cihangir, Taksim, 34433 **Tel** *(0212) 293 91 44*   **Map** *1 B5*

This is a highly regarded fish restaurant in an attractive area. Everything is friendly and comfortable here. *Mezes* are freshly prepared and colourful, and there is a daily set menu available. The salads are masterful. Domestic wines are available but *rakı* goes best with the many fish selections.

FURTHER AFIELD Mezzaluna   €€€€€
Abdi İpekçi Cad 38/1, Nişantaşı, 80400 **Tel** *(0212) 231 31 42*   **Map** *2 A3*

Mezzaluna attracts shoppers and strollers at lunch and a serious social set in the evenings. With branches in other Turkish cities also, they cater for the upwardly mobile who crave well-cooked continental dishes. The accent is on Italian cooking and the mussels are first rate. Finish a refined meal with a potent *grappa*.

THRACE AND THE SEA OF MARMARA

BURSA Çiçek Izgara   €
Ünlü Cad 7 **Tel** *(0224) 221 46 15*

This restaurant comes highly recommended by the locals, combining three floors of white linen tablecloths and impeccable service with the bright casualness of a cafeteria. Menu items include *peynerli köfte* (meatballs with cheese), *kabak dolmasi* (stuffed zucchini), and *cacik*, a refreshing yogurt soup.

BURSA Kebapçı İskender

Ünlü Cad 7 **Tel** *(0224) 221 46 15*

This venue is the birthplace of the famous ıskender Kebab, an artery-clogging delight that symbolizes Turkish food. It was in 1867 that young ıskender thought of grilling meat vertically on a spit, and then serving it with yogurt and melted butter on flat bread.

BURSA Kitap Evi

Kavakli Cad 21, Bursa, 16040 **Tel** *(0224) 225 41 60*

A local landmark and one of the oldest kebab restaurants in Bursa, everybody comes here and all are welcomed almost like family. The restaurant is known for kebabs and they serve nothing else. Try the *patlican kebabı* (aubergine kebab) for the most satisfying main course. No alcohol is served.

BURSA Sehir Lokantasi

Inebey Cad 85 **Tel** *(0224) 222 62 03*

For over 30 years, this unpretentious and friendly restaurant has delighted its customers with a good selection of well-prepared traditional Turkish specialities. A range of kebabs are on the menu, but its most popular dishes are based on home cooking.

BURSA Uludag Kebapçısı

Garaj Karşısı, Şirin Sok 12 **Tel** *(0224) 254 72 64*

They may not have invented it, but they've had four decades to perfect their own recipe. As a result, their ıskender kebab is second to none. The venue itself is quite small, and little attention has been paid to the decor. But the photos on the wall testify to the popularity of this restaurant.

BURSA Safran Hotel

Ortapazar Cad, Arka Sok 4 **Tel** *(0224) 224 72 16*

Located in the old part of Bursa, away from the industrial modern city, this restaurant is part of a small boutique hotel. The building is a restored Ottoman townhouse, painted a pretty saffron colour. It has a bar, and the restaurant serves grilled meat, mezes and vegetables in olive oil. Popular with tourists.

BURSA Red Zone Restaurant & Pub

Yeni Yalova Yolu 12, Bursa **Tel** *(0224) 261 60 85*

Families visit this restaurant at weekends to savour the *kuzu tandır* (lamb baked in a special oven until very tender). The place is simple and unassuming, but the service is efficient and the meat succulent. Grilled meats, as well as salads and vegetables in olive oil, are also on the menu.

BUYUKADA Ali Baba

Gülistan Cad 20 **Tel** *(0216) 382 37 33*

Fish restaurants line the waterfront in Büyükada, the largest of the Princes' islands. This venue is one of the oldest and occupies a spot that Atatürk is said to have frequented regularly. The fish and mezes are very fresh, and the rakı plentiful. Perfect place for a relaxing meal, before or after a ride in a horse-drawn carriage.

ECEABAT Maydos Restaurant

Ismet Paşa Mah, Kilitbayır Yolu üzeri **Tel** *(0286) 814 14 54*

A short distance away from the ferry station in Eceabat, this restaurant prepares excellent Turkish food. Part of a small hotel, it is an ideal starting point to visit the battlefields on the peninsula. There is plenty of beer, wine and liquor to satisfy visitors. The hotel has its own beach.

EDİRNE Çınar Et ve Balık Lokantasi

Karaağaç Yolu üzeri, iki Köprü Arası, Bülbül Adası 13 **Tel** *(0284) 214 32 36*

The green environment makes this large venue, slightly outside town, very attractive to weekend visitors who enjoy the terrace and the garden. People come here mainly to enjoy the local specialities, lamb baked in the oven and Edirne liver. But fish is also on the menu, best enjoyed with a glass of *rakı*.

EDİRNE Ağa Köşkü

Sarayiçi, Kırkpınar Alanı Yanı **Tel** *(0284) 213 76 59*

Wood panelling contributes to create a warm and comfortable atmosphere in this family restaurant, but in the summer, customers prefer to enjoy their food in the large garden. Set near the Mehriç river, this venue serves fish and meat specialities. At weekends, tables are set around the pool for brunch.

EDİRNE Villa Restaurant

Karaağaç Yolu üzeri **Tel** *(0284) 223 40 77*

From the outside it looks more like an official building than a villa, but the interior is spacious and the decor pleasant. There is a large terrace, with wooden platforms right on the river. The food is the standard selection of grills and *mezes*. Popular venue for weddings and group meetings.

EDİRNE Lalezar

Karaağaç Yolu, Edirne **Tel** *(0284) 213 06 00*

This is one of the most pleasant places in Edirne. It is a little way out of town but, after visiting local sights, there is nothing better than to sit here on the banks of the Meriç River and enjoy one of their fine dishes. Try to get a waterside table. Food is not exotic but the *mezes*, kebabs and main courses are well cooked, with good service.

GALLIPOLI Ilhan Restaurant 🎵 ♿ 🍴 🔲 🆅 €

Balıkhane Meydanı **Tel** *(0286) 566 11 24*

This pleasant venue occupies a prime spot in Gallipoli harbour, where fisherman can be seen mending their nets. The food is the standard fish and seafood fare, but it is fresh and well prepared. There is a good range of *mezes*, which can be enjoyed with a glass or two of *rakı*.

GALLIPOLI Yarımada Osmanlı Mutfağı 🍴 🔲 🆅 €€

Atatürk Cad 34 **Tel** *(0286) 566 12 25*

In the centre of Gallipoli, this large restaurant serves a very wide range of home-style cooked vegetable casseroles and meat stews. The usual kebabs and grills are also on the menu. This is not a place where customers linger, but it serves simple and healthy food in a clean and pleasant environment.

GALLIPOLI Gelibolu Liman Lokantası/ Vehbi Ustanin Yeri 🎵 ♿ 🍴 🔲 🆅 €€€

İç Limanı 20 **Tel** *(0286) 566 11 25*

This harbour-side venue provides welcome respite after a visit to the WWI battlefields. Focused on seafood, it serves interesting dishes: fish grilled in vine leaves, stuffed sardines or sardine salad. The place has a pleasant old-fashioned feel. If you want to make a night of it, the adjacent disco-bar stays open until dawn.

HEYBELIADA Göksin's Ambrosia 🎵 ♿ 🍴 🔲 🆅 €

Heybeliada **Tel** *(0216) 351 13 88*

This friendly restaurant by the water has a loyal clientele, drawn by the quality of the food. The fish soup is a classic and the olive oil used for vegetables is the best from the Aegean region. The friendly ambiance is another reason why this venue is popular. Creative selection of *mezes*. Live music at weekends.

HEYBELIADA Merit Halki Palace Hotel 🍴 🔲 🆅 €€€€

Heybeliada **Tel** *(0216) 351 00 25*

Stylish hotel on a quiet island where cars are banned, only a short ferry ride away from central Istanbul. Its restaurant serves mainly à la carte Turkish cuisine, beautifully presented to suit the fancy decor. Beautiful sea views and a nostalgic atmosphere. In the summer, tables are arranged around the swimming pool for dinner.

İZNİK Çamlik Restaurant 🍴 🔲 🆅 €

Sahil Cad 22 **Tel** *(0224) 757 13 62*

This lakeside restaurant, with a capacity of 150, combines a cosy atmosphere indoors and a green environment outdoors. Visitors to this historical town find excellent *mezes* and a relaxed atmosphere in this venue, which is popular for weddings and banquets. Try the fresh-water fish and the locally grown olives, which are renowned.

İZNİK Kenan Çorba ve ızgara Salonu ♿ 🍴 🔲 🆅 €

Atatürk Cad 93 **Tel** *(0224) 757 02 35*

There is nothing fancy about this basic, but friendly, restaurant. Soup is the main speciality here, and it comes in several varieties. Grilled kebabs and meat are also on the menu. Four or five meat and vegetable casseroles are prepared every day. The place is clean and welcomes families.

İZNİK Çamlık Motel ♿ 🔲 €€€

Sahil Yolu, İznik **Tel** *(0224) 757 16 31*

İznik is beautiful with lakes and mountains and wonderful undiscovered gems begging to be explored. Çamlık Motel is one gem that visitors want to keep all to themselves. It is a tranquil and simple countrified retreat with a secluded garden. The local speciality, *İnegöl köfte* (meatballs) will tempt you to return.

POLONEZKÖY Leonardo Restaurant 🔲 €€€€

Köyiçi Sokak 32, Polonezköy **Tel** *(0216) 432 30 82*

Leonardo has been going for years and seems to have become ever more popular. There is a wonderful garden, and also picnic areas and a small swimming pool. The food combines French and Austrian cuisine. They do a generous open-buffet brunch on weekends. It gets very crowded because it is so close to the city centre.

POLONEZKÖY Stella'nin Evi ♿ 🍴 🔲 🆅 €€€€

75 Yil Cad 59 **Tel** *(0216) 432 30 28*

This pension and restaurant has attained an authentic feel. Weekend breakfasts are particularly enjoyable: the jams are home-made and the eggs free range from the farm. There is a large garden and the forest is nearby. Meals are cooked on a wood oven. Aside from the buffet breakfast, they serve grilled meat, salads and fresh vegetables.

SILIVRI Garden Et Lokantasi 🎵 🍴 🔲 🆅 €€€

E-5 karayolu **Tel** *(0212) 723 68 40*

This vast restaurant, within the Istanbul catchment area, welcomes weekend visitors who come here to spend a relaxing family day. The atmosphere is different in each of its salons, but the marble fountain in the lobby sets the tune. Meat, in dozens of different guises, is the main item on the menu. Large garden and playground.

TEKIRDAĞ Özcanlar €

Hüseyin Pehlivan Cad 5 **Tel** *(0282) 261 29 76*

This is a cheap and basic venue that specializes in meatballs. In short, it is fast-food, Turkish-style. The company that runs it has perfected the art since 1953 and now operates several branches around town. Different recipes have been developed: meatballs with cheese, meatballs butcher-style and, of course, the local Tekirdağ variety.

Key to Price Guide *see p352* **Key to Symbols** *see back cover flap*

THE AEGEAN

AYVACIK Biber Evi

Assos, Ayvacik **Tel** *(0286) 721 74 10*

Facing the island of Lesbos, the ancient village of Assos has become a haven for select visitors. This beautifully decorated boutique hotel and restaurant offers refined food, both Turkish and international. The terrace overlooking the Aegean is perfect for a leisurely drink at sunset. The owner, a whisky buff, has a good collection of single malts.

BODRUM Gemibaşi Restaurant

Neyzen Tevfik Cad 17A **Tel** *(0252) 316 12 20*

Opposite the yacht harbour, on the corner of Firkaylen Sok and Neyzen Tevfik, this restaurant is cheap and cheerful but with wonderful, freshly prepared Turkish fare. Tables overflow onto the street and it is always full. Single women can comfortably come here for an evening meal.

BODRUM Hong Kong Marina Restaurant

Neyzen Tevfik Cad 204/A **Tel** *(0252) 316 85 37*

In this venue, open from 8:30am to 10pm, the menu is mainly Chinese, as is the decor, but Mexican options, seafood and steaks are also available. There is even a children's menu. The owner, who runs several Far Eastern restaurants in Turkey, travels to China every year to discover new tastes and buy new ingredients.

BODRUM Kocadon

Saray Sokak 1 **Tel** *(0252) 316 37 05*

Located in a 19th-century stone house, with tables also set in the pretty courtyard, Kocadon serves consistently good quality Turkish and Mediterranean cuisine. The buffet of cold *mezes* makes a delicious starter, followed by a classic Ottoman dish such as *hunkar begendı* (lamb with pureed aubergines). Open for dinner only. Closed Nov–Apr.

BODRUM Antique Theatre Hotel Restaurant

Kıbrıs Şehitleri Cad 243 **Tel** *(0252) 316 60 53*

Romantic dining by the poolside, overlooking Bodrum bay. The gourmet restaurant of this luxury boutique hotel is a member of the Chaine des Rotisseurs. Menu includes mussels Florentine with a white wine sauce, tiger prawns topped with a ginger and soy sauce, and duck breast. À la carte dining or four-course set menu for €35.

BODRUM La Jolla Bistro

Neyzen Tevfik Cad 174 **Tel** *(0252) 313 76 60*

A blend of Mediterranean and Californian fusion food is served at this trendy venue, which also has a sushi bar and boasts an impressive selection of local and foreign wines. Salads, pasta, seafood and juicy steaks are on the menu. The cheesecake is a popular after-dinner choice. Iced sangria and frozen margaritas are best-sellers at the bar.

BODRUM Café La Vela

Neyzen TevfikCad 5, Bodrum Marina **Tel** *(0252) 316 12 29*

One of three restaurants at Bodrum's exclusive Marina Yacht Club, this venue offers an eclectic selection, which ranges from sandwiches to baked seabass fillet. But the main theme is Italy. Pizzas are baked in a wood-fired oven and the cannelloni come highly recommended. Live jazz or latin music every night.

BODRUM Tuti Restaurant

The Marmara Bodrum Hotel, Yokusbaşı Mah, Suluhasan Cad 18 **Tel** *(0252) 313 81 30*

Fine dining in the elegant atmosphere of this 100-room hotel, selected one of the top hotels of the world. Tuti restaurant is on the second floor, and offers a breathtaking view over the bay from its open-air terrace. The Turkish and international dishes on offer are prepared by some of Turkey's best chefs and are beautifully presented.

BODRUM PENINSULA Musti's Steakhouse

Plaj Cad 28, Yalıkavak **Tel** *(0252) 385 52 30*

Popular with tourists, attracted by the bar, the good food and the welcoming staff, this venue features a quiz night on Wednesdays and karaoke evening on Fridays. The place is usually packed. The food is international. As its name suggests, steaks are a speciality of the house, but vegetables and salads are also on offer.

BODRUM PENINSULA Deniz Restaurant

Gerişaltı Mevki 58, Yalıkavak **Tel** *(0252) 385 42 42*

In the fancy environment of Bodrum, this is a refreshingly simple and unpretentious venue by the sea. A good place to relax and watch the sunset while savouring a few *mezes* and freshly caught fish. Service is friendly and the food excellent. Specialities include stuffed courgette flowers and herb *mezes*.

BODRUM PENINSULA Denizhan Restaurant

Atatürk Bulvarı 277, Konacık **Tel** *(0252) 363 76 74*

Customers immediately feel welcome in this family-owned meat restaurant, housed in a pretty stone building. The meat is specially chosen for its tenderness and the vegetables are home grown in an organic garden. The Denizhan Kebab, wrapped in flat bread with cheese, pistachio nuts and sesame seeds, comes highly recommended.

BODRUM PENINSULA Yakamoz Restaurant

Gümüşlük Yalı Mevkii **Tel** *(0252) 394 33 14*

One of several fish restaurants nestling in Gümüşlük harbour, this reasonably priced venue offers simple but delicious food. The waiters are chatty and friendly, and the atmosphere cosy. Crisp *calamar*, tender grilled octopus and sole in butter are among the delights on offer in this simple eatery. Time a visit to catch the sunset.

BODRUM PENINSULA Mey Restaurant

Atatürk Cad 62, Türkbükü **Tel** *(0252) 377 51 18*

This trendy seafood venue has been a Türkbükü classic for over 20 years and is a favourite of Istanbul visitors who descend on the peninsula in the summer. If you book in advance, you can eat on a deck suspended over the water. Rich selection of *mezes* and interesting seafood dishes. Ask the chef for fresh fish caught in the bay.

BOZBURUN Orfoz Restaurant

Orfoz Restaurant **Tel** *(0252 456 2337) / 456 22 09*

Very exclusive, this out-of-the way restaurant, reached by sea or on foot, only has five tables. The place is usually full because those who have tried it always come back. The setting is spectacular and the food exceptional. Try the smoked eel or the seafood soup. The restaurant opens for the season in May.

ÇANAKKALE Doyum Pide Ve Kebap Restaurant

Cumhuriyet Meydanı 13, Çanakkale, 17100 **Tel** *(0286) 217 48 10*

Pide (flat bread) with various baked toppings and döner kebabs are very serious business here. Simple, delicious and filling foods, on which Turkey practically runs, are cooked to perfection with enormous pride and traditional skill. No alcohol is served. If no tables are available, ask them to make up a tasty takeaway instead.

ÇANAKKALE Anzac Hotel

Saat Kulesi Meydanı 8 **Tel** *(0286) 217 17 17*

This is a cheap and cheerful place. Open to hotel guests as well as non-residents, they serve a buffet breakfast, light snacks and a few more substantial meals, such as grilled fish and meats, which appeal to a global range of hungry backpackers.

ÇANAKKALE Yalova Liman Restaurant

Gümrük Sokak 7, Çanakkale, 17100 **Tel** *(0286) 217 10 45*

Overlooking the harbour in Çanakkale, this restaurant is popular with locals who come for the stews and soups for lunch and then fill the place for more formal grills, fish and steaks in the evening. Alcohol is served and they have a separate bar area below ground. Yalova Liman is recommended for great dining.

ÇANAKKALE Çanakkale Balık Restaurant

Atatürk Cad, Pirireis Çeşmesi Karşısı **Tel** *(0286) 218 04 42*

Typical fish restaurant set by the water, it has a capacity of 400 including outside seating. The menu is fairly standard, but the food is good. Rich selection of traditional appetizers, made of vegetables or sea food, and fresh fish, which can be served grilled or fried. Service is friendly and efficient.

ÇEŞME Ildır Balık Restaurant

ıldırı Köyü, Çayağzı Mevki, Çeşme **Tel** *(0232) 725 13 22*

In this little village, which claims to be the birthplace of the philosopher Homer, the sound of the waves will provide the background to your meal. Start with appetizers made of wild greens found in the region or artichokes in olive oil, and follow with a grilled çipura, or seabream, which is the local fish.

ÇEŞME Balıkçı Hasan

Liman Cad 4255, Dok 2 Dalyan Köyü **Tel** *(0232) 724 02 02*

Don't be deceived by the somewhat tatty décor, this seaside restaurant is well-known for its good food and is a favourite of Turkish celebrities. Upon demand, they produce a delicious fish soup. Other specialities include seafood crepe, fish cooked in milk and grilled octopus. Their seafood pasta is also good. The background music is Greek and Turkish.

CUNDA ADASI Bay Nihat

Cunda Adası, Ayvalık **Tel** *(0266) 327 10 63*

Customers always come back, this restaurant boasts, and it's easy to see why. You're unlikely to find a wider selection of *mezes* anywhere else. They claim to serve more than 100 appetizers, cold and hot, among them shrimps in garlic butter and octopus with soy sauce. The fish selection is equally broad, and the atmosphere friendly.

DATÇA Mehmet Ali Ağa Mansion

Resadiye Mah, Kavak Meydanı **Tel** *(0252) 712 92 57*

This stone mansion, transformed into a boutique hotel, is a member of the select Relais et Chateaux. The exquisite food it serves in its restaurants attracts customers from far afield. Fine Ottoman and Mediterranean cuisine is on the menu for candle-lit dinners in the garden. On Saturdays, live music adds to the romantic atmosphere.

DIDIM Big Ben Restaurant

Yalı Cad 20, Altınkum **Tel** *(0256) 813 40 01*

To tourists who are tired of the local food, this venue brings a taste of home cuisine with international staples such as hamburgers, pasta, bangers and mash or fish and chips. You can even have a full English breakfast, unless you prefer beans on toast or a baked potato. Particularly popular with young visitors.

Key to Price Guide *see p352* **Key to Symbols** *see back cover flap*

FOÇA Fokai Balık Restaurant

Atatürk Mah, 131 Sok 8, Eskifoça **Tel** *(0232) 812 21 86*

This family-friendly restaurant is tastefully decorated and is in the oldest part of Foça, which has a nice Aegean atmosphere. The main focus of the menu is fish, but Chinese, Mexican and Italian dishes, are also on offer. Vegetable *mezes* and pasta are popular with tourists. Closed during the winter months.

GUKÇEADA Kalimerhaba

Kaleköy **Tel** *(0286) 887 36 48*

This friendly island, also known under its Greek name, Imroz, has retained a lot of its Greek atmosphere. In this venue, both a motel and restaurant, the food has a typically Aegean feel and is prepared daily by the owners. Sitting in their garden, you can taste 20 different types of vegetables cooked in olive oil or savour a freshly grilled fish.

GUKÇEADA Meydan Restaurant

Atatürk Cad 26 A–B **Tel** *(0286) 887 23 93*

Particularly well suited for long, lazy meals with friends, this friendly restaurant offers a rich menu, which evolves with the seasons. On average, 22 fish and seafood specialities are on offer at any time, including lobster, crab and sea urchins. Plenty of fresh vegetable appetizers are also on offer, as well as home-grown wines and cheeses.

İZMİR Antepli Ramazan Usta

Süvari Cad 36 **Tel** *(0232) 342 53 03*

A friendly, popular meat restaurant serving kebabs from South-east Anatolia. Liver on skewer, spicy *Adana* kebab and lamb cubes with aubergines are among the specialities on offer. Several types of Turkish pizza, known as *lahmacun*, are also on the menu as well as *baklava* and other Turkish sweets. The restaurant also delivers.

İZMİR Akçaabat Köftecisi

Mithat Paşa Cad 291, Balcova **Tel** *(0232) 259 58 57*

A 200 seat restaurant serving Black Sea food on the Aegean. Often listed among the best in Turkey for local specialities such as *mihlama* (cheese and corn flour-based dish), anchovies, lentil soup and *Akçaabat* meatballs. On Saturdays, a band plays the *kemençe*, a traditional three-string violin from the Black Sea.

İZMİR Vejetaryan Restaurant

Şehit Nevres Bulv 9/A, Alsancak **Tel** *(0232) 464 11 03*

Organic produce is used in this vegetarian restaurant, which offers a wide variety of vegetables baked in the oven and salads. Sardines and salmon are also on the menu. Soybean products are used as a substitute for meat in pasta dishes. Organic products are also on sale in the store adjacent to the restaurant.

İZMİR Kordon Ocakbaşı

Atatürk Cad 174/B, Alsancak **Tel** *(0232) 463 46 06*

A simple and friendly restaurant focusing on grilled meat. Kebabs, cooked on an open-charcoal fire, come in numerous varieties, some made of mince, others of cubed meat. Lamb chops, ribs and small pieces of meat sautéed with mushrooms and tomatoes are also on the menu. Open all day from 8.30am until 1am in the morning.

İZMİR Asansör

Şehit Nihat Bey Cad 76/A, Karataş **Tel** *(0232) 261 26 26*

The food, French and Italian, is excellent here, but it is mainly for its spectacular setting and unbeatable views that this restaurant, perched at the top of a cliff, is popular. It is reached via a lift, the Asansör, built in 1907, in the old Jewish quarter. A bridge leads to the restaurant, which has two open terraces.

İZMİR Brasserie Lamia

Alsancak Şehit Nevres Bulvari 5/A **Tel** *(0232) 463 58 58*

Brasserie Lamia is one of the best restaurants in Turkey and hard to fault. Food, decor and presentation are perfect. The gourmet Turkish and Mediterranean food mean that reservations are essential. Air conditioned, and children are welcome.

İZMİR Mezzaluna

Atatürk Cad 19, Konak Pier **Tel** *(0232) 489 69 44*

This slick and glamorous Italian restaurant at the end of Konak Pier is ample proof of İzmir's culinary supremacy. Snacks and salads are served all day but the chef's talents shine in the evening. The decor is nautical outside, with upmarket Italian furnishings inside. Air conditioned.

KUŞADASı Café Seyhan

Sağlık Cad 63 **Tel** *(0256) 614 79 85*

Centrally located in an old part of town, this venue is usually crowded. The menu borrows dishes from all over the world: Mexico, Italy, India and China among others. There is also a salad bar for the diet-conscious. Live guitar and popular Turkish tunes contribute to the romantic atmosphere in the garden.

KUŞADASı Rigolo Café Restaurant

Atatürk Bulvarı 42 **Tel** *(0256) 614 76 08*

Popular with tourists, this à-la-carte restaurant is located next to the Hotel Andic and serves good quality world cuisine, such as pasta, steaks and salads. Indoors, the decor has a pub flavour, but guests can also enjoy their meals outdoors during long summer evenings. Jazz music every night.

KUŞADASı Kazım Usta

Dağ Mah, Liman Cad 11 **Tel** *(0256) 614 12 26*

This harbour restaurant has won several prizes for the quality of its food and its relaxed atmosphere. Sitting by the sea, diners really feel on holiday. Service is friendly and the olive oil and seafood *mezes* outstanding. Fish, fresh from the sea, are grilled over charcoal. Prices vary according to weight.

KUŞADASı Tarihi Çınar Balık

Afyar Mevkii Kismet Hotel Yanı **Tel** *(0256) 618 18 47*

In a seaside resort, there is no shortage of fish restaurants but this one stands out. Located at the entrance of Kuşadası, it boasts a splendid sea view. The garden provides plenty of shade for those who prefer to stay out of the sun. Vegetable *mezes*, fish, and seafood dishes like stuffed *kalamar* are on the menu.

MARMARIS Çağlayan Pınarbaşı Restaurant

Çetibeli Köyü **Tel** *(0252) 426 00 79*

Located outside Marmaris, this venue provides a nice escape on a hot summer day. The tables are shaded by trees and hidden in the greenery – there is even a stream. Plenty of fresh produce is on offer: wonderful salads, fish and seafood, as well as traditional Turkish dishes. Breakfast includes home-made jams, olives and village bread.

MARMARIS Mona Titti Restaurant

Gölenye Mah, Ortapınar Cad. 23, ıçmeler **Tel** *(0252) 455 40 46*

Run by a self-described 60s hippy, this friendly restaurant was originally located in town, before relocating to a quieter spot in 2000. Art pieces and antiques are displayed around the restaurant; classical and jazz music complete the atmosphere. The food is Turkish but the recipes are the owner's. Free transportation is provided. Just give them a call.

SELÇUK Hotel Kalehan

Selçuk **Tel** *(0232) 892 61 54*

This hotel, with its beautiful garden and swimming pool, has long been a favourite of Ephesus visitors. The ancient ruins are close by. The lobby is tastefully decorated with antiques and hand-woven *kilims*. The restaurant, open all day, offers tasty Turkish and international dishes, prepared with fresh, organically grown produce.

ŞIRINCE Artemis Restaurant and Wine House

Eski okul binası **Tel** *(0232) 898 32 40*

Set in a picturesque Greek village among olive groves, this restored 19th-century school building has been turned into a restaurant and wine house with a total capacity of 700, indoors and outdoors. The menu includes local greens, salads, kebabs and other local specialities. Village bread and, of course, local wines make perfect accompaniments.

TIRE Tire Babaoğlu Kebapcısı

Gümüş Palas Cad, Hasır Pazarı Sok 16 **Tel** *(0232) 512 01 16*

This is a very basic, but friendly place to visit if stopping in Tire. Lamb kebab and a hearty meat soup made from the broth are the only foods available. This family-friendly venue has been in operation for 90 years. It opens at 5:30am, in time to catch the truck drivers on their way to work.

MEDITERRANEAN TURKEY

ADANA Kebap 52

Kurtuluş Mah, Sinasi Efendi Cad, Subhi Ramazanoğlu Apt. 6 **Tel** *(0322) 363 15 85*

This quiet and unassuming venue serves a mean *Adana* kebab, a spicy mix of ground lamb meat and fat from the animal's tail. Chicken, other types of grilled meat as well as *pide*, a kind of bread with a meat or cheese topping, are also on the menu in this restaurant, which boasts an outdoor terrace.

ADANA Unal Et Lokantası

Dörtyol Ağzı, Teknosa arkası, Çınarlı ışhanı 32 **Tel** *(0222) 363 15 85*

This simple restaurant has achieved local fame with its Konya *tandır* kebabs. Lean lamb shank is used for this dish, slowly oven-baked for seven hours and left to rest for another six. The end result is served on rice with onion and tomatoes. Other grilled kebabs are available, as well as vegetables in olive oil and salads.

ADANA Guest

Cemal Paşa Mah, Etem Ekin Sok, Arsava Apt **Tel** *(0322) 459 20 28*

After travelling internationally, the owner of this restaurant brought a taste of world cuisine to Adana. The menu includes dishes from Russia, France, the US and Italy. The restaurant's best-selling speciality is Guest chicken, with tropical fruit. The decor is elegant but cosy, and a garden allows outdoor dining in the summer. Live jazz at weekends.

ADANA Halikarnas

Güzelyali Mah, Uğur Mumcu Bulvarı 54/B **Tel** *(0322) 234 57 83*

Some of the best fish *mezes* to be found in Turkey are served in this friendly fish restaurant. Numerous Turkish celebrities have visited this venue to sample its cured *lakerda* and its seafood cocktail. There is a wide selection of fish to choose from. The seabass in apple vinegar is a perennial favourite.

Key to Price Guide *see p352* **Key to Symbols** *see back cover flap*

ALANYA Bistro Bellman

*Iskele Cad 40 **Tel** (0242) 512 19 92*

After dark, this venue turns into one of the hottest spots of Alanya's night life with disco music lasting well into the night. But earlier in the evening, it is a pleasant place to eat and enjoy a spectacular view. The menu is mainly Mexican, with some items borrowed from Western and Turkish cuisine.

ALANYA Kervansaray Ocakbaşı

*Saray Mah. Atatürk Cad 63/A **Tel** (0242) 519 03 49*

Unlike many of the eateries in Alanya, which are geared to tourists, this is an authentic grill frequented by local residents. The decor is oriental and the menu focuses largely on meat, which is grilled on the large open barbecue, although a vegetarian casserole is also on offer as well as *pide*, a kind of Turkish pizza.

ALANYA Mahperi Restaurant

*Rıhtım Cad 17 **Tel** (0242) 512 54 91*

Mahperi has occupied this spectacular spot on the waterfront since the 1940s. Originally mainly a seafood restaurant, it has expanded its range to suit the tastes of foreign visitors. The menu now includes French, Mexican and Chinese food, and a rich selection of steaks. The seafood is still the best choice. Try the Red Sea Lobster Thermidor.

ALANYA Ottoman House

*Damlataş Cad 31 **Tel** (0242) 511 14 21*

Live music is played every weekday in this cheerful venue, set in an old Ottoman house. Visitors can dine outdoors in the leafy garden, and enjoy the excellent service. The well-balanced menu combines old Turkish cuisine and international favourites. Specialities include Ottoman kebab and lamb with pureed aubergines.

ANTAKYA Antakya Evi Restaurant

*Silahlı Kuvvetler Cad 3 **Tel** (0326) 214 13 50*

The only restaurant in town to hold a special license, this venue is located in a restored 19th-century house. Menu and service are in line with the surroundings: traditional local food and warm hospitality. In this part of Turkey, very close to Syria, the food has an Arabic flavour. Here, it has a home-made feel, too. Closed on Sundays.

ANTAKYA Sultan Sofrası

*ıstiklal Cad 20/A **Tel** (0326) 213 87 59*

The menu here draws on a rich local food culture. There is plenty to feast on, including several kinds of *pilav*, made of rice or pounded wheat. Many of the dishes are specific to the region and are based on pulse or dough with vegetables. Simple but elegant decor in a renovated stone mansion.

ANTALYA Deniz Restaurant

*Karaalioğlu Parkı 2, Gençlik Mah, 1211 Sok 7/A **Tel** (0242) 241 57 99*

Huge venue in the middle of a park, seating up to 1,000 in the summer when the garden is open. Open all year round and very popular with local residents. The view is spectacular, the food is good Turkish fare and prices are very reasonable. At weekends, there is live music and entertainment.

ANTALYA Parlak Restaurant

*Elmalı Mah, Kazım Özalp Cad Zincirlihan 7 **Tel** (0242) 241 91 60*

For over half a century, this popular venue with a capacity of 300 has been delighting customers with an impressive selection of *mezes* made of wild greens. Their focus is on Ottoman cuisine, but their best-known dish is the charcoal-grilled chicken. Very reasonable prices for good quality food. If you have a sweet tooth, try their pumpkin dessert.

ANTALYA Marina Restaurant

*Mermerli Sok 15, Kaleiçi **Tel** (0242) 247 54 90*

Upscale restaurant in a renovated 18th-century Ottoman mansion turned boutique hotel in the heart of the old city. The garden and swimming pool provide a splendid backdrop. Piano music and an aquarium further contribute to a relaxing and romantic atmosphere. The cuisine is international and Mediterranean, prepared by top chefs.

ANTALYA Zen Café Bistro

*Metin Kasapoğlu Cad, Ayhan Kadan iş Merkezi 31 **Tel** (0242) 321 04 04*

This cheerful and elegant locale, inspired by Zen philosophy, serves international food in a red and black decor. The eclectic menu mixes Italian pastas with Mexican *fajitas* and juicy steaks, as well as a good range of desserts. There is jazz music at the bar on Thursdays, Fridays and Saturdays. Indoor and outdoor seating.

ANTALYA Yedi Mehmet

*Atatürk Kültür Parkı 333 **Tel** (0242) 238 52 02*

The restaurant, a legend in Antalya, serves Turkish specialities for lunch and dinner. It began more modestly in 1948. Set on a gentle hill, surrounded by greenery and with a spectacular sea view, it is a good choice for a tasty meal. The menu offers a mix of meat and fish dishes.

ANTALYA Antalya Balık Evi

*Eski Lara Yolu **Tel** (0242) 323 18 23*

The sound of the waves provides a gentle musical accompaniment to your meal in this sophisticated seafood restaurant. The garden and terrace have a capacity of 300, and the food is everything expected in a top-class venue. A rich selection of appetizers and a wide variety of fresh fish and seafood is available.

ANTALYA Club Arma

Kaleiçi Yat Limanı **Tel** *(0242) 244 97 10*

Discotheque, concert hall and restaurant, Club Arma offers entertainment for everyone. The complex, in a restored old building, is near the sea, but also benefits from beautiful mountain views. The food is Ottoman and French, and the presentation is refined. Meat and fish are both on the menu together with pasta, salads and vegetable *mezes*.

ANTALYA Tuti
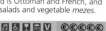

Marmara Hotel **Tel** *(0242) 249 36 00*

Contemporary Turkish and Mediterranean fusion cuisine, prepared by prize-winning chefs, and served in a space that is as innovative as the food. Part lounge, part activity ground, part restaurant, with a high ceiling and huge pillars, it is an unusual but spectacular venue. This luxury hotel also has revolving rooms.

ANTALYA Villa Perla

Hesapcı Sok 26, Kaleiçi **Tel** *(0242) 248 97 93*

Romantic atmosphere in this boutique hotel set in an Ottoman mansion. Reached through the narrow alleys of the walled old city, its restaurants serves refined Turkish and Ottoman food under orange trees. Rabbit, which cannot be found anywhere else in town, is on the menu as well. Good vegetarian options.

ASPENDOS Belkis Restaurant

Belkis Köyü, Serik **Tel** *(0242) 735 72 63*

The spectacular Antique Theatre at Aspendos is a compulsory stop for any tourist visiting the region. This friendly restaurant, right by the river, is a good place to stop for a cooling meal afterwards. The food is Turkish and the main speciality is the *güveç* (stew baked in a clay dish).

FETHIYE Cem & Can Restaurant

Hal ve Pazar Yeri 57 **Tel** *(0252) 614 30 97*

To experience the authentic atmosphere of a bustling fish and produce market, this is the place to do it. This unassuming venue is full of local ambiance. Customers choose a fish from the display and have it cooked in this no-frills, family-friendly restaurant. They also serve Turkish pizza and grills.

FETHIYE Şamdan

Tütün Sok 9 **Tel** *(0252) 614 28 68*

Simple and friendly place serving inexpensive Turkish food. The lunch menu rotates, and several vegetables in olive oil, meat and chicken dishes are on offer every day. Options for dinner include grilled fish and meat. Their speciality is *ınegol* meatball. For dessert, their crème caramel is particularly popular with customers.

FINIKE Altin Sofra Restaurant

Yacht Marina, Finike **Tel** *(0242) 855 12 81*

Located in Finike's yacht marina, close to the entrance, is this restaurant in an old wooden building. The garden is shaded by plane and acacia trees and makes a pleasant setting for a delicious meal of cold *mezes*, followed by one of the restaurant's famed lamb or lambs' liver dishes. Or, choose from the full menu that includes fresh fish dishes.

GÖCEK Can Restaurant

Skopea Marina **Tel** *(0252) 645 15 07*

One of several fish restaurants in the area frequented by yacht owners, this venue is good value for money. The menu is fairly standard seafood fare, but the quality is good and the atmosphere very inviting. The *mezes*, especially the courgette fritters, are delicious. Vegetarians will enoy the vegetable casserole.

KALKAN Korsan Marina

Kalkan Yacht Limanı yanı **Tel** *(0242) 844 36 22*

One of three eateries owned by the same family, Korsan Marina benefits from an unbeatable location at the entrance of the harbour. The friendly waiters make sure customers are having a good time. The food combines traditional Turkish food with western favourites such as beef fillet. There is also a lively bar.

KAŞ Erís Restaurant

Uzun Çarşı, Gürsoy Sok 13 **Tel** *(0242) 836 10 57*

Modestly-priced and inviting, this restaurant occupies an old Ottoman house that has been restored. The focus is on seafood and Turkish food, but the menu includes non-seafood items and other specialities such as *güveç* (casserole), crêpes and pasta. Fish is served grilled, fried, on a skewer (swordfish) or accompanied by tasty sauces.

KAŞ Dolphin Restaurant

Sandıkcı Sok 7 **Tel** *(0242) 836 35 38*

Located in an old Greek house overlooking the marina, this restaurant is among the best in Kaş. From its outdoor terrace, diners can observe the fishermen while enjoying a taste of their catch. The selection of seafood *mezes* includes some original creations not available elsewhere. Lobster is often on the menu.

KAŞ Mercan

Balıkçılar Barınağı, Hükümet Cad, Cumhuriyet Meydanı **Tel** *(0242) 836 12 09*

This waterside restaurant has been operating in the harbour for half a century, owned by the same family. The atmosphere is friendly, the service efficient and the food excellent. The fresh swordfish kebab is worth a try. If meat is preferred, the speciality here is lamb marinated in wine and spices.

Key to Price Guide *see p352* **Key to Symbols** *see back cover flap*

KAŞ Chez Evy

Terzi Sok 12 **Tel** *(0242) 836 12 53*

This classy restaurant is owned by a French woman, who gives her customers a warm welcome in her colourful garden. The food, French country cooking at its best, attracts customers from all over the coast. Whether you choose steak, rack of lamb or *calamari provençale*, portions are generous. Reservations essential.

KEMER Şelale

Ulupınar Köyü, Havuzbaşı **Tel** *(0242) 825 00 25*

When the heat gets too stifling, a visit to this spectacular mountain venue will cool visitors off. In this trout farm outside Kemer, customers eat fresh fish sitting on comfortable cushions laid out on decks above a running stream, shaded by trees. Grilled chicken or meat are also on offer.

KEMER La Paz Bistro Bellman

Liman Cad, 119 Sok 119 **Tel** *(0242) 512 19 92*

Close to the shopping area of this booming sea resort, La Paz is an informal and pleasant venue with a menu offering enough choice to suit all palates: omelettes, soups and salads for light lunches, or steaks, pasta, seafood for more substantial meals. The menu is mostly international, but also includes Turkish classics.

MERSIN Özkan-Tantini

Camiserfi Mah Cemalpaşa **Tel** *(0324) 231 50 62*

This is more a fast-food joint than a place suitable for a long leisurely meal. But here customers can sample a local delicacy: *tantuni* (meat, usually sauteed with onions and spices, served in flat bread, like a wrap). Each restaurant has its own recipes, and this one is among the best.

MERSIN Sarıta íras Restaurant

Çağlarca (Sunturas) Köy **Tel** *(0324) 476 70 01*

Outside Mersin, this trout farm and kiwi orchard is a perfect destination for a relaxing day out in nature, amid waterfalls and luxuriant vegetation. Trout features prominently on the menu, of course, but there is also chicken, quail, various cheeses and *mezes*, as well as a good selection of local wines.

MERSIN Göçtü

Ismet ınönü Bulvarı 1 **Tel** *(0224) 326 12 87*

This large kebab restaurant is one of the oldest in Mersin, and a good place to taste the local fare. Locals insist their Mersin kebab, which contains chopped parsley, onion and red pepper, stands out among other types of grilled meat. Vegetarians may opt for a vegetable or mushroom stir fry.

ÖLÜ DENIZ Çin Bal

Turabi Mevkii, Kaya Köyü **Tel** *(0252) 618 00 66*

The place is simple and friendly, but its rustic setting in the ghost village of Kaya makes it worth a visit. You can even hike from the beach. This is a place for carnivores, who can grill meat on their own barbecue, and eat it with a few *mezes*. There is plenty of space for children to run around.

ÖLÜ DENIZ Buzz Beach Bar and Grill

Deniz Camp **Tel** *(0252) 617 04 50*

Excellent Turkish cuisine in a seafront restaurant set in a shady vineyard garden. Open for breakfast and snacks such as wraps, pastas, paninis and salads throughout the day and pasta, pizzas, seafood dishes and grilled meats in the evening. Comprehensive cocktail menu and wine list. Air conditioned

ÖLÜ DENIZ Meğri

Ordukan Eski Cami Geçidi, Likya Sok 8–9 **Tel** *(0252) 614 40 46*

One of the best in the market area, this venue is a favourite of the locals. It serves classic Turkish cuisine, with the accent on seafood. Fish in salt is one of the specialities most often requested, but you could also opt for leg of lamb or one of the traditional stews. Friendly atmosphere and outdoor seating.

ÖLÜ DENIZ Oba

Oba Motel Restaurant **Tel** *(0252) 617 04 70*

Close to the beach, this motel provides accommodation in small wooden bungalows, and good Turkish and English food in its leafy garden. There is also a bar. The rattan furniture is comfortable and inviting, and the service friendly. The menu includes fish, meat, chicken and vegetables. The chef's pride is *Oba* steak.

ANKARA AND WESTERN ANATOLIA

ANKARA Mangalcı

Bayındır Sok 2, Kızılay **Tel** *312 435 52 26*

In this airy and friendly meat restaurant in the heart of Ankara, customers get a chance to grill their own kebabs, chops or chicken on a charcoal fire, right at the table. The restaurant is also known for specialities such as stuffed beef ribs, which feed two to three people. Good selection of *mezes* with a distinct South-eastern flavour.

ANKARA And Evi €€

ıçkale Mahallesi 29, Kale **Tel** *(0312) 312 79 78*

A good spot to watch the sun set over the city, this restaurant located inside the citadel serves mainly Turkish food. Its speciality is *saç kavurma* (a mix of meat and vegetables served on a hot sizzling pan). Meals are served on the terrace in the summer. Open until 9pm in winter and 10pm during summer months.

ANKARA Gaziosmanpaşa Gar Lokantası €€

Filistin Sok 35, Gaziosmanpaşa **Tel** *(0312) 447 29 96*

This restaurant enjoys a solid reputation for good traditional Turkish food. The menu includes stews as well as grilled meat and fish. There is also a broad selection of *mezes*. In the summer, whole lambs are grilled on a spit in the garden on Fridays evenings and döner kebab is on offer on Thursdays.

ANKARA Quick China €€

Uğur Mumcu Sok 64/B, Gaziosmanpaşa **Tel** *(0312) 437 03 03*

This stylish restaurant employs seven international chefs and serves Chinese, Japanese and Thai cuisine. Aside from sushi, the Japanese section includes a tepanyaki table where chefs cook the food in front of the clients. The menu offers more than 250 different dishes. Chinese duck in pastry, Thai soups and fried ice cream are among the favourites.

ANKARA Agora Asmalı Konak Restaurant €€€

Kale Kapısı 14, Ulus **Tel** *(0312) 311 35 11*

A friendly restaurant in a renovated old house, this is the perfect place for lunch or a light meal. In the summer, food is served under the vines in a small but pretty garden. Specialities include *saç kavurma* (meat served on a sizzling pan) and fish baked in a crust of sea salt. Turkish music every evening.

ANKARA Boxer by Wok €€€

Uğur Mumcu Cad 8/2, Gaziosmanpaşa **Tel** *(0312) 446 19 92*

A trendy and upscale night spot, with a terrace overlooking the city. Dark walls and mirrors decorate the main room. The bar serves various cocktails, including frozen margaritas. Food is international, with an Asian flavour. There is also a sushi bar. Live ambiance, with jazz music at weekends on the upper floor.

ANKARA Budakaltı €€€

Budak Sok 6, Gaziosmanpaşa **Tel** *(0312) 427 85 45*

A haven of peace in the city centre, this airy restaurant is located in a duplex villa, with a conservatory and garden. Favoured by diplomats, politicians and businessmen for lunch, it offers world cuisine and Turkish dishes with a modern twist. Good selection of salads for the calorie-conscious and wide variety of desserts for those with a sweet tooth.

ANKARA Chez le Belge €€€

Sahil Cad 24, Gölbaşı **Tel** *(0312) 484 14 78*

Located outside of Ankara on the banks of a small lake, this restaurant is a favourite destination for weekend outings. Its upstairs room has a cosy atmosphere and a nautical decor. The food is French, and includes chicken and meat dishes as well as salads. Their *Crêpe Suzette* is particularly popular. Closes at 10pm.

ANKARA Hatipoğlu Konağı €€€

Sevinç Sok 3, Ulus **Tel** *(0312) 311 36 96*

A historic mansion inside Ankara's citadel houses this large restaurant with several dining rooms. The menu is Turkish and French, and includes both meat and fish dishes as well as plenty of vegetables. Live Turkish music on Wednesdays, Fridays and Saturdays. Spectacular terrace overlooking the city. Popular with tourists. Reasonable prices and good service.

ANKARA Kalbur  €€€

Oran Sehri Çarşı Merkezi, C 3 Blok 23, Oran **Tel** *(0312) 490 50 01*

Often crowded, this restaurant, member of the Chaine des Rotisseurs, offers a lively taverna atmosphere, perfect for a long evening with friends. The menu includes over 40 different kinds of appetizers, such as stuffed squid and asparagus with salmon, as well as many hot starters and main dishes, mostly fish and seafood based.

ANKARA Merkez Restaurant €€€

Çiftlik Cad 72 **Tel** *(0312) 211 02 50*

This venue, inaugurated by Atatürk in 1933, is part of Turkey's history. When Ankara residents want to escape from their urban environment, they come to this area known as the Atatürk Farm to enjoy the outdoors. The restaurant itself has a huge garden, and it serves perennial Turkish favourites, such as *su böreği* and beans.

ANKARA Schnitzel €€€

Mega Residence Hotel, Tahran Cad 5, Kavaklidere **Tel** *(0312) 468 54 00*

Serves international food, with a strong accent on Austrian cuisine, in a chalet atmosphere. Aside from schnitzels, including a vegetarian version, fish and steaks are also on the menu. Live music every day except Sundays. The restaurant is also well known for its rich open-buffet breakfast. Open daily from noon to midnight.

ANKARA Sushico/Chinese in Town €€€

Attar Sok 10, Gaziosmanpaşa **Tel** *(0312) 426 25 26*

Set in a quiet street, this bright and friendly restaurant serves food from China, Japan and Thailand, cooked by chefs from each country. Its sushi, prepared with fresh fish, is particularly popular with Ankara residents. Lunch specials and sushi menus are very good value. Food is also available to take away.

Key to Price Guide *see p352* **Key to Symbols** *see back cover flap*

ANKARA Ege Restaurant

Büklüm Sok 54/B, Kavaklidere **Tel** *(0312) 428 27 17*

The name means "Aegean" and accurately describes this two-storey restaurant. The sea is a prominent element here: the decor is nautical and the menu focused on seafood, although they serve a couple of meat and chicken dishes too. The *mezes* are mainly seafood. Fish is served either grilled, fried or in a sauce with vegetables.

ANKARA Fige

Abdullah Cevdet Sok 15, Çankaya **Tel** *(0312) 438 07 21*

International cuisine in a romantic decor of wood and antiques. This restaurant offers a wide selection of meat, pasta and fish, including dishes from Cambodia and Mexico. Local specialities include *Kayseri mantı* (ravioli) and stuffed vine leaves. Its popular bar has jazz on Wednesdays, Fridays and Saturdays. Open until 2am weekdays, 4am weekends.

ANKARA Kale Washington

Doyuran Sok 5–7, Kale, Ulus **Tel** *(0312) 445 02 12*

Panoramic views over Ankara and excellent food have kept this venue popular for nearly half a century. Located in two old Ottoman houses, it has hosted countless foreign dignitaries and celebrities who have enjoyed its wide selection of traditional Turkish dishes. Vegetables cooked in olive oil is a house speciality.

ANKARA Köşebaşı

Kuleli Sok 32, Gaziosmanpaşa **Tel** *(0312) 446 59 59*

A very good address for dedicated carnivores, it is part of a prize-winning chain that has grown rapidly in the past decade. This is a kebab restaurant with a difference. The meat, specially marinated, is incredibly tender. The restaurant is airy and friendly, with a trendy decor. There is a large garden for summer dining.

ANKARA Mezzaluna

Turan Emeksiz Sok 1, Kavaklidere **Tel** *(0312) 467 58 18*

The Ankara branch of a small US-based Italian chain, this popular restaurant provides quality Italian food at affordable prices. Their pizzas, baked in a wood oven, have a thin crust. Good selection of salads, fresh pasta dishes and risottos as well as mouth-watering desserts. Local and foreign wines available to accompany the meals.

ANKARA RV

Atatürk Bulvarı 243, A Blok, Kavaklidere **Tel** *(0312) 427 03 76*

Favoured by politicians and diplomats, who often lunch here, this centrally located restaurant serves international cuisine. Beef ribs, slow-cooked for 15 hours, are a house speciality. Duck and Italian dishes are also on the menu. The restaurant seats 190 people and also has a separate bar section.

ANKARA Spice Restaurant

Çayhane Sokak 30/A, Gaziosmapaşa **Tel** *(0312) 446 68 35*

Situated in one of Ankara's most upmarket areas, combining modern decor and a relaxed atmosphere, Spice serves authentic South Asian cuisine. A vast window allows diners to see the chef preparing a wide range of dishes, such as aromatic meat or vegetable curries and fresh naan breads. Both alcoholic and non-alcoholic Indian drinks are available.

ANKARA Yosun

Iran Cad 27/A, Gaziosmanpaşa **Tel** *(0312) 467 54 64*

This fish restaurant has been around for just over a decade, but it already feels like an institution. Its location is very central and the food reliably good. Service is also excellent and friendly. There is a rich selection of *mezes* on offer and the fish is always very fresh. Fish cooked in milk or in a crust of sea salt are among specialities served here.

ANKARA Zenger Paşa Konağı

Doyuran Sok 13, Kale, Ulus **Tel** *(0312) 311 70 70*

Worth a visit for its atmosphere and its location at the heart of Ankara's citadel, this restaurant serves a wide range of traditional appetizers, stews, grilled meat and fish in a restored 18th-century house. It is a favourite among tourists, who also enjoy the bar at the entrance. Open daily.

ANKARA Bistro Niki

Iran Cad 27/1, Kavaklidere **Tel** *(0312) 426 54 90*

This small and cosy restaurant in a fashionable corner of Ankara serves international food with an emphasis on the Mediterranean. Try the seabream in pomegranate sauce or the pepper steak. A complimentary glass of sangria is served to all customers. Wide selection of foreign wines available. Food served on the verandah in the summer.

ANKARA Liman

Cinnah Cad, Ahenk Sok 2, Çankaya **Tel** *(0312) 440 15 47*

Plush decor and a cosy atmosphere. Expect international and Ottoman cuisine with the emphasis on seafood and fish, but the menu offers plenty of alternatives, including chicken, salads, pasta and venison. Broad range of appetizers and good wine list with local and foreign brands. There is also a separate bar. Open until 2am.

ANKARA Papermoon

Tahran Cad 2, Kavaklidere **Tel** *(0312) 428 74 74*

This Italian restaurant has been a favourite of the Istanbul elite for the past decade. Food presentation is refined and the decor chic. This is fine Italian dining. Pizzas are baked in a wood-fired oven to produce a thin, crisp crust. Risottos, pasta and meat dishes are also succulent.

ANKARA Park Fora

Nenehatun Cad 97, Gaziosmanpaşa **Tel** *(0312) 447 73 00*

This is a branch of a well-established Istanbul fish restaurant. Favoured for business lunches and receptions, it uses only the freshest ingredients. There is a wide selection of fish and seafood appetizers. Specialities include fish baked in dough (allow 90 minutes) and Sole Cardinal, stuffed and baked in a clay dish.

ANKARA Trilye

Hafta Sok 11 B, Gaziosmanpaşa **Tel** *(0312) 447 12 00*

Upscale seafood restaurant housed in a small villa with a comfortable garden. Serves a broad range of seafood and fish dishes as well as Turkish and international cuisine. Seabass in a bamboo basket and seafood spring rolls have an Asian flavour. Traditional *meze* have been given a twist. Good dessert selection, including hot chocolate soufflé.

ESKİŞEHIR Chinatown

Kızılcıklı Mahmut Pehlivan Cad, Eti Plaza altı 13 **Tel** *(0222) 221 13 20*

Chinese chefs prepare the food in this authentic Far Eastern restaurant, located by the Porsuk river. The decor is elegant and the service friendly. Specialities include fowl and spicy chicken. A VIP room is available for business lunches or private functions. Between noon and 5pm, a discount menu is available. Closed on Sundays.

ESKİŞEHIR Hayal Kahvesi

Ismet Inönü Cad 115/A **Tel** *(0222) 320 82 20*

Part of an entertainment complex located in a renovated wine factory, this restaurant serves international and Turkish cuisine in a comfortable setting. Rock music concerts are regularly scheduled in the adjacent hall. There is also a café, and a conference and banquet hall. Open from 7pm to 4am.

KONYA Akyokuş Restaurant

Orman içi Dinlenme Tesisleri, Akyokuş Mevkii **Tel** *(0332) 324 43 43*

Located in a wooded recreational area, this locale enjoys a spectacular view over Konya. This is where city residents come at weekends to get fresh air and enjoy a relaxing meal. The food is Turkish/Ottoman and includes specialities like Orman Kebab, a tasty combination of meat, beans, mushrooms, vegetables and cheese.

KONYA Köşk Mutfağı

Piri Esad Cad, Konya **Tel** *(0332) 352 85 47*

This small, popular restaurant is located just behind the Mevlana Museum, in a renovated historical mansion. It serves traditional Turkish cuisine. Start with a refreshing salad and then try a *tandir* dish (cooked in a special clay pot) or Konya's favourite *arapasi* (chicken) soup. Finish off with some honey-soaked *baklava* and a Turkish coffee.

KONYA Mevlevi Sofrasi

Civar Mah, Şehit Nazım Bey 1, Karatay **Tel** *(0332) 353 33 41*

Sufi philosophy is an important influence in this restaurant. Food is meant to feed the soul as well as the body. The specialities here are okra soup and *kiymali su boregi* (ground meat layered with filo pastry). There is an oriental corner where guests sit on cushions. Whirling dervishes perform on special days. Indoor and outdoor seating.

KÜTAHYA Germiyan Konağı

Meydan Mah, Pirler Sok **Tel** *(0274) 224 55 52*

Meticulously restored and beautifully decorated with local artifacts, this Ottoman house successfully recreates a past atmosphere. The restaurant serves specialities from the region, including vegetables cooked in olive oil. Suitable for groups. Live Turkish music on Mondays, Tuesdays, Fridays and Saturdays. Open from 9am to 11pm.

KÜTAHYA Kütahya Konağı

Ulucami arkası Kurşunlu Sok 13 **Tel** *(0274) 224 55 52*

Turkish food is served in this picturesque Turkish restaurant, set in a six-room mansion. *Mantı* (Turkish ravioli) and *güveç* (stew served in a clay dish) are specialities of the house. Food can be served at the table or, Turkish style, on a *sofra*, on the ground. Opening hours 9am to midnight.

THE BLACK SEA

AKÇAABAT Cemil Usta Köfte & Balık

Sahil Park Alanı **Tel** *(0462) 228 91 04*

The restaurant looks like a white flying saucer, stranded on the seaside. The futuristic decor contrasts with the quaint atmosphere of this sleepy Black Sea area, but the food is very much in line with local tradition. Turks take their meatballs seriously, this popular venue prepares the local version very successfully.

AKÇAABAT Nihat Usta

Liman Mevkii **Tel** *(0462) 228 20 50*

A popular eatery, which has been in operation for over 30 years. The place is clean and modern, the waiters wear white uniforms. Meatballs are the main speciality: the local version is round and flat, and very tasty. Nihat Usta, the owner, has won prizes for his food. Grilled chops and fish are also available.

Key to Price Guide *see p352* **Key to Symbols** *see back cover flap*

AKÇAKOCA Hamsi Balık Lokantası

Balıkçı Barınağı Yanı **Tel** *(0380) 611 82 91*

The anchovy is king in this Black Sea venue, but other fish, freshly caught, are also displayed in the refrigerated cabinet. Hazelnut oil is used to fry fish and *calamari*. Accompanied by a crisp salad, it makes a wonderful, if simple, meal by the sea. For dessert, they serve a delicious hazelnut *helva*.

AMASRA Çeşm-ı Cihan Restaurant

Büyük Liman Cad 21 **Tel** *(0378) 315 10 62*

This restaurant on three floors commands a spectacular view over the beautiful harbour. The food is equally inviting. Customers can choose among the impressive selection of fish on display; try the special fish soup or opt for meat. There are also many cold and hot *mezes*, including fried mussels and *calamar*.

AMASRA Öz Canlı Balık Restaurant

Küçük Liman Cad 8 **Tel** *(0378) 315 26 06*

This venue, founded in 1945, is the oldest fish restaurant in Amasra. Right by the water, it has an attractive atmosphere and a rich menu that includes fish, fried or grilled, and meat. Their special salad contains 28 different vegetables and herbs. For dessert, try the creamy home-made yogurt, served with honey and chopped nuts.

ARDEŞEN Pınar Alabalık Tesisleri

Camlihemşin Yolu üzeri **Tel** *(0464) 752 42 25*

This trout farm offers pleasant surroundings for a delicious meal. There is a stream running nearby and the air is fresh. Aside from trout, they serve regional delicacies such as *Akçaabat* meatballs, rice with *hamsi* and stuffed savoy cabbage leaves. Vegetarians can opt for the egg-based *mıhlama*. Open from 7am until midnight.

ARTVIN Teras Restaurant

Cumhuriyet Cad 42 **Tel** *(0466) 212 84 76*

On the way to a spectacular mountainpass, this restaurant and motel provides a perfect spot to enjoy the lush green landscape of the Black Sea highlands. The venue is simple, but made cosy by wood panels. After a walk in the great outdoors, customers can enjoy traditional home style cooking, in beautiful surroundings.

GIRESUN Çavuşlu Dinlenme Tesisleri

Sahil Cad 10, Çavuşlu Görele **Tel** *(0454) 523 00 31*

This is a roadside venue, located almost exactly half-way between Trabzon and Giresun. It is a good place to stop for a rest and for a quick meal near the sea. The fish, meat and vegetable dishes on offer are simple but good, and the restaurant is clean. Open 24 hours a day.

GIRESUN Çerkez Restaurant

Gemiler Çekeği Mah, Çerkez Mevkii **Tel** *(0454) 216 31 39*

Local specialities are served in this seaside restaurant, which faces a small island. This is the land of hazelnuts and wild greens. Some of them are on the menu, which is predominantly fish-based. Their *tel kadayif* (a dessert made of thread like pastry) is said to be the best in the region.

KASTAMONU Toprakcılar Konakları

ısmailbey Mah Alemdar Sok 2 **Tel** *(0366) 212 18 12*

This elegant restaurant occupies a restored Ottoman mansion, which turned into a boutique hotel a few years ago. The ornate ceiling decorations, and the atmosphere, have been successfully preserved. The local speciality is a rich rice *pilav* dish, but the restaurant also serves fish, grilled meat and a good selection of vegetable *mezes*.

ORDU Vonalı Celal'ın Yeri

Ordu-Samsun karayolu üzeri, Perşembe'nin Ramazan Köyü, Vona mevkii **Tel** *(0452) 587 21 37*

Frequented by politicians and artists, this restaurant is renowned for its 101 different kinds of pickles and for its 30 local recipes, many of which use anchovies. With its unequalled selection of food, cosy setting and nice view, this restaurant is definitely a good choice. Try *kuymak* (a melted concoction of cheese and corn flour).

RİZE Evvel Zaman

Emineddin Mah, Atatürk Cad, Eski Devlet Hastanesi Karşısı

Customers may be forgiven for thinking they have stepped into an antique store. Objects collected by the owner over 30 years are on display here. But it is for the excellent Black Sea specialities that customers visit this venue. Savoy cabbage soup, corn bread, anchovy bread, rice with anchovies are all prepared to high standards here.

RİZE Sevimli Konak

Atatürk Cad, Valilik Binası Karşısı **Tel** *(0464) 217 08 95*

This inviting venue has classical or Turkish music on Wednesdays and Fridays, but the food itself is enough to draw the clientele. A perennial favourite here is their own creation, the Konak steak, which is topped with vegetables and baked with cheese in a clay pot. They also serve the famous local dessert, the *Laz böreği*.

SAFRANBOLU Kadıoğlu Şehzade Sofrası

Çeşme Mah Arasta Sok 1 **Tel** *(0370) 712 50 91*

People come to this little town to see its unique architecture and a get a glimpse of a past lifestyle. This restaurant, linked to a beautifully renovated hotel, serves local delicacies in a nostalgic environment. Meat features heavily on the menu, but there are also vegetable dishes and delicious home-made Turkish desserts.

SAFRANBOLU Havuzlu Köşk

Bağlarbaşı Mah, Dibekkonu Cad 32 **Tel** *(0370) 725 21 68*

The name of this restaurant refers to the pool that is found inside many of the historical houses in this district. This one is 300 years old and has retained its old charm. The restaurant serves local specialities, kebabs and meat sautéed on a sizzling iron pan. Customers can also relax with a drink at the bar.

SAMSUN Canlı Balık Restaurant
Liman içi Mevkii, Yakakent **Tel** *(0362) 611 23 62*

Visitors here will find a long stretch of beach with waterfront restaurants in a pretty little harbour. The name of this one, which means "Live Fish", says it all. This is a simple seaside restaurant, where you can relax, enjoy the smell of the sea and savour the simple pleasure of a grilled fish, with *mezes* and a salad.

SAMSUN Maide Et Lokantası
19 Mayıs Sanayi Sitesi, Atatürk Bulvarı 25, Kutlukent **Tel** *(0362) 266 74 72*

This is a restaurant that started small over a decade ago, and grew rapidly due to popular demand. It has now expanded into catering. The food is tasty and the staff friendly and welcoming. The focus is on grilled meat, and casseroles, which are different every day, and Turkish pizzas are also on offer.

SAMSUM Sofram Restaurant
19 Mayıs Mah, Kışla Sok 7 **Tel** *(0362) 435 05 25*

The place is simple and unpretentious, but it serves good, honest food. *Keşkek* (a local wheat stew cooked for hours) is on the menu alongside grilled meat, fried *böreks* and home-cooked vegetables in olive oil. The restaurant is open-plan, so you can see your meal being prepared in the kitchen.

SAMSUN Körfez Restaurant
Körfez Mah., Atatürk Bulvarı 110, Kurupelit **Tel** *(0362) 457 53 29*

In this friendly restaurant, popular with local families, there is music and a lively atmosphere at weekends. The garden seats up to 500 people and you can admire the sea view from the roof-top bar. The menu offers a good range of fish, meat, and *pides* (Turkish pizza) with various toppings.

SİNOP Deniz Restaurant
Yalı Mah, Ömer Seyfettin 8, ıskele Meydanı **Tel** *(0368) 613 51 06*

A simple and inexpensive waterfront restaurant located in a pretty natural harbour of the Black Sea. Deniz serves fresh fish, naturally, which can be ordered grilled or fried, but also a good range of meats and kebabs. Meals can be enjoyed outside, while watching the fishermen go about their business.

SURMENE Hancıoğlu Restaurant
Çamburnu Mevkii **Tel** *(0462) 752 26 50*

Wooden panels create a cosy interior in this waterfront restaurant, which enjoys a splendid view. With its wide garden, it can accommodate up to 1,000 guests, who come here to savour fresh fish and meat. Aside from the standard kebabs, this restaurant also serves local specialities like *Akçaabat* meatballs and *mihlama*.

TRABZON Balıkçı Dede Restaurant
Devlet Karayolları altı Akyazı Beldesi **Tel** *(0462) 221 03 98*

This waterfront venue is famous for its anchovies, a local delicacy, which are served fried, grilled or in a casserole. Vine leaves in olive oil, and other vegetable dishes are also popular. In total, they have 15 different types of *mezes*. On Saturdays, guests can enjoy classical Turkish music while they eat.

TRABZON Kadakal Sahil Tesisleri
Yalı Mah, Sahil Yolu Cad, Balıkçı Limanı yani Faroz **Tel** *(0462) 229 83 44*

This large beach facility is popular with families because children can run around the vast garden while the parents eat. Choosing from the vast selection of food on offer is not easy. Savoy cabbage soup, stuffed anchovies or rice with anchovies are among regional dishes served in this restaurant, also famous for its baked beans.

TRABZON Roksalana Restaurant
ıskenderpaşa Mah, Sıramağazalar 5/E **Tel** *(0462) 322 40 08*

Suleyman the Magnificent was born in this region and the restaurant is named after his Ukranian-born consort. This small, cosy venue serves many variations on the *hamsi* (anchovy) theme. In *Hamsi Kaygana*, fried anchovies are combined with corn flour, another regional staple. Casseroles and grilled meat are also on the menu.

TRABZON Suleyman Restaurant
D.Dere, 100. Yıl Parkı, Olimpik Havuzu Yanı **Tel** *(0462) 325 05 50*

This comfortable and friendly seaside venue serves all the local specialities, but it has also expanded its range to include pasta and other Italian and French dishes. There is a nice view, and a bar where customers can enjoy a relaxing drink. Locals particularly enjoy the live Turkish music on Saturdays.

TRABZON Galanima Restaurant
Adnan Kahveci Bulvarı, 2 Sok 2, Söğütlü **Tel** *(0462) 248 71 27*

The main focus is on fish in this seaside restaurant, which has live classical Turkish music performances on Fridays and Saturdays. Located in an old mansion with a large garden, it also serves local specialities such as stuffed savoy cabbage. Many of their vegetable *mezes* are prepared with home-grown produce.

CAPPADOCIA AND CENTRAL ANATOLIA

AMASYA Ali Kaya Restaurant
 €

Çakallar Mevkii **Tel** *(0358) 219 15 05*

Perched on a cliff, high above the town, this restaurant has an impregnable view of Amasya and its meandering river. Aside from this obvious asset, this venue also has a broad menu that includes a good selection of *mezes*, grilled meat, soups and *pide* (Turkish pizzas). Indoor and outdoor dining.

AMASYA Şehir Külübü
 €

Karşıyaka Mah Tevfik Hafiz Sok **Tel** *(0358) 218 10 13*

Overlooking the river, the City Club, is a popular restaurant in this picturesque little town of great architectural interest. The food consists of local dishes and grilled meat, as well as vegetables and *mezes*. It is simple but good, and the ambiance is friendly. There is also a bar, and the place is open from 8am to 1am.

AVANOS Bizim Ev Restaurant
 €

Orta Mah, Baklacı Sok 1 **Tel** *(0384) 511 55 25*

In the old part of town, two old houses have been combined to create this large restaurant with an ethnic feel. Four sections provide different atmospheres, but local specialities, fish, meat and vegetable *mezes* taste equally good in all four. There is an enclosed terrace and an oriental corner with cushions and low tables.

AVANOS Altinocak Restaurant
 €€

Yeni Mah, Hasankalesi Mevkii **Tel** *(0384) 511 43 57*

This cosy underground facility is carved out of soft rock and boasts a wonderful view over the Cappadocian landscape. Guests come here mainly for the entertainment: belly dancing, folk dances, classical Turkish music and whirling dervishes. The tasty fixed menu comprises of 15 hot and cold mezes and a main course.

ÇORUM Katipler Konağı
 €

Karakecili Mah 2, Sok 50 **Tel** *(0364) 224 96 51*

This historical mansion surrounded by a large garden not only provides a good example of local architecture, it has also become one of the best restaurants in the region. The menu consists of regional dishes, prepared to perfection. While eating in the green room, you can admire the antiques on display.

GÖREME Ottoman House
 €

Orta Mah, Uzundere Sok 25 **Tel** *(0384) 271 26 16*

The view over the fairy chimneys from the terrace is, in itself, worth a visit to this elegant hotel with well-appointed rooms. The beautiful landscape is best enjoyed at breakfast, but the restaurant serves fine Ottoman and Turkish cuisine for lunch and dinner in a decor that incorporates local artifacts and *kilims*.

GÖREME A'la Turca Restaurant
€€€

Göreme **Tel** *(0384) 271 28 82*

You can find almost anything that the heart desires here: excellent Turkish food, but also hamburgers, soups, salads and sandwiches. They even serve English breakfast and, in the evenings, wine and cocktails aplenty. The restaurant is chic and spread over a vast area that includes a garden, terrace and two bars.

GÖREME Orient House
€€€

Göreme **Tel** *(0384) 271 23 46*

The organic vegetables and herbs are fresh from the garden in this upscale restaurant that serves Cappadocian and international cuisine. Elegant decor with a local ethnic touch. The food is beautifully presented and the portions generous. There is also an impressive wine list to choose from to accompany the meal and liquors for afters. Recommended.

KAYSERİ Kaşıkla Mantı Restaurant
€

Anbar Mah Zafer Cad 4 **Tel** *(0352) 326 30 75*

Kayseri manti (local ravioli-like dumplings) are a staple in this 800-seat restaurant, which started with eight tables in 1985, and now has branches in Istanbul and Izmir. Expect to find kebabs as well as regional delights baked in in clay dishes, yogurt soup and casseroles on their menu.

KAYSERİ Tuana Restaurant
€

Sivas Cad, Mehmet Alemdar ış Merkezi, Kat 2 **Tel** *(0352) 222 05 65*

This spacious venue, opened by two university graduates in 1998, seats up to 600 people. Its menu consists of local Kayseri specialities and traditional Ottoman recipes as well as a selection of international favourites. Popular for banquets and weddings, this centrally located restaurant has music at weekends. Spectacular view of Mount Erciyes.

MUSTAFAPAŞA Old Greek House
 €€

Sinasos Village **Tel** *(0384) 353 53 06*

Built in 1887, this mansion was turned into a hotel in 1992, but it has lost none of its original authenticity. *Kilims* adds a touch of colour to rooms with high ceilings, stone walls and elegant arches. The food, Turkish, is served *sofra*-style on low tables and eaten sitting on cushions.

MUSTAFAPAŞA Gül Konakları
Sümer Sok **Tel** *(0384) 353 54 86*

The elegant Rose Mansions, originally Greek houses, have been meticulously restored and turned into a charming boutique hotel and restaurant. The name comes from the fragrant flowers in the garden. The food served here is local and well-prepared. Oven-roasted lamb and vine leaves are among the dishes on the menu.

SİVAS Sofa Ev Yemekleri
ıstasyon Cad Örülü Pınar Mah Akgül Apt **Tel** *(0346) 224 08 15*

The place is tiny, with only 25 seats, but customers are happy to wait in line to get a chance to taste the delicious home-style regional dishes served here. These include the nourishing Erzincan soup prepared with yogurt and meat, and potato dumplings. There is also a good selection of sweets.

UÇHISAR Elai Restaurant
Eski Göreme Cad **Tel** *(0384) 219 31 81*

This restaurant was once a coffee house. Partly carved out of sandstone, it now offers very elegant dining in an intimate cave-like setting. The food, contemporary Turkish and European, is refined and the presentation exquisite. A roof terrace with teak furniture provides a perfect viewpoint to admire the spectacular Cappadocian landscape.

ÜRGÜP Şömine Restaurant
Merkez Pasajı üzeri 9 **Tel** *(0384) 341 84 42*

The central piece in this venue is the large fireplace which creates a romantic ambiance. Meals can also be eaten in the garden or on the terrace. The menu, mainly Turkish, contains interesting dishes such as *kiremits* (vegetables or meat cooked on clay tiles). *Testi* kebab is baked in a clay amphora, sealed with dough, then broken open.

ÜRGÜP Micro Restaurant
Cumhuriyet Meydanı 11 **Tel** *(0384) 341 51 10*

In the heart of Cappadocia, this inviting family-run locale attracts tourists and local customers alike. Aside from regional specialities such as meat baked in a sealed clay pot and stuffed vine leaves, they also serve dishes with a more international flavour such as spinach crêpe and stuffed steak rolls. Desserts include stuffed figs, served with clotted cream.

EASTERN ANATOLIA

BITLIS Beş Minare Lokantası
Kale altı çarşısı, Kazım Dirik Cad 30 **Tel** *(0434) 226 37 00*

In the centre of town, this no-frills venue, which can accommodate up to 150 customers, serves honest and solid food. Their range includes various grilled kebabs, including döner and *iskender*, served with yogurt. They also have meat and vegetable casseroles. Opens 6am to 9pm.

DIYARBAKıR Ka-Mer'ın Mutfağı
Aliemri 3. Sok, Dişkale Apt. **Tel** *(0412) 229 04 59*

This venue, run by a women's association, was founded to provide job opportunities and financial resources for victims of domestic violence. It has grown into a popular restaurant serving excellent home-cooked food from various parts of the South-east. The range is broad and the menu changes often according to market availability. Worth a visit.

DIYARBAKıR Mezopotamya Konağı
Mezopotamya Konağı **Tel** *(0412) 223 10 40*

If you want a taste of authentic South-east atmosphere, this restaurant, which occupies a renovated old mansion, is a good choice. Local delicacies are served by friendly and welcoming staff. Meat is a main feature on the menu, with kebabs and the local favourite *kaburga dolması* (stuffed lamb rib). Pasta and salads are also on offer.

DIYARBAKıR Selim Amca'nın Sofra Salonu
Aliemri Cad 22/B **Tel** *(0412) 224 44 47*

This place is a Diyarbakir classic and no visitor comes to the city without stopping here for *kaburga dolması* (stuffed lamb rib), served with a tasty rice. Other local delicacies are also on the menu, such as *bumbar* (a local sausage). For dessert, the *irmik helvasi* (a semolina sweet served lukewarm) is worth a try.

DIYARBAKıR Asmin Restaurant
Doktor Selahaddin Yazıcıoğlu Cad, Binevs Apt Altı Yenişehir **Tel** *(0412) 224 31 97*

This fancy restaurant has rapidly grown in popularity thanks to its delicious food and inviting atmosphere. Violin music accompanies the meals here. The food is local with an international flavour. As in most venues in this region, the focus is on meat, but there are also *mezes* and even seafood and fish.

DIYARBAKıR Gurme
Aliemiri Sok 18/A, Yenişehir **Tel** *(0412) 228 51 55*

This classy and quiet family-run restaurant offers a very broad selection of international, Italian, French and Turkish dishes. The owners are friendly and helpful. The menu has a vegetarian section, and a salad bar provides fresh vegetables every day.The best-selling item on the menu is the leg of lamb with oregano.

Key to Price Guide *see p352* **Key to Symbols** *see back cover flap*

ERZURUM Güzelyurt Restaurant

Cumhuriyet Cad 42 **Tel** *(0442) 234 50 01*

This stylish restaurant, open since 1928, offers an impressive menu combining Turkish and international cuisine. The decor, wood panels and white tablecloths, is slightly formal. Casseroles and other specials are on offer for lunch. In the evenings, the menu is à la carte. The food is beautifully presented in contemporary style.

GAZIANTEP ımam Çağdaş Restaurant

Eski Hal civarı, Uzun Çarşı 49, Şahinbey **Tel** *(0342) 231 26 78*

Gaziantep is said to have 150 kinds of kebabs. Many of them are served in this restaurant, which has been in operation for 120 years. Now run by the third generation, it offers excellent value for money in a friendly atmosphere. The meat, specially chosen and cooked on an open fire, is lean and tender, and the local *mezes* particularly tasty.

GAZIANTEP Memo Restaurant

23 Nisan Mah, Üniversite Bulvarı 249/1 **Tel** *(0342) 360 13 13*

This unpretentious kebab venue offers a good selection of grilled kebabs, chicken and lamb chops, with a spicy South-eastern twist. A few *mezes* and salads are also on the menu. A guitarist and a singer provide entertainment most nights. Families are welcome in this restaurant, which is open from 10am to midnight.

GAZIANTEP Doğan Usta Balık Restaurant

Doğan Usta Balık Restaurant **Tel** *(0342) 339 56 56*

This venue focuses on fish, unlike most restaurants in this part of the country, although meat and chicken are also available. For a party of four or more, they'll prepare a delicious *buğlama* (a sort of fish casserole). Trout topped with cheese and mushroom is also a popular dish here. Quiet, cosy atmosphere.

KÂHTA/ADıYAMAN Akropolian Restaurant

Baraj Kenarı, Kahta **Tel** *(0416) 725 51 32*

Next to the Kahta dam, this restaurant, seating up to 1,200 in the summer, is used by tour groups as a staying post on the way to Nemrut Dag. Fish, caught in the lake and baked on a clay tile, is the main item on the menu, but chicken, meat and vegetable *mezes* are also available.

MARDIN Turistik Et Lokantası

Cumhuriyet Meydanı 49 **Tel** *(0482) 212 16 47*

No alcohol is served here, but this friendly restaurant with an ethnic touch more than makes up for it with delicious food. The menu reflects Turkish, Kurdish, Arab and Assyrian influences. Meat is prominent in most of the dishes, which are flavoured with unusual spice combinations. The menu also includes vegetables in olive oil and salads.

MARDIN Cercis Murat Konağı

Birinci Cad 517 **Tel** *(0482) 213 68 41*

This outstanding restaurant, one of the finest in Turkey, serves local specialities cooked with ingredients such as cinnamon, herbs or dried fruit. Add the spectacular terrace view over the Mesopotamian plain from the terrace of this stone mansion, and a glass of local cherry wine, and you have a memorable culinary experience.

MARDIN Erdoba Konakları

Birinci Cad 135 **Tel** *(0482) 212 76 77*

Turned into a successful hotel and restaurant, these renovated stone mansions offer fine examples of the local architecture. The food they serve matches the surroundings – best enjoyed from the beautiful terraces. Meat features heavily on the menu, but there are vegetarian alternatives such as vegetables baked in a clay dish.

ŞANLIURFA Hotel Harran

Atatürk Bulvarı **Tel** *(0414) 313 28 60*

Centrally located, this hotel restaurant serves traditional local specialities. The decor is plush and slightly formal, but the staff are very friendly. There is a swimming pool, and a terrace where you can enjoy your meal on summer evenings, Turkish musicians perform most evenings. Popular with local residents for weddings and other functions.

TATVAN Şimşek Lokantası
Cumhuriyet Cad 152 **Tel** *(0434) 827 15 13*

Good, solid Turkish food is served in this two-storey restaurant, decorated with wood pannels, which can accommodate up to 100 guests. A good selection of casseroles and grills are on the menu, but the main speciality here is *büryan pilavı* (a local rice and meat dish). No alcohol is served. The restaurant closes at 9pm.

VAN Aşiyan Ev Yemekleri
Kazım Karabekir Cad, Dervişoğlu ış Merkezi 3 **Tel** *(0432) 212 41 90*

In this friendly and simple locale, which seats 55, eastern hospitality is very much evident. The food is mainly of the home-cooked variety: rice with meat, casseroles, lentil soup or baked beans. For tour groups, they also produce more sophisticated local delicacies on request. The environment is family friendly. No alcohol.

VAN Day Süphan Dinlenme Tesisleri
Adilcevaz, Ercis Yolu üzeri **Tel** *(0434) 311 28 07*

This venue, outside the city, is a favourite of local families who enjoy the lakeside terrace and garden. The menu offers plenty to choose from: casseroles, kebabs and even grilled trout. Their best-known dish is the *saç kavurma* (a mix of meat and vegetables served sizzling on an iron pan).

SHOPPING IN TURKEY

Even if you are not a shopper by nature, the varied and unusual selection of gifts found in Turkey's markets will easily tempt you. The grand shops and teeming streets of Istanbul are a world away from the ateliers and craft shops of smaller towns in rural areas. Outside Istanbul, you will also find bargaining (*see p130*) a less cut-throat pursuit. However, you are

Colourful Kütahya ware

sure to encounter high-pressure sales pitches wherever you travel. The weekly market is a unique aspect of regional shopping. These markets are a holdover from the days of trading caravans, when shops as we know them did not exist. Traders still pay taxes to have a market stall, as they did 400 years ago. And the *zabıta* (municipal market police) still control weights, measures and prices.

Upmarket clothing boutique in Bodrum

OPENING HOURS

In large cities, shops are usually open from 9am to 7 or 8pm. But hours can be much extended in tourist and coastal areas, where many shops will stay open until midnight, seven days a week, particularly in summer, when the daytime heat discourages all but the most dedicated shoppers. Out of season, these places often close for extended periods so that the owners can relax after the long hours of summer trade.

In general, opening hours are much more flexible in rural areas. If you find a shop closed, you can ask where the owner is and it will not take long before someone tells him/her that there is a potential customer. Note that some shops may close during Muslim religious holidays.

HOW TO PAY

Most shops that cater to tourists will be happy to accept foreign currency. If you can pay in cash, you can

usually get a discount on most goods. Exchange rates are often displayed in shops, and also appear in daily newspapers.

Credit cards are widely accepted for purchases (except in markets and smaller shops), and most vendors do not charge a commission. Visa, MasterCard and American Express are the most common, Diners Club less so.

Vendors who accept credit cards may try to tell you that they will not be reimbursed for the transaction for several days, and ask you to pay a small compensatory commission. Resist this, and insist on paying without a commission. It is common for a vendor to ask you to go to the bank with him to draw the money out on your credit card. There is nothing wrong with this, but you will pay interest on your card for a

cash advance. Note that very few shops in Turkey now accept travellers' cheques.

In rural markets, you will be expected to pay in cash. Some merchants will happily accept foreign currency.

Merchants in bazaars and markets expect customers to bargain. If you see something you want to buy, offer half the asking price. Increase the offer slightly if the merchant resists. He will then indicate whether he thinks that the bargaining should continue.

VAT EXEMPTION

If you spend at least 118 TL in one shop, you can claim back the 18 per cent VAT (KDV in Turkey). VAT exemption is now widely available – look for the Tax Free Shopping logo. The retailer gives you a Global Refund Cheque, which you should present to customs officials with your invoices and purchases for a cash refund when leaving Turkey.

Fresh herbs and spices, sold by weight at Kadıköy Market in Istanbul

Locally produced copper and brassware in the old quarter of Safranbolu

BUYING ANTIQUES

Before purchasing antique items, it is important to know what can and cannot be taken out of Turkey. The rule is that objects which are over 100 years old may be exported only with a certificate stating their age and granting permission to remove them from the country. Museums issue these certificates, as does the Culture Ministry in Ankara, who will also authenticate the correct age and value of an object, if necessary. The shopkeeper from whom you bought your goods will often know which

Ornate ceramic vase and saucer

museum will be authorizing your purchases for export. In theory, a seller should register with a museum all goods that are over 100 years old. In practice, sellers usually only seek permission after a particular item has been sold. In the past, antiques could be removed from Turkey without a certificate. Although this has changed, the export of antiques is not forbidden, as some believe. If the relevant authorities permit your purchase to be exported, you can either take it with you or send it home, whether or not it is over 100 years old. Do take note, however, that

taking antiques out of Turkey without proper permission is regarded as smuggling, and is a punishable offence.

Van cats and Kangal dogs are now also included in this category.

HOW TO SEND PURCHASES HOME

If you have bought items from a reputable and trustworthy supplier, he will have an arrangement with an international courier company who can ship goods to your home address. Try to get your own copy of any shipping documents and an air waybill number. Do not use the post office (PTT) to send such items. Be aware that there are also some disreputable dealers, especially in carpets, who will either substitute an inferior item in place of the one you have bought or who will fail to send the goods. Beware of traders who advise you to ignore official rules.

SIZES AND MEASURES

Turkey uses continental European sizes for clothes and shoes. Food and drink are sold in metric measures.

DIRECTORY

VAT EXEMPTION

Global Refund
Teşvikiye, Ferah Sok 19/A-2, Istanbul.
Tel (0212) 232 11 21.
www.globalrefund.com

ANTIQUES

Motif Handicrafts
Sirince Koyü, Selcuk, Izmir.
Tel (0232) 898 30 99.
www.motiftr.com

HANDICRAFTS AND GIFTS

Deli Kizin Yeri
82 Halicilar Cad,
Grand Bazaar, Istanbul.
Tel (0212) 526 12 51.
www.delikiz.com

Çeşni Turkish Handicrafts
Tunalı Hilmi Cad, Ertuğ Pasajı 88/44, Ankara.
Tel (0312) 426 57 87.

Evcim
Netsel Marina Shopping Mall D-03, Marmaris.
Tel (0252) 412 06 26.
Fax (0252) 411 13 55.

Galeri Sarpedon
Hotel Pirat, Marina, Kalkan.
Tel (0242) 844 28 49.

Gallery Anatolia
Hükümet Cad, Kaş.
Tel (0242) 836 19 54.
www.sibelduzel.com

JEWELLERY

Topika Jewellery
Bahçe Sokak 6/F, Kaş.
Tel (0242) 836 23 63.
topikajewellery@yahoo.com

CARPETS/KILIMS

Gallery Shirvan
Halıcılar Sok 50, Kapalıçarşı (Grand Bazaar) Istanbul.
Tel (0212) 522 49 86.

Kaş and Carry
Liman Cad 10, Kaş.
Tel (0242) 836 16 62.
Fax (0242) 836 23 89.
www.kascarry.com

Tribal Collections
Müze Yolu 24/C, Goreme, Nevşehir.
Tel (0384) 271 24 00.
www.tribalcollections.net

HAND-WORKED COPPERWARE

L'Orient
İçbedesten, Şerif Ağa Sok 22–23, Kapalıçarşı (Grand Bazaar), Istanbul.
Tel (0212) 520 70 46.

LINENS

Özdilek
Bursa.
Tel (0224) 211 52 00.
Fax (0224) 211 52 44.

Afyon (on main highway junction of Ankara and Afyon road).
Tel (0272) 252 54 00.

SPICES AND HERBS

Ayfer Kaun
Mısır Çarşısı (Spice Market) 7, Istanbul.
Tel (0212) 522 45 23.

Ucuzcular Kimya Sanayii
Mısır Çarşısı (Spice Market) 51, Istanbul.
Tel (0212) 520 64 92.

What to Buy in Turkey

When it comes to shopping, nothing can compare with Istanbul's bustling bazaars, markets, shops and stalls. In contrast, the rural markets have an unhurried feel and unique products that often don't travel much beyond provincial boundaries, such as stout walking sticks made in Devrek (near Zonguldak), ceremonial pipes produced in Sivas and the angora goat-hair bedspreads and rugs made in Siirt. Markets are lively and colourful, and the best places to find handmade items that are produced in small quantities.

Meerschaum pipe head

Copper goblets

Copperware

Antique copperware can be very expensive. Newer items, however, are also available, at more affordable prices.

Antique copper water ewer

Pipes

Classic, beautifully crafted nargiles (bubble pipes) are still used by some Turkish men. They can make very attractive ornaments, even if you do not smoke.

Box inlaid with mother-of-pearl

Evil-eye pendants

Box with painted scenes on bone inlay

Jewellery

Turkey produces stunning gold jewellery in original designs. Silver is also popular, and rings and necklaces are often set with precious stones. A simple blue glass eye (boncuk) is said to ward off evil.

Inlaid Wood

Jewellery boxes crafted from wood or bone, and then inlaid or painted, make unusual souvenirs. Backgammon players will be delighted at the delicate, inlaid rosewood backgammon (tavla) sets available in markets and shops around Turkey.

Green jugs from Çanakkale

Blue and white decorated ceramic plate

Ceramics

Ceramics are an important artistic tradition. The style varies according to the area of origin. İznik, Kütahya and Çanakkale are famous for ceramic production, but Avanos is also known for hand-painted pottery and porcelain.

Leather Goods

Shoes, handbags, briefcases and other leather accessories are good buys, as are jackets. For high-fashion, Istanbul is the place. Desa Deri is a good name all over Turkey. For accessories, look for the Matraş or Tergan brands.

Glassware

This elegant lamp is an example of the blue and white striped glassware called çeşmibülbül, *which is made in the famous Paşabahçe works. The firm makes many utilitarian designs as well as an up-market range in fine lead crystal. Paşabahçe glassware makes a wonderful gift.*

Textiles

Hand-woven cloths, including ikat *work (where the cotton is dyed as it is woven), and fine embroidery are just some of the range of textiles that can be bought. Turkey is also a leading producer of top-quality garments and knitwear. Bathrobes and towels are of high quality. Look for the Altınyıldız label for finest woollens and fabrics by the metre or yard.*

Çeşmibülbül lamp

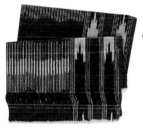

Cotton *ikat* work

Embroidered scarves known as oyalı

Hand-printed *yazma* (shawls) from Tokat

Local Delicacies

Delicious sweets such as halva, Turkish delight and baklava are always popular. Many fragrant spices, as well as dried fruit and nuts are sold loose by weight in most markets and tourist shops throughout Turkey.

Halva

Nuts in honey

Turkish delight

Dried red peppers and aubergines

Mulberries

Sunflower and pumpkin seeds

Apricots

Chickpeas

Almonds

Pistachios

Turkish Carpets and Kilims

The ancient skill of weaving rugs has been handed down from generation to generation in Turkey. Rugs were originally made for warmth and decoration in the home, as dowry items for brides, or as donations to mosques. There are two main kinds of rug: carpets *(halı)*, which are knotted, and kilims, which are flat-woven with vertical (warp) and horizontal (weft) threads. Many foreign rugs are sold in Turkey but those of Turkish origin come in a particularly wide range of attractive colours. Most of the carpets and kilims offered for sale will be new or almost new; antique rugs are rarer and far more expensive.

A carpet may be machine-made or handmade. Fold the face of the rug back on itself: if you can see the base of the knots and the pile cannot be pulled out, it means that it is handmade.

Wool is the usual material for making a rug, although some carpets are made from silk.

Weaving a Carpet
Wool for rugs is washed, carded, spun and dyed before it is woven. Weaving is a cottage industry in Turkey; the women weave in winter, leaving the summer months for farming duties.

RUG-MAKING AREAS OF WESTERN TURKEY

The weaving industry in Turkey is concentrated into several areas of production, listed below. Rug designs are traditional to their tribal origins, resulting in a wide range of designs and enabling a skilled buyer to identify the area of origin.

CARPETS
① Hereke
② Çanakkale
③ Ayvacık
④ Bergama
⑤ Yuntdağ
⑥ Balıkesir
⑦ Sındırgı
⑧ Milas
⑨ Antalya
⑩ Isparta

ISTANBUL• ①
② ⑥
③
④
⑤ ⑦
⑫
⑪ ⑩ ⑬
⑧ ⑨

ANKARA •

KILIMS
⑪ Denizli
⑫ Uşak

CARPETS AND KILIMS
⑬ Konya

CARPET
This reproduction of a 16th-century Uşak carpet is known as a Bellini double entrance prayer rug.

Indigo

Madder

Camomile

Dyes
Before chemical dyes were introduced in 1863, plant extracts were used: madder roots for red; indigo for blue; and camomile and other plants for yellow.

The **"prayer design"** is inspired by a *mihrab*, the niche in a mosque that indicates the direction of Mecca *(see pp32–3)*.

The **tree of life** motif at the centre of the kilim is symbolic of immortality.

BUYING A RUG

Before you buy a rug, look at it by itself on the floor, to see that it lies straight – without waves or lumps. Check that the pattern is balanced, the borders are of the same dimensions, and the ends are roughly the same width. The colours should be clear and not bleeding into one another. Bargaining is essential *(see p130)*, as the first price given is likely to be at least 30% higher than the seller really expects.

Buying a good-quality old rug at a reasonable price, however, is a job for an expert. The age of a rug is ascertained from its colour, the quality of the weaving and the design. Check the pile to make sure that the surface has not been painted and look for any repairs – they can easily be seen on the back of the rug. The restoration of an old carpet is acceptable but the repair should not be too visible. Make sure the rug has a small lead seal attached to it, proving that it may be exported, and ask the shop for a receipt.

KILIM

Kilims are usually made using the slit-weave technique by which a vertical slit marks a colour change.

The **width** of a rug is limited by the size of the loom. Most rugs are small because a large loom will not fit into a village house.

Kilim pieces are used to make a variety of smaller craft objects, also for sale in carpet shops.

Burdock motif

Chest motif

Motifs

The recurring motifs in rugs – some of them seemingly abstract, others more figurative – often have a surprising origin. For instance, many are derived from marks that nomads and villagers used for branding animals.

Motif from wolf track, crab or scorpion

Modern motif of a human figure

ENTERTAINMENT IN TURKEY

Almost every town and village in Turkey enjoys an annual celebration – be it grease wrestling, bull butting or simply an agricultural festival where farmers can show off their new tractors. Some of these events hark back to ancient seasonal rites, such as the Giresun Aksu Festival on the Black Sea in May. Even though most of these activities are aimed at locals, you are sure to be made welcome or even be a guest of honour.

Football souvenir

Spectator sports have a very long history in Turkey. In classical times, the many amphitheatres of Anatolia hosted wrestling matches, circuses and risqué theatricals, which were entertainment as much as sport. Today, the average Turk identifies more with football (soccer) than any other type of sport. Visitors will soon notice the coloured banners and car horns blasting in support of favourite teams such as Beşiktaş, Galatasaray and Fenerbahçe.

ENTERTAINMENT GUIDES

A number of magazines list events and entertainment in Istanbul and elsewhere in the country. Visitors to Istanbul, Antalya and Bodrum should look for *The Guide*, while *The Gate* magazine is available for free at airports. Turkish Airlines also has its own publication, *Skylife*. *Jazz*, the quarterly Istanbul magazine, is a good source of information on various local jazz clubs, events and musicians.

Bodrum events guide

CINEMA, THEATRE AND MUSIC FESTIVALS

Turkey has a large cinema-going public. Most films are shown in their original language with Turkish subtitles. The **Golden Orange Film Festival** is held annually in Antalya *(see p218–19)*.

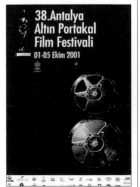

Golden Orange Film Festival poster

Other items on the arts calendar are the **International Opera and Ballet Festival** *(see p35)* held at Aspendos, as well as an exciting series of Istanbul events that focus on theatre, classical music, film and jazz. Among these is the Istanbul Theatre Festival, which is held in May *(see p132)*.

Music festivals include the Akbank Jazz Festival, held in April and May in Istanbul, Ankara and other cities; the touring Efes Pilsen Blues Festival, held in the autumn, and the Fuji Film World Music Days, held in Istanbul. There are occasional concerts in the amphitheatre at Ephesus.

DISCOS, NIGHT CLUBS AND BELLY DANCING

You will find huge, open-air discos in most summer resorts – Bodrum's Halikarnas *(see p194)* is the best known, with pillars and torchlight reminiscent of ancient times.

Despite a somewhat seedy reputation – especially in the back alleys of Istanbul – belly dancing *(see p23)* is outdoor family entertainment for Turks at seaside resorts in summer, and this is where you are likely to see the most authentic displays.

Special tourist floor shows at hotels and holiday villages in season frequently include folk dancing and traditional music. Folkloric whirling dervish performances are

Halikarnas disco in Bodrum

frequently staged but these are not the authentic troupe who perform during the Mevlâna Festival in Konya in December *(see p37)*.

SPECTATOR SPORTS

Although football *(futbol)* is hugely popular, grease wrestling, or *yağlı güreş*, is Turkey's most time-honoured sport *(see p152)*. The main event is the four-day festival at **Kırkpınar**, near Edirne, in June. Wearing nothing but *kıspet* (black leather trousers soaked with olive oil), up to 1,000 men compete according to weight groups.

Camel wrestling *(see p37)* takes place every January and February. The biggest camel wrestling festivals are in Selçuk and around İzmir.

The Camel Classic Motor Racing series, which is held in the summer months, starts in Istanbul and follows a circuit that includes most of the western resort areas.

The major events on the horse racing calendar include the Gazi Race, held at the **Veli Efendi Hippodrome** in

Istanbul at the end of June, and the Presidential Cup in Ankara at the end of October.

The Mediterranean coastal town of Alanya *(see p226)* is the venue for the **Alanya International Triathlon** (swimming, cycling and foot races) in October. Istanbul has a state-of-the-art Grand Prix racing circuit on the Asian side of the city which hosts a leg of the prestigious **Formula One** car race *(see p35)*.

THEME PARKS

Theme parks are growing in popularity in Turkey. **Minicity Antalya** *(see p218)* is a cross-cultural attraction that enchants visitors of all ages.

Some of the big holiday villages around Kemer or Alanya even have their own mini theme parks tucked away within the hotel complex, but access to these is usually reserved for resident guests only.

At **Antalya Dolphin Parks**, the aquaparks, with their many slides, are popular with children of all ages.

TRADITIONAL TURKISH MUSIC AND DANCE

Traditional Turkish music is regularly performed at the Cemal Reşit Rey Concert Hall in Istanbul. In summer, recitals of Turkish music are occasionally organized in the Basilica Cistern *(see p86)*, which has wonderful acoustics.

Folk dancers performing at Ephesus

Traditional *Fasıl* music *(see pp22–3)* is best enjoyed live in *meyhanes* (concert halls) such as Ece, Kallavi and Hasır in Istanbul. *Fasıl* is performed on instruments which include the violin, *kanun* (zither), *tambur* and *ud* (both similar to the lute).

CHILDREN

Children are welcome and will be fussed over almost everywhere. However, there are relatively few attractions that have been planned with children in mind. Beaches and theme parks are good bets, and holiday villages always have programmes for children. In Istanbul, there are large parks at Yıldız *(see pp124–5)* and Emirgan *(see p141)*. Also near Emirgan is Park Orman, with picnic areas, a pool and theatre.

Miniature versions of Turkey's sights at Minicity Antalya

DIRECTORY

CINEMA, THEATRE AND MUSIC FESTIVALS

Ankara International Music Festival
Tel (0312) 427 08 55.
Fax (0312) 467 31 59.
www.ankarafestival.com

Ankara Theatre Festival
Tel (312) 419 83 98.

Aspendos International Opera & Ballet Festival
Ankara.
Tel (0242) 243 76 46.
Aspendos Theatre:
Tel (0242) 735 73 37.

Golden Orange Film Festival
Kültür Parkı İçi, Antalya.
Tel (0242) 238 54 44.
Fax (0242) 247 10 13.
festival@altinportakal.org.tr
www.altinportakal.org.tr

International Istanbul Music Festival
Tel (0212) 293 31 33.
Fax (0212) 249 55 75.
www.istfest.org

SPECTATOR SPORTS

Alanya International Triathlon
Alanya Municipality.
Tel (0242) 513 10 02.

Fax (0242) 513 05 02.
www.triathlon.org.tr

Formula One
Karaaliler Mevkii,
9–10–11 Pafta 1935
Parsel, Tepeören Yolu
Akfırat Beldesi, Tuzla,
Istanbul.
www.formula1-istanbul.com
www.f1grandprix
turkey.com

Kırkpınar Grease-Wrestling
Edirne tourism office.
Tel (0284) 213 92 08.
www.kirkpinar.org

Veli Efendi Hippodrome
Türkiye Jokey Kulübü,
Osmaniye, Bakırköy,

Istanbul.
Tel (0212) 543 70 96.
Tel (0212) 444 08 55.

THEME PARKS

Antalya Dolphin Parks
Several locations.
www.antalyadolphinland.com

Minicity Antalya
Arapsu Mahallesi,
Konyaaltı,
Antalya.
Tel (0242) 228 92 28.
Tel (0242) 229 45 45.
Fax (0242) 228 92 29.
www.miniatureart.com.tr
Internet booking:
www.biletix.com

Music and Dance

Turkish music and dance are deeply rooted in history and tradition, having been influenced by Ottoman classics, mystical Sufi chants and Central Asian folk tunes, as well as jazz and pop. The result is a vibrant mosaic of old and new culture, an eclectic mixture of styles. In Turkey, visitors are treated to variety, from the meditational trance of Whirling dervishes and the merry twirling of folk dancers to the steady beat of Mehter bands, undulating rhythms of belly dancers and the stirring strains of *zurna* buskers. The country offers a musical and dance extravaganza second to none.

Zither-like kanun

The zurna *(shawm) is a member of the oboe family. Its characteristic, strident sound features strongly in Turkish folk music.*

Davul

TRADITIONAL INSTRUMENTS

Turkish instruments can be classified into three main groups. Stringed instruments include the *saz* and *ud*, winds the *kaval* and *ney*, and percussion the *davul* and *darbuka*.

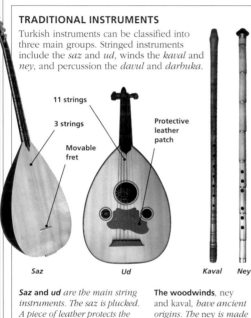

11 strings

3 strings

Movable fret

Protective leather patch

Saz   Ud   Kaval   Ney

Saz and ud *are the main string instruments. The saz is plucked. A piece of leather protects the belly of the ud from the strokes of the plectrum.*

The woodwinds, *ney and kaval, have ancient origins. The* ney *is made from reed, while the* kaval *is carved from the wood of the plum tree.*

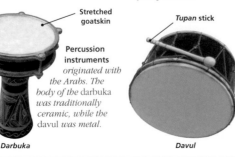

Stretched goatskin

Tupan stick

Percussion instruments *originated with the Arabs. The body of the* darbuka *was traditionally ceramic, while the davul was metal.*

Darbuka   Davul

A saz player *entertains villagers in this 1950s photograph. Although tastes have changed, Turks remain proud of their musical traditions.*

Sufi music *uses the sounds of the ney, ud and* kanun *to interpret secular pieces based on the mode system and accompany poems that are chanted by a chorus. Through whirling motions, the dancers attain a trance-like state* (see p255).

The *Kılıç Kalkan, or spoon dance, of the Black Sea region is performed to the rhythmic beating of two wooden spoons. Traditional folk dancing is an important part of Turkish culture, as are colourful regional costumes.*

Low G clarinet

Belly dancing *is popular in Turkey and remains a firm favourite with tourists. The sensuous rippling body movements, and gyrations of the hips, require impressive muscle control.*

Bagpipes *(tulum)* made from goatskin

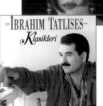

***Arabesque** and pop music are big business in Turkey, its heroes and heroines attaining cult status. Ibrahim Tatlıses is a much-loved performer of* arabesk, *Oriental-style music with lyrics that bemoan human hardship, while art-music trained Sezen Aksu is one of the top-selling pop stars.*

ASIL MUSIC

Fasıl music is considered semi-classical and is performed in *meyhane (see p347)* or concert halls. Its distinctive single harmony is similar to gypsy *(Çingene)* music, and both display a masterful control of traditional wind, string and percussion instruments. Fasıl music is intended to be listened to, but gypsy music is often accompanied by dancing.

MEHTER: MUSIC OF THE JANISSARIES

Mehter performance

From 1299 until the dissolution of the Janissary corps in 1826, *mehter* music accompanied the armies of the Ottoman empire into battle, with a distinctive marching step to the rhythm of the words, "Gracious God is good. God is compassionate." Today the revived Mehter band performs at the Istanbul Military Museum *(see pp120–21)* and at Topkapı Palace.

OUTDOOR ACTIVITIES AND SPECIALIST HOLIDAYS

Turkey's geographical and climatic diversity presents almost limitless possibilities for outdoor enthusiasts. Anatolian winters are ideal for skiers and mountaineers, and the long, hot Mediterranean summers are perfect for yacht cruises, diving and windsurfing. Although

Lycian Way marker

spring and autumn are quite short, the temperate conditions are pleasant for walking and cycling. Turkey also has many options for themed holidays suitable for individuals or groups with particular interests, or those who prefer a more in-depth slant on historic events or sporting activities.

WALKING AND TREKKING

Turkey's spectacular basalt and limestone mountain ranges provide ample opportunity for hiking. The first marked long-distance trek, the Lycian Way, was opened in 1999 along the Mediterranean coast (see p206). In central Turkey, the landscape of Cappadocia, with its celebrated "fairy chimneys" (see pp280–81), also has several signposted walks. A lack of detailed maps makes solo ventures difficult elsewhere.

Among the best areas for day walks and treks are the mountains of Lycia on the Mediterranean coast, as well as the Turkish Lake District around Eğirdir (see p254) and the Bolkar and Aladağlar ranges (part of the Taurus Mountains). In the northeast, the Kaçkar Mountains, with glaciers, lakes and peaks rising to 3,932 m (12,900 feet), offer excellent longer treks, albeit for a short season. The highest peak in Turkey is Mount Ağrı (Ararat) (see p314–15), near the eastern border with Armenia, rising to 5,165 m (16,945 feet). Mount

Ağrı has been reopened after being off-limits for some time. Adventure outfits like **Exodus**, **Trekking in Turkey** and **World Expeditions** can organize guided treks. **Türkü Tourism** offers high altitude trekking expeditions in the Kaçkar Mountains south of Rize (see p274).

MOUNTAINEERING, CLIMBING AND CANYONING

Turkey's mountain ranges offer excellent opportunities for serious climbers. Deep snow makes ski mountaineering in the Aladağlar and Kaçkar regions a good option for ski mountaineering. **Bukla Tour** can organize treks and guides. **Bougainville** and **Get Wet** offer canyoning excursions.

SKIING

Turkey's most popular ski centre is Uludağ, near Bursa (see p159). It has many lifts, a range of runs and views over the Sea of Marmara. Kartal, between Istanbul and Ankara, offers newer facilities and less

crowded runs. Near Isparta, the Davraz ski centre has a 50-bed hotel and a 1-km (0.5-mile) chairlift. Erciyes, near Kayseri has hotels, reliable snowfalls and long runs. Palandöken (see p319) near Erzurum, combines a long season with good runs and accommodation. **İçem Tour** will make bookings at most ski resorts and at Palandöken.

The rapids of the Çoruh River are only for experienced rafters

WHITEWATER RAFTING

In the northeast, the Çoruh River has Grade-5 rapids and is the ideal testing ground for serious rafters. Several overseas agencies offer trips. In contrast, day trips on the Köprülü River (between Antalya and Side) are suitable for families and novices. Many local agencies operate through the hotels or from Antalya city centre. Both **Alternatif Turizm** and **Adrift** offer Çoruh rafting tours; **Mithra Tourism** and others run day tours on the Köprülü River.

PARAGLIDING

Few activities combine the serenity and high altitude scenery of paragliding. Babadağ Mountain, above the coastal resort of Ölü Deniz

The popular Palandöken ski resort near Erzurum

Paragliding above the Mediterranean coast near Ölü Deniz

(see p212) and the mountain ridge above Kaş *(see p214)* both have the ideal updrafts, vistas and landing pads needed for this breathtaking sport. **Skysports** is an experienced and reputable company, offering expert tuition and equipment hire.

HORSE RIDING AND PONY TREKKING

Cappadocia's trails weave through valleys and uplands. **Bagana Ranch** near Antalya offers excellent accommodation, lessons and trail riding. In Istanbul, the **Klassis Golf and Country Club** has an indoor ring and jumping facilities. The best place for trail riding is the Equestrian Centre at Daday, a village near Kastamonu *(see p264)*.

SAILING AND CRUISING HOLIDAYS

The Aegean and western Mediterranean coasts are perfect for cruises aboard comfortable *gulets* (traditional wooden sailing vessels). One- or two-week cruises (called "blue voyages") are an excuse to relax, swim and sunbathe, with occasional forays ashore for shopping or dining. Those with a historical bent can combine one of these cruises with visits to the many fascinating ancient sites along the coast, guided by an expert in Greek and Roman history. The chain of marinas, each about a day's sailing apart, also offer secure moorings and facilities for private yachts. **Arya Yachting** in Bodrum

or the UK's **Alternative Travel Group** offer cruises. **Westminster Classic Tours** have cruises with lectures and site visits. **Gino Group** in Marmaris rents and sells new and good-value reconditioned sailing yachts.

DIVING

Marmaris, Bodrum, Fethiye Kaş and Alanya are all leading diving resorts, offering warm water and perfect conditions with excellent visibility. Here, qualified scuba instructors who are accredited to the Professional Association of Diving Instructors (PADI) offer tuition which takes novices as well as more experienced divers through an internationally recognized diving certificate course.

The **European Diving Centre** in Fethiye and **Ayışığı Diving** in Istanbul both offer high quality tuition and can be recommended.

BEACHES

Turkey's Mediterranean, Aegean and Black Sea coasts have many beaches, offering a wide range of seaside pursuits.

Conditions are generally warm, though the Black Sea can be rough at times, with big waves. The Bodrum peninsula has ideal conditions for sailing and dinghy racing. Water-skiing, water parasailing and jet skiing are offered at major beachside hotels and resorts.

The best place near Istanbul for swimming and watersports such as water-skiing and windsurfing is the Princes' Islands *(see p158)*.

HOTEL-BASED SPORTS

Five-star hotels in the major resorts have good hard tennis courts. Most four- and five-star hotels also organize table tennis, billiards, archery, step dancing and aerobics; even some three-star hotels offer beach volleyball and excellent swimming pools.

GOLF

The mild winter and early spring make golf a year-round sport in Turkey. There are four purpose-built courses at Belek, east of Antalya *(see p224)*. **Pamfilya Travel Agency** can arrange tailor-made tours for amateurs or championship golfers. Near Istanbul, the **Kemer Golf and Country Club** has a championship course.

Diving school in Marmaris, offering courses at all skill levels

HISTORICAL AND CULTURAL TOURS

Given Turkey's wealth and variety of historic sites, it is no surprise that these are what attract most visitors to the country. Tourists who wish to visit ancient and classical sites can do so in the company of an expert in the field. The classical sites of the west and south, Ephesus *(see pp182–3)* and Pergamum *(see pp176–7)* in particular, draw large crowds of visitors, especially in the summer months. Others under excavation, such as Sagalassos and Aphrodisias *(see pp188–9)*, are also very impressive and may be less congested. Some sites, such as Patara and Xanthos *(see p214)* – whose chief tombs are on view in the British Museum – can be visited as part of a *gulet* tour *(see p385)*.

Marble head of Athena

Istanbul deserves careful exploration, particularly its churches, mosques and museums. Since the major sites in Istanbul and around Göreme in Cappadocia are situated fairly close together, walking tours are an attractive option.

Much more recent history is movingly commemorated on the Gallipoli peninsula *(see pp168–9)*, site of some of the fiercest and most tragic battles of World War I.

British Museum Traveller and **Andante Travels** run tours of the classical sites. Andante and **Martin Randall** offer cultural tours of Istanbul. **Troy-Anzac** have been arranging tours to the Dardanelles and Gallipoli for 30 years.

Memorial cemetery, Gallipoli

WILDLIFE TOURS

Turkey's diverse habitats support many endemic plant species, especially of orchids and bulbs, with tulips being perhaps the best-known examples. This diversity, coupled with the country's pivotal position along migration routes between Europe, Asia and Africa, assures the presence of numerous bird species from three continents. In spring and autumn, over 200 species can be spotted in the course of a two-week holiday. DHKD, a local conservation group, records observations and works to preserve habitats such as wetlands. In-depth birding holidays are available from **Greentours**.

The House of the Virgin Mary, near Ephesus *(see p182)*

RELIGIOUS TOURS

Modern-day pilgrims can follow in the footsteps of the Apostle Paul, whose faith led him from Tarsus to Ephesus and beyond. Visitors can tour the "Seven Churches" founded by Paul, and see the small house near Ephesus where the Virgin Mary is said to have spent her last days.

There are also quite a few Armenian and Greek Orthodox churches in Istanbul *(see p114)* that are still active. In southeastern Turkey, there are haunting Syrian Orthodox churches and monasteries.

Pacha Tours offer specialist itineraries for pilgrims who would like to trace the wanderings of St Paul.

A bird hide in the Göksu Delta, near Silifke

RAIL TOURS

Turkey's rail network *(see pp404–05)* is extensive, but has slow trains and outdated rolling stock. However, the old-fashioned couchettes and dining carriages offer a relaxed, interesting way to see the country.

For rail buffs, there is an open-air rail museum at Çamlık, near Selçuk *(see p180)*, with well-marked displays and fine examples of vintage steam locomotives.

The most popular rail trips are from Istanbul to Kars, close to the Armenian border, and from Istanbul to Van in the southeast (which includes a ferry crossing of Lake Van). Both journeys take around three days, and are better undertaken in shorter hops. The Dutch company **SNP Reiswinkel** offers tours of the Istanbul–Kars route, with day breaks for exploration on foot.

OTHER SPECIALIST HOLIDAYS

Several operators offer more specialized holidays that involve particular pursuits such as photography, or painting and sketching. **Kaş Eflatun Art Camp** in Antalya, for example, runs weekly residential painting courses.

Several other companies have begun to use Turkey's relaxed holiday atmosphere and natural beauty to offer breaks which include such activities as yoga, massage, tai chi and meditation. For details on active holidays try **Exclusive Escapes**.

DIRECTORY

MINISTRY OF TOURISM
(For general information)
İsmet İnönü Bul 5,
Bahçelievler, Ankara.
Tel (0312) 212 83 00.
Fax (0312) 213 98 00.
www.kulturturizm.gov.tr

ADVENTURE TRAVEL COMPANIES

Bougainville
İbrahim Sercin Cad 10, Kaş.
Tel (0242) 836 37 37.
www.bougainville-turkey.com

Exodus
Grange Mills, Weir Road,
London, SW12 ONE, UK.
Tel (44) 020 8675 5550.
Fax (44) 020 8673 0779.
www.exodus.co.uk

Türkü Turizm
İnönü Cad 47,
Çamlihemşin, Rize.
Tel (0464) 651 72 30.
Fax (0464) 651 75 70.
www.turkutour.com

WALKING AND TREKKING

Exodus
(see Adventure Companies)

Trekking in Turkey
www.trekkinginturkey.com

World Expeditions
Level 5, 71 York St,
Sydney, NSW 2000,
Australia.
Tel (61) 2 2870 84 00.
www.worldexpeditions.com

MOUNTAINEERING, CLIMBING AND CANYONING

Bukla Tour
Yeni Çarşı Cad 28/11, Galatasaray, Beyoğlu, Istanbul.
Tel (0212) 245 06 35.
www.climbararat.com
www.bukla.com

Get Wet Turizm
Eski Lara Yolu 198/1,
Şirinyalı, Antalya.
Tel (0242) 324 08 55.
www.getwet.com.tr

SKIING

İcem Tour
Mimar Mehmet Aga Cad
34, Sultanahmet, Istanbul.
Tel (0212) 638 19 86.
www.icemtour.com

WHITEWATER RAFTING

Adrift
127 High St,
Hungerford RG17 0DL, UK.
Tel (44) 1488 684 509.

Alternatif Turizm
Çamlık Sok, Marmaris.
Tel (0252) 413 59 94.
www.alternatifraft.com

Mithra Tourism
Kılıçaslan Mah,
Hesapçı Sok 7.
Tel (0242) 248 77 47.
www.mithratravel.com

PARAGLIDING

Sky Sports
Deniz Camp, Ölüdeniz,
Fethiye, Muğla.
Tel (0252) 617 05 11.
www.skysports-turkey.com

HORSE RIDING AND PONY TREKKING

Bagana Ranch
Kemer, Antalya.
Tel (0242) 425 22 70.
Fax (0242) 425 20 55.
www.baganahorseclub.com

Klassis Golf and Country Club
Seyman Köyü, Altıntepe
Mevkii, Silivri (W of Istanbul).
Tel (0212) 710 13 00.
Tel (0212) 748 46 43.

SAILING AND CRUISING HOLIDAYS

Alternative Travel Group
69–71 Banbury Road,
Oxford OX2 6PE, UK.
Tel (44) 1865 315 678.
Fax (44) 1865 315 697.

Arya Yachting
Caferpaşa Cad, Mildos
Elveri 25/1, Bodrum.
Tel (0252) 316 58 54.
www.aryatours.com

Gino Group
Netsel Marina, Marmaris.
Tel (0252) 412 52 20.
www.ginogroup.com

Westminster Classic Tours
Suite 120, 266 Banbury
Road, Summertown,
Oxford OX2 7DL, UK.
Tel (44) 1865 728 565.
Fax (44) 1865 728 575.

DIVING

Ayısığı Diving
Bagdat Cad, İçlaiye Apt
24/4, Kızıltoprak, Istanbul.
Tel (0216) 418 22 44.
www.ayisigidiving.com

Bougainville
(see Adventure Companies)

European Diving Centre
PK 26, Fethiye.
Tel (0252) 614 97 71.
www.europeandiving.co.uk

GOLF

Kemer Golf and Country Club
Göktürk Beldesi,
Kemerburgaz, Istanbul.
Tel (0212) 239 77 70.

Pamfilya Travel Agency
Isıklar Cad 57/B, Antalya.
Tel (0242) 243 15 00.
www.pamfilya.com.tr

HISTORICAL AND CULTURAL TOURS

Andante Travels
Winterbourne Dauntsey,
Salisbury SP4 6EH, UK.
Tel (44) 1980 610 555.
Fax (44) 1980 610 002.

British Museum Traveller
46 Bloomsbury St, London
WC1B 3QQ, UK.

Tel (44) 20 7323 88 95.
Fax (44) 20 7580 86 77.

Martin Randall
Barley Mow Passage,
Chiswick, London W4, UK.
Tel (44) 120 8742 3355.
www.martinrandall.com

Troy-Anzac Tours
Yalı Cad 2, Çanakkale.
Tel (0286) 217 58 90.
www.troyanzac.com

WILDLIFE TOURS

Greentours
Gauledge Lane, Longnor,
Buxton SK17 0PA, UK.
Tel (44) 1298 83563.
@ enquiries@greentours.co.uk

RELIGIOUS TOURS

Pacha Tours
5757 Wiltshire Bd, Suite
645, Los Angeles, USA.
Tel (800) 722 4288 (US).
@ information@pachatours.com

RAIL TOURS

SNP Reiswinkel
Groesveekseweg 181,
Nijmegen, Netherlands.
Tel (30) 024 360 52 22.
Fax (30) 024 360 14 22.

OTHER SPECIALIST HOLIDAYS

Fotografevi
(photographic tours)
Tütüncu Çikmazı 4,
Galatasaray, Beyoğlu.
Tel (0212) 251 05 66.

Kaş Eflatun Art Camp
Çukurbag, Kaş, Antalya.
Tel (0242) 839 54 29.
www.kasartcamp.com

Exclusive Escapes
Alexander House, 15
Princes Road, Richmond,
TW10 6DQ, UK.
Tel (44) 20 8605 3500.
www.exclusiveescapes.co.uk

Spas and Hot Springs

Dervis copper bowl

Turkey's geophysical matrix, which occasionally causes earthquakes and tremors, has an unexpected upside seen in the geothermal springs on which the country seems to be floating. Over 1,000 thermal hot springs (and some icy cold ones) bubble from deep seismic fissures at high temperatures and under great pressure. Roman armies soothed battle wounds in the rich, therapeutic mineral pools. Turkish families have taken the waters for decades. Medical tourism in Turkey is on an upward curve and is marvellously rejuvenating.

Bathers in the rehabilitating calciferous pools at Pamukkale

GEOTHERMAL SPRING RESORTS

Turkey's most potent thermal springs have a high mineral content. There are springs all over the country but very few have accommodation facilities; these are among the best.

Reputed to have soothed the wounds of Agamemnon's Greek soldiers, **Balçova Thermal Hotel** was a pioneer in thermal tourism. The 70°C (158°F) geothermal springs have an exceptional mineral count.

Bursa is one of Turkey's most venerable spa cities. The **Yeni Kaplıca** complex is historic and hot, 85°C (185°F). The spa for men is a traditional 16th-century domed building. Mineral baths and treatments for families are also available.

Of the many geothermal areas north and west of Ankara, Kızılcahamam is best suited to accommodate visitors. Among these are the **Kaplıca Otel** and **Hotel Ab-ı Hayat**.

The mineral waters at **Yalova Thermal Hot Springs** bubble up

at 65° C (149°F) from a deep volcanic source and are considered to be the most remedial in Turkey. The cascading calciferous pools at Pamukkale *(see p186)* are very popular and a short distance away at Karahitit, the waters contain iron and the source is much hotter. **Pam Thermal Hotel** is one of the most professional and well-run of the thermal hotels.

FIVE-STAR SPAS

Turkey's leading spa hotels are located in Istanbul, Ankara and near Bodrum. None has geothermal springs but all offer a sensual and invigorating experience.

The **Kempinski Hotel Barbaros Bay** is a renowned Six Senses Spa, the only in Turkey. Eastern traditions and remedies meet Aegean atmosphere at this fine spa.

One of the country's most spiritual spas is at **Hôtel Les Ottomans**, which adheres to oriental Feng Shui concepts.

Ankara's impressive **Swissôtel Amrita Spa and Wellness Centre** is huge and

combines heavenly, healthy and wholesome treatments.

At the **Ritz Carlton's Laveda Spa**, staff are superbly trained and the focus is on inner health and harmony. The healthy regime promotes relaxation and rejuvenation.

HAMAMS

The traditional Ottoman Turkish bath, or *hamam (see p77)*, was an integral part of the Ottoman social structure, and scrubbing and massages were a ritual procedure. Top spa hotels all have *hamams*. Look for quality in the central stone – it should be transparent, smooth and highly polished. Bursa's **Çakır Hamam** is simple but friendly and dates from 1484. The **Cağaloğlu Baths** in Istanbul are very popular. On the Aegean coast, **Bodrum Hamam** *(see p194)* has a hotel pick-up service.

THERAPEUTIC SPAS

Medical tourism is popular in Turkey and several spas concentrate on specific health problems. **Natur-Med Thermal Springs & Health Resort** is close to the Aegean city of İzmir and offers treatments for, amongst others, chronic disease, weight loss and detoxification. Near Sivas *(see p295)* in the secluded hills are the **Kangal Fish Springs**, a healing centre for psoriasis. The hot springs contain selenium and support a type of fish that nibbles affected skin. Documented since Roman times, **Ayaş İçmece ve Kaplı-caları** is noted for cures and rehabilitation. There are two spas here sharing a thermal source. The waters are so hot

The Turkish hamam at the luxury Hotel Les Ottomans

Clients taking the healing waters of Natur-Med Thermal Spring

and heavily mineralized that drinking and bathing are done under medical supervision.

RURAL SPAS

Ayder is a well-known Black Sea thermal centre, with hot springs ideal for physical therapy and rehabilitation. The facilities bask in pastoral high-altitude surroundings, with about 20 simple pensions.

A delightful spa village of small streams, gardens and rustic bridges forms the backdrop for the thermal waters of **Hamamayağı**. The healing spring contains radon in therapeutic quantities.

A remedial watering hole since the Phrygia era (800 BC), the **Hüdai** thermal waters relieve many of life's modern twinges.

Set in a tranquil, rural location on the banks of the Meander River,

Umut Thermal Resort and Spa is ideal. Standards are high and the atmosphere is clinical but friendly.

Located on the Meander River embankment, **Yenice Ilıcası Kamara İşletmesi** offers 15 basic rooms; however, clientele return regularly for its uncomplicated charm.

AQUA ACCESSORIES

Beautiful spa and *hamam* products can be found in specialist shops. **Derviş Bath Accessories** has two outlets in Istanbul's Grand Bazaar. Close by is another favourite, **Abdullah Natural Products**. On Turkey's Mediterranean coast, **a la turka** has a treasury of delicious bath treats.

Derviş Bath Accessories' products

TOURIST INFORMATION

TRADITIONAL HOT SPRINGS

Balçova Thermal Hotel
Vali Hüseyin Öğütcen Cad 2, Balçova, İzmir.
Tel (0232) 259 01 02.
www.balcovatermal.com

Hotel Ab-ı Hayat
Kazım Karabekir Cad, Kızılcahamam, 06890.
Tel (0312) 736 56 20.
www.ab-ihayat.com

Kaplıca Otel
Yenice Mah, Soğuksu Cad 1, Kızılcahamam, 06890, Ankara.
Tel (0312) 736 16 44.

Pam Thermal Hotel
Beytur Turizm İşletmeleri A. Ş., Karahayıt, Pamukkale.
Tel (0258) 271 41 40.
www.pamhotel.com

Yalova Thermal Hot Springs
Yalova Termal, 77400.
Tel (0226) 675 74 00.
www.yalovatermal.com

Yeni Kaplıca
Kükürtlü Mah, Yenikaplıca Cad 6, Osmangazi, Bursa.
Tel (0224) 236 69 68.

FIVE-STAR SPAS

Hôtel Les Ottomans
Muallim Naci Cad 168, Kuruçeşme, Istanbul.
Tel (0212) 359 15 00.
www.lesottomans.com

Kempinski Hotel Barbaros Bay
Kızılağaç Köyü, Gerenkuyu Mevkii, Yalıçiftlik, Bodrum,
Tel (0252) 311 02 80.
www.kempinski-bodrum.com

Ritz-Carlton
Süzer Plaza Elmadağ, 34367, Şişli, Istanbul.
Tel (0212) 334 44 44.
www.ritzcarlton.com

Swissôtel Amrita Spa and Wellness Centre
Yıldızevler Mah, Jose Marti Cad 2, Çankaya, Ankara.
Tel (0312) 409 36 66.
www.amritaspa.com

HAMAMS

Bodrum Hamam
Cevak Şakir Sok, Fabrika Sok, Bodrum.
Tel (0252) 313 41 29.
www.bodrumhamami.com.tr

Cağaloğlu Baths
Cağaloğlu, Istanbul.
Tel (0212) 522 24 24.
www.cagaloglu hamami.com.tr

Çakır Hamamı
Atatürk Cad 101, Osmangazi, Bursa.
Tel (0224) 221 25 80

THERAPEUTIC SPAS

Ayas İçmece ve Kaplıcaları
Fizik Tedavi Rehabilitasyon Merkezi A.Ş, İçmeler Mevkii Ayaş, Beypazarı, Ankara.
Tel (0312) 718 31 01.
www.ayasicmece.com.tr

Kangal Fish Springs
Sivas. *Tel (0346) 469 11 51.* www.balikli.org

Natur-Med Health Resort
Davutlar, Kuşadası.
Tel (0256) 657 22 80.
www.naturmed.biz

RURAL SPAS

Ayder Turizm A.Ş.
Tel (0464) 657 21 02/03.

Hamamayağı Tesisleri
Between Havza and Ladık.
Tel (0362) 782 00 01/02.

Hüdai Yeni Thermal Hotel
Sandıklı, Afyon.
Tel (272) 535 73 30.
www.hudai.sandikli.bel.tr

Umut Thermal Resort and Spa
Eski Aydın Yolu, Hasköy Tekke Köyü Yolu üzeri 9 km, Kokar Hamam Mevkii, Sarayköy, Denizli.
Tel (0258) 426 10 14.

Yenice Ilıcası Kamara İşletmesi
Yenicekent, Buldan, Denizli.
Tel (0258) 434 6097.

AQUA ACCESSORIES

a la turka
Uzunçarşı, Kaş, Antalya.
Tel (0242) 836 44 47.

Abdullah Natural Products
Halıcılar Cad 58/60, Kapalıçarşı, Istanbul.
Tel (0212) 522 90 78.
www.abdulla.com

Derviş Bath Accessories
Kesiciler Cad 33–35 Kapalıçarşı, Istanbul.
Tel & Fax (0212) 514 45 25. www.dervis.com

SURVIVAL GUIDE

PRACTICAL INFORMATION

Many first-time visitors to Turkey expect the country to be sedate and reserved due to the influence of Islam, so the exuberant and lively character of Turkish life comes as a pleasant surprise. Observing a few customs and learning some basic Turkish words or phrases will get you off to a good start. Show respect for the laws of the country,

Official sign to a tourist sight

as well as for religious differences, culture and class structure. Although you may not agree with the beliefs or politics, opinions are the least acceptable way to promote friendships. With very few exceptions, Turks are uninhibited when it comes to friendship and hospitality and will welcome any effort to appreciate their lifestyle and respect their traditions.

VISAS

Visa requirements change frequently, depending on political circumstances. Most tourist visas are issued for three calendar months, and bar the holder from working at any job. Overstaying the three-month limit incurs a fine, which can escalate alarmingly. Most tourist visas can be obtained at the airport or overland entry point, but the visa process is more complicated if you arrive by sea. Citizens of some countries need to obtain visas before arrival. For up-to-date requirements, contact the Turkish consulate or embassy in your country.

CUSTOMS

Only airports and main road entry points offer full customs service. At major ports or marinas, customs hours are 8:30am–5:30pm weekdays. If you arrive or leave outside these hours in your own yacht or on a ferry, where a visa is required, you will have to pay a fee to activate a customs official.

Import limits are generous, with a few exceptions. You can buy duty-free items at the airport on entering Turkey. However, it is often more economical to buy cartons of cigarettes and local spirits from retail stores rather than from the duty-free shops.

Visitors over 18 years can bring in generous amounts of coffee, perfume (5 bottles),

spirits (5 litres/180 fl oz) and cigarettes (500).

There is no limit on the amount of foreign currency or Turkish lira you can bring into the country, but on leaving you may take out a maximum of US$5,000 (or Turkish lira equivalent). In practice, though, this rule is rarely enforced.

Turkey is extremely strict regarding drugs. Sniffer dogs are in use at Atatürk Airport in Istanbul and will be used at other airports in the future.

Customs service emblem

You need to have a permit if you wish to take antiquities out of Turkey (see p375). Visitors on a three-month tourist visa can bring personal items, including electronics, laptops and their own car. Rules for foreign residents, however, are different. Contact the Turkish consulate or embassy in your country for full details on what can and cannot be brought into Turkey.

ETIQUETTE

Turks tend to dress smartly. In eastern areas, women usually cover their arms and legs in public. Although it is a matter of choice, many women cover their heads. Visitors are not expected to follow suit, but some Turks may be offended at exposed limbs. Mosques are less strict now about covering your head and often supply disposable plastic cover-alls to put over shoes. However, skimpy clothing is unwelcome.

Traditional rules of etiquette and hospitality play an important part in Turkish society. Carpet sellers can be annoying, but always try to remain polite but firm. Always show respect for Atatürk (see p394), whose picture you will see often.

Gay and lesbian visitors are unlikely to experience problems, but overt displays of affection are best kept to a minimum. Homosexual culture is not new to Turkey, and Istanbul in particular has a lively gay scene.

Covering the head is a matter of personal choice for Turkish women

◁ **Boats in the harbour at Alanya, with the 13th-century Red Tower in the background**

Bazaar shops in Kayseri, Cappadocia

LANGUAGE

Even if you learn only a few Turkish words, the effort will be worth it. Turks will respect any attempt at their difficult language. In cities, English-speakers can always be found. Menus are printed in several languages, and most shopkeepers can speak one other language.

PUBLIC CONVENIENCES

Public toilets are marked *Bay* for men and *Bayan* for women. A fee is usually charged for their use. If you are squeamish about using the old-fashioned squat toilets, you can go to any restaurant, hotel or café and ask to use their modern flush toilets. Motorway service areas have pristine washroom facilities for which there is no charge.

SMOKING

Smoking is now prohibited in government offices, on public transport, including dolmuşes and intercity buses, on all Turkish Airlines domestic flights and inside airport terminals. Restaurants are beginning to have sections for non-smokers and some hotels maintain non-smoking rooms or floors.

OPENING HOURS

Turkey generally follows western working hours. Banks and offices are open from 9am to 5pm, although half-hour variations are common. Government offices close between noon and 1pm; so do some banks. Most official businesses are closed on weekends. In tourist areas, however, post offices often stay open seven days a week and until late at night.

Officially, museums in Turkey are open from 9am to 5pm, but in practice opening hours vary considerably, as does the statutory closure day during the week. Some smaller establishments close for an hour at lunch time. Major museums are usually open all year round, but some small sites may close during the winter months. Local tourist offices have access to the latest information and it is recommended that visitors double-check opening times before setting out on any sightseeing expedition.

TIME

Turkey is two hours ahead of Greenwich Mean Time and British summer time. New York is 6 hours behind and Los Angeles is 9 hours behind.

ELECTRICITY

Turkey's electrical current is 220–240 volts AC. Plugs have two round pins, but two separate diameters, which fit all local sockets and most European two-pin plugs. Bring a universal adaptor for other voltages.

Power cuts are a fact of life, particularly outside the cities and also during periods of very hot weather, when the increased demand for air conditioning causes problems.

Personal Security and Health

Emblem of the Turkish police

For the sensible visitor, Turkey is as safe to visit as anywhere else. Bear in mind that the country has undergone rapid social change in a relatively short period, and urban centres bulge with people who have recently abandoned traditional ways of life. Unemployment is high, and there is a huge gap between rich and poor. Health care is of a high standard, with a thriving private health sector alongside the state-run system. It is essential to keep basic immunization up to date before you travel. Turkey is not as hygiene-conscious as you might expect an Islamic country to be.

POLICE

There are a number of police forces in Turkey, with responsibilities varying from traffic control to rapid response motorcycle units (Dolphin Police). The Jandarma, who are attached to the army, are responsible for policing rural areas. Special tourism police *(Turizm Polisi)* operate in Istanbul. In smaller towns, the *Emniyet Polisi* (Security Police) carry out law-enforcement duties.

It is obligatory to carry some form of identification with you in Turkey. Police or Jandarma carry out spot checks on cars, buses and trucks. A passport or driving licence is usually sufficient.

Police officers are usually very helpful, but should you need help, the first place to contact is your embassy. Most countries have missions in Ankara and some have consulates in Istanbul *(see p369)*, İzmir or Antalya.

Badge of Dolphin rapid-reaction unit

PERSONAL SECURITY

Do not wander off into lonely places, wherever you are. Do not pick up hitchhikers or offer to take people you don't know across the border. Never act as a courier for anyone else, into or out of Turkey.

As Turkey continues to adopt Western standards, petty crime has also risen. Ankara is the safest city but in other areas you should be vigilant. Picking pockets and snatching purses are growth industries, often from speeding vehicles. Walk on the inner area of the pavement and use a large, secure purse, as Turkish women do.

It is not a good idea to leave valuables lying around at any time in your hotel. Police are helpful but petty criminals are rarely apprehended. Whether you are male or female, you should avoid lonely areas. This includes some tourist attractions. It is always best to travel with others in a group if you are planning to visit remote areas.

TURKISH TRADITIONS

The army, Atatürk and the Turkish flag are three of the fundamental symbols of Turkish identity. Disrespect towards any of these is seen as an insult to the state.

PHOTOGRAPHY

Always ask permission before taking photographs in any public places or of individuals. Taking photos of military installations is strictly forbidden.

HEALTH AND HYGIENE

Bottled spring water

Before arriving in Turkey, be sure that your basic inoculations (diphtheria, polio, typhoid and tetanus) are all up to date. Check with your doctor about hepatitis A and hepatitis B. Mosquitoes are an annoying problem along most of the south coast. Few appear to spread malaria but many people are allergic to bites. Use mosquito repellent.

Some visitors experience digestive upsets due to the amount of oil used in Turkish cooking. Try to eat lightly for the first few days and keep alcohol intake to a minimum.

Bottled water is safer to drink than tap water. Grilled meat is sometimes served lightly cooked. Ask for it *iyi pişmiş* (well cooked) and avoid foods that may have been sitting in the sun.

Security policeman   **Traffic policeman**   **Dolphin policeman**

Turkish Security Police *(Emniyet Polisi)* patrol car

State ambulance in Istanbul

HOSPITALS

The Turkish health system has public and private hospitals. Private hospitals are well equipped and staffed, and are more comfortable than the state hospitals. Private hospitals may run their own ambulance services. Doctors at private hospitals are more likely to speak foreign languages. Go to http://ankara.usembassy.gov/consular/acdoclist for lists of hospitals.

It is strongly recommended that you take out both travel and medical insurance before you leave, or a policy that incorporates both. It may also be useful to have a policy that covers repatriation in an emergency. The state health system has few reciprocal agreements with other countries. You have to pay for treatment and then claim the amount back from your insurance company. State and private medical facilities accept major credit cards.

PHARMACIES

Most non-prescription medications are available from an *eczane* (pharmacy or chemist) at reasonable prices. Visitors are allowed to bring into the country sufficient

Typical sign for a pharmacy in Istanbul

quantities of medications that are required regularly. Turkish pharmacists are well-trained and professional; most are also trained to give *iğne* (injections). Every area district has a *nobetci eczane* (duty pharmacist) outside normal business hours. The name is usually posted in a pharmacy window or displayed prominently in a public place.

Condoms are readily and easily available in almost all pharmacies, even if not on display. Ask for a *prezervatif*.

ANIMALS AND INSECTS

By far the worst pests are mosquitoes, particularly in coastal areas. Many local repellents are available, such as Esem-Mat. Immunization clinics are the best place to buy anti-mosquito supplies. The Turkish for mosquito is *sivrisinek* (sharp fly).

At the seaside, watch out for a sea anemone known as *karadikiş* or *deniz kestanesi* (sea chestnut) clinging to the rocks. If you step on one, do not try to extract the quills; seek medical attention right away. In rocky terrain, look out for scorpions and snakes.

Don't approach, encourage or pet stray animals. If you are hiking in remote areas, you may come across shepherd dogs. These look fierce but are rarely aggressive unless you come between the dog and his flock.

Banking and Currency

There is no limit on the amount of currency (foreign or Turkish) you can bring into Turkey. By 2004 the inflation rate dropped from 100 per cent to about 9 per cent, and it remains in single figures. A new currency, the New Turkish Lira (TL), was introduced in 2005, a source of pride for all Turks, as the many zeros that humbled the old currency were eliminated. Exchange rates have also stabilized but, for a higher rate, try to change money once you are in Turkey. Most trading establishments accept cash in major foreign currencies. Visitors will have few problems in paying by credit card or using automated teller machines (ATMs).

Cash dispenser with instructions in a range of languages

BANKS

Banking hours run from Monday to Friday, 9am to 12:30pm, and from 1:30 to 5:30pm. Some banks, such as Garanti Bankası, remain open over the lunch hour and are experimenting with Saturday trading. Queues are usually quite long in banks and you have to take a number and wait for service, so you will need to be patient and allow extra time for carrying out any banking transactions.

Several Turkish banks have outlets at airports, offering a full range of banking services. If you are leaving Turkey by air, do note that some airports have no banking facilities after you have passed through the customs and security check.

CHANGING MONEY

Exchange bureaux (*döviz para*) are found in most towns, and this is the most reliable way to change money at a reasonable rate of exchange. These offer the best rates for foreign currencies, usually without the tedium of queuing at a bank. Rates are displayed daily on an electronic board. Exchange bureaux are usually open Monday to Saturday, but if you go before about 10am you will get the previous day's exchange rate.

Hotels, some shops and other retail outlets will change money for you, but the rate will not be to your advantage. If you are bargaining for an item, remember that foreign currency is acceptable, if not preferable, and makes a good bargaining lever. It is always a good idea to bring some foreign notes with you to Turkey for such eventualities.

CREDIT CARDS AND DEBIT CARDS

ATMs are found all over Turkey, even in remote, small towns. They are often located at an outer entrance to a bank, to provide 24-hour service. Machines accept Visa and MasterCard (Access) and American Express, as well as debit cards for many international banks, such as HSBC and Citibank. Before leaving, ask your bank if its card is accepted internationally. It may be necessary to activate this service if you have not used it before.

The most versatile ATMs are those with the Cirrus or Plus interbank logo. Some banks, like Yapı Kredi, have an 800 TL daily withdrawal limit at ATM cash dispensers. If your daily withdrawal limit is less than this, however, don't exceed it, or your card might be blocked.

You can use credit cards all over Turkey to pay for almost anything, including intercity bus tickets, car rental and meals. Be aware, however, that smaller establishments may not take cards in winter, even if they do so in summer.

There is no commission on credit cards; even places that used to charge it, such as petrol stations, now display signs saying *kredi kartı komisyonu sıfırdır* (without commission). If you buy an airline ticket from a travel agent, however, they will charge about 3 per cent commission on the fare.

TRAVELLER'S CHEQUES

ATMs have practically made the use of traveller's cheques obsolete. The only place to cash traveller's cheques without fuss is at the arrivals terminal at Atatürk International Airport. Some banks (though not all) will cash traveller's cheques, but will almost certainly charge a hefty commission.

DIRECTORY

EXCHANGE BUREAUX

Bamka Döviz
Cumhuriyet Cad 23,
Taksim, Istanbul.
Tel (0212) 253 55 00.

Çetin Döviz
İstiklal Cad 39, Beyoğlu,
Istanbul.
Tel (0212) 252 64 28.

Para Döviz
Nuruosmaniye Sok 36,
Kapalı Çarşı,
Istanbul.
Tel (0212) 513 16 43.

CREDIT CARD HOTLINES

American Express
Tel (0212) 283 22 01.

Diners Club, MasterCard and VISA
Tel (0212) 211 59 60.

TAX

Value-added tax (KDV in Turkish) is included in all prices. It is currently 18 per cent. If you need a receipt for purchases, ask for a *fiş*; if you require an invoice, ask for a *fatura*. For information on tax refunds, see p354.

CURRENCY

The currency of Turkey is known as the Turkish Lira, abbreviated to TL or, more officially, TRY (credit card statements will show the latter).

The coins are made of nickel and are similar to the Euro. They are known as *kuruş*. The higher denomination notes contain many advanced and high technology security features that are not visible to the naked eye. The old-style notes ceased to be legal tender on 1 January 2006.

Banknotes

The Turkish banknotes come in seven denominations: 200 TL, 100 TL, 50 TL, 20 TL, 10 TL, 5 TL and 1 TL, and each denomination has its own distinctive colour. All the notes display the familiar image of the head of Atatürk on one side, with some of Turkey's most important touristic highlights on the reverse side.

1 lira

5 lira

10 lira

20 lira

50 lira

100 lira

Coins

There are six coins now in circulation, ranging in value from 1 kuruş, 5 kuruş, 10 kuruş, 25 kuruş, and 50 kuruş to 1 TL (100 kuruş). Those shown here (at their actual sizes) are for 1 lira and 50 kuruş.

50 kuruş   1 lira

Communications

PTT sign on a letter box

The telephone and postal services in Turkey used to operate as a single unit until 1996, when they were split up to create Türk Telekom (telephone) and the PTT (the postal service). To prepare for privatization, the telephone monopoly has made tremendous improvements. Over 80 per cent of Turkey has fibre optic technology and major cities enjoy high-speed Internet access and broadband connections. Many businesses have numbers beginning with '444' and you can call one contact office in any local area.

Post Offices, or PTT, can be used for sending letters; service is slow, though reliable. Making phone calls from their counter-top metred phones is economical. Many PTT outlets change foreign currency and have Western Union service for sending and receiving money.

USING A CARD PHONE

1 Lift the handset and wait for the dialling tone.

2 Insert your card.

3 Select instructions in the language of your choice and then dial the telephone number you require, using the key pad above the card slot.

4 To make another call press the follow-on button (second from left). If you have finished, replace the handset and the card will be ejected.

USING PUBLIC TELEPHONES

Telephone calls can be made either from public call boxes, post offices or small but convenient telephone "boutiques". Mobile (cellular) phones have helped to relieve some of the congestion at public call boxes, which are usually grouped in main squares, at transport hubs or near post offices. The most economical way to telephone locally or internationally is by using a phonecard.

The phonecards have a concealed scratch-off code and this allows you to make phone calls locally and internationally from any land line in Turkey. Cards come in units of 30, 60, 100, 120 and 180. These can be purchased from all post offices and, for an additional charge, from street sellers and kiosks. After you pick up the receiver, the display screen will prompt you to select the language of

Logo found on Turkish phonecards

your choice, and insert your card. A panel then shows the number of units remaining on your card.

Some telephones in airports or luxury hotels will accept credit cards such as Visa and MasterCard. Generally, however, local telephones are programmed to accept local credit cards only.

Note that if you are calling from a mobile (cell) phone or calling a number in a different province, you must dial 0 first, followed by the appropriate area code, then the seven-digit phone number.

MOBILE PHONES

Turkey has many mobile (cellular) phone operators but the main one is Turkcell. Turkcell has GSM roaming agreements with 180 countries on three different MHz bands, which means that most people can use their existing cellphone as they would at home. The exception is North America, where wireless standards and frequencies are less integrated with global ones, even if you have a triband mobile phone. To contact Turkcell call 444 0 532. Alternatively, try TurkTelekom on 444 1 444.

With few formalities, visitors have a flexible option of prepaid SIM cards from all the local mobile operators and these can be used with any handset (but you must use the telephone number assigned to individual cards). Units can be topped up at many convenient kiosks, bufés and teleboutiques. These cards self-cancel if not used within three months.

Mobile phone company logo

Some companies offer a GSM phone rental service, which can usually be arranged at hotels. Calls are likely to be expensive.

COUNTRY DIRECT SERVICE

If your local telephone company has a direct-access calling card, you can use this from Turkey (including pay telephones and hotels) to contact an operator in your own country. Calls will be billed to your home number at your local international tariff (and discount) rate. As Turkish telephone rates are relatively expensive, it is well worth obtaining details about country-direct services from your telephone provider.

REACHING THE RIGHT NUMBER

• Istanbul is divided into two area codes:
0212 (European side)
0216 (Asian side)
• To call a number on the same side of Istanbul, dial only the seven-digit number. To call the other side, dial as intercity.
• To call another city in Turkey, dial the four-digit area code before the seven-digit number, for example, 0224 for Bursa.
• To call Turkey from abroad, the country code is 90, omit the zero of the local area code, followed by the seven-digit number.
• For international calls, dial 00 followed by the country code: Canada 1; Republic of Ireland 353; United Kingdom 44; US 1; South Africa 27; Australia 61; New Zealand 64.

OPERATOR SERVICES

Directory Enquiries
Tel 11811.

Inter-City Operator
Tel 131.

International Operator
Tel 115.

Wake-Up Call Service
Tel 135.
Note: only international operators are guaranteed to speak English.

An Internet café in İzmir, one of thousands all over Turkey

INTERNET ACCESS

Internet cafés have sprung up all over Turkey. If you need to find one, ask at the local tourist office. Charges are only a few dollars for an hour of browsing; for e-mail access, you will be charged for the time used. Travel agents will sometimes let you use their Internet facilities.

Foreign newspapers and magazines on sale in Ankara

NEWSPAPERS AND MAGAZINES

Many English-language publications are available in major centres in Turkey via newsagents or Dünya outlets. Foreign-language newspapers are available the following day from newsstands. Weekly magazines such as *Time* and *Newsweek* are readily found, even if less prominently, outside Istanbul and Ankara.

POSTAL SERVICES

Postcards or letters sent from Turkey to Europe or North America automatically go via air mail. Letters, postcards and smaller packages are weighed at post offices and charged according to a price scale which may or may not be on display.

The PTT has a monopoly on all mail, and post offices are the only places to send and receive any mail. Outside Istanbul, the PTT acts for the customs office by collecting duties on parcels. Fees are levied arbitrarily on incoming mail and parcels, and even sometimes on *poste restante* letters. If you are sending a package, leave it open for inspection. Mail is delayed for weeks when items have to be opened, inspected and signed by customs. Do not send anything valuable or urgent by post. Tourist offices sometimes receive mail for visitors; this option usually ensures that such items are received promptly and intact.

Letters between Turkey and Europe average 7–10 days in transit. For other continents, count on 14 days or more. A recorded delivery service (called APS) is available from post offices, with delivery in three days within Turkey. Local courier companies deliver inland letters and parcels in a day or so at a comparable price.

Old-style postage stamps in 500,000, 300,000, 250,000 and 750,000 lira denominations

TRAVEL INFORMATION

The easiest way to get to Turkey is to fly directly to Istanbul. Turkish Airlines (THY) has regular, direct flights from 113 destinations in Europe, North America and Asia. Several major European carriers, including Lufthansa and KLM, also fly direct to Istanbul. Most air traffic uses Atatürk airport on the European side of Istanbul, but a handful of char-

Emblem of Turkish Airlines

ter firms now use the second international airport, Sabiha Gökçen, near Pendik on the Asian side of the city.

Turkish Airlines operates an extensive domestic network, with routes focused on Istanbul or Ankara. Flights between İzmir and Antalya, or Erzurum and Samsun, for example, will invariably go via Istanbul or Ankara.

ARRIVING BY AIR

Most visitors will arrive at Istanbul's Atatürk Airport (Atatürk Havalimanı). For onward travel within Turkey, you will have to change to a domestic **Turkish Airlines**' (THY) flight or, alternatively, use one of the new low-cost domestic carriers *(see opposite)*. Atatürk Airport has a separate terminal for domestic flights.

Major European carriers, such as **Lufthansa, KLM, Austrian Airlines** and **British Airways**, all have at least one flight daily to Istanbul. **American Airlines**, Qantas and other international carriers also serve Istanbul, though not always by direct flight.

May to October is peak season, but flights tend to fill up during school or religious holidays (including the annual Muslim pilgrimage to Mecca, the date of which varies with the lunar calendar).

ATATURK AIRPORT

Passengers arrive at the *dış hatları* (international) terminal. If you are travelling

The spacious modern arrivals hall at Atatürk Airport

on to another destination in Turkey, you will be taken as a transit passenger to the *iç hatları* (domestic) terminal.

Depending on which airline or charter company you are flying with, you will clear customs *(gümrük)* either in Istanbul or at your final destination. There are few customs formalities for foreigners entering Turkey for short stays of up to three months. Remember that you can buy duty-free goods upon entry. For further details on customs allowances, see p368.

If you have cleared customs in Istanbul and are continuing your journey as a domestic passenger, a shuttle *(minibüs)*

service is provided to take you to the domestic terminal. There is a small charge for the inter-terminal shuttle bus. It is sensible to use this service as taxis are more expensive and are generally reluctant to make the five-minute journey.

CHARTER FLIGHTS AND PACKAGE HOLIDAYS

Arriving on a charter flight is generally a cheaper option. Most charter flights land in Istanbul, many of them at Sabiha Gökçen Airport. Sun Express and Öger Tours, fly direct to Bayındır International Airport in Antalya. Sun Express runs regular direct charter flights with Turkish Airlines to Antalya from Frankfurt and London. Öger Tours operates from Hamburg, with a stop at Munich.

The western Mediterranean region is served by Dalaman Airport, which handles mainly short take-off and landing (STOL) charter flights from western Europe. The south coast airport, Bodrum-Milas, also handles many charter flights for the surrounding Aegean region.

Taxi rank outside the domestic terminal at Atatürk Airport

DOMESTIC AIR TRAVEL

All major centres in Turkey are linked by the **Turkish Airlines**' network. The national carrier runs summer and winter schedules to its 35 local destinations and adds extra flights for the busy summer season. Bookings can be made via travel agents or online via their website.

A Turkish Airlines Airbus A-340 taking off

Almost all internal air traffic is routed in and out of Ankara or Istanbul. Flights between other cities can involve extended connection time in either of these hubs. Smaller cities have fewer flights and, off-season, only on certain days of the week. Check shedules carfully.

There are many low-cost carrier companies which compete with Turkish Airlines on domestic routes. Three companies in particular are very reliable: **Fly Airlines, Atlas Jet** and **Onur Air**, all of which have daily flights to and from the major cities in Turkey at much reduced rates. Their fleets are brand new and have good safety records. You will see many agents selling tickets for these and other new airline companies, particularly in Istanbul and Ankara. Budget carriers all post lower off-season fares (November-April).

FLYING WITHIN TURKEY

If you are taking a domestic flight, you have to be at the airport an hour before the flight leaves. If you have no baggage to check, you can arrive later. If this the case, go to the counter displaying the *el bagajı* (hand luggage) sign. Try to go through the security check as early as possible, as this gets extremely busy. For security reasons, you will be required to identify your bags to the baggage handling crew before being allowed to take your seat on the aircraft.

On domestic flights, there is little difference between business class and economy. If economy is full, you can usually buy a ticket in business class at a higher price, but both classes offer identical three-abreast seating and a boxed snack. There is no smoking on any domestic flight, and usually no alcohol is served.

AIRPORT TRANSFERS

To get to and from Atatürk Airport or Sabiha Gökçen Airport and Istanbul, a shuttle bus service run by **Havaş** *(see p387)* operates from both domestic and international terminals to and from Taksim Square *(see p111)*. The Metro *(see p410)* also links Atatürk Airport with the city centre. Travel five stops to Zeytinburnu, then change to the tramway to the main tourist area of Sultanahmet Square. The tramway operating between Atatürk Airport and Aksaray is the cheapest way of reaching Istanbul. Taxis, plentiful at both airports, are a more expensive option. All major car rental companies have offices grouped around the Arrivals Lounge. For information on car rental, see p382.

Major hotels will send a private driver if you request this in advance.

DIRECTORY

TURKISH AIRLINES

Atatürk Bulvarı 154,
Kavıklıdere, Ankara.
Tel *(0312) 428 02 00.*
Fax *(0312) 428 16 81.*
www.thy.com
@ abayka@thy.com

Cumhuriyet Cad 199–201,
3rd floor, Harbiye, Istanbul.
Tel *(0212) 225 05 56.*
(ticket sales)
Tel *(0212) 663 63 63.*
(reservations)

125 Pall Mall, London,
SW1Y 5AE.
Tel *(020) 766 93 00.*
Fax *(020) 796 17 38.*
www.thy.com

OTHER CARRIERS SERVING TURKEY

Atlas Jet
Tel *(0216) 444 03 87 (24 hrs).*
www.atlasjet.com

American Airlines
www.americanairlines.
com

Austrian Airlines
www.aua.com

British Airways
www.britishairways.com

Fly Airlines
Florya Cad, Cevizli Sokak
No. 2, Florya, Istanbul.
Tel *(0212) 424 38 37, 444 43 59.*
www.flyair.com

KLM (Royal Dutch Airlines)
www.klm.com

Lufthansa
www.lufthansa.com

Onur Air
Tel *(0212) 662 97 97.*
www.onurair.
com.tr

AIRPORT INFORMATION

Atatürk Airport
Tel *(0212) 663 64 00.*
www.ataturkairport.com

Lost and Found *(not luggage)*
Tel *(0212) 663 25 50.*

Bayındır International Airport
Antalya.
Tel *(0242) 330 36 00.*
Tel *(0312) 398 01 00.*
www.aytport.com

Esenboğa Airport
Ankara.
Tel *(0312) 428 02 00.*

Havaş Airport Bus (Shuttle Service)
Tel *(0212) 465 47 00.*
www.havasturizm. com.tr

Sabiha Gökçen Airport
Pendik, Istanbul.
Tel *(0216) 585 50 00.*
www.sgairport.com

Travelling By Bus and Dolmuş

Varan bus company logo

Few enterprises in Turkey are as well-developed or efficient as its intercity bus travel service. Bus or coach is the most comfortable way of getting to just about any destination in the country, and even beyond. For a more informal travelling experience, and over shorter distances, a *dolmuş* (shared taxi or minibus) is the most cheerful, versatile and cheapest way to get around. Travelling in a dolmuş may seem a bit intimidating, but if you state your destination clearly to the driver, you should enjoy the journey.

Bus passengers visiting a roadside craft stall in Cappadocia

TRAVEL BY BUS

The profusion of coach or long-distance bus companies gives the impression that bus travel is a highly competitive business. In fact, the entire industry operates on a franchise system: bus companies maintain relatively uniform fares based on petrol (gas) prices and the inflation rate. The system ensures that bus operators share revenue.

The leading intercity coach firms are **Kâmil Koç, Varan** and **Ulusoy**. They run regular schedules with teams of well-trained drivers, comfortable vehicles, on-board refreshments and videos. Most buses stop for 30 or 40 minutes every four hours or so, and some companies even operate their own immaculate service areas. Journeys of more than 10 hours tend to be made overnight.

Kâmil Koç, the oldest of these three companies, enjoys a reputation for reliability and safety. Ulusoy have linked up with Dedeman Hotels to offer a 50 per cent discount to their passengers who stay at a

hotel in the Dedeman chain. As you move eastwards in Turkey, the intercity bus network becomes sparser, with services offered by just a few local firms. These buses are just as comfortable, but the distances are greater and the passengers and their parcels decidedly "eastern".

BOOKING AND SPECIAL SERVICES

When travelling by bus, it is essential to book your tickets in advance, particularly on weekends or during any school or religious holidays (*see p36*). Several bus firms have now set up facilities for online booking and payment.

Varan run regular services to Athens and other European destinations such as Bologna,

Innsbruck, Salzburg and Vienna. Varan have also teamed up with the Greater Istanbul Metropolitan Council to co-ordinate services with the Istanbul Sea Bus Service (IDO). This makes it possible to book either through Varan, the ferry services or their combined services. You can book online in English on the company website. Details of schedules and seasonal fares are also available. You can use your mobile phone to get booking and schedule information via WAP protocol.

ON THE BUS

Seating on buses is allocated on a same-sex basis, with exceptions made for married couples. Alcohol and smoking (*see p393*) are not allowed. The only person exempt from the no-smoking rule is the bus driver, but the modern air-control systems mean that you will probably not notice.

Intercity bus interior, with reclining seats

INSURANCE

The leading bus companies offer travel insurance, but the proverbial small print, in fact, details a limit on claims.

BUS STATIONS

In almost all Turkish cities, the *otogar* (bus station) is now located well away from the city centre. Typically, the

Luxury bus operated by Kâmil Koç

Bodrum bus station, with buses from several different companies

company you are travelling with provides a free shuttle service from city-centre pick-up points to the main *otogar*. The exception is in Bursa, where the municipality runs a shuttle service to and from the central terminal from convenient points all over the city.

The main intercity *otogar* in Istanbul, **Esenler**, is 10 km (6 miles) northwest of the city. In Istanbul, coach companies ferry passengers to and from their own terminals (close to the motorway) on the Asian and European sides of the city. There is also a bus terminal in **Harem** on the Asian side.

Sign for a dolmuş stop

TRAVEL BY DOLMUŞ

In Istanbul, a dolmuş means two things: a shared taxi that follows a fixed route and departs when full *(see p408)*, and the cream-coloured (or sometimes blue) minibuses which follow fixed routes according to hectic schedules and are generally chock-a-block with passengers. These are particularly convenient for getting to areas outside the city centre. In the past, dolmuş passengers would travel in huge 1950s-vintage Chrysler or Chevrolet cars. Today minibuses or sport utility vehicles (SUVs) have largely replaced these enormous, fuel-hungry dinosaurs.

Outside Istanbul, however, a dolmuş simply means a minibus. These tend to be cream-coloured, and serve numerous points in the city centre. Dolmuş stops are indicated by rectangular blue signs bearing a large "D" on a white panel. Destinations are also shown on the front or side of the vehicle, and these relate to *mahallesi* (districts) rather than streets.

Dolmuş fares are cheaper than the normal bus prices. Payment is by Turkish lira in cash, not tickets or electronic smart tickets. Note that if you sit in the front, you will be responsible for passing fares and change to and fro from passengers to the driver.

The best thing about travel by dolmuş is that you can usually alight wherever you want. Say "Müsait bir yer'de" (at the next convenient point) or "İnecek var" (somebody wants to get off). Dolmuşes can often get uncomfortably crowded, but drivers know city areas intimately and can generally drop you off right at your required stop.

Typical dolmuş as seen on routes in all large towns and cities of Turkey

DIRECTORY

BUS STATIONS	BUS COMPANIES	Kâmil Koç	Tel 444 0 562
Esenler	**Ulusoy**	Genel Müdürlük, İnönü Cad, Kâmil Koç, İş Merkezi 16, Kat 4, Bursa.	*(throughout Turkey).*
(International Istanbul Bus Terminal, NW of city centre) Bayrampasa.	**Tel** *(0212) 471 71 00*		**Varan**
☐ *5am–midnight daily.*	*(Istanbul).*	**Tel** *(0212) 658 20 00 12 11 (Istanbul).*	**Tel** *(0212) 444 89 99 (Istanbul).*
Tel *(0212) 658 00 36.*	**Tel** *(0242) 331 13 10*	**Tel** *(0224) 261 50 00 (Bursa).*	**Tel** *(0312) 224 00 43 (Ankara).*
Harem	*(Antalya).*	**Tel** *0252 614 19 73 (Fethiye).*	**Tel** *(0232) 472 03 89-90 (Izmir).*
(International Istanbul Bus Terminal, Asian side).	**Tel** *444 18 88*	**Tel** *(0242) 836 19 49 (Kaş).*	**Tel** *(0242) 331 11 11 (Antalya).*
☐ *5am–midnight daily.*	*(throughout Turkey).*	**Tel** *(0252) 412 06 30 (Marmaris).*	**Tel** *(0252) 316 78 49 (Bodrum).*
Tel *(0216) 333 37 63.*	**www**.ulusoy.com.tr		**www**.varan.com.tr

Travelling by Train and Ferry

Insignia on a TDİ ferry

Turkey's state-owned railway system is not as up-to-date as other European rail networks, but train travel is worth considering, especially if you have time. Most of Turkey's boat traffic is centred on Istanbul's busy waterways. Going by ferry, however, is not the same as a genuine cruise with a private yacht company (see p385). Car ferries from ports in Italy go to several Turkish coastal towns. Arriving by ferry from Brindisi or Venice is a leisurely, if not overly luxurious, experience, but for those who enjoy longer journeys a ferry can be a more memorable and relaxing option than travelling by the usual road or air routes.

Haydarpaşa Station, terminus for trains from Anatolia

TRAVEL BY TRAIN

Turkey's national railway system is run by **Turkish State Railways** (**TCDD** or Türkiye Cumhuriyeti Devlet Demiryolları). It is not necessary to travel far in Turkey to see that the country is ideally suited to train travel, and that there is excellent potential for sightseeing and touring by train. However, the country's rail network has suffered from a lack of new investment. There are a number of scenic tours to Kars, Lake Van, the Southeast Anatolian Project (GAP) and the Black Sea, but these have generally not been planned with the needs of tourists in mind. If time is not a factor and you want to experience a bit of nostalgic meandering, luxuriating in the old-fashioned couchettes and dining cars, then you

Side plate of a locomotive

will be quite delighted by this mode of travel.

Remember that rail travel, like the rest of Turkey, is divided into Thrace (Europe) and Anatolia (Asia). For the bulk of journeys to and from Istanbul, you will be arriving and departing from Haydarpaşa Station (see p125) on the Asian shore of the Bosphorus. Trains serving European destinations leave from

Sirkeci Station (see p76) near the Galata Bridge.

All rail trips can be booked on the TCDD website. However, tickets must be collected from the departure station by the end of the same day. Credit cards are accepted at most intercity train stations.

RAIL ROUTES

The Turkish State Railways network consists of main and regional lines. There are rail links between all of the major cities. However, apart from the upmarket Mavi Tren (Blue Train), which travels between Istanbul and Ankara, most train services are slow and atmospheric.

The Taurus Mountains, which slice Turkey laterally, presented an insurmountable barrier to railway engineers, so there is no rail line along the southern Aegean and Mediterranean coasts. If you want to go to Antalya by train, for example, you have to get off the train at Burdur and continue the 100 km (62 miles) or so to Antalya by bus or taxi. Although much cheaper than other forms of travel, train journeys are also generally much slower.

SERVICE

Meals on Turkish trains are delightful. TCDD dining carriages often have white linen and silver service, and so deserve more than a brief mention. Food is impeccably presented, delicious and, unlike airlines, there are no restrictions on the serving of alcohol. When you purchase

Sleeper carriage on the Ankara–Istanbul express

Car ferry crossing the Dardenelles from Çanakkale

your ticket, make sure that it includes the meal service, if it is available. You can choose the time you want to eat and, once on board, your dining time will be announced.

If you plan to travel to the eastern provinces, note that certain services may be scaled down or not available at all. When you book, make sure you check what services will be provided on the train.

RAIL TOURS

Several foreign tour group operators offer interesting and scenic rail package tours through the Anatolian interior. Such tours combine visits to the major tourist sights with the use of bus and air travel to provide variety and save time where necessary. For more details on specialized rail tours, see p386.

FERRIES

Ferry services are operated by the government-owned **Turkish Maritime Lines** (**TDİ** or Türkiye Denizcilik İşletmesi). TDİ ferries follow routes between the ports of Alanya, Brindisi, Çeşme, Girne (Northern Cyprus), Istanbul, İzmir, Taşucu and Venice. Contact TDİ or one of its authorized agents for the most up-to-date information.

In addition to TDİ, there are a number of local ferries, often privately owned, which operate on the following routes: Istanbul to Trabzon (Mondays only); Marmaris to Rhodes (many services daily by catamaran or hydrofoil); Bodrum to

Kos; Bodrum to Datça; Antalya to Girne (Northern Cyprus); Fethiye to Rhodes; Finike to Rhodes (day visits only, with obligatory same-day return). Note that these are commuter ferry services used by locals and are not necessarily scenic or tourism-oriented. Local tourist offices can provide the latest information.

ISTANBUL FERRIES

Whether they are commuter ferries, high-speed catamarans (sea buses) or car ferries, all of Istanbul's ferry services are run by the Greater Istanbul Municipality in partnership with Turkish Maritime Lines (TDİ) or other operators. For information on ferry services in and around Istanbul, see p409.

Sea bus (Deniz Otobüs) at a ferry dock in Istanbul

DIRECTORY

TRAIN INFORMATION

Turkish State Railways (TCDD)
Talat Paşa Bulvarı,
06330 Gar, Ankara.
Tel (0312) 309 0515, ext 336 and (0312) 311 06 20.

Istanbul (7am–midnight)
Tel (0216) 348 8020, ext 336.
www.tcdd.gov.tr
Information on rail routes, timetables, services, fares, authorized ticket agents, discounts, contact details and many special features in Turkish.

TRAIN RESERVATIONS

Istanbul
Haydarpaşa Station,
8am–6pm (trains to Asia).
Tel (0216) 336 04 75.

Sirkeci Station
7am–midnight (trains to Europe).
Tel (0212) 527 0050/1.

Ankara
Tel (0312) 309 0515.

FERRY INFORMATION

Turkish Maritime Lines (TDİ)
Rıhtım Cad, Merkez Han 4, Karaköy, Istanbul.
Tel (0212) 251 50 00 (with English menu options).

FERRY RESERVATIONS

Tel (0212) 249 92 22 and 293 74 54 (Istanbul).
Tel (0212) 244 02 07 (general information).
Tel (0242) 241 11 20 and 241 26 30 (Antalya).
Tel (0232) 413 02 30.

TDİ AGENTS OUTSIDE TURKEY

Logistic Transport Services srl
c/o Agenzia Marittima Adriatico, Via Provinciale Per Lecce 33, Brindisi, Italy.
Tel (39) 0831 54 83 40.
Fax (39) 0831 54 09 03.

Pacha Tour
61 bis rue du Faubourg Saint-Denis, 75010, Paris, France.
Tel (33) 1 40 22 04 20.
www.beytours.com

Sun Tours
Rossmarkt 6 D 63739, Aschaffenburg, Germany.
Tel (49) 602 125 642 and 602 125 655.
@ info@sun-tours.com

GENERAL TRAVEL INFORMATION AND BOOKINGS

www.neredennereye.com
Rail and ferry timetables and booking information. Also covers bus and air travel. Six languages.

Travelling by Car and Bicycle

Rental agency logo

Both in terms of independence and convenience, you will see far more of the country by car than any other method of touring, although Turkey's high road accident rate may deter some drivers. You can rent a car from one of the international rental firms or bring your own vehicle or caravan.

Turkey is a large country, and places that may appear close on a map can take much longer than expected to reach. Apart from the Trans European Motorway (TEM) system around Istanbul and Ankara, and a motorway network around İzmir, there are few fast highways.

The rugged terrain and long distances make cycling a strenuous way to see the country. However, cyclists will benefit from their curiosity value, and are certain to encounter helpful, friendly people during their journey.

CAR RENTAL

Before contacting one of the well-known car rental agencies, inquire about fly-drive options. These are often more economical than local car rental, and you can pay in your own currency before you depart for Turkey.

To rent a car, you need to have a local driving licence (or an international one) and your passport. To avoid having to pay a large deposit, use a credit card. Drivers must be over 18 years of age.

Make sure you read the fine print on the rental contract: insurance cover may exclude windscreen damage or even theft. Keep your vehicle's *rhusat* (documents) with you at all times and do not leave them unattended in the car. The car will be given to you with an empty tank and you return it the same way. Most hotels can arrange car rental for you.

BRINGING YOUR OWN VEHICLE

If you enter Turkey in your own vehicle, you need to have a valid driving licence and a Green Card to denote international insurance coverage. Documents relating to the car, such as proof of purchase or chassis number, are not required but can be useful. Officially, cars can be brought in for a period of six months, but customs officers often apply arbitrary decisions. On all major motorways and Bosphorus bridge crossings, you will pay a fee, usually taking a ticket at the entry point and paying as you exit. You will see lanes labelled OGS, where tolls are deducted electronically. Foreign visitors cannot use these, so avoid these lanes.

FUEL

Petrol (gas) is easily obtainable, and is sold in leaded octanes of normal and super, and *kurşunsuz* (unleaded). Filling stations do a full service and will usually wash the windscreen too. There are few self-service facilities. Credit cards are accepted without commission *(see p396)*.

Many vehicles now run on Otogaz (liquid petroleum gas), which is cheaper than regular petrol. Top-up outlets have mushroomed, usually at established petrol stations and motorway service areas.

Truck refuelling at a large petrol station near Konya

RULES OF THE ROAD

Vehicles drive on the right and distances are shown in kilometres. Turkish road signs and icons conform to the international standard. It is compulsory to wear a seatbelt. Heavy motoring fines have helped to bring down the accident rate. The police frequently stop cars to check identification; showing a passport or driving licence usually suffices.

TÜRKİYE — Urban and motorway speed limits

Look out for pedestrians, animals, tractors and vehicles without lights. Vehicles often reverse on the motorway hard shoulder if they have overshot their exit. Drivers making a left turn often veer to the right and wait for traffic to pass. Don't assume that you have the right of way: drivers often give way to vehicles entering from the right, even on minor roads. As in many countries, truck drivers rule the road. Park only in designated areas. Tow-away zones are indicated by a break-down-van sign.

Intercontinental traffic crossing the Bosphorus Bridge

EMERGENCIES

If you have an accident, call the police and do not move your vehicle, even if others tell you to do so. Ambulances arrive less quickly than the police, and heavy city traffic can slow their progress. Many Turks display blood group details prominently; in case of a serious accident, this is a sensible precaution.

On secondary roads, local people will generally be very helpful if you have a flat tyre or breakdown. On the motorway system around Istanbul, there are emergency callboxes located every few kilometres, and these will connect you to the police. A local firm called Tur Assist handles recovery services. The **Touring and Automobile Association of Turkey** (TTOK), known simply as Turing, can provide detailed advice on driving in Turkey, transit documents and assistance with breakdowns, accidents and insurance. Your consulate or embassy can be helpful in the event of even a minor emergency.

REPAIRS

Although spare parts can be hard to get in Turkey, Turks are renowned for their ability to fix almost anything (this goes for bicycles, too). Most towns have a designated Sanayi area (industrial zone) or a specialized Oto Sanayi (automotive repair zone) to handle repairs. The standard may not be what you are used to, but it will be enough to get you on your way again.

CYCLING IN TURKEY

It is not difficult to bring a bicycle to Turkey. It can be brought in freely as a personal possession without customs formalities. It is a good idea to bring extra inner tubes and any spares that may be required, particularly for a long-distance tour. It is possible to rent bicycles in

Mountain biking in Kalkan, on the Mediterranean coast

Roadside emergency telephone

Turkey, but this is generally a seasonal activity which is only found in the busier coastal areas.

GETTING AROUND

Because detailed, small-scale maps of Turkey have largely been phased out, your biggest problem will be how to find your way on country roads or to out-of-the-way places. While rural roads make for great adventures, the potholes can be a hazard. Villagers can advise on road conditions in their region, but try to base yourself in a large town where information may be more reliable and available in your own language. Tourist offices or travel agents will also be able to help.

Aegean and Mediterranean coastal areas are the best for cycling; even if you have a stiff uphill climb, there are exhilarating opportunities for freewheeling. Cappadocia is less well known for cycling, but the off-road trails and tracks are more accessible than the coastal areas and the terrain is flatter. Finding your way on unmarked routes will likely present the greatest challenges. Most cycling tours are arranged by travel agents and local tour operators. Bougainville of Kaş *(see p384)* offers mountain biking tours locally and in Cappadocia.

Keep in mind that Turkish drivers may show very little consideration for cyclists.

GETTING AROUND ISTANBUL

There can be few cities in the world that enjoy the variety and choice of transport that is available in bustling Istanbul. However, chronic traffic congestion can make it difficult to get around quickly. The city stretches some 150 km (93 miles) from Tekirdağ in the west almost to İzmit in the east. However, visitors rarely appreciate the real extent of the sprawling metropolis, as most of

Street sign at a junction in central Sultanahmet

the major tourist attractions are confined to compact districts like Sultanahmet, Beyoğlu and Taksim.

Travelling on Istanbul's various modes of public transport can be an exhilarating experience. For instance, the number 40 bus follows a route from Taksim to Tarabya along the Bosphorus, and reveals a side of the city not shown by a Bosphorus boat tour *(see pp126–7)*.

ISTANBUL ON FOOT

The development of semi-pedestrianized areas, such as İstiklâl Caddesi and central Sultanahmet, has made it possible to walk with ease in parts of Istanbul. Visitors can also tour some of the city's less central areas – the antiques shops of Çukurcuma, near Galatasaray, or Eyüp *(see p120)* – without meeting too much traffic.

Wherever you walk in Istanbul, bear in mind that traffic only stops at pedestrian crossings controlled by lights; always make use of pedestrian overpasses and underpasses.

Istanbul, like any major city, has parts that visitors should avoid. If you want to walk through neighbourhoods that are off the usual tourist track, seek the advice of locals and try to avoid walking in unfamiliar streets after dark.

Sign for a pedestrian underpass

TAXIS

Taxi cabs are ubiquitous in Istanbul, and fares are reasonable in relation to other major European cities. Taxis

operate day and night, and can be hailed in the street or found at taxi ranks. Restaurant and hotel staff can always phone for a taxi.

Cabs are bright yellow, with the word "taksi" on a sign on the roof. They take up to four passengers. In all licensed taxis the fare is charged according to a meter. The daytime *(gündüz)* fare applies between 6am and midnight; the night-time *(gece)* rate is 50 per cent higher. If you cross the Bosphorus Bridge in either direction the bridge toll will automatically be added to the fare. The normal procedure for tipping taxi drivers is just to round up the fare to the nearest convenient figure.

Most taxi drivers do not speak much English, if any. You may also find that some drivers are not familiar with routes to lesser-known sights, so it is a good idea to know which part of the city you want to visit and to carry a map with you at all times. It is also advisable to have the name and address of your destination written down in Turkish for you to show.

DOLMUŞES

Dolmuşes are a useful way of getting around outside the city centre. These are the shared taxis with fixed routes. They are cheaper than regular taxis and more frequent than the buses. The word *dolmuş* means "full", because drivers usually wait until every seat is taken before they set off.

Dolmuş ranks are marked by a blue sign with a black "D" on a white background. A main centre for dolmuşes is Taksim. Unlike taxis, they do not add bridge tolls to the standard fare.

For more information on dolmuş travel, see p403.

USEFUL DOLMUŞ ROUTES IN ISTANBUL

Taksim – Ataköy
(from Mete Caddesi)
Taksim – Eminönü
(from İnönü Caddesi)
Taksim – Kadıköy
(behind Atatürk Kültür Merkezi)
Beşiktaş – Taksim
(from Beşiktaş Caddesi)
Eminönü – Topkapı
(from Sobacılar Caddesi)
Kadıköy – Üsküdar
(from Haydarpaşa Rıhtım Caddesi)
Kadıköy – Bostancı
(from Kumluk Meydanı)
Üsküdar – Beykoz
(from Paşa Limanı Caddesi)
Beşiktaş – Sarıyer
(from Barbaros Bulvarı)
Yedikule – Edirnekapı
(the underpass beneath the city walls at Kale İçi)

Licensed Istanbul taxi cab with its registration number on the side

Large commuter ferries docked at the Eminönü ferry piers

FERRIES

Passenger and car ferries ply the Golden Horn and the Bosphorus, linking the Asian and European sides. These are known as *vapur*, and are operated by **Turkish Maritime Lines** (TDİ) *(see p405)*. Fast catamarans, or Deniz Otobüsü (sea buses), also use these routes. These services are operated by the municipal-owned **Istanbul**

Sea Bus Service (İDO). There are ferry terminals at Karaköy, Eminönü, Beşiktaş and Ataköy on the European side. The quays at Üsküdar, Harem, Kadıköy and Bostancı serve the Asian side *(see map below)*. Commuter ferries run every 15 or 20 minutes, and sea buses less frequently. To explore other alighting points along the Bosphorus, be sure to look at a timetable from TDİ or İDO, as stops along

the upper reaches of the Bosphorus can be infrequent. Don't rule out taking a boat up one side of the Bosphorus and coming back by bus.

From the western side of the Galata Bridge, there are a number of firms offering short, inexpensive excursions up the Bosphorus. These are full of local people, and make for a thoroughly rewarding experience. If you decide to book a private cruise through a tour company, be sure to use a reputable one, such as **Hatsail Tourism** or **Sultan Kayıklari**.

FERRY TICKETS

For all local ferry journeys, you can purchase a flat-fare ticket *(jeton)* from the booth *(gişe)* at the ferry pier or at a slightly higher price from the street vendors who sit nearby. AKBIL electronic tickets can also be used.

To enter the pier, simply put the *jeton* or ticket into the slot beside the turnstile.

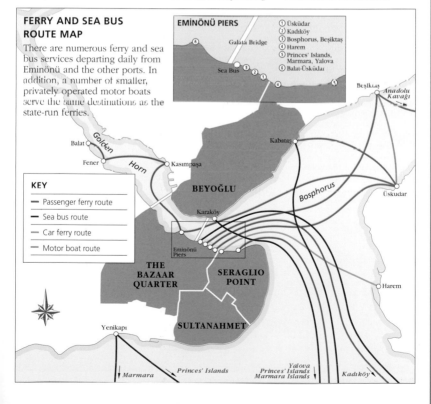

FERRY AND SEA BUS ROUTE MAP

There are numerous ferry and sea bus services departing daily from Eminönü and the other ports. In addition, a number of smaller, privately operated motor boats serve the same destinations as the state-run ferries.

EMİNÖNÜ PIERS

① Üsküdar
② Kadıköy
③ Bosphorus, Beşiktaş
④ Harem
⑤ Princes' Islands, Marmara, Yalova
⑥ Balat-Üsküdar

Galata Bridge

Sea Bus

KEY

— Passenger ferry route
— Sea bus route
— Car ferry route
— Motor boat route

Balat
Fener
Golden Horn
Kasımpaşa
BEYOĞLU
Karaköy
Eminönü Piers
THE BAZAAR QUARTER
SERAGLIO POINT
SULTANAHMET
Yenikapı
Kabataş
Bosphorus
Beşiktaş
Anadolu Kavağı
Üsküdar
Harem

Marmara   Princes' Islands   Yalova
Princes' Islands
Marmara Islands   Kadıköy

Municipal buses at the Eminönü bus station

GETTING AROUND BY BUS

Istanbul's two inner-city bus companies, IETT and Halk Otobüsü, are both run by the Istanbul Transportation Company. IETT alone has over 2,600 buses covering hundreds of routes. Both companies operate from strategic, central terminals, and routes serve suburbs as much as 50 km (31 miles) outside the city core. Destinations are marked on the front of the bus, with the route shown on the side. Bus shelters are located all over the city. Few bus drivers speak English, but they are invariably patient and polite – even in the worst traffic jams.

Halk Otobüsü services require a cash payment upon entry; IETT buses require a ticket, which you must buy before you alight. Tickets can be bought from the small square booths near the main areas, or at a small premium from the many street sellers or kiosks. Buy a *tam bilet* (full-fare ticket) for your journey. Double-decker buses, which are usually green and much more comfortable, require double fare, as do any routes over the Bosphorus bridges. Both IETT and Halk Otobüsü services accept cash or the electronic ticket, AKBIL, which can be purchased at bus terminals and topped up at strategic points. Note that you cannot top up electronic tickets at street kiosks.

METRO

Istanbul's underground system, known as the Metro, opened in 2000, and runs from Atatürk Airport to Şişhane. Although it currently has only ten stops, the Metro relieves some of the pressure on the streets north of Taksim. Tokens, purchased upon entry, operate the turnstiles. The line runs deep underground, and there are at

Sign for the Metro

least two escalators before you reach the platform. Wait in the middle of the platform to board the carriages, as the train takes up only a fraction of the platform length. A southern extension from Taksim to Yenikapı is under construction.

TRAMWAYS

Istanbul's tramway system is clean, modern and comfortable, and is highly recommended as the speediest way to get around the city. The tramway and its branch lines are popularly known as the Raylı Sistemi.

The main overland line runs from Kabataş, across Galata Bridge (*see inside back cover*), up through the main tourist area of Sultanahmet to Aksaray. Feeder lines go above and below ground, linking to the *otogar* (bus station) at Esenler and to the World Trade Centre as well as Atatürk Airport. Cars are fully air conditioned.

The tramway line is currently being extended on the Asian side from Kadiköy to Kartal.

TUNEL AND İSTIKLAL STREET TRAM

A pulley-operated cable car, known simply as Tünel, runs underground from the Galata Bridge at Karaköy up to the Tünel end of İstiklâl Caddesi in Beyoğlu.

Built by French engineers and opened in 1875, it

Modern tram at a stop in Sultanahmet, the heart of historic Istanbul

The vintage İstiklâl Street tram at Taksim Square

requires a token *(jeton)* purchased from the stall at the entrance. The Tünel is open until 9pm.

From Tünel, you can board a refurbished trolley car to take you the 1 km (just under a mile) up to Taksim Square.

TRAIN

The suburban train network is lacking in romance and has been superseded by more efficient (and cleaner) means of transport.

On the European side, one line follows the Sea of Marmara coast from Sirkeci Station down to Florya. On the Asian shore, services run from Haydarpaşa Station out to Izmit. You can cross the Bosphorus by ferry and alight at Haydarpaşa to step directly onto the train.

Suburban trains depart every half hour or so, and are used mainly by commuters.

FUNICULAR AND TELERIFIK

A funicular route now operates along a 0.6 km (0.4 mile) stretch from Taksim to Kabataş, from where it is easy to board the tram.

A télérifik service operates from Eyüp Sultan mosque up the steep ascent to the Pierre Loti Café *(see p120)*.

AIRPORT TRANSFERS

Options for getting to and from Atatürk Airport (and on the Asian side of the city Sabiha Gökçen Airport) to central Istanbul are convenient and economical. A shuttle bus service, **Havaş**, runs between Taksim Square (next door to DHL) and the domestic and international terminals of each airport. The Atatürk Airport service runs half-hourly from 5am until 1am, stopping at Bakırköy Sea Bus Terminal and Aksaray. The 25 km (15 mile) journey takes 30–40 minutes, longer in rush hour.

The Havaş bus goes less frequently from Atatürk Airport to the *otogar* (bus station) at Esenler but will not pick up passengers from the *otogar* to the airport.

Another option is city bus number 96T from Taksim Square to Atatürk Airport. Note that it stops near the airport entrance, not at the terminals.

The Metro links Atatürk Airport with the city centre *(see p401)*, but is hard to beat catching the tramway from the airport (marked at both terminals). Change at Merter to the line with final destination Kabataş. Passengers can alight at Sultanahmet, or continue to Kabataş, connecting with the futuristic funicular that delivers them directly to Taksim Square.

Taxis are plentiful, if frenetic, at both airports

Airport shuttle bus bearing the Havaş logo

DIRECTORY

FERRY INFORMATION

Turkish Maritime Lines (TDİ)
Rıhtım Cad, Merkez Han 4, Karaköy, Istanbul.
Tel (0212) 251 50 00
(with English menu options).
Fax (0212) 249 53 91.
www.tdi.com.tr

SEA BUSES

Istanbul Sea Bus Service (İDO)
Kennedy Cad, Yenikapı Feribot İskelesi, Eminönü.
Tel (0212) 455 69 00.
(Information line)
Tel (0266) 444 44 36
(Bandirma).
www.ido.com.tr

PRIVATE CRUISES

Hatsail Tourism
Cumhuriyet Cad, Erk Apt

14, Elmadağ, Istanbul.
Tel (0212) 241 62 50.
Fax (0212) 246 70 03.
www.hatsail.com

Sultan Kayıkları
Cumhuriyet Cad Kat 3, Harbiye, Istanbul.
Tel (0212) 296 52 40.
www.sultankayiklari.com

METRO/TRAMWAY INFORMATION

Hızlı Tramvay
Tel (0212) 568 99 70.

TRAIN INFORMATION

Haydarpaşa Station
Tel (0216) 336 04 75.

Sirkeci Station
Tel (0212) 527 00 51.

AIRPORT TRANSFERS

Havaş
Tel (0212) 465 47 00.

General Index

Acknowledgments

Dorling Kindersley would like to thank the following people whose contributions and assistance have made the preparation of this book possible:

Main Contributor

Suzanne Swan graduated from Queen's University in Kingston, Ontario, Canada, and has lived in Turkey since 1990. She was contributing editor of *Antalya, the Guide* for two years and contributed to many articles and books on Turkey, including *Globetrotter Travel Guide to Turkey* and *Insight Guide to the Turkish Coast*. She is the Turkish correspondent for a trade publisher.

Contributors and Consultants

Dominic Whiting, a freelance writer-photographer, lived in Turkey for four years. He wrote *Footprints Turkey Handbook*, was a co-author of Time Out's *Istanbul City Guide*, and updated the *DK Eyewitness Guide to Istanbul*.

Dr Caroline Finkel is an Ottoman historian and academic researcher.

Dr Bianka Ralle has an MA in German Studies and worked in journalism as well as teaching and training programmes for developing countries. She was a consultant on Turkey for the Organization for Economic Cooperation and Development (OECD). Her doctoral thesis was on migration and modernization in Turkey.

Kate Clow was educated in the UK, but completed her MBA at Istanbul University in 1991 and stayed in Turkey. She has contributed to the *Rough Guide to Turkey*, *Top Treks of the World* and *Cornucopia Magazine*, and is the originator of the Lycian Way and St Paul Trail walks.

Terrance Duggan walked from Greece to Egypt in 1988–89, in the footsteps of Alexander the Great. A scholar and painter, he has written widely on Islamic and Turkish culture and art. His paintings of Seljuk and Ottoman designs have been exhibited in London, Istanbul and Italy.

Terry Richardson studied classics at Sheffield University, England. He has contributed to *Rough Guide to Turkey* and *Footprints Guide* and photographed for *Cornucopia Magazine* and *The Lycian Way*.

Nilüfer Tünay has a degree in Communication Technology, worked in the Turkish media sector and represented *Sea Trades Magazine* in Turkey. She is now retired.

Molly McNailly-Burke was Turkish correspondent for the *Irish Times* and a contributor to the *Insight* and *Columbus Guides*. She now lives in Hertfordshire, England.

Ronnie Askey-Doran edited a satirical broadsheet in Istanbul and now lives in her native Australia.

Christopher Gardner is a botanist and horticulturist who lives in England.

Rosie Ayliffe lived in Turkey for three years while working as a freelance writer in Istanbul. She was one of the authors of *Rough Guide to Turkey*, and contributed to the *Rough Guide to France*, *Time Out's* London guides and the *DK Eyewitness Guide to Istanbul*.

Rose Baring is a travel writer who has spent many months exploring Istanbul. She was co-author of *Essential Istanbul* (AA) and *DK Eyewitness Guide to Istanbul*.

Barnaby Rogerson has travelled and lectured extensively in the eastern Mediterranean. With Rose Baring he co-wrote *Essential Istanbul* (AA) and contributed to other AA and Cadogan guides, as well as *DK Eyewitness Guide to Istanbul*.

Canan Silay was a journalist on the Turkish daily, *Hürriyet*, and then editor of *Istanbul, The Guide* for many years. She has contributed to several books on Turkey, including the Insight guides to Istanbul, Turkey and the Turkish coast.

Additional Contributors

Sean Fraser, Lisa Greenstein, Alfred LeMaitre.

Additional Cartography

Globetrotter Travel Maps; Haluk Inci, İki Nokta.

Design and Editorial Assistance

Emma Anacootee, Claire Baranowski, Tarryn Berry, Sonal Bhatt, Leizel Brown, Pure Content, Jo Cowen, Lellyn Creamer, Claudia Dos Santos, Karen Fitzpatrick, Rhiannon Furbear, Emily Hatchwell, Jacky Jackson, Priya Kukadia, Simon Lewis, Irene Lyford, Ian Midson, Helen Peters, Nicole Pope, Marisa Renzullo, Gerhardt van Rooyen, Reinette van Rooyen, Conrad van Dyk.

Proofreader and Indexer

Pat Barton.

Additional Photography

DK Studio/Steve Gorton, Dave King, Ian O'Leary, Clive Streeter.

Publishing Manager

Kate Poole

Managing Editor

Helen Townsend

DTP Designer

Jason Little

Cartographer

Casper Morris

Special Assistance

Dorling Kindersley would like to thank staff at museums, mosques, churches, government departments, shops, hotels, restaurants, transport services and other organizations in Turkey for their help.
    Particular thanks are due to: Dr Oğuz Alpözen, Bodrum Museum; Ibrahim Baştutan; Emine Bilirgen, Topkapı Palace, Istanbul; Erol Çakir, İzmir Archaeology Museum; Süleyman Çakır; Sühelya Demirci, Sivas Museum; Hikmet Denizli; The Museum of Anatolian Civilisations, Ankara; Ercihan Düzgünoğlu, TÜRSAB, Istanbul; Veysel Ediz, Çorum Museum; Dr Donald Frey, Institute of Nautical Archaeology, Bodrum; Iclal and Muzaffer Guler; Ali Harmankaya, Side Museum; Kaili Kidner and Lars-Eric Möre, Göreme; Joanna March and Hülya Soylu, Turkish Tourist Office, London; Güney Paksoy, Yedikule and Rumeli Hisar Museums; Feyza Sürücü, Ministry of

Tourism, Ankara; Ertan Tezgör, Turkish Grand National Assembly, Ankara; Feridun Ülker, Presidential Palace, Ankara; Ürcel Üzerin, Bursa Archaeological Museum; Varan Turizm; Üsküdar Folklore and Tourism Society (ÜFTUD), Kırklareli region; Neco Yoksulabakan.

The following staff of provincial tourist offices were very helpful: Reşit Akgüneş, Diyarbakır; Nebahat Alkaya, Bodrum; Bülent Aslan, Amasya; Ayten Aydın, Dalyan; Mustafa Aydın, Kaş; Nurten Celikkaptan, İzmir; Polat Cengis, Çeşme; Ali Fuat Er, Amasya; Fadime Hanim, Sivas; Yaşar Gül, Kastamonu; Yücel Güneş, Nevşehir; Mehmet Hacıağaoğlu, Side; Hüsnü Küçükaslan, Tokat; Murat Keleş, Amasya; Mustafa Kurt, Amasya; Ferhat Malcan, Kaş; Halis Öğüt, Konya; Şentürk Özdemiş, Erzurum; Sare Özdemir, Safranbolu; Safiye Portal, Safranbolu; Kadir Savçı, Çanakkale; Cennet Tazegül, Kars; Ahmet Tazegül, Erzurum; Yüksel Unal, Samsun; Mevlut Uyumaz, Afyon; Erdal Uzun, Kütahya; Zübeyir Yılmaz, Antakya; İbrahim Yakup, Çorum; Garip Yıl, Osmaniye; Zeki Bey, Işak Paşa Saray, Doğubeyazıt.

Other associations and individuals whose assistance was invaluable. Faik Akın, Turkish Airlines, Istanbul; Çetin Akant, Pedasa/Bodrum; Baki Akpınar, Göreme; Ali Baba Rent a Car, Kaş; Dr Şakir Aktaş, Kaş; Ali Baysan, Foto Ali, Kaş, Ahmet Burcu, Istanbul; Ahmet Büyük Yilmaz, Director, Turkish State Mint; Hasan Dağlı, Kaş, Fatih Demirhan, Istanbul Ulaşim A.Ş.; Zafer Emeksiz, Payas/Yakacık Municipality; Ali and Nazife Gülşen, Kaş; Cengiz Güzelmeriç, Kaş; Prof. Dr Wilhelm Gernot, Würzburg University; Hülya Gürkan, Minitcity Antalya; Kamil Koç Otobüs İşletmeleri A.Ş., Bursa; Ahmet Karaşahin, Adana; Lars-Eric Möre, Kapadokya Balloons, Göreme, Kerim Mat, Alanya, Abdullah Muslu, Kaş; Myriam Hanim, St Polycarp Church, İzmir, Dr Munise Ozan, Kaş; Muhammed Özcan, Kaş; Aydın Özmen, Turkish Central Bank, Ankara; Cihat Şahin, Fethiye; Diler Şaşmaz, DHL, Antalya; Mustafa and Sultan Soylu, Kaş; Tahsin Bey Konak Hotel, Safranbolu; Ismail Tezer, Kayseri Governor's Office; Ömer Tosun, Ottoman House, Göreme; Tuğrul Bilen Unal, Turkish State Mint, Istanbul; Osman Uvuç, Kayseri Esnaf; Veysel Bey, İznik Municipality; Bayram Yıldırım, Bodrum; Özkan Yaşar, Kaş; Yenişehir Palas Hotel, Istanbul; Sevilay Yilmaz, İzmir Kültür ve Turizm Müdürlüğü; Hüsnü Züber, Bursa.

Photography Permissions

Dorling Kindersley would like to thank the following for their kind permission to photograph at their establishments: General Directorate of Monuments and Museums; Ministry of Culture; Ministry for Religious Affairs; İstanbul Valiliği İl Kültür Müdürlüğü; İstanbul Valiliği İl Müftülüğü; Milli Saraylar Daire Başkanlığı and Edirne Valiliği İl Müftülüğü.

Picture Credits

Stone/ Travelpix Ltd 11tl; Ara Güler: Mosaics Museum 87c; Topkapı Palace Museum 71cr, 91tr, 161bl; 379t; Şems/ Güner: 123tr.

Sonia Halliday Photographs: Bibliothèque Nationale, Madrid 51tr; engraved by Thomas Allom, painted by Laura Lushington 71br; Topkapı Palace Museum 86b; Robert Harding Picture Library: David Holden 150; Michael Jenner 69br; J.H.C. Wilson 123br; Adam Woolfitt 19tr, 21cl, 33cl, 101tr, 151; Hotel Les Ottomans: 388br; Hulton Getty Images: 22br, 23tl, 59tc; The Hutchison Library: © Robert Francis 27bl, 403b; © Maurice Harvey 410b; © John Hatt 62tl; © Jeremy Horner 26bl; © Joan Klatchko 186b, 233b; © Tony Souter 28b, 29bl, 134.

Hanan Ischar: 183b; Istanbul Library: 76b.

Michael Jenner Photography: 183cr.

Ali Kabbas: 7c, 26tr, 29tc, 30b, 37b, 121tl, 255t; Museum of Turkish and Islamic Arts, Istanbul, from *Hadiqat al-Su'ada* (17th century), Baghdad 29br; Gürol Kara: 104cl; İzzet Keribar: 1, 4–5, 12, 14b, 15tr/c, 18cl, 20bl, 25b, 26tl/cr/br, 28ba, 28–9, 31tr/bl, 44cl, 60–61, 62bl/br; 64, 66tl, 72tr, 118tl, 122tr, 128br, 133t, 146–7, 149tl, 167c, 182tr, 193b, 205, 206b, 218tl/tr, 228b, 255cbr, 263t/b, 266–7, 272tr/bc, 277, 281cr, 294tr, 307bl, 310–11, 312-3, 346bl, 386c, 390–391; Kippa Nature Photo Agency: H. Glader 21bra; J. van Holten; 21bc; E. Pott 21br.

José Luczyc-Wyhowska: 378cr, 379cl/cr/bl/blc/brc/br.

Magnum: Topkapı Palace Museum/Ara Güler 63c, 69tl; Alberto Modiano: 19br, 26cl, 157b; with approval of ÜFTUD (Üsküdar Folklore and Tourism Society, Kırklareli region) 27bcr, 34tc; Museum of Anatolian Civilizations, Ankara: 41tc, 41bl, 41br, 42tc, 42cr, 42bl, 42br, 43tc, 43bl, 43br, 44bl, 44bc, 45bc, 45br, 47ca, 48tl, 48br, 49ctc, 242tr/ bc, 243tl/cr/cl, 296tr.

Natural History Museum, London: 213b. Natur-Med thermal Springs and health resort: 389tl; Network Photographers: Gerard Sioen/Rapho 7tr, 215c, 222–223, 315t.

Dick Osseman: 308clb, 308tr, 309br, 309ca; Güngör Özsoy: 6br, 157tl/tr, 300, 301. Pera Museum: 109cb; Photo Access Photographic Library: Harvey Lloyd 22–3; Photobank: Adrian Baker 56bl, 170, 406bl; Jeanetta Baker 14t, 34cb, 184–5, 190t, 191tr, 191b, 198cl, 386bl; Peter Baker 27tr, 174t, 176tr, 177b, 182cl/bl, 192b, 320–1, 347bl, 405t; Pictures Colour Library Ltd.: 24bl, 173t, 224bl, 378cl; Planetary Visions Limited: 11b.

Neil Setchfield: 94, 148bl, 194cl, 274b, 347cr, 374cl; George Simpson: 37cr; Jeroen Snijders: 13b, 15bl, 116tr, 374b, 410tl; Remy Sow: 322cl; Jeff Spiby: 211b.

Golkhan Tan: 22tl/cl/c/cr/r/bl/bc, 196cbl, 197cbr; Travel Ink: Marc Dubin 23b, 187b, 192t, 325b; Abie Enock 324tl; Ken Gibson 171; Simon Reddy 37t; Trip Photographic Library: 153; Turkcell: 398bc; Turkish Airlines: 401t, Turk Telekom: 398tr.

Andrew Wheeler: 31cl, 54tl, 346cl, 375t; Peter Wilson: 70c, 85cl, 85tr, 89tl, 118cl.

Front endpaper: all special photography except Robert Harding Picture Library: David Holden tl; Güngör Özsoy: br; Photobank: Adrian Baker tcl.

JACKET

Front - 4Corners Images: SIME/ Schmid Reinhard main image; Alamy Images: Turkey Alan King clb. Back - DK Images: bl; tl; Francesca Yorke clb; Izzet Keribar: cla. Spine 4Corners Images: SIME/ Schmid Reinhard t; DK Images: Francesca Yorke b.

All other images © Dorling Kindersley. For further information, see: **www.dkimages.com**

SPECIAL EDITIONS OF DK TRAVEL GUIDES

DK Travel Guides can be purchased in bulk quantities at discounted prices for use in promotions or as premiums. We are also able to offer special editions and personalized jackets, corporate imprints, and excerpts from all of our books, tailored specifically to meet your own needs.

To find out more, please contact:
(in the United States) **SpecialSales@dk.com**
(in the UK) **TravelSpecialSales@uk.dk.com**
(in Canada) DK Special Sales at **general@tourmaline.ca**
(in Australia) **business.development@pearson.com.au**

Phrase Book

Pronunciation

Turkish uses a Roman alphabet. It has 29 letters: 8 vowels and
21 consonants. Letters that differ from the English alphabet are:
c, pronounced "j" as in "jolly"; ç, pronounced "ch" as in "church";
ğ, which lengthens the preceding vowel and is not pronounced;
ı, pronounced "uh"; ö, pronounced "ur" (like the sound in
"further"); ş, pronounced "sh" as in "ship"; ü, pronounced "ew"
as in "few".

In an Emergency

Help!	İmdat!	eem-dat
Stop!	Dur!	door
Call a doctor!	Bir doktor	beer dok-tor chah-
	çağrın!	ruhn
Call an	Bir ambulans	beer am-boo-lans
ambulance!	çağrın!	chah-ruhn
Call the police!	Polis çağrın!	po-lees chah-ruhn
Fire!	Yangın!	yan-guhn
Where is the	En yakın telefon	en ya-kuhn
nearest	nerede?	teh-leh-fon
telephone?		neh-reh-deh
Where is the	En yakın hastane	en ya-kuhn
nearest	nerede?	has-ta-neh
hospital?		neh-reh-deh

Communication Essentials

Yes	Evet	eh-vet
No	Hayır	h-'eye' uhr
Thank you	Teşekkür ederim	teh-shek-kewr
		eh-deh-reem
Please	Lütfen	lewt-fen
Excuse me	Affedersiniz	af-feh-der-see-neez
Hello	Merhaba	mer-ha-ba
Goodbye	Hoşça kalın	hosh-cha ka-luhn
Good morning	Günaydın	gewn-'eye'-duhn
Good evening	İyi akşamlar	ee yee ak-sham-lar
Morning	Sabah	sa-bah
Afternoon	Öğleden sonra	ur-leh-den son ra
Evening	Akşam	ak-sham
Yesterday	Dün	dewn
Today	Bugün	boo-gewn
Tomorrow	Yarın	ya-ruhn
Here	Burada	boo-ra-da
There	Şurada	shoo-ra-da
Over there	Orada	o-ra-da
What?	Ne?	neh
When?	Ne zaman?	neh za-man
Why?	Neden	neh-den
Where?	Nerede	neh-reh-deh

Useful Phrases

How are you?	Nasılsınız?	na-suhl-suh-nuhz
I'm fine	İyiyim	ee-yee-yeem
Pleased to	Memnun oldum	mem-noon ol-doom
meet you		
See you soon	Görüşmek üzere	gur-rewsh-mek
		ew-zeh-reh
That's fine	Tamam	ta-mam
Where is/are ...?	... nerede?	...neh-reh-deh
How far is it to ...?	... ne kadar uzakta?	...ney ka-dar
		oo-zak-ta
I want to go to ...	... a/e gitmek	... a/eh geet-mek
	İstiyorum	ees-tee-yo-room
Do you speak	İngilizce biliyor	een-gee-leez-jeh
English?	musunuz?	bee-lee-yor moo-
		soo-nooz?
I don't	Anlamıyorum	an-la-muh-yo-room
understand		
Can you help me?	Bana yardım	ba-na yar-duhm
	edebilir misiniz?	eh-deh-bee-leer mee
		-see-neez?

Useful Words

big	büyük	bew-yewk
small	küçük	kew-chewk
hot	sıcak	suh-jak
cold	soğuk	soh-ook
good/well	iyi	ee-yee
bad	kötü	kur-tew
enough	yeter	yeh-ter
open	açık	a-chuhk
closed	kapalı	ka-pa-luh
left	sol	sol
right	sağ	saa
straight on	doğru	doh-roo

near	yakın	ya-kuhn
far	uzak	oo-zak
up	yukarı	yoo-ka-ruh
down	aşağı	a-shah-uh
early	erken	er-ken
late	geç	gech
entrance	giriş	gee-reesh
exit	çıkış	chuh-kuhsh
toilets	tuvaletler	too-va-let-ler
push	itiniz	ee-tee-neez
pull	çekiniz	cheh-kee-neez
more	daha fazla	da-ha faz-la
less	daha az	da-ha az
very	çok	chok

Shopping

How much is this?	Ne kadar?	ney ka-dar
I would like ...	... istiyorum	... ees-tee-yo-room
Do you have ...?	... var mı?	...var muh?
Do you take	Kredi kartı	kreh-dee kar-tuh
credit cards?	kabul ediyor	ka-bool eh-dee-yor
	musunuz?	moo-soo-nooz?
What time do	Saat kaçta	Sa-at kach-ta
you open/	açılıyor/	a-chuh-luh-yor/
close?	kapanıyor?	ka-pa-nuh-yor
this one	bunu	boo-noo
that one	şunu	shoo-noo
expensive	pahalı	pa-ha-luh
cheap	ucuz	oo-jooz
size (clothes)	beden	beh-den
size (shoes)	numara	noo-ma-ra
white	beyaz	bay-yaz
black	siyah	see-yah
red	kırmızı	kuhr-muh-zuh
yellow	sarı	sa-ruh
green	yeşil	yeh-sheel
blue	mavi	mu-vee
brown	kahverengi	kah-veh-ren-gee
shop	dükkan	dewk-kan
till	kasa	ka-sa
bargaining	pazarlık	pa-zar-luhk
That's my last	Daha fazla	da-ha faz-la
offer	veremem	veh-reh-mem

Types of Shop

antiques shop	antikacı	an-tee-ka-juh
bakery	fırın	fuh-ruhn
bank	banka	ban-ka
book shop	kitapçı	kee-tap-chuh
butcher's	kasap	ka-sap
cake shop	pastane	pas-ta-neh
chemist's/	eczane	ej-za-neh
pharmacy		
fishmonger's	balıkçı	ba-luhk-chuh
greengrocer's	manav	ma-nav
grocery	bakkal	bak-kal
hairdresser's		
(ladies)	kuaför	kwaf-fur
(mens)	berber	ber-ber
leather shop	derici	deh-ree-jee
market/bazaar	çarşı/pazar	char-shuh/pa-zar
newsstand	gazeteci	ga-zeh-teh-jee
post office	postane	pos-ta-neh
shoe shop	ayakkabıcı	'eye'-yak-ka-bub-jub
stationer's	kırtasiyeci	kuhr-ta-see-yeh-jee
supermarket	süpermarket	sew-per-mar-ket
tailor	terzi	ter-zee
travel agency	seyahat acentesi	say-ya-hat
		a-jen-teh-see

Sightseeing

castle	hisar	hee-sar
church	kilise	kee-lee-seh
island	ada	a-da
mosque	cami	ja-mee
museum	müze	mew-zeh
palace	saray	sar-'eye'
park	park	park
square	meydan	may-dan
theological	medrese	med-reh-seh
college		
tomb	türbe	tewr-beh
tourist	turizm	too-reezm
information	danışma	da-nuhsh-mah
office	bürosu	bew-ro-soo
tower	kule	koo-leh
town hall	belediye sarayı	beh-leh-dee-yeh
		sar-'eye'-uh
Turkish bath	hamam	ha-mam

Transport

airport	havalimanı	*ba-va-lee-ma-nuh*
bus/coach	otobüs	*o-to-bewss*
bus stop	otobüs durağı	*o-to-bewss doo-ra-uh*
coach station	otogar	*o-to-gar*
minibus	dolmuş	*dol-moosh*
fare	ücret	*ewj-ret*
ferry	vapur	*va-poor*
sea bus	deniz otobüsü	*deb-neez o-to-bew-sew*
station	istasyon	*ees-tas-yon*
taxi	taksi	*tak-see*
ticket	bilet	*bee-let*
ticket office	bilet gişesi	*bee-let gee-sheb-see*
timetable	tarife	*ta-ree-feh*

Staying in a Hotel

Do you have a vacant room?	Boş odanız var mı?	*bosh o-da-nuhz var muh?*
double room	iki kişilik bir oda	*ee-kee kee-shee-leek beer o-da*
room with a double bed	çift kişilik yataklı bir oda	*cheeft kee-shee-leek ya-tak-luh beer o-da*
twin room	çift yataklı bir oda	*cheeft ya-tak-luh beer o-da*
for one person	tek kişilik	*tek kee-shee-leek*
room with a bath	banyolu bir oda	*ban-yo-loo beer o-da*
shower	duş	*doosh*
porter	komi	*ko-mee*
key	anahtar	*a-nab-tar*
room service	oda servisi	*o-da ser-vee-see*
I have a reservation	Rezervasyonum var	*reb-zer-vas-yo-noom var*
Does the price include breakfast?	Fiyata kahvaltı dahil mi?	*fee-ya-ta kab-val-tuh da-heel mee?*

Eating Out

A table for ...please	... kişilik bir masa lütfen	*... kee-shee-leek beer ma-sa lewt-fen*
I want to reserve a table	Bir masa ayırtmak istiyorum	*beer ma-sa 'eye'-uhrt-mak ees-tee-yo-room*
The bill please	Hesap lütfen	*beb-sap lewt-fen*
I am a vegetarian	Et yemiyorum	*et yeh-mee-yo-room*
restaurant	lokanta	*lo-kan-ta*
waiter	garson	*gar-son*
menu	yemek listesi	*ye-meklees-teb-see*
fixed-price menu	fiks menü	*feeks meb-new*
wine list	şarap listesi	*sha-raplees-teb-see*
breakfast	kahvaltı	*kab-val-tuh*
lunch	öğle yemeği	*ur-leh yeh-meb-ee*
dinner	akşam yemeği	*ak-sham yeb-meb-ee*
starter	meze	*meh-zeh*
main course	ana yemek	*a-na yeb-mek*
dish of the day	günün yemeği	*gewn-ewn yeh-meb-ee*
dessert	tatlı	*tat-luh*
rare	az pişmiş	*az peesh-meesh*
well done	iyi pişmiş	*ee-yee peesh-meesh*
glass	bardak	*bar-dak*
bottle	şişe	*shee-sheh*
knife	bıçak	*bub-chak*
fork	çatal	*cha-tal*
spoon	kaşık	*ka-shuhk*

Menu Decoder

badem	*ba-dem*	almond
bal	*bal*	honey
balık	*ba-luhk*	fish
bira	*bee-ra*	beer
bonfile	*bon-fee-leh*	fillet steak
buz	*booz*	ice
çay	*ch-'eye'*	tea
çilek	*chee-lek*	strawberry
çorba	*chor-ba*	soup
dana eti	*da-na eb-tee*	veal
dondurma	*don-door-ma*	ice cream
ekmek	*ek-mek*	bread
elma	*el-ma*	apple
et	*et*	meat
fasulye	*fa-sool-yeb*	beans
fırında	*fub-rubn-da*	roast
fıstık	*fubs-tuhk*	pistachio nuts
gazoz	*ga-zoz*	fizzy drink
hurma	*boor-ma*	dates
içki	*eech-kee*	alcohol
incir	*een-jeer*	figs
ızgara	*ubz-ga-ra*	charcoal grilled
kahve	*kah-veh*	coffee
kara biber	*ka-ra bee-ber*	black pepper
karışık	*ka-rub-shuhk*	mixed
karpuz	*kar-pooz*	water melon
kavun	*ka-voon*	melon
kayısı	*k-'eye'-uh-suh*	apricots
kaymak	*k-'eye'-mak*	cream
kıyma	*kuby-ma*	minced meat
kızartma	*kub-zart-ma*	fried
köfte	*kurf-teh*	meatballs
kuru	*koo-roo*	dried
kuzu eti	*koo-zoo eh-tee*	lamb
lokum	*lo-koom*	Turkish delight
maden suyu	*ma-den soo-yoo*	mineral water (fizzy)
meyve suyu	*may-veh soo-yoo*	fruit juice
midye	*meed-yeb*	mussels
muz	*mooz*	banana
patlıcan	*pat-lub-jan*	aubergine
peynir	*pay-neer*	cheese
pilav	*pee-lav*	rice
piliç	*pee-leech*	roast chicken
şarap	*sha-rap*	wine
sebze	*seb-zeh*	vegetables
şeftali	*shef-ta-lee*	peach
şeker	*sheb-ker*	sugar
su	*soo*	water
süt	*sewt*	milk
sütlü	*sewt-lew*	with milk
tavuk	*ta-vook*	chicken
tereyağı	*teb-reh-yab-ub*	butter
tuz	*tooz*	salt
üzüm	*ew-zewm*	grapes
vişne	*veesh-neb*	sour cherry
yoğurt	*yob-urt*	yoghurt
yumurta	*yoo-moor-ta*	egg
zeytin	*zay-teen*	olives
zeytinyağı	*zay-teen-yab-ub*	olive oil

Numbers

0	sıfır	*suh-fubr*
1	bir	*beer*
2	iki	*ee-kee*
3	üç	*ewch*
4	dört	*durt*
5	beş	*besh*
6	altı	*al-tuh*
7	yedi	*yeb-dee*
8	sekiz	*seb-keez*
9	dokuz	*doh-kooz*
10	on	*on*
11	on bir	*on beer*
12	on iki	*on ee-kee*
13	on üç	*on ewch*
14	on dört	*on durt*
15	on beş	*on besh*
16	on altı	*on al-tub*
17	on yedi	*on yeb-dee*
18	on sekiz	*on seb-keez*
19	on dokuz	*on doh-kooz*
20	yirmi	*yeer-mee*
21	yirmi bir	*yeer-mee beer*
30	otuz	*o-tooz*
40	kırk	*kubrk*
50	elli	*eb-lee*
60	altmış	*alt-muhsh*
70	yetmiş	*yet-meesh*
80	seksen	*sek-sen*
90	doksan	*dok-san*
100	yüz	*yewz*
110	yüz on	*yewz on*
200	iki yüz	*ee-kee yewz*
1,000	bin	*been*
100,000	yüz bin	*yewz been*
1,000,000	bir milyon	*beer meel-yon*

Time

one minute	bir dakika	*beer da-kee-ka*
one hour	bir saat	*beer sa-at*
half an hour	yarım saat	*ya-ruhm sa-at*
day	gün	*gewn*
week	hafta	*baf-ta*
month	ay	*'eye'*
year	yıl	*yubl*
Sunday	pazar	*pa-zar*
Monday	pazartesi	*pa-zar-teb-see*
Tuesday	salı	*sa-luh*
Wednesday	çarşamba	*char-sham-ba*
Thursday	perşembe	*per-shem-beh*
Friday	cuma	*joo-ma*
Saturday	cumartesi	*joo-mar-teb-see*

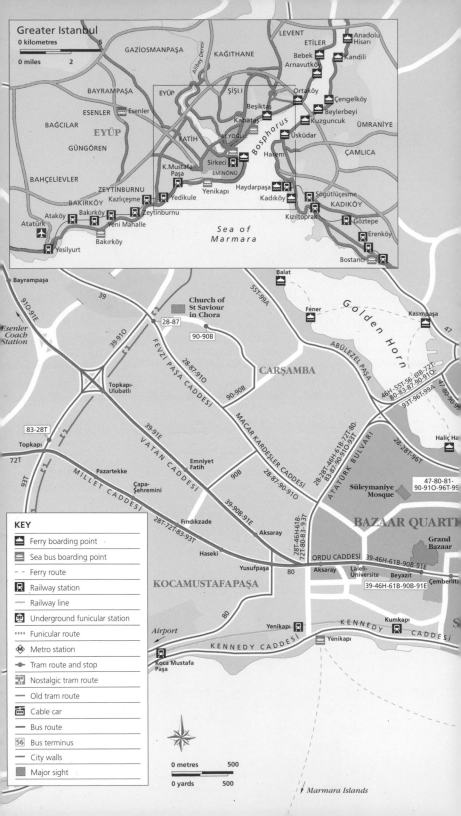